is the first full-length study of Spanish attitudes toward death and afterlife in the peak years of the Counter-Reformation. It contains an analysis of the death rituals requested in sixteenth-century Madrid testaments, as well as a detailed account of the ways in which the "good" deaths of King Philip II and St. Teresa of Avila were interpreted by contemporaries. Though focused on death, it also aims to analyze the ethos of Spanish Catholic piety and belief in an age of profound transformations. This is a history of mentalities that combines quantitative and qualitative methods and analyzes the symbiotic relation between beliefs and cultural structures. It is a study of the relation between popular piety and elite theology, between paradigms and deeds, myth and ritual, art and craft. Though concentrating exclusively on Spain, this study places the early modern Spanish mentality in the wider context of the European Reformation and Counter-Reformation and of Western attitudes toward death.

From Madrid to Purgatory

CAMBRIDGE STUDIES IN EARLY MODERN HISTORY

From Madrid to Purgatory

The art and craft of dying in sixteenth-century Spain

CARLOS M.N. EIRE

University of Virginia

CAMBRIDGE
UNIVERSITY PRESS

PUBLISHED BY THE PRESS SYNDICATE OF THE UNIVERSITY OF CAMBRIDGE
The Pitt Building, Trumpington Street, Cambridge, United Kingdom

CAMBRIDGE UNIVERSITY PRESS
The Edinburgh Building, Cambridge CB2 2RU, UK
40 West 20th Street, New York NY 10011–4211, USA
477 Williamstown Road, Port Melbourne, VIC 3207, Australia
Ruiz de Alarcón 13, 28014 Madrid, Spain
Dock House, The Waterfront, Cape Town 8001, South Africa

http://www.cambridge.org

First published 1995
First paperback edition 2002

A catalogue record for this book is available from the British Library

Library of Congress Cataloguing in Publication data
Eire, Carlos M. N.
From Madrid to purgatory: the art and craft of dying in sixteenth-
century Spain / Carlos M. N. Eire.
p.   cm. – (Cambridge studies in early modern history)
Includes bibliographical references and index.
ISBN 0 521 46018 2
1. Death – Religious aspects – Catholic Church – History of
doctrines – 16th century.   2. Catholic Church – Doctrines –
History – 16th century.   3. Catholic Church – Spain – History – 16th
century.   4. Spain – Religious life and customs.   I. Title.
II. Series.
BX1584.E57   1995
236′.2′094609031–dc20   94-39716   CIP

ISBN 0 521 46018 2 hardback
ISBN 0 521 52942 5 paperback

Partial funding for the publication of this book has been provided by
The Program for Cultural Cooperation Between Spain's Ministry of Culture
and United States Universities.

for Jane

Contents

Contents

Acknowledgments

In the summer of 1983, somewhere between Avila and Madrid, I overheard a most peculiar conversation on a train. At the time, I had not yet fastened onto this project in earnest and still harbored some doubts about the wisdom of switching the focus of my research from Protestant Europe to Catholic Spain. Across the aisle from me, a boy of about ten years of age was talking to his mother about heaven as if he had an intimate knowledge of the place. He not only informed her that St. Peter could not hold any keys "because people in heaven have no bodies, and no hands" but also led her through a celestial language drill. "Do you know what this is called in heaven?", he asked his mother repeatedly, pointing to objects inside and outside the train and then naming them in some incomprehensible tongue. I cannot recall how long this continued or how his mother reacted to it, but I do know that by the time I stepped off the train I had decided to embark on this project.

More than ten years later, I realize that this was a most unusual exchange and that it was no more representative of the Spanish mentality than another dialogue I heard some months later in a smoky Madrid bar about the shape of Coca-Cola bottles. Nonetheless, I am glad that I allowed this boy's eccentric fixation on the afterlife to confirm my hunches about the intrinsic merits of this project. I have him to thank for decisively pulling me away from Calvin's Geneva and planting me firmly in the history of death.

I have many others to thank as well, of course, and for far more substantial assistance. First, I would like to thank John Elliott, who eased my move to Spain in innumerable ways through his support, advice, and encouragement. I am also deeply indebted to Sara Nalle and James Amelang, who have guided me with their erudition and insights through the most difficult parts of this project, especially in its latter stages. William Monter, a fellow traveler on the road from Geneva, and Miriam Usher Chrisman and Thomas Brady, from the world of the Reformation, offered sage advice and sorely needed reassurance that I had not wandered down some wrong path. In Madrid, the director and staff of the Archivo Histórico de Protocolos ensured through their congenial professionalism that every afternoon I spent there was both profitable and enjoyable. In Charlottesville, as ever, Erik Midelfort generously shared his wisdom and friendship. James Childress, my chairman in Religious Studies, steadily offered his backing and served as a splendid advocate at the heavenly courts of funding and research leaves. Elizabeth Brennan McManus, my research assistant, deserves special thanks for her work on the bibliography, the index, and the final round of proofreading.

This brings me to those who have placed their trust in me but cannot easily be thanked by name. The U.S.–Spain Joint Committee for Educational and Cultural Affairs got this project off the ground with a fellowship for research in Madrid in 1984. The University of Virginia funded me generously and patiently: with seven summer fellowships 1983–91; a Sesquicentennial Associates Fellowship in 1986–7; an Alumni Association Teaching Award that provided me with a semester's research leave in 1991; and finally an appointment to the Center for Advanced Study in 1992–3. The School of Historical Studies at the Institute for Advanced Study in Princeton has played a pivotal role in the writing of this book by offering me a Membership in 1986–7, and a Visitorship in 1992–3. It was there that I first began to assemble my notes and there that I finished my writing, nourished by its rarefied intellectual atmosphere and its graciousness. Those who have enriched my work at the Institute would make a very long list.

Which, in turn, brings me to another lengthy roster. The hundreds of long-dead Madrileños whose wills I read deserve some apologetic thanks, for I am certain that not a single one of them ever suspected that their choices would be so closely analyzed or that their words would be made so public by a total stranger. Perhaps they would take some comfort in knowing that although I have intruded and eavesdropped, I have also learned much from them. One of the toughest and most valuable lessons conveyed to me by their wills came to me in my sleep when I was about one-third of the way into the writing. I dreamt I was poring over a list that contained the names and death dates of my sixteenth-century testators. Suddenly, much to my surprise, *my* name appeared on the roster, with a blurry date next to it that I could not make out. At that instant I became aware of my own mortality in a most immediate way. Moreover, from that point forward, my sources ceased being mere names and became flesh-and-blood people with whom I shared a common predicament.

Fortunately, I have loved ones to thank for keeping such dreams and lessons in perspective. Antonio Nieto Cortadellas, my father, would have been quite drawn to the subject of this book, and he is in large measure responsible for bringing me to it. May it cheer him in that *otro mundo* where he now dwells. My mother, Maria Azucena Eire de Nieto, has imparted her faith to me many times over and has continued to believe in my work all these years even though I write in a language she cannot read. May this gladden her in the here and now. My children, John-Carlos, Evelyn Grace, and Bruno Rowan, all born in the midst of this project, are too young to know how much they help me each day and how they have made this a better book. My wife, Jane Ulrich, knows her part in this fully well. Without her wisdom and love I could not have written this book. So it is that on her birthday, I finish it and dedicate it to her.

Abbreviations used in footnotes

Libraries and archives

AHN	Archivo Histórico Nacional, Madrid
AHPM	Archivo Histórico de Protocolos, Madrid
BNM	Biblioteca Nacional, Madrid
IVDJ	Institutuo Valencia de Don Juan, Madrid

Printed works

FHM	*Fuentes Históricas sobre la muerte y cuerpo de la Santa Teresa de Jesús (1582–1596)*, ed. by J. L. Astigarraga, E. Pacho, and O. Rodriguez (Rome, 1982).
OCASB	*Obras Completas de la Beata Ana de San Bartolomé*, 2 vols., *Monumenta Historica Carmeli Teresiani*, 5 (Rome, 1981).
OCST	*Obras Completas de Santa Teresa de Jesús*, ed. by Efrén de la Madre de Dios, O.C.D., 3 vols., *Biblioteca de Autores Cristianos* (Madrid, 1954).
PBC	*Procesos de Beatificación y Canonización de Santa Teresa de Jesús*, ed. by Silverio de Santa Teresa, O.C.D., 3 vols., *Biblioteca Mistica Carmelitana*, 18–20 (Burgos, 1934–35).
Tejada	*Colección de Cánones y de todos los concilios de la Iglesia Española*, ed. by Juan Tejada y Ramiro, 5 vols. (Madrid, 1855).

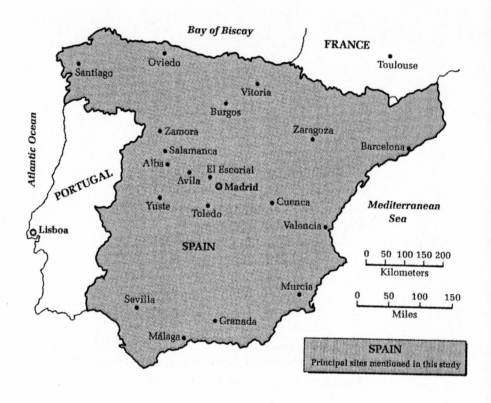

Bay of Biscay

FRANCE

Toulouse

Santiago

Oviedo

Vitoria

Burgos

Zamora

Zaragoza

Salamanca

Barcelona

Atlantic Ocean

Alba

El Escorial

PORTUGAL

Avila

Madrid

Yuste

Cuenca

Toledo

Mediterranean Sea

Valencia

Lisboa

SPAIN

0 50 100 150 200
Kilometers

0   50   100   150
Miles

Murcia

Sevilla

Granada

Málaga

SPAIN
Principal sites mentioned in this study

PROLOGUE

Death and the sun

Death and the sun cannot be stared at.
– La Rochefoucauld, *Maxims* (1665)[1]

In the cheapest seats at a Spanish bullring, two things are unavoidable: death and the sun. Yet Spaniards have been flocking to such seats for centuries, week after week, year after year, down to the present, staring down the unavoidable and the unendurable. What does this mean, aside from suggesting that the sixth duke of La Rochefoucauld failed to consider customs beyond the Pyrenees? Certainly it cannot mean that the Spanish are immune to mortal fright and retinal damage; no, for they have long admitted that the bullfight is itself a ritual theater of the deepest human fear, and they also know that seats in the shade command a higher admission price. What it means is that Spanish culture has long confronted mortality in its own ways and that, contrary to the advice proffered in La Rochefoucauld's maxim, it has even fixed its gaze on discomforting realities, with unique results.[2]

A striking example of this Spanish propensity for gazing at death in

[1] François VI, duc de La Rochefoucauld, *Maximes et réflexions diverses* (Paris, 1975), maxim 26, p. 28.

[2] Ernest Hemingway's eloquent appreciation of this fact might have further popularized the notion that Spain is more at home with death than other cultures: "They think a great deal about death," he wrote of Castilian peasants, "and when they have a religion they have one which believes that life is much shorter than death. Having this feeling, they take an intelligent interest in death and when they can see it being given, avoided, refused, and accepted in the afternoon for a nominal price of admission they pay their money and go to the bullring." *Death in the Afternoon* (New York, 1953), p. 266.

I

the full light of day – and therefore also an apt illustration with which to begin this book – is Francis Borgia, a man who had his own peculiar encounter with death and the sun. In May 1539, Francis unexpectedly lost one of his dearest friends to death: the Empress Isabel, wife of Emperor Charles V and mother to the future King Philip II. Francis joined the cortege that ferried Isabel's remains from Toledo, where she had died, to Granada, where she was to be buried with Charles's grandparents at the royal chapel. One of the wealthiest and most powerful men in Spain and Europe, scion of the notorious Italian Borgias, Marquis of Lombay, Duke of Gandía, Viceroy of Catalonia, close friend of the emperor, Francis would relinquish his titles and vast fortune and become a Jesuit because of his involvement in this funeral. When the cortege reached Granada after a fifteen-day journey in the blazing Spanish sun, Isabel's lead coffin had to be opened so that, according to law and custom, her remains could be identified by some witnesses. This task proved to be the undoing of Francis, who was very fond of the empress, and already had been deeply affected by her death. The corpse was a horrific sight and an assault upon the senses, for the heat of the sun-baked coffin had hastened its putrefaction; the witnesses fell back, nauseated, except for Francis, who remained composed. For him, the dissolving tissues of Isabel were as much an epiphany as a horror: "Are you really my Lady the Empress?" he asked himself. Francis's hagiography would later seize on this moment as the most pivotal in his life:

He was illumined by a divine light in such a way, that in that brief instant he was given to behold the wretched result of our first parents' disobedience upon the human race, and the severe punishment of God on all their descendants, along with the vanity of all that can be gained and esteemed by human beings. At that moment he apprehended what deceit and disillusionment lay in the allure of the flesh; there he saw clearly the full horror and grief of hell. . . . This same light stamped upon his heart disdain and loathing for everything that could estrange him from God, and a powerful, vibrant desire to know and love eternal and divine things, which are not subject to death or corruption.[3]

---

[3] Juan Eusebio Nierenberg, S. J., *Hechos políticos y religiosos del que fué Duque Quarto de Gandía, Virey de Cataluña y despues tercero General de la Compañia de Jesús, el Beato Francisco de Borgia* (1643). Later edition (Barcelona, 1882), 2 vols., vol. 1, p. 61. Pedro Suau, S. J., disputes tradition, arguing that Francis's conversion occurred at the moment of Isabel's death rather than at the burial in Granada. See *Historia de San*

Death and the sun

Back in his lodgings a few hours later, overcome by a fit of weeping, Francis threw himself on the ground and asked: "What are we doing, my soul? What are we searching for? How long shall we continue to chase shadows?" Sighing, groaning, meditating on death, he arrived at a melancholy awareness of his own need to prepare for the inevitable:

If this is how death deals with earthly majesty and power, what army shall we send to contend with it?, what authority shall challenge it?, who shall be able to resist it? This same death which struck the Imperial Crown now bends its bow and aims its arrow at me. . . . Would it not be better to die to the world while living, in order to live with God after death? . . . Grant me my Lord, grant me my God, your light, your spirit, and your assistance. . . . I vow that if you do so, I shall never again serve a Lord who can die.[4]

Though it took him nearly eleven years from the time of this vow to disentangle himself from worldly affairs and to apportion his estate among his eight sons, he finally abandoned all titles and property and entered the Society of Jesus in 1550. That he again rose to prominence and power when he was named general of the Jesuits is immaterial: As far as he and his contemporaries were concerned, he had died to the world and had done so with heroic virtue.

Surely, St. Francis Borgia had somehow been conditioned to react in a particular way to this traumatic experience, for the language of his conversion mirrors that of much of the devotional literature of his day and shares common points of reference with it. His conversion might have been sudden, but it was not as a bolt out of the blue; on the contrary, it was the culmination of a long process of introspection, the logical endpoint for a mentality that had been shaped by certain aspects of Spanish culture. But Francis did more than mirror certain paradigms. He embodied them. He verified their significance. Francis himself, in turn, became a paradigm and a mirror for others, including his close friend Emperor Charles V, who appointed him co-executor of his will, along with the heir to the throne, Philip II. It is no mere coincidence that when the world-weary Charles abdicated in 1556, he retired to a monastery to contemplate his own death and that, as tradition has it, he re-

Francisco de Borja, tercer General de la Compañia de Jesús (Zaragoza, 1963), esp. pp. 59–65.

[4] Nierenberg, *Borgia*, p. 62.

hearsed his own funeral, all under the bright, blinding sunlight of Extremadura: Francis and Charles both partook of a certain mentality and also contributed to it.[5]

This book analyzes the attitudes toward death shared by St. Francis and the Emperor Charles, the mentality that compelled them to fix their stare upon death. Like Francis looking back upon Empress Isabel's sunbaked coffin, but with a much lighter heart, I too can recall the moment when I decided to gaze upon death. It began with my reading *The Hour of Our Death* by Philippe Ariès, a work that introduced me to the history of mentalities and thrust my mind into a peculiar dialectic. Inspired and irritated, challenged by his insights and generalizations, I found myself drawn to the subject but also opposed to much of what he had to say. About midway through the book, one generalization in particular captured my attention. Purgatory, he claimed, was

a dogma that was long limited to a small elite of theologians such as Saint Thomas Aquinas or philosophical writers such as Dante . . . [it] rarely appears in popular writing before the middle of the seventeenth century; one seldom finds references to it in Parisian wills before 1640.[6]

It was a bold assertion, and it irked me. So much of what I had read before that summer of 1981 pointed toward the opposite conclusion: Purgatory had not been a trivial elitist concept in the age of the Reformation but, rather, one of the chief focal points of popular religion. Above all, it was Ariès's sanguine reductionism that prompted me to linger over the theme of death and to ponder the meaning of the history

---

[5] For a description of the funeral rehearsal see José de Siguenza, *Historia de la Orden de San Jerónimo* (1605), Bk I, chap. 39; modern edition: *Nueva Biblioteca de Autores Españoles*, 8 and 12 (Madrid, 1907), p. 158. The bibliography on the emperor's final days is quite lengthy. The most significant studies are: Francisco de Irarrazábal y Andia, Marqués de Valparaiso, *El perfecto desengaño. Relación de la abdicación de Carlos V y sus ultimos dias en Yuste* (Madrid, 1638); Louis-Prosper Gachard, *Sur le séjour de Charles Quint au Monastère de Yuste* (Brussels, 1843); William Stirling Maxwell, *The Cloister Life of the Emperor Charles V* (London, 1853); François A. A. Mignet, *Charles Quint, son abdication, son séjour, et sa mort au monastère de Yuste* (Paris, 1854); Adolf Poschman, *Kaiser Karl V in Yuste* (Leppstadt, 1960); Felipe Jimenez Vasco, *Como nace un monasterio y muere un César* (Caceres, 1969).

[6] Philippe Ariès, *L'homme devant la mort* (Paris, 1977), trans. Helen Weaver, *The Hour of Our Death* (New York, 1981), p. 306. For a more detailed critique see my review in *Catholic Historical Review* 69 (1983): 3.

of mentalities, for his sundering of society into the two self-contained worlds of the elite and nonelite struck me as a wrongheaded approach to history and religion.

Attracted to the topic but piqued by his methodology and conclusions, I set out to survey a much smaller portion of the same terrain as Ariès, with an eye toward integrating what he had bifurcated, that is, the attitudes of the elites and the nonelites. Once this project began to take shape, its scope and content made Ariès recede into a distant horizon; nonetheless, as is the case with most sources of inspiration, that faraway speck remained a constant point of reference.

The more I read in the history of death, the more I was drawn to the subject. I was soon convinced that attitudes toward death and the afterlife are indeed a barometer of faith and piety, and a unique manifestation of the interrelationship between belief and behavior, between the abstract world of theology and the practical world of deeds and gestures. For death is not only a universal phenomenon common to all human beings; it is also that crucial moment when the here and the hereafter supposedly intersect for every human being. In the case of Catholic Europe before the Enlightenment, death was the moment when salvation was decided, the instant when the soul began its journey into the unseen spiritual realm that was the church's special dominion. Hence, death was the unique moment, common to all, when the church could make the ultimate claim over each individual and over society as a whole; it was arguably the consummate Catholic experience, the ultimate expression of a society's beliefs, and also the ultimate opportunity for shaping and controlling a society's behavior.

Also, I was especially captivated by the way in which historians of death questioned their own enterprise and acknowledged its difficulties and shortcomings. Michel Vovelle, for instance, admitted after having researched the subject himself, that the study of collective attitudes toward death had become one of the greatest problems faced by the history of mentalities, for its scope and methodology remained indeterminate.[7] Joachim Whaley, also drawn to the subject, confessed it was

---

[7] Michel Vovelle, "Les attitudes devant la mort: Problèmes de méthode, approches et lectures différentes," *Annales, E.S.C.* (1976): 120. See also his essay, "L'histoire des hommes au miroir de la mort," in *Death in the Middle Ages*, ed. Herman Braet and Werner Verbrecke (Louvain, 1983), pp. 1–18.

5

"bedeviled by obscurity and confusion."[8] Their intellectual honesty not only convinced me that this field of inquiry was still wide open and much more than simply "à la mode" but also gave me a sense of direction.[9]

Once I had decided to pursue the history of death, my first challenge was how to improve upon its scope and methodology. In regard to scope, the challenge was greater, for death is a truly boundless subject that touches upon nearly all aspects of human existence. Because any human activity connected with death was open to investigation, no exhaustive list could ever be drawn up. Moreover, the central claim made by the historians of death was itself an obstacle: the proposition that the study of attitudes toward death is one of the best means – perhaps even the best way – to judge the character of civilizations. The immensity of such a claim seemed to undermine any attempt to delimit either the range of questions one could pose or the material one could examine. As far as methodology was concerned, I needed to resolve what Vovelle had seen as an unfortunate divorce between the study of infrastructural problems (i.e., demography, economics, social structures) and ideological super-structures (i.e., theology, philosophy, political theory).

I began to narrow my focus by choosing the sixteenth century, a period dismissed by Ariès as having scant bearing on attitudes toward death, and Spain, a region largely overlooked by him. But why Spain? And why the sixteenth century? Convinced that attitudes toward death and the afterlife must have been a major divergence between Protestants and Catholics in the Reformation, I settled on Spain, the staunchest defender of the Catholic faith in the sixteenth century, because I had read enough Spanish devotional literature to know that heaven, hell, and purgatory were as much a part of that nation's topography as Madrid, Gibraltar, and the Pyrenees. Spanish ascetics from this time, I knew, had fused self-denial with a desire for death to a degree unseen elsewhere in Europe. This apparent fascination with death was evident not only in mystics who explicitly linked spiritual ecstasy to death but also

---

[8] Joachim Whaley, ed., in his introduction to *Mirrors of Mortality: Studies in the Social History of Death* (London, 1981), p. 3.

[9] A decade ago Jacques Le Goff declared "la mort est à la mode," in his foreword to Jacques Chiffoleau, *La comptabilité de l'au delà: Les hommes, la mort et la religion dans la région d'Avignon à la fin du Moyen Age* (Rome, 1980).

among artists, writers, theologians, and monarchs. While Teresa of Avila exclaimed, *"Me muero porque no me muero"* (I am dying to die), El Greco dispensed with boundaries when painting scenes that included the hereafter, and King Philip II built the great palace of the Escorial with a floor plan based on the outline of the grill on which the martyr St. Lawrence had been roasted alive. The Escorial was to serve as a combined residence, monastery, and family mausoleum, and Philip spent his final days much as had his father Charles, contemplating death with his own coffin at his bedside. I also suspected that this apparent fascination with death and the hereafter drew upon the collective psychology of the nation, for I knew that at this same time popular demand for devotional manuals on the art of dying was increasing in Spain. Furthermore, I knew of the reputation that Spain had in popular and learned circles as a nation obsessed with death. The closer I looked at Spain, the more aware I became of the pervasiveness of this notion, even among the Spanish themselves. Américo Castro, for one, had trumpeted the notion that the Spanish had a lust for life – a *vivir desviviéndose* – that encompassed death as well.[10] Federico Garcia Lorca had been more dramatic:

In all countries death is the end. It arrives and the curtain falls. Not so in Spain. In Spain, on the contrary, the curtain only rises at that moment, and in many Spanish poems there is a ramp of flowers of saltpeter over which lean a people who contemplate death.[11]

Whether it was Hemingway musing on the rituals of the bullring in *Death in the Afternoon,* or Miguel de Unamuno philosophizing about mortality in *The Tragic Sense of Life,* or Bartolomé Bennassar analyzing

---

[10] "Vivir Desviviéndose," Américo Castro, *España en su historia: Cristianos, moros y judíos* (Buenos Aires, 1948), pp. 25–45. In "The Meaning of Spanish Civilization," his inaugural lecture at Princeton University (1940), Castro said: "For a Spaniard, living is always an open problem, and not a solution, to be confined in a slogan. To live or to die are for him equivalent points of departure, which today, less than ever, cannot be considered an impertinence." *An Idea of History, Selected Essays of Américo Castro,* ed. S. Gilman and E. L. King (Columbus, OH, 1977), p. 159.

[11] Cited by Bartolomé Bennassar, *L'Homme Espagnol: Attitudes et mentalités du XVIe au XIXe siècle* (Paris, 1975), trans. Benjamin Keen, *The Spanish Character* (Berkeley, CA, 1979), p. 237.

the significance of the "good death" for the Spanish character, the commentary pointed toward some unique relation between death and Spanish culture.[12]

Having chosen a time and place, I gradually developed a sharper focus in regard to the topic and my methodology. This process of narrowing does not now need describing; what needs to be explained is the end result. On an analytical level, this is a history of mentalities that combines qualitative and quantitative methods, what Michel Vovelle has called *approches qualitatives* and *approches serielles*.[13] It is a study that juxtaposes the actual and the ideal and analyzes the way in which belief shapes society and culture and how in turn society and culture define and express belief. Though I draw upon the pioneering work of French historians of death, I have not limited myself to their methodology and have eschewed their dichotomizing of elite and popular mentalities.[14] Eager to fuse social and intellectual history, and guided by some approaches in the social-scientific study of religion, I have written a history of mentalities in which apparent dichotomies in faith and piety are viewed as dynamically interrelated rather than as diametrically opposed.

This is a study of the relation between the *art* of dying well and the actual *craft* of dying, between elite theology and popular piety, between paradigms and deeds, between myth and ritual, between the sacred and the profane: It is an attempt to plumb the social, political, and cultural functions of Catholic theology in the Counter-Reformation Spain. In it I analyze the model "good" deaths of the two chief social types, the monarch and the saint – King Philip II as the apex of secular authority and St. Teresa of Avila as the apex of sacred power – and juxtapose these paradigms with the attitudes of more mundane social types as revealed in last wills and testaments from sixteenth-century Madrid.

But why this particular triad of testament, king, and saint? The use of

---

[12] "It would be absurd to deny that Spaniards over the centuries have been preoccupied with the thought of death." Bartolomé Bennassar, *The Spanish Character*, chap. 9, "Mourir bien," p. 237.

[13] Vovelle, "Problèmes," *Annales* (1976): 124. See also the essay by Jacques Le Goff, "Les mentalités, une histoire ambigue," in *Faire de l'histoire: nouveaux problèmes*, ed. J. Le Goff and P. Nora (Paris, 1974), pt. 3, pp. 76–94.

[14] For a synopsis of this historical genre see Joachim Whaley, ed., *Mirrors of Mortality*, especially the introduction by Whaley, pp. 1–14; and "Death and the French Historians" by John McManners, pp. 106–30. Also by McManners: "The history of death," review article, *Times Literary Supplement*, 14 December 1979, p. 111.

testaments was a given, dictated by necessity and precedent, for, as the French historians had proven, these documents were indispensable for the study of popular attitudes.[15] To set these mundane popular attitudes in context, as related to more abstract beliefs, I turned to the mythopoeic process whereby models of faith and behavior are constructed and affirmed. As anthropologists have known for some time, paradigms offer unparalleled access to the study of mentalities. Victor Turner has claimed, for instance, that paradigms not only have reference to the ever-fluid social relations of people but also to "the cultural goals, means, ideas, outlooks, currents of thought, patterns of belief" that determine and interpret those relationships and incline them toward cohesiveness or divisiveness. Paradigms are not, he says, "precision tools of thought" but, rather, a means of intuiting and apprehending axiomatic values, mostly through myth and symbol. As such, they can influence the vital actions of societies more profoundly than logically arrayed ethical guidelines.[16] But where does one look for the paradigmatic "good" death?

The paradigmatic cases of the king and the saint seemed obvious choices as points of reference in the bipolar social structure of early modern Spain, that nation where church and state worked hand in hand to control thought and behavior: the king as the summit of secular authority, the saint as the apex of sacred power.[17] Kings represent law and authority. They are the ultimate earthly power, the apex of temporal lay society. To study the myth of the "good" death of the king, I thought, would be to peer into the ultimate lay paradigm. Saints represent holiness and spiritual authority. Though saints are not always necessarily at the summit of the church hierarchy, their alleged nearness to God enables them to embody that sacred power from which the church itself

---

[15] Using wills as a gauge of a community's mentality was suggested principally by the following works: Pierre Chaunu, *La Mort à Paris, XVIe–XVIIIe siècles* (Paris, 1981); Jacques Chiffoleau, *La comptabilité de l'au delà: Les hommes, la mort et la religion dans la region d'Avignon à la fin du Moyen Age* (Rome, 1980); and Michel Vovelle, *Piété baroque et déchristianisation en Provence au XVIIIe siècle* (Paris, 1973), and (with Gaby Vovelle), *Vision de la mort et l'au-delà en Provence du XVe au XXe siècle,* (Paris, 1970).

[16] Victor Turner, *Dramas, Fields, and Metaphors: Symbolic Action in Human Society* (Ithaca NY/London, 1974), pp. 64, 96.

[17] The idea of focusing on models was suggested to me by R. C. Finucane's essay, "Sacred Corpse, Profane Carrion: Social Ideals and Death Rituals in the Later Middle Ages," in Whaley, *Mirrors of Mortality,* pp. 40–60.

claims to derive its authority. They are the ultimate confirmation of divine power on earth, the very apex of sacred ecclesiastical society. To study the myth of the "excellent" death of the saint, I thought, would be to examine the ultimate ecclesiastical paradigm. Myths, after all, derive from transitions such as death: They are "liminal" phenomena told at a time of passage.[18] In speaking of myth, I am speaking of sacred narrative, of myth as a historical construct. I am not speaking of fictions or legends (though myths can contain invented and imagined elements and can be narrated as legends) but of culturally conditioned core beliefs imbued with profound social, political, and religious significance: myth as the symbolic synthesis of a people's ethos at a specific time and place and as the conceptual foundation of their major social institutions.[19]

But even if the prototypical "good" deaths of King Philip and Saint Teresa do reveal to us the ideals of their society, what kind of correlation can one seek between the elite mythopoeic literature that idealizes them and the gritty, mundane requests left behind by dying testators in Madrid? Is this juxtaposition of paradigmatic myths and notarial records perhaps a comparison of apples and oranges? In response, I shall first allude to the medieval tradition of the *danse macabre*, or Dance of Death, that artistic genre that delighted in representing the Grim Reaper as the great leveler, snatching away the entire spectrum of unwilling social types into the great beyond. Insofar as death is the great leveler, the common fate of all human beings from kings to paupers, it offers the historian a unique opportunity. Kings and paupers may share no common experiences throughout life, but they will inexorably be drawn toward the common predicament of death. The moral axiom of the *danse macabre* – that all people are equal in the face of death – also pertains to the structure of this study. Although it is true that I have chosen two very different types of documentation and that they highlight distinct aspects of attitudes toward death, it is also true that they are concerned with the

---

[18] The concept of myth is central to the socioscientific study of religion and is interpreted in various ways. For an overview that stresses the understanding of myths as liminal phenomena see Victor Turner, "Myth and Symbol," *International Encyclopedia of the Social Sciences*, ed. D. L. Sills (New York, 1968), vol. 10, pp. 576–82.

[19] The notion that myth is "not merely a story told but a reality lived . . . not an idle tale, but a hard-worked active force" is in Bronislaw Malinowski's "Magic, Science, and Religion" (1925), in *Magic, Science, and Religion, and Other Essays* (Glencoe IL, 1948), pp. 100–1.

same phenomenon and that instead of proving to be incompatible or discordant, these various documents actually complement one another and shed light from different angles on a common problem. Shifting from the metaphor of vision to that of sound, the total effect of these disparate documentary voices is very much like a three-part harmony wherein the congruity of different tones makes for a consistent and pleasing whole that is more than the mere sum of the parts.

But figurative speech alone cannot sufficiently adduce the confluence of testaments and elite paradigms. The structure of this study is not derived from metaphor but from a certain perception of religion and its place in the shaping of mentalities. Profound affinities exist between the history of mentalities and the social-scientific study of religion, particularly the ethnographic and anthropological approaches of that discipline known as history of religions.[20] Essential to these approaches is the view that myth and ritual are irreducible categories of human experience through which ultimate values are formulated and expressed. The realm of symbol, myth, and ritual, as described by the social scientist Clifford Geertz, seems prime hunting ground for "mentalist" historians. Sacred symbols, he avers, synthesize a people's worldview – "the picture they have of the way things in sheer actuality are, their most comprehensive ideas of order." Because myth is expressed through symbol, much the same can be said of myth. Rituals, Geertz proposes, are "consecrated behavior," an enactment, a materialization, a realization of the worldview encapsulated in myth and symbol – a fusing of "the world as lived and the world as imagined."[21] Moreover, according to the anthropologist Victor Turner, ritual does more than encapsulate a worldview; it instigates social action. "Symbolic behavior," he says, "actually 'creates' society for pragmatic purposes."[22] In other words, symbol, myth, and

[20] Jacques Le Goff has observed: "Proche de l'ethnologie, l'historien des mentalités doit aussi se doubler d'un sociologue. . . . L'historien des mentalités se rencontre tout particulièrement avec la psychologie social." *Faire de l'histoire*, "Les mentalités," pt. III, p. 78.

[21] Clifford Geertz, "Religion as a Cultural System," in *Anthropological Approaches to the Study of Religion*, ed. Michael Banton (London/New York, 1966), pp. 3, 28–9. The study of ritual is not without controversy. Edmund R. Leach observed in 1968 that "the widest possible disagreement" exists among social scientists "as to how the word ritual should be used and how the performance of ritual should be understood." *International Encyclopedia of the Social Sciences*, "Ritual," vol. 13, p. 526.

[22] Turner, *Dramas, Fields, and Metaphors*, pp. 55–6.

ritual are the stuff of which mentalities are constructed. This applies as much to Christian Europeans of the sixteenth century as to the non-Christian, non-European peoples among whom anthropologists and ethnographers have developed their theories in modern times.

I have here conceived of religion much along these lines, as "a humanly constructed system of meaning, based on notions of transcendent realities, that gives ultimate value to the experiences of life through mythic and ritual forms."[23] By juxtaposing the testamentary record from Madrid with the paradigmatic "good" deaths of the king and the saint, I have aimed to include *both* myth and ritual: As the paradigms disclose the myth, the testaments unveil the ritual. This is not to say that the testaments deal exclusively with ritual and the paradigms with myth. The symbiotic interpenetration of myth and ritual is far too dynamic and complex to allow for such a reduction. Nonetheless, inasmuch as the testaments are principally concerned with death rites, they speak of ritual – and its relation to myth. Conversely, inasmuch as the paradigms speak of archetypes, they speak of myth – and its relation to ritual. By juxtaposing testaments and paradigms, then, I have neither sought to segregate myth and ritual nor attempted to trace any causal relation between the two. What I have attempted to do is to highlight the ways in which myth and ritual relate to each other in the formation of collective attitudes at various social levels.

Similarly, I have also sought to probe the relation between the "sacred" and the "profane," two other categories that are central to the study of religion and of mentalities and that were very much a part of sixteenth-century Spanish thought and piety, albeit in an inchoate manner. The sacred/profane dichotomy, though problematic, especially if understood in a metaphysical sense, is still employed as an analytic concept by many anthropologists and certainly merits use by historians.[24] As long as this dichotomy is attributed to "the structure of the

---

[23] This is the broad definition of religion favored by Benjamin C. Ray, *Myth, Ritual, and Kingship in Buganda* (New York/Oxford, 1991), p. 15.

[24] On the formulation of this dichotomy see Emile Durkheim, *The Elementary Forms of Religious Life*, trans. J. S. Swain (New York, 1912); and Mircea Eliade, *The Sacred and the Profane: The Nature of Religion*, trans. W. R. Trask (New York, 1959). For criticism see Jack Goody, "Religion and ritual: The definitional problem," *British Journal of Sociology* 12 (1961): 148–62; E. E. Evans-Pritchard, *Theories of Primitive Religion* (Oxford, 1965), pp. 64–5.

thoughts and imagery of the people under study" rather than to some ontological reality,[25] it can be used to better understand the ways in which people approach their own myths and rituals, especially in regard to death, the ultimate passage to the realm of the sacred. For if sixteenth-century Spanish attitudes toward death and the afterlife are to be understood in the context of that age, one must be willing to accept it as a given that religion at that time was *much more* than a social reality, that the world was at certain points invested with "sacredness."[26] This is not to make any metaphysical claims for the supernatural character of religion but merely to observe that believers can indeed find sacredness in the most seemingly profane things, even when they have no clearly defined categories of "sacred" and "profane." This seems especially true in the case of rites of passage such as death ritual, in which, as Victor Turner has noted, "We find not merely the sacred but the most sacred. And paradoxically this is where we also find the most human, indeed, the all-too-human."[27] The juxtaposition of testaments and paradigms in this study aims to highlight the intensity of this paradox in the early modern Spanish mentality.

Each of the three sections of this study has been devised as a discrete entity and has been partitioned into distinct books, following a classical model. This is no mimetic artifice but, rather, a deliberate strategy, a means of sharpening my focus and gaining control of a vast, amorphous subject. Since it is my contention that mentalities are ever in flux, shaped through a constant dynamic correlation of polarities – between the elites and nonelites, between the ideal and the actual, between the novel and the traditional, between the temporal and the eternal, between the sacred and the profane – I thought it best to arrange the material in a way that would allow the reader to see the distinct outlines of these discrete elements and also, in an analogous manner, to witness the ways in which they define one another. In other words, by circumscribing each set of documents to its own concerns and by letting the documen-

---

[25] Ray, *Myth, Ritual, and Kingship*, pp. 153–4.

[26] James R. Banker has observed, "Religion need not be conceived as supernatural to recognize that it is *not* just another social reality. It is grounded in recurring individual relationships but is perceived by participants as that and, more fundamentally, as beyond mundane reality." *Death in the Community: Memorialization and Confraternities in an Italian Commune in the Late Middle Ages* (Athens GA/London, 1988), p. 8.

[27] Turner, "Myth and Symbol," pp. 579–80.

tation speak with its own voice, I have aimed at isolating the various processes whereby attitudes are molded and affirmed. Though each of the books is self-contained and could be read in some order other than as here arranged, their full meaning comes from reading the whole.

On a narrative level, this is also a history of death and of early modern Spanish religion; it is a history of sainthood, of Spanish kingship, and of funeral practices in Madrid. It is not, however, an exhaustive account of Spanish attitudes toward death and the afterlife during the sixteenth century. This is but a limited foray into a vast and largely uncharted landscape; many of its features remain to be explored. To begin with, this study focuses on the "good" death and attempts to attain it; consequently, the "bad" death has been excluded, principally because it is a subject unto itself. The execution of heretics and criminals was an integral part of public life in early modern Spain, but unfortunately it was also a crucial element in the development of the Black Legend among other European nations. For centuries, nothing seemed to confirm the inherent cruelty of Spain more convincingly for its enemies than its prisons, torture chambers, and *autos-da-fé.*[28] The "bad" death in Spain, then, has as much to do with perceptions abroad as with Spanish attitudes, making it a topic that requires a different approach. Another public spectacle omitted here because of its immensity is bullfighting, that quintessential Spanish death ritual.[29] The same could be said of that other spectacle that so vividly expresses Spanish attitudes toward death, Holy Week celebrations in Andalusia, which, like bullfighting, began to assume its modern forms in the sixteenth century.[30] Death from plagues and the death of children – two constant horrifying realities for sixteenth-century Spaniards – have also been excluded here because they are subjects unto themselves. Furthermore, this study takes little account of regional differences, focusing as it does on Cas-

---

[28] One representative example is James C. Fernald, *The Spaniard in History* (New York, 1898), pp. 54–5: "By making terrible suffering an enjoyable spectacle, which no one must fail to attend, and at which no one, on peril of his life, must manifest a thrill of pity, the Inquisition trained a nation to delight in cruelty for its own sake." See William Maltby, *The Black Legend in England* (Durham, NC, 1971).

[29] See Timothy Mitchell, *Blood Sport: A Social History of Spanish Bullfighting* (Philadelphia, 1991).

[30] See also by Timothy Mitchell, *Passional Culture: Emotion, Religion and Society in Southern Spain* (Philadelphia, 1990).

tilian centers of secular and spiritual power where paradigms were established (Madrid/El Escorial and Avila/Alba); and it is chronologically limited for the most part to the latter years of the reign of Philip II.[31] Finally, one of the deepest reservoirs of attitudes remains largely untapped here: the art, literature, and theater of Golden Age Spain.[32]

The title of this book, *From Madrid to Purgatory*, is an allusion – and counterpoint – to the boast made by proud Madrileños for generations, *De Madrid al Cielo* ("From Madrid to Heaven"), which vaunts that to live and die in that city is to prepare oneself for paradise, for only heaven can rival Madrid.[33] Whereas the mentality revealed by this maxim is that of ultimate optimism, the one disclosed by the book's title is that of historical circumspection, for it is a summation of Spanish attitudes toward death and the afterlife in the sixteenth century. Purgatory loomed large and near in the mentality of early modern Spain, contrary to Ariès's expectations. Though eager for heaven, most sixteenth-century Spaniards hoped, at best, for a stint in purgatory. They also lived cheek by jowl with purgatory: It was as near to them as their own graves and those of their dearly departed and was as much a part of their reality as the churches in which they were buried and the coins with which they paid for masses. Only the souls of the holiest men and women, always few in number, could hope to enter heaven directly. For most people – elites and nonelites alike – death was not a journey from Madrid to heaven, so to speak, but from Madrid to purgatory. How they confronted that prospect is the subject of this inquiry.

[31] Throughout this study I refer to these very Castilian foci as "Spanish" not because they encapsulate the ethos of an entire people but because they are a specific part of a multifarious whole known to itself and the outside world as "Spain."

[32] No study has yet focused exclusively on the sixteenth century or on the Golden Age as a whole. On literature see José Vives Suria, *El tema de la vida y la muerte a través de algunos de nuestros principales literatos* (Folletones de Mision, s. d., s. l.); Juan Ayuso Rivera, *El concepto de la muerte en la poesía romantica española* (Madrid, 1959); Eduardo Camacho Guizado, *La elegía funeral en la poesía española* (Madrid, 1969); Maria del Rosario Fernandez Alonso, *Una visión de la muerte en la lírica española: La muerte como amada* (Madrid, 1971). On art see Manuel Sanchez Camargo, *La muerte y la pintura española* (Madrid, 1954); Juan José Martín Gonzalez, "En torno al tema de la muerte en el arte español," *Boletín el Seminario de Estudios de Arte y Arqueología* 38 (1972): 267–85; and Jonathan Brown, "Hieroglyphs of Death and Salvation," in *Images and Ideas in Seventeenth Century Spanish Painting* (Princeton, 1978).

[33] See Antonio Casero, *De Madrid al Cielo* (Madrid, 1968).

BOOK ONE

Eager for heaven

Death and the testamentary discourse in Madrid, 1520–99

I feel I am dying very quickly, sirs: leave all joking aside, and bring me a priest to hear my confession and a notary to write my testament; for at a grave moment such as this no man should jest with his soul; and, so, I beg you, that as soon as the priest is done with my confession, you bring the notary.

– Don Quixote on his deathbed[1]

[1] Miguel de Cervantes Saavedra, *El ingenioso hidalgo don Quijote de la Mancha* (1615), Bk. II, chap. 74. Modern edition by Alberto Sanchez (Barcelona: Noguer, 1975), p. 1035. This edition is used for all subsequent citations.

~~~~~~

Wills and the history of death
in Madrid

Legal documents for this world and the next

At death's door in the world of Cervantes, a notary could be as indispensable as a priest and a testament as crucial as a confession. In the heat of August 1589, a Spanish nobleman clearly explained in his will, through a notary's pen, the nature and purpose of such a document:

I, Don Martin Cortés, Marquis of the Valley of Guaxaca, residing in this city of Madrid, beset by infirmities and lacking in health, but unaffected in my intellect, fearing that since death is a certainty but its hour an uncertainty, I might be taken while I am unprepared in those things that are necessary for salvation, and wishing to make perfectly clear to my wife and children how they are to inherit my belongings, so that there will be no discord or quarreling among them, do hereby order and execute this my last will and testament in the following manner: . . .[2]

Two distinct yet inseparable functions of the will are mentioned here by the marquis. These two objectives are listed in order of importance:

[2] AHPM 1398.493. Published in Antonio Matilla Tascón, *Testamentos de 43 personajes del Madrid de los Austrias* (Madrid, 1983), p. 83. This description of the purpose of the will is by no means unique. Many other Madrid testators felt compelled to include this kind of explanation, albeit in less detail, as did one married couple in their joint will of 1594: "Deseando disponer de los bienes que su divina majestad nos tiene prestados, por su bondad y clemencia infinita, para evitar diferencias y pleitos que por ellos podria aber, y resultar, moriendo ab intestate, y deseando poner nuestras animas en carrera de salvacion, habemos y ordenamos este testamento" (AHPM 620.226).

First, the will serves as a salvific instrument, as one of "those things that are necessary for salvation"; second, it controls the distribution of his estate and lessens the possibility of "discord and quarreling" among his survivors. This particular ordering of the two functions is customary and quite deliberate. In fact, it refers specifically to the two separate sections into which every will was divided: first, the so-called pious clauses, which dealt with the spiritual estate of the deceased; second, the distributive clauses, which apportioned the material belongings.

In this preamble, the marquis tells us much about the way in which the function of wills was perceived in Madrid and most of Western Europe during the sixteenth century. In Roman antiquity, as in our own day, the will was simply a private legal document that sought to regulate the transmission of property from the dead to the living. It is no accident that this practical function, which would seem to be the primary reason for writing such a document, is ranked second in importance by the marquis. When the written will reappeared as a common practice in the twelfth century, as a Christianized version of an ancient Roman procedure that had not been totally forgotten but had generally fallen into disuse for half a millennium, its primary function was no longer strictly the regulation of property.[3]

In the late medieval and early modern period, when the sacred was yet inextricably joined to the profane, wills could be imbued with a transcendent religious purpose. The Roman Catholic Church required a will from each of its members, from the richest to the poorest – at least in principle if not in actual practice. In Spain, as in most of Western Europe, those who died without wills faced special difficulties. Hence the urgency of Don Quixote's request for a priest *and* a notary: Dying without a testament would be as risky as dying without confession and the last rites. Consider, for instance, the rule laid down by the Synod of Zaragoza in 1357 forbidding the burial of anyone who died without a will, *ab intestato*. The only way such a person could obtain a proper Christian burial in consecrated ground was for his natural heirs to con-

---

[3] For a more detailed history of the rebirth of wills in twelfth-century Europe, consult Chiffoleau, *Comptabilité*, pp. 35 ff. For a brief summary of the history of wills see Marion Reder Gadow, *Morir en Málaga: Testamentos Malagueños del siglo xviii* (Málaga, 1986), pp. 5–13. An outdated but somewhat useful history of wills in Spain, supplemented by an ample bibliography, can be found in *Enciclopedia Universal Ilustrada Europeo-Americana* (Madrid, 1928), vol. 61, pp. 101–50.

tribute part of the inheritance to the church for the establishment of pious bequests on his behalf "according to the quality and quantity of his belongings."[4]

The significance that this decree placed on the writing of a will was immense. By denying burial to anyone who died *ab intestato,* the church was making it clear that without a will there could be no salvation. The denial of a proper Christian burial was normally reserved for excommunicates, heretics, and hardened criminals. To rank an intestate Christian alongside with the most obviously damned was to place a nearly sacramental value on the will, or at least on that part of it that made provisions for certain postmortem devotions.[5]

Yet, wills could not be demanded of *all* Christians. Naturally, wills were of greater concern for those who had some property to redistribute; those of lesser means, who in our period were a substantial part of the population, normally dispensed with such formalities. Estimates from Spanish cities where the total number of deaths can be compared to the total number of testaments show that in the early modern period only about one-quarter to one-half of the population wrote wills; the figures are lower for rural areas.[6] Since burial could not thus be denied outright to all who died intestate, it was denied conditionally until certain obligations had been met. Those who lacked property could make a formal declaration of poverty as a substitute for a will and provide for a few alms and pious bequests. What really mattered was not so much the will itself, then, but something it was supposed to contain: the ordering of alms and

---

[4] Federico Rafael Aznar Gil, *Concilios provinciales y sinodos de Zaragoza de 1215 a 1563* (Zaragoza, 1982), p. 155, also points out that this decree was no local idiosyncrasy but very much in keeping with similar statutes enforced in other Spanish dioceses.

[5] Along with intestates, the Council of Madrid in 1473 forbade church burials to all thieves and those who died in duels and also ordered that the corpses of known thieves already buried in consecrated ground be unceremoniously exhumed and discarded (Tejada, 5, pp. 25–6). For more on this subject, see A. Orlandis, "Sobre la elección de sepultura en la España medieval," *Anuario de Historia del Derecho Español* (1950), pp. 5–49; and A. Bernard, *La sepulture en droit canonique du Décret de Gratien au Concile de Trente* (Paris, 1933).

[6] The estimate on Oviedo and Gijón at the turn of the sixteenth and seventeenth centuries ranges between 25 and 48 percent. Roberto J. Lopez Lopez, *Comportamientos religiosos en Asturias durante el Antiguo Régimen* (Gijón, 1989), pp. 38 and 41, claims that these figures are similar to those found throughout the Iberian peninsula and cites studies of localities in Catalonia, Galicia, Andalusia, and León.

pious bequests. Once these were arranged for by surviving relatives, burial was possible. In Madrid, almost all declarations of poverty contained some minimal provisions for pious bequests. We also know that the parish clergy who buried these poor people in Madrid as acts of charity would often sell their meager belongings and use the proceeds for masses.[7] The primary function of the will, therefore, from a theological and pastoral perspective, was to provide the faithful with the opportunity to request suffrages for their passage to the hereafter. As far as the church was concerned, no one could harbor hopes for a Christian burial – or for salvation – without at least a requiem mass and alms for the ecclesiastical coffers.

This is made evident by other decrees of the Synod of Zaragoza (1357). One stipulated that even those who had written a will and arranged for their pious bequests could not be buried until the funds needed to carry out these bequests had been turned over to the curate. Another ordered the heirs to inform the corresponding ecclesiastical authorities about all the clauses that referred to the church or to pious bequests. In addition, all pastors were required to keep a very careful record of their parishioners' wills.[8]

Undoubtedly, what made the writing of a will so important in the eyes of the church and invested it with a quasi-sacramental quality was its function in the arrangement of those liturgical rites that helped ensure salvation. But there was much more to writing a will than the listing of pious bequests. Other factors also contributed to the way in which the testamentary act came to be endowed with salvific qualities. The writing of a will was considered a penitential act and a rehearsal for death, an exercise that could help the faithful accept death and detach themselves from the things of this world. Expert advice had it that it was much better to write a will while in good health rather than at the final moment, for to let go of one's possessions and to contribute to charity

[7] M. F. Carbajo Isla, *La población de la villa de Madrid desde finales del siglo XVI hasta mediados del siglo XIX* (Madrid, 1987), pp. 12–14; *Madrid en el Archivo Histórico de Protocolos*, ed. Ana Duplá del Moral (Madrid, 1990), pp. 151–2.

[8] Aznar Gil, *Concilios provinciales*, pp. 114, 155. Philippe Ariès, drawing primarily upon his acquaintance with French funerary practices, claims that throughout medieval Europe wills were drafted and preserved by the curate as well as the notary and that it was not until the sixteenth century that they became the exclusive responsibility of the notary. *The Hour of Our Death* (New York, 1981), p. 189.

without the threat of imminent death was an act that could lessen one's time in purgatory. Expert advice also had it that a constant periodic reading of one's own testament was a highly meritorious form of devotion, not only as a preparation for death but also as a means of enhancing the efficacy of the will's pious bequests, for if one renewed one's assent to the will over and over again, it could increase one's charitable disposition. A full charitable assent to one's will counted much more in the afterlife than a troubled or grudging acceptance. These periodic reviews were considered even more meritorious if done in a state of grace, immediately after confession, without the stain of mortal sin.[9] Moreover, because the will was ostensibly the final public statement of every person, it assumed a confessional quality. At the end of one's life, even after one had departed from this world, when others read the will – or, more likely, had it read to them – one could confess one's faith, acknowledge one's sins, and attempt to redeem them by making certain statements and arranging for certain liturgies and public gestures. The church reciprocated all this by granting forgiveness to the sinner and allowing for a burial in consecrated ground.

The writing of a will thus came to be viewed as a spiritual exercise that was not only a sober meditation on death but also on the whole of one's life and on one's hopes for the hereafter. As the stock phrase repeated by many testators put it, writing a will was a way of placing one's soul on the road to salvation – *en carrera de salvación*. At century's end Luis de Rebolledo warned that "writing a testament is called putting one's soul in order; wretched is the soul that is not well ordered at that hour."[10] This is why the pious clauses in the first part of every will occur in a nearly unchanging, almost ritualistic order, and why Ariès was probably correct in suggesting that the religious portion of the will must have developed as part of a long oral tradition before it became fixed in written form.[11]

The religious function of the testament can perhaps be more fully

---

[9] Alexo Venegas, *Agonía del tránsito de la muerte. Con avisos y consuelos que cerca della son provechosos* (1536). I have used the 1565 Alcalá edition, reprinted in *Escritores Místicos Españoles*, ed. Miguel Mir, vol. I, which is vol. XVI of the *Nueva Biblioteca de Autores Españoles* (Madrid, 1911), pp. 129–33.

[10] Luis de Rebolledo, *Primera parte de cien oraciones fúnebres en que se considera la vida, y sus miserias: la muerte y sus provechos* (Madrid, 1600), fol 318v.

[11] Ariès, *Hour*, p. 189.

appreciated when one considers its place in the death ritual itself, for the majority of wills were written by ailing people from their deathbeds and the remainder by people who were prudently contemplating their own demise. If one understands how most wills were written – or at least how it was thought that they should be ideally drafted – and how most people were advised to confront that awful moment, one may more easily comprehend their transcendent significance for many dying Madrileños of the sixteenth century.

The art of dying in early modern Spain

When a notary came to prepare someone's testament at the bedside anywhere in sixteenth-century Spain, he would be drawn into an intimate ritual, both as participant and spectator, for most people died at home then, in their own beds, and had their bodies prepared for burial by their relatives. Moreover, the process of dying was itself marked by many conventions and expectations to which the writing of the will was inextricably linked. To try to understand the mentality of these documents, one must first contemplate the death ritual itself, or at least some idealized portrayal of it.

In the sixteenth century it was taken for granted by most Catholics that one should prepare for death throughout one's life, so that when the inevitable moment arrived, one would know how to act. Crossing over into the afterlife, to a timeless state in which one faced existence in purgatory, hell, or heaven, was far too important a moment to approach unprepared. This was the assumption made by the genre of *Ars Morienai* literature. After all, to promote the act of dying as an "art" in which one should become skilled was to assume that, as in any other art, success would be impossible without the proper training.

Ars Moriendi texts were a genre of practical, devotional literature aimed at the laity that first appeared in the early fifteenth century. Though often mentioned in the same breath with the *danse macabre* and other aspects of late medieval interest in funereal realism, the *Ars Moriendi* did not share in the grotesque spirit of dancing skeletons and rotting corpses. The tenor of most of these texts was one of comfort: The *moriens*, or dying person, was seen as a Christian who needed to be prepared for the experience beyond the grave by the assurances of a loving God. On the whole, this literature emphasized the doctrines of grace and forgiveness over those of punishment and damnation but insisted that these benefits could be gained only through deliberate effort and preparation.[12]

These were detailed instruction booklets. The more traditional texts were divided into six sections: (1) a collection of questions on death from Christian authorities; (2) advice to the dying person on ways of resisting the five sins of faithlessness, despair, impatience, pride, and worldliness; (3) catechetical questions that had to be answered correctly in order to gain salvation; (4) prayers and rules to assist in the imitation of the dying Christ; (5) advice to those who were present around the deathbed; (6) prayers to be said by those who were present at the moment of death.[13]

The basic structure and content of these texts remained largely unchanged until the sixteenth century, when the forces of humanism and the Catholic Reformation gave rise to some innovations. The key assumption of the earlier literature had been that one's eternal fate was decided at the moment of death: As the Latin adage put it, *Salus hominis in fine consistit.* The purpose of the manual was to allow the dying to escape hell, or even purgatory, by helping them to repent as deeply and thoroughly as possible. Although retaining the central assumption of *salus hominis in fine consistit,* the Renaissance added an extra dimension: The art of dying should not only open the gates of heaven at the moment of death but also show one how to live a good Christian life. The *Ars Moriendi,* then, was transformed into an art of living, or *Ars Vivendi,* and became a manual to be read not just at the moment of death but throughout the course of one's life. This theme assumed great importance in Erasmus of Rotterdam's *De praeparatione ad mortem* (1534) and in a popular book written by a Spanish Erasmian from Toledo, Alejo de Venegas, *The Agony of Crossing Over at Death* (1537): "Let him who still

---

[12] For an overview of this genre of literature, see my article, "Ars Moriendi," in the *Westminster Dictionary of Christian Spirituality* (London/Philadelphia, 1984), pp. 21–2. For more detailed information consult the following: Roger Chartier, "Les Arts de Mourir, 1450–1600," *Annales, E.S.C.,* 31: 51–76 (1976); Sister M. C. O'Connor, *The Art of Dying Well: The Development of the Ars Moriendi* (New York, 1942); N. L. Beaty, *The Craft of Dying: A Study in the Literary Tradition of the* Ars Moriendi *in England* (New Haven, 1970); and A. Tenenti, *Il Senso della morte e l'amore della vita nel Rinascimento (Francia e Italia)* (Turin, 1957).

[13] M. C. O'Connor, *Art of Dying,* p. 157.

25

has time today take advantage of the present moment, and not wait until tomorrow," he advised. "The greatest folly any man could commit, we must therefore conclude, is to live in a state in which he does not want to die; and the remedy for such madness is none other than a good, constant preparation for death."[14]

By the late sixteenth century, Counter-Reformation writers were producing a type of *Ars Moriendi* that combined the Renaissance focus on the *Ars Vivendi* with a Tridentine reinterpretation of the traditional motifs of the art of dying. Using the old themes and dramatic forms (and liberally citing classical authors alongside the Church Fathers), these newer treatises placed greater emphasis on the freedom of the will, the power of the sacraments, and the intercessory role of the church and the saints.[15]

Although books on the art of dying had never been as popular in Spain throughout the fifteenth and early sixteenth century as they had been elsewhere in Western Europe,[16] Spanish interest in this type of literature slowly began to increase in the late 1530s and built up considerable momentum after midcentury. The renowned Erasmus was the first to appear in print in 1535, with two speedy Castilian translations of his *De pareparatione ad mortem*, which he had sent to Cristobal Mexia of Seville less than a month after its publication in Basel.[17] Though this quickly became an immensely popular book throughout Europe (twenty Latin editions 1534–40, plus translations into French, German, Dutch, and English), it did not fare as well in Spain, for it appeared at a time when anti-Erasmianism was in full swing.[18] Of the two translations, the one published at Burgos seems to have enjoyed a wider circulation, but

---

[14] Venegas, *Agonía*, pp. 125, 127. Venegas chose a most appropriate title for his work. The Spanish word *agonía* can refer specifically to the throes of death but in a general way also express a deep, unfulfilled yearning.

[15] For a more detailed bibliography on this subject, consult my article, "Ars Moriendi," p. 22.

[16] Roger Chartier, "Les Arts de Mourir," *Annales* 31: 51–76 (1976).

[17] Erasmus, *De pareparatione ad mortem* (Basel, 1534); *Libro del aparejo que se deve hazer para bien morir* (Burgos, 1535); *Aparejo de bien morir* (Valencia, 1535). The Latin text can be found in *Opera Omnia Desiderii Erasmi Roterodami* (Amsterdam/Oxford, 1969), Ordinis V, vol. I, pp. 321–92.

[18] On the persecution of the Spanish Erasmians, see Marcel Bataillon, *Erasme et l'Espagne* (Paris, 1937), 3rd ed. 3 vols. (Geneva, 1991), vol. 1, pp. 467–532.

this stemmed from the fact that it was a sanitized version that left out much of the original text. The reception of Erasmus's treatise might be more accurately judged from the fate of the unexpurgated translation published in Valencia, which was totally obliterated after being listed in the 1559 *Index of Forbidden Books*.[19]

Yet, some of Erasmus's influence survived in Spain. As mentioned, he had a follower in Alejo Venegas, author of *The Agony of Crossing Over*. Venegas embraced his Christocentrism and also emphasized the *Ars Moriendi/Ars Vivendi* dialectic but without Erasmus's disdain for external forms of piety.[20] Overall, the tone of the two works is quite different. In fact, publication of *The Agony* signaled quite clearly the rejection of Erasmian piety. Whereas Erasmus had declared that true charity and faith in Christ were more important than Catholic death rituals – going as far as to say that the sacramental last rites were no guarantee against the flames of hell – Venegas emphasized the traditional significance of these rituals with a reverent vengeance.[21] Venegas's *The Agony* went through ten editions before losing popularity in the latter part of the century when other treatises apparently took its place.[22]

Venegas had tapped a deep well: Interest in treatises on death and the art of dying grew steadily in the second half of the sixteenth century. In 1555 Pedro de Medina, the well-known author of a manual of navigation, further popularized Venegas by borrowing heavily from him for his *Book of Truth*. Though not a manual on dying *per se*, Medina's work contained a lengthy discussion of death and the afterlife and attracted a

---

[19] Bataillon, *Erasme et l'Espagne*, vol. I, p. 604. See also the bibliography, vol. II, p. 406, where Bataillon lists some later editions of the expurgated translation of Erasmus (Seville, 1551; Antwerp, 1549 and 1555).

[20] See vol. I. Adeva Martín, *El maestro Alejo Venegas de Busto, su vida y sus obras* (Toledo, 1987). See also "Los Artes de Bien Morir en España antes del Maestro Venegas," *Scripta Teologica* (1984); 405–16, where Adeva Martín summarizes how Venegas's *Agonía* differs from that of Erasmus. See also Bataillon, *Erasme et l'Espagne*, vol. I, pp. 608–613.

[21] "Equidem arbitror multos nec absolutos a sacerdote, nec percepta eucharistia, nec unctos, nec ecclesiastico ritu sepultos demigrare in requiem, quum alii ceremoniis omnibus solemniter peractis atque etiam in templo iuxta summum altare sepulti, rapiantur ad inferos." Erasmus, *Opera Omnia*, vol. I, p. 377.

[22] Martín, *Alejo Venegas*, p. 186, indicates that after 1583 there were no further editions of the *Agony* for another hundred years.

large reading public.[23] Another treatise that was not as complete a manual as *The Agony* but overtook it in popularity was Alonso de Orozco's *Victory of Death*.[24] Orozco's work proved to be influential not only for its own merits but also because of its author's reputation. An ascetic Augustinian who had refused several bishoprics, including the primal see of Toledo, Orozco had earned a reputation as a living saint and had become a chaplain to King Philip II, who revered him and credited him with having cured some members of his household.[25] Less well-known authors also fed the growing appetite for this sort of literature: Jaime Montañes, Hector Pintor, and Juan Raulin.[26]

The founder of the Jesuits, Ignatius Loyola, was among the first to emphasize innovative kinds of meditations on death and the afterlife in his *Spiritual Exercises* (1548). Before long other Jesuits followed – many of them Spanish – and with such vigor that by the seventeenth century they came to dominate the genre, producing a veritable flood of *Ars Moriendi* texts.[27] At the end of the sixteenth century in Spain, however, the Jesuits were not yet at the forefront of the art of dying. One of their company, Juan Polanco, had written a manual to be used by priests, *Rule*

---

[23] Pedro de Medina, *Libro de la Verdad* (Valladolid, 1555), went through thirteen editions, 1563–1626. Modern edition by Angel Gonzalez Palencia, *Obras de Pedro de Medina, Clasicos Españoles*, vol. I (Madrid, 1944). Medina's other works were *El Arte de navegar* (1545), which was translated into every major European language, and *El Libro de grandezas y cosas memorables de España* (1548).

[24] Alonso de Orozco, *Victoria de la Muerte* (Burgos, 1583). Modern editions by Gil Blas (Madrid, 1921 and 1975).

[25] Orozco was known as "el santo" at court. He was beatified in 1881. See Tomás Camara y Castro, *Vida y escritos del Beato Alonso de Orozco* (Valladolid, 1882). Trans. W. A. Jones (Philadelphia, 1895).

[26] Hector Pintor, *Imagen de la vida Cristiana, ordenada por dialogos* (Madrid, 1573), which contained an entire dialogue on the "memoria de la muerte"; Jaime Montañés, *Libro intitulado espejo de buen vivir. Con otro tratado para ayudar a buen morir, en el incierto dia y hora de la muerte* (Madrid, 1573); Juan Raulin, *Libro de la muerte temporal y eterna* (Madrid, 1596), translated from the Latin.

[27] Numbers of *Ars Moriendi* titles written by Jesuits: 1540–1620: 20; 1621–1700: 139; 1701–1800: 101. See listings in A. De Backer and C. Sommervogel, *Bibliographie de la compagnie de Jesus*, 12 vols. (Brussels, 1890–1960), vol. X, cols. 510–19. Also O'Connor, *Art of Dying*, and Tenenti, *Il senso della morte*, pp. 80 ff. For a thorough statistical analysis of the impact of this literature in France, consult D. Roche, "La Mémoire de la Mort. Recherche sur la place des arts de mourir dans la Librairie et la lecture en France aux xvii et xviii siècles," *Annales, E.S.C.* 31 (1976): 76–119.

and Order for Helping Those Who Are Departing from This Life to Die Well (1578), in Latin and in Castilian Spanish, which, though not aimed at the laity, was at least accessible to them in the vernacular.[28]

But what, exactly, did these treatises have to say about dying well? The step-by-step instructions were clear and detailed, the advice easy to comprehend. Because dying was considered to be a social process, the advice was aimed not just at the dying person but at family and neighbors as well. Piecing together the advice given in this literature and information gathered from other sources, the following picture emerges about the process of dying well in sixteenth-century Spain.

Once someone's illness or injury was determined to be serious enough to threaten death, a notary and a priest would be sent for, a will would be drawn up, and preparations for the death watch would begin. But this was no passive vigil. Helping one's relatives and neighbors to die well was considered a serious obligation, for the temptations that the dying person faced were considered to be the most awful and terrifying of all, and it was generally believed that one could aid the dying to resist them. To assist the dying, in fact, was considered a highly meritorious act of charity: It was better than offering suffrages for those who were already dead.[29] Friends and relatives would arrive. Some would begin to assist the dying person in the recitation of prayers; others would read devotional literature, possibly from an *Ars Moriendi* book. Confraternities might be summoned to pray for the soul of the *moriens*, or dying person. If he or she belonged to a confraternity, their fellow members were obliged to come and remain throughout the ordeal; if not, the confraternity could be paid to come. Their procession and arrival were often underscored in the streets with the tolling of bells and the chanting of hymns.[30] The priest, too, would often make a ceremonial approach and entrance, carrying the consecrated host through the streets, as in a small-scale Corpus Christi procession, causing bystanders to drop to their knees and sometimes even drawing out people from the churches. The priest administered to the dying three indispensable sacraments

---

[28] Juan Polanco, S. J., *Methodus ad eos adiuvandos, qui moriuntur* (Burgos, 1578); *Regla y orden para ayudar a bien morir a los que se parten de esta vida* (Zaragoza, 1578).

[29] Venegas, *Agonía*, p. 137, argued that the souls in purgatory were already saved but that every dying person faced the possibility of eternal damnation.

[30] Francisco J. Lorenzo Pinar, *Actitudes religiosas ante la muerte en Zamora en el siglo xvi: Un estudio de mentalidades* (Zamora, 1989), p. 28.

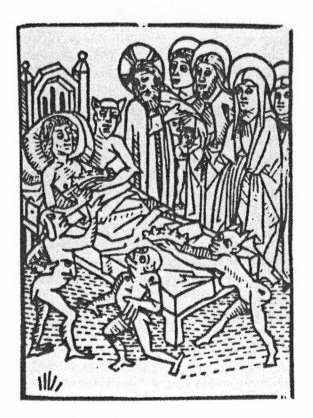

Deathbed Temptation. From *Arte de Bien Morir* (Zaragoza, 1484). Reproduced in *Estampas: Cinco siglos de imagen impresa* (Madrid: Minesterio de Cultura, 1982), plate 146.

This *Ars Moriendi* illustration depicts the dying man being tempted by demons. The crowns being offered to him represent the sin of vainglory. Christ and the saints offer him assistance, forming a phalanx against the tempters from hell. In this instance, the powers of heaven have enabled the *moriens* to resist, for Christ shelters the man's soul (depicted as a small naked figure) within his robes.

known as the last rites and served other functions as well.[31] First, he heard their final confession and granted them absolution, allowing them to face death with a clean soul: This was supposed to be the most

---

[31] Evidence from Cuenca's parish registers indicates that reception of the last rites was nearly universal and that the few exceptions were always carefully explained by the clergy. Sara T. Nalle, *God in La Mancha* (Baltimore, 1992), p. 182. The same

thorough and most contrite confession of one's whole life. For many people it was not only their last confession but the first one they had made in years, and it could take a considerable amount of time to do it well. Next, the priest gave them communion, their last one on earth, known as the *viaticum*, literally the "take-it-with-you," which fortified them for the final death struggle and helped ensure a safe passage into the hereafter. Many apparently believed that the bringing of the *viaticum* to the dying was more important and meritorious than the celebration of the mass itself.[32] Foreign visitors to Spain were often surprised by the devotion shown to the *viaticum* in the streets, which seemed unusually intense to some of them.[33] This fervor extended to the royal family: Emperor Charles V and King Philip II routinely humbled themselves in the presence of these eucharistic processions, even to the point of kneeling in muddy puddles.[34] Popular belief in the holiness supposedly needed to receive the *viaticum* apparently ran deep, for condemned prisoners in Spain were routinely denied this sacrament before being executed, even if they had confessed. Reform after Trent was slow. St. John of Avila complained in his advice to the 1566 Council of Toledo, "It is truly reprehensible that, at the time of greatest need, a Christian should be denied his strongest remedy." Only after Pope Pius V's nuncio in Spain instructed King Philip II to discontinue this abuse did it gradually begin to disappear in the latter part of the sixteenth century.[35] Finally, at the very last possible moment, just before death but while the

evidence has been gleaned from Madrid's few surviving parish records: M. F. Carbajo Isla, *La población de la villa de Madrid*, p. 11, n. 30.

[32] José Luis Gonzalez Novalín, "Religiosidad y Reforma del Pueblo Cristiano," in *Historia de la Iglesia en España*, ed. Ricardo García-Villoslada (Madrid, 1980), vol. III.1, p. 361. This form of popular devotion gradually diminished after the reforms of the Council of Trent were implemented in Spain.

[33] José Garcia Mercadal, *Viajes de extranjeros por España y Portugal*, 3 vols. (Madrid, 1952–62), vol. I, p. 469. In 1501 the Burgundian Antoine de Lalaing was surprised by the crowds that followed the viaticum and by the way in which even kings and nobles would dismount and kneel before it.

[34] Juan de Salazar, *Politica Española* (1619), p. 70; Jerónimo de Sepulveda, *Documentos para la historia del monasterio de San Lorenzo del Escorial* (Madrid, 1924, 1964–65), vol. 4, p. 183; Javier Varela, *La muerte del rey: El ceremonial funebre de la monarquía Española, 1500–1885* (Madrid, 1990), p. 75.

[35] Juan de Avila, *Obras*, 6.303; Garcia-Villoslada, "Religiosidad," *Historia de la Iglesia en España*, III.1, pp. 359–61.

dying remained conscious, the priest administered the sacrament of extreme unction, reciting prescribed prayers and anointing the five senses of the dying with sacred oil as these began to fade away in the final stages of the separation of soul and body. This last sacrament, which was believed to guarantee entrance at least to purgatory, was approached with some trepidation, for it was also widely believed that those who recovered after receiving it had to lead a semimonastic existence for the remainder of their lives and, among other things, abstain from sex and refrain from walking barefoot.[36] Priests were supposed to remain with the *moriens* until death arrived or at least to visit them frequently if they lingered for days.[37] Under ideal circumstances, priests would also have read from the Bible to the dying, particularly from the penitential psalms and from the passion narratives in the gospels, and would have continually encouraged them to resist temptation and to have confidence in the saving power of Christ's sacrificial death and resurrection. In addition, they would have led the *moriens* and those assembled at bedside in the recitation of intercessory prayers addressed to the Virgin Mary, Michael the Archangel, and local and personal patron saints.[38]

Popular and official belief in the presence of demons at the deathbed was apparently quite strong, and helped shape much of the death ritual. As the body of the *moriens* deteriorated and its five senses began to fail, it was believed, the soul now could catch glimpses of the spirit world. Because the soul was now nearly out of the body, literally at the door to the hereafter, but the *moriens*'s reason remained unimpaired, the devil would make one final terrifying assault and turn the final hours of life into a pitched battle.[39] This contest, or *agonía* (a term derived from the Greek word for struggle, *agon*), was described in graphic detail in the devotional literature of the day, not only in regard to the appearance of

[36] Gonzalez-Novalín, "Religiosidad," *Historia de la Iglesia en España*, III.1, p. 359. Popular belief also dictated that the priest anoint the kidneys of the dying person, p. 361.
[37] This duty was especially emphasized in the Tridentine reform, as reflected in the Synod of Santiago, 1565 (Tejeda 5, p. 345) and the Synodal Constitutions of Zaragoza, 1589.
[38] Venegas, *Agonía*, pp. 139–40.
[39] Pedro de Medina, *Libro de la Verdad* (1555), in *Obras de Pedro de Medina*, ed. Angel Gonzalez Palencia, *Clasicos Españoles*, vol. I (Madrid, 1944), p. 453, said of the *agonía*: "Es la mayor batalla y contienda, dolor y tristeza que nunca el hombre jamás a tenido."

the demons but also in regard to specific areas of temptation. The typology of these temptations varied little in *Ars Moriendi* handbooks. Venegas numbered the chief temptations at seven: desire for a longer life, impatience with suffering, attachment to one's family, attachment to riches and honors, false confidence in one's merits, fear of hell and punishment, and denial of one's faith.[40] Medina numbered them at nine, but his list was nearly identical.[41] According to one spiritual writer, these temptations were so powerful, especially the temptation to be angry with God for one's death, that it was better to lose consciousness immediately after receiving extreme unction.[42]

Prayer was the most immediate recourse against this onslaught. This is where the assistance of the priest, of the confraternities, and of one's relatives and neighbors was crucial: It was their responsibility to recite the prescribed prayers and to encourage the *moriens* to resist the devil's temptations. Reciting the creed over and over, and invoking the power of "the sacrosanct union of the Holy Mother Catholic Church militant" was recommended as one of the most efficient means of driving off the devils who hovered around the deathbed "like bees around a hive."[43] Acts of charity were another recourse: Poor adults and children were invited to the bedside, given alms by the dying person, and asked to remain there, praying for him or her, until the struggle ended in death. These final charitable gestures might even affect the testament itself and further engage the notary in adding alms and pious bequests not previously ordered, either in a codicil or hastily inserted, out of place, at the very end of the will.[44]

At the moment of death, which was believed to be the instant when the soul was decisively sundered from the body, the soul of the *moriens*

---

[40] Venegas, *Agonía*, pp. 169–70.

[41] Medina, *Libro de la Verdad*, pp. 455–60: (1) desire for a long life; (2) impatience; (3) attachment to honor and riches; (4) attachment to loved ones; (5) despair over one's sins; (6) vainglory; (7) unfaithfulness and superstition; (8) self-love; (9) obstinacy in sin.

[42] Alonso de Orozco, *Victoria de la Muerte* (1583). Modern edition (Madrid, 1921), p. 138. Orozco knew of an Augustinian monk who prayed to God for such a loss of consciousness and was granted his wish, "porque no usando de razón, no le afligiría el demonio con escrupulos," p. 112.

[43] Venegas, *Agonía*, p. 140.

[44] Ibid., pp. 140, 170–2. A good number of the Madrid wills used in this study contain such last-minute pious bequests and alms.

was taken by his or her guardian angel to the hereafter. For baptized Christians there were three possibilities: two eternal and one temporary. The eternal abodes of the blessed and damned were heaven and hell. Immediate entrance into heaven was restricted to the exceptionally pure, holy, and virtuous (believed to be a very small number of the faithful at death). Hell was for those who died with the stain of mortal sin on their souls (a very real possibility for most people). The temporary place was purgatory, a place of cleansing for those who had availed themselves of the last rites but who still needed to be purified before being admitted into heaven (the most likely possibility for all). A fourth place was limbo, which was reserved for the souls of those infants and children who had died unbaptized.[45]

In the midst of all of this, one could say near the very center, stood the writing of the will, for it was a document that not only helped one prepare for the struggle of death but also could ostensibly ensure that one's stay in purgatory would be substantially shortened. It was a passport to the afterlife, drawn up by a notary as the dying person stood on the rim of eternity, poised between heaven and hell. It was filled with instructions for the *moriens's* executors and heirs and was dutifully filed away for safekeeping. The surviving documents give us, centuries later, the privilege of peering into the hearts and minds of those who knew they were about to die.

The nature and function of the will

Written wills are usually divided into two categories: (1) *holographic* wills, which are written by the testator's own hand, and (2) *nuncupative* wills, which are written by a notary in the presence of witnesses. The vast majority of surviving wills are of this latter sort, which means that the notary in early modern Spain played a key, intimate role in the process of dying.

By the sixteenth century, the notarial profession had been clearly defined in Spain and was closely regulated by royal decrees. Notaries (*escribanos*) served various functions and were divided into different cat-

---

[45] Medina, *Libro de la Verdad*, p. 464. None of this literature made mention of the fact that, unlike the case of purgatory, the church's teaching on limbo had not been doctrinally confirmed by any church council.

egories. The most significant types were the following: (1) *escribanos reales*, who produced and managed the mountains of paperwork required in the governing of Spain's vast empire; (2) *escribanos de provincia o del crimen*, who worked for municipal governments and courts; (3) *escribanos eclesiásticos y apostólicos*, who concerned themselves with church documents; and (4) *escribanos de número*, who were so called because there were only a fixed number of such posts allowed by law and who oversaw the writing of private contracts. It was these *escribanos de número* who prepared testaments in the cities and towns of Spain; in the countryside and in remote villages priests often served this function.[46]

The formulaic composition of notarial documents, including wills, was as closely regulated as the notarial profession itself, and it was the notaries' responsibility to ensure that their paperwork met the prescribed guidelines. Although many notaries learned their craft by serving apprenticeships, as *escribientes* or *papelistas*, some purchased their offices without any prior experience. But it was never too difficult, even for the greenest novice, to find expert guidance in printed manuals that contained examples of testaments and other documents, such as F. Diaz de Toledo's *Las notas del Relator* (Valladolid, 1493); H. Diaz de Valdepeña's *Summa de notas copiosas* (Toledo, 1543); and Lorenzo de Niebla's *Suma del estilo de escribanos* (Seville, 1565), among others.[47] These Spanish guidelines conformed, for the most part, to models established in the later Middle Ages throughout Catholic Europe.[48]

Those relatively few testators who drew up their wills while still healthy usually came to do so at the notary's residence; those many who waited until death seemed imminent, in contrast, had the notary come to

---

[46] On the history of the notarial office in Spain, see J. Bono y Huerta, "Los formularios notariales españoles de los siglos xvi, xvii, y xviii," *Anales de la Academia Matritense del Notariado*, 22.1 (1978); and the introduction by Agustin G. Amezúa y Mayo, *La Vida Privada Española en el Protocolo Notarial* (Madrid, 1950), pp. ix–xli; as well as Antonio Matilla Tascón, "Escribanos, notarios y Archivos de Protocolos en España," *Archivum* 12 (1962).

[47] The number of these apprenticeships was also fixed by law, but as the paperwork increased, their numbers were expanded. In 1588 each *escribano* could hire no more than three such assistants, but by 1610 they were allowed to have up to nine. Amezúa y Mayo, *La Vida Privada Española*, pp. xxi–xxiv.

[48] Chiffoleau, *Comptabilité*, p. 107: "Ce n'est pas dans l'Europe tridentine, ou post-tridentine que le testament a pris ses formes baroques mais bien pendant la crise de la fin du Moyen Age."

them. Whether at the notary's or at their deathbeds, testators depended on the *escribano's* expertise to determine the precise configurations of their document, which never varied from the following outline.

   I. Preliminaries: Approaching the Divine Tribunal
     A. Invocation
     B. Identification
     C. Preamble
       1. Supplication
       2. Meditation on death
       3. Meditation on judgment
       4. Profession of faith
     D. Encommendation
  II. Disposing of the Body: The Funeral
     A. Place of burial
     B. Burial dress
     C. Vigil and immediate suffrages
     D. Cortege and funeral procession
 III. Saving the Soul: Pious Bequests
     A. Suffrages
     B. Charity
 IV. Dividing Up the Estate: Distributive Clauses
  V. Closing: Work for the Survivors
     A. Naming of testators
     B. Identification of funds to be used
     C. Witnessing and signing

First comes the declaration of faith, a free rendering of the *confiteor* in which the testators express their beliefs and confirm the fact that they are obedient members of the church. This credal proclamation also invokes various members of the Celestial Court (God in three persons, the angelic hosts, the Virgin Mary and all the saints) to come to the testators' aid at the moment of death and in the afterlife.

After this catechetical exercise comes the petition for forgiveness, a general confession of sins in which the testators meditate upon their own failings in life and seek to redress wrongs or forgive the injuries caused by others before the judgment of their souls takes place.

Finally, after the needs of the soul have been addressed through a confession of faith and a plea for mercy, the needs of the body are taken up. If properly approached, this section could serve as a *memento mori*, or profound meditation on death. Here, the testators have to choose a burial place and arrange all the details of their own funeral, from the number of masses to be said and candles to be lit to the amounts to be spent as alms for the poor. Testators who arranged all the proper details could in effect experience the details of their own death by going through the steps of their burial and even through the ceremonies observed by their survivors. To go through such an exercise was more than to remind oneself of one's mortality; it was to actually experience death and the hereafter vicariously while still alive and in this world.

The church also invested the second, practical part of the will with spiritual value. In addition to serving the functions just mentioned, the will also discharged a necessary ethical function in the eyes of the church. The redistribution of one's estate, not only *ad pias causas* but among one's heirs, became a duty and a matter of conscience.[49] To arrange for the disposition of one's belongings had a positive spiritual value, beyond the practical reason of avoiding "dissension and quarreling" among one's survivors, as the marquis pointed out in his testamentary preamble. Many Madrileños were conscious of this when they wrote their wills, as one of them attested in 1584:

In order to enjoy the eternal glory for which we have been created . . . it is necessary for me first to dispose of all the belongings which God saw fit to give me in this life, so that when He deigns it proper to take me from it, I may be able to discharge my conscience.[50]

Medieval and early modern Catholicism made detachment from this world one of the principal Christian virtues. Avarice was a very broadly defined vice: Any desire for or attachment to temporal wealth as good in itself was frowned upon. The monastic ethic of poverty, embraced most rigorously by the mendicant orders (and most immoderately by the Waldensians and the Spiritual Franciscans), was not only commended to those who took vows but also to all Christians. It was, after all, one of the counsels of perfection prescribed by Jesus himself when he said: "If you

---

[49] Ariès, *Hour of Our Death*, p. 196.   [50] AHPM 1015.289.

would be perfect, go sell what you possess and give it to the poor," and "Truly, I say to you, it will be hard for a rich man to enter the kingdom of heaven."[51]

In a very real sense, the will functioned as an extension of the counsel of poverty to all Christians. Although it would hardly seem meritorious to part with one's belongings at death – since it is an involuntary and ultimately unavoidable divestment for all human beings, whether heathen or baptized, godly or reprobate – the act of voluntarily redistributing one's earthly possessions in the will came to be regarded as a demonstration of the proper detachment required from those who hoped to join the saints in heaven.

The fact that such a redistribution was unavoidable made the conscious acceptance of it no less meritorious. So it is that the will became a quasi-sacramental means of obtaining an eternal reward without altogether losing the temporal goods one enjoyed in this life. According to Phillipe Ariès, the will became a way of combining wealth with the work of salvation: "It was an insurance policy contracted between the individual and God, through the intermediary of the Church."[52] As "insurance," the will guaranteed two benefits. First, as Jacques LeGoff has indicated, it served as a "passport to heaven."[53] Second, it guaranteed eternal wealth in the hereafter in exchange for premiums paid in temporal currency, that is, the pious bequests.[54]

The will was also a permit for use of one's temporal goods in this life. Of course, for those who wrote wills on their deathbeds – often the majority of all testators – this was a moot point. Still, for all testators, whether deathly ill or healthy, the will seemed to legitimize and condone the fact that one acquired and used temporal wealth throughout one's lifetime. Possessions that would normally be suspect were sanctified, in effect, at the moment in which they became provisionally detached from their owner. For those who were close to death, the will legitimized their enjoyment of earthly goods retroactively; for those who still had time remaining in this world, the will rehabilitated the continued enjoyment of their temporal fortune.

---

[51] Matthew 19.21–23.   [52] Ariès, *Hour of Our Death*, p. 190.
[53] J. LeGoff, *La Civilisation de l'Occident Médiéval* (Paris, 1964), p. 240.
[54] Ariès, *Hour of Our Death*, p. 190.

And it was not enough to simply write a will with a charitable, clean heart and to let go of the world: One also had to see to it that all of one's requests (*mandas*) would be carried out, especially in regard to the pious bequests and the almsgiving. The best of wills, if unfulfilled, could become the worst of wills. Everything depended on one's heirs and especially on one's designated executors, or *albaceas*, whose duty it was to present the testament to a judge within a month of the testator's death and to implement all of its requests. The executors played a spiritual as well as a juridical role, because it was up to them to ensure "relief from the pain of purgatory." The amount of time it would take for one to be released from purgatory could be seriously lengthened by lax or negligent executors. Experts advised selecting the executors carefully and not trusting simply to familial duty or friendship to ensure the fulfillment of one's will, for even the closest relatives and friends could fail to perform their duties. The optimal number of *albaceas* was two or three. According to one popular guidebook on dying, it was always best to name at least one good priest and one married man who was neither too rich nor too poor as executors.[55]

Because wills served so many important practical functions in the late medieval and early modern world, they were indispensable to the maintenance of social order. Surely, the fact that testaments *could* be imbued with a religious dimension and that devotional writers encouraged such an attitude toward them does not mean that all testators saw the writing of their will as a profound religious experience. Common sense dictates that not each and every will can be approached as a document composed in the manner suggested by the devotional literature. Nonetheless, the fact that every will was supposed to address certain religious concerns makes the sum total of the testamentary record open to interpretation as an expression of a prevailing religious mentality. In Spain, as elsewhere in Western Europe, a varied multitude of voices can still be heard speaking through the wills of the dead. Though much of the original testamentary record from Madrid has been lost, enough material remains to allow us to hear what many Madrileños were saying about death and the afterlife in the age of Philip II as they prepared for the end of their earthly existence.

[55] Venegas, *Agonía*, pp. 135, 222.

Wills and the history of mentalities

Over the past two decades, historians of mentalities have argued that notarial documents offer a revealing glimpse into the practices and beliefs of any given society. More specifically, these same historians have also firmly established the place of the will as a *speculum mortis,* or mirror of popular attitudes toward death and the afterlife.[56]

The will has been compared to a rich mine that can yield many different kinds of gems, or valuable pieces of information that can enrich the history of religion and, on a grander scale, the history of mentalities.[57] What Pierre Chaunu said about Paris wills in particular could also be said of other European wills from the late medieval and early modern period: Through these documents all testators have left behind a record of their thoughts, their fears, and their hopes as they entered the vestibule of death.[58]

From its credal statements and invocations, which are open to many kinds of thematic analyses, to its most mundane functions, such as the ordering of funeral ceremonies, liturgies, works of charity, and the distribution of property, the will reveals an intricate network of exploitable elements for the historian. Because wills contain specific instructions about all sorts of funerary practices, which in and of themselves are formalized social gestures developed in part from ever-fluid popular customs and in part from more rigid philosophical and theological concepts, they allow the historian to reconstruct – albeit with caution – the structures of the process of crossing over from this world to the next at any given time in any given place. What has been said of royal rituals also applies to testaments: They allow one to analyze "the working of ceremonial *in* society" and "the working of society *through* ritual."[59]

Moreover, because wills serve as a unifying link between generations and as instruments that seek to impose a certain sense of order and continuity on the potentially chaotic experience of transition caused by every death, they also illustrate the way in which any given society

[56] Chiffoleau, *Comptabilité,* p. 33. [57] Vovelle, *Piété baroque,* p. 27.
[58] Pierre Chaunu, *La Mort à Paris,* p. 288.
[59] David Cannadine and Simon Price, *Rituals of Royalty* (Cambridge, 1987), p. 14.

constructs its ultimate values and beliefs and the way in which it approaches the relation between the living and the dead.[60]

Those who have used wills to analyze attitudes toward death and the afterlife have also been cautious about the limitations of this kind of documentation. Wills may be good mirrors of death, but all mirrors distort reality to some extent. In the first place, wills were not written by an entire cross section of early modern Spanish society; they were limited for the most part to the more stable and prosperous socioeconomic sectors of the urban populace. In cultural terms, then, this means that wills tended to be drawn up by those sectors that were prone to have formal education and literacy. Which means, in turn, that though wills may provide a somewhat faithful image of the values and beliefs of the propertied class of any given population, this image will always be an incomplete, secondary representation of the total social reality. It may be the least distorted image anyone could hope for, but it will be distorted nonetheless.[61]

Moreover, no matter how faithfully any will expresses the desires of any individual, the means of expression are rigidly formalized by the structure and language of the document, which is itself a juridical, standardized representation of accepted social conventions. Much of what one finds in wills is strictly *pro forma*, written in a carefully regulated and codified language that is limited by a specific number of acceptable choices. Words as well as gestures are fixed; both the notary and the testator have only a predetermined range of expression. The organization of the document, its wording, the types of choices to be made by the testator, and the ways in which an estate is to be redistributed – these are all circumscribed by the standardization required of most legal documents.

Regarding this point, Michel Vovelle asked: "Is the will a legal formula, a fixed and unyielding stereotype . . . or a sensitive index of changing ideas, those of the notary, as well as of his clients?" The answer he had for his own question, after reading thousands of eighteenth-century wills from Provence, was that although wills lacked a certain degree of

---

60 For more on the value of wills, see Chiffoleau, *Comptabilité*, p. 32; and Vovelle, *Piété baroque*, p. 28.

61 Vovelle, *Piété baroque*, p. 22.

spontaneity or personal effusion, they could not be judged as inflexible stereotypes. He concluded that there was plenty of room for individuality in the writing of a will, saying: "There are almost as many formulas as there are notaries."[62] Moreover, as one Spanish scholar has observed, the formal structure and language of testaments allow the historian to contextualize individual requests by framing them within the boundaries of larger social patterns of behavior.[63]

Within the limits imposed on each individual will by law and social convention, there is room for individuality. An outsider from another culture or another time may view the range of choices as limited but will not be able to deny that the possibilities for variation within these limits, trivial as well as substantial, can seem nearly infinite, much like the hues within one color range of the light spectrum.

This means that the mentality expressed by each individual, confined as it is within certain boundaries, is but part of a larger whole and that each individual choice is in the final analysis a reflection of the social mentality. Though wills can reveal much about individual testators, the usefulness of a single isolated will for a historian of mentalities is severely limited. It is only when many wills from a given time and place are studied as a group that the larger patterns begin to emerge, revealing the structures of the social mentality. So, although it is true that a will can seldom rival a personal diary, or even a letter, in terms of the capacity of any document to reveal the inner self of any individual, it is also certainly true that a will, when analyzed as a personal expression of certain social conventions, can reveal much about the larger sociocultural superstructure of which it is a component.

Thus far, no historian has been foolish enough to assert that individual belief can be unerringly gauged through a will. Neither has anyone claimed that wills can be used empirically to measure mentalities with quantitative certainty – especially in view of the fact that testaments were written by only a segment of the population in early modern times. Although wills can sometimes be used to determine the actual material wealth of an individual or of a segment of the population, they cannot ever be used to measure belief in the same way. At the very least, wills

---

[62] Ibid., pp. 56–7.
[63] B. Morell Pequero, *La contribución etnográfica del Archivo de Protocolos* (Salamanca, 1981), p. 158.

can reveal certain *patterns* of belief and behavior for particular segments of a given society; at most, they can disclose the ways in which a certain mentality is expressed on a personal and social level by a certain individual.

Wills can reveal "mental representations": As juridical acts, they speak in a very formalized way about the meaning of death for the individual and for society.[64] In the world that historians seek to analyze, wills serve a practical social and economic function by arranging for the disposal of the dead and their belongings. But in the very act of giving shape to the final wishes of each testator, each will speaks for the society that produced it.

This is not merely a passive phenomenon. As each will reflects the values of the society within which it is written, so does it also act reciprocally on that same society. It could be argued that wills define and modify the social mentality as much as they reflect it. The rigidly formalized structure and carefully codified language of each will helps to define and even impose certain models of social conduct. No set of social practices is ever truly static. As minor and major changes in attitudes toward death develop within a society, they are reflected in wills. Moreover, to some extent, the changes themselves are not only implemented but also actually caused by wills. Since the thirteenth century, when the practice of the writing of wills began to be diffused throughout all social classes in Western Europe, the will has played a vital, active role in the evolution of attitudes toward death and the hereafter.

Ultimately, what is done at a funeral is largely determined by the will of the deceased. Although much of what is requested in a will may be *pro forma* and restricted by convention, it is still possible that, within the limits established by tradition, a will can forge a new path. This is not to say that a single will can bring about profound changes. Cultural change is much too complex a phenomenon to allow for such assumptions. Nonetheless, changes *do* take place, and they do begin with individuals. The cumulative effect of a gradually increasing number of wills that begin to express new kinds of requests for funeral or postmortem devotions can be tremendous, leading eventually to the redefinition of what is acceptable. In cases where one can see some new type of request appear

---

[64] Chiffoleau, *Comptabilité*, p. 35.

for the first time in one or two wills from a given year, and then in several more the year after that, and even more two or three years later, doubling, tripling and quadrupling in quick succession, one is in fact viewing how process of change is effected.

Recent studies of Spanish wills

The historical study of wills pioneered by French scholars has become very popular among Spanish scholars in the past decade. When this project was first conceived in the early 1980s, practically nothing had been published on Spanish testaments.[65] Beginning in the mid-1980s, however, studies began to appear in great numbers.[66] The overwhelming majority of these studies have focused their attention on the seventeenth, and especially the eighteenth, century, driven, as most of them were, by a desire to find out whether the "de-Christianization" that Vovelle had documented in France could also be found in Spain. Though these studies prove that there was a high degree of uniformity throughout the Spanish kingdoms in testamentary customs and that demand for pious bequests continued at a very high pitch well into the age of Enlightenment, the vast majority begin *in medias res*, without any

[65] Miguel del Arbol Navarro, *Spanisches Funeralbrauchtum unter Berücksichtigung Islamischer Einflüsse* (Bern/Frankfurt, 1974) was in many ways a pioneering work, but it did not rely on testaments. Regrettably, it seems to have been overlooked by the later scholarship.

[66] Two of these have already been cited: López López, *Comportamientos religiosos en Asturias* (1989); and Lorezo Pinar, *Actitudes religiosas ante la muerte en Zamora* (1989). Other significant monographs are: Marion Reder Gadow, *Morir en Málaga: Testamentos málagueños del siglo XVIII* (Málaga, 1986); Fernando Martinez Gil, *Actitudes ante la muerte en el Toledo de los Austrias* (Toledo, 1984); O. Lopez i Miguel, *Actituds colectives davant la mort i discurs testamentari al Mataro del segle XVIII* (Mataro, 1987); M. J. de la Pascua, *Actitudes colectivas ante la muerte en el Cádiz de la primera mitad del siglo XVIII* (Cádiz, 1984); Antonio Peñafiel Ramón, *Testamento y buena muerte: Un estudio de mentalidades en la Murcia del siglo XVIII* (Murcia, 1987); José A. Rivas Alvarez, *Miedo y Piedad: Testamentos Sevillanos del siglo XVIII* (Seville, 1986). Numerous articles have appeared in anthologies, most notably in: *La documentación notarial y la historia: Actas del Segundo Coloquio de metodología historica aplicada* (Santiago de Compostela, 1984); *Primer Encuentro sobre religiosidad popular* (Seville, 1987); and *La religiosidad popular*, ed. C. Alvarez Santaló, M. J. Buxó, and S. Rodriguez Becerra, 3 vols. (Barcelona, 1989), vol. II, *Vida y Muerte: La imaginación religiosa*, pp. 205–397.

substantial consideration of developments in the sixteenth century, that period during which were forged so many of the attitudes and customs of the baroque era. Those few studies that use wills from the earlier period – our area of concern – have tended to lump the entire testamentary record together, making no distinction between decades within that century[67] or simply dividing it into fifty-year segments.[68]

These studies as a whole show a great disparity in criteria for the selection of documents, in terms both of chronology and of the total number of wills chosen for the sample. For example, one study analyzed a mere forty-five wills for all of the sixteenth *and* seventeenth centuries, making no distinction between years and decades, and another published in the same volume used nearly 1,200 wills for the years 1705–1825, exhausting the archival record for six whole years during this period, at twenty- to twenty-five-year intervals.[69]

As of early 1993, only two published studies had focused substantially on sixteenth-century wills: one for Madrid and one for Cuenca. Leonor Gomez Nieto has recently analyzed 100 Madrid wills from the period 1452–1558, but, as in all other Spanish studies, she lumps the entire sample together, making no distinctions among the years and decades of that long time span. Though useful as a descriptive narrative, this study is short on analysis and is rendered tentative by the small number of its

[67] López López, *Comportamientos religiosos en Asturias*, covers the period 1550–1600 through a relatively small testamentary sample, as part of a much larger study that ranges at times to mid-nineteenth century. Martinez Gil, *Toledo*, used 100 wills from the sixteenth and seventeenth centuries but did not specify any chronology and did not quantify any of his findings.

[68] Lorenzo Pinar, *Actitudes Religiosas ante la muerte en Zamora*, studied 229 testaments for the sixteenth century but divided the data into two equal chronological halves, as "first half" and "second half" of the century. Ricardo Garcia Carcel took a sounding of 300 from Barcelona, 1540–56, but his published findings encompassed a mere ten pages: "La muerte en Barcelona del Antiguo Régimen," in *La documentación notarial y la historia*, pp. 115–24.

[69] Lourdes Mateo Bretos, "Actitudes ante la muerte de la población de Sitges en los siglos XVI y XVII," used twenty-one wills for the sixteenth century, from no single year or decade, and twenty-four for the seventeenth, all from 1690–9. In contrast, Anastasio Alemán Illán, "Sociabilidad, muerte y religiosidad popular: Las cofradias de Murcia durante el siglo xviii," plumbed 1,153 testaments. Both appear in *La religiosidad popular*, vol. II, pp. 261–72 (Sitges); 361–83 (Murcia).

sample, as well as by its lack of attention to chronology.[70] In contrast, Sara Nalle's splendid study of religious life in and around Cuenca during the sixteenth and seventeenth centuries makes extensive and judicious use of sixteenth-century testaments, weaving that evidence into a larger tapestry, both chronologically and thematically. In many ways, her findings complement and reinforce those of this study without any substantial overlap or duplication – a most gratifying surprise for both of us, since we conceived and carried out our research independently without knowledge of each other's work until the data had all been gathered.

Madrid's wills

On a short and quiet street in Madrid that runs from the rear of the Prado Museum to the leafy oasis of Retiro Park, a nineteenth-century building with crumbling brickwork houses the Archivo Histórico de Protocolos, the depository for all Madrid wills. This archive contains more than 20 million legal documents bound in 34,496 thick volumes (known as *protocolos*) from the years 1504–1889.[71]

No one really knows for sure how many wills are stored there, because the cataloguing is still in process. There is no doubt that much has been lost and that many documents have suffered from centuries of neglect. It is estimated that only about one-fourth of the original notarial record from the sixteenth century has survived, making it impossible for anyone to carry out a truly exhaustive study of these documents.[72] Given the history of this archive, however, it is remarkable that even this much has survived and that so much of it is still in decent shape.[73]

---

[70] Leonor Gómez Nieto, *Ritos funerarios en el Madrid medieval* (Madrid, 1991). The exact chronological proportions of the testamentary sample are never revealed, but the references to post-1520 wills far outnumber all others.

[71] See *Madrid en el Archivo Histórico de Protocolos*, pp. 7–9; 151–7; 165–9. Earlier wills can be found at the Archivo General de la Villa de Madrid. Leonor Gómez Nieto employed an unspecified number of these in *Ritos funerarios en el Madrid medieval*.

[72] Matilla Tascón, p. vii.

[73] Amalio Huarte Echenique has written a brief but detailed history of this archive: "Origenes del Archivo de Protocolos de Madrid," *Revista de la Biblioteca, Archivo y Museo del Ayuntamiento de Madrid* 7 (1930):194–9. The Archivo de Protocolos was founded by a royal decree of King Charles III, on 5 March 1765, who ordered that all existing and future notarial documents be filed in a central archive. Before this, all

Because the cataloguing is incomplete, it would be extremely difficult and time-consuming at present for any one person to gain access to all the surviving documents. About 1,400 wills from the sixteenth century had been identified and catalogued at the time that this study was carried out, and it appears that many more remain to be discovered. Thus far, this archive remains relatively underused by early modern historians.[74]

By 1984, when I was searching for wills in Madrid, the archive had produced three partial catalogues: one published (1980), two unpublished. Of the 9,000 wills listed in the published catalogue, only 460 dated from the sixteenth century.[75] Nearly 1,000 more were listed in the two unpublished catalogues available at the archive. While culling through *protocolos* I had called up from the stacks, searching for some of the wills listed in these catalogues, I often found others that had not yet been identified or listed. As a result, I was able to catalogue about 200 additional wills for my own use, raising to nearly 1,600 the total number of identifiable and accessible documents.[76] The following list shows the exact number of catalogued testaments for each decade of the sixteenth century.

1500s	*1510s*	*1520s*	*1530s*	*1540s*	*1550s*	*1560s*	*1570s*	*1580s*	*1590s*
—	—	63	205	82	159	116	293	331	339

notarial records were scattered throughout the city, in the cellars, attics, and spare rooms of the notaries and their families, or else in uninhabited houses and the outbuildings of monasteries and convents. The present archive was organized in the 1930s during the Spanish Civil War.

[74] Agustín Dieguez Delgado has studied testaments from a later period in his *tésis de licenciatura* (Universidad Complutense, 1980), "Religion y sociedad en la segunda mitad del siglo XVII segun los protocolos notariales de Antonio Bravo." Unfortunately, I did not see a reference to this thesis until 1993 and was unable to consult it.

[75] Archivo Histórico de Protocolos de Madrid, *Indice de Testamentos y Documentos Afines*, Primera Serie, ed. by Antonio Matilla Tascón (Madrid, 1980).

[76] The catalogues of the archive are not chronologically arranged. Instead, the wills are listed by family name, in alphabetical order. Although some of the sixteenth-century wills are in surprisingly good condition, many are badly damaged and cannot be used. This means that the actual number of exploitable documents is less than the total number of accessible wills. A rough estimate of the percentage of illegible wills, based on the protocolos I examined, would be somewhere around 10 to 15 percent. In addition, any researcher must also contend with another 10 to 20 percent of the undamaged wills that offer a serious paleographical challenge.

Some incongruities in the testamentary record are revealed by these numbers. To begin with, hardly any documents are available for the first two decades of the sixteenth century, and relatively few are accessible from the 1520s and 1540s. The decade of the 1530s, which was not singularly prosperous for the city, yields nearly twice as many wills as the 1560s, which was the initial boom decade for Madrid, when its population began to increase by leaps and bounds. Obviously, this indicates that the actual number of accessible documents is not directly related to the demographics of the period but to the vagaries of record keeping in the notarial archives over five centuries. Otherwise, for instance, how could one explain the fact that there are almost as many wills catalogued for the one decade 1590–9 as for the five whole decades of 1500 to 1549? Although Madrid's population did increase significantly in the 1590s, the growth rate was certainly not so overwhelming.

In spite of the fact that the notarial record for the sixteenth century is incomplete, few other Spanish cities offer such a wide range of possibilities for studying attitudes toward death and the afterlife in the age of Philip II. This is due to a particular set of circumstances, not the least of which is the fact that during the sixteenth century Madrid was alternatively both a small, unexceptional town and also a rapidly expanding metropolis – home to the most ordinary urban and semirural sorts of people and also the seat of the royal court.

For slightly more than the first half of the sixteenth century, Madrid was a small and relatively prosperous central Castilian *villa*, with few eminent noble families. It had grown steadily throughout most of the fifteenth century, due in part to the irregular presence of the court and in part to its fairs, which were licensed by the monarchy. A report on Madrid given to the Catholic kings referred to it as "principally agricultural." Yet, it had a fair number of artisans who worked in textiles, metals, and leather, and it also had a robust construction industry. As could be expected, Madrid had its share of servants and functionaries tied to the royal Alcazar, and a sprinkling of lawyers and bureaucrats.[77]

Madrid might have been urban, with its fortified Alcazar that served

---

[77] Manuel Montero Vallejo, *El Madrid Medieval* (Madrid, 1987), pp. 299–302; 322. His estimate for Madrid's population growth, 1474–1500, is 50 percent.

as a sometime royal residence, but Madrid manifested a nearly rural atmosphere before 1561 and for some time after that. In the opening year of the century, 1501, when most of the city streets were still unpaved, its council had to contend with the uncertain boundaries between the town and the countryside. Consider, for instance, the following decree from one of the council's sessions:

The council members have agreed that since there are already laws that forbid swine from roaming through the streets helter-skelter, and that since these laws have been repeatedly proclaimed in public, and been ignored, that within three days all swine must be henceforth penned up. If after the aforementioned period of time someone neglects to obey this order, permission is herewith granted to anyone who finds a loose pig to take it as his own, kill it, or make any other use of it without any penalty.[78]

Three months later, on the same day that it ordered Madrileños to stop throwing their refuse onto the streets – an order that had already been proclaimed in 1496, along with another that forbade Madrileños from slaughtering chickens on their doorsteps – the council had to issue another decree concerning animals:

The councilors have agreed that water carriers should henceforth cease from running through the streets with their donkeys, under penalty of ten days in chains, because they often bump into many people and knock them over, creating much havoc.[79]

Apparently, Madrid remained in much the same condition fifty years later, for in 1551 the city council was still contending with roving swine and still trying to pave some of the major streets. The following year, 1552, the council once again had to repeat its proscription against live-

---

[78] *Libros de acuerdos del Consejo Madrileño (1464–1600)*, 4 vols. (Madrid, 1932), vol. 4, p. 297. From the meeting of 17 May 1501.

[79] For 1496: ibid., vol. 3, pp. 213–14; for 1501: ibid., vol. 4, pp. 313 and 325. The 1496 decree leveled a fine of 24 *maravedis* for emptying latrines (*servidores*) onto the street, 12 to 24 *maravedis* for throwing dirty, smelly water out of a window or door (*agua suzia que hieda*), and 12 *maravedis* for *echar gallinas muertas en la calle*. The decree against littering the streets with garbage was proclaimed in late August 1501, and again in October of the same year.

stock in the streets and squares.[80] In 1588, it was still trying to cope with all the dead animals found in its streets.[81]

The sanitation habits of the old, smaller Madrid became a nightmare for the new capital city and its booming population after 1561. Ambassadors and foreign visitors were often shocked by what they saw. Henry Cock, a Batavian who lived in Madrid from 1574 to 1584, griped that each time he ventured into the streets the stench would nauseate him, especially in the mornings.[82] A decade later, the papal nuncio Camilo Borghese (the later Pope Paul V) had similar complaints about Madrid's "intolerable odor."[83] Lambert Wyts, a servant of Anne of Austria at court, described the cause of this foulness in graphic detail:

Madrid is the dirtiest and filthiest city in all of Spain, for you see nothing but *servidores* (as these chamber pots filled with urine and feces are called) being emptied out onto the streets, turning them into an incredibly foul and viscous ooze. If you walk in this slime – and there is no way to avoid it – your shoes are burned black and red . . . this has happened to me many times. After ten at night it is best not to walk about the city, for at that hour they start to hurl their *servidores*, and that's when the ordure begins to fly.[84]

Another visitor in the early 1590s observed that the dry, baking heat of summer made matters worse, because the filth turned into a choking dust that blew on everything and everyone.[85]

---

[80] "E mandaron los dichos señores . . . que maten los puercos que estuvieren por las plazas y calles desta dicha villa, conforme a la carta de Su Majestad e ordenanza desta villa." Archivo de la Villa, *Libro de Acuerdos*, XI, fol. 89v (23 November 1551); and XIII, fol. 385 (June 1552). Cited by Manuel Fernández Alvarez, *Madrid bajo Felipe II* (Madrid, 1966), pp. 20–21.

[81] In that year the Ayuntamiento contracted the services of a certain Miguel del Rei for 6 *ducados* a month to dispose of all dead birds, dogs, and cats. Apparently there were also large animals to pick up, for it is mentioned that they were not to be his responsibility. This contract is reproduced in *Madrid en el Archivo Histórico de Protocolos*, pp. 144–45.

[82] For a summary of these reports see Alfredo Alvar Ezquerra, *Felipe II, la corte y Madrid en 1561* (Madrid, 1985), pp. 62–77. On Cock's impressions see "El Madrid de Felipe II visto por el humanista holandés Enrique Cock," *Madrid en el Siglo XVI* (Madrid, 1962), vol. I, pp. 5–45.

[83] José García Mercadal, *España vista por los extranjeros*, 3 vols. (Madrid, 1917–21), vol. 2, p. 271.

[84] José García Mercadal, *Viajes de extranjeros por España y Portugal*, vol. I, p. 1174.

[85] Gianbattista Confalonieri (1592–3), in García Mercadal, *España vista por los extran-*

The point is that for over half of the sixteenth century Madrid was a small city that was still very much tied to the agricultural society that surrounded it and that even after it became the seat of the court it could not change its character and habits overnight. As such, it offers the historian who reads its wills an opportunity to examine the attitudes toward death of a sample of people in an ordinary town located in the heart of New Castille, an area that many might consider the most typically "Spanish" region of the Iberian peninsula. Because of this, Madrid can perhaps reveal more faithfully the mentality of urban and rural Castille as a whole than other large cities that were more powerful, prosperous, or exceptionally rich in culture, such as Toledo, Salamanca, Burgos, or Valladolid.

Furthermore, since Madrid was also an occasional residence for the royal court and never too far removed from the pulse of life among the truly powerful, it also perhaps more clearly reflects those social values that were being promoted as normative by the ruling elite. Because one of the principal aims of this book is to plumb the relation between popular belief and practice and the models of behavior officially proposed by church and state, it will be most advantageous to stay as close to the royal court as possible.

This brings us to a second consideration: After 1561 Madrid gradually became a very different city, one that offers the opportunity to study the influence of the court and the impact of social and cultural changes upon attitudes toward death. Suddenly, in 1561, Madrid had greatness thrust upon it when the city was chosen as a new, permanent capital for the Spanish kingdoms by Philip II.[86] What had once been a dusty Castilian town was now to be the very hub of a vast global empire, the seat of government for the richest, most powerful nation on earth. It did not take long for people from all parts of the peninsula, and even other

jeros, vol. 2, p. 259: "Se suele decir como proverbio que aquello que se caga en invierno se bebe en verano, porque aquella porquería se convierte en polvo y en verano el hombre se llena de el cuanto quiere."

[86] See J. I. Gutierrez Nieto, "En torno al problema del establecimiento de la capitalidad de la monarquía hispanica en Madrid," *Revista de Occidente*, special issue, "Madrid, villa, y comunidad," 1983, pp. 53–65; and M. Fernández Alvarez, *El establecimiento de la capitalidad de España en Madrid* (Madrid, 1960). Also the two works by F. C. Sainz de Robles, *Motivos que determinaron la exaltación de Madrid a capitalidad de España* (Madrid, 1932); and ¿*Porqué es Madrid capital?* (Madrid, 1961).

nations, to flock to Madrid, swelling its population and gradually changing its complexion. From 1561 onward, Madrid had a stable nucleus of older families and various strata of newcomers, from the very rich to the utterly destitute. It also attracted its share of *pícaros* and criminals.[87] Estimates of Madrid's sixteenth-century population vary and are not too reliable, but they agree on one thing: Before 1561 the city was not large.[88] One estimate for 1513 places the number of residents at 3,000.[89] A recent study points at slow, steady growth up to 1561, followed by a population explosion:[90]

1528	*1542*	*1561*	*1572*	*1597*
4,700	18,000	20,000	40,000	60,000

Another estimate calculates a larger population for 1597 of somewhere between 83,000 to 90,000, not including the clergy, the military, or those in welfare institutions and hospitals. If these figures are correct, this places Madrid among the twenty most populous European cities of that time.[91]

Statistics from the baptismal records of six Madrid parishes confirm the dimensions of the sudden population boom, showing an increase between 1560 and 1562 of 174 percent.[92] Though some of the higher estimates overstate the increase (such as that which assigned 250,000 to 300,000 residents to Madrid by 1600 – an impossible average of thirty-five residents per house), there is no denying that the city was quickly flooded with newcomers, many of whom were directly tied to the court. On the more cautious side, for instance, it has been estimated that by

---

[87] David Ringrose, "Imigración, estructuras demográficas, y tendencias económicas en Madrid a comienzos de la Epoca Moderna," *Moneda y Credito*, 138, pp. 9–55.

[88] See M. F. Carbajo Isla, *Población*, pp. 115 ff.

[89] Julián Paz, "Noticias de Madrid y de las familias madrileñas de su tiempo, por Gonzalo Fernández de Oviedo," *Revista de la Biblioteca, Archivo, y Museo del Ayuntamiento de Madrid* (1947), pp. 273–326. Another 3,000 residents were estimated for the surrounding area.

[90] Annie Molinié-Bertrand, *Au siècle d'or. L'Espagne et ses hommes: La population du royaume de Castille au XVIe siècle* (Paris: 1985), pp. 207–18, esp. p. 208.

[91] M. F. Carbajo Isla, *Población*, pp. 137–8. On p. 227, Madrid is placed in the same category as Rome, Genoa, Florence, Palermo, and Antwerp.

[92] Alfredo Alvar Ezquerra, *Felipe II, la corte y Madrid en 1561* (Madrid, 1985), p. 22.

1600 Madrid was host to 1,200 personal servants at court, 1,400 soldiers attached to the court, and hundreds of government functionaries.[93]

With the royal court firmly anchored at the Alcazar and court officials, ambassadors, merchants, soldiers, artists, and hangers-on steadily moving in, the social, economic, and cultural structure of Madrid was gradually transformed. As is true of most capital cities, much of life in Madrid began to revolve around the business of government. Power and influence became highly prized commodities; courtiers and bureaucrats tried to out-impress one another in the same streets and squares, some newly paved, where only a few years before stray pigs had been slaughtered.

The Madrid of King Philip II's court offers the historian an opportunity to analyze change and continuities in attitudes toward death. The old, simple Madrid never simply vanished. Much of what commends it as a good representative Castilian town before 1561 continues to be true for the rest of the century – albeit in different and sometimes diminishing ways. Between 1561 and 1599 Madrid was in transition. Many of those who wrote wills in the 1590s were newcomers, but they were still outnumbered by native Madrileños who had grown up in the days when the court came to town only occasionally.

As a court city, Madrid still retained many of its old ways while it incorporated new influences, some brought by the new arrivals, others simply engendered by new events and the passage of time. It is good to keep in mind that about the same time the court moved to Madrid, the Council of Trent held its final sessions, ushering in a period of religious reform and renewal. The Madrid of Philip II, then, is also the Madrid of the Catholic Reformation.

This means that the documentation from Madrid after 1561 brings the historian closer to the models proposed by king and church. At the same time, however, this documentation never ceases to reveal the beliefs and practices of more ordinary people. Some of these Madrileños were newcomers with different perceptions and modes of behavior, but most others were native residents who continued to face death much as their forebears had. All of them, regardless of their place of origin or social status, were members of the newly reformed Catholic Church,

---

[93] Alvar Ezquerra, pp. 17–22, includes a detailed list of these officials.

and as such they were influenced by the decrees of the Council of Trent. All of them, too, were near the king and his court.

The advantages offered by this juxtaposition of conditions in Madrid make it an excellent place in which to study the history of mentalities in the age of Philip II.

The demographics of Madrid's testators

Given that the notarial archive holdings for sixteenth-century wills is so incomplete, it would be foolish to attempt to speak in absolutes about the testamentary evidence. The documentation we have for this period is far too fragmentary and too unevenly distributed among the corresponding decades to warrant any kind of exhaustive analysis.

Even if one were to study every surviving will, the results of the findings would still be but a sampling based on a relatively small portion of the original whole. Furthermore, if one were to rely on the whole of this surviving portion for a sample, the results would probably be adversely affected by the fact that the holdings for some decades are disproportionately related to one another. For instance, how could evidence from the sixty-three wills of the 1520s be compared to evidence from the 205 wills of the 1530s. In turn, how could the 1530s be compared to the next decade, from which we have only eighty-two accessible wills? Worst of all, how could the paltry dozen or so wills from the first two decades be used in any significant manner?

An obvious solution to this dilemma is to try to control the sample not only by reducing it to a manageable size but also by making it more evenly distributed among the different decades and more representative of the different social types that inhabited sixteenth-century Madrid. This is precisely what was done. Of the nearly 1,600 wills available for the sixteenth century, a sample of about 450 was chosen for study. This representative sample group was not chosen at random, although in the case of each individual will, the final choice was determined by chance to some extent.

The 450 wills selected for this study date from 1520 to 1599. These chronological boundaries encompass the whole of King Philip II's life (1527–98). This range of years also very neatly divides into two equal periods of four decades each: one before Madrid became a capital city and the decrees of the Council of Trent were promulgated, one afterward. The period from 1520 to 1599 thus spans the whole of Philip's life, the whole of Madrid's early transformation, and the whole of the most crucial period of the Catholic Reformation.

This particular sample was chosen with an eye toward obtaining as wide a range of different social types as possible. Of the 450 wills, fourteen proved unusable for various reasons, ranging from the illegibility of key phrases to incorrect photocopying. The final number actually used was 436, and the distribution of numbers among the decades came out as follows:

1520s	*1530s*	*1540s*	*1550s*	*1560s*	*1570s*	*1580s*	*1590s*
50	51	50	48	50	76	54	57

As is evident, the distribution is fairly even with one exception. Although most decades have around fifty representative wills, one (the 1570s) has seventy-six. This slightly higher number was chosen as a control to see what difference if any would be made by a greater or lesser sample. Any noticeable deviations in patterns would then show that the sample group as a whole needed some adjustments and that perhaps more wills would be needed for each decade. As it turned out, this modest asymmetry had so little effect on all the curves that it indicated no adjustments were necessary. For each of the different problems analyzed, the percentages remained in relation to one another and in proportion to the greater pattern.

Nonetheless, caution must always be exercised when dealing with representative samples. If even professional pollsters in our own day calculate a slight margin of error for the results of "scientific" surveys based on responses to simply phrased yes or no questions, so much more should interpreters of the past do the same when eliciting complex information from more intractable sources. Although wills allow us to analyze attitudes toward death by means of quantitative judgments, the numbers never tell the whole story or necessarily reveal what may be most important. There is something very qualitative about this quantitative type of analysis: It can provide a fairly accurate rendering of the whole picture, but no one should expect it to be photographically precise. The situation in this case may be compared to the difference between a painting of a Paris street scene by an Impressionist and a photograph of the same location taken at the same time. Though the resemblance between the two pictures would be apparent to all, so would the differences. Having said this much, let us now see what kind of picture emerges when we analyze the salient characteristics of this sample group.

Notaries in sixteenth-century Madrid were not always very concerned with the kinds of details that would please a historian. All the information required for the writing of a will was limited to a person's name and health status: "I, so-and-so, being healthy (or sick) . . ." Any other detail beyond this was listed gratuitously. Some details, such as age, are hardly ever mentioned. Consequently, it is difficult to arrive at a detailed understanding of the social makeup of any sample of wills. In the earlier part of the century, for instance, notaries seldom listed the testator's profession. Although this changed in the latter decades of the century, it never became a universal practice among notaries.

One piece of information that was never hidden from view was the testator's gender, which is easily identifiable in the person's Christian name. Consequently, it is easy enough to determine with absolute certainty how many testators were men and how many were women. In the total number of wills that I catalogued, the proportional relation between genders fluctuates substantially. Although men almost always outnumber women, the proportion varies wildly from one decade to the next. In the sample I chose, the proportions are closer together, with some exceptions. The breakdown is as shown in Table 1.1.

Because the fluctuations in the total number of indexed wills are so irregular from 1520 to 1569, it is difficult to determine how well the figures reflect the actual proportions between male and female testators in sixteenth-century Madrid. The fluctuations are more regular between 1570 and 1599, hovering near the average of 67 percent and 33 percent, respectively, but one should not assume that this constancy is a true reflection of the demographic reality. The notarial record is far too incomplete to make such assumptions.

For women testators, it is very difficult to determine social status. A woman's status in society was largely determined through her relationship to men as wife, widow, or daughter. The few women who were recognized as having an independent status were either at the very top or the very bottom of the social scale. At the top were the titled noblewomen, at the bottom servants and prostitutes. Between these two extremes there was little room for a woman's identity beyond her association with a husband or father. Occasionally, the notary might indicate

Table 1.1. *Percentages of male and female testators*

	1,576 indexed wills		In sample of 436 wills	
	Men	Women	Men	Women
1520s	56	44	54	46
1530s	49	51	54	46
1540s	66	34	64	36
1550s	54	46	64	36
1560s	53	47	46	54
1570s	66	34	52	48
1580s	67	33	50	50
1590s	68	32	73	27

the profession of a woman's husband or father, but more often than not there is total silence concerning the status or profession of the male who determined her identity. It seemed enough to say she was a wife, widow, or daughter.

Throughout the sixteenth century, only one designation was used for women with enough regularity to give us some idea of their social condition. This special category was that of widow. Since notaries in the first half of the century were not always thorough, it is quite likely that many widows were not even listed as such before 1550. In our sample, widows made up a substantial part of the female population (see Figure 1.1 and Figure 1.2).

It is relatively easier to identify males by their profession or status, but the situation here is still far from ideal. During the first half of the century, notaries were not much interested in identifying a male testator's profession or rank. At no time during this period did the notaries list more than 35 percent of testators' titles or occupations. After the court moved to Madrid in 1561, it appears that the question of social rank or position began to matter more to the notaries and their clients. Suddenly, there is a sharp increase in the number of wills that list the occupations of males (see Figure 1.3). Skilled tradesmen, merchants, soldiers, and different types of professionals, as well as some nobles, make up the vast majority of those whose occupation or status is listed (see Table 1.2). Still, few laborers or servants identified themselves as

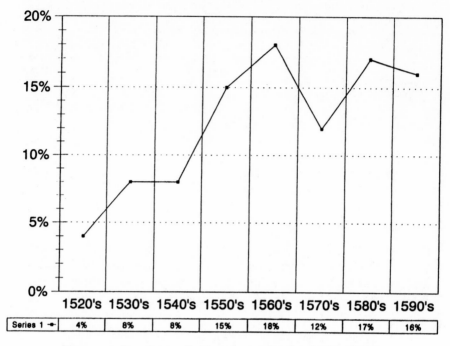

Figure 1.1. Percentage of widows in sample of 436 Madrid wills.

such. The one group that is by far best represented throughout the century are the artisans, both in terms of sheer numbers and in terms of distribution over every decade. Court functionaries are also well represented throughout the century – showing that the court made its presence felt in the city before 1561 – but are disproportionately distributed in the last three decades, after the court moved to Madrid. In terms of numbers, the clergy come in third, far behind the court functionaries, followed by merchants, nobles, and physicians. In terms of distribution over the decades, however, the physicians are next in constancy after the artisans. In each decade there is at least one will from a physician.

The nobles make their presence felt in the second half of the century, as do the soldiers and civil administrators, indicating the changes that were taking place in Madrid's population. Merchants are fairly constant and somewhat numerous, especially after 1561. Again, the influence of

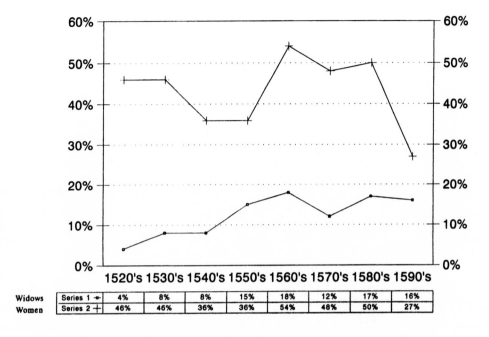

		1520's	1530's	1540's	1550's	1560's	1570's	1580's	1590's
Widows	Series 1 ◆	4%	8%	8%	15%	18%	12%	17%	16%
Women	Series 2 +	46%	46%	36%	36%	54%	48%	50%	27%

Figure 1.2. Widows and single women in sample of 436 Madrid wills.

the court on the city appears to make this difference. In contrast, the number of lawyers and their distribution over the decades remain basically the same throughout the century. The same is true of simple laborers and servants. Prostitution, represented by three *mujeres enamoradas*, makes a bashful appearance in the 1530s and 1540s but quickly vanishes thereafter to hide perhaps under a more respectable guise.

This sample is not representative of the actual demographics of sixteenth-century Madrid and should not be construed as an unequivocal measuring device of the views of all of its citizens. Given the incompleteness of the archival record, it is not likely that such a sample could ever be obtained. Nonetheless, this sample represents a fairly wide spectrum of people from sixteenth-century Madrid. Although the proportional distribution of different types of people in the sample itself may not ultimately be representative of the original distribution of people in

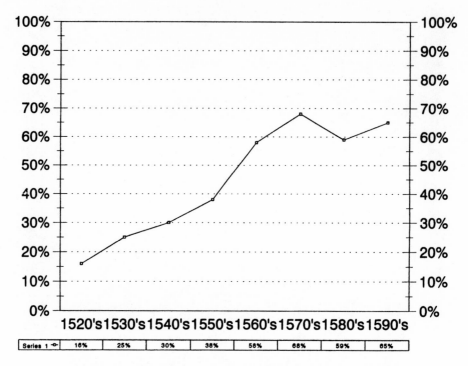

Figure 1.3. Percentage of testators declaring profession or status.

Table 1.2. *Profession or status of testators from sample of 436 Madrid wills, 1520–99*

	1520's	1530's	1540's	1550's	1560's	1570's	1580's	1590's
Clergy	1	2	–	3	–	3	5	4
Nobility	–	–	–	1	2	3	2	5
Civil Administrators	1	–	–	–	2	2	1	2
Court Functionaries	–	2	1	2	9	16	8	11
Soldiers	–	–	–	–	4	3	1	–
Lawyers	–	1	–	1	1	2	–	1
Physicians	1	1	1	2	1	2	1	2
Merchants	–	1	–	1	3	5	5	–
Artisans	5	2	10	7	4	11	8	8
Laborers	–	1	1	–	3	3	–	1
Servants	–	1	1	1	–	2	1	3
Prostitutes	–	2	1	–	–	–	–	–
Subtotals	8	13	15	18	29	52	32	37
Not Specified	42	38	35	30	21	24	22	20
Total	50	51	50	48	50	76	54	57

Madrid, or even of the total number of wills written at that time, it is certainly representative of the variety that could have been found in Madrid's testamentary record. The sample was designed to include as many different kinds of people from as many different social strata as the nature of the documentation would allow. Though it was difficult to determine with exactness the social and economic position of all testators, it was not impossible at least to establish broad categories for them. Often, the inventories of the testators' estates provided significant clues about their status or economic level, even when the notaries had omitted such information from the document. Considered individually, each will speaks not only for the testator but also for the social group to which he or she belongs. Taken as a whole, these 436 voices from men and women who have never been heard from before – and who surely never dreamed of acting as mouthpieces for their era – can bring us ever so much closer to the mentality they shared. We may not ever know with scientific exactitude what the sum total of the testamentary record would tell us, or what those who were too poor to write wills would have told us, but through an act of historical eavesdropping we can at least allow these carefully selected few to give us a fairly detailed description of what it was like to die and be buried in Madrid during the lifetime of King Philip II.

2

Approaching the divine tribunal

We now begin our analysis of these wills, taking each section of the wills in order, from beginning to end, focusing on those that reveal something about attitudes toward death and the afterlife. In this chapter, we begin with the preliminary statements in which testators carefully identified themselves before God and neighbor through ritual phrases.

Invocation

At the very beginning of each will, testators place all that is going to be said under the protection of God. The most common expression found in all wills throughout the sixteenth century (and up to the late eighteenth) is the Latin phrase "In Dei Nomine, amen." The use of the Latin phrase is a holdover from the time in the Middle Ages when the entire will was written in Latin. The fact that this is the only surviving trace of previous forms of expression in the will indicates a quasi-liturgical function. In no small way, this opening prayer is an echo of the mass: It is a ritualistic incantation that calls upon God in the language normally reserved for public worship. It is a notarial convention that also clearly shows how much of the style of the will is strictly *pro forma*, an adherence to tradition.[1]

[1] This invocation was widely used in Catholic Europe. For instance, medieval Italian account books, business letters and *ricordanze* also began "In Dei Nomine." I am indebted to Lauro Martines for sending me a copy of his forthcoming paper, "Ritual Language in Renaissance Italy: The Worldly Aspect," to be published as part of the conference proceedings (Erice, Sicily, 1990): *Rites et rituels dans les sociétés médiévales*

In some cases, the Latin phrase is repeated in Castilian Spanish. This duplication seems to indicate that the Latin phrase was used by some notaries and testators as a formula and that its integration in the will was at times not so much for its cognitive meaning as for its ritualistic language. The meaning had to be affirmed by the Castilian equivalent.

In the few wills in which the Latin invocation is not used, the most common replacement is a longer, more detailed trinitarian confession in the vernacular, such as: "In the name of the Most Holy Trinity, Father, Son, and Holy Spirit, three persons in one True God, who lives and reigns forever and ever, amen." Ines Tomilla was one of a few who appealed directly to the second person of the trinity, not without some sign of confusion. Her will begins with the invocation "In the name of God Our Lord Jesus Christ."[2] A small number of people included the Virgin Mary in the invocation.[3] An even smaller number dispensed with the invocation altogether, but such cases were extremely rare.[4] The invocation served to make the will a religious document, which was written in the presence of God and in His name. Through the power of this prayer – enhanced in most cases by the mysterious, liturgical power of Latin – both notary and testator sought to endow the document with a transcendent value. By doing all in the name of God, those who were writing the will were bringing it to God's attention, as it were, making sure that it would be as valid in heaven as they hoped it would be on earth. The adoption of such a formalized prayer shows that belief in God and in His control of the person after death could not be publicly or officially questioned: It was a foregone conclusion.

Identification

Immediately after the invocation, the testator identifies himself or herself. First comes the name: "Let all who read this testament know that I

(XIII–XVIe siècles), ed. A. Paravicini Bagliani and J. D. Maire-Vigeur. He cites, among others: A. Castellani, *Nuovi testi fiorentini del Dugento*, 2 vols. (Florence, 1952), I, 207, 210, 291; II, 459, 604, 623, 804. Also in V. Branca, *Mercanti Scrittori* (Milan, 1986), pp. 3, 103.

[2] AHPM 542: 676 (1568).

[3] AHPM 73.294 (1538) is a good example. Pedro Espinosa, who held the position of "Reparador de las camas de la reina," began his will by saying: "En el nombre de Dios todopodersoso, Padre, Hijo y Espiritu Santo, un solo Dios verdadero y en nombre de la bienaventurada Virgen Maria."

[4] AHPM 73. s.f. (1542).

. . . [name]," followed by other descriptive identifying elements, such as titles, honors, profession, or familial relationships. For women, as has already been mentioned, the predominant form of identification is that of their relation to some male, either the father or the husband. A few men who might have been too young to have a status of their own were listed as sons of some other male. Because age is hardly ever listed, however, it is difficult to ascertain whether this is due to youth in all cases. The identification of women with their husbands and fathers increases slightly in the second half of the century when the listing of professions becomes more normative. From 1561 to 1599 the husband's profession or status is listed in some women's wills.

Although notaries did not always list the profession or status of the testators, especially before 1561, they almost always listed their physical condition under two simple categories: "healthy" or "sick." This little bit of information lets us know much about attitudes toward the writing of the will itself, because the testator's health was an indication of his or her acceptance of the inevitability of death. Obviously, those who wrote wills while still healthy were preparing ahead of time for their passage to the next world. This not only showed prudence but true piety as well: It was a sign that an individual had willfully meditated on death and its consequences. Throughout the sixteenth century, most Madrileños wrote their wills while seriously ill. Nonetheless, it is possible to see a gradual increase in the number of healthy testators (see Figure 2.1). Temporary fluctuations aside, it is possible to draw an upward curve in the percentage of healthy testators and a downward curve in the percentage of sick ones. By the 1590s, for the first time in the century, the situation was reversed: There were more healthy than sick testators. This change is most probably a result of the acceptance of a new attitude toward making a will as something not reserved exclusively for one's final moments, and it is an indication that more testators were willing to prepare for a good death while still in possession of good health.

Those who were sick seldom described their ailments. There were some exceptions, however, such as the unfortunate Juan de Vitelo, who had been wounded in the head, and the worried Ana de Valencia, who was experiencing difficulties with childbirth.[5] Surprisingly few wills allude to the seriousness of the illness. Most statements are as general as

[5] Vitelo: AHPM 96. s.f. (1556). Valencia: AHPM 147.215 (1552).

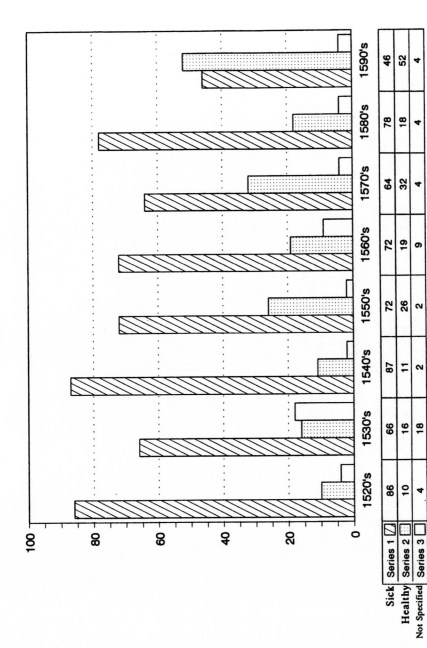

	1520's	1530's	1540's	1550's	1560's	1570's	1580's	1590's
Sick · Series 1	86	66	87	72	72	64	78	46
Healthy · Series 2	10	16	11	26	19	32	18	52
Not Specified · Series 3	4	18	2	2	9	4	4	4

Figure 2.1. Sick and healthy testators.

the one made by Diego de Madrid in 1549, who described himself as "suffering from some maladies," or Pedro de Olivares, who was described as "sick in his body with a grave illness."[6] In the case of people who were very old, it sometimes seems enough to mention that fact, as if age itself were a fatal disease. For instance, Francisco de Vargas, *viejo* (old man), described himself as "seemingly healthy in body, although beset by infirmities."[7] Most often, it seems to be assumed that the testator's illness could prove fatal. "If it is the will of God to take me from this life to the other . . . ," add many wills, confirming the fears of the sick person.[8] In many cases, it is clear that the testator is still at home, in his or her own bed, and not in a hospital. In other cases the phrasing sometimes makes it difficult to determine the location of the sickbed with certainty.[9]

Another convention observed in the wording of this information is that which ascribes the illness to God's will. Two very common ways of phrasing this throughout the entire century were to say the testator was "sick in bed with the illness that God Our Lord saw fit to give," or "bodily ill with the malady that God willed to give."[10] This formal resignation to illness and death as God-given, which appears too often and in much too contrived a formation to be an expression of genuine, personal sentiment, is an example of the way in which certain accepted models of behavior toward death and dying were presented to every individual in society. It is also an example of the way in which ritual language conveyed these paradigms. Because the will was a legal contract that was as binding in heaven as on earth – as well as a ritual invocation – it was considered most prudent to voice the proper, acceptable attitude toward death. A willing acceptance of disease and death had long been considered to be a "proper" Christian attitude. Resignation to one's fate as

---

[6] AHPM 314.1012 (1564).

[7] AHPM 412.311. Another aged testator, Inés Alvarez, was described as "muy vieja . . . ya pasionada de enfermedades." AHPM 139.474.

[8] AHPM 73.87 (1541) is but one of many wills that make this statement.

[9] Two of the relatively rare examples of testators who identify themselves as patients in a hospital are Maria Calderón (AHPM 571.15) and Francisco Hernández (AHPM 543.83).

[10] AHPM 1015.92: "Enfermo en la cama de la enfermedad que Dios Nuestro Señor fue servido de dar." One unusual will ascribes the illness to Jesus Christ specifically: "Enferma del cuerpo de la dolencia que Dios Nuestro Señor Jesucristo me quiso dar" (AHPM 139.137).

willed by God and as accepted through ceremonial phrasing was the mark of a good death.

No illness should be so incapacitating, however, as to impede the testator's judgment. For if the illness were to be described in such a way as to give the impression that the testator was not thinking clearly or rationally, then the will itself could have been called into question. Because a last will or testament ostensibly reflects the final wishes of an individual (a function clearly revealed in the English world "will"), it is necessary that this individual's will and intellect be functioning properly. Otherwise, it would be difficult for the heirs to accept as final whatever redistribution is made by the testator. It would also be difficult to accept such a person's final religious confession. Cervantes alluded to this in his narration of Don Quixote's death, when he had the priest proclaim after hearing the hero's confession: "Alonso Quijano el Bueno is truly dying, and he is truly sane; surely, we can now go in and have him draw up his will."[11]

To avoid any possible misunderstanding, a commonsense clause testifying to the testator's clarity of mind and purpose was inserted into the vast majority of Madrid wills. Most often it claimed that the testator was "of sound mind and judgment" or simply "of sound mind."[12] This one tidbit of information in Madrid wills reveals, first of all, that most sixteenth-century Madrileños wrote wills on their deathbeds – or at least on what they feared might be their deathbeds. These wills are, for the most part, the voices of the dying. For those who are healthy, the realization of death is forced upon them; for the sick, acceptance of their condition is forced upon them. All in all, whatever is said after this point shows what the dying person is thinking or at least what limits are imposed on these thoughts.

The preamble

The identification is always followed by an introductory statement that explains the reasons and intent of what is to follow. This preamble can

---

[11] *Don Quixote*, Bk II, chap. 74 (Barcelona, 1975), p. 1035.

[12] One of many possible examples is Isabel Calderón, who declared she was "en my sano juicio y seso natural" (AHPM 1015.103). Maria Santander linked her clarity of mind directly to her ability to confess her faith: "En mi entero juicio creyendo como firmemente creo en la Santisima Trinidad" (AHPM 1015.92).

vary immensely in content and length but generally consists of four parts: (1) the supplication; (2) the meditation on death; (3) the meditation on judgment; (4) the profession of faith.

Supplication

After calling directly on God in the invocation, the testator could continue beseeching Him in other ways. The supplication was essentially a plea for mercy and a call for assistance at the hour of death. Although addressed principally to God, as a continuation of the invocation, this appeal was quite often extended to other intercessory powers, most notably the Virgin Mary, the angels, and the saints who surrounded the throne of the divine majesty.

In the supplication, testators revealed much about their attitudes toward death and the afterlife in general and about their conception of heaven in particular. In brief, what is revealed in this section of sixteenth-century Madrid wills is a belief in death as a moment of judgment, and of heaven as a "court," in the sense of its being both a place where the Highest Sovereign and all His retinue reside and a place where ultimate justice is administered. This conception of the organization and function of the heavenly court was not very imaginative or otherworldly but rather mundane. In many ways, it was little more than a projection of the sociopolitical order of an earthly monarchy, where no favor can ever be received from the king, as supreme ruler and judge, without the aid of influential intercessors. Consider, for example, the petition made in the detailed preamble of Francisco de Berestegui, a knight of the military order of San Juan (1568):

I beseech God my Lord as our merciful Heavenly Father not to disown or reject my soul . . . and I call on his only begotten son, Jesus Christ, who with the Holy Spirit is of the same essence as the Father . . . through the power of his blood on the cross . . . and I pray to the Virgin Mary to be my personal intercessor, and also to the choirs of angels and especially to the one who is my guardian . . . and finally to all the saints of the celestial court, particularly the blessed John the Baptist, to whom I am very devoted, I beg of them to come to my aid and intercede for me, so that through their influence and mediation my soul may be forgiven its sins and may thus come to enjoy with them the perpetual glory that they already possess.[13]

[13] AHPM 542.501.

Here we have a court where power and influence get things accomplished. No doubt, Don Francisco knew the way the court functioned in Madrid. To have the king come to someone's assistance usually required the cooperation of others close to him, who could bring special cases to his attention or even sway his opinion. Here, certain parties in the heavenly court are being called upon for assistance, so that through their influence and mediation (*favor y intercesión*) the Supreme King may be moved to act in the testator's favor.

Those with whom the testator claims to have a special relationship are urged in a special way to perform this task. In this case, Don Francisco called upon the patron saint of the order to which he belonged, St. John, to whom he was "very devoted." The fact that this devotion should be mentioned at all, as if the written clause in the will would somehow be binding on the saint's conscience in heaven, shows how the will itself could be perceived: It not only had a binding legal power on earth but also in heaven.

The double image of the Celestial Court as a place of residence for God and His retinue and as a place of judgment is reflected in the language used to describe the intercessors. For Don Francisco, as just shown, the saints were more like courtiers soliciting favors from their king. For many others, the intercessors most often acted as attorneys pleading their case before a judge. Gaspar de Berlanger, himself a member of the royal court, knew he needed a heavenly lawyer's assistance in 1530: "I call upon all the saints of the celestial court to act as my attorneys before my Lord Jesus Christ," he said, "so that he may forgive my guilt and my sins."[14]

The image of the saint as advocate for the testator at the hour of judgment appears in Madrid wills throughout the entire century but with only moderate frequency. Most often, it is the Virgin Mary who is called upon to fulfill this function. In these cases, she is asked to act in her role as mother of Jesus. Francisco Yepes de Peralta (1530) echoed the plea of many of his contemporaries when he asked for "divine assistance through the intercession of the Virgin Mary, Mother of God, mediatrix and advocate for sinners."[15] Isabela Diaz, a servant at Philip's court, focused precisely on Mary's motherhood to place a claim on her intercessory powers. In her preamble, Mary is not only referred to as

[14] AHPM 55.841.   [15] AHPM 69.94.

"the mother of God's most holy son, our redeemer, true God and true man," but also, in a very physical sense, as "the reliquary of the angels."[16] The use of this uncommon title for Mary shows that it could be difficult for sixteenth-century Madrileños to conceive of heaven in an immaterial way. The assumption made here by Isabela is that the angels in heaven worship much as Catholics do on earth, using objects of veneration and focusing their attention on the physical fact of the Incarnation of the second person of the Trinity. The assumption that Mary should be revered by the angels in heaven as a "reliquary," that is, as a receptacle containing the physical presence of something holy (in this case the entire body of Jesus in her womb) shows how difficult it could be for anyone to separate the heavenly and earthly spheres, even when trying to conceive of heaven itself.

If Mary was capable of interceding for the living on earth and for those who were dying, she was also certainly able to plead for the dead in the afterlife.[17] It is not surprising, therefore, to find invocations to Mary at the moment of death and judgment. Some wills specifically asked Mary to help the testator to die a good death.[18] Many others asked her to lead the testator's soul to heaven and plead on its behalf with her son Jesus, the judge. To some testators, it seemed inconceivable that any act of divine mercy should take place without the assistance of Mary. Her role as mediatrix was so firmly entrenched in the minds of some that it seemed for them as if the redemptive work of Jesus was not sufficient by itself for salvation. Francisco Martinez, for instance, asked Mary to remind her Son of what He had accomplished on the cross: "I take as my guide and advocate the Virgin Mary, so she can intercede for me before Jesus Christ and ask Him to forgive my sins . . . through the merits of His most holy passion."[19]

For others, such as Ines de Arroyo (1550), Mary could serve more than one function: she could be both a courtier with an influential position and a legal counselor, both the Queen of Mercy and her advocate (*abogada*). The same double function could be performed by other saints in heaven. In the same will, for example, St. Francis and St. Clare were asked to serve as "patrons" and "defenders."[20]

[16] AHPM 1015.289.
[17] Venegas thought that invoking the name of Mary along with that of Jesus was an especially potent defense against the devil at the moment of death. *Agonía*, p. 66.
[18] AHPM 139.375.   [19] AHPM 141.264.   [20] AHPM 107. s.f.

Though she did not appear in every will, the Virgin Mary was by far the most popular intercessor in this testamentary sample (see Table 2.1). Most of the intercessors listed under the category of "Other saints" were requested only once or twice with the exception of Saint Francis (requested by five testators 1550–99), and Saint John the Baptist (requested by five testators 1520–99). The remainder, especially those invoked in the 1570s, 1580s, and 1590s, do not constitute a long list.[21]

Aside from verifying the popularity of the Virgin Mary, these figures reveal something remarkable: the relatively modest role played by her in the wills and the minuscule role played by other intercessors. Though Mary and the saints were routinely approached for assistance within the realm of earthly existence, it appears that they had not yet been universally perceived as testamentary patrons. The highest percentage of testators who sought Mary's aid (54 percent in the 1540s) is still a relatively low figure when compared to other indexes of popular devotion, such as chapels, shrines, images, and vows.[22] The figure of about 28 percent for the 1580s seems remarkably low. When one looks at the relative absence of other intercessors and at the paucity of requests for those few who are invoked, there is no denying the fact that saintly intercession (especially by saints other than the Virgin Mary) was not considered crucial within the testament. And these figures for Madrid are similar to those elsewhere in Spain.[23]

This does not necessarily mean that saintly intercession was considered unimportant when it came to death and the afterlife. It only means that the invocation of the saints had not made its way universally into the document of the will itself, and that compared with other indexes of popular devotion, the number of invocations seems low. The saints remained important. We know that the *Ars Moriendi* literature recommended the intercession of the saints during the death struggle. Also,

---

[21] The other intercessors can be divided into the following categories: (1) Biblical: Andrew, John the Evangelist, Simon, Jude, Joseph, Mary Magdalene; (2) Patristic: Gregory, Jerome; (3) Mendicants: Dominic, Clare, Catherine of Siena, Anthony of Padua; (4) National patrons: George; (5) Angelic: Michael the Archangel, and the Guardian Angels.

[22] See William Christian, *Local Religion in Sixteenth-Century Spain*, esp. pp. 70–5; 181–3; 201–3.

[23] Lopez Lopez has similar findings for the area of Oviedo and Gijón in the second half of the sixteenth century, in *Comportamientos religiosos en Asturias*, p. 57.

Table 2.1. *The Intercession of the saints:*
Number of invocations in the sample of 436 Madrid wills
(Number of wills sampled per decade in parentheses)

	Virgin Mary	Celestial court	Saint James	Sts. Peter & Paul	Other saints
1520s (50)	5	2			1
1530s (51)	16	2			
1540s (50)	27	1			
1550s (48)	23	5	2	1	5
1560s (50)	23	3			2
1570s (76)	28	3	2	2	9
1580s (54)	1	2	4	3	7
1590s (57)	26	6	1	4	12

as will be seen later, many of the Madrid testators who requested perpetual masses chose to have them celebrated on the feast days of their patron saints. Moreover, in Madrid one can see a subtle change taking place at midcentury, and especially after the arrival of the court and the reforms of the Council of Trent. The number of invocations does not increase markedly, but the number of saints addressed does increase. What this means is that more testators began to appeal to their personal patrons instead of to popular socially accepted intercessors (Mary, the Celestial Court, Santiago, Peter and Paul). Whether this change is attributable to the presence of the court or to the Tridentine reforms cannot be easily or conclusively determined from the wills alone.

Whether it was Mary who was called upon at the moment of death, then, or some specific patron saint, or even the entire heavenly court, one thing is certain: Some Madrileños believed that intercession was as necessary in heaven as it was on earth. Those who inserted the saints into their wills might have been thinking of life at court. Just as no one on earth would have the presumption to approach the king directly, without the assistance of a powerful patron at court, so should no one expect to deal with God on a one-to-one basis. Consequently, it is possible to find supplications such as the one made by Diego de Herrera in 1544: "I call forth as my advocates all the saints of the heavenly court, so that they may come to my aid, and so that through their favors my soul will find the way of salvation."[24]

The meditation on death

Immediately following the supplication, almost every single preamble includes a brief, *pro forma* meditation on death. This statement usually reads as follows, with relatively little variation: "Nothing is more certain in life than death, and nothing more uncertain than its hour."

Through this statement the testator affirms that certain kind of resignation to death that is expected of each good Catholic Christian and also pointedly reminds all who read the document that if it were not for death, the will itself would be unnecessary. As one of the more eloquent testators put it, he was drawing up a will "in consideration of human frailty, and of the inconstancy of human nature, knowing that nothing is more certain than death, and nothing more uncertain than its day, or its hour."[25]

This brief *memento mori* reveals what the testator thought to be the proper attitude toward death, an attitude promulgated by the devotional literature of the age.[26] There is no noticeable change in this attitude throughout the century. The vast majority of all wills express a personal fear of death and a grudging acceptance of death as a natural phenomenon. There is relatively little philosophizing and even less theologizing about death. Very few testators hazard a true meditation on the meaning of death from a Christian perspective. Whereas accepted doctrine taught that death was not part of God's original creation but a punishment for the sin of Adam and Eve, it is far more common to find the fear of death described simply as "a natural thing, common to all creatures." That death might be a punishment for sin or a release from a less desirable state of existence is seldom mentioned. Normally, most testators make a commonsense observation, such as that made by a lawyer in 1540: "I

---

[24] AHPM 139.375.   [25] AHPM 620.226.

[26] See, for instance, Luis de Granada, *Libro de la oración y meditación* (1554), modern edition (Madrid, 1979), p. 72: "Piensa, pués, primeramente cuán incierta es aquella hora en qué te ha de asaltar la muerte, por que no sabes en qué día, ni en qué lugar, ni en qué disposicion te tomará. Solamente sabes que has de morir, todo lo demás es incierto."

Death, the Great Leveler. From *Cordial de las quatro cosas postrimeras* del Cartujano Dionisio (Zaragoza, 1499). Reproduced in Agusti Duran-Sanpere, *Grabados Populares Españoles* (Barcelona, 1971), plate 154.

"Nemini parco qui vivit in orbe": Death's banner proclaims, "I spare no one who lives on earth." The victims depicted here are wearing the insignia of the secular and clerical elite. Below and to the right: crowned heads. To the left: a papal tiara, a bishop's mitre, a cardinal's hat, and two tonsured monks. Here, Death is holding an arrow in his left hand. Death could be depicted with either an arrow or a scythe.

know that all men living in this life must submit to death, and that it is a debt from which no one can escape."[27]

Still, one can now and then find testators who voice the official teaching of the church with conviction, such as Juan de Galarca (1562), who confessed that death sometimes arrived unexpectedly as a result of one's "sins and demerits."[28] Even more correct was the meditation of the priest Francisco Sanchez, who said: "I believe I am under that universal law of mortality from which no one can escape, which is decreed by God, and under which it is necessary for each creature to die and pass on from this world by means of a corporeal death to an eternal heavenly life."[29]

The meditation on judgment

The fear of death expressed in Madrid wills is tempered by resignation; one could no more escape from anxiety than from death itself. The wording of most Madrid wills throughout the sixteenth century is intentionally ambiguous in one respect. As the often-used formula put it, each testator wrote his or her will "fearful of death, which is something natural" (*temiendo de la muerte que es cosa natural*). This statement has a double meaning: It refers both to death and the fear of death as being "something natural."

Although the thought of death itself was frightful enough when considered on a strictly material level, as the disintegration of one's earthly body, it was even more terrifying when viewed from a spiritual perspective. The wording of most Madrid wills makes it clear that death was not regarded as the *end* of life but, rather, as its most significant transition point. Above all else, death was a moment of judgment. It was the most crucial phase in one's existence, the instant at which the merits of one's life were closely examined by God and when one's eternal fate was decided. As one testator said in the 1490s, death was "that uncertain day in which each of us is required to account for all the good and evil that one has done in this world, to obtain the reward or punishment that one deserves."[30]

Undoubtedly, the moment of reckoning was viewed with apprehension in Madrid wills, and at times it seemed to be feared more than

[27] AHPM 105. s.f.   [28] AHPM 85.866.   [29] AHPM 78.394.   [30] AHPM 1407.244v.

75

death itself. In some wills, the testators openly admit to a fear of judgment at the moment of death. One soldier, for instance, changed the formula slightly to reveal his deepest concern. Instead of saying he was "fearful of death," he said he was "fearful of the divine judgment, since there is nothing more certain than death and nothing more uncertain than its hour."[31] Another testator, Inés de Arroyo, expressed her anxiety more bluntly. "When I think about divine justice," she said, "I feel a great dread and terror."[32]

Such anxiety appears to have been caused as much by the inevitability of death as by its unpredictability. Since God's final judgment over an individual's eternal fate was based on the state of each individual soul at the moment of death, it was of supreme importance not to be unprepared at the moment one was summoned to appear before the divine judge. As Francisco de Rojas and his wife declared in their joint will, written at the royal court in 1540, it was necessary to be always prepared for death and to have one's soul "clean from sin" because one never knew the exact moment when God would "call us from this life to the next."[33] Juan de Galarca, a secretary of Philip II, summarized these sentiments succinctly. "Death often comes suddenly," he said, "and puts an end to one's life without giving one the chance to ponder how one's time has been spent, or to unburden one's soul and conscience, or to even plead mercy for one's salvation from Him who created the soul for eternal life."[34]

The vast majority of Madrid wills express uneasiness over the hour of death precisely because so much was at stake during this particular moment. No other single instant in one's life was as important as the hour of one's death, for without a "good death" one could not hope to gain heaven. Isabela Diaz, who left the court of Philip II to become a Franciscan nun in 1584, had taken this belief to heart and voiced her conviction unequivocally: "There is no other moment that matters as much as the hour of death, because if it is a good one, it will serve as a door through which we can come to enjoy the eternal glory for which we have been created."[35]

If such an attitude was normative in sixteenth-century Madrid, it should come as no surprise that the wills from this period exhibit a

[31] AHPM 567.2230.
[32] AHPM 107. s.f.: "Aunque pensando en la divina justicia he muy gran pavor e temor."
[33] AHPM 136.216.   [34] AHPM 85.866.   [35] AHPM 1015.289.

marked apprehension about death and the afterlife, and particularly about the moment of judgment. This anxiety, though pervading, could not be expressed in entirely negative terms. The surest way *not* to have a "good death" would be to despair or to doubt God's mercy and goodness. Consequently, most testators display a mixture of hope and fear when speaking about their own final hour. Inés de Arroyo, the woman who said she felt "great dread and terror" when she contemplated the divine justice, also declared that she looked forward to the moment when she would be freed from the "many dangers and labors" of this life:

Confident of God's infinite kindness, I firmly hope to enter upon the road to salvation, not trusting in my own deeds or merits, but rather in the unique passion and death that He suffered for us . . . believing and trusting in the power of even a single drop of the most precious blood that He shed on our behalf.[36]

Still, in spite of such a testimony, this same woman could not help but tremble before the divine majesty at the moment of judgment. Her will expressed an overwhelmingly judicial concept of God. This confession of faith, though intensely personal, was a clear reflection of the beliefs expressed less succinctly in most other wills. She believed in a God, she said, "who is triune in persons and one in essence, and who is the ruler of those who are good, and the chastiser of those who are evil." God's primary function, according to Inés, was to dispense justice: to reward the just and punish the wicked. Although she expressed confidence in God's benevolence, she also despaired of her own goodness and of her ability to withstand the scrutiny of the divine magistrate. Her profession of faith is at the same time a plea for mercy. "I beg that at the hour of my death God may place His passion and death between my soul and His judgment," she implored. As if this were not enough, she also appealed to the Virgin Mary for assistance at the hour of her death, as Queen of Mercy and as her personal advocate (*abogada*), to the archangel Michael and all the saints, and especially to Saint Francis and Saint Clare to serve as her "patrons and defenders."[37]

[36] AHPM 107 s.f.
[37] AHPM 107. s.f. Although this will has been singled out as an example for its eloquence, it is by no means unique in terms of its contents. Many other wills throughout the century express similar beliefs, even if stiffly constrained by notarial conventions.

Fear of death and fear of judgment were thus inseparable for sixteenth-century Madrileños. All of one's existence hung in the balance at that one moment when the self passed from this life to the next, a moment that was all the more frightful because it was as unpredictable as it was inevitable. In many wills, an undeniably profound fear of God's justice was often juxtaposed with a firm profession of confidence in God's mercy and benevolence. For most, there existed an uneasy equilibrium between dread and hope, between the notions of God as judge and God as father. On the one hand, God had to punish sin in order to be just, and the testators felt compelled to tremble before His majesty. On the other hand, God had to forgive sins in order to be merciful, and the testators felt obliged to remind Him of this. It was a complex dialectic fueled by raw emotion but controlled by carefully measured thinking expressed in dogmatic phrases.

We should not think that this willing acceptance of conflicting dispositions, which always appeared couched in the legalistic prose of notaries and theologians, concealed some other less bewildered extraecclesiastical attitude toward death. Sixteenth-century Madrid wills clearly expressed both fear and hope concerning death and the afterlife, showing that the prevailing attitude of the people was far from simple. Though such a dialectical attitude might seem befuddled, or even insincere, it was not lacking in integrity. After all, if sixteenth-century Spanish society demanded belief in an eternal afterlife that consisted either of eternal bliss or everlasting torment, and in a moment of judgment during which everyone's ultimate fate would be decided on the basis of their previous behavior on earth, it is only reasonable to expect that the members of that society would feel somewhat bewildered and intimidated by the prospect of death.

The profession of faith

Every preamble ended with a credal statement that affirmed the testator's orthodoxy, and confirmed his or her right to receive a proper

Another will that expresses similar sentiments in a highly personal way is that of Francisco de Berestegui, a knight of the Order of St. John. He, too, despairs of his own goodness, calling himself a sinner with a stained soul, and begs for mercy from "Dios mio señor como nuestro padre celestial y misericordioso," asking Him not to disown him at the hour of judgment, in the name of Christ, "y por su sangre en la cruz" (AHPM 542.501).

sacramental burial. Here, perhaps more than in any other part of the will, there was little room for individual expression. Above all else, what all testators sought to do through their profession of faith was to show their conformity to the teachings of the Catholic Church or, as many of the wills call it, their "Holy Mother Church." There could be a great variation in the number of doctrinal points that were affirmed by each individual, but as far as the actual doctrines were concerned, the last thing anyone would have wanted to do was to express creativity.[38]

The length and comprehensiveness of these credal statements varies immensely. At one extreme there are hurried, perfunctory summaries that border on impatience, such as the one made by Hernando de la Parra, a priest, in 1528: "I affirm everything that any Catholic Christian is supposed to believe."[39] At the other extreme there are nearly interminable dogmatic inventories that rival the Niceno-Constantinopolan Creed in their attention to detail. Somewhere in between there are several variations of the same modest confession, in which the vast majority of testators profess their faith in all the teachings of Holy Mother Church.

Even if only perfunctorily, the profession of faith was included in every will. The single most important item to confess, it seems, was to voice assent with the teachings of the Catholic Church. If one acknowledged one's willingness to be a faithful member of the church, it was assumed that one's heart was in the right place, and that even if one did not know about certain specific doctrines, one would want to believe in them.

So important was this credal consent, that many wills also contained a cautionary clause to protect the testator in the case of grave illness. "If I am unable to use my mouth to say anything [about my faith] due to the seriousness of some malady, I will say it nonetheless with my heart, and say it continuously, as a true son and member of the Catholic Church."[40]

---

[38] The confession of faith began to appear regularly in Spanish wills at the beginning of the fifteenth century. According to Idelfonso Adeva, the popularity of this practice can be attributed to *Ars Moriendi* treatises: "Los Artes de Bien Morir en España antes del Maestro Venegas," *Scripta Theologica* 1–2 (1984): 414.

[39] AHPM 55.728.   [40] AHPM 1390.609.

The encommendation

After making this profession of faith, which closed the preamble, testators placed their destiny in God's hands. Again, much of the structure of this was *pro forma*, couched in standard notarial formulae. Its stiffness notwithstanding, this final public gesture of surrender to God served three purposes. First, as the ultimate act of submission, it confirmed the faith that the testator had just expressed in the credal statement. Second, as a declaration of trust, it demonstrated that the testator conformed to the norms of surrender considered necessary for a "good death." Third, as a plea for mercy, it reminded God in no uncertain terms of the work of redemption He had accomplished through the blood of Jesus Christ.

The encommendation deserves close attention. Of all the parts of the will, few others reveal as much about popular perceptions of Catholic eschatology. Since this section addresses the question of the fate of the individual at the moment of death, explicit reference is made to the very essence of the self, particularly as pertains to the relation between body and soul.

What do sixteenth-century encommendations from Madrid tell us? Without exception, Madrileños publicly accepted and reinforced the notion that the human self is composed of two elements, one material (the body) and one spiritual (the soul), which are sundered at death.[41] The prevailing attitude toward the way in which these two components actually define the self leans decidedly in favor of a dualistic understanding. Here is an example of the most typical formulation as it appears in almost every single will from 1520 to 1599, with little variation:

First, I commend my soul to God, Our Lord, who created and redeemed it through His most precious blood, and I commend my body to the earth from which it was formed.[42]

---

[41] The definition of death itself depended on such a conception, as in the case of Venegas, *Agonía*, p. 121: "La muerte no es otra cosa que un apartamiento del cuerpo y del alma." Pedro de Medina also employed this definition, *Libro de la Verdad*, III, p. 447. One Madrid testator, Inés de Arroyo, explains death in her 1550 will as that time "despues que el Señor placiere que la mi anima sea apartada deste cuerpo a que está unida y allegada" (AHPM 107 s.f.).

[42] "Primeramente encomiendo mi anima a Dios nuestro señor que la crió y redimyó por

Although orthodox Catholic doctrine taught that the redemption worked by Jesus benefited the total human person, in body as well as in soul, the encommendations from Madrid reflect the nearly universal tendency of Western Christendom to overlook this teaching.[43] Little mention is ever made of the promised resurrection of the body. Only three wills out of the entire sample take the Resurrection into account, but two out of the three place more emphasis on the terror of the Day of Judgment than on the delights of an everlasting embodied existence.[44] Antonia de Ayala (1538) offers her body to the earth "until Our Lord be pleased to resurrect it on Judgment Day." In 1585 Juan Zapata de Cardenas, a *Comendador* of the Order of Santiago, mentions the final judgment but not the Resurrection: "I offer my body to the earth, where it shall be deposited until the day of universal judgment." Hernando de Vireysa, keeper of the king's jewels, stands alone in 1580 when he expresses some hope for a resurrection without judgment: "I commend my body to the earth, from which it was formed, and where it shall be deposited until the day of Our Lord's kingdom."[45]

Overall, what one finds is an overwhelmingly spiritualized view of salvation. It is the soul – and *only* the soul – that is created and redeemed by the blood of the Lord. The body simply dissolves into the earth and disappears.[46] The encommendation heightens this juxtaposition of body and soul by focusing directly on the redemptive value of the blood of Jesus: The soul of the testator is promised salvation because the incarnate God freely offered His human body for sacrifice. It is the

su preciosisima sangre, y el cuerpo a la tierra de que fue formado." Only seven out of all the wills sampled for this study failed to include an encommendation.

[43] Commending one's body to the earth and one's soul to the eternal realm was an ancient practice absorbed by Christianity. It is found in epitaphs dating back to the sixth century B.C.E. See Lopez Lopez, *Comportamientos religiosos en Asturias*, p. 56.

[44] Near the century's end an entire treatise was devoted to this topic, with a title aimed at a general readership: Nicolás Diaz, *Tratado del juyzio final en el cual se hallarán muchas cosas provechosas y curiosas* (Valladolid, 1588).

[45] Ayala (AHPM 69.102); Zapata de Cardenas (AHPM 580.511v); Vireysa (AHPM 412.756).

[46] This attitude is most clearly revealed in the will of Felipe Marichal, a servant of King Philip II (1595), where the relation of God to the self is not only limited to the soul but is even explained according to different functions of each person in the Holy Trinity: "Ofrezco mi anima al padre que la crío, al hijo que la redimío, y al espiritu que la alumbró" (AHPM 1407.105).

spilling of Christ's blood, the very act of draining His human body of life, that makes the redemption of all human souls possible.

Moreover, a different origin and destiny are proposed for body and soul, as if they were essentially incompatible. The lower part, the body, returns to the earth from which it was fashioned, where it decomposes, disintegrates, and turns to dust. In contrast, the higher part, the soul, returns to the God by whom it was created and redeemed. Several wills add that the soul must return "to the glory of the paradise for which it was created," implying a totally disembodied existence in the afterlife.[47] One will goes as far as to use phrasing reminiscent of Plato's *Phaedo:*

I trust that the Divine Majesty will save my soul through His mercy and passion. Therefore, whenever He sees fit to *free my soul from the prisonhouse of the flesh* [emphasis added] I order that my body be deposited in the monastery of San Domingo el Real.[48]

These are faithful echoes of what could be found in the devotional literature of the day. Alejo Venegas spoke of the good death as something very much to be desired. It was

a release from prison, an end to exile, a cessation of the body's labors, a safe haven from storms, the final destination of our journey, a discarding of a massive burden, an exit from a crumbling edifice, an evasion of dangers, a detachment from all evils, a payment of the debt owed to nature, a homecoming, and, finally, a passage and entrance into glory.[49]

Since the 1530s, Alejo Venegas's highly popular *Ars Moriendi* treatise had trumpeted the notion that the resurrected bodies of the just would reside for eternity with God in heaven, not on a reconstituted earth.

---

[47] AHPM 73.115 (1541) is but one of nearly two dozen such examples. One will goes as far as to posit that God created only the soul "con su imagen y semejanza," forgetting completely about the body (AHPM 73.294).
[48] AHPM 85.866 (1562).
[49] Venegas, *Agonía*, pp. 121–2.

(*Opposite*) The Horrors of Hell. From *Cordial de las quatro cosas postrimeras* del Cartujano Dionisio (Zaragoza, 1499). Reproduced in Agusti Duran-Sanpere, *Grabados Populares Españoles* (Barcelona, 1971), plate 153.

Demons here inflict everlasting tortures on the damned, including a monk (upper left), a king, and a bishop (both in a cauldron, beneath the monk).

Only the damned, trapped forever in the abyss of hell, which was located at the very center of the earth, would remain on earth. There amidst the flames, their bodies would be eternally tortured by demons – a fitting punishment, he thought, for those that had so loved their earthly pleasures.[50] At midcentury, Venegas's highly spiritualized conception of the resurrected body was further popularized by Pedro de Medina in his *Book of Truth*.[51] By the early 1580s, Alonso de Orozco was giving voice to an already familiar vision when he, too, spoke in highly dualistic terms of the uncoupling of body and soul and of the "true" destination of the human self.

This is a great mystery we ought to ponder: that our body, though engendered in the earth, has an inclination and a natural appetite for being in heaven . . . and since God created it to be a resident and citizen of the empyrean heaven, which is the highest and most excellent of all, its proper homeland should be in heaven.[52]

In 1598, at the funeral exequies for King Philip II held at Seville, the preacher Juan Bernal seconded Orozco's sentiments and added a curious twist. As there is a purgatory for the soul, he proclaimed, so is there a purgatory for the body. As the soul is purified through suffering in purgatory, so is the body "spiritualized" in the grave. If all souls need cleansing, he asked, should not our "gross animal bodies" need much more? His dualism untempered, Bernal concluded: "The body deserved to be jailed in the prison of the grave for all of the contradiction it offered to the soul in its service of God and its journey to heaven, and for being so burdensome and unwieldy."[53] At century's end, Luis de Rebolledo summed up the prevailing attitude by means of a social analogy that could be understood by all, both high and low. Because the body came from the soil of the earth, he said, it was of "low birth," as rustic and boorish as a peasant. In contrast, the soul being from heaven, was "of high descent" and as noble as *hijodalgo*.[54]

If Madrileños seemed less than clear about their notion of the self and

---

[50] Ibid., pp. 201–2.   [51] Medina, *Libro de la Verdad*, III, pp. 493–500.

[52] Orozco, *Victoria de la Muerte*, p. 242.

[53] Juan de Bernal, funeral sermon for Philip II, published as an appendix to Francisco Ariño, *Sucesos de Sevilla de 1592 á 1604*, *Sociedad de Bibliófilos Andaluces*, series I (Seville, 1873): 533–4.

[54] Rebolledo, *Oraciones funebres*, fol. 30: "El cuerpo es de baxo nacimiento, y es por esta

their attitude toward the body, it was because they had been taught a highly paradoxical eschatology. The body was not believed to be absolutely essential for existence: Though it housed the soul in this world and would house it again for eternity after the Resurrection (either in eternal bliss or everlasting torment), there was believed to be an intermediate time during which the soul would exist disembodied.[55] This was the span of time between the individual's death and the Resurrection, the remaining historical time before the return of Jesus Christ and the Last Judgment. As Venegas explained it, at the very instant that the soul ceased to vivify the body, "without any intervening time, it will be in one of four places, and they are heaven, purgatory, limbo, or hell."[56] This meant that the soul could easily be perceived as the true self, for it was the one constant existing entity, and most significantly it was the self that persisted immediately after death, the self that needed intercessory prayer. But the body was also somehow intimately part of the self, for it would exist eternally after a relatively brief interlude of nonexistence. Compared with eternity, the historical time between death and the Resurrection seemed infinitesimally small. But no matter how brief, this disembodied state was believed to be imminent for all, and this belief made attitudes toward the body very complex.[57]

At best, then, the body was a temporal husk for the soul; at worst it was an awful burden and a great risk. The intensity of the disdain shown for the "lower" part of the human self could indeed be extreme: A dozen wills fail to mention the body altogether when commending the soul to God.[58] Fear of contagion from Jewish and Islamic influences might have

parte villano, destripaterrones, y en una palabra: es hijo de la tierra; pero el alma es hijodalgo, de alta descendencia; porque es resuello de Dios y participación en su divina naturaleza."

[55] For a history of the development of this eschatological geography in the West see Jacques Le Goff, *La naissance du purgatoire* (Paris, 1981), trans. Arthur Goldhammer, *The Birth of Purgatory* (Chicago, 1984).

[56] Venegas, *Agonía*, p. 196. Medina (*Libro de la Verdad*, p. 464) added that the soul would be escorted to the appropriate place by the individual's guardian angel.

[57] Medina, *Libro de la Verdad*, pp. 465, 476–7, could not see his way clear of this complexity. Though he argued that the soul alone was responsible for moral choices, and therefore deserving of reward or punishment in a disembodied state before the final judgment, he also made much of the fact that it would again be embodied in eternal bliss or torment.

[58] AHPM 55.728 is one example. In contrast, only two wills offer the body to God instead of to the earth (AHPM 1410.673; 1410.718).

further increased this scorn for the body in Spain, leading to the common practice of not washing the corpse for burial. Throughout Spain, the Inquisition paid close attention to cases of corpse washing, for this practice came to be viewed as one of the surest signs of false belief, ritual proof of an un-Christian concern for the body.[59] Yet, a complex dialectic remained at work in regard to the body. Despite the disdainful language employed in their testaments, Madrileños expressed belief in an essential connection between body and soul that continued after death. This belief was most intensely expressed in their funeral practices and postmortem devotions, to which we shall presently turn our attention.

[59] See Miguel del Arbol Navarro, *Spanisches funeralbrauchtum*, pp. 52–60.

3

Relinquishing one's body

The tendency to view body and soul as distinct entities with temporarily separate destinies is clearly revealed in the structure of the will itself, which pays attention separately to each component of the self. Immediately following the encommendation, in which the body has been offered to the earth, the will takes up the task of detailing how the testator wishes to be buried. First, one must attend to the corpse.

Reading the meanings of death ritual

The disposal of the body is an occasion fraught with meaning for most human societies. Though dead and decomposing, the corpse is still somehow the "person" it recently embodied: It does more than signify that person; it *is* that person, albeit in a liminal state of transition. It is neither entirely that person nor something altogether *other* than that person. Moreover, the corpse is a threat and a symbol of danger. It is a tangible reminder of the fact that death is a certainty and an omnipresent menace to all members of society.

As soon as a death occurs, the corpse becomes the focus of activity by those who knew the deceased person, from the most intimate, who usually take care of its disposal, to the less intimate, who participate in the ritual, for the death of an individual affects all those who knew him or her. Over the centuries in human society, one of the chief functions of funeral ritual has been to close the circle of community that death has broken. Death ritual is a means for those who knew the dead person to bring themselves – as well as the deceased – through a transition stage by means of private and public symbolic gestures.[1] Another ancient dimension of death ritual has been its prophylactic function: It is a complex act of self-protection on the part of individuals and society, a way of coping with the threat posed by death. Social scientists have long argued, in fact, that all ritual is part of a system of beliefs and gestures that are espoused and performed in response to danger.[2]

Modern scholars of death ritual have made much of something that was already evident to some in the sixteenth century: the fact that ritual actions and behaviors associated with funerals pertain more to the survivors than to the deceased. As Antonio de Guevara put it in 1523: "I have often said, and have often written and preached that church bells toll not for the dead, but for the living."[3] Viewed from this perspective, as complex semiotic displays carried out by those who survive, funerals become symbolic events that very self-consciously cry out for interpretation. One recent study has approached death rites as a form of symbolic behavior that objectifies relations between individuals and social groups, interpreting them as a set of gestures that construct and communicate "a variety of social and cultural categories and understandings, ranging from definitions of kinship and gender roles to forms of patronage and political domination."[4]

But this is only one perspective in the social-scientific study of religion, and it is tied to the functionalism of Emile Durkheim, which tends to view ritual principally as an instrument for achieving specific ends, as a societal control system, and a medium of social interaction.[5] For

[1] Arnold Van Gennep continues to exert his influence over the socioscientific study of death ritual. See his *Les rites de passage* (1909), trans. M. B. Vizedom and G. L. Caffee, *The Rites of Passage* (London, 1960). For commentary on Van Gennep see M. Gluckman, "Les rites de passage," in *Essays on the Ritual of Social Relations*, ed. M. Gluckman (Manchester, 1962); and Jack Goody, *Death, Property, and the Ancestors* (Stanford, CA, 1962).

[2] Edward Sills, "Ritual and Crisis," in *Center and Periphery: Essays in Macrosociology, Selected Papers of Edward Shils*, vol. II (Chicago, 1975), p. 155.

[3] Antonio Guevara, *Epistolas familiares*, Ep. 57 (1523), p. 172. An observation also made later by La Rochefoucauld, *Maximes*, n. 612: "La pompe des enterrements regarde plus la vanité des vivants que l'honneur des morts," p. 105.

[4] Sharon T. Strocchia, *Death and Ritual in Renaissance Florence* (Baltimore, 1992), pp. xiv–xv.

[5] For a synopsis of the impact of Durkheim's *Elementary Forms of the Religious Life* (1912), see Nancy D. Munn, "Symbolism in a Ritual Context," *Handbook of Social and Cultural Anthropology*, ed. J. J. Honigmann (Chicago, 1973).

Durkheim and his followers, ritual regulates relations between individuals within a realm of "sacredness," but this realm is a human construct, and it is constructed for the practical purpose of binding societies together according to their agreed rules.[6] This perspective can open remarkably large windows onto social and political relations, as two brilliant historical studies of Italian death ritual have recently proven.[7] This perspective, however, has a tendency to overlook belief, and that is its major shortcoming for historians of mentalities.[8]

But one could not take a functionalist approach to Madrid's sixteenth-century death rites even if one wanted to. To adequately interpret the sociopolitical and economic dimension of funerals from the past in a functionalist framework, one needs to reconstruct them; to reconstruct, one needs adequate documentation. Unfortunately, in the case of Madrid the documents are far too fragmentary to allow for a detailed analysis of the social, political, and economic dynamics of death rites. The approaches of Strocchia on Florence and Cohn on Siena simply cannot be undertaken in Madrid, where the notarial and parochial archives are incomplete. Nonetheless, this does not mean that funerals cannot be reconstructed to a considerable extent from the surviving testamentary record, at least in regard to the structure of the ritual itself. The sociopolitical and economic dimensions of death remain indeterminable for most testators, but the structure of the ritual itself remains for us to examine as an encoded language.

A perspective more advantageous than functionalism for the history of mentalities is that favored by Victor Turner. Abandoning the functionalists' reliance on the concept of abstract social forms (which he calls the "reinforced concrete" of social theory), Turner has instead called attention to the constant flux of social structures and to the profound complexity of religious symbolism. Focusing on the subjective experience of participants in ritual behavior, he has argued that sacred symbols and rites are much more than means to practical ends: They are the

---

[6] Mary Douglas, *Implicit Meanings: Essays in Anthropology* (London, 1975), pp. xii–xix.

[7] Strocchia, *Death and Ritual;* Samuel S. Cohn, Jr., *Death and Property in Siena, 1205–1800. Strategies for the Afterlife* (Baltimore, 1988).

[8] Hans H. Penner, "The Poverty of Functionalism," *History of Religions*, vol. XI.1 (1971): 91–97. Penner observes (p. 95) that the problem with functionalism "is not that it 'reduces' religion, or explains religion away, but that it does not explain religion at all."

code that enables societies to coalesce and that renders social life intelligible.[9]

According to this perspective, which is favored by other social scientists, ritual behavior not only discloses mundane, practical realities, it is also a lively theater of the collective psychology and one of the richest expressions of the ideology and beliefs – the mentality – of a society.[10] After all, as anthropologists have noted, religion is more than a pattern of social relations: It is an expression of the human capacity to imagine the structure of reality.[11] Religious ritual is not simply a cultural construct: It is a form of cognition that constructs models of reality and paradigms of behavior. And within this process whereby reality is defined, death ritual plays a key role.

Because of their centrality in the ritual life of most societies and their close relation to other forms of symbolic expression, funerals can become a window onto the inner workings of almost any culture. In Spain, as in all of Christian Europe, funerals conveyed their social messages by means of systems of repeated analogies. Elements of the structure and symbolism of death ritual were common to other types of symbolic behavior. Death rites, then, partook of and contributed to an encoded language. Their intelligibility was derived from a commonly understood set of symbols and also gave shape to and confirmed this means of communication.[12] As Edward Shils has observed, "Logically, beliefs could exist without rituals; rituals, however, could not exist without beliefs."[13] Which means that historians of mentalities must go beyond an analysis of the social dimension of funeral rites. Sharon Strocchia has elegantly argued that death rites "realized their many purposes and

---

[9] Victor Turner, *Dramas, Fields, and Metaphors*, pp. 23–59. See also *The Forest of Symbols* (Ithaca, NY, 1967), *The Ritual Process* (Chicago, 1969). For a synopsis of Turner's work see the obituary article by Lawrence E. Sullivan, "Victor Turner 1920–1983," *History of Religions*, 24 (1984): 160–3.

[10] See Michel Meslin, *Aproximación a una ciencia de las religiones* (Madrid, 1978), p. 174.

[11] Edward Shils, "Ritual and Crisis," *Center and Periphery*, p. 154, defines ritual as "a stereotyped, symbolically concentrated expression of beliefs and sentiments regarding ultimate things." A similar observation is made by Maria Jesús Buxó i Rey in "La inexactitud y la incerteza de la muerte: apuntes en torno a la definición de religión en antropología," in *Religiosidad Popular*, vol. 2 (1989): 205–23.

[12] Buxó i Rey, "Inexactitud," *Religiosidad Popular*, vol. 2 (1989): 208–9: "La elaboración simbólica de la muerte delimita las fronteras significativas del fenómeno religioso."

[13] Shils, "Ritual and Crisis."

meanings only within the total field of their social environment."[14] Although this is certainly true, it must be kept in mind that the rites themselves gained their intelligibility from beliefs and that the social environment and the encoded symbolic language were defined by – and also gave shape to – certain ways of thinking and feeling. And it is through their detailed planning for their own funerals that Madrid's testators most clearly reveal this mental and spiritual dimension.

Place of burial

The first detail to be handled in the wills is where to dispose of the body. To some extent, all testators are left in charge of their remains in sixteenth-century Madrid, for they are given the opportunity to state exactly where to be buried or at least to indicate a range of choices. In most wills, testators usually express some kind of personal preference. Relatively few people leave the funeral arrangements to their executors and survivors (see Figure 3.1).

In sixteenth-century Madrid the only acceptable place of burial for a Catholic Christian was in consecrated ground. Without exception, this involved being buried in a parish church, a monastery chapel, or, in some rare cases, a cloister. Like so many other Spanish cities, Madrid had no outdoor graveyards or cemeteries in the sixteenth century.[15] Of the 436 Madrid testators in our sample, 435 ask for burial inside the church *dentro de la iglesia*. The single exception is Juan Sandyno, who asked in 1524 to be buried *en la iglesia o cementerio de la parroquia donde yo falleciere*[16] (in the parish church or cemetery where I might die).[17] Sandyno might have been thinking about the possibility of dying outside Madrid and of being buried in some parish church that had an outdoor cemetery.

[14] Strocchia, *Death and Ritual*, p. 51.

[15] Various localities and regions in the Iberian peninsula had cemeteries outside the churches and different burial preferences. Sitges, in Catalonia, is one such place. In a small sample of sixteenth-century wills from Sitges, testators preferred the cemetery over the church interior by a margin of two to one. Lourdes Mateo Bretos, "Actitudes ante la muerte de la población de Sitges en los siglos XVI y XVII," in *Religiosidad Popular*, vol. 2 (1989): 268.

[16] It is possible that courtyards, such as the one at San Ginés, might have been considered "dentro de la iglesia," as is suggested in *Madrid en el Archivo Histórico de Protocolos*, p. 153.

[17] AHPM 55.635.

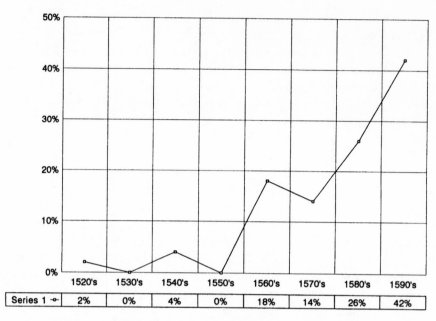

Series 1 ⊸	2%	0%	4%	0%	18%	14%	26%	42%

Figure 3.1. Percentage of testators leaving funeral plans to others.

Elsewhere in Spain, especially in areas with substantial numbers of Jewish and Moslem converts, outdoor cemeteries seem to have caused problems for the church. The provincial Church Council of Granada (1565) decreed that although "it was an ancient custom among faithful Christians to bury some in blessed cemeteries," the practice had to stop. Henceforth, as long as there was still room, all Christians were to be buried inside the city's churches. This rule sought to prevent Moriscos (Moorish converts) from holding their own Islamic funeral ceremonies in unguarded cemeteries. To ensure universal adherence to this rule, the council proclaimed that it was to be observed by both old and new Christians. Foreseeing that the churches could not serve as burial grounds indefinitely, the council also dictated that if churches found it necessary to extend burials to the outdoors, their cemeteries were to be

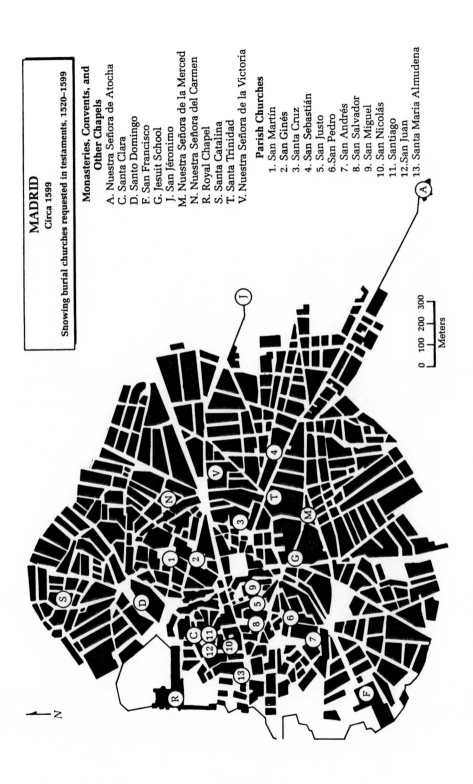

MADRID

Circa 1599

Showing burial churches requested in testaments, 1520–1599

Monasteries, Convents, and Other Chapels

A. Nuestra Señora de Atocha
C. Santa Clara
D. Santo Domingo
F. San Francisco
G. Jesuit School
J. San Jéronimo
M. Nuestra Señora de la Merced
N. Nuestra Señora del Carmen
R. Royal Chapel
S. Santa Catalina
T. Santa Trinidad
V. Nuestra Señora de la Victoria

Parish Churches

1. San Martín
2. San Ginés
3. Santa Cruz
4. San Sebastián
5. San Justo
6. San Pedro
7. San Andrés
8. San Salvador
9. San Miguel
10. San Nicolás
11. Santiago
12. San Juan
13. Santa María Almudena

0 100 200 300

Meters

N

"blessed, walled in, and locked, with a cross in the center."[18] By century's end in 1591, the situation was still touchy enough to prompt Philip II to order that all Moriscos be buried inside the churches, regardless of local customs.[19]

Some parish churches in Madrid, especially San Ginés, San Miguel, and Santa Cruz, constantly serviced the dead. The vaults beneath the parish churches were cities of the dead. These church buildings became true houses of the communion of the saints, where the dead and the living shared the same space. For those families that had long resided in Madrid, the presence of several generations within the sacred space of the churches must have produced an intense feeling of endurance and continuity. The newcomers who flooded the city after 1561 did not seek to join their ancestors but, rather, to be joined by their descendants when they, too, established their own claims to these sacred spaces.

Throughout the sixteenth century the vast majority of the dead in Madrid were buried by the secular clergy in parish churches. The monasteries and convents of the regular clergy also served as burial grounds but were not used as frequently (see Table 3.1 and Figure 3.2). The parish church of San Ginés was one of the most popular locations for burial. Although the church building itself had been reconstructed in 1493–6, this parish was one of the oldest in the city.[20] If one considers the frequency with which burials were requested at this location, it does not take much imagination to realize that this building was not only a church but also a charnel house and that it must have been in a nearly constant state of disrepair as its paving stones and walls made way for an unceasing number of *rompimientos* (grave openings) and *traslados* (transfers of remains). Throughout the century the dead keep flowing into San Ginés in a steady stream, filling a vast reservoir with bones. The magnitude of burials in busy Madrid churches, such as San Ginés, is hinted at in a funeral sermon preached at the royal chapel of the Alcazar on 20 December 1597, in which Father Aguilar de Terrones spoke of "those parishes where they have five hundred burials in a single year."[21]

[18] Tejada, vol. 5, p. 390.

[19] AHN, leg. 1263, fol. 276. See M. del Arbol Navarro, *Spanisches funeralbrauchtum*, pp. 21–48.

[20] *Diccionario geografico-estadisco-histórico de España y sus posesiones de Ultramar* (Madrid, 1848), p. 197.

[21] *Sermones funerales en las honras del Rey Nuestro Señor don Felipe II, recogidos por Juan*

Table 3.1. *Places of burial requested in Madrid wills, 1520–99*

Location	Percentage of testators by decade							
	1520's	1530's	1540's	1550's	1560's	1570's	1580's	1590's
Number of Wills	(50)	(51)	(50)	(48)	(50)	(76)	(54)	(52)
Parish Churches: subtotal	58%	56%	56%	57%	52%	66%	48%	40%
San Gines	30%	24%	22%	16.5%	14%	20%	13%	10%
San Miguel	6%	6%	10%	6%	6%	8%	13%	8%
Santa Cruz	8%	12%	6%	16.5%	14%	6%	5%	7%
San Justo	2%	4%	4%	2%	0%	1%	2%	2%
San Pedro	12%	2%	6%	0%	2%	1%	4%	0%
S. Maria Almudena	0%	4%	6%	4%	6%	4%	0%	3%
San Andres	0%	0%	2%	4%	2%	6%	0%	0%
Santiago	0%	0%	0%	6%	4%	1%	7%	8%
San Nicolas	0%	0%	0%	0%	2%	1%	0%	0%
San Juan	0%	0%	0%	0%	0%	4%	4%	0%
San Sebastian	0%	0%	0%	2%	0%	0%	0%	0%
San Salvador	0%	4%	0%	0%	2%	0%	0%	2%
Monasteries: subtotal	16%	14%	22%	29%	16%	13%	31%	16%
San Francisco	10%	0%	14%	6%	4%	5%	5%	2%
N. S. de Atocha	4%	4%	2%	2%	0%	0%	2%	0%
San Felipe	0%	0%	2%	13%	2%	4%	7%	2%
San Geronimo	2%	10%	2%	6%	0%	0%	2%	2%
Victoria	0%	0%	0%	0%	6%	1%	2%	2%
N. S. de la Merced	0%	0%	0%	0%	0%	1%	9%	3%
San Martin	0%	0%	0%	2%	2%	2%	4%	0%
Sta. Trinidad	0%	0%	2%	0%	2%	0%	0%	5%
Convents: subtotal	0%	0%	0%	6%	4%	2%	7%	11%
Sta. Catalina	0%	0%	0%	2%	0%	0%	0%	2%
Sta. Clara	0%	0%	0%	4%	2%	1%	2%	2%
Sto. Domingo	0%	0%	0%	0%	2%	1%	5%	2%
Carmen	0%	0%	0%	0%	0%	0%	0%	5%
Others:								
Italian Hospital	0%	0%	0%	0%	0%	0%	0%	2%
Jusuit School	0%	0%	0%	0%	0%	0%	0%	2%
Unspecified: subtotal	26%	30%	22%	8%	28%	19%	14%	29%
Nearest Parish	2%	2%	0%	0%	0%	1%	2%	3%
Wherever is best	0%	2%	2%	2%	6%	4%	4%	7%
Nearby Town	14%	6%	8%	0%	12%	2%	4%	5%
Elsewhere in Spain	0%	2%	4%	2%	8%	6%	4&	14%
Foreign Country	0%	0%	0%	0%	0%	1%	0%	0%
Unclear Request	10%	18%	8%	4%	2%	5%	0%	0%

Iñiguez de Lequerica (Madrid, 1601). Aguilar de Terrones, Predicador de Su Majestad, "Sermon predicado en las honras de la Infanta Doña Catalina," fol. 283r. Father Terrones was trying to get his congregation to meditate upon the overwhelming presence of death in Madrid.

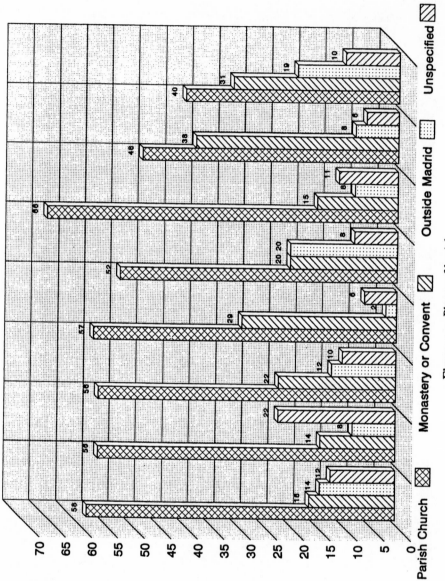

Figure 3.2. Places of burial.

The same might be said of San Miguel and Santa Cruz, the other two parish churches most frequently requested as burial places in our sample. Those who worshiped in this church could not help but notice that the dead surrounded them and could scarcely avoid treading on the resting places of their relatives and neighbors. It is not hard to imagine many of these living parishioners pondering their own fate as they gazed at the very spot where their own remains would one day be buried, or even as they sat directly over it.[22] Alejo Venegas knew that the burial of the dead within the churches could have a profound psychological impact. In fact, he thought it was precisely because of the didactic value of these ever-present dead that such burials were first allowed by Christian bishops.[23]

As the city grew in the latter half of the century, crowding became a serious problem. The creation of new parishes and the building of new churches seemed to offer only temporary relief. By 1593 we can find one testator asking that he be buried in the church of Santiago, "in the central nave, wherever there is the most room."[24]

It is difficult to determine where, exactly, the poor were buried in Madrid and how they fared in view of such overcrowding. We do know that some of the most destitute, including those found dead on the street, could receive a decent burial through the Confraternity of Our Lady of Charity, which had been founded by King Juan II in 1421 at the Hospital del Campo del Rey.[25] The parish clergy in Madrid routinely buried the poor – even those who had died in charity hospitals – and

---

[22] One fifteenth-century testator who was not part of our sample asked to be buried "dentro de la iglesia, en el coro, en San Nicolás, donde yo me acostumbro a sentar." Alfonso Gonzalez (1478) AGVM Sa. 2-362-8, cited by Leonor Gomez Nieto, *Ritos funerarios en Madrid medieval*, p. 65.

[23] Venegas, *Agonía*, p. 233: "Creo que a esta causa se permitió que se hiziesen los enterramientos en las iglesias, porque las sepulturas nos traigan a la memoria la muerte, que también vendrá por nosotros como vino por aquellos cuyas sepulturas pisamos." In contrast, Antonio de Guevara thought that it was the laity who had pushed for church burials rather than the clergy: "Y es de creer que mas fué por la devoción de los fieles, que por algún interés de los eclesiasticos." *Epistolas Familiares*, Ep. 61 (1534), in *Biblioteca de Autores Españoles*, vol. 13, *Epistolario Español*, ed. Eugenio de Ochoa y Ronna (Madrid, 1850), p. 184.

[24] AHPM 1404.316. This is the will of Aganon Carlier, a Flemish cook at Philip II's court.

[25] Gomez Nieto, *Ritos funerarios*, p. 37, citing José Amador de los Rios, *Historia de la villa y corte de Madrid* (Madrid, 1978), vol. II, p. 77 ff. In Toledo, the Confraternity of

kept records of all such *sepulturas de limosna* (charity burials).[26] Elsewhere in Spain, it was common to bury the poor in outdoor cemeteries rather than inside the churches.[27] Some ecclesiastics, like Bishop Antonio de Guevara, saw this as a reversal of Christian charity but preferred to leave the outcome in the supremely just hands of God. Although there are many rich people who are burning in hell, he said, "there are many poor people buried in cemeteries, whose souls are resting in heaven."[28]

The increased demand for limited space made burial sites a prized commodity not only in Madrid but elsewhere in the same diocese. The Council of Toledo (1582) found it necessary to decree that grave sites were not to be bought and sold by the laity. Apparently, a black market in burial places had been created by enterprising families that sold their graves to others for the highest possible price.[29] This practice was deemed incorrect not only because of its mercenary nature but also because burial sites were never technically "sold" by the church to anyone.

According to ecclesiastical law, burial space in consecrated ground should be made available to all deserving Christians. In Madrid, the money that exchanged hands between the laity and the clergy for burial rights at a specific location inside a church was not a purchase price for the grave itself but a *limosna*, or alms, given as an act of charity to atone for the sins of the deceased. The amount of the *limosna* varied from place to place, according to local custom. The wills from Madrid simply state that the family should "pay what is customary" (*que paguen lo que se acostumbra*). Nonetheless, as the decree of the Council of Toledo indicates, families could come to regard the alms as a purchase price and the

Charity not only buried the poor but also took their corpses on procession through the streets of the city, begging for alms so masses could be said for them.

[26] See Martinez Gil, *Toledo*, p. 75. M. F. Carbajo Isla, *Población*, p. 14.

[27] In the seventeenth century, some of the few surviving parish records suggest that the poor of Madrid were relegated to cemeteries. The parish of San Sebastián began a book entitled "Pobres de Cimenterio" in March 1678. M. F. Carbajo Isla, *Población*, p. 14, n. 40, which cites Claude Larquie, "Une approche quantitative de la pauvreté: Les madrilénes et la mort au XVIIe siècle," *Annales de Démographie Historique*, pp. 175–96.

[28] Guevara, *Epistolas familiares*, Ep. 61 (1534), p. 183.

[29] Tejada, vol. 5, pp. 417–435.

grave site as their personal property.[30] A good example is the case of the priest Pedro de Reballos, who instructed his executors to "purchase a burial place for 3,000 *maravedis* . . . and make sure that it is never sold again to anyone else."[31] Some people even drew up contracts for the purchase of their *sepultura,* as did the Alcalde Gregorio López Madera with the Dominican friars at Our Lady of Atocha in the suburbs of Madrid. In exchange for a perpetual rent of 1,000 *reales* a year – and a valuable sword given by Pope Pius V to Don John of Austria for the Battle of Lepanto – Don Gregorio secured for himself and his family the right to use the chapel of St. Dominic as a burial space, a most prestigious location, facing the main chapel of Our Lady.[32]

Because the burial places within the churches were cramped, the competition became keen for favorable grave sites such as that just mentioned, especially after 1561, when church building could not keep pace with the growth of the city. Although all graves within the church partook of the same sacredness, it is evident that they did not share in this equally and that the testators accepted a certain hierarchy of space within the church building. The closer one could be to the eucharist, the better.

The choicest spot was the main altar, where the expiatory sacrifice of the mass was offered regularly. Proximity to this altar was customarily reserved for the most influential, both lay and clerical. For the few who could afford it, a side chapel with its own altar ensured a similar privilege. Consequently, privileged testators often requested burial near an altar. Antonio Josepfe, Viscount of Milan and founder of the Italian Hospital in Madrid, could claim the spot nearest the altar because he was paying for the construction of the hospital chapel.[33] Cristina de Almendares, wife of a court attendant, asked to be buried in the crypt under the main altar at San Miguel.[34] Catalina de Arceo requested a

---

[30] Apparently, this problem was not limited to the diocese of Toledo, or even to Spain proper. The Council of Mexico (1555) had earlier deemed it necessary to spell out clearly the law forbidding the sale of church burial sites by the laity (Tejada, vol. 5, p. 139).

[31] AHPM 107 s.f. (1549).

[32] This contract is from 1606, slightly beyond our period. AHPM 1606.889–900, published in *La vida privada Española en el protocolo notarial,* pp. 302–10.

[33] AHPM 1412.737 (1597).   [34] AHPM 566.198v (1579).

spot "next to the steps leading to the main altar."[35] Although it is difficult to ascertain her specific social status, since she is simply listed as "a widow," it is evident from her other requests that she had a good deal of property at her disposal.

Those who could not obtain the choicest spot often requested other specific locations. Hernando Pereira, who had offered his services as an attorney to the Jesuit fathers on several occasions, left them very clear instructions about exactly where he was to be buried in their school chapel: "just outside the gate that adjoins the *capilla mayor*, at the foot of the altar on the Gospel side."[36] Catalina Palacios, the widow of a porter, wanted to rest beneath a specific image of the Virgin Mary in the parish church of Santa Cruz.[37] Similarly, Alonso Nuñez de Toledo requested burial "directly under the wall," beneath a painting of St. Christopher he had commissioned at the Franciscan chapel of Santa Clara.[38]

Others, in the meantime, settled for locations such as "to the right of the choir,"[39] or "next to the holy water font."[40] In the complex hierarchy of sacred space, some of these apparently humble locations could have an exalted rank. Being buried next to the holy water font, for instance, had definite advantages. Because so many worshipers would necessarily tread on the grave and cross themselves over it, its occupant could gain great recognition and some unexpected prayers, along with a generous and constant sprinkling of spilled holy water. But not everyone had a chance to choose a location. Those at the very bottom of the social scale, such as the indigent Francisco Hernandez, could ask only for a general location, such as "wherever it is that the poor people who die in this Royal Hospital are customarily buried."[41]

Burial was very much a family affair because hardly anyone in sixteenth-century Madrid ever expected to be buried alone. For all practical purposes, the concept of a single, inviolate, and permanent burial place for each individual did not exist. Generally, entire families were buried in the same cramped location, even though burial sites could not legally become anyone's property. Most often, one finds testa-

---

[35] AHPM 69.66 (1538).

[36] AHPM 1403.770 (1592). Pereira reminded the Jesuit fathers that they owed him this favor, "porque saben que yo siempre e acudido a los negocios de su orden en todo lo que me an querido mandar."

[37] AHPM 542.213 (1568).   [38] AHPM 543.435 (1569).   [39] AHPM 566.225 (1579).

[40] AHPM 69.35 (1537); and 78.527 (1556).   [41] AHPM 543.83 (1569).

tors demarcating their burial place not so much by the location but by the identity of some other relative already buried there, typically either a parent or a spouse. For example, all the testators mentioned earlier requested burial with spouses or parents. Requests for burial with other relatives, such as uncles, aunts, brothers, sisters, cousins, or even in-laws, also appear regularly. Throughout the sixteenth century, the number of testators who simply ask to be buried in their own grave remains relatively small (see Table 3.2). This meant, of course, that the dead were routinely exhumed and their bones gathered and compressed into smaller receptacles to accommodate the new arrivals.[42] Since one often literally joined one's family in a single grave, it seemed quite natural to try to exercise proprietary rights over a certain spot, regardless of what canon law proscribed.

For those wealthy few who could afford it, the establishment of a family chapel in a parish or monastery church secured a permanent and prominent resting place. This was a very expensive proposition because it not only entailed the construction and decoration of a chapel but also the establishment of a salaried chaplaincy. For example, Francisco de Berestegui, a knight of the Order of San Juan, set up a family chapel in 1568 at the cost of 30,000 *escudos*. This fee was simply for masses that were to be offered for him and his family in the chapel and did not include the cost of construction or of decoration. (De Berestegui commissioned an elaborate altarpiece, indicating exactly which saints were to be included.) The chaplain's salary was set at 30,000 *maravedis* a year, over and above the 30,000 *escudos*.[43]

Aside from the elegant Capilla del Obispo, erected for the family of a bishop of Palencia, Madrid does not have many surviving chapels from the sixteenth century. Though rich and powerful families like De Berestegui's lavished attention on their graves, relatively little has survived. We know that the amount of money expended on funerary monuments throughout Spain at this time was viewed as a problem by bishops and devotional writers who thought it un-Christian. Bartolomé de Carranza, the troubled Archbishop of Toledo, lashed out against those who

---

[42] The dead in Madrid were usually buried in wooden coffins, and many wills testify to this. Apparently, some coffins fell apart. One couple was careful enough to ask for coffins "chapeados de manera que no se puedan deshazer"; AHPM 457.1116.

[43] AHPM 542.501–504.

Table 3.2. *Graves requested in Madrid wills, 1520–99*

Descriptive Reference	Percentage of Testators by Decade							
	1520's	1530's	1540's	1550's	1560's	1570's	1580's	1590's
Number of testators	(50)	(51)	(50)	(48)	(50)	(76)	(54)	(57)
Self:								
Own grave	2%	6%	2%	2%	2%	3%	9%	3.5%
Grave to be purchased	0%	2%	14%	15%	0%	1%	4%	0%
Family:								
With Parents	14%	10%	14%	12.5%	14%	22%	17%	17.5%
With Spouse	12%	16%	16%	12.5%	12%	13%	17%	12%
With Other Relatives	14%	12%	20%	20%	8%	9%	18%	19%
In Chapel	2%	2%	2%	8%	6%	16%	7%	16%
Place:								
Wherever seems best	0%	6%	14%	19%	18%	13%	13%	14%
Specific Location	0%	2%	2%	2%	10%	6%	4%	7%
Unspecified:								
No Indication	56%	44%	16%	9%	30%	17%	11%	11%

wasted money on corpses and neglected the needs of the poor.[44] Antonio de Guevara, Bishop of Mondoñedo, poked fun at those who purchased fine Italian marble and alabaster for their tombs "just so they could have a splendid chapel and a luxurious tomb in which to bury their bones and have their entrails gnawed by worms."[45] Similarly, Alonso de Orozco devoted an entire chapter of his *Victory of Death* (1583) to criticism of extravagant tombs.[46]

Such warnings notwithstanding, it is not at all surprising that as more nobles, courtiers, and bureaucrats began to take up residence in Madrid after 1561, there was a noticeable increase in the number of testators who set up chapels or requested to be buried in them. (Roughly an average of 11.25 percent of all testators from 1560 to 1599, versus an average of 3.5 percent from 1520 to 1559; see Table 3.2.)

Another discernible change that took place during the sixteenth century was an increased concern on the part of testators to specify their place of burial. In the 1520s about 56 percent of the wills make no stipulations about location. In the 1530s the figure remains high but has dropped to 44 percent; in the 1540s it drops much further, to 16 percent; and in the following decade to 9 percent. A temporary rise to 30 percent in the 1560s is offset by rather constant low percentages in the 70s, 80s, and 90s. After 1570, it becomes uncommon to encounter wills in which the testator does not state a preference for some specific location or at least leaves the choice to the executors.[47] This increased concern to lay claim to a specific grave may indicate how serious the overcrowding had become in the churches.

But it was not only the parish churches that took in the dead. The chapels and cloisters of Madrid's monasteries and convents also served as burial places. Personal piety guided many such choices: Apparently,

---

[44] Bartolomé de Carranza, *Comentarios sobre el catecismo Cristiano* (1558), ed. J. L. Tellechea, 2 vols. (Madrid, 1972), vol. 2, p. 474: "No se justifica la ambición que muchos tienen de hacer suntuosos sepulcros, los cuales gastan en cubrir los cuerpos muertos de sus padres y los suyos, lo que habían de dar para que se vistiesen los cuerpos de los pobres. Para el cuerpo muerto, la propria vestidura es la tierra."

[45] Guevara, *Epistolas Familiares*, Ep. 61 (1534), pp. 183–4.

[46] Alonso de Orozco, *Victoria de la muerte* (1583); modern ed. (Madrid, 1921), Chap. 30.

[47] One such rarity is the widow Maria de Cabrera, who not only failed to make a choice but also asked that if her wayward son did not come back to Madrid within ten years, the entire proceeds from her estate were to be used for masses on her behalf. AHPM 1407.704 (1595).

some testators felt a special affinity with a certain saint's order. A good example is Francisca Henriquez de Albaniza, the Marquesa of Posa, who asked to be buried in Santo Domingo because she had "a special devotion" to St. Dominic.[48] Similarly, Francisco de Guara, a knight of the Order of Santiago, specifically requested to be buried in a Dominican church, no matter in what city or country.[49] Generally, however, such a choice was reserved for the more privileged families of Madrid.

Because the wills from 1520 to 1549 rarely mention the testator's profession or social status, it is very difficult to discern any clear patterns about the relationship between privilege and monastic burial places for the first half of the sixteenth century. From 1550 to 1599, in contrast, a clearer picture emerges. Many of those who asked to be buried in monasteries and convents after 1550 were nobles, royal officials, and servants at court. The list of those who requested a monastic location includes several members of the four military orders, some titled nobles, the widow of Hernán Pizarro, the widow of a cook to the Duke of Alba, a buyer for King Philip II, a smith for the royal weapons factory, a royal scribe, a court lawyer, and a court physician. Side by side with these court people, nonetheless, are a few less exalted royal subjects, including a shoemaker, the widow of a barber, and the wife of an innkeeper. Curiously enough, some of the secular clergy chose monastic burial places over their own parishes.[50]

Throughout the sixteenth century the number of testators who requested burial in a monastery or convent remained relatively constant, fluctuating between 14 and 38 percent (see Figure 3.2). In the first half of the century, testators favored San Francisco (Franciscans), Nuestra Señora de Atocha (Dominicans), and San Jerónimo (Hieronymites). In the 1540s, for instance, San Francisco was chosen by as many as 14 percent of all testators in my sample. However, some of the oldest monastic institutions in Madrid, such as Santo Domingo (Dominicans) and San Martín (Benedictines), were not requested during this time. In the 1540s and 1550s, possibly as a result of crowding in the other

---

[48] AHPM 1810.1209 (1597). The marquesa also left specific instructions to offer 100 *ducados* for the grave and to pressure the Prior to grant her request.

[49] AHPM 457.1072.

[50] One of several examples is Pedro de Madrid, a parish priest at Santa Cruz, one of the most popular burial churches in Madrid, who asked for burial at San Jerónimo, the Hieronymite monastery. AHPM 78.436 (1554).

churches, requests began to appear for Santo Domingo and San Martín. The same is true for the convents of Santa Clara (Poor Clares), and Santa Catalina (Dominicans).

When new religious houses were founded in the latter half of the century, the distribution among the various orders evened out. New establishments such as San Felipe (1547, Augustinians), Nuestra Señora de la Merced (1564, Redemptorians), and Nuestra Señora de la Victoria (1561, Minims), received as many requests for burial in the 1590s as did the older monasteries.[51]

Burial dress

Testators could choose not only where to be buried but also how to be dressed for burial. Throughout the sixteenth century, lay people could elect to be dressed in one of three ways: in a linen shroud, a habit from a religious order, or a confraternity tunic. Secular clergy were normally buried in their vestments, the members of religious orders in their habits.[52]

Sixteenth-century Madrid wills say much about popular attitudes toward burial dress. In the first place, it is clear that many lay people considered it advantageous to be buried in a religious habit. The most popular habit was that of the Franciscans, which in the 1540s was requested by as many as 59 percent of all testators. In fact, the most constant pattern in burial dress from 1520 to 1599 was the Franciscan habit. Whereas the linen shroud, the confraternity tunic, and the habits of other orders virtually disappeared from wills toward the end of the century, the Franciscan habit was still being requested by many testators (see Table 3.3), a trend that apparently grew in popularity from that time forward. Recent research has shown that the use of the Franciscan habit

---

[51] After Madrid became the capital city of Spain in 1561, church building did not keep pace with population growth. Although the regular clergy established several new churches in Madrid during the second half of the sixteenth century, the secular clergy did not enlarge the city's parishes. The establishment of San Sebastián as a new parish in 1550, to handle the overflow from Santa Cruz, was the only concession made to Madrid's growing population. Yet, this took place long before the city's phenomenal growth. For a chronology of religious establishments in Madrid, see Ramón de Mesonero Romanos, *El Antiguo Madrid* (Madrid, 1861), pp. xlvi–xlvii.

[52] One priest asked to be buried "en un ornamento de lizo, como es costumbre de enterrar los sacerdotes"; AHPM 107 s.f. (1549).

Table 3.3. *Types of burial dress requested in Madrid wills, 1520–99*

Burial Dress	Percentage of Testators by Decade							
	1520's	1530's	1540's	1550's	1560's	1570's	1580's	1590's
Linen shroud	24%	6%	20%	28%	6%	11%	4%	0%
Clerical vestments (clergy)	0%	2%	0%	11%	0%	0%	10%	0%
Habits of religious orders:								
Franciscan	42%	39%	59%	39%	32%	33%	18%	19%
Dominican	4%	2%	0%	0%	0%	0%	6%	2%
Jeronimite	0%	14%	0%	0%	0%	0%	2%	0%
Benedictine	0%	0%	0%	0%	2%	0%	0%	0%
Carmelite	0%	0%	0%	0%	0%	0%	2%	2%
Trinitarian	0%	0%	0%	0%	0%	0%	2%	0%
Mercedarian	0%	0%	0%	0%	0%	0%	4%	0%
Habits of military orders:								
Santiago	0%	0%	0%	2%	0%	1%	4%	0%
San Juan	0%	0%	0%	0%	2%	0%	0%	0%
Alcantara	0%	0%	0%	0%	0%	1%	0%	0%
Confraternity tunic	2%	2%	4%	4%	6%	3%	0%	0%
No specific request	28%	35%	17%	16%	52%	51%	48%	77%

for burial became immensely favored throughout all regions of Spain in the seventeenth and eighteenth centuries.[53]

But why should a lay person request to be buried in a Franciscan habit, and why should the friars be so willing to accommodate the desires of the laity on this account? Even more important, what does all this reveal about attitudes toward death and the afterlife?

Some wills provide us with answers. Inés de Arroyo, for instance, left no doubt as to why she chose the habit of the Franciscan friars: She said she was doing it "so that St. Francis may serve as my advocate [*abogado*] before the Son of God."[54] Two decades later, Isabel Morejón could still ask for "the habit of Saint Francis, whom I have chosen as my advocate."[55] In the minds of these women, as in those of their contemporaries, the Franciscan habit ensured the intercession of St. Francis himself. This conclusion is further indicated by the fact that many wills specifically asked for "*el abito del Señor San Francisco*" or "*el abito del Serafico Señor San Francisco*," but never for "*el abito* de la orden *de San Francisco.*"

The personal, contractual nature of this advocacy was unintentionally made clear by another testator, Catalina de Palacios, the wife of a porter. As she was dictating the will to her notary, this woman started to say she wanted to be buried "*en el abito del Señor San Francisco*" but apparently changed her mind and made him cross out the partly written name "*Francisco*" and replace it with the name *Antonio de Padua*. Obviously, she wanted burial in a Franciscan habit, because St. Anthony of Padua belonged to the Franciscan order, but she suddenly realized it would be more advantageous to lay claim to her special advocate. For her, it was

---

[53] Lopez Lopez finds the Franciscan habit nearly universal in late baroque Asturias (*Comportamientos religiosos*, p. 62). Other findings: Reder Gadow, 57 percent of testators in Malaga, plus another 22 percent who request other habits (*Morir en Malaga*, p. 101); Rivas Alvarez, 54 percent of testators in Seville, plus another 14 percent who request a Carmelite habit (*Miedo y piedad*, p. 119); Peñafiel Ramon, 59 percent of testators in Murcia, plus another 20 percent who request other habits (*Testamento y buena muerte*, p. 76); García Fernández, 63 percent of testators in Valladolid, plus another 27 percent who request other habits ("Vida y muerte en Valladolid," *Religiosidad Popular*, vol. 2 (1989): 241–2); Martinez Gil, 42 percent of testators in Toledo, plus 9 percent who request other habits (*Toledo*), p. 51.

[54] AHPM 107. s.f. (1550). In modern Spanish usage, *abogado* has a much less formal meaning, identical with the English "lawyer" or "attorney."

[55] AHPM 457.1098 (1573).

not so much a Franciscan habit she wanted but the habit worn by a specific Franciscan (St. Anthony) who would come to her aid in the afterlife.[56]

Some testators sought even more security by asking for two habits. If a habit could somehow procure assistance in heaven, would it not be more advantageous to wear more than one? Luis Diaz, a physician, certainly thought so, asking to be dressed in the tunic of his confraternity, "*con el abito del Señor Santo Domingo encima*" (with the habit of St. Dominic on top).[57] Notice, again, how it is the habit of St. Dominic himself – not of his order – which is requested. Juana Gomez, the wife of a *corregidor* (a court official), also agreed, asking that her body be dressed "in the habit of the blessed St. Francis, with the habit of the Holy Trinity on top, the habit that is commonly given to the sisters that belong to the order of the Holy Trinity." In her case, the association with the person of St. Francis was not sufficient; she also wanted to associate with an entire order and redundantly specified exactly what she meant.[58]

For some, being buried in one habit or two was not sufficiently prudent. Some of those who wrote their wills while in good health also indicated that they wanted to wear a specific habit during their final illness. Juan Zapata de Cardenas, a knight of the Order of Santiago, made this request: "Before I expire, I want to be dressed in the white tunic I usually wear when I take communion."[59] Pero Nuñez de Toledo asked "to be dressed in the habit of Saint Francis at the time of my death, which I want to wear as I die and when I am buried."[60] Juan de Roja, a porter to the Princess of Portugal, similarly hedged his bets by asking to die in a Benedictine habit and then to be changed into a Franciscan habit for burial.[61] These wills and others like them lead one to think that many of those who wrote wills on their deathbeds might have been wearing some habit, perhaps the one they requested for burial.

Undoubtedly, this custom provided some religious orders – especially the Franciscans – with a steady income, because the habits used for burial had to be the genuine article and could be obtained only from

---

[56] AHPM 542.213 (1568).   [57] AHPM 541.139 (1567).

[58] AHPM 580.164 (1585).   [59] AHPM 580.511v (1585).

[60] AHPM 85.266 (1544). Other similar examples can be found in 55.748 (1528); 55.865 (1530); 141.623 (1546); and 144.678 (1549).

[61] AHPM 542.339 (1568).

them. Although the price is seldom mentioned in wills, it seems to have remained somewhat steady throughout the century, somewhere around 20 *reales*.[62]

The origin of these practices can be traced to early medieval monasticism. In monastic lore, the cowl, or habit, assumed a special significance. Because the habit symbolized in a very palpable manner the monk's renunciation of the world, it naturally came to be regarded as a physical manifestation of the vows of poverty, chastity, and obedience. As a funerary gesture, the habit was an external sign of humility, especially in cultures where sumptuous dress was part of the death ritual.[63] But there was more to this practice than attempted humility: Throughout the Middle Ages, it was commonly believed that anyone who died in a monastic habit would gain preferential treatment in heaven.

Many medieval *exempla* told stories about monks and their habits at the moment of death. One such tale recounted how a Cistercian who was delirious from a high fever took off his habit, only to die moments later. When he arrived at the gates of heaven, he was forbidden entrance by St. Benedict, the author of the Rule so strictly observed by the Cistercians, because he could not identify the monk without his habit. All that this wretched monk could do was to peer through the gates to see how his brethren enjoyed paradise, fully dressed in the proper monastic garb. Finally, St. Benedict granted him a chance to live on earth again for a while, so he could prove himself worthy by properly wearing his habit.[64]

---

[62] AHPM 136.470 (1540); 542.573 (1568); 1392.926–928v (1584). This is a practice that continued well into the twentieth century in Spain and that has given rise to some popular misconceptions. When I inquired about this practice, a prominent Spanish historian mistakenly said that all who were buried in Franciscan garb were members of the third, or lay, order. A Gallegan poet informed me that the habits were provided by undertakers in the modern age, and, as was common with commercial mortuary garb, did not have any backs to them. He remarked that he was looking forward to the Resurrection when all those buried in backless Franciscan habits would discover, much to their surprise, that they had to face the Heavenly Judge *con el culo al aire* (bareassed).

[63] Sharon Strocchia, *Death and Ritual in Renaissance Florence,* p. 41, points out that the Franciscan habit was at first a stark contrast to the customary funeral garb in Florence, which included elaborate dress and costly hats.

[64] Caesarius of Heisterbach, *Dialogus Miraculorum,* dist. 11, c. 36; cf 12.39. For more on this see G. G. Coulton, *Five Centuries of Religion,* 4 vols. (Cambridge, 1936; New York, 1979), vol. 3, pp. 16–17.

Such tales were not limited to audiences of poorly educated monks or lay people. Some of the most learned minds of medieval Christendom, such as St. Bonaventure and St. Thomas Aquinas, also shared in this attitude toward the monastic habit. In his *Major Life of St. Francis*, Bonaventure took pains to point out that although Francis had wanted to die naked, in keeping with his desire to observe total poverty and imitate Christ in all things, he was prevailed upon at the last minute by one of his companions to accept a habit as a loan. This companion, who was "inspired by God," thus made it possible for Francis to enter heaven with the proper attire.[65] Thomas Aquinas went as far as to imbue the habit with a sacramental significance, referring to it as a "second baptism" that restored sinners to the state of innocence they had enjoyed when first baptized.[66]

Given that such attitudes were not only accepted by the common people but also vigorously promoted by the elite, it is not surprising that the laity should seek to be buried in monastic garb. This phenomenon shows how far the monastic ideal had penetrated the popular consciousness and how it was perceived. The sacred powers associated with monastic habits, especially their alleged ability to gain one direct entrance into heaven, are based upon a series of interdependent assumptions, all of which reveal much about attitudes toward death and the afterlife.

First, it is assumed that one must be holy or especially pure to enter into heaven and that this holiness can be achieved only through a total renunciation of the world.

Second, it is also assumed that the outward sign of this renunciation, the habit, is itself a mark of holiness and is absolutely indispensable for gaining entrance into heaven.

Third, it is also assumed that some holiness is directly conveyed by the habit to any wearer, or that at least it can provide the wearer with a special identity at death, even if the wearer had no direct association with that identity in life.

For all of this to work, one must accept a fourth assumption: that the

---

[65] Marion A. Habig, ed., *St. Francis of Assisi, Writings and Early Biographies: English Omnibus of the Sources for the Life of St. Francis* (Chicago, 1973), p. 739.

[66] Thomas Aquinas, *Summa Theologica*, II, II, 111.2–2; 120.2–3; *Commentary on the Four Sentences of Peter Lombard*, 38.1.2.3–2; Roland Bainton, *Here I Stand: A Life of Martin Luther* (New York, 1950), p. 33.

habit actually crosses over into the afterlife with its wearer or that those in heaven can somehow see that a person's corpse is wearing it. The acceptance of this notion also prompted the secular clergy to request burial in their vestments. One Madrid priest, Father Pedro de Raballos, made it clear he did not want to cross over into the afterlife poorly dressed, saying he wanted to be buried "in one of my vestments, the oldest and the best."[67]

None of this was very carefully thought out or systematically developed into a coherent theology. By the sixteenth century, lay burial in a monastic habit was an ancient practice, deeply embedded in the fabric of social customs. Because it had a life of its own, it needed no learned explication and thus failed to become a topic of discussion in the religious literature of the time. Whatever meaning and purpose this custom may have had in sixteenth-century Madrid, then, is best revealed to us by those who requested its observance in their wills.

What the wills tell us most clearly is that those who chose to be buried in a monastic habit were hoping to secure the intercession of some saint in heaven, most often St. Francis, and that the principal reason lay people thought they needed such assistance was the fact that they did not consider themselves holy enough to enter heaven. As Inés de Arroyo put it in 1550, she wanted to place a claim on St. Francis so that he would "serve as her attorney before the Son of God."[68] If she was not holy enough herself, then perhaps the habit of the holy man St. Francis would gain her access to holiness, one way or another.

The image of the afterlife that emerges from the will of Inés de Arroyo is not very otherworldly. This helps to explain why she sought to prepare for the afterlife through something as mundane as having her corpse dressed in a particular garb. At the entrance to the afterlife, she expected to find a court of law presided over by Jesus Christ, a just but stern judge who had the power to punish her for her sins.[69] She also expected to need a lawyer to defend her, as in an earthly courtroom, and even more, she hoped that her lawyer could somehow convince the judge to be lenient. The way she solicited the services of her chosen

---

[67] AHPM 107 s.f. (1549).
[68] AHPM 107 s.f.
[69] This was perhaps the most common image of the entrance to the afterlife. One testator went as far as to call God's abode "el altísimo tribunal." AHPM 457.1072 (1573).

attorney was through a particular gesture that would make him feel some obligation toward her. This gesture, of course, was her burial in his habit.

If in an earthly court it is most advantageous to be defended by a well-connected, influential lawyer, then why not also do the same in heaven? Who could best convince Jesus to be lenient? Undoubtedly, Inés de Arroyo believed that St. Francis could help her most ably. After all, St. Francis was universally regarded, even in his own day, as the man who had most faithfully imitated Jesus.[70]

Although many testators specified their choice of burial dress, others passed the responsibility of choosing to their executors. In these cases, which increase dramatically after 1560, it is impossible to learn what choice was finally made (see Table 3.3). Does the dramatic increase in the number of testators who do not choose their own burial dress reveal a declining interest in this matter? Perhaps. On the one hand, when as many as 77 percent of the testators leave the choice up to their relatives or friends, as is the case in the 1590s, one must refrain from assigning too much meaning to these practices. On the other hand, however, other evidence suggests that the question of burial dress may not have become trivial.

The continued popularity of monastic burial garb is indicated by the fact that although fewer and fewer testators took the time to specify their burial dress, a good number still asked specifically for the Franciscan habit. For instance, in the 1550s, when only 16 percent of the testators refrained from making a request, slightly more than a third (39%) asked for the Franciscan habit. In contrast, two decades later, in the 1570s, a full third of all testators were still asking for the Franciscan habit, even though one-half of all testators refrained from making a specific request. If this is compared to the figures for the 1550s, it is possible to see a relative *increase* rather than a decrease in requests for the habit among those who actually specified their choices (as opposed to all testators).

---

[70] St. Bonaventure summed up this attitude in the *Major Life* by saying: "Surely he was the most Christ-like of men! His only desire was to be like Christ and imitate him perfectly . . . in his life he imitated the life of Christ and in his death he imitated his death, and he wished to be like him still when he was dead." *Omnibus of Sources*, pp. 739–40. On the seventeenth-century cult of Francis as a "death saint" see Martinez Gil, *Toledo*, pp. 149–154.

The increase in the number of testators who do not request a specific kind of burial dress in the second half of the century is part of a larger pattern. Beginning in the 1560s, as will be seen in the next section, funeral practices in Madrid become increasingly elaborate. As the complexity of the funerals increases, testators find it more expedient, perhaps even prudent, to leave the arrangements to someone else, most often a spouse, parent, or child. One must keep in mind that many, if not most wills, were written when the testator was ill or on the verge of death. In many cases, the testator's wishes might have been expressed verbally but not dictated in detail to the notary.

4

~~~~~~

Impressing God and neighbor

Funeral ceremonies are social expressions of grief on the part of survivors. The deceased, who are unable to feel or act in any functional sense, take no active part in the funeral and exercise no real control over the fate of their remains. At any funeral, an empirical observer would have to admit that all gestures related to the disposal of the body, then, are performed by the survivors for their own benefit, as a means of coping with their loss. Christian societies are no exception to this rule, even if Jesus once advised that it would be better for the dead to bury the dead.[1]

Preparing the funeral

In Madrid, as elsewhere in Spain, it could be said that most people did not die alone, for their funerals (especially the kind requested in wills) removed privacy from their deaths and made them a public spectacle.[2] Moreover, when it came to the funeral, death was anything but the "great leveler" that carried off all members of society equally, regardless of status. On the contrary, because they typically separated people on the basis of status, affirming distinctions in the processional order of the cortege, funerals could easily become public statements regarding the status, rank, privilege, and wealth of the dead and their families.[3]

---

[1] *Luke* 9.60.
[2] "Nadie muere solo": Lopez Lopez, *Comportamientos religiosos en Asturias*, p. 69.
[3] Strocchia, *Death and Ritual in Renaissance Florence*, p. 7.

Funerals in sixteenth-century Madrid surely need to be analyzed from an empirical perspective, but much would be missed if they were to be considered exclusively as political rites that reveal and legitimize power relations between individuals and groups. Most sixteenth-century Madrileños did not seem to have a purely physical attitude toward death and burial. To many of them, perhaps to most, funeral ceremonies were much more than grieving or status-affirming gestures on the part of the living; they were a key step in the passage to the afterlife. Every gesture performed by the survivors in a funeral could be viewed as an intercessory act on behalf of the dead, a necessary spiritual formality that aided their entrance into heaven, and there is reason to believe that for many Madrileños the transcendent and mundane functions could be indistinguishable and inseparable. Furthermore, funeral rituals were an integral part of the mentality of Madrileños: They were an enactment, materialization, and realization of their beliefs. Through funeral ritual, Madrileños attained their faith as they portrayed it. These rituals were models *of* their beliefs and also models *for* those beliefs.[4]

Although it is true that much of what went on in the funeral served very practical earthly needs (such as disposing of the corpse, or affirming a family's social status through pomp), and that most participants were quite eager to benefit from these mundane functions, it is also true that these same gestures were imbued with a transcendent, otherworldly purpose. Certainly, no one denied the fact that much had to be done by the living or that they benefited in some way by participating in the funeral, but most believed that the dead themselves played central, active roles in all these ceremonies. The first was by their presence, which was not only physical but also spiritual, and the second was through the planning of the funeral itself, which the deceased often detailed beforehand in his or her will.

To plan for one's own funeral was to take an active part in a crucial set of ceremonies: It was not only prudent but also necessary. The funeral instructions left behind by sixteenth-century testators served the purpose of extending their presence into the period after their deaths, when they would be unable to express their desires. Even though there was not much room for originality, because so many of the gestures were rigidly

---

[4] Clifford Geertz has said this is true of all ritual: "Religion as a Cultural System," in Banton, *Anthropological Approaches*, p. 29.

codified, every individual could select which of those available gestures he or she wished to have performed.

Sixteenth-century Madrileños could plan their entire funeral in detail before dying, if they so wished, and it appears that many considered it a duty rather than a choice. In the first half of the sixteenth century, nearly all testators exercised this prerogative, specifying exactly what kind of funeral they wanted. After 1561, however, fewer and fewer testators made the effort to be specific in their wills, leaving decisions about funeral details to their closest survivors instead, simply saying they wished to be buried "in whichever way seems best to the executors."

The change that takes place after 1561 is dramatic. In the wills sampled from 1520 to 1560, almost all testators (96 to 100%) make an effort to plan their funeral in detail. Suddenly, in the 1560s, the figure drops to 82 percent. By the 1580s it is down to 74 percent; in the 1590s, it reaches only 58 percent (see Figure 3.1). What could be the reason for this sudden change in attitude among so many Madrileños? Does this mean that funeral ceremonies were suddenly devalued?

An answer is provided by those testators who continue to observe tradition. With few exceptions, the funerals requested after 1561 become increasingly elaborate. After the 1560s, each passing decade brings with it a noticeable increase in the size of funeral corteges and the number of ceremonies requested. It is no accident that the beginning of this trend toward increased pomp coincides with the establishment of a permanent royal court in Madrid. It is also no accident that as funerals become more complex and more difficult to arrange (especially on a deathbed), a greater number of testators leave the burial details in the hands of their executors.

Elaborate funerals suggest a more rigid codification of what is considered proper for people in certain social stations. In other words, as concern for status increases in any society, so does the need for gestures that convey a sense of rank. This was especially true of early modern European court societies, where questions of rank and privilege became an indispensable component of the function of government.[5] When the royal court moved to Madrid in 1561, the city immediately began to feel the effect of this preoccupation with rank and status. Because funerals

---

[5] For a synthesis of this phenomenon see Norbert Elias, *Die Höfische Gesselschaft*, English tr. *The Court Society* (Oxford, 1983).

were one of the central status-affirming rituals of court life, it did not take long for Madrid's funerals to be transformed according to a new set of conventions.

These changes may not have been caused single-handedly by the court. Some evidence suggests that urbanization itself could have been a factor. The sudden growth of Madrid may have also forced it to catch up with other cities, adopting patterns of behavior in the second half of the sixteenth century that had already existed for a long time in the more sophisticated urban areas of Castille.

In her study of funeral practices in medieval Valladolid, Adeline Rucquoi observes that whereas hardly any testators failed to plan their own funerals in the fourteenth century, many chose to leave the task to their executors in the fifteenth century.[6] According to her findings, the number of testators who planned their own funerals decreased from 100 percent in 1278–1399, to 83 percent in 1400–1449, and only 62.5 percent in 1450–1503. In Madrid, the figures do not dip to 82 percent until the 1560s, or to 58 percent until the 1590s – a full century behind Valladolid!

Rucquoi's interpretation of this phenomenon in late medieval Valladolid helps to explain developments in early modern Madrid. Is it possible that this change could have been produced by a lack of interest in ritual or an increased desire for humility and simplicity, she asks? Not necessarily. On the contrary, it is more likely the result of an increased concern with status. Rucquoi concludes that this phenomenon "is symptomatic of a society that has so carefully codified its funeral rites that it is no longer necessary to specify them, since every person is entitled to a certain number of 'gestures,' according their status."[7]

The marked increase in the number of testators who do not plan the details of their funeral in fifteenth-century Valladolid and sixteenth-century Madrid does not signify a declining interest in ritual but an increased codification of ritual based on status. The evidence from Madrid helps prove Rucquoi's theory, because there seems to be a correlation between the increased complexity of funerals and the increase in the number of testators who simply ask to be buried "in

---

[6] Adeline Rucquoi, *Valladolid en la Edad Media: La Villa de Esqueva* (Valladolid, 1983), pp. 103–14.

[7] Ibid., p. 110.

whichever way seems best." If the increasingly complex funeral instructions are not specified by all testators, it is quite likely that certain practices are routinely assumed to be necessary for certain people.[8]

Exactly how much of this is caused by the process of increased urbanization and how much by the influence of the court cannot be precisely ascertained. Similar developments have been traced elsewhere in Europe. Late medieval Avignon saw a remarkable escalation in funeral pomp and in requests for postmortem liturgies, a "numeric delirium," or delight in ever larger corteges and ever higher numbers of masses. Jacques Chiffoleau has attributed this phenomenon to demographic restructuring, more specifically to the urban dislocation caused in Avignon by a sudden influx of outsiders who were separated from their kin and from the burial grounds of their ancestors.[9] Florence, too, was gripped by a wave of conspicuous consumption and ceremonial largesse in the late fourteenth century, as well as by a numeric delirium in regard to postmortem masses. Sharon Strocchia attributes this development to the urban environment but mildly disagrees with Chiffoleau, saying that it was "the particular quality and impact of the urbanization process, rather than the urban experience itself" that caused these changes.[10] The parallels with post-1561 Madrid are striking: This was a period in Florence of social fluidity, a time during which funerals assumed a strategic importance in the identification of social rank, especially for the *gente nuova*.[11] Could this Florentine phenomenon help us better understand Madrid's own plunge into funerary inflation?

There is no denying the impact of certain changes in the urban environment on Madrid's death rites, but caution should be exercised in

---

[8] This is further confirmed by the findings of Lopez Lopez for Asturias, where leaving the details to others increased from 46 percent of all testators in 1550–1600 to 70 percent in 1830–45. He argues: "No indica una pérdida del valor de la manda, o un desinterés por los sufragios." *Comportamientos religiosos en Asturias*, p. 135.

[9] Chiffoleau, *Comptabilité de l'au-delà*, pp. 153–207; 429–35. The expression "délire numerique" comes from Jacques Le Goff, in his preface to Chiffoleau, p. ix. See also Chiffoleau's article, "Ce qui fait changer la mort dans la région d'Avignon à la fin du moyen âge," in *Death in the Middle Ages*, pp. 117–33.

[10] Strocchia, *Death and Ritual*, p. 67.

[11] Ibid., pp. 67, 70–1, 106, 128–9, finds that funeral pomp becomes a means of deepening social cleavages once this period of fluidity comes to an end in Florence, when lavish funerals are restricted to a cluster of the wealthiest households in the fifteenth century.

determining an exact cause for these phenomena. One must never forget that funeral ceremonies were also imbued with a transcendent value. Could there be more at work here than the codification of gestures in a time of demographic dislocation and social fluidity? Could it be that this growing preoccupation with complexity in ritual is not only related to factors of increased urbanization and social stratification but also to a corresponding change in attitude toward the religious value of specific funeral ceremonies?

Other evidence seems to suggest this possibility, because the increased complexity of funerals was also accompanied by an increased demand in postmortem devotions (a development that will be analyzed in the next chapter). The inflation in funeral gestures and the inflation in the number of masses requested – Madrid's own numeric delirium – coincide with the closing of the Council of Trent (1563) and the beginning of a great renewal in the Spanish Catholic Church.

One must not overlook the fact that the period immediately following 1563 was one in which many traditional religious practices were vigorously promoted, particularly those that were opposed to the Protestant challenge. Because the Protestants had rejected much of Catholic eschatology, funeral practices became an especially intense focus of attention in the Catholic Reformation. The Protestant denial of the salvific value of ritual, their repudiation of intercessory prayer, and worst of all, their rejection of purgatory had to be answered through the reaffirmation of the value of well-established burial customs and postmortem devotions.

Given such a set of circumstances, it seems appropriate to suggest that some close affinity exists between the changes caused after 1561 by the arrival of the court in Madrid, and the changes caused after 1563 by the implementation of the Tridentine decrees. These different factors worked hand in hand to produce some remarkable changes in attitudes toward death, burial, and the afterlife. We now analyze the exact nature of these changes.

Death and vigil

"To give up the ghost" is one of the many euphemisms employed in the English language for the act of dying. This ancient expression conveys the notion that death occurs at the instant that body and soul are separated and that the true self of any person ceases to reside in the body after that moment. One reason that sixteenth-century Madrileños did not use any such expression in their wills is that, despite commending their bodies to the earth and their souls to God, they seemed convinced that the body continued to have some sort of bond with the soul of the deceased after death, not only during the funeral ceremonies but even after burial.

Francisco de Guara, a high-ranking member of the king's Council of War, seemed to have no doubt that his funeral ceremonies were spiritual in nature and that all gestures concerned with the disposal of his corpse would aid in his salvation:

As regards all things related to the suffrages that should be made and celebrated for my soul, I ask that they be performed in accordance with the decency of my own person, with all brevity, so that my soul may be helped immediately, without any procrastination or delay. . . . For this reason, I am not detailing exactly what should be done on the day of my death regarding such things as confraternities or novenaries, or any other devotions. All I want is for my wife and brother to take pity on my soul, and aid it with the greatest possible alacrity.[12]

Don Francisco reveals much in this statement. First, that he considered all funeral gestures to be "suffrages" for his soul: He saw no substantial difference between the presence of confraternities at his burial and the offering of novenary masses. The arrangement of his funeral cortege (the use of confraternities) and the devotions offered after the burial service (the novenaries) were all of one piece. Both were gestures that focused on the presence of his corpse – at the funeral procession and at the burial – but both were also intensely related to his soul.

Second, it seems clear that Don Francisco thought that brevity and alacrity were important. He was most interested in having the funeral services performed quickly. Whatever his wife and brother did for him as his corpse was being interred would have an *immediate* effect on his soul. Body and soul were still intimately linked, temporally as well as spatially; so were heaven and earth. The gestures performed by Don Francisco's survivors in Madrid, in the immediate vicinity of his corpse,

[12] AHPM 457.1072 (1573).

during the first few hours following his death, somehow affected the fate of his soul as it faced God in the heavenly tribunal.[13]

Third, this request proves that those who left their funeral arrangements in the hands of their relatives could be, in fact, intensely concerned with these rituals. Moreover, since Don Francisco simply requests a funeral *"conforme a la decencia de mi persona"* (in accordance with my social status), he reveals to what extent these gestures could be codified and demonstrates that such codification could indeed be a symptom of an increased interest in funeral ceremonies.

Don Francisco was not alone in desiring a quick, effective burial. Most other Madrid wills also conform to this pattern. In the vast majority of cases, not more than twenty-four hours elapsed between death and burial.

Immediately after a person's death, the presence of others around the corpse became immensely significant. First came the washing and dressing of the corpse, and the *velada* (vigil) when family, close acquaintances, and some clergy gathered around the corpse to pray. The vigil was usually very brief because burial was carried out so quickly. Those who died before noon were normally buried that same day, in the afternoon or evening. Those who died after noon could enjoy a slightly longer vigil (especially if they died in the early afternoon), because burial could not take place until the next morning. The *velada* is not mentioned in wills, but it is always assumed. It is one of those important functions that, by nature of being universally observed, do not need to be specifically requested.[14]

The cortege

After the *velada*, the corpse had to be taken from the house of the deceased (or the hospital) to the church for burial. Again, the presence of others around the corpse is deemed essential. Although in most cases the church was never very far, this final trip for the deceased required a cortege. In the early part of the century, the cortege was a relatively simple procession, but after 1561 it became increasingly complex and crowded.

[13] Don Francisco's own term: "en el altísimo tribunal." AHPM 457.1072.
[14] A similar observation about the *velada* in medieval times is made by Rucquoi, *Valladolid*, p. 110.

It appears that in most cases the means of conveyance for the corpse depended on the distance that had to be covered and that the standards for measurement were flexible. Father Juan Zorilla de Alfaro, for instance, left the following instructions: "If the road leading from the city to the shrine of Atocha seems too long for my executors, let them not carry my body on foot, but rather in a cart."[15] In those funerals where the corpse was taken on foot, it was carried in a pall-covered coffin that rested on a litter, or bier (*andas*).[16] Normally, relatives or friends and neighbors shouldered the *andas* all the way to the church, but some Madrileños had to hire strangers to act as pallbearers.[17]

Social scientists have identified a nearly universal pattern to funeral processions. Madrid's funerals adhered to this typical three-cluster configuration, with the corpse at the center and two distinct and hierarchically ranked groups arranged in front and behind.[18] Marching first, holding a cross aloft at the head of the procession, were the clergy, society's protectors, aiding not only in the disposal of the body but also in the passage of the soul. The clergy could be assigned ranks according to their position in the cortege. The very front of the procession was a place of honor and could become the source of contention. Behind the clergy came the confraternities, lay associations devoted to acts of charity and intercessory gestures. Trailing behind the corpse came the mourners, the family, friends, and acquaintances of the deceased, along with poor people and orphans who had been paid to join the cortege.

Theologians did not incorporate the issue of rank and status into their idealization of the funeral; they nonetheless built upon social convention, providing a spiritualized interpretation of existing death ritual. In this way, they not only legitimized certain practices; they also encouraged some types of behavior and determined the boundaries of propriety. Social conventions and theology were mutually interdependent, and it was the clergy who mediated this interchange. When it came to death

---

[15] AHPM 78.524 (1556). The shrine of Atocha was outside the city walls, about one kilometer from the center of sixteenth-century Madrid.

[16] AHPM 1410.389: "Se lleve mi cuerpo en un ataud con varas de litera."

[17] AHPM 1412.953 (1597). This will asks that four men be hired, at 1 *real* each, in the event that no friends could be found to act as pallbearers.

[18] Clifford Geertz, "Centers, Kings, and Charisma: Reflections on the Symbolics of Power," in *Culture and Its Creators*, ed. J. Ben-David and T. N. Clarke (Chicago, 1977), pp. 150–71.

rites, sixteenth-century Spanish theologians relied heavily on notions of communal responsibility as an interpretative focus. Viewed from a strictly theological and devotional perspective, that is, according to the idealizing advice proffered in *Ars Moriendi* treatises, the function of the cortege was supposed to be an intercessory one. The presence of others in the burial ceremonies ensured that the deceased would not be alone in death and that others in the community would share the responsibility of lessening the spiritual burdens of the dead, beseeching God for mercy as a group. And when it came to intercession, the prevailing opinion seemed to be that there was safety in numbers: the larger the cortege, the more effective the prayer. Alejo Venegas, for instance, promoted a nearly mathematical formula: the larger the cortege, the shorter one's time in purgatory.[19] As we shall presently see, many Madrileños took this advice to heart when it came time to assemble their own cortege.

The parish clergy

The presence of the clergy in the funeral was perhaps more important than that of family and friends. From the moment of death, the clergy hovered around the corpse constantly, uttering prayers and accompanying it every step of the way from the deathbed to the grave.

In the first half of the century, the clergy who were summoned to the deathbed were the secular parish priests. Normally, it was the clerics from the burial church who were asked to take charge of the funeral. It was they who would pick up the corpse and escort it to the grave, leading the cortege through the city streets with their cross held aloft. All along the way, beginning at the deathbed, these clerics would intone a certain number of prayers for the deceased. Apparently, the presence of the parish funeral cross was as important as that of the clergy, for the vast majority of wills mention that the testator requests the presence of "the cross and clergy" (in that order) from a certain parish. Those who do not

---

[19] Venegas, *Agonía*, p. 252: "El que con su autoridad atrae más número de prójimos que concurren a su enterramiento, allende que de la oración de muchos gana algo de la qutiación de su pena, gana gloria accidental en el cielo, es ocasión con la estima de su persona de la obra de caridad e misericordia que cumplen los que caritativamente se hallan en su enterramiento."

make this request simply assume that it will be part of the funeral arrangements made by their survivors.

The wording of these requests reveals exactly what the clergy were expected to do. Juan Lopez Garavato, for instance, summoned the clergy from his deathbed in 1530: "I ask that the cross and clergy from the aforementioned church come to collect me at the house of my mother in law, where I am now ill, and that they pause three times to say responses and a vigil on the way to the church."[20] For him, the clergy served a dual function. As far as Don Juan was concerned, the clergy were not only conveying his body to the church but also ferrying his soul to a favorable resting place. This attitude toward the clergy as ministers to *both* components of the human self is reflected in the wording of the instructions. It is interesting to notice how he and many others ask the clergy "to collect *me*," or "to carry *me*," rather than to "collect my body" or "carry my body," inadvertently revealing how they refused to consider a complete separation of body and soul at death.

Ritual forms were so complex that they sometimes seemed to escape the grasp of testators and notaries. At times, testators did not know exactly which rites the clergy should perform. Some requests were unspecific: "I ask that the cross and clergy carry my body from the house to the church, praying with litanies and responses."[21] Some requests were more detailed but still somewhat vague: "I ask that the clergy carry me to the church with their cross and clamors, and that they perform nine-prayer ceremonies with their litanies."[22] Still, those who were familiar enough with the ritual dictated very specific instructions: "Before the clerics take my body from the house, I ask that they perform a vigil for me, with a litany and nine readings . . . and that they pause three times between my house and the church to make three receptions [*recibimientos*] . . . and that they offer a sung mass for me, with deacon and subdeacon, once my body is interred in the church."[23]

The *recibimientos* just mentioned were an integral part of the funeral

---

[20] AHPM 55.894.

[21] The Spanish asks for "mysterios rezados con sus responsos," suggesting a sense of awe and reverence toward these rites that cannot be correctly or adequately conveyed by the English "mysteries." AHPM 69.72 (1538).

[22] AHPM 69.40 (1537).

[23] AHPM 314.308. A similar request is made in AHPM 314.765, which is written in the same notarial hand. It is quite likely that the notary suggested these specific requests.

procession. These were pauses made by the cortege on the way to church and were more often referred to as *posas* or *posadas*, during which a response would be intoned by the clergy. These ritual punctuations of the funeral procession evolved from necessity, it appears, as a means of relieving the pallbearers, who had to stop and rest, or change places in shifts, depending on their stamina and the distance that had to be covered. The exact number of these pauses does not appear to have been rigidly prescribed, because some testators requested different numbers of them.[24] Most testators simply asked "that the clergy perform the customary number of *posas* with their clamors and responses."[25] Some, however, asked for three; others for four or six.[26]

Overall, there is no discernible pattern in the number of *posas* requested throughout the century. When it comes to the number of parish clergy, however, a clear pattern is evident: As the century progresses, testators request the participation of more and more of them.

In the first half of the century, the majority of all testators request burial in their parish church and therefore simply ask for the presence of the clergy from this single parish (see Table 4.1). When burial did not take place in the testator's parish, the participation of the parish clergy could be requested, over and above that of the clergy from the burial church.[27] From 1520 to 1540, however, no more than 8 percent of all testators made such a request – which means that up to 1540, there were hardly any funerals in Madrid with clerics from more than one parish church.

This situation begins to change around 1540. In the following decade,

[24] Nonetheless, some restrictions had been placed on this ritual elsewhere in Spain. Leonor Gomez Nieto cites the *Constituciones sinodales* of Valladolid (1529), which stipulated that the total number of *posas* be determined by the amount of rest needed by the pallbearers. *Ritos funerarios en Madrid medieval*, pp. 57–8.

[25] AHPM 73.87 (1541).

[26] AHPM 55.894; 1403 s.f.; 746.138. I have not found any specific cost assigned to these ritual stops in Madrid. In Toledo, each *posa* cost 10 *maravedis* in 1583: Martinez Gil, *Toledo*, p. 70, n. 164. Grayson Wagstaff promises a thorough analysis of this and other Spanish funerary music in his forthcoming dissertation: *Music for the Dead: Settings of the Missa and Officium Pro Defunctis by Spanish and Latin American Composers Before 1700* (University of Texas).

[27] In other parts of Castille, the presence of the parish clergy was obligatory. For instance, the Council of Salamanca (1565) ordered all pastors to accompany their parishioners in the funeral cortege. See Tejada 5, p. 345.

Table 4.1. *Funeral corteges requested in Madrid wills, 1520–99*

Number of testators for each decade in ( ) **PARTICIPANTS**	(50) 1520's	(51) 1530's	(50) 1540's	(48) 1550's	(50) 1560's	(76) 1570's	(54) 1580's	(57) 1590's
Secular clergy								
From burial church	54%	64%	52%	56%	52%	58%	37%	40%
From own parish	8%	8%	18%	38%	38%	28%	31%	32%
From additional church	0%	2%	0%	2%	2%	8%	17%	9%
Mendicant Friars								
From one order	0%	0%	0%	0%	2%	4%	9%	7%
From two orders	0%	0%	0%	0%	0%	5%	4%	9%
From three orders	0%	0%	0%	0%	0%	3%	11%	2%
From four orders or more	0%	0%	0%	0%	0%	0%	4%	10.5%
Unspecified Number of Orders	0%	0%	0%	0%	0%	4%	0%	2%
Confraternities								
One Confraternity	28%	22%	32%	24%	38%	20%	24%	3.5%
Two Confraternities	6%	18%	8%	12%	20%	25%	17%	14%
Three Confraternities	0%	0%	2%	8%	2%	12%	11%	10.5%
Four or more Confraternities	0%	0%	0%	2%	6%	1%	7.5%	12%
Poor People								
2–9 poor people	4%	10%	24%	52%	36%	47%	35%	24%
10–12 or more	0%	2%	8%	4%	6%	14%	13%	16%
Charity Children	0%	0%	0%	10%	48%	53%	53%	42%
Unspecified								
"However seems best"	2%	0%	4%	0%	18%	14%	26%	42%

*Note: Total percentages do not add up to 100% in each column because testators requested multiple participants.

the number of those requesting the presence of clerics from their parish, in addition to those of the burial church, increases to 18 percent. By 1550–60, the figure has risen to 38 percent. For the remainder of the century, this figure remains more or less the same, showing that from 1550 to 1599, more than a third of all testamentary funerals in Madrid included clergy from two parish churches.[28]

A similar but less dramatic increase can be seen in the number of testators who request the participation of clerics from a third parish church. From the 1520s to the 1560s, hardly any wills contain such a request (never more than 2 percent during these five decades). In the 1570s, at least 8 percent of all testamentary funerals include clergy from three parish churches. In the 1580s the number rises to 17 percent; in the 1590s, it dips to 9 percent. If one takes into account two other factors, namely, that many testators failed to specify such requests when they left funeral arrangements in the hands of their survivors and that this was a period during which funerals tended to become more elaborate, it becomes possible to speculate that the actual number of funerals with clergy from three parish churches was probably even higher.

No explanation is ever given in the wills of those who ask for clergy from three parishes as to why such a request was made. The participation of clergy from two churches is easy enough to justify in cases when the burial did not take place in the testator's parish, but the presence of clergy from an additional church is not so easily explained. In general, this phenomenon seems to be part of a larger pattern: In the second half of the sixteenth century, Madrileños seemed to be taken with the idea that, in death as in life, *more* was always *better*. As will be presently seen, Madrileños not only requested more clerics at funerals; they also requested more confraternities, more poor people, more orphans, more candles and torches, more prayers, and more masses, plunging into a grand numerical obsession.

---

[28] Although there are no indications that this caused any trouble in Madrid, such a practice had led to numerous street brawls in medieval Valladolid. It appears that these conflicts were caused by the clergy, who often looked upon their crosses as symbols of status and privilege. The fiercest scuffles were those between parish priests and mendicant friars, in which the clerics physically attacked one another and even destroyed each other's crosses. See Rucquoi, *Valladolid*, p. 111.

Mendicant friars

One of the more startling changes in the second half of the sixteenth century is the sudden appearance of mendicant friars in funeral processions (see Table 4.1). Before 1561, not a single request for mendicant friars could be found in any of the wills in this sample. In 1564, an isolated request is made (roughly 2 percent of all testators for that decade). Then, suddenly, after 1570 the mendicants begin to show up in increasing numbers. In 1570–9, 12 percent of all testators request some kind of mendicant presence at their funeral; in the next two decades, 1580–99, the number of such requests remains consistently at about 28 percent. The actual number of funerals attended by the mendicants must have been much higher, because these requests, it must be remembered, occur despite a precipitous increase in the number of testators who leave all final arrangements to their executors. More than one-quarter of the wills from the 1580s (26%) and nearly *half* (42%) from the 1590s simply ask for "the company of crosses, clerics, *and friars*, etc., however seems best [emphasis added]."[29]

The participation of mendicants in funerals became so widely accepted in the 1590s, that even the secular clergy would ask for them. One such example was Juan Gomez Martinez, a parish priest who asked for twelve Franciscans and twelve Minims.[30] These figures appear even more surprising when closely examined. Throughout the final three decades of the sixteenth century, Madrileños not only began to request mendicants in addition to secular clerics but also asked them to appear in higher and higher numbers (see Table 4.2).

At first, in the 1570s, most people who requested mendicants asked for the presence of only one or two orders. In the next decade, as many

---

[29] Such was the request of Francisca Pizarro, the widow of Hernando Pizarro. AHPM 1810.734 (1598).

[30] AHPM 1412.953. This practice was not universally accepted in Spain. For instance, in the diocese of Santiago the regular clergy were not allowed to take part in the funeral procession after 1565. As the Council of Salamanca ordered: "Los religiosos que recibieren un cadaver para darle tierra, no saldrán fuera de la puerta del monasterio o al cementerio llevando la cruz." See Tejada, vol. 5, p. 345. This might have been an attempt to curb the kind of disturbances described by Rucquoi, where the secular and regular clergy fought each other in the streets during funeral processions. Rucquoi, *Valladolid*, p. 111.

Table 4.2. *Friars requested for funeral corteges in Madrid wills, 1520–99*

Number of testators for each decade in ( ) **House & Number of Friars requested**	Percentage of Testators by Decade			
	(50) 1560's	(76) 1570's	(54) 1580's	(57) 1590's
San Francisco (Franciscans)				
4	2%	0%	0%	0%
6	0%	1%	2%	5%
12 or More	0%	9%	17%	18%
Subtotal	2%	10%	19%	23%
La Victoria (Minims)				
4	0%	0%	2%	0%
6	0%	0%	2%	0%
12 or More	0%	4%	13%	12%
Subtotal	0%	4%	17%	12%
La Merced (Mercedarians)				
4	0%	0%	0%	0%
6	0%	3%	4%	0%
12 or More	0%	1%	6%	5.5%
Subtotal	0%	4%	10%	5.5%
La Trinidad (Trinitarians)				
4	0%	0%	0%	0%
6	0%	0%	2%	5.5%
12 or More	0%	4%	4%	9%
Subtotal	0%	4%	6%	14.5%
El Carmen (Carmelites)				
4	0%	0%	2%	0%
6	0%	1%	2%	5.5%
12 or More	0%	3%	6%	9%
Subtotal	0%	4%	10%	14.5%
San Felipe (Augustinians)				
4	0%	0%	0%	0%
6	0%	1%	2%	5.5%
12 or More	0%	4%	9%	11%
Subtotal	0%	5%	11%	16.5%
Atocha (Dominincans)				
4	0%	0%	0%	0%
6	0%	0%	2%	0%
12 or More	0%	0%	2%	0%
Subtotal	0%	0%	4%	0%
Total Number of Requests	1	23	40	48

as 11 percent were asking for three orders, and some were even beginning to request four. By the 1590s, almost 11 percent were asking for four mendicant orders at their funeral.

In addition to such an escalation in requests for multiple orders, there was also a corresponding increase in the number of friars solicited from each order. The friars were normally requested in specific even numbers: four, six, and twelve being the most popular. Between 1570 and 1599, there is a greater increase in the number of testators who request twelve or more friars than in those who request six. Requests for four, though infrequent in 1570–89, disappear altogether in the 1590s. This means that in the 1590s, as many as one out of every ten funerals in Madrid (or perhaps more) could include a procession of forty-eight friars! (See Table 4.2.)

As is generally true in all situations that involve choice, there were distinct preferences among the testators concerning which order to request. Because burial in a Franciscan habit was so popular in Madrid, it is not surprising to see that the Franciscans were more frequently requested than any other order. The Augustinians and Minims came in second, followed by the Mercedarians, Trinitarians, and Carmelites. Surprisingly, the Dominicans hardly figure at all; they were requested in only two wills from the 1580s (see Table 4.2).

It is clear that the testators were much more interested in the orders themselves than in the churches where these mendicants resided. The vast majority of testators phrased their requests as did Maria Barreda and Geronima de Heredia, who asked specifically for "Augustinian friars" rather than "friars from San Felipe."[31] One testator who wanted to ask for Augustinians even made the mistake of saying she wanted the friars from "San Agustín" rather than "San Felipe."[32]

Although it is relatively easy to prove that these changes did in fact take place and that they occurred rapidly, it is not so easy to account for their sudden appearance or to arrive at a constructive interpretation of their significance.

One of the keys to this puzzle can be found in the history of this practice. What seemed new to Madrid in the 1570s was not really new: Mendicant friars had participated in the funerals of the nobility and royalty in medieval Castile. In fourteenth-century Valladolid, for instance, as many as half of all nobles requested the presence of friars at their funerals.[33] The same is true for Toledo, where the three major orders (Franciscan, Dominican, and Augustinian) routinely participated in noble funerals. The hooded, gaunt-looking friars who play such a

---

[31] AHPM 1403.793 (1592); and 1407.234 (1595).
[32] AHPM 567.1950 (1579).   [33] Rucquoi, *Valladolid*, p. 112.

prominent role in El Greco's masterpiece, *The Burial of the Count of Orgaz*, may in fact be good likenesses of the friars seen in Toledan funerals by the artist, but they are not an anachronism. By 1584, when El Greco was commissioned to paint this medieval scene for an altarpiece, friars had long been a part of Toledan noble funerals.[34]

But how does this help explain the fact that friars are conspicuously absent from all wills in Madrid before 1570, including those of nobles? Or that those who suddenly begin to request friars in Madrid after 1570 are *not*, for the most part, nobles?

One possible answer to the first question is that Madrid lacked a significant number of noble families, because of its relatively small size. It is difficult to overlook the fact that for the entire period 1520–69, hardly any noble wills show up in the Archivo Histórico de Protocolos or in our sample. This sample contains no nobles from 1520 to 1549 and only four knights of Santiago from 1550 to 1569, two of whom ask to be buried without pomp.[35] Since the remaining two knights do not request friars, however, the question remains partly unanswered.[36] Perhaps, as in the practice of leaving funeral details to one's survivors, Madrid was simply slow in catching up to customs already prevalent in more cosmopolitan cities such as Valladolid and Toledo.

The second question may be answered in part by the fact that almost all the noble wills included in our sample from 1570 to 1598 leave the funeral arrangements to survivors, and therefore they do not specify the presence of friars. Because the two nobles who leave specific funeral instructions *do* request the presence of friars, it is fairly safe to speculate that the executors of the other nobles also followed suit, "as it seemed best."[37] This helps account for the relatively low number of nobles who ask for friars. But if most nobles leave funeral arrangements to their

---

34 Sarah Schrott, "The Burial of the Count of Orgaz," *Studies in the History of Art*, vol. 11 (Washington, DC, 1982), p. 1. See also Martinez Gil, *Toledo*, pp. 68–9; 77–82.

35 AHPM 107 s.f. (1550), Felipe de Guevara; and 147.64 (1552), Juan de Castilla.

36 AHPM 107 s.f. (1550), Fernan Perez de Lujan; and 542.501 (1568), Francisco de Berestegui.

37 The only two who request friars are Ladron de Guevara, a knight of Santiago, who asked for eight Franciscans on horseback [AHPM 1410.389 (1596)], and Maria de Barreda y Sotomayor, the widow of a knight of Santiago, who asked for a total of forty-eight friars [AHPM 1403.793 (1592)].

executors, who, exactly, is making all those requests for friars after 1570?

A good number of those who make such requests are connected with the royal court, often as servants of the king or queen. Out of the number of requests for friars, court people make up for six out of eleven (55%) in the 1570s, seven out of fifteen (47%) in the 1580s, and six out of fourteen (43%) in the 1590s. The remainder of these requests come from seven artisans, one priest, and twelve testators who fail to indicate their profession or status. Among the artisans, there are three gold-smiths, one furrier, one shoemaker, one carpenter, and one blacksmith. The goldsmiths and the furrier conceivably found clients for their luxury crafts among the royal family and the nobility. The other artisans could also have served the court, but we have no way of knowing for sure.

It is quite possible that the abrupt appearance of the friars in non-noble Madrid wills indicates how intensely the question of status became related to public gestures such as funerals. Such a conclusion seems to be suggested, in the first place, by the high incidence of court people and luxury artisans among those who request friars. Because such a practice had been previously restricted to nobles and the royal family, it seems reasonable to suspect that some at court sought to affirm their own status by mimicking or approximating the gestures of their superiors.

In the second place, it is somewhat peculiar that none of those who request friars explain why they want their company. Obviously, it does not take much effort to deduce the intercessory role of friars. As ostensibly "holy," these men could offer prayers that had a better chance of being heard. Also, much like the habit worn as burial dress, the presence of these friars also invoked the assistance of some powerful patron in heaven. However, unlike the case of the burial dress, when testators reveal why the request is being made, the function of the friars has to be guessed. As will be seen presently, these same testators did not hesitate to explain the function of other cortege participants, such as the con-fraternities or the orphan children. Why this silence regarding the function of the friars? Could it be that the gesture was observed and imitated without its ever being fully explained?

Two major public events may have helped to change funeral practices in Madrid and to foster a climate of imitation: the funerals of the prince,

Don Carlos, and of the queen, Elizabeth of Valois in 1568. These funerals were the first major displays of royal ceremony in the new capital of Madrid. It is quite likely that those citizens who witnessed these elaborate ceremonies were not only deeply impressed by them but also were inspired to emulate their pomp as much as possible.

Fortunately, it is possible to reconstruct these funerals in detail. The funeral of Don Carlos, eldest son of King Philip II, was chronicled by Juan Lopez de Hoyos. It was a monumental spectacle that awed all of Madrid.[38] One of the most extraordinary aspects of this funeral was the size of the cortege, which consisted not only of the royal family and all the appropriate nobles, prelates, courtiers, servants, and officials, but also of all the confraternities and clergy from Madrid. As Lopez de Hoyos tells it:

The cortege of friars and clerics was so lengthy, that as they filed out from the palace, in order, with their candles in hand, they reached the church of Santo Domingo el Real – which is a considerable distance – before the prince's body had even left the palace. All of this in spite of the fact that they processed in a very tight formation.[39]

This great procession was so immense that not all of these "innumerable" clergy were able to enter the convent church of Santo Domingo, where the prince was to be buried. Instead, they filed past the main portal, finally allowing the clergy from the royal chapel to enter with the body.[40]

A similar display took place that same year when Queen Elizabeth of Valois died. In her case, some members of each religious order were asked to come to the palace to keep vigil over her body. The following morning another colossal cortege was assembled, consisting of all the

---

[38] Juan Lopez de Hoyos, *Relación de la muerte y honras funebres del Principe Don Carlos* (Madrid, 1568), in Jose Simon Diaz, ed., *Fuentes para la historia de Madrid y su provincia*, vol. 1 (Madrid, 1964).

[39] Ibid., p. 10.

[40] Ibid.: "Y la gente ynnumerable ningun cabildo ni parrochia ni orden alguno entro en el monasterio, sino en llegando a la puerta passavan de largo hasta que llego la cruz y capilla real con el cuerpo de su Alteza, entraron todos los que yvan en su siguimiento."

clergy and confraternities in Madrid. Lopez de Hoyos relates that this funeral was witnessed by great numbers of people, most of whom wept openly as the cortege passed by.[41]

It is no mere coincidence that soon after these royal burials took place all funeral corteges in Madrid become increasingly elaborate. This is not to say that these spectacular ceremonies alone changed funeral customs in Madrid, but we can surmise that they must have made some impact on a city that was adapting to the presence of the court. After all, some of the testators in our sample may have seen these funerals themselves. And many of those who saw these immense processions were the same people who began to request the presence of increasingly large groups of mourners at their own funerals.

Confraternities

The funerals of Don Carlos and Queen Elizabeth of Valois not only employed all of Madrid's clerics but also all of its confraternities (*cofradías*). Throughout the Middle Ages, confraternities had played an important role in funeral services.[42] One of the chief functions of confraternities was to help bury the dead. In essence, many confraternities were burial clubs of sorts, since they were intensely concerned with the task of burying their members, an obligation they normally fulfilled by offering prayers for the deceased and taking part in the funeral cortege. By belonging to a confraternity, a layperson would not only become involved in the charitable task of helping to bury the dead but himself also be ensured a proper funeral, with the requisite number of inter-

---

[41] *Hystoria y relación verdadera de la enfermedad, felicissimo tránsito y sumptuosas exequias funebres de la Serenísima Reyna de España doña Isabel de Valoys nuestra señora* (Madrid, 1569). In: Jose Simón Díaz, ed., *Fuentes para la Historia de Madrid y su Provincia*, vol. 1, pp. 24–5.

[42] The bibliography on confraternities is vast and ever growing. For an overview of their place in the Counter-Reformation see: Louis Châtellier, *L'Europe des devots* (Paris, 1987), tr. J. Birrel, *The Europe of the Devout: The Catholic Reformation and the Formation of a New Society* (Cambridge, 1989). On Spain (Zamora) see Maureen Flynn, *Sacred Charity: Confraternities and Social Welfare in Spain, 1400–1700* (Ithaca NY, 1989). Much of the research has focused on Italy: R. F. Weissman, *Ritual Brotherhood in Renaissance Florence* (London/New York, 1982); James R. Banker, *Death in the Community* (Athens GA/London, 1988); and Christopher F. Black, *Italian Confraternities in the Sixteenth Century* (Cambridge, 1989).

cessory prayers. In an age when it was believed that to die alone was most frightful, confraternities protected individuals from that fate. So deep was the anxiety about dying alone that confraternities were established for the sole purpose of assisting condemned criminals in their death and burial.[43]

To have these benefits, one need not go as far as to face the gallows; one did not even have to join a confraternity. Madrid's *cofradías* routinely participated in the funerals of nonmembers, lending their services for a set fee.[44] This practice served the dual purpose of filling confraternity coffers and providing them with the opportunity to perform more meritorious acts of charity.

The increasing complexity of Madrid funerals deeply affected the city's confraternities. Throughout the century, the number of testators who declared membership in a confraternity remained fairly constant, somewhere between 20 and 30 percent of the total sample. However, as the century progressed, and especially after 1560, the number of requests for confraternities gradually increased (see Figure 4.1). The most obvious change is the practice of requesting the presence of multiple confraternities. In the 1520s, for example, only 6 percent of the testators requested more than one confraternity, and none requested more than two. By the 1550s, after a steady, gradual increase, the figures changed dramatically: 12 percent requested at least two confraternities, and 8 percent requested three. The upward spiral of requests continued to bring more and more confraternities into the picture, so that by the 1590s hardly anyone seemed satisfied with a single confraternity (only about 3 percent of the testators), and as many as 12 percent requested the presence of four or more confraternities! Even before the end of the century, it was not too unusual for some testators to request the pres-

---

[43] The city of Oviedo, for example, expressed pity when it established the Confraternity of Mercy to help condemned prisoners to die well and be properly buried: "Parece que el que muere e padece va tan desconsolado yendo tan solo e sin personas que le animen a morir." Ciríaco Miguel Vigil, *Colección histórico-diplomática del Ayuntamiento de Oviedo* (Oviedo, 1889), p. 477, cited by Lopez Lopez, *Comportamientos religiosos*, p. 193.

[44] These fees are difficult to ascertain from the wills, which simply instruct the executors to "pagar lo acostumbrado." One will from 1529 specifies the sum of 1 *ducado* (11 *reales*) for a confraternity. AHPM 55.800. Another from 1571 specifies 12 *reales*. AHPM 317.216v.

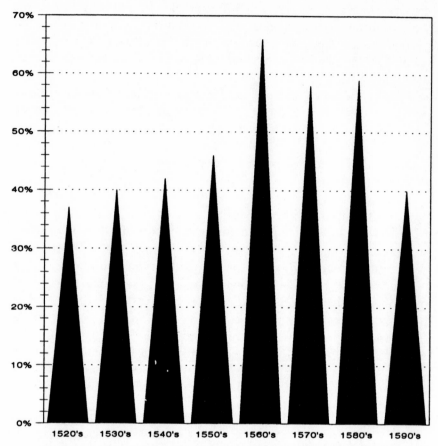

Figure 4.1. Percentage of requests for confraternities in funeral cortege.

ence of *all* of the city's confraternities at their funeral.[45] Again, we see a marked increase in the number of confraternity participants, an inflation that closely parallels that which also occurred for priests and mendicants.

Throughout the sixteenth century, the number of requests for confraternities was always higher than actual membership, but as the century progressed, the gap widened (see Figure 4.2), showing that confraternities became involved in a greater number of nonmember funerals,

[45] AHPM 567.2230 (1576).

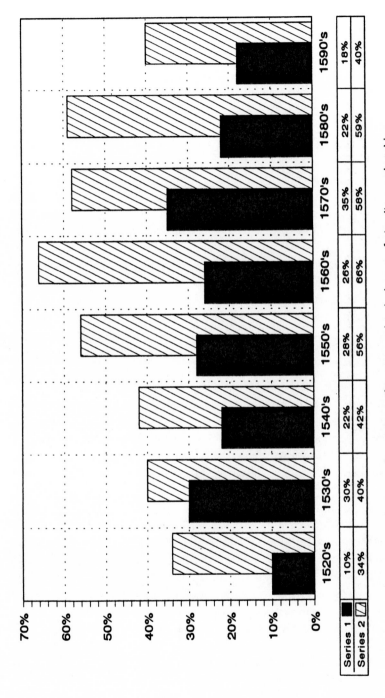

	1520's	1530's	1540's	1550's	1560's	1570's	1580's	1590's
Series 1	10%	30%	22%	28%	26%	35%	22%	18%
Series 2	34%	40%	42%	56%	66%	58%	59%	40%

Series 1: Percentage of testators who declare confraternity membership

Series 2: Percentage of testators who request participation of confraternities in funeral cortege

Figure 4.2. Confraternity membership compared to requests for confraternities.

especially as testators requested the presence of more than one confraternity. The slight dip in the total number of requests in the 1580s and 1590s was not a real decline in requests or membership but simply a reflection of the increased complexity of funerals, and of the practice of not specifying one's funeral requests and leaving them in the hands of one's survivors.

As was the case with priests and mendicants, it is quite likely that the actual, final number of requests for confraternities was much higher than that reflected in the wills. With a high percentage of all testators leaving arrangements to their executors and simply asking for the presence of "as many confraternities as seems best," it is possible that perhaps as many as one-third to one-half of all funerals in Madrid had at least two confraternities by 1590.

In nearby Toledo, a similar phenomenon was also taking place. Faced with an ever-growing confraternity system, the Council of Toledo sought to place a limit on membership in 1582. The principal reason for this reform was that "since they [the confraternities] create such immense crowds, they cause great inconveniences."[46] Apparently, Madrid was not the only Castilian city in which confraternities could clog the streets.

But what is at work here? Why this increased interest in confraternities? The testators tell us themselves. Most often, the confraternities were requested so that the deceased would have certain intercessory prayers and gestures performed on their behalf. The silversmith Francisco de Tapia, for instance, gave the following instructions to the two confraternities to which he belonged: "I ask the aforementioned confraternities to come to my funeral, and entrust them with the task of escorting my body and pleading with Our Lord, and of saying the prayers and masses that they normally say for all their members."[47]

Obviously, there were benefits to membership. This silversmith could be sure to have the prayers of these confraternities because he was a member and could lay a claim to their services. The constitutions of many confraternities clearly stated that one of their chief functions was to offer intercessory prayer. One such constitution from Oviedo (1528) reminded the confraternity members that their prayers were "the key

[46] Tejada, vol. 5, p. 426. See also Martinez Gil, *Toledo*, pp. 72–6.
[47] AHPM 542.11 (1568).

that can open the gates of heaven," and that they were duty-bound to rescue suffering souls from purgatory. This constitution outlined four reasons for the confraternity's intercessory duties. First, the agony of the souls in purgatory was too immense to ignore; second, since they were fellow Christians who shared in redemption, these afflicted souls deserved to be rescued; third, after being freed from their torment, these souls would undoubtedly intercede in heaven on behalf of those who had prayed for them; fourth, the work of prayer itself earned merit in heaven for the confraternity members.[48] Guided as much by self-interest as by concern for their neighbors, confraternities thus offered fellowship and helped to allay fear of suffering in the afterlife.

Many testators specified that they were members of certain confraternities and asked their executors to remind these confraternities that they had an obligation to perform their duties. Most of these requests were rather perfunctory and read very much like this: "I ask the aforementioned confraternity to render me the honor of their presence, as they are required to do, since I am a member."[49] Some testators carefully indicated that their spouses were members of certain confraternities and that they were entitled to the same treatment as a full member.[50]

Although confraternities routinely participated in the funerals of non-members, they did have the right to refuse such requests, and many testators knew this. One, for instance, asked for the confraternity of San Felipe, "if it wishes to come."[51] An illiterate man who could not sign his own will urged his executors to rush through his application to a certain confraternity and pay his entrance fee "as quickly as possible" so that he could be considered a member.[52] Another tried to make a confraternity feel a sense of obligation, even though he was not a member, by pointing out that he had taken part in some of their functions and was "immensely devoted" to it.[53] Those who were not members or who had little

---

[48] AHN Clero, libro 9203, cited by Lopez Lopez, *Comportamientos religiosos en Asturias*, p. 190.

[49] AHPM 800.243 (1588).

[50] AHPM 107 s.f. (1549).

[51] AHPM 1410.673.

[52] AHPM 542.631 (1568): "Pido me acompañe la cofradia de la soledad de Nuestra Señora, en la cual he pedido que me reciban por cofrade y si me recibieren, acompañen mi cuerpo y paguenles la entrada lo mas presto que se pueda y si no me recivieren acompañenme la cofradia que pareciere."

[53] AHPM 457.1108 (1573).

chance of joining, simply had to take their chances. Francisco Hernandez, a poor cavalryman who was dying in the court hospital and who did not belong to any confraternity, took to pleading with a sense of urgency: "I beg the brethren of the confraternity of this hospital, for the love of God, that they try to do as much for my soul as they can."[54]

This last statement clearly reveals what was perceived to be the function of the confraternities: By escorting the body and saying certain prayers in its vicinity, these laypeople aided the soul of the deceased. Confraternities were but another important link in the chain of intercession that linked all human beings and that strengthened the position of any single individual before the divine tribunal.

Can we assume, however, that every testator sincerely believed in the necessity of intercession or that all requests for confraternities were as heartfelt as that of the poor cavalryman? Certainly not, but conviction makes little difference in explaining the inflationary spiral of increasingly complex gestures. As significant as the theological reasons may be, they do not alone explain the phenomenon. The increased participation of these lay associations in Madrid funerals resulted as much from the peculiar social dynamics of the city as from religious convictions. These gestures, much like those surrounding the participation of clerics, were couched in a richly symbolic religious language, but they were also laden with all sorts of claims to status and privilege and could be simultaneously used to impress other humans as much as God.

The fact that people requested more and more confraternities as the sixteenth century progressed, along with more and more priests and friars, would be hard to disprove. What is difficult to prove is that some specific reason, or set of reasons, was responsible for this phenomenon. On the one hand, this ever expanding preoccupation with intercessory gestures could be seen as the result of a proportionate increase in anxiety over death and the afterlife, or of an intensified insecurity over questions of status, or a combination of the two factors. In other words, it is possible that this increased need to impress God and neighbor reflected a growing uncertainty about what was truly adequate. All of this could also be interpreted as resulting from an increased confidence in the value of certain gestures, on a divine as well as a human plane. It is

[54] AHPM 543.83 (1569).

also possible that this apparent desire to show off and have as many prayers as possible reflected a secure reliance on the specific value of certain gestures.

Poor people and orphans

Relief of the poor was a significant component of Spanish funerals throughout the Middle Ages.[55] As a final act of charity, testators could offer alms to several poor people, provide them with a meal, and ask them to join the cortege. These poor strangers, who were neither friends nor relations, would escort the body to the grave, intoning prayers on behalf of the deceased.

This practice was considered beneficial for two reasons. First, as an act of almsgiving, it earned the deceased a certain degree of merit and helped them face the divine tribunal with more points in their favor.[56] Second, it also functioned as an intercessory act, much like that performed by the priests, mendicants, and confraternities. The prayers of the poor were deemed to be especially powerful, not only because they reminded God of the charity of the testator but also because they carried a special weight. As a well-known psalm has it: "A cry goes up from the poor man, and the Lord hears, and helps him in all his troubles."[57]

Throughout the Middle Ages, the most common form of funeral almsgiving was the meal offered to the poor.[58] In sixteenth-century Madrid wills, meals for the poor are occasionally mentioned in the early decades of the sixteenth century.[59] In some cases, the food offering for the poor became part of the funeral cortege, as in the case of Francisco Franco, who requested that two lambs, six arrobas of wine, and four

---

[55] Teofilo Ruiz, "Feeding and Clothing the Poor: Private Charity and Social Distinction in Northern Castile Before the Black Death." Unpublished paper.

[56] The Catechism of the Council of Trent, Part IV, chap. 8, question 9, laid out this lesson clearly.

[57] *Psalm* 34:6.

[58] T. Ruiz, "Feeding and Clothing the Poor," pp. 12 ff.

[59] These few requests usually read as follows: "Le den de comer a diez pobres de carne o pescado." AHPM 55.642 (1525). AHPM 69.46 (1538) asks "Le den de comer a siete pobres por tres dias despues de mi entierro." Leonor Gomez Nieto cites several such requests from the fifteenth century, *Ritos funerarios en Madrid medieval*, pp. 66–70.

fanegas of wheat be carried along with his corpse.[60] Such requests disappear from the wills after about 1540. Occasionally, testators ask that the poor receive some of their clothing.[61] The vast majority simply ask that the poor "be paid the customary alms" (*le paguen lo acostumbrado de limosna*). Here, the choice of the verb "to pay" is somewhat revealing: The money given to the poor, while still technically considered as alms (*limosna*), is also regarded as a fee that is *paid* for services rather than freely *given*.[62]

Although the amount of *limosna* is not usually specified, some wills do mention exactly how much each poor person should receive. Apparently, there was no set fee but, rather, a generally accepted range of prices. In the 1540s, for instance, Francisco Rojas paid 1 *real* to each of the twelve poor people he requested.[63] A few years earlier, Juan Lopez Garavato had offered each poor person the paltry sum of 1 *maravedi* for additional prayers to be said over his grave and that of his parents.[64] In the 1550s, Catalina de Arceo, a widow, paid 4 *maravedis* (about one-eighth of a *real*) to each poor person, but Juan de Castilla, a knight of Santiago, paid 1 *real*.[65] In the 1570s, 1580s, and 1590s prices fluctuate considerably, ranging from 10 *maravedis* (about one-third of a *real*) to half a *ducado* (about 5 *reales*), but the most common price seemed to be about 1 *real* for each poor person.[66]

---

[60] AHPM 69.42 (1538). In the 1520s and 1530s, the food offering was an accepted gesture that did not need to be specified, because it was linked to one's social status. One testator simply asked: "Que el dia de mi enterramiento lleven las ofrendas que se acostumbra a llevar por las pesonas de mi manera." AHPM 69.94 (1538).

[61] Some combine both feeding and clothing: "a los pobres . . . le den de comer, beber, y zapatos." AHPM 55.700 (1528). Some merely mention clothing: "le den a cada pobre una camisa de las mias." AHPM 543.435 (1569). This gesture is different from another that will be discussed presently: dressing the poor in mourning clothes.

[62] One will, for example, indicated exactly what the poor were to do for the small sum of 1 *maravedi*: "Que salgan sobre mi sepultura y sobre la de mis padres . . . y ruegen a Dios por todos los difuntos y mi anima." AHPM 55.894 (1530).

[63] AHPM 136.216 (1540).

[64] AHPM 55.894 (1530): "Un maravedi . . . para que salgan sobre mi sepultura al fin del novenario, y sobre la de mis padres . . . y ruegen a Dios por todos los difuntos y mi anima."

[65] AHPM 96 s.f. (1556); and AHPM 147.164 (1552).

[66] 10 *maravedis*: AHPM 746.25 (1570), and 746.100 (1571); 17 *maravedis* (0.5 *real*): AHPM 746.79 (1570), and 412.943 (1597); 34 *maravedis* (1 *real*): 746.166 (1570),

The trend toward larger funeral corteges is also proven by the number of poor people requested in Madrid wills. In the early part of the century, such requests are rather uncommon, but with every passing decade there is a marked increase both in the number of testators who ask for poor people and in the number of poor people requested (see Tables 4.1 and 4.2). Although no more than 4 percent of all testators made such a request in the 1520s, nearly two-thirds (61%) did so in the 1570s. Whereas only one will (2%) asked for more than six poor people in the 1520s, nearly a third (30%) did so in the 1590s. This means that by the end of the century, almost one out of every three funerals in Madrid included at least six poor people. Again, there is an upward spiral in requests for funeral participants in spite of an increasing number of testators who leave all arrangements to their survivors.

Regarding the number of poor people requested, even numbers were greatly favored. The number six seemed to be the most popular, though four and eight were also often requested. Some testators attached a symbolic significance to the numbers. One asked for "twelve poor people, in memory of the twelve apostles."[67] Another asked for thirty-three poor people no doubt because of the number of years supposedly spent on earth by Jesus.

Although most wills do not specify the gender of these poor people, some ask for specific numbers of men or women. Francisco Rojas and his wife requested exactly seven men and five women.[68] Maria de Madrid wanted six men and two women.[69] Another testator specified that he wanted twelve men but would be willing to accept women if enough men could not be found.[70] This kind of attention to detail reveals an attitude of genuine concern over the exact meaning and purpose of funeral gestures.

Undoubtedly, this form of charity must have become indispensable for many of the needy. Although the wills do not usually indicate how or where these poor people could be located, a few do indicate that this kind of relief was administered through the parish churches. One will, for instance, specifies that the total sum of 66 *reales* is to be given to the

---

and 800.1168 (1581); 68 *maravedis* (2 *reales*): 1412.379 (1597); 170 *maravedis* (5 *reales*): 317.312 (1571).

[67] AHPM 147.164 (1552).   [69] AHPM 575.418 (1583).

[68] AHPM 136.216 (1540).   [70] AHPM 800.1168 (1581).

pastor of the church of Santa Cruz for distribution to the thirty-three poor people requested at 2 *reales* each.[71] Another specifies that the poor people should not be "of the sort that go begging from door to door."[72] Regardless of how they were chosen or how often they were asked, many of Madrid's poor could benefit from funerals. By the end of the century, this custom had become an unofficial but well-established means of relief for the poor of the city.

It also seems clear that this gesture, perhaps more than any other, could serve the additional purpose of confirming the social status of the deceased. It was more than simple almsgiving. It was a public display of largesse and patronage in which the beneficiaries walked through the city streets in a distinctive, encoded apparel that affirmed the prestige of the deceased and confirmed the dependency of the needy. The mere presence of the poor at someone's funeral established that the deceased was not poor but affluent enough to engage in charity. The poor, after all, were always on the receiving end; they could seldom afford to be generous.

The mourning garb worn by the poor seems to have been fairly standardized but still open to variations. Those wills that specify how the poor are to be dressed all ask that they be given capes and hoods (or pointed caps), but the names used for these articles vary quite a bit, indicating some variety.[73] As far as the fabric and color were concerned, there seemed to be room for choice. Some were dressed in black, some in white, others in gray or brown. One testator left the final choice of color to his executors.[74]

In addition to being dressed according to the will of the deceased or the wishes of executors, the poor also carried torches and candles. Most often, the poor are asked to carry torches. Some of those testators who carefully plan every detail of their funeral go as far as to specify how many poor people should carry torches and how many should carry

---

[71] AHPM 1412.379 (1597).   [72] AHPM 96 s.f. (1556).

[73] AHPM 542.501 (1568) asks for "sotanas y caperuzas"; 147.164 (1552) for "caperuzas y camisas"; 571.714 (1571) for "capa y bonete"; 1015.93 (1579) for "ropillas y caperuzas"; 800.1168 (1581) for "quirroza y caperuza."

[74] AHPM 542.501 (1568) asks for "soyal negro"; 1015.93 (1579) for "ropillas y caperuzas blancas"; 800.1168 (1581) for "paño pardo"; 1407.105 (1595) for "frisa blanca"; 571.714 (1571) for "paño del color que pareciere."

candles.[75] The wording of these requests indicates that their function as bearers of light must have been considered important, because the poor are hardly ever requested without their torches and candles. In fact, the exact wording in the vast majority of wills asks for the torches and the poor people in the same breath, as if the function of each were of equal importance. In many cases, the torches are mentioned first, as in "I request six torches with six poor people," suggesting that the torches may be more important. A few testators indicate that the function of these lights is to "honor the cross," which means that the poor served as acolytes to the clergy who carried the cross.[76] The deep liturgical symbolism of the lights themselves undoubtedly made them significant as reminders of the Easter promise. In a Christological context, they represented the triumph of light over darkness and life over death.[77] Another reason that the lights sometimes seemed more important than the poor who carried them may be that they were placed over the grave and remained there through the funeral services and postmortem devotions until they burned out, whereas the poor people simply went away after the funeral.[78]

Another major change in funerary practices that occurred about mid-century was the addition of orphan children to the cortege. Suddenly, in the 1550s, testators begin to request the presence of *los niños de la doctrina*. These children were orphan pupils at the charity school known as the Colegio de Doctrinos.[79] Although this school had existed in

[75] AHPM 107 s.f. (1549) asks for twenty poor people, two of whom should carry torches, eighteen of whom should carry one-pound candles. A similar request is made in 542.501 (1568). A *pragmatica* of Ferdinand and Isabella limited the number of lights to twenty-four for titled nobles and twelve for all others: *Libro de las bulas y pragmaticas delos Reyes Catolicos* (2 vols., facsimile edition, Madrid, 1973), vol. 2, fol. 309v. On decrees concerning excess torches and candles see Gomez Nieto, *Ritos funerarios*, p. 74, and Lopez Lopez, *Comportamientos religiosos*, p. 74.

[76] AHPM 343.656 (1576); 1390.139 (1584).

[77] Venegas, *Agonía*, p. 222: The candles and torches were believed to represent Christ and the faith of the believer, as in the Gospel of John 8:12, "I am the light of the world; anyone who follows me will not be walking in the dark; he will have the light of life."

[78] AHPM 412.388 (1579); 96 s.f. (1556).

[79] Charles E. Kany, *Life and Manners in Madrid, 1750–1800* (Berkeley, CA, 1932), p. 371, n. 84; José Antonio Alvarez de Baena, *Compendio histórico de las grandezas de la*

Madrid since 1470, it is not even mentioned in any wills from the first half of the sixteenth century.[80] (Children from the orphanage of Santa Catalina apparently also attended funerals in Madrid, but they are not requested by any of the testators in this sample.)[81]

The function of these children was similar to that of the poor adults: They escorted the deceased to the grave and offered prayers on their behalf. Cristobal de Madrid, for instance, requested these children "so that they may attend my vigil, burial, and mass." He also made it clear that they had a specific function to perform in exchange for a set fee: "Since they are poor, I ask that they receive 3,000 *maravedis* in alms, so that they will pray to God for my soul."[82] Luisa de Medina put it more succinctly, without mentioning any specific sums of money: "Give some alms to the pupils of the doctrine, so that they will come to my funeral and pray to God on my behalf."[83] The orphans thus fulfilled a dual function. First, as was the case with the poor adults, they provided the deceased with an opportunity to perform a final act of charity. Second, they could offer very powerful prayers on behalf of the deceased because they were not only poor but also pure. After all, it was common knowledge that the prayers of children were heard more readily in heaven.[84] Some wills, such as that of the priest Gregorio de Oviedo, explained the purpose of the orphans through specific instructions: "They should attend my funeral, both in the morning and afternoon, and should say a litany for my soul both coming and going, as they come to my house and as they go to the church."[85]

The abrupt appearance of these children in Madrid wills after 1550 is in keeping with the general trend toward more elaborate funerals. At first, in the 1550s, they are requested by no more than 10 percent of all

---

coronada villa de Madrid, corte de la monarquía de España (1786), modern edition (Madrid, 1978), pp. 182–3.

[80] Leonor Gomez Nieto, *Ritos funerarios*, pp. 54–5 probably contains a typographical error, for she says that requests for the *niños* begin to appear in Madrid wills in the second half of "siglo XIV."

[81] On these orphans see: Juan Ramón Romero, "Asistencia a los pobres y caridad en Madrid en la segunda mitad del siglo XV," *Anales del Instituto de estudios Madrileños* (1987), pp. 123–31; and Jerónimo de la Quintana, *Historia de la antiguedad, nobleza, y grandeza de la villa de Madrid* (Madrid, 1954), pp. 1010–11.

[82] AHPM 78.381 (1554).   [84] Venegas, *Agonía*, p. 140.

[83] AHPM 542.443 (1568).   [85] AHPM 457.1219 (1573).

testators. By the next decade, the figure jumps to nearly one-half of the wills (48%) and remains around that level for the remainder of the century. Again, keeping in mind that more and more testators leave their executors in charge of the funeral details as the century wears on, it seems quite likely that many more such requests must have been made by the *albaceas*. It would be safe to say that after 1570 as many as three out of every four testamentary funerals could have included these orphans.

For this service, the children were provided with torches and candles and clothed in distinctive garb. Their function as light bearers seemed to be taken very seriously. In some wills, as was the case with the poor adults, the children and the lights are mentioned in the same breath. One will asked for twenty-four orphans "dressed in red flannel, each carrying his own torch."[86] Another summed it all up by asking that "they march along, praying and commending my soul to God, each one holding a burning candle in his hand."[87]

Since the *niños* took part in so many funerals during the latter part of the century, this practice must have become an important source of revenue for the Colegio de los Doctrinos. The amount of *limosna* (alms) given to the school is seldom mentioned, but it could apparently fluctuate quite a bit. One will simply offered to buy shoes for all the children who came to the funeral.[88] Some offered as little as 3 *reales*; others 6, 8, 10, or 12 *reales;* or – more rarely – as much as 44 *reales*, or 3,000 *maravedis* (about 88 *reales*). One magnanimous testator donated 20 *ducados* to the school (220 *reales*)![89] Occasionally, the orphans would earn extra money for the school by attending the anniversary masses that were celebrated a year after the funeral.[90]

Even from childhood, then, the poor came to depend on funerals in sixteenth-century Madrid. Whether as *niños* from the Colegio de la Doctrina, or as *pobres* selected by some pastor, the needy turned a profit

---

[86] AHPM 88.866 (1562).   [87] AHPM 543.435 (1569).   [88] AHPM 412.388 (1579).

[89] 3 *reales:* AHPM 61.671 (1563); 6 *reales:* AHPM 314.231 (1564); 746.113; 746.118 (1571); 8 *reales:* AHPM 542.339 (1568); 746.25 (1570); 10 *reales:* AHPM 746.100 (1571); 1412.953 (1597); 12 *reales:* AHPM 317.216v (1571); 44 *reales:* AHPM 457.1154 (1568); 88 *reales:* AHPM 78.381 (1554); 220 *reales:* AHPM 457.1208 (1573).

[90] AHPM 457.1219 (1573). The *limosna* was 4,000 *maravedis* in this case (about 118 *reales*)!

from the business of death. Granted, no one spoke of it as a business but as charity. The monetary transactions that took place between the poor and those who requested their presence were always carefully called *limosnas*. Technical niceties aside, however, the fact remains that funerals became an increasingly important part of the city's economy and of its system of relief for the poor. In addition to generating income for artisans and merchants, particularly those who made and sold the coffins, mourning clothes, and candles, funerals also created a safety net for the poor. In the sixteenth-century story of *Lazarillo de Tormes*, the character of Lazaro fends off starvation in Toledo by attending funerals. Working as a lackey for a priest who does not feed him, Lazarillo visits the dying when the priest goes to administer the last rites. At each bedside, as the priest asks for intercessory prayers, Lazarillo petitions God to let the ailing person die so he can get some food at a funeral meal. His words might not at all be fictional hyperbole:

On those days when there were no deaths, I returned to my daily hunger, and felt it all the more acutely. . . . Thus I could find no comfort in anything, save for death, which at times I wished upon myself, as well as upon others; but I avoided it, even though it was ever with me.[91]

We will return to this subject presently when we take up a discussion of the connection between funerals and relief for the poor.

Funeral meals

Ritual banquets were normally the culmination of burial ceremonies throughout early modern Spain. When Lazarillo de Tormes spoke of gorging himself at funerals, he was not speaking of a meal served only to the poor. All those who had attended a funeral, including the clergy, could be invited to celebrate at graveside. The feasting could at times become both lavish and raucous. And the practice was not limited to burials, for ritual feasts could also be celebrated in the church on the anniversaries of the dead and on All Soul's Day. During the first half of the sixteenth century, church authorities in some Spanish localities found it necessary to speak out against such behavior. In Asturias two

[91] Anonymous author, *La vida de Lazarillo de Tormes y de sus fortunas y adversidades* (1552–54), tratado segundo. Modern ed. Alberto Blecua (Barcelona, 1982), pp. 34–5.

synods tried to tone down the scale of these banquets, apparently without much success, first in 1511 and again in 1553. The second of these synods, which sought to bring down the cost of burials by scaling down on banquets, spoke of funerals at which the entire estate of the deceased was literally gobbled up in feasting. The synod complained that this practice not only left the heirs destitute but also prevented the testator's bequests from being fulfilled.[92] Antonio de Guevara, Bishop of Mondoñedo, proclaimed in 1541 that churches in his diocese could no longer be used for funeral banquets. He knew what he was banning, for he had seen it up close: "They eat and drink, and put up tables within the churches; and, even worse, set plates and pitchers on the altars, turning them into sideboards."[93] That such feasting could take place in a sacred space in the company of the dead indicates how difficult it could be to separate the mundane from the transcendent in Spain and how familiar the living had become with the dead.

Funeral meals show up in Madrid's testaments obliquely, through requests for the *ofrenda* (food offering) that was to be brought to the church for the funeral or the anniversary mass. Most testators throughout the century paid little attention to this; many do not even mention it, especially in the second half of the century. The majority of those who asked for it simply requested the customary *ofrenda* (*lo que se acostumbra*), leaving the details to their executors. Those who were more specific requested certain amounts of foodstuffs for the feast – grain or bread, meat, and wine. Sometimes the wax needed for the candles was listed as part of the *ofrenda*. The relatively low interest shown toward this custom by most testators and the modest amounts of food requested by those who bothered with the details might indicate that the funeral meals were not as popular in Madrid at this time as they were elsewhere. Testaments from Cuenca, for instance, show a much greater interest in the food offering, which they usually called the *añal*.[94] The contrast is

---

[92] Lopez Lopez, *Comportamientos religiosos en Asturias*, p. 76.

[93] *Constituciones sinodales hechas por el Ilustre Señor Don Antonio de Guevara, Obispo de Mondoñedo* (1541). Cited by Americo Castro, *España en su historia* (Buenos Aires, 1945), p. 646. He discusses the custom of funeral meals on pp. 645–7. See also R. Coster, *Antonio de Guevara, sa vie* (Bordeaux, 1925), p. 58.

[94] Leonor Gomez Nieto found both terms, *añal* and *ofrenda*, in Madrid wills from the fifteenth century, *Ritos funerarios*, pp. 69–70. I was able to find only *ofrenda* in the sixteenth century.

sharp. Whereas mention of the *ofrenda* decreases and details about it dwindle in Madrid wills during the second half of the sixteenth century, requests for the *añal* in Cuenca begin to increase at that same time, becoming larger and more expensive.[95] One must be cautious, however, for the absence of the *ofrenda* from Madrid wills does not conclusively prove its lack of popularity. Though there is precious little other evidence – such as complaints about excess or statutes against it – for all we know, funeral meals might have become more lavish in Madrid. The silence of the wills on this subject might simply mean that the funeral banquet became one of those carefully codified gestures that did not need to be spelled out by the testator.

The clergy in Madrid undoubtedly benefited from the *ofrenda*, even if it was not as popular there as in other places, for it was not limited to banqueting. Food offerings were also brought to the clergy strictly for their use, especially in cases where priests were being asked to say specific numbers of masses for the dead within a specified period. This was not a uniquely Spanish custom. Elsewhere in Europe, the clergy also received such offerings and in some cases had come to depend on them for their survival.[96] In fact, during the early years of the Protestant Reformation, clerical dependency on the cult of the dead became a favored topic among propagandists and pamphleteers.[97] In some parts of Spain, it was customary for priests who were saying cycles of thirty masses for the dead over thirty consecutive days not to leave their churches and to be fed during the entire period. This led to many abuses, including card playing and gambling among the priests while they were not saying masses.[98] Bishop Antonio de Guevara attempted to

---

[95] Nalle, *God in La Mancha*, pp. 185–7. Lopez Lopez found very few requests for the food offering in sixteenth-century Oviedo and Gijón but noticed a steady increase in such requests in the following century. *Comportamientos religiosos*, pp. 107–17.

[96] Strocchia (*Death and Rituals*, p. 225) points out that Florentine clerics, especially the mendicants, reaped great benefit from this custom. In November 1528, for instance, twenty-one out of the thirty-one dinners eaten by the friars of Santa Maria Novella came from funerals, and during the next eight months, funeral food offerings accounted for 36.6 percent of their meals.

[97] Nicholas Manuel's play *Die Totenfresser*, which ridiculed the clergy in Bern as "those who feed upon the dead," is but one example. *Niklaus Manuels Spiel Evangelischer Freiheit: Die Totenfresser. "Vom Papst und Seiner Priestschaft," 1523*, ed. F. Vetter (Leipzig, 1923).

[98] Nalle, *God in La Mancha*, pp. 190–1. These so-called *Trentanarios cerrados* were

reform this practice but maintained a sense of humor about it. Writing in 1524 to a friend who was hiding in a church and was planning to stay there indefinitely (this man had disobeyed a royal order and feared punishment), Guevara teased him. Like it or not, said Guevara, his friend would now be constantly exposed to death, for he would have to witness many funerals and hear many masses for the dead. But there was a good side to all this. Perhaps a rich man would die and ask for a *trentanario* (a thirty-mass cycle) to be said for his soul. "In that case," Guevara joked, "you will be able to join the priests who say these masses, and help them eat the food offerings, and even gamble with them for their earnings."[99]

Mourning gestures

Even though funerals became increasingly complex throughout the sixteenth century, some restraint continued to be exercised in regard to mourning gestures. This may be due, in part, to the fact that certain laws distinguished between those gestures that benefited the dead and those that affected only the survivors.

Intercessory gestures, such as the participation of priests, friars, confraternities, and poor people, were deemed not only acceptable but meritorious. Non-intercessory gestures, such as the wearing of mourning clothes or the lighting of a certain number of candles, had long been deemed tolerable but unessential – or even worse, un-Christian. In Spain, the fear of contagion from Jewish or Moslem influences made the question of mourning gestures a delicate issue.[100]

For instance, the Synod of Toledo in 1323 had issued strict injunctions against what it called "lugubrious excesses," "execrable abuses," and "indecencies" practiced at funerals, that betrayed a sense of desperation and a lack of faith in the Christian doctrine of the Resurrection. Among such practices that "tended to imitate the rites of the pagans," this synod singled out "the horrible cries" of mourners and the wearing of mourning clothes by large numbers of people. In addition, this synod

expensive. In Cuenca, they cost 66 *reales* in 1531, the equivalent of an artisan's salary for two months.
99 Antonio de Guevara, *Epistolas familiares*, p. 197.
100 M. del Arbol Navarro, *Spanisches funeralbrauchtum*, pp. 66–77.

warned the clergy not to wear any mourning garb, even for their immediate family, under pain of excommunication.[101]

Such restrictions were apparently disobeyed, because over a century
and a half later we find another synod near Madrid issuing very similar
proscriptions. In 1480, the Synod of Alcalá saw fit to forbid the clergy
from observing any of the "excessive" grieving practices of the laity. The
rationale for this prohibition was clearly explained:

The testimony of sacred scripture teaches us that those who are greatly saddened by the deaths of their friends and relatives . . . really seem to deny the
resurrection, and to lose hope in that promise that all Catholics hold dear of
being brought back to life on the Last Day. Since faith and hope in this teaching
should be more certain and firm among those who are well versed in the sacred
scriptures and the precepts of the law, that is, the clergy and all ecclesiastics, it
seems most reprehensible and dangerous that they should give in to such grief,
inducing others into great error.[102]

As this document reveals, those who governed the church perceived
the grieving gestures of the laity as contrary to Christian ideals and very
much wanted to have the clergy abstain from them to provide an example of what the elite deemed acceptable. Some other details disclosed by
this synod show how much of a gap may have indeed existed between
official theology and popular practice. Aside from reaffirming the proscriptions of 1323 regarding the wearing of mourning clothes by the
clergy, this synod also prohibited certain forms of mutilation. Among
other things, the clergy were reminded that they were not allowed to
scratch their faces, pull out their hair with their hands, or do any other

---

[101] José Sanchez Herrero, *Concilios provinciales y sinodos toledanos de los siglos XIV y XV:
La religiosidad cristiana del clero y pueblo* (Laguna, 1976), p. 178. Sinodo diocesano de
Toledo, 1323. De sepulturis: "Quanquam pietatis affectu et humanitatis intuitu
liceat mortuous deplorare, excessus tamen lugubris prohibetur, quia desperationem
videtur future resurrectionis habere, illum ergo execrabilem abusum, ut cum aliquis
moritur, homines et mulieres ululando per vicos et plateas incendant, voces hor-
ribiles in ecclesiis et alibi emittant, ac quedam aliam indecencia faciant ad gentilium
ritum tendencia, que non solum fidelium corda pungunt, sed divine occulos maiestatis offendunt, penitus repprobamus. Expressius autem ea clericis sub pena ex-
communicationis interdicentes precipimus, ne, tempore dumtaxat exsequiarum ex-
cepto, vestes lugubres portent, nisi pro patre, matre, fratre, domino aut sorore."
[102] Herrero, *Concilios Provinciales*, p. 308.

damage to themselves, "according to the customs of the laity." Apparently, these immoderate gestures were still commonly practiced in the diocese of Toledo at the end of the fifteenth century, even by some of the clergy, in spite of the ecclesiastical legislation against them. This was no small concern, for the penalty to be imposed on any priest who broke these laws was rather stiff: suspension of benefices for three months and imprisonment for two months in an ecclesiastical jail.[103]

Other evidence points to the fact that the models of behavior proposed by the synods did not easily displace the ancient grieving customs actually practiced by parish priests and their congregations. In 1502, the Catholic Monarchs Ferdinand and Isabella saw fit to try to correct mourning abuses throughout their kingdoms by means of civil rather than ecclesiastical law. The wording of the sumptuary laws enacted by them is quite similar to that of the synods of Toledo and Alcalá and indicates a strong desire to bring public behavior in line with official church teachings.

Ferdinand and Isabella made a clear distinction between mourning gestures that aided the deceased and gestures that "were only invented as signs of grief by people who did not believe in the resurrection, but instead believed the soul died with the body." Among the customs excoriated by their pronouncement, the following received the most attention: excesses in the wearing of mourning clothes, excesses in the use of candles, and uncontrolled "dolorous crying." According to the preamble to this law, such practices were very common throughout Spain and had led to "much disorder" and "inordinate superfluous spending." Assuming a paternalistic stance, the monarchs proclaimed that because God was not pleased by such behavior and their subjects thus ran the risk of being damned, it was their duty to put an end to these excesses.

All these gestures of weakness and dolorous cries were devised only for the solace of the living. But we Catholic Christians believe that there is another life beyond this, where our souls will enjoy eternal life; and we should endeavor to earn this life through meritorious works, not through vain and transitory gestures such as excessive spending on mourning clothes, or the inordinate burn-

---

[103] Ibid. The revenue from any condemned priest's benefice was to be divided in half between the priest's accuser and his church.

ing of candles. . . . Instead, it would be much better for all that money so vainly spent to be used for masses, alms, and other meritorious works.[104]

To correct the kind of behavior they considered un-Christian, Ferdinand and Isabella prescribed very specific guidelines. First, mourning clothes were to be worn only by the immediate family or servants of the deceased, and no garment was to be made from *jerga* (a rough cloth) or worn for more than six months. Women were never to dress entirely in black except for the death of a husband or of a royal person. Specific instructions were given as to what types of dress men and women should wear.[105] Mourning decorations on the walls of homes and churches were also forbidden.[106] The penalty for disobeying this law would be the confiscation of all mourning clothes involved, which were then to be divided equally in thirds between the accuser, the court, and a hospital or poor house.

Exact limits were also placed on the number of candles that could be used in a funeral and on the number of days during which they could burn. Titled nobles were allowed twenty-four candles, those "of a lesser state" no more than twelve. The use of candles was restricted to the day of the funeral, the services on the ninth day after burial, and the anniversary mass.[107] Though the rationale for these laws was expressed in theological terms as the desire to bring public grieving gestures in line with Christian hopes for eternal life (albeit a disembodied life, according to the wording of the document), more mundane factors were also at work. The mourning laws sought to aggrandize royal power and to control public displays of status as much as they sought to make the people better Christians. The mundane dimension of these laws is disclosed by two facts.

[104] "De la manera que se puede traer luto y gastar la cera por los defuntos" (1502), *Libro de las bulas y pragmaticas de los Reyes Catolicos* (2 vols., facsimile edition, Madrid, 1973), vol. 2, pp. 308–9.

[105] *Libro de bulas*, fol. 309. "Por personas reales, los hombres han de traer luto de lobas cerradas por los lados con falda y capirotes todo de paño tundido. Las mujeres han de traer tocas negras y habito con manto con gulla. . . . Por personas grandes, prelados, y nobles de titulo, los hombres han de traer lobas cerradas, sin falda y capirote, todo de paño tundido, y por las otras personas lobas largas con vaneras abiertas por los lados que no allegen mas de fasta el suelo, y que no rastren, y sayos y capirotes de paño tundido. Las mujeres han de traer abitos de paño negro tundido, que no arrastren, que lleguen los mantos al suelo, no mas falda que sin luto."

[106] *Libro de bulas*, fol. 309.   [107] *Libro de bulas*, fol. 309v.

First, and most important, regulations were put into effect for the royal family. In case of a royal death, all citizens were allowed to wear mourning garb. Whereas no one was to be permitted to dress this way for any death beyond one's immediate family, a special exception was made for royal personages. For example, as previously mentioned, a woman could dress totally in black only for the death of her husband or of a royal person. In this way, the monarchs tried to assume a privileged position, reserving for themselves a place in every Spanish family. These very special grieving gestures dramatically signified the power of the monarchy over every single subject. The entire nation was to mourn for a royal person as for a mother, father, husband, brother, or sister (or as for a master, in the case of servants). No one else could demand such gestures, not even grandees, prelates, or titled nobles. Universal public grieving for a royal person was one way of displaying and reaffirming the exclusive, privileged dominion of the king and his family. Such privileges could be claimed, but they could not be easily monopolized by the monarchy. A law (*pragmatica*) issued by Philip II in 1572 also excluded anyone outside the royal family from erecting catafalques (*tumulos*) in churches or covering the church walls with black bunting, a practice that could be afforded only by the wealthiest titled families and was apparently very much to their liking. This law had to be re-promulgated in 1610, but infractions continued to take place. In 1633, the Duke of Infantado was temporarily banished from his estates and fined 10,000 *ducados* for having erected a catafalque for his wife's funeral.[108]

Second, the restrictions applied to the number of candles and to catafalques also show that the question of mourning gestures was inseparable from the question of status. Titled nobles were allowed twenty-four candles, twice as many as all other subjects. Obviously, this carefully measured distinction relates more directly to the issue of power and privilege than to any so-called Christian attitude toward grieving. The twenty-four candles at a duke's funeral were a coded sign of his station in the social hierarchy, not necessarily a sign of any greater hope for eternal life. The same was true of catafalques and their symbolism. Some Madrid testators were well aware of this relation between the gestures allowed to them and the question of status. One, for instance,

---

[108] This law was finally relaxed by Charles II in 1696. See Varela, *Muerte del rey*, pp. 122–33.

asked for as many candles as the law would permit and asked that his servants be given mourning garb "according to what the law allows."[109]

As the infractions of the ban on nonroyal catafalques indicate, it was no easier to enforce sumptuary mourning laws in the sixteenth and seventeenth centuries than it had been in the preceding two. By looking far outside Madrid, in Navarre we can see proof for this conjecture. When Philip II tried to impose on the subject kingdom of Navarre his *Pragmatica de los lutos,* a set of mourning laws similar to those of Ferdinand and Isabella, the results were disastrous. Philip's *Pragmatica* of 1562 sought to supplant the long-established elaborate mourning practices of the Navarrese, which were very similar to those criticized earlier in Castille, with the more restrained gestures demanded by law elsewhere in Spain.[110]

Again, the wording and content of these laws are very similar to those of the proscriptions of 1323, 1480, and 1502: Distinctions are made between necessary and superfluous funeral gestures; strict guidelines are established for the wearing of mourning garb, which is limited to immediate family members and servants; and special prerogatives are established for the royal family.

These laws were generally disobeyed in Navarre, first by the more powerful (*algunas personas constituidas en dignidad*), who wanted to continue enjoying elaborate public displays of grief, and then by others further down on the social scale (*y asi otras gentes a imitacion suya*), who seemed eager to promote their own status through imitation of their betters. As late as fourteen years after the enactment of this *pragmatica,* in 1576 a special petition was made to Philip II so he would waive the penalties imposed on the more than 100 individuals who had violated its laws.[111] After consulting with the viceroy of Navarre, his councilors,

---

[109] AHPM 542.501 (1568).

[110] *Quaderno de las leyes, ordenanzas, provisiones y pragmaticas hechas a la suplicación de los tres estados del Reyno de Navarra, 1562* (Pamplona, 1563) BNM R–2968. These laws had been petitioned in 1558 at the meeting of the Cortes at Tudela. See *Las leyes del Reyno de Navarra, hechas en Cortes Generales a suplicación de los tres estados del, desde el ano 1512 hasta el de 1612,* ed. Pedro de Sada and Miguel de Murillo y Ollacarizqueta (Pamplona, 1614), BNM R–14748, fols. 263v–264.

[111] *Quaderno de las leyes, ordenanzas, provisiones y pragmaticas hechas a la suplicación de los tres estados del Reyno de Navarra, 1576* (Pamplona, 1576) BNM R–2968. Provisión 25, "De la remision de penas en los lutos," fol. 54 ff.

and members of the Cortes, the king decided to grant this petition, cautioning the Navarrese: "We remit and pardon the penalties only for this time, so that the aforementioned law, or *pragmatica* may be obeyed from now on."[112]

Although Philip II demanded a new public proclamation of this law through town criers and a stricter enforcement of its proscriptions, it appears that infractions continued to take place. Among the documents related to this episode that are bound together at the Biblioteca Nacional, there is a manuscript copy of the same *pragmatica* from 1595, which was reissued for use by a town crier in the city of Estela. This document explains why the law was still being promulgated so many years after its initial enactment:

Even though this said law was established as required for the reform of the excesses which were then common in mourning, the penalties required by this law were not enforced, so that experience teaches us that there has been *and there continues to be* [emphasis added] a great excess and disorder in these matters. . . . All of this has done great injury to the universal good of our subjects in this Kingdom, because they squander their estates in the gross excesses and expenditures made for the funerals and burials of their dead, through which they seek not to benefit and aid the souls of these deceased but, rather, to increase their own station.[113]

The fact that the definition of "excess" hinged on questions of status may have made it all the more difficult for ecclesiastics to draw firm theological lines of distinction between what was Christian and un-Christian. The royal family was allowed expressions of grief that were deemed inappropriate for ordinary Christians. It was well known that Juana "la Loca" had gone mad with grief over the death of her husband Philip the Fair and would not part with his corpse. Similarly, when her son Charles V lost his wife Isabel, he found it necessary to retire to a monastery to get away from the loud weeping and depressive grieving of others at court. Loud laments were an integral part of royal funerals. In 1539 "great weeping and wailing" accompanied Isabel's burial at Gra-

---

[112] *Quaderno de las leyes, 1576*, fol. 55.

[113] BNM 2968, fol. 7, s.f. The crier, Joan de la Cunha, was instructed to proclaim this law "a son de trompetas . . . por las calles y cantones acostumbrados de la dicha ciudad de Estela, al tiempo que habra en ella mucho concurso de gente."

nada. When Charles V died at Yuste in 1558, his servants cried out loud, "shouting, wailing, slapping their faces, and knocking their heads against the wall."[114] In 1569 the same thing occurred at the funeral of Philip II's wife, Elizabeth of Valois: Loud, uncontrollable weeping seized the ladies at court and bystanders on the streets, and the grieving cries emanating from the Alcazar could be heard at some distance.[115]

Some ecclesiastics and devotional writers from the sixteenth century took aim against this kind of grieving. The reports of two such men give us glimpses of what was considered excessive. Alejo Venegas decried the "superfluous tears" and "sad sighs" of some mourners, and warned against apparently common practices such as "the delay in eating again, the rejection of consolation, and the perpetuation of vigils." He also counseled against "remaining pensive."[116] Antonio de Guevara inserted the following warning in a letter to a bereaved husband:

Do not be like your neighbor and my friend Rodrigo Sarmiento, who began wearing a hood and a long trailing cape after his wife died, and refused to use tablecloths or silver tableware when eating, and would not sit in a chair, or open a window, or wash his face for two months, and also slept fully clothed for half a year.[117]

In another letter, Guevara scolded one of his nieces for grieving over a dead dog. This young woman had reportedly taken to her bed and was disconsolate and had even said that the death of this pet grieved her as much as the death of a close relative. This irked Guevara, who lashed out:

To tell you the truth, it does not surprise me that you weep, but I am shocked at your reason for weeping; for it would be much more honorable and profitable for you to weep for just a single sin, than to weep for a dog. . . . To behave in this manner and to show such affection for a little bitch exceeds, I believe, the limits of propriety for an honorable lady and a Christian woman, because Christians ought to weep for their offenses rather than for something they have lost. . . . What ought to grieve you the most about your little bitch is that you

---

[114] Varela, *Muerte del rey*, pp. 30–5.
[115] Lopez de Hoyos, "Hystoria y relación," pp. 24–5.
[116] Venegas, *Agonía*, p. 227. He also warned that excessive grieving gestures saddened rather than consoled the survivors.
[117] Guevara, *Epistolas familiares*, Ep. 57 (1523), p. 172.

did not ask the Confraternity of Mercy to come to her funeral, for if you had, they could have absolved her with a bull of indulgence, and all prayed together for her.[118]

In *Lazarillo de Tormes* a humorous glimpse is offered into the kinds of public excess that were officially condemned, yet allowed by the church. In one scene, the starving Lazarillo sees a funeral cortege coming toward him in one of Toledo's narrow streets. Pinning himself against a building to make way, he watches as a throng of clerics and mourners pass by him. Following immediately behind the corpse on its *andas*, the wife of the deceased, laden down with mourning garb and accompanied by similarly dressed ladies, cries out the most un-Christian lament in a loud voice: "My husband and lord! Where are you being taken? To the house of sorrow and misery, to the house of gloom and shadow, to the house where no one ever eats or drinks!" Thinking that this is a fitting description of his own dwellings and that the dead man is being taken there, Lazarillo then runs home and bolts the door in panic.[119]

Further proof that friction existed between the ideal and the actual – between popular customs and the gestures allowed by law – comes to us from the area around Madrid, through two sets of documents from the archives of the Inquisition at Toledo. These are two trials (*procesos*) that deal with mock funerals, the records of which reveal much not only about death rites and mourning customs but also about the uneasy relationship that could exist between lay piety and official religion.

The first of these mock funerals, or *entierros burlescos*, took place in 1538 in Guadalajara, about forty miles northeast of Madrid, when a group of youths took down a roadside cross and staged a mock funeral procession. According to one of the accused, the whole affair began innocently enough as some sort of prank among a few friends, but it quickly got out of hand as more people joined in and the wine began to flow. These youths claimed that they began their horseplay by simply staging an impromptu Palm Sunday procession, in which they knocked on the doors of some friends' houses with the roadside cross, saying "*attollite portae*" (open the door). At the house of one youth, however, after a round of drinking, one of them pretended to fall dead. The others immediately wrapped him up in a sheet "and they carried him

---

[118] Ibid., Ep. 17 (1524), pp. 220–2.
[119] *Lazarillo de Tormes*, tratado tercero. Barcelona 1982 ed., pp. 52–3.

out, singing, with the cross, using a cooking pot and a broom as an *hysopo* (an aspergillum, or sprinkler of holy water), banging on a cowbell, while some pretended to weep." Offended by all this, a neighbor ran to notify his parish priest. When the curate arrived at the scene, he quickly brought the celebration to a halt and notified the Inquisition that a sacrilege had been committed.[120]

The Inquisitors at Toledo seemed puzzled by this event. One of their immediate reactions was to suspect that such a sacrilege could have been committed only by new Christians, so they asked if there were any *moros* (Moors) or *judios* (Jews) among them. Much to the tribunal's surprise, all of the youths claimed to be old Christians. The Inquisitors also expressed an interest in finding out exactly what had been sung, but when questioned about their singing, the youths' answers varied. Some claimed to have sung liturgical chants; others insisted they had sung only "profane" songs. Eventually, one of the accused offered the Inquisitors an honest explanation for the whole charade, saying "he had not done this to offend God," but "just to pass the time."

Unable to acknowledge this event as an acceptable relief for boredom, the Inquisitors declared the youths guilty of sacrilege and required them as penance to take part in a real procession, marching barefoot and bareheaded to the scene of their crime, with a priest and a cross, where they were to kneel and express the proper devotion. In addition, they were ordered to pay for a new stone cross to be erected on that same spot to replace the one they had taken down and used in their farce.[121]

An even more dramatic incident took place that same year during a festival in the village of Hita. In this case, ten men were accused of performing the sacrilege of an *entierro burlesco*. Nine of the culprits were young, in their early to midtwenties; one of them was about forty-five years old. Two were listed as *clerigos*, though apparently neither had yet been ordained as a priest at the time of the incident. Unlike the youths at Guadalajara, who seem to have stumbled upon the idea of holding a mock funeral, these men carefully planned their parody.[122]

Because the testimonies of all the accused agree, it is possible to reconstruct this elaborate affair in detail. The sacrilege at Hita took place during a public joust, or *corrida de la sortija*, when horsemen

---

[120] AHNM, Inquisición, Legajo 225, n. 8, fol. 16v.
[121] Ibid., n. 8, fol. 16v. [122] Ibid., Leg. 226, n. 12, fol. 5 ff.

proved their riding skills by spearing rings at full gallop. On this particular occasion, the joust was part of some unidentified festival in which the riders were asked to don masks and dress in the costume of their choice. The leader of this group, a certain Antonio de Sandoval, began the "funeral" by riding up to his place in line for the *corrida* dressed as a corpse, wearing a white shirt that looked very much like the *mortaja*, or linen shroud, used on the dead. Behind him rode the two clerics, dressed in black and carrying candles. The rest of the cortege was made up of a horseman who carried a cross draped in black cloth (or red cloth, according to one witness); another who had wrapped himself up in a chain and carried a bell; two others dressed as friars, singing responses; and finally, three who dressed as women, one of whom repeatedly cried out, "Woe is me! . . . he has left me all alone with four children! . . . Just because he gorged himself on a breast of lamb!" Another cried out "as if they were carrying a corpse."[123]

As the assembled townspeople watched, the entire cortege proceeded to spear the rings, beginning with Sandoval, the "corpse." Having completed their run, four (the two clerics and the two who were dressed as friars) turned their costumes inside out, "and they revealed painted skulls and bones of the dead, and said they were the horsemen of death." Finally, they reared up on their horses and galloped away after sweeping past the astonished crowd.[124]

Eight years elapsed before this case came to be tried by the Inquisition at Toledo. This long delay had not made it any easier on the accused, however, since it is reported that one of them, a priest, appeared before the tribunal "in tears." After taking all the usual depositions and carefully recording the accounts of witnesses and participants, the tribunal found all ten men guilty of sacrilege. In pronouncing their sentence, the Inquisitors let these men know exactly why they were being condemned:

Because they profaned the offerings and rites that the Church has ordained for the assistance of the dead and the devotion of the Christian faithful, and for having misused such things in contempt and scorn of Holy Mother Church, giving scandal to the people.[125]

As penance, each of these men was ordered to pay for one mass for the dead and to kneel during that entire liturgy. In addition, each of

[123] Ibid., n. 12, fols. 5–7v.   [124] Ibid., n. 12, fols. 8–9.   [125] Ibid., n. 12, fols. 6, 10.

them was also to say one rosary, fast one Friday, feed one poor person, and distribute 200 *maravedis* to the indigent. As in the case at Guadalajara, the Inquisition imposed a very light sentence with an eye toward teaching the offenders a lesson in true piety.

What can we learn from these two similar events? In the first place, through the sentences imposed by the Inquisition, we have evidence of the value officially placed on certain funeral rituals. In each case, the Inquisition decided that a sacrilege had indeed taken place because the rites in question were considered beneficial to the dead and therefore unworthy of ridicule. The formal teaching of the church, here protected by the Inquisitors and by those who denounced the offenders, invested these gestures with an otherworldly value.

Second, we also learn that some of the exaggerated grieving gestures forbidden by law must have been commonly observed. In both cases, some of the men pretended to weep loudly; at Hita, the lament of the "widow" was particularly shrill. To some extent, these men were promoting the teachings of the church rather than mocking them, because they poked fun at some of the exaggerated mourning gestures condemned by civil and ecclesiastical law. Oddly enough, the Inquisitors paid little attention to this point. Even though the law distinguished between proper and improper rituals, these men were condemned for *all* their gestures, as if each of them called into question the valid rites of the church. This may show us not only how inseparable certain illicit mourning gestures were from all other funeral rites but also how even the clergy could fail to distinguish between them.

Third, through the mocking gestures of these men we learn how familiar and how standardized funeral customs were in central Castille at this time. The two burlesque funerals are not only similar to each other but also to the funerals requested in Madrid wills. In both, the cross and the clergy play a central role; in both, mourners follow the corpse intoning prayers and singing responses. These men were all obviously familiar with funeral rites and knew exactly what to do when they decided to stage their own parodies. The men at Hita carefully planned their satire, but those at Guadalajara had no time for rehearsal. Theirs was a purely spontaneous and genuine reenactment of the funerals they had no doubt witnessed.

If it is indeed true that familiarity breeds contempt, then these men were indeed intimately acquainted with the funeral gestures of their society. Although it does seem a rather odd thing to mock, at least by our modern standards, it may not have been all that peculiar in the sixteenth century. Good satire requires good timing, for its edge is sharpest when it addresses an issue of immediate concern. Satire requires recognition. It requires familiarity with the things being mocked, not only on the part of the satirists but also of their audience. The fact that two such cases came before the Toledan Inquisition in one year indicates that these funeral details were second nature to many sixteenth-century Castilians.

This brings us to a fourth and final point. The tension between the ideal and the actual that is mocked in these two burlesque funerals must have been rather strong. Satire most often takes aim against behavior that seems inordinately pompous or that falls short of the ideals proposed by society. Satire aims to reveal unresolved tensions in human behavior. In these two mock funerals, the offenders were taking aim against ritual gestures that their society had invested with profound, overlapping values. Whether they were poking fun at them because they seemed inadequate or grossly inflated did not matter to the Inquisitors. They knew well enough that to mock is to question and that such behavior could not be condoned. As defenders of the status quo, the Inquisitors had to remind these men that the church saw no tension between the ideal and the actual in these funeral gestures, that the very things that had been mocked were in fact immensely valuable. Hence, the penance imposed in both cases required the offenders to pay due reverence to what they had ridiculed. Still, the fact that funerals could be mocked and that such behavior could be worthy of the attention of the Inquisition shows that the official religious explanation of funeral gestures may not have been universally accepted.

But what do Madrid wills reveal about mourning gestures and the tension that may have existed between ideals and actual practices? For the most part, the wills are silent on this point. Out of nearly 500 wills, only about three dozen refer specifically to some aspect of grieving. It is safe to assume that this is not due to a lack of interest but to the fact that so many of these gestures were standardized and did not need to be specified. If the youths at Guadalajara could spontaneously mimic such gestures without any instructions, it seems more than plausible that the same could be done by most other people.

It is not too surprising that the only substantial meditation on mourning found in this sample should come from a priest and that it should be a clear, eloquent summary of the official teaching of the church:

I command, implore, and advise that no one don mourning garb for me, not even a cap, or any other such sign; because through death we are freed from prison, and it is the will of the Lord our creator that we be born to die this death, and pass through it to eternal life. Not to conform to His will, and to express undue grief is therefore unfitting; so let those who love me express their affection through prayers to the Lord for my soul. Anything else is of little use, either to those who depart from this life, or to those who remain behind.[126]

Through his protestations against mourning gestures, Father Pedro de Reballos hoped to instill in his survivors a proper, acceptable attitude toward death. By preaching and teaching about the meaning of death in his will, he hoped to change the minds of his survivors, to make them accept the official teaching of the church about death and the afterlife, and to persuade them to view his death as something good, as the escape of his soul from the prisonhouse of the body, as the beginning of eternal life instead of something mournful. The fact that he had to "command, implore, and advise" shows that he knew that their impulses would be just the opposite, that he suspected they would grieve openly, and use all those mourning gestures which were "of little use."

This one statement suggests that the prevailing attitude among the laity may have been far from the ideals proposed by priests such as Father Reballos and that the routine, fitting reaction to death was one of grieving rather than rejoicing. Hence the fact that mourning is so seldom mentioned in Madrid wills: In most cases, the "proper" gestures (those that Father Reballos rejected) were universally understood and practiced.

Such a conclusion also seems to be indicated by the fact that only one other will in the entire sample makes a similar request and that it too seems to be struggling against a very strong tide of convention. In this other case, Juan de Castilla, a knight of the Order of Santiago, had to use strong language – and a bit of leverage – to force his children *not* to wear any mourning garb for him, saying "under the penalty of losing my blessing . . . I command my children not to dress in mourning for me."[127]

[126] Father Pedro de Reballos, AHPM 107, s.f. (1549).   [127] AHPM 147.164 (1552).

In contrast, the few other wills that mention mourning gestures are concerned primarily with making sure that the appropriate garments be worn by certain people and that the law be obeyed. One testator, for instance, simply asked that his servants be dressed in mourning garb on the day of his death.[128] Another asked that his servants and heirs dress for mourning as soon as he died "according to what the law allows."[129] A third asked that no one wear mourning clothes for more than nine days.[130]

An additional concern for a few testators was the manner in which the coffin should be presented at church. Apparently, it was customary to hang black bunting on the walls of the church and to place the coffin on a raised platform during the funeral services. A handful of testators made it known that they did not want these customs observed at their funerals but merely wanted to have their coffins displayed at ground level over a black rug.[131] One priest suggested that the confraternity carry a black velvet cloth on which to rest his coffin but also indicated that they had the right to refuse this request and that he would be satisfied with a plain black baize rug.[132] A couple of testators also asked specifically to have only two candles instead of the number allowed to them by law.[133]

All in all, then, relatively few testators sought to simplify mourning gestures for their funerals. In some cases, it is clear that the reason for such requests was financial rather than spiritual or ideological. One widow, for example, asked for a funeral "without any pomp whatsoever, because I am poor and that is the way I wish to be buried."[134] One man also put it bluntly, saying that since he did not know how much money he really had, he wanted to be buried "with the pomp and cortege that will cost the least."[135]

---

[128] AHPM 1410.624 (1596).   [129] AHPM 542.501 (1568).

[130] AHPM 55.982 (1532).

[131] AHPM 85.266 (1544): "Y mi cuerpo se ponga en la dicha iglesia de Santa Clara en el coro, en una alfombra negra de paño sobre qual se ponga el ataud." Similar requests are made in AHPM 457.1160 (1573), 286.412 (1579), 1390.139 (1584), and 1412.943 (1597).

[132] AHPM 1412.953 (1597).   [133] AHPM 85.266 (1544) and 541.13 (1567).

[134] AHPM 541.13 (1567).

[135] AHPM 1407.449 (1595). This testator left the final funeral arrangements in his brother's hands, and asked: "Al qual pido . . . gaste y tenga cuydado de lo que tocare

In a few other cases, however, there seems to be a genuine desire to cut back on those gestures that were officially deemed to be non-intercessory. Maria de Gribaja knew exactly where to draw the line between necessary and superfluous gestures in 1573. Although she asked for the parish clergy, four poor people, and the orphan children from La Doctrina to join her cortege, she still insisted she wanted a funeral "without any pomp whatsoever, and with all humility."[136] Obviously, as far as she was concerned, her cortege was humble and without pomp, even though a cortege of this size would have been unusual thirty years earlier. Her understanding of "pomp" as non-intercessory gestures suggests that some people regarded the cortege as a necessity and all else as luxury. It also implies that "pomp" could be understood to be any of those gestures that the civil and ecclesiastical authorities sought to repress.

A few other wills make similar requests, always vaguely worded: "I greatest amount of charity possible."[137] Or, "I implore that my burial take place without pomp and with great moderation."[138] However, in a period of inflated gestures, as in the latter third of the sixteenth century, such vague instructions could be variously interpreted. A so-called moderate funeral in the 1590s, for instance, could easily have been more complex than an elaborate one in the 1540s. When Francisco de Zamora, physician to the king, asked to be buried in 1594 "without any more pomp and ostentation than that with which a man is *ordinarily* [emphasis added] buried," he was still probably expecting a funeral in keeping with his status.[139] Since he was a court physician, it is safe to conjecture that the "ordinary" pomp he requested was not the same as that which one would have found at most funerals forty years earlier or at the funeral of a poor widow during his own time.

After reading more than 500 wills, it is still enormously difficult to speak of a prevailing attitude toward grieving in sixteenth-century Madrid, as if there were some unanimity or agreement among all testators.

---

al dicho entierro y misas y obras pias por mi alma lo qual no dejo declarado en particular por no saber la hacienda que al presente tengo."

[136] AHPM 457.1160 (1573).   [137] AHPM 566.225 (1579).

[138] AHPM 580.511 (1585). Similar requests are made in AHPM 1392.366 (1584) and 620.36 (1594).

[139] AHPM 626.539 (1594): Sin pompa ni aparato ninguno mas de como se entierra un hombre ordinariamente.

What does seem clear is the fact that some tension existed between the models of behavior proposed by church and state and those gestures commonly performed by the majority of the people. Ecclesiastics had been insisting since the Middle Ages that death was not to be grieved over by good Christians because anyone who believed in the Resurrection should be hopeful about the afterlife.

In the early sixteenth century, the state tried to enforce the theological distinctions made by the church between proper intercessory funeral gestures and improper non-intercessory ones. Few wills reveal an acceptance of these distinctions. Rare was the testator who would willingly accept the notion that one should differentiate between those gestures that affected the dead in the afterlife and those that had an impact on only the survivors in this world. The careful, measured instructions of Francisco de Guevara, a member of the king's Council of War, are a clear reflection of official ideals, but they are hardly representative of the tenor of most Madrid wills:

Above all I call upon my wife and brother, as earnestly as I can, because of the love they have for me, to make sure that whatever ought to be done for my soul be performed without impiety or a desire to follow the external pomp of this world, but rather with a sound, righteous intention that aims purely at God, towards the true assistance of my soul, because nothing else is acceptable in that highest tribunal.[140]

[140] AHPM 457.1072 (1573).

5

~~~~~~

Planning for the soul's journey

According to the formula used in almost every Madrid will, the body was offered up "to the earth from which it was formed," whereas the soul returned "to God who created it and redeemed it." This dualistic understanding of the human self was not some pure theological abstraction but, rather, a functional organizing principle for funeral customs. Although in burial services, a substantial concern was expressed for the body of the deceased as the visible focus of many intercessory gestures, it tended to be viewed as a temporary material husk that remained behind and disintegrated while the true eternal self, the soul, entered a new sphere of existence. The teaching of the church, sustained by the civil law of the Spanish kingdoms, affirmed this conception of selfhood through the distinction made between intercessory and non-intercessory gestures, and even in the burial itself, that ritual concerned with the body's disposal, only those gestures that affected the soul of the deceased were deemed legitimate.

Pious bequests

As we have just seen, there could be some tension between ideals and actual practices, but no testator was ever allowed to stray too far from the ideal norms when writing a will. The very structure of each testament was determined by law, and this law was in turn shaped by the official ideals of Spanish society. According to the letter of the law, every will had to contain certain provisions for the soul of the deceased, beyond those that pertained to the funeral. All testators had to make arrangements for their burial, then, not only to dispose of their corpse but also to place their soul, as the testaments said, *en carrera de salvación*. They had to ensure the soul's safe passage to the afterlife.

More important than the manner of burial, which principally concerned the corruptible body, were those devotions that assisted the soul in crossing over to the afterlife: prayers, vigils, and masses. These devotions that began with the funeral itself but continued after the corpse was interred were known as *obras pias*, or *sacrificios pios*, and the law required that they be requested in every will, directly after the burial plans.[1] The law also allowed testators to use up to one-fifth of their entire estate for these pious bequests.[2] In this way, the structure of the will reflected official church teaching: Because the true self continued to live on eternally, long after the body decomposed, and the redemptive power of the church could continue to affect the self in the afterlife, specific provisions had to be made to aid it after the funeral was over.

A great deal is revealed about attitudes toward these devotions by the difference between the Spanish terms *obras pias* and *sacrificios pios* and their English equivalent. In English, they are commonly referred to as "pious bequests," but this term does not convey the true meaning of the Spanish used by sixteenth-century Madrileños. The English term "bequest" implies a gift or, more specifically, something that is distributed from the testator's estate. The Spanish word *obra* means a "work," or "action." The word *sacrificio* means "sacrifice." Both of these terms are more active than "bequest" and imply more than simple giving on the part of the testator: These are gestures – works, sacrifices – performed on behalf of the testator. In myriad ways, the Spanish terms reveal a deep acceptance of certain beliefs about salvation and the way in which it may be obtained. Consequently, these terms also serve as a clear testi-

---

[1] Since the Middle Ages, even those who died without a will had to fulfill this requirement before they could obtain a Christian burial. The Synod of Zaragoza (1357), to cite but one example, required all heirs of those who had died intestate "ad faciendam aliquam ordinationem supra corpus in operibus piis," according to the net worth of the estate in question. This same synod also required the clergy to refuse burial to anyone whose heirs had not yet paid them for these required masses. See: Federico Rafael Aznar Gil, *Concilios provinciales y sinodos de Zaragoza de 1215 a 1563* (Zaragoza, 1982), p. 155.

[2] Venegas, *Agonía*, p. 134, encouraged his readers to keep this in mind when writing their wills.

mony of the ways in which sixteenth-century Madrileños believed in the affinity between this world and the hereafter.

Salvation and the mass

The soteriology of the Catholic Church found expression in an elaborate network of beliefs and practices, most of which had gradually evolved during the first millennium of Christian history. By the sixteenth century, this soteriological system had become a vast, well-oiled machine. If contemporaries had been able to think of it in such mechanical terms, they might have described it as some sort of perpetual motion apparatus. According to official doctrine, it was a system started in the distant past by Jesus Christ that would be maintained by Him through the agency of the church until the end of time.

From the deathbed to the grave and even thereafter, Catholics depended upon the sacraments offered by their church for salvation. And no sacrament was more important for their ultimate redemption than the Eucharist because its beneficial, timeless effects applied both to this life and the next. Although all the other sacraments were crucial, their power was restricted to terrestrial time, to specific moments in the earthly life of believers. Baptism, for instance, marked that single instance when an individual was incorporated into the church; penance forgave only the sins committed up to the time of confession and absolution; confirmation, marriage, and orders marked precise moments when one's status as a believer underwent some change; extreme unction served its function only at the end point of terrestrial existence. The Eucharist, however, aided individuals in another dimension, beyond earthly time. Because every celebration of the Eucharist was regarded as a reenactment of Christ's timeless sacrifice on the cross, the spiritual benefits of every mass could be applied not only to the living on earth but also to the dead in the hereafter. Best of all, it could be repeated and multiplied: It could be quantified.[3] This was the traditional Catholic belief reaffirmed in the mid–sixteenth century at the Council of Trent.[4]

A rather simple but effective way of summarizing the prevailing Catholic viewpoint before and after Trent would be to say "no mass, no

[3] Chiffoleau, *Comptabilité*, p. 432.
[4] Council of Trent, session 22, chapter 2, canon 3.

salvation." This belief was so inextricably linked to the doctrine of purgatory that it would be difficult to conceive of one without the other. Obviously, the souls of the saints and martyrs who enter heaven are in no need of spiritual assistance. What more could be offered to them than eternal bliss? For the mass to be considered as an act that can benefit the dead, one must first believe that some souls do not fully enter the eternal joys of heaven or the eternal torments of hell but are somehow suspended between the two in a temporary state. Second, one must also believe that these souls are still capable of obtaining salvation beyond the grave, that they can somehow make up whatever they lack through the reception of spiritual benefits occasioned by others still on earth.

Although such beliefs continued to be upheld in sixteenth-century Spain without substantial change, elsewhere in Europe they were seriously challenged by the Protestant Reformation. The denial of purgatory and of the salvific value of the mass was a central part of the attack launched against Catholic soteriology by Martin Luther, Ulrich Zwingli, John Calvin, and many other Reformers. Generally, Protestants opposed Catholic soteriology on three fronts. First, by denying the redemptive value of any human actions and insisting instead that humans were saved only by faith in Christ, Protestants denied the possibility of human intercession and the existence of any "pious works." Second, by insisting that Christ's sacrifice on the cross could never be reenacted in the eucharist, they repudiated all salvific claims for the Catholic mass. Third, by teaching that humans were incapable of true purification and that salvation was a free gift of God given only to those He chose during their life on earth, the Reformers denied the possibility of purification in the hereafter and demolished the principal rationale for the existence of purgatory.

Only in the light of this challenge can the reaffirmations of the Council of Trent be fully understood. What Trent attempted to do in the mid–sixteenth century was to defend traditional Catholic doctrine and piety and to call for a more vigorous promotion of these beliefs. The council fathers themselves put it this way:

Since the Catholic Church, instructed by the Holy Ghost, has, following the sacred writings and the ancient tradition of the Fathers, taught in sacred councils and very recently in this ecumenical council that there is a purgatory, and that the souls there detained are *aided by the suffrages of the faithful* and *chiefly by the acceptable sacrifice of the altar,* the holy council commands the bishops that they strive diligently to the end that the sound doctrine of purgatory, transmitted by the Fathers and the sacred councils, be believed and maintained by the faithful of Christ, and be everywhere taught and preached [emphasis added].[5]

Regarding these matters, sixteenth-century Madrid wills can serve as a very good gauge of popular belief before and after Trent. These documents can help us do much more than simply determine how deeply certain teachings were accepted; they can also shed light on the process of cultural transmission, showing us how it was possible for individuals simultaneously to participate in and contribute to the structures of belief promoted by a Catholic society. By analyzing the ways in which sixteenth-century Madrileños requested *obras pias* before and after Trent, we can gain a better understanding of that complex relationship between ideals and actual practice that gave shape to Spanish attitudes toward death and the afterlife.

The picture that emerges from these wills is that of a giant redemptive apparatus kept in motion by social convention. After reading more than 500 wills, it becomes clear that the construction and maintenance of this machinery was not exclusively in the hands of the elite and that it was not simply a question of getting the clergy to impose a certain system of belief and practice on the laity, as the council fathers of Trent apparently believed. It was a system fueled by fear of death and the hereafter, a fear that ran deep in Spanish society, cutting across all ranks from top to bottom. Even though it was controlled, promoted, and sustained by the clergy (working in close association with civil authorities), it was perhaps as much a reflection of popular beliefs as of elite ideals. What these wills indicate is that the church sanctioned and promoted an ancient redemptive system that was deeply ingrained in the social consciousness and that this liturgical apparatus was eagerly kept in motion by Spanish society as whole.

Inevitable suffering, indispensable suffrages

The sixteenth century marked the beginning of a "golden age of purgatory" in Spain.[6] The expectation that purgatory would follow imme-

---

[5] "Decree Concerning Purgatory," Twenty-Fifth Session, December 1563. *Canons and Decrees of the Council of Trent,* trans. by H. J. Schroeder (Rockford, 1978), p. 214.
[6] Nalle, *God in La Mancha,* p. 191.

diately after death was deeply ingrained in the early modern Spanish mentality: It was a message subliminally encoded into all thought and piety regarding the afterlife. Alejo Venegas, for instance, assumed that a good death would lead to purgatory, not heaven, and made this clear in an unreflexive offhand manner when he said that the intercessory prayers of priests "ensured that what was being done on our behalf would benefit us in our dying, and later *in purgatory*" (emphasis added).[7]

Many Madrileños were convinced of the reality of purgatory, but how did they conceive of it and of the suffrages required there? Catholic eschatology was highly complex but not totally incomprehensible to the laity. Because this theology was part and parcel of the piety surrounding the cult of the dead, it was at least minimally understood in an inchoate manner through the rich symbolism of death rites. It could also be learned about through sermons and through devotional literature. Literate Madrileños did not need to know how the doctrine of purgatory gradually developed over the centuries, to be definitively affirmed by the Councils of Lyons (1274) and Florence (1439), nor did they need to read the works of Aquinas or of other learned theologians.[8] All they needed to know could be found in highly accessible language in the devotional manuals such as those of Venegas, Medina, and Orozco. If we turn to these treatises, which were also widely read by the clergy and undoubtedly influenced their sermons, we can get a clear glimpse of the teachings made available to the laity. We can also learn, as could sixteenth-century Madrileños, many details about this realm of the hereafter, its place in the cosmos, and its relation to the sacrifice of the mass.

Purgatory was the temporary abode of souls that needed cleansing before being admitted into heaven. Its existence was demanded by a concomitant belief in the retributive nature of divine justice, that is, the belief that each sin incurred an inescapable penalty. These penalties, which had to be endured even after the sinner had confessed the sin and received absolution, could be paid through suffering in this life. But because the penalties incurred in the life of the ordinary Christian were considered to be so great in number and magnitude, it was not thought possible for anyone but a saint to be sufficiently cleansed within an

---

[7] Venegas, *Agonía*, p. 139.
[8] No history has yet surpassed Le Goff's *The Birth of Purgatory*.

earthly lifetime. Those penalties that remained unpaid at the moment of death had then to be paid in the hereafter, in purgatory. Located within the earth, directly above hell and fanned by its fires, purgatory was a place of torment where souls received the punishment still due to forgiven sins.[9] Deprived of the vision of God but aware that they were being gradually purged and would one day gain heaven, the souls in purgatory endured excruciating pain. This torment was gradual and lessened with the soul's progressive cleansing, for it derived principally from the soul's awareness of its distance from God.[10] Yet, this pain, no matter how gradual and spiritual, was supposedly greater than any pain on earth, so great as to be beyond comparison. Moreover, a lack of proportion existed between the penalties paid in this life and those paid in the hereafter. Suffering in this life, though lesser in degree, counted more in the eyes of God and therefore had a greater time-related redemptive value. One theologian calculated that one day of suffering in this life could count for a year or more in purgatory and advised his readers to avoid venial sins and to do as much penitence as possible before dying. An average Christian, he reckoned, would have to spend about one or two thousand years in purgatory.[11]

But there were ways to lessen the time of one's purgation, through acts known as suffrages. Venegas defined suffrages as "the work of one or many persons done in the true spirit of love, or at least containing sufficient grace to pay for part or all of the debt of a neighbor." He also identified four different kinds of suffrages: prayer, fasting, almsgiving, and the mass. Of these, the mass was the best (*el que más vale*).[12] There were many reasons for assigning such a function and such value to the mass, but none ranked higher than the notion that the sacrificial redemptive work of Christ, offered anew in each celebration of the mass, could be applied directly toward the lessening of penances. In other words, the suffering of Christ could be selectively applied toward the suffering any Christian soul still owed in purgatory. This was a piety

[9] Venegas, *Agonía*, pp. 201–2. Descriptions of the geography of the hereafter proliferated in the seventeenth century. See Ana Martinez Arancón, *Geografía de la eternidad* (Madrid, Tecnos, 1987).

[10] Rebolledo, *Oraciones funebres*, fol. 328.

[11] Alonso de Orozco, *Victoria de la muerte*, pp. 170–2; 181.

[12] Venegas, *Agonía*, p. 210; Medina copied Venegas almost word for word, *Libro de Verdad*, III, p. 465.

steeped in accounting, shaped and governed by numbers, focused squarely on debts and credits, driven by the desire to transfer specific amounts from one ledger to another. It was, as Chiffoleau has observed, a piety constructed on the model of marketplace accounting.[13] For instance, Alonso de Orozco explained the superiority of the mass over other forms of suffrage by saying that it counted twice, as Christ's sacrifice (as if this were not enough by itself) *and* as almsgiving, because the money paid to have masses said for the dead was a contribution toward the upkeep of the clergy.[14] Pedro de Medina argued that one always earned merit for oneself when ordering masses for the dead, for this was an act of charity. Moreover, he also thought there was always extra, unexpected merit earned by suffrages for the dead. According to him, whenever one freed a soul through suffrages, one was also benefitting the other souls in purgatory because this caused them to feel joy. This shared gladness, though indirectly caused, also earned one merit.[15]

Theological rationalizations for the liturgical suffrage system were intricate, complex, and overlapping. Guided at various levels by the principle of "the more the better," theologians and devotional writers piled argument upon argument while urging their readers to pile mass upon mass. And through their efforts to explain, they affirmed and encouraged a hierarchy of values and an overabundance of distinctions, such as the following, to list but a few: masses were better than bulls of indulgence[16]; masses said at indulgenced altars were better than masses said at other altars[17]; perpetual masses were better than masses said immediately after one's death; Sunday and feast day masses were better than requiem masses; masses said during Advent, Lent, and Holy Week were better than masses said during other times of the year; masses said by a priest in a state of grace were better than those said by a priest in a state of sin.[18]

Furthermore, the souls in purgatory eagerly hung their hopes on these fine distinctions and knew what was being done or *not* being done for them. In medieval monastic literature and in sermon *exempla*, accounts

---

[13] Chiffoleau, *Comptabilité*, p. 345. He also argues (pp. 434–5) that this phenomenon was created by the laity in an attempt to gain more control of their piety: It was the infusion of the "rationalité des marchands" into religious ritual.

[14] Orozco, *Victoria de la muerte*, p. 176.   [15] Medina, *Libro de la verdad*, III, p. 468.

[16] Ibid.   [17] Orozco, *Victoria de la muerte*, p. 178.   [18] Venegas, *Agonía*, pp. 210–17.

of visits from purgatory had been commonplace.[19] Though by the six-teenth century it was believed that souls in purgatory were very rarely allowed by God to visit the living or relay messages to them – especially to the laity – it was still believed that these souls felt an immense gratitude for those who offered suffrages on their behalf and that, once in heaven, they would eventually reward their benefactors by interceding for them.[20]

We shall presently see in detail how this swarm of minute distinctions shaped the mentality of Madrid's testators and how in turn they ex-pressed their numeric delirium in pious bequests.

The arithmetic of salvation

If one simply looks at the sheer number of masses requested by Madrid testators throughout the sixteenth century, one can easily be led to conclude that purgatory was a very real place for them – and that they thought they could do something to lessen the time they would spend there after death.

One constant, unchanging pattern is the simple fact that without exception all who write wills ask for masses to be said. Because this was required by law, it should come as no surprise. However, one noticeable change is the fact that with each passing decade, there is a gradual, substantial increase in the number of masses requested.

Because these postmortem masses are intended primarily to free souls from purgatory, it seems safe to conclude that sixteenth-century Ma-drileños displayed a certain amount of fear of purgatory. Although most wills exhibit a pronounced ambivalence toward death and the hereafter, one often has to read between the lines. Every will was supposed to contain some statement showing the testator's resignation over death, which usually read "I, so and so . . . fearing death which is a natural

---

[19] Sharon Farmer, "Personal Perceptions, Collective Behavior: Twelfth-Century Suf-frages for the Dead," in *Persons in Groups: Social Behavior as Identity Formation in Medieval and Renaissance Europe*, ed. Richard Trexler (Binghamton NY, 1985).

[20] Venegas, *Agonía*, pp. 203–6; Medina, *Libro de la Verdad*, III, pp. 470–1. The clear emphasis on the rarity of such visions in Spanish *Ars Moriendi* tracts confirms William Christian's thesis that lay visions came to be distrusted and discouraged in sixteenth-century Spain. See *Apparitions in Late Medieval and Renaissance Spain* (Princeton, 1981), pp. 150 ff.

thing," but no such statement was ever made concerning purgatory. Though most wills insert some statement expressing hope for salvation, it is clear that this hope was cautious. This ambivalence is best displayed in the concern testators showed over ceremonies and masses and more specifically in the actuarial compulsion to request specific numbers of specific kinds of masses at specific times in specific places, to aid one's soul and the souls of the previously departed.

There can be little doubt that an inflationary spiral affected requests for masses in sixteenth-century Madrid.[21] Whereas the average number of masses requested by an individual in the 1520s was ninety, the figure had grown to 777 by the 1590s. A quick glance at the overall pattern immediately reveals that this inflation was constant throughout the century but most intense in the final three decades (see Figure 5.1). Between the 1520s and 1540s, the number doubles, from nearly 100 to nearly 200. Then, it remains more or less steady around that same level for three decades. Suddenly, in the 1570s and 1580s, the numbers more than double, rising to more than 400. In the 1590s, the figures double once more, skyrocketing to nearly 800.

If the figures are broken down more specifically, the contours of these changes become even more dramatic (see Table 5.1). In the 1520s, only one-tenth of all testators (10%) requested more than 150 masses each, and nearly half (48%) requested no more than sixty. Eight percent asked for no more than ten masses each, the lowest possible request. The greatest number of masses requested was 639, and this seemed an odd request, contained in only one will (2%). In the 1590s, by contrast, only 15 percent asked for less than 150 masses, whereas nearly half (40%) requested 500 or more, and one-quarter (26%) requested more than 1,000! This contrast may be highlighted in another way: In the 1520s the single highest concentration of testators (32%) were those who asked for one to sixty masses; in the 1590s the single highest concentration (19%) was composed of those who requested one to two thousand masses!

---

21 A parallel increase has also been detected in Cuenca, where the completeness of the parochial archives has allowed Sara Nalle to count not only the masses requested in wills but also those requested by those who were too poor to write wills. Her conclusion: "Testators and nontestators alike, even the propertyless, upped the number of masses they wanted said for themselves and the souls in purgatory." *God in La Mancha*, p. 188.

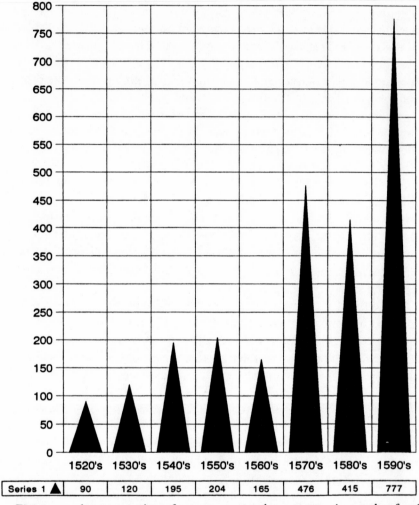

| Series 1 ▲ | 90 | 120 | 195 | 204 | 165 | 476 | 415 | 777 |

Figure 5.1. Average number of masses requested per testator in sample of 436 Madrid wills.

A quick glance at another set of figures serves as a final confirmation of the inflation that took place in requests for masses during the sixteenth century and of the way in which lower numbers seemed to become less and less satisfactory and higher numbers gained popularity:

Percentage of Testators Who Request Fewer Than 90 Masses

1520s	1530s	1540s	1550s	1560s	1570s	1580s	1590s
70	46	54	37	41	21	30	7

Percentage of Testators Who Request More Than 500 Masses

1520s	1530s	1540s	1550s	1560s	1570s	1580s	1590s
2	2	11	11	4	23	26	37

Table 5.1. *Number of masses requested in Madrid wills, 1520–99 (number of testators for each decade in parentheses)*

(Number of Testators for each decade in parentheses)

Number of Masses	Percentage of Testators							
	(50) 1520's	(51) 1530's	(46) 1540's	(46) 1550's	(47) 1560's	(70) 1570's	(49) 1580's	(42) 1590's
1–10	8%	2%	2%	2%	0%	0%	0%	0%
11–30	8%	10%	9%	7%	4%	0%	8%	0%
31–60	32%	18%	17%	11%	24%	12%	16%	2%
61–90	22%	16%	26%	17%	13%	9%	6%	5%
91–120	8%	12%	13%	17%	15%	6%	8%	5%
121–150	10%	16%	9%	9%	11%	4%	4%	8%
151–180	4%	6%	0%	9%	6.5%	7%	0%	5%
181–210	0%	10%	2%	7%	2%	6%	8%	10%
211–240	0%	6%	4%	2%	6.5%	9%	2%	2%
241–270	0%	0%	0%	0%	0%	6%	2%	0%
271–300	0%	0%	0%	0%	4%	1%	4%	5%
301–330	4%	2%	7%	0%	4%	6%	2%	2%
331–360	0%	0%	0%	2%	0%	1%	0%	8%
361–390	0%	0%	0%	0%	0%	0%	2%	0%
391–420	0%	0%	0%	4%	2%	6%	0%	5%
421–450	0%	0%	0%	0%	4%	1%	2%	2%
451–510	0%	2%	0%	0%	0%	0%	8%	4%
511–600	0%	0%	2%	4%	0%	1%	4%	2%
601–700	2%	0%	2%	7%	2%	7%	4%	2%
701–800	0%	0%	0%	0%	0%	0%	2%	0%
801–900	0%	0%	0%	0%	0%	1%	4%	5%
901–1000	0%	0%	0%	0%	2%	0%	0%	2%
1001–2000	0%	0%	7%	2%	0%	10%	8%	19%
2001–3000	0%	0%	0%	0%	0%	1%	0%	2%
3001–4000	0%	0%	0%	0%	0%	0%	0%	0%
4001–5230	0%	0%	0%	0%	0%	3%	4%	5%

It would appear that the spiritual value of each mass declined relatively among testators in this period, very much like the purchasing value of currency. Whereas over one-half of all testators before 1570 thought it sufficient to ask for fewer than ninety masses, only a third found that number appropriate in the 1580s, and only about one-tenth seemed to find it satisfactory in the 1590s.

How is this phenomenon to be explained? Is it possible that these increasingly large requests for masses reflect a disagreement over the spiritual value of masses rather than a devaluation of their worth? Although many people requested high numbers of masses in the 1570s, 1580s, and 1590s, a corresponding number continued to ask for much fewer. For instance, in the 1570s roughly the same number of testators asked for eleven to thirty masses (12%) as asked for one to two thousand (10%). In the 1580s the same percentage (8%) asked for fewer than thirty masses as asked for one to two thousand! When one considers that a parallel inflation in requests for masses has also been detected in Cuenca, Toledo, Zamora, Oviedo, Gijón, and Barcelona – though with lower overall amounts than in Madrid – the numbers seem to be shouting out something.[22] What, if anything, can they be saying?

Although it is true that some people continued to seem satisfied with modest numbers of masses toward the end of the century, it is impossible to deny a gradual, perceptible move by the majority of testators toward increasingly high requests for masses. The fact that some remained content with thirty, ninety, or 100 masses while many others were requesting five, eight, or 1,500 does not necessarily point to a disagreement over the value or usefulness of a single mass but perhaps to a reevaluation of the mass as a commodity in the spiritual marketplace.

Masses and the inflationary economy

Much can be gained by comparing the inflation in mass requests and mass prices to the general inflation that gripped the Spanish economy in the sixteenth century.

---

[22] Lorenzo Pinar, *Zamora*, pp. 67 ff.; Lopez Lopez, *Asturias*, pp. 117 ff.; Garcia Carcel, "Barcelona," *Documentación notarial*, pp. 122–3; Nalle, *La Mancha*, pp. 171 ff. The amounts for Cuenca offer the best possibility for a comparison, where the average

Although some aspects of the theory of a "price revolution" in the sixteenth century have been challenged, no one has yet denied that prices rose throughout the century and that this was a new, startling development for contemporaries.[23] The evidence for price increases comes from many different sources and is too overwhelming to ignore. A common factor is the surprised reaction of contemporaries and their inability to fathom the reasons for this phenomenon.

It is generally agreed that prices began to rise very rapidly and sharply in Spain about 1500. By 1513, it is possible to find some Spaniards making statements such as the following: "Today a pound of mutton costs as much as a whole sheep used to, a loaf of bread as much as a *fanega* of wheat, a pound of wax or oil as much as an *arroba* did in former days, and so on."[24] The statistics provided by Earl J. Hamilton confirm these complaints. According to him, the price of mutton doubled in New Castile between 1520 and 1550 and then almost doubled again in the second half of the century.[25] Despite some minor local variations in rates, the impact of this inflation was uniformly severe throughout Spain.

At first glance, it is tempting to speculate that the inflation in mass requests must be directly related to rising prices. It seems sensible to conjecture that mass prices might not have risen as rapidly as those for other commodities and that as the rate of inflation grew and people generally came to have more and more currency, they could simply pay for more masses. The first question that needs to be asked, then, is whether the price of each mass became relatively cheaper throughout the century.

The answer to this question is somewhat surprising. In sixteenth-

number of masses requested are as follows: before 1535, under 100 masses; 1545, 136 masses; 1585, 173 masses; 1595, nearly 500 masses. Nalle, *La Mancha*, p. 188.

23 The tone for discussion of this topic was set by Earl J. Hamilton in his magisterial *American Treasure and the Price Revolution in Spain 1501–1650* (Cambridge MA, 1934). He was challenged principally by Carlo M. Cipolla in "La prétendue 'révolution des prix,' réflexions sur l'experience italienne," *Annales, E.S.C.*, Oct.-Dec., 1955, pp. 513–16; and J. Nadal Oller in "La revolución de los precios españoles del siglo XVI," *Hispania* 19 (1959):503–29.

24 G. Alonso de Herrera, a sixteenth-century agriculturalist, cited by Ferdinand Braudel, *The Mediterranean in the Age of Philip II*, trans. Siân Reynolds (New York: 1972), vol. I, p. 519.

25 Hamilton, *Price Revolution*, appendixes III and IV.

century Madrid, mass prices kept rising with inflation or even out-stripped its average pace. This means, of course, that masses did not become relatively cheaper; in some cases, it was just the opposite. How-ever, because the price structure for masses and the general rate of increase became somewhat complex in this period, it would be wise to exercise caution before reaching any conclusions.

From the 1520s until the 1550s, each mass requested in Madrid wills cost about half of 1 *real*. It is not until the 1550s that some wills reflect a price increase, asking for masses at 25 *maravedis* (three-quarters of 1 *real*), or 1 *real*. This price increase is gradual and somewhat haphazard, and it takes another full decade for it to be universally accepted. By the 1570s, when the lowest price paid for any mass has become 1 *real*, the highest price has doubled to 2 *reales*. This price difference results in part from a new sliding price scale for different types of masses. Simple, recited masses (without any singing) generally cost 1 *real*. Novenary, feast day, anniversary, requiem, and high (sung) masses tended to cost 2 *reales*, which was four times higher than the price in the first half of the century. At this time, a new and more expensive type of mass seems to have been introduced. This was the *misa del anima*, or mass of the soul, which could cost anywhere from 4 *reales* to 2 *ducados* (22 *reales*)![26]

Throughout the 1580s and 1590s, this price scale remained in effect, with the cost at about 1 or 2 *reales*, depending on the type of mass or the church where it was to be said. In the 1570s, 1580s, and 1590s, how-ever, it is possible to find isolated instances of testators who offer much more than the accepted price, paying as much as 7, 8, or 22 *reales* for feast day and anniversary masses.[27]

When such exceptions are discounted, the increases in mass prices seem to be about on a par with the nominal price averages for other basic commodities, such as wine, wheat, beef, mutton, wax, and olive oil (see Figures 5.2 and 5.3). Comparisons cannot be exact if one simply speaks of "masses" without taking the sliding price scale into account. The prices for masses were more complex than the prices for basic commod-ities. Whereas wine, meat, wax, wheat, and oil normally sold for rela-tively uniform unit prices set in the marketplace, masses could cost

[26] Four *reales*: AHPM 586.500 (1586); 2 *ducados*: AHPM 1403.793 (1592).
[27] Seven *reales*: AHPM 457.1160 (1573); 8 *reales*: AHPM 571.10v (1581); 2 *ducados*: AHPM 566.253v (1579).

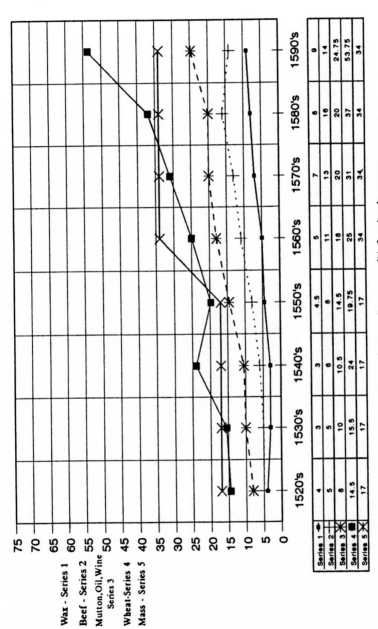

	1520's	1530's	1540's	1550's	1560's	1570's	1580's	1590's
Series 1 ◆	4	3	3	4.5	5	7	8	9
Series 2 ✛	5	5	6	6	11	13	16	14
Series 3 ✳	8	10	10.5	14.5	18	20	20	24.75
Series 4 ■	14.5	15.5	24	19.75	25	31	37	53.75
Series 5 ✕	17	17	17	17	34	34	34	34

Wax - Series 1
Beef - Series 2
Mutton, Oil, Wine
  Series 3
Wheat- Series 4
Mass - Series 5

Figure 5.2. Comparison of prices (in *maravedis*) for simple masses.

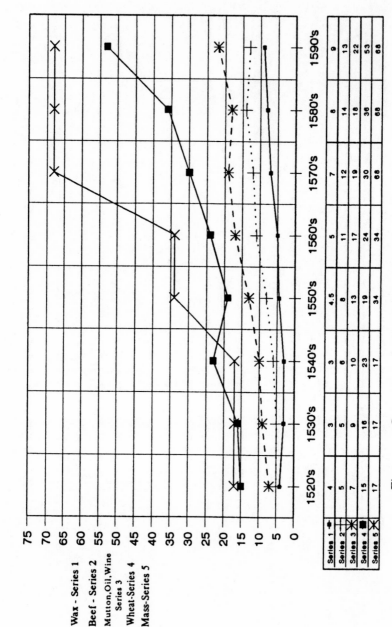

Figure 5-3. Comparison of prices (in *maravedis*) for special masses.

varying prices after 1550. If one considers only the lower cost mass (0.5 *real* or 1 *real*), then it is possible to say that this price increase was more or less in step with the general inflationary curve. When one considers the masses of higher cost (1 *real* and 2 *reales*), however, it seems that this increase was slightly above the norm. All in all, the increase in mass prices reflected in Madrid wills seems to match the general pattern suggested by the economic historian Earl J. Hamilton. According to his calculations, Spanish prices quadrupled in the sixteenth century.[28] The increase from 0.5 *real* to 1 *real* and then 2 *reales* is exactly fourfold. However, the figures proposed by J. Nadal Oller, the man who "disproved" Hamilton's theories, suggest only a doubling of prices over the entire century. If these calculations are correct, then mass prices seem to have increased much faster and higher than almost anything else.[29]

The total picture becomes even more complex when one takes account of what happened to wages during this time. According to Ferdinand Braudel, wages did not keep pace with the price rise, making the life of those at the bottom of the economy increasingly difficult. Though nominal wages rose relatively rapidly along with prices – or even remained high in times of recession – the purchasing power of the currency, that is, the real wages, took a beating. The figures cited by Braudel testify to the severity of the crisis faced by the lower-paid workers.

Real Wages in Sixteenth-Century Spain

1510	*1530*	*1550*	*1560*	*1570*	*1580*	*1590*	*1600*
127.8	91.4	97.6	110.7	105.7	102.9	105.8	91.3

Taking the years 1571 to 1580 as an index of 100, Braudel estimates that the real wages that had been at an index of 127.84 in 1510 fell to 91.4 in the next twenty years. By 1550, real wages stood at 97.6; thereafter, they rode a roller coaster but stayed generally low, hitting bottom at 91.31 at the end of the century. Overall, Braudel concludes, the "price revolution" brought little comfort to wage earners and even less to artisans.[30]

[28] Earl J. Hamilton, *Price Revolution*, appendixes III, IV, V.

[29] J. Nadal Oller, "La revolución" *Hispania* 19:503–29 (1959). This study suggests a 2.8 percent average yearly increase from 1501–62 (or about 171%), and a 1.3 percent average yearly increase for 1563–1600 (another 48%).

[30] Braudel, *Mediterranean*, vol. I, pp. 524–25. See also Hamilton, *Price Revolution*, pp. 278–9, esp. tables 29 and 30, and chart 19.

Table 5.2. *Comparison of wages and mass prices*[a]

Decade	Daily wage	Cost of simple mass	Cost of special mass
1520s	35.4	17	17
1530s	17.5	17	17
1540s	31.0	17	17
1550s	53.4	25–34	34
1560s	44.0	34	34
1570s	68.0	34	68
1580s	60.0	34	68
1590s	85.0	34	68

[a]Wages and prices listed in *maravedis*.

The effect of inflation was visible in the currency, for the medium of exchange used for the wages of the poor and their daily purchases was hardly ever gold (*escudos*) and only occasionally silver (*reales*). For the most part, the poor were limited to copper currency (*ducados* and *maravedis*).[31] In Madrid, mass prices were most often quoted in *reales* – silver coins – showing that a mass was a relatively expensive commodity that was beyond the ordinary daily exchange of the poor and dispossessed. A brief comparison of average wages and average mass prices shows how the purchasing power of a day laborer generally declined through the century (see Table 5.2).[32]

If Hamilton's figures are correct, it does appear that the prices for masses actually remained steady while wages increased in 1570–99, which may account in part for the higher number of masses requested in those three final decades of the century. However, this development does not fully explain the inflation in mass requests, because Madrileños

[31] Braudel, *Mediterranean*, vol. I, p. 525.
[32] Source for average wages: Hamilton, *Price Revolution*, pp. 278–9. See also Manuel Fernández Alvarez, *El Madrid de 1586* (Madrid, 1962), p. 11. According to Fernández Alvarez, a bricklayer in Madrid earned about 1.5 *reales*, or 102 *maravedis*, per day in 1562. Counting for Sundays and holidays, which makes 300 real working days, this would amount to about 450 *reales*, or 30,600 *maravedis*, per year. A street sweeper was paid 2 *reales* a day by the city in 1586. If he worked 300 days, he would have earned about 600 *reales*.

spent a relatively higher proportion of their estates on masses during this period.[33]

To be more specific, let us take a look at the cases of three sample laborers (or their relatives) from Madrid, and see how their mass requests might have been affected by inflation. In 1538 Pedro Gonzalez, a farm worker, requested twenty masses at 0.5 *real* (17 *maravedis*) each. If he had been earning the average wage of 17.5 *maravedis* per day computed by Hamilton, this means that the twenty masses required the income from almost twenty full working days.[34]

In 1567 Maria de Torres, the widow of a carpenter, requested a total of fifty-one masses at 1 *real* (34 *maravedis*). At the average wage of 44 *maravedis* per day, it would have required her husband to work about forty days to pay for her masses.[35]

In 1592 Gaspar Garcia, a weaver, asked for 166 masses, a relatively low number for his day. Two of these were special 2-*real* (68 *maravedis*) masses, the rest cost 1 *real* each. Working at a daily wage of 85 *maravedis*, these masses would cost him the income from about sixty-seven working days.[36]

These are but three isolated cases, chosen at random. Although they may not be the most typical, they can be taken as illustrative of the kind of requests made by laborers in Madrid. Two things can be noticed when the three are compared. First, all of them make mass requests that are on the low end of the scale, far below the average for their time. Second, although these requests remain below average, they do increase, in spite of the shrinking purchasing power of wages.

What these figures suggest is that the inflation of mass requests may have been related in part to the inflation of the Spanish economy but that other factors must also have been at work. Although it appears that masses may have become relatively cheaper in the 1570s, 1580s, and 1590s, the lower price does not match the increase in mass requests. Also, it is quite possible that masses did not become relatively cheaper for everyone as a result of the "price revolution." In some respects –

[33] Nalle's findings in Cuenca (*God in La Mancha*, p. 202) are very similar, and she sees "an enormous conversion of wealth into the cult of the dead." Her conclusion: "Testators, however, were not content to spend what their parents and grandparents had spent on suffrages. . . . Instead, the inflation of the cult of the dead rose at twice the rate of inflation in general."

[34] AHPM 69.30 (1538).   [35] AHPM 541.145 (1567).   [36] AHPM 1403.93 (1592).

especially when the purchasing power of wages is taken into account –
masses could have very well become more expensive because mass
prices rose at the same pace as the general inflationary curve. As the
century progressed and testators requested more and more masses, a
proportionately larger percentage of their income or estates had to be
spent on these pious bequests.

Anxiety over the hereafter and confidence in masses

In looking for reasons other than economic to explain the inflation of
mass requests in sixteenth-century Madrid, one is inexorably drawn
toward more subjective explanations, toward the minds and hearts rather than the purses, of the testators.

To begin with, it is quite possible that the inflation in the Spanish
economy could have had a profound psychological effect on most Madrileños, altering the way they looked at the value of anything that could
be purchased. If the cost of all material goods increased, then why not
also of spiritual goods? If more *maravedis* were needed for the wine and
wax used at a funeral, or even for the mass, then why not assume that it
would also require more masses to gain release from purgatory? In the
case of the mass, the likelihood of a psychological impact was doubled by
its unique character, for the mass was not only a commodity, something
to be purchased for a price; it was also a currency, a unit of value with a
certain purchasing power. Could it be that masses, considered as a
spiritual currency (used to procure some reduction in the amount of
time spent in purgatory) underwent a devaluation parallel to that of the
monetary currency? Or that some testators may have become uncertain
and confused about the exact value of masses? For instance, when Maria
Herrera requested 100 masses for the soul of her husband "who is in
glory," was she aware of her mistake?[37] If she thought her husband was
in heaven, why offer 100 masses for his soul? Did she make this request
because 100 masses were no longer considered much in 1588? Or was
this a slip of the tongue that reveals a certain confusion about masses
and the afterlife?

Moreover, since the precipitous numerical increase in pious bequests

[37] AHPM 800.1122 (1588).

accompanied a parallel increase in funeral pomp, could this not also be another manifestation of the reevaluation of public ritual gestures in reference to social status? Other European cities had previously experienced these twin phenomena of larger funerals and larger numbers of masses (though the numbers of masses in Madrid are much greater than any other cities). In three such cases, Chiffoleau's Avignon, Cohn's Siena, and Strocchia's Florence, the ritual inflation has been closely linked to the status question.[38]

A clue to what may have really been affecting the minds of sixteenth-century Madrileños may be found in another development that took place in the latter part of the century. One of the more notable changes that takes place in mass requests about midcentury is the increase in the number of testators who request an unspecified number of masses. Before 1540, no testator would ever leave the total number of masses to be said to anyone else's discretion, not even a wife's or a parent's. After 1540, however, perhaps as customs become more rigidly codified and it becomes easier to determine what is "proper" for certain persons according to their status, a small but significant percentage of testators (between 4 and 9%) leave the question of numbers to others in 1540–90 (see Figure 5.4). Many testators also begin to request a specific number, plus an unspecified number on top of that.

Though many of these unspecified requests leave the choice of numbers of masses to others, perhaps giving the impression that some testators simply could not be bothered with liturgical accounting, a good number remain unspecific for a very different reason. After 1540, a fluctuating percentage of testators (as low as 1 percent in the 1570s, and as high as 6 percent in the 1580s) request that their entire estate be used to pay for masses. These cases, in which testators who had no direct heirs make their soul the *heredero universal* (sole heir), reveal an obsessive concern over the afterlife.[39]

By making their soul the only beneficiary, these individuals expressed

[38] Chiffoleau, *Comptabilité*, p. ix; Cohn, *Death and Property*, pp. 166–82; Strocchia, *Death and Ritual*, pp. 55–104. The average mass amounts calculated by Cohn for Siena seem puny in comparison to Madrid: 1551–75, 39 masses; 1576–1600, 8 masses; 1601–25, 31 masses; 1626–50, 46 masses.

[39] See Maldonado y Fernández del Torco, *Herencias a foavor del alma en el derecho español* (Madrid, 1944).

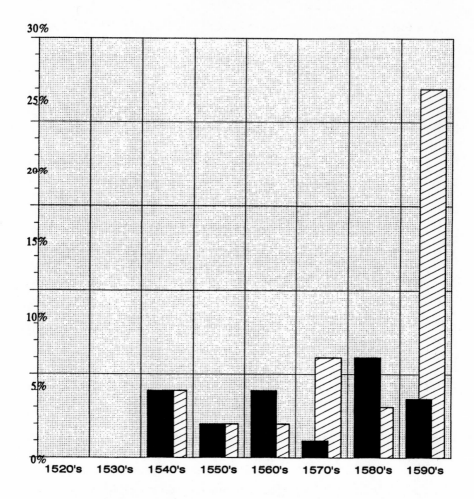

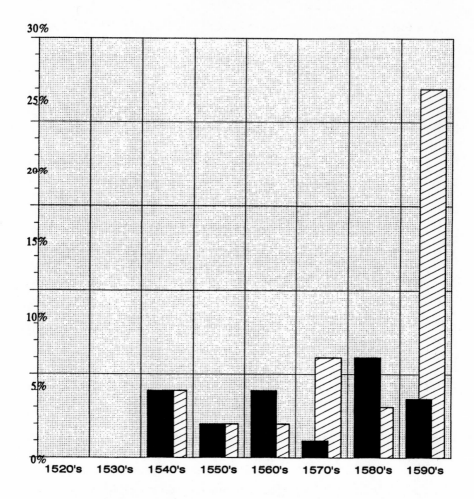 Total % requesting unspecified number of masses

  % of those who request that their entire estate be used to pay for masses

Figure 5.4. Requests for unspecified number of masses in relation to naming of testator's soul as "universal heir."

a mixture of anxiety and confidence.[40] First, by showing an all-consuming interest in themselves and in postmortem masses, they expressed concern with the immediate future state of their existence in the hereafter – perhaps even an undisguised fear of punishment. Second, however, they also showed a supreme confidence in the power of the mass, or more specifically, in the power of sheer volume and quantity. By using their entire estate to purchase great numbers of masses, these testators showed that they believed, or at least hoped, that such a gesture would help them escape from punishment. Of course, not every single instance in which the soul was named universal heir can be taken at face value as a *purely* spiritual concern. Spanish ritual life was too complex to make such an assumption. One can never discount the social forces at work, especially the desire for memorialization as a status symbol. But even if in some of these cases the testators had questions of status in mind, the gesture of making their souls the universal heir reveals a certain mentality and a certain hierarchy of values in Madrid society. Why use up one's estate in this manner? Why not, for instance, leave one's estate for charity?

This mixture of anxiety and confidence shows through very clearly in many of the wills that request unspecified numbers of masses. A good number of wills simply ask for "all the masses that could possibly be said."[41] Often, it is clear that such requests are not prompted by indifference but, rather, uneasiness over not having enough money left over in the estate to spend on a high number of masses.

One testator, for instance, asked for "all that could be done for my soul . . . according to my estate"[42]; another urgently pleaded with his wife to aid his soul as much as she could with their limited resources[43]; a third requested that all his belongings should first be sold to pay off his debts and that "whatever might be left over, should be spent on masses."[44] Alonso de Ruselga asked his wife as he lay dying to arrange for "as many masses and sacrifices" as she deemed best, adding "and I beg

[40] This may be an inescapable emotional dialectic, as La Rochefoucauld observed (*Maximes*, n. 515, p. 94) "L'esperance et la crainte sont inséparables, et il n'ya point de crainte sans esperance, ni d'esperance sans crainte."

[41] Two such examples: AHPM 575.527 (1583); 1392.612 (1584).

[42] Alonso Hernández, AHPM 105, s.f. (1540).

[43] Francisco Hernández, AHPM 543.83 (1569).

[44] AHPM 139.33 (1544); and the same request in 139.715 (1544).

that she look after my soul as much as I would have looked after hers."[45] Obviously, these were not careless requests but, rather, earnest attempts to obtain the highest possible number of masses.

Some of those who were short of funds looked for every means possible to pay for masses or to add an unspecified number to those they had already requested. One pharmacist asked that the money owed to him by several clients be used for masses.[46] Another man, Pedro de Olivares, specified he wanted 155 postmortem masses, but he added two pages later, near the end of the will, that he wanted his executors to sell some of his silver spoons and use the money for as many additional masses as possible.[47] The same concern seemed to have gripped Mariana de Castro, a woman who made her soul the only beneficiary in her will. After specifying where she wanted forty masses said, she listed her meager belongings, one by one (a rug worth 40 *reales*, a gold cross, a bed, some blankets, hats, and clothes) and asked that they be sold so the money could all be used for masses, "to do some good for my soul."[48]

As could be expected, those who bequeathed their entire estate to their souls showed the greatest concern over salvation and the greatest amount of trust in the forbearance and honesty of their executors. Inez de la Cruz, a woman who claimed to have no relatives, left her entire estate in the hands of her parish priest, saying she wanted him to "spend all my belongings on masses and pious sacrifices for my soul."[49] Apparently, others who had interested relatives could act this way only if they fended off all other claimants to the estate. One such case was Mariana de Castro, who stated clearly in her will that no questions should be asked by anyone about how her money was spent for masses.[50]

Although it may be surmised that these extreme measures were promoted by the clergy solely as a means of increasing church revenue or of increasing their control over the laity, there is sufficient evidence to deny such suspicions. For the most part, it appears that many priests themselves actively participated in these beliefs and practices and that they could be even more enthusiastic about its benefits than the laity. Several

---

[45] AHPM 746.91 (1570). [46] AHPM 78.444 (1554). [47] AHPM 314.1012 (1564).
[48] AHPM 61.417 (1563). [49] AHPM 1412.91 (1596).
[50] AHPM 61.417 (1563). This testator made a certain Maria Fraidos her executrix and asked her to arrange for as many masses as possible, adding: "Lo qual por efecto de hazer bien por mi anima . . . no le pidan cuenta de como los gastó ny distribuyó."

wills show that it was not so much a case of the clergy controlling the laity or of imposing certain "elite" beliefs on them from above as it was of the clergy and laity participating *together* in a certain shared conception of what can be done for the human soul in the hereafter. To a great extent, the priests controlled this system not so much by calculation and persuasion as by their active participation and support. It should not seem too surprising, then, that the most revealing and eloquent statements about these matters should be found in the wills of priests.

No testator showed a more profound mixture of anxiety over the afterlife and confidence in the power of masses than Father Gregorio de Oviedo. Calling himself an "unworthy priest," this curate sat down with a notary while he was still healthy, long before he needed to worry about death, and then went on to write an obsessively detailed will, paying attention to every aspect of his funeral and postmortem devotions, focusing entirely on the business of saving his soul from punishment. In addition to listing all possible contingencies and alternate plans for his burial, Father Gregorio left his soul as *heredera universal*, requesting at least 875 masses (all to be said at meticulously specified churches, at carefully specified times), plus certain other clusters of masses. In addition, he asked with customary redundance that after the appropriate fees had been paid for these, the remainder of his estate "all be spent in pious works and alms for my soul. . . . I want it all spent on masses, sacrifices, and pious works." As if this were not enough, he closed his will with more compulsively exacting requests for specific numbers of masses, at specific churches, at specific times.[51] Without a doubt, Father Gregorio sought no profit from these obsessive gestures other than the salvation of his soul in the hereafter.

A similar case was that of Father Pedro de Reballos, another curate who named his soul as *heredera universal*. He requested an exact number of 1,526 masses and then ordered that all his remaining belongings be used to pay for as many additional masses as possible.[52] Such manifestly self-centered preoccupation on the part of the clergy may indeed show how deep the anxiety over purgatory extended in Spanish society. The will of yet another priest reveals more clearly how these obsessive gestures could be wholeheartedly accepted and justified by one of those

[51] AHPM 457.1219 (1573).   [52] AHPM 107 s.f. (1549).

who ostensibly controlled the salvific system. The *apologia* offered by Father Juan de Talavera Salazar, canon of the cathedral of Siguenza, and administrator of the hospital for the poor students of the University of Alcalá (*hospital de San Lucas y San Nicolás*) makes it clear that he thought he had every right to care exclusively for his own salvation:

I declare that I wish to make my soul the heir of all that remains of my possessions . . . because I have worked for fifty-three years, toiling and struggling along diverse roads and towns, and I have done all I could for my brothers and sisters, out of my own sweat and the income I earned through it. And as Our Lord well knows, I never shrank back from labor in order to maintain my honor, because I did not inherit a single *real* from my parents. Therefore, it is fitting that my soul . . . should now enjoy the fruits of this labor, and that my earnings all be spent in masses and sacrifices, so that through these devotions and through His mercy, God my redeemer may desist from damning me, and save me.[53]

The way Father Juan saw things, he was entitled to his income even in the afterlife, and this income could be literally used to purchase his salvation. His *apologia* betrays much more than a bristling impatience with whatever claims his relatives may have wanted to place on his estate; it discloses an earnest concern with salvation, an ardent confidence in the redemptive power of the mass, and an unshakable certainty in the compatibility of the here and the hereafter. After all, did he not seem certain that God would spare him punishment and "save" him if all these masses were said for his soul? And were not these masses to be performed by the living and paid for with the money he earned in this life?

To some extent, by calmly writing his will this way, in full health rather than under the threat of imminent death, Father Juan was making an investment in his future, and he seemed to do it with optimism, as if he fully expected a return for his investment, very much like present-day wage earners who divert part of their salaries into retirement plans. This means, of course, that he feared purgatory as a real possibility and sought to allay this anxiety through planning for a high number of postmortem masses.

[53] AHPM 586.790 (1587).

The complexity of requests for masses

The emotion and energy expended on these postmortem masses seems even more intense when one considers the complexity of the liturgical system and the vast array of different kinds of masses that were requested.

In sixteenth-century Madrid it was not enough simply to ask for masses in one's will: One also had to know exactly which types of masses one wanted, where and when they were to be said, and for which intentions they were to be offered. To make these requests, testators were expected to be somewhat knowledgeable about the options available to them. Although notaries helped by letting testators know what was deemed proper, ultimately it was always the testator's responsibility to choose what seemed best. Because masses were believed to accomplish so much, this was no small responsibility.

The nearly obsessive attention paid to these further details in postmortem devotions again reveals an uneasy dialectic between anxiety and confidence, a dialectic that gave shape to the economy of salvation and that fueled its complex machinery.

On the one hand, the complexity of the system itself and the familiarity which most testators seemed to have with it point to a heightened sense of foreboding about the afterlife, not just for the self but also for all the dead. The fact that the structure and meaning of the liturgy had become so finely nuanced, tailored to meet a seemingly infinite set of circumstances and contingencies in the afterlife, much like a science, shows that much thought had gone into the matter. The fact that so many testators seemed to be quite adept at making use of this complex system – and that they used it so intensely – suggests that a good number of them were genuinely preoccupied with the hereafter.

On the other hand, the dexterity with which testators could manipulate the liturgical system and the magnitude of their investment in it also hint at a certain degree of security, ease, and comfort on their part. Often, especially when faced with a will in which the testator is making complex, detailed arrangements for all sorts of postmortem masses, it is not at all difficult to think that this elaborate liturgical system could have been perceived as a powerful, well-oiled machine that ensured passage into heaven.

At best, this liturgical system could be perceived as a spiritual insurance policy that allayed fears about the hereafter, as a means of protecting the self and relatives from possible punishment in the afterlife according to accepted doctrine and practice. At worst, it could be perceived as an intelligible commercial system that could be exploited to one's advantage, as no more than one final set of transactions through which those with the most knowledge and the most money could buy the appropriate commodities needed for entry into heaven.

Moving from the abstract to the concrete, however, we consider exactly what was involved in this grand liturgical obsessiveness, and we provide a brief outline of the different types of masses most commonly chosen by Madrileños in the sixteenth century.

Type of mass	Explanation
Misa Rezada	Low mass, in which the priest simply recites the liturgy, most often celebrating whichever feast is indicated for that day by the liturgical calendar.
Misa Cantada	High mass, in which the priest chants the liturgy, assisted by a deacon and subdeacon.
Misa de Requiem	Requiem mass: the special liturgy indicated for funerals in the missal, usually chanted rather than recited.
Novenario	A cycle of nine masses, to be said on nine consecutive days, usually recited, celebrating the feasts indicated by the liturgical calendar.
Treintanario Llano	A cycle of thirty masses, celebrated on thirty consecutive days, usually recited, celebrating the feasts indicated for those days by the liturgical calendar.
Treintanario Revelado (such as *Misas del Conde; Misas de Amador*)	A cycle of thirty masses, celebrated on thirty consecutive days, usually recited, celebrating special feasts. The exact arrangement of these feasts and the rubrics varied according to which set of masses one requested. Each of these particular combinations of feasts was believed to have been revealed by some saint or angel.
Cinco Llagas	A cycle of five masses celebrating the Five

	Wounds of Jesus, on five specific days of the year, according to the calendar.
Nueve Fiestas	A cycle of nine masses celebrating the nine major Marian feast days, on nine specific days of the year, according to the liturgical calendar.
Misa del Anima	Requested only after 1570: a special mass for the soul of the deceased, to be said at specific, indulgenced altars.
Misas Perpetuas	Specific masses celebrating certain feasts during the year, chosen by the testator, which were to be said "forever and ever" every year on those designated days.

Madrileños also requested several other types of masses not included in this list, such as the *misas de Santiago,* the *misas del angel, misas de la luz,* and a few others, but requests for them were infrequent (see Table 5.3).

To illustrate how these masses were requested and to provide some sense of the ways in which testators used this system, we look at two sample wills, one from the 1520s and one from the 1590s, chosen at random. First, we consider the will of Ramiro Martinez, which was written in June 1529, while he was suffering from a serious illness. The requests made in this will are rather typical for the time but do reveal some confusion on the part of Ramiro, showing that he was not entirely familiar with the liturgical services available for the dead. First, he asked for the abbot and monks of the suburban monastery of San Benito to come to his house, claim his body, and take it to their church, where he was to be buried. Then, mistakenly, he asked for the monks to form a cortege, carrying their cross and candles, "saying plain masses along the way, as is their custom." What Ramiro had failed to realize was that the monks could not say masses on the street as they accompanied his body to the grave. The "custom" he refers to is the reading of responses, not the saying of masses. Through this error, his will exposes two significant trends. First, by asking for masses so hurriedly, he shows how deep the people's conviction in the power and significance of the mass could be; second, by mistaking the responses for masses, he also reveals that misunderstandings were not uncommon and that the liturgical system was not always properly understood by the laity.

Ramiro, like everyone else, was forced to outline two different scenar-

Table 5.3. *Types of masses requested in Madrid wills, 1520–99*

SPECIAL MASSES	Percentage of Testators by decade							
	1520's	1530's	1540's	1550's	1560's	1570's	1580's	1590's
Novenario (9)	90%	82%	59%	57%	30%	31%	35%	21%
Trentanario llano (30)	34%	39%	35%	17%	13%	8%	0%	2%
Trentanario revelado (30)	10%	12%	0%	0%	0%	0%	0%	0%
Misas del Conde (30)	26%	8%	9%	0%	0%	0%	0%	0%
Misas de San Amador (30)	18%	18%	31%	20%	9%	3%	2%	2%
Five wounds of Jesus (30)	6%	2%	11%	4%	9%	3%	0%	0%
Nine feast days of Mary (9)	6%	8%	7%	0%	0%	4%	4%	0%
Misas del anima	0%	0%	0%	0%	0%	13%	55%	62%
Misas Santiago	2%	0%	0%	0%	0%	0%	0%	0%
Misas del San Miguel (10)	2%	0%	0%	0%	0%	0%	0%	0%
Misas del San Andres (10)	2%	0%	0%	0%	0%	0%	0%	0%
Misas del Angel	0%	2%	0%	0%	0%	0%	0%	0%
Misas de Luz	0%	0%	2%	0%	0%	0%	0%	0%
Misas del Angel de Guardia	0%	0%	0%	0%	0%	0%	2%	2%
Passion of Jesus (15)	2%	6%	0%	4%	0%	1%	2%	0%
Four Evangelists	0%	0%	2%	0%	0%	0%	0%	0%
Holy Spirit	0%	0%	0%	0%	2%	0%	2%	2%
Thirty-three years of Jesus	0%	0%	0%	0%	0%	0%	0%	2%
Nine months of Mary	0%	0%	0%	0%	2%	0%	0%	0%
TOTAL Number of Wills Sampled	50	51	50	48	50	76	54	57

* Note: Percentages do not add up to 100% in each column because testators made multiple requests.

ios for his funeral. If he died in the morning, he was to be buried immediately. If he died after noon, he was to be buried the next morning, after a vigil consisting of responses. In either case, he was to be buried with a requiem mass. After his burial, he requested three sets of "accumulative" masses, that is, mass cycles to be said quickly after his death, over a specified number of days.[54] Because it was commonly believed that the soul was judged and sent to purgatory immediately after death, it was also believed that these accumulative masses had the speediest possible impact on the lessening of one's stay in purgatory.[55] Ramiro asked for a *novenario*, a set of nine masses to be said over nine consecutive days. In addition, he asked for a *treintanario revelado*, a cycle of thirty "revealed" masses known as the *Misas del Conde* (which will be explained shortly). On top of this trental he asked for another *treintanario revelado*. A year later, on the anniversary of his death, his heirs were to arrange for two more requiem masses. All in all, he had asked for a total of seventy-three masses, slightly below the average for his day.

Next, we turn to the will of Alonso del Hoyo, also written on what the testator believed to be his deathbed, in 1596. First, his body was to be retrieved by his parish clergy from a small village near Madrid and taken there for burial with three sets of responses. If he died in the morning, he was to be buried immediately; if at night, the next morning, after a vigil consisting of responses. In either case, he wanted to be buried with a high requiem mass. Like Ramiro, he too asked for a *novenario* to be said for the first nine days after his funeral. Unlike Ramiro, he asked for no *treintanarios*, requesting instead a single *misa del anima* (also to be explained shortly) at the church of San Francisco. In addition, he asked for eighty plain masses for his own soul, forty of which were to be said in his parish church outside the city and the other forty in Madrid, at San Francisco.

For the souls of his parents and grandparents, he requested ninety more low masses, which were to be divided in half between the churches of La Trinidad and Nuestra Señora de Atocha. For the souls in purgatory he also requested four high masses at his parish church. Almost as an afterthought, he added two more high masses to be said for his soul at his parish church. Finally, he requested that the anniversary of his death

---

[54] The term *misas acumulativas* is used by L. Gomez Nieto, *Ritos funerarios*, p. 86.
[55] Venegas, *Agonía*, p. 134.

be marked by the celebration of another *novenario*, just as at his funeral. Altogether, he had requested 195 masses, far below the average for his decade.

Aside from the mistakes made by the first testator, neither of these wills contains anything out of the ordinary. Although both convey a good, clear sense of the types of masses chosen made by Madrid testators in these two decades, neither as a whole contains the entire range of choices available to them.

Perpetual masses

One of the more important types of masses overlooked by both of these wills were the *misas perpetuas,* or perpetual masses, which were to be said at specified intervals *por siempre jamas* (forever and ever), down through the generations, long after the death of the testator. For those who could afford them, these masses apparently offered a singular kind of spiritual security. According to the complex ranking assigned to different kinds of masses by theologians, perpetual masses were considered the best kind of suffrage.[56]

Few other special liturgies reveal the obsessive attitude of Madrileños toward the mass as well as these perpetual masses. Moreover, few others also expose as clearly that dialectic between fear and confidence that drove testators to request so many masses. To begin with, Madrileños seemed content to overlook the logical incoherence behind the concept of the perpetual mass. If masses did indeed help to spring souls from purgatory, thereby ensuring salvation, then why insist that masses be said on specific feast days "forever," for the rest of human history? Would not many of those masses be redundant? (Especially when one considers that most of those who requested perpetual masses usually asked for many other masses as well.) And how, exactly, did such masses add merit to one's account, stretched as they were over the years, when requested alongside with *novenarios* and *treintanarios,* especially since it

---

[56] Venegas, *Agonía,* p. 134, gets very technical at this point and says that perpetual masses are best, even though they do not have as swift an effect as cumulative masses. A full discussion of this theology is beyond our scope here. Suffice it to say that in this intricate reckoning *novenarios* and *treintanarios* gained "accidental" merit, whereas chaplaincies and perpetual masses gained "essential" merit, which was deemed better.

was commonly believed that judgment followed immediately after death and that it was a good strategy to ask for a high number of masses to be said as soon as possible after one's death? Apparently, Madrileños were not interested in asking such questions. Also, none seemed eager to raise a further question: Just exactly how do masses said "forever" in earthly time affect any soul's length of stay in purgatory? In other words, by requesting perpetual masses until the end of earthly time, does one necessarily imply that one's soul will remain in purgatory that long? Were some of these testators expecting to remain in purgatory until the end of earthly time? Had they taken seriously that timetable which estimated that the average soul would have to spend one or two thousand years in purgatory?[57] Or were they seeking control over memorialization and over time itself, as is evidenced by the one testator who asked that perpetual masses be said not only for his soul but also those of his wife and all his descendants, even those not yet born?[58]

Clearly, those who requested perpetual masses did not ask such questions. Their requests seemed to be informed more by emotion than logic. At bottom, the perpetual mass was an extreme gesture, an indication of some residual uncertainty about the afterlife that no number of masses – even an unusually high number – could ever completely efface. It is quite likely that those who requested perpetual masses were ensuring themselves against the worst possible scenario, against the possibility that all the other masses would be insufficient, and that more and more would have to be said, until purgatory itself ceased to exist at the end of the world.

It is also possible that many testators were simultaneously stockpiling merits for themselves and their loved ones, for it was commonly believed that suffrages offered for those already released from purgatory were not wasted. Venegas spoke about investments in the treasury of merit with the confidence of a successful stockbroker: Nothing was ever lost, and it always promised a high dividend. Those souls who had already advanced to heaven would gratefully acknowledge any suffrage offered on their behalf by the living (that is, by the relatives or executors who actually arranged for them on earth). Even better, these rescued souls would pray in heaven for those they wished to thank and thus help to reduce *their* time in purgatory later. All of which meant, of course, that

[57] Orozco, *Victoria de la muerte*, p. 173.   [58] AHPM 69.46 (1538).

one could never request too many suffrages, for their merit could felicitously rebound upon others.[59] These promises could also prompt executors to perform their duties competently.

The act of requesting masses to be said for one's soul for an indefinite amount of time, "forever and ever," shows as much confidence as anxiety. In the first place, such an investment, which had to be very carefully planned, was not something to be taken lightly. Those who requested perpetual masses had to set up chaplaincies and plan for all sorts of contingencies to ensure that there would be a succession of priests down through the generations who would make these masses their responsibility. Such planning requires a great degree of faith not only in the power of the mass but also in the stability of the church and society.

Conclusions must be cautiously drawn. It should never be assumed that every one of these testators sincerely believed in the power of perpetual masses or that this gesture had a purely spiritual function. To some extent, the perpetual mass was intended for the survivors as much as for the souls of the dead. It was a social convention that also served as a legitimate earthly memorial to the deceased, much like a monument, as something that reminded the living of their ancestors and that confirmed their social status. It is not outside the realm of possibility that some (or perhaps many) of the testators who asked for perpetual masses had precisely this function in mind, either as their primary or secondary motivation. This gesture increased in popularity toward the end of the century, along with other elaborations in pomp, as funeral practices became increasingly linked to questions of status.

Still, this great admixture of anxiety and confidence points eventually to uncertainty at both levels, the theological and the social. Those who requested perpetual masses were those who wanted to place their trust in the redemptive machinery of the church – for the benefit of their status as well as of their souls – but at the same time suspected that even the grandest gestures might not suffice to free them from purgatory or make them seem important enough in the eyes of others. We now look at perpetual mass requests in closer detail to see how they actually reflected such a dialectical attitude toward the afterlife.

[59] Venegas, *Agonía*, pp. 210, 217: "Ningun bien queda sin renumeración." For the same reasons, Venegas also advised his readers to take out as many indulgences as possible. Medina borrowed freely from Venegas on this point, *Libro de la verdad*, III, pp. 466–8.

The simplest kind of perpetual mass was that celebrated once every year on the anniversary of the testator's death, usually at the altar nearest to the grave. This kind of request is generally found in the early part of the century.[60] As the century progresses, it becomes increasingly common to see more complex requests, such as the one that asked in 1538 for three masses every month, "perpetually and forevermore" at Santa Cruz.[61]

These simpler requests merely asked for masses to be said at certain intervals, with no concern for any specific kind of liturgical celebration. Many of these requests simply state that they want "whatever masses the church is celebrating"; a few ask for a certain liturgy, such as the mass of the five wounds of Jesus, to be celebrated at specific intervals.[62]

A more common practice, however, was that of asking for masses on specific feast days in order to gain the intercession of certain heavenly patrons. Diego de Madrid, for example, asked for one mass every year on the feast of the conception of Mary.[63] Isabel Morejón, also asked for this same feast but added others that honored her *abogados* (advocates), St. Francis, St. Peter, and St. Paul.[64] Maria de Gribaja went further in seeking the intercession of her favorite saints, asking for yearly celebrations of the nine feasts of Mary and the feasts of St. Idelfonso, St. Isidro, St. Peter, St. Catherine, and St. Jerome. Wishing to gain as many advocates in heaven as possible, she also asked for the feast of All Saints.[65] Instead of seeking the assistance of specific saints, others sought special recognition by requesting the most important feasts of the liturgical calendar, such as those of the Annunciation, the Conception of Jesus, the Name of Jesus, Christmas, Pentecost, Ascension, and Corpus Christi.[66] Some, like Diego Ortega, combined the feasts of patrons with major liturgical feasts, an optimal blend according to experts on these matters.[67]

An anxious, obsessive edge can be detected in many of these requests. Cristobal de Madrid Roman, for instance, showed the intensity of his concern by tripling the number of masses to be said on the feasts that his

[60] AHPM 55.651 (1526) is but one example.   [61] AHPM 69.42 (1538).
[62] AHPM 78.394 (1554).   [63] AHPM 69.46 (1538).   [64] AHPM 457.1098 (1573).
[65] AHPM 566.296 (1579).   [66] AHPM 457.1160 (1563).
[67] AHPM 800.1168 (1581). This testator requested the feasts of St. James, St. Michael, St. John the Baptist, All Saints, and the Ascension. See Venegas, *Agonía*, p. 215.

wife had earlier requested. One mass per day apparently did not seem sufficient to him.[68] Pedro de Torres and Maria Hernandez, another married couple, expressed their apprehension through an obsessively detailed list of instructions. To them, it did not seem enough to request the nine feasts of Mary, plus three weekly masses (a total of 165 masses per year, every year, forevermore!), they also had to stipulate exactly where and how these masses should be said, asking for additional responses and even for different altars during certain days of the week.[69] As obsessive as these requests may seem, they look relaxed next to those of Francisco de Avila Carbajal, who, in addition to requesting a mass during each day of the year and specifying exactly where and how these 365 liturgies should be celebrated, down to the end of time, also drew up a precise schedule that took account of seasonal changes, demanding 10:00 A.M. masses in fall and winter, and 11:00 A.M. masses in spring and summer.[70]

The most obsessively detailed request in this sample, which was made by Francisca Henriquez de Albaniza, the Marquesa of Poza, dwarfs all others and betrays a mind filled with apprehension. First, in addition to requesting a total of 5,320 accumulative masses immediately after her death (3,000 for herself, and the remainder for the souls of others), the marquesa made the following special plea concerning those masses that were to be said for her soul:

I ask my executors, with all my love, that they do as much as possible to ensure that all of these masses be said within nine days of my death, so that Our Lord Jesus Christ may be pleased to accept me with great alacrity into the joy of his presence.

Even though she hoped that these 3,000 masses would get her into heaven within nine days, the marquesa hedged her bets by also setting

[68] AHPM 78.381 (1554).   [69] AHPM 1410.673 (1596).

[70] AHPM 1407.222v (1595). This testator's obsession with his perpetual masses went much further, down to specifying the smallest details of how his grave was to be decorated on nine special feast day liturgies (the kind of cloth, the number of candles); and by whom ("an honest woman"); and how this custodian was to be chosen (by the chaplain); and how much she was to be paid (3 *reales* for each mass, or 27 per year). Not wanting to leave any detail unplanned, he also stipulated how much should be paid to the sacristan for ringing the bell during these masses (500 *maravedis* a year, or about 15 *reales*).

up three perpetual masses a year, to be said *"perpetuamente para siempre jamas,"* on the feasts of St. John, All Souls, and the Assumption. This is a relatively small request for someone of her standing. After all, Pedro de Torres, the man who requested 165 masses a year, had been a mere carpenter, and Francisco de Avila Carbajal, the man who asked for masses every day of the year, had been only an *alcalde* (mayor). What is most unusual about the marquesa's request is her attention to detail and her apparent concern over these three yearly masses.

Although she requests nothing out of the ordinary, so little is left to chance by the marquesa's instructions that it seems almost as if she wanted to be present at these liturgies. For each of the masses she ordered that her grave be covered with a black cloth and that it be surrounded by candles. Then, she asked for a vigil on the evening before the feast, a solemn requiem mass the next day (with deacon and subdeacon), and, finally, a set of sung responses over her grave.

Her greatest concern, however, was reserved for the financing of these masses, which she orchestrated very meticulously. After carefully listing which properties should be used to pay for the masses, she repeatedly urged her executors to arrange for the masses as quickly as possible and constantly reminded them of their duty to honor her requests, much like some unreasonably nagging parent. Yet, this was not enough. Finally, she still felt compelled to add:

If all this is insufficient, then sell whatever you have to sell in order to ensure that, under no circumstances whatsoever, these masses fail to be instituted, said, and performed forever, because this *is* my last will and testament.[71]

This request indicates that the marquesa was genuinely interested in the spiritual benefits offered by these masses, which she considered crucial to her salvation. However, in the requests of other wealthy and powerful testators, especially those who built family chapels, it is more difficult to draw the line between spiritual and worldly concerns.

Family chapels were the ultimate investment in the redemptive system of the church, both in spiritual and material terms. These private chapels, which were constructed within parish or monastic churches, served a dual purpose. In both cases, the chapel altar was the functional focus. First, these niches within the church building served as mausoleums,

[71] AHPM 1810.209–10 (1597).

providing a single, exclusive altar around which entire families could be buried. Second, this private mausoleum with its own altar served as a liturgical center from which perpetual masses could be offered. Without exception, this was a gesture that required an enormous expense and an exalted status. As such, it could be afforded only by those at the apex of the social structure.

The family chapel thus ensured two privileges to those who could afford them. From a worldly perspective, it offered the elite a chance to display their status. From a spiritual perspective, it provided a secure, exclusive place where perpetual masses could be said without interruption. Families with chapels did not have to go begging for their perpetual masses, as did the marquesa. Those who requested perpetual masses without the benefit of a private chapel not only had to find priests who would say them but also a place in which to say them. Often, as will be seen presently, these arrangements proved to be fragile, and the masses would go unsaid. By claiming a specific *locus* within the church building, those who built chapels created a visible reminder of their requests in a functional as well as symbolic sense for both the priests and their neighbors. In every family chapel, the symbolism was as rich as the family buried in it.

As the ultimate privilege, the family chapel fostered the privatization of salvation: It was an institution through which the elite tried to seize their share of redemption in an exclusive manner. In most requests for family chapels, the testators reveal a certain clannishness. As the royal *contador* Diego Alderete and his wife put it, their chapel at the Merced monastery was to be "for us and our descendants . . . and let no one else ever have dominion over it."[72]

At times, however, it is difficult to discern when this exclusiveness relates to anxieties over the afterlife and when it involves more mundane desires. Diego Alderete and his wife displayed an intense interest in the spiritual function of their chapel, asking for an incredibly large number of perpetual liturgies: two masses each day, three requiem masses each week, the nine Marian feast days, and the feast of St. Francis, a total of 896 masses each year! Yet, this same couple also showed a marked interest in having a functional, aesthetically pleasing monument: "The aforementioned chapel should have a vault beneath," they said, "and a very good altarpiece in proportion to its size." Apparently, what mattered most to them was not the content of the altarpiece or its liturgical function but its decorative value.[73] The same was true of Francisco de Avila Carbajal, who left detailed instructions on how, when, and by whom his altarpiece should be cleaned and renovated.[74]

In contrast, Francisco de Berestegui, a knight of the Order of San Juan who also requested a private chapel and a high number of masses, found it impossible to separate the decorative and liturgical dimensions of his altarpiece. In this case, the testator was not content with simply asking for an altarpiece; he left very specific instructions about its contents:

The central figure should be a crucifix . . . and to the right should stand the Virgin Mary, and to the left St. John the Baptist, indicating *ecce agnus dei* [behold the lamb of God]. Next to Our Lady, in the remaining space on this altarpiece, should stand St. Mary Magdalene, St. Ynes, and St. Claire; next to St. John the Baptist should stand St. John the Evangelist, St. Peter, St. Paul, St. Fermin, St. Dominic, St. Anthony, St. Lawrence, and the martyrs St. Cosmas and St. Damian; and on whatever space is then left over in this altarpiece, as many other saints as possible.[75]

To read his instructions for this altarpiece is to come face to face with Don Francisco's belief in the intercessory power of the saints and in the effectiveness of the liturgy. This is much more than an attempt to impress with a large altarpiece: It is an effort to enlist the aid of certain *abogados,* or even "as many as possible," through their symbolic presence at that one physical location where masses are continuously offered for the soul of the deceased.

Should all of this apparent fervor be automatically taken at face value as an expression of genuine devotion or anxiety? To some extent, perhaps, but never unequivocally. Even in the most seemingly devout wills, the interweaving of spiritual and material concerns was far too intense to allow for such conclusions. By the same token, it would also be foolish to single out any gesture as insincere or purely mundane. These were gestures that functioned on two levels simultaneously, as status symbols

---

[73] AHPM 457.1116 (1573). [74] AHPM 1407.244v (1595).
[75] AHPM 542.501–14 (1568).

and redemptive acts. To focus on one dimension at the expense of the other, as if they were antagonistic or mutually exclusive, would be short-sighted.

Nothing points out this interdependence more clearly than the practice of assigning chaplaincies to relatives. By requesting perpetual masses one could not only aid oneself in the afterlife but also one's family on earth. The best way to ensure that perpetual mass requests would be fulfilled was to contract a priest (or priests) to serve as chaplain(s) and assume responsibility for these liturgies. Under such an arrangement, the chaplain would draw a steady income from the estate of the deceased in exchange for his services. In the case of extremely large requests, such as that of Diego Alderete, a single chaplaincy could easily provide a comfortable income for one or two priests. It was a system that benefited both testator and priest: Testators ensured compliance with their requests by putting a specific priest (or priests) in charge of their masses, and the priests enjoyed a steady income from these obligations.

Because chaplaincies could be lucrative, it is not at all surprising that many chaplaincies were assigned to relatives as a means of providing for some priest in the family, usually a son or nephew. In this respect, the request for perpetual masses was a *bequest* in two senses, for two spheres of existence: something given to an heir in this world and something given to one's soul in the hereafter. Such arrangements not only kept the money in the family but also drew on the more immediate sense of obligation shared by relatives. After all, a brother, son, or nephew would be more likely to fulfill these duties than a stranger.

A good example is Isabel Rojas, who asked for one mass per day "forever and ever," and appointed her son as chaplain, designating an income of 4 *reales* for each of these daily masses, an amount totalling 1,460 *reales* a year.[76] This was a decent income, more than twice the amount earned by the average laborer at that time. In other wills, such as that of Inés Manrique, the daughter of the Marques de Cañete, the same amount of money could be used to support two priests. Under the terms set up in her will, two chaplains would serve one week on and one week off, alternatingly, and say one daily mass plus some feast day

---

[76] AHPM 412.388 (1579). This testator very carefully ordered that one of her houses be sold and a trust fund set up to pay for these masses.

masses. Their income from this bequest was to be 25,000 *maravedis* a year each, or 735 *reales*, almost exactly the same as Isabel Rojas's chaplain, only divided between two priests.[77]

Choosing the right priest was no small concern for many of these testators, especially since the chaplaincy was supposed to last until the end of time. To ensure continuity through the ages, most of these testators left complex instructions for their descendants on how exactly to choose these chaplains. Some simply stipulated that the chaplaincy should always go "to the nearest relative."[78] Others tried to foresee every possible situation. One, for instance, dealt with the possibility of having two or more equally close relatives available for this post. In such a case, the post was to be awarded to the eldest.[79] Another testator who faced the possibility of having no priests available in the family was careful enough to stipulate that in such a case, a nonrelative could be selected but that he had to be "an honest priest, who lives a good life, has a good reputation, and is truly pious."[80]

Planning for chaplaincies that would endure forever, *perpetuamente y por siempre jamas*, could get rather complicated for those testators who paid close attention to details. For instance, how would chaplains be chosen by succeeding generations? Selecting someone who could later choose future chaplains was also a great concern. Most often, a *patrono* would be named to choose the chaplains, who could also name his own successor, and so on, down to the end of time. Pedro de Torres considered this problem carefully and decided to choose the prior of San Jerónimo as his *patrono*. This was not enough for him, however. In addition, he also left detailed instructions telling the prior how to watch over the behavior of these chaplains, how to select substitutes in case of illness, and even how to remove them in case of "scandalous behavior."[81]

In such a way, many Madrileños sought to extend their concern for propriety even into the afterlife. This intense preoccupation with chaplaincies and perpetual masses may have been informed by a certain ambivalence toward the power of the mass. This uncertainty, however,

[77] AHPM 286.430v (1579). [78] AHPM 1407.222v (1595).
[79] AHPM 586.500 (1587). The income for this chaplaincy was set at 14,000 *maravedis* a year, or about 412 *reales*, to be derived from the rent on a certain property. The chaplain's duties consisted of three simple masses and one high mass per week.
[80] AHPM 1403, s.f. (1592). [81] AHPM 1410.679 (1596).

was no passive thing but, rather, a strong positive force that invested certain gestures with an increasingly complex value, both in a spiritual and material sense.

Mass intentions

The complexity of this redemptive system was further heightened by the belief that postmortem masses were said not just for the self but also for others. In addition to distinguishing between the different kinds of masses that one could request, testators also had to consider for whom they wanted these masses said. This was a great responsibility, perhaps even a burden, that could not be taken lightly.

In the traditional Catholic theology reaffirmed at the Council of Trent, the doctrine of the communion of saints was inseparably linked to belief in the redemptive power of the mass. As Trent defined it, the souls detained in purgatory were "aided by the suffrages of the faithful and chiefly by the acceptable sacrifice of the altar."[82] In other words, the saints in heaven were not the only available patrons and advocates: Sinners on earth also had the power to help each other escape purgatory, and this power resided in their ability to request masses with a specific intention. Furthermore, since this kind of intercession was so crucial for salvation, and all Christians were commanded to love and assist one another, it was a *duty* enjoined on all good Catholics.

In this manner, the communion of saints involved complex responsibilities. To be saved one not only had to request masses for oneself but also for others. Concern for one's own salvation included concern for the salvation of others, because no one could hope to enter heaven without such works of mercy. Consequently, one was under the *obligation* of looking after the welfare of other souls. Most often, this obligation extended no further than one's own family, but on occasion it could also include nonrelatives, such as benefactors, servants, or neighbors.

Throughout the sixteenth century the list of mass intentions remained more or less the same, with some subtle changes. As could be expected, masses for the self remained the primary concern of most testators. Many also sought to cover all bases at once by requesting masses under

---

[82] "Decree Concerning Purgatory," Twenty-fifth Session, December 1563. *Canons and Decrees of the Council of Trent,* trans. H. J. Schroeder (Rockford, 1978), p. 214.

the catchall category "for myself and my deceased relatives." After the self, testators expressed most concern for parents and spouses. All other possible relations crop up in mass intentions; sometimes they are listed individually, at other times in groups. Nonrelatives are always mentioned by name, without any reason given for their inclusion.[83]

Sixteenth-century Madrileños also requested a more general category of mass intentions. Many a will contains mass requests intended for the "souls for which I am responsible" (*animas que tengo en cargo*).[84] Usually, these were nonrelatives to whom one had promised masses for one reason or another, or other people to whom one was indebted. One shoemaker, for instance, requested masses "for the soul of Juan Marcos, to whom I am under a special obligation because of all the favors he did for me."[85] No other request reveals the continuum of responsibility as clearly. Everyone took on the task of offering masses for the dead, and they also passed on a similar duty to the living. In this system, one took on the burdens of others but simultaneously became a burden for someone else. Those who requested masses for a benefactor, for instance, had the comfort of knowing that the same would be done for them by those they had themselves helped.

Apparently, many testators took this duty very seriously. Quite often, Madrileños displayed their concern by requesting masses "for those who are my responsibility, but whose names I cannot remember."[86] This request shows that what really mattered was not remembering those to whom one was obliged but merely acknowledging that one might be under obligation. This was an attempt to fulfill the letter of the law. Somehow, because God was omniscient and kept His records

---

[83] It was important to mention such people by name, or at least to try to identify them. Francisco del Pino, for instance, seemed disturbed by the fact he could not remember the names of two servants for whom he was requesting masses. About the first, for whom he requested twenty masses, he indicated that all he knew was that this servant was a Basque. For the second, who received ten masses, he indicated he could not even remember a place of origin. AHPM 69.58 (1538).

[84] Some testators showed little patience with this system and tried to cover as much ground as possible with a single request. One such example was Sebastian Martinez de Roguera, Captain General of the Galleys of Spain, who hurriedly requested 100 masses "por mi anima, por mi madre, por mi padre y mujer y difuntos y por animas que tengo a cargo." AHPM 542.71 (1568).

[85] AHPM 1404.492 (1593).

[86] Two of many such possible examples are AHPM 61.338v (1563) and 1403.93 (1592).

straight, it was assumed that these masses would benefit some specific person or persons and that the proper credit would be assigned to the testator. This type of request discloses a palpable anxiety. It seems quite clear that those who made such requests believed that their own souls would be imperiled if they did not meet their obligations to the dead, that they would suffer punishment themselves regardless of how many other masses were said on their behalf. The fact that this is a very formal, impersonal request tells us that the real concern here was not the souls of the deceased but the soul of the self.

Many testators also requested masses "for the souls in purgatory," to include all those who were not specifically mentioned in the will. Some are more specific, reserving their intention strictly "for the neediest souls in purgatory."[87] Basically, this was an act of charity, because it included strangers to whom one was not obliged in any way. The charitable dimension was clearly revealed by Elvira Hernandez, who requested fifty masses "for those souls in purgatory that need them the most, and who are receiving the least amount of assistance."[88] This request reveals two important things. First, through its conception of needy souls in the afterlife who have no advocates among the living, it reveals a genuine conviction in the redemptive power of the mass. Second, as an attempt to earn more merit through a good deed, it further discloses the same anxiety exposed by the other mass requests.

Are there any discernible changes in mass intentions during the sixteenth century? Yes, but of only a limited nature. The most noticeable change is a moderate decline in the number of wills requesting masses for "self" alone: from nearly all testators (96%) in the 1520s to around three-quarters (70%) in the 1590s (see Table 5.4). The same is true of requests for "self and relatives," which decline, with fluctuations, from 26 percent in the 1520s to 16 percent in the 1590s.

At first it would seem that the general trend throughout the century was one in which concern for "self" became slightly less intense, and concern for others increased. Among those intentions that increased, the greatest gain was made (again, with fluctuations) by the "souls under obligation," a category requested by hardly anyone (2%) in the 1520s and by nearly a third of all testators (32%) in the 1590s. It is interesting to note that masses for "the souls in purgatory" increased and decreased

87 AHPM 139.449 (1544).   88 AHPM 541.500 (1581).

Tables 5.4 and 5.5. *Intentions of mass requests in Madrid wills, 1520–99*

Number of testators for each decade in ( ) Intention	Percentage of Testators by decade							
	(50) 1520's	(51) 1530's	(46) 1540's	(46) 1550's	(47) 1560's	(76) 1570's	(54) 1580's	(57) 1590's
For self	96%	96%	90%	92%	90%	80%	81%	70%
For self & deceased relatives	26%	18%	22%	10%	14%	18%	9%	16%
For parents	18%	24%	32%	37.5%	24%	29%	35%	25%
For spouse	2%	8%	18%	12.5%	20%	11%	11%	9%
For other relatives	12%	30%	22%	35%	22%	34%	30%	32%
For non–relatives	6%	12%	20%	8%	4%	7%	0%	9%
For soul under obligation	2%	22%	22%	40%	36%	25%	17%	32%
For souls in purgatory	18%	14%	14%	10%	34%	28%	41%	21%

Intention	Total number of masses and (average) number of masses requested by decade							
	1520's	1530's	1540's	1550's	1560's	1570's	1580's	1590's
For self	2,701 (56)	3,633 (76)	6,580 (146)	5,507 (125)	4,743 (105)	16,657 (273)	12,617 (286)	15,110 (378)
For self & deceased relatives	1,102 (84)	543 (60)	534 (49)	1,381 (276)	924 (132)	10,972 (784)	1,827 (365)	7,678 (853)
For parents	254 (28)	424 (35)	330 (21)	1,148 (64)	367 (31)	713 (32)	1,863 (98)	1,302 (93)
For spouse	30 (30)	122 (30)	414 (46)	173 (29)	153 (15)	349 (44)	662 (110)	1,305 (261)
For other relatives	211 (35)	455 (30)	253 (23)	466 (27)	299 (27)	1,780 (68)	1,008 (63)	3,868 (215)
For non–relatives	20 (8)	60 (10)	156 (16)	20 (5)	50 (25)	380 (76)	0 (0)	373 (75)
For souls under obligation	50 (50)	424 (39)	566 (51)	604 (32)	804 (45)	816 (43)	1,005 (112)	1,580 (88)
For souls in pugatory	103 (11)	90 (13)	113 (16)	68 (14)	368 (22)	843 (40)	539 (25)	358 (30)

quite a bit through the decades but were not much more popular in the 1590s (21%) than they had been in the 1520s (18%), revealing, perhaps, the most constant pattern in sixteenth-century mass intentions.

If one looks at another set of figures, however, the apparent increase in concern for others appears less dramatic (see Table 5.5). When it came to actual *numbers of masses* requested for the various intentions, it seems that masses were not evenly distributed and that the "self" continually reaped the greatest benefits.

In the 1520s the average number of masses requested for "self" was fifty-six. By the 1590s, this number had climbed to 378, nearly a *sevenfold* increase. Similarly, the number of masses for "self and relatives" increased *tenfold*, from eighty-four in the 1520s to 853 in the 1590s. In contrast, the number of masses offered for parents rose from twenty-eight to only ninety-three in the same period, a comparatively slight *three-fold* increase. A quick glance at the actual figures will immediately reveal that, in spite of increases, the quantity of masses offered for other relatives or nonrelatives always lagged far behind those that included "self." Even the masses for "spouses," which enjoyed nearly a *ninefold* increase between 1520 and 1599, still lagged far behind "self" and "self and others" in actual numbers by the 1590s (261 for "spouses" as opposed to 378 for "self" and 853 for "self and others").

So, although relatively more testators requested masses for others besides themselves, the actual number of masses offered for these "others" remained relatively low, indicating a continued preoccupation with the "self" throughout the century. The great increase in the number of masses requested for "self and others" shows that Madrileños were interested in covering as many bases as possible through their mass intentions. By aiming the highest number of masses at an intention that simultaneously included the "self" and one's relatives, many of these testators hoped to profit from the mass in two ways. First, they hoped to be the object of all these mass intentions. Second, they also hoped to gain the merit needed for entrance into heaven, the merit that flowed from the act of meeting their obligations.

The actual numbers of masses intended for "nonrelatives," for "souls under obligation," and the "souls in purgatory" remained very low throughout the century, suggesting perhaps a comparative *decrease* in their value rather than an increase. Masses for the "souls in purgatory" were the lowest of all, numbering an average of eleven in the 1520s and no more than thirty in the 1590s. When one compares these thirty masses to the 853 offered for "self and others," it seems fair to conclude that at best these were a grudging act of charity, at worst little more than a token gesture.

What does all this reveal, if anything? First, the patterns of mass intentions tell us something important about the social context of the redemptive system accepted by most Madrileños. To some extent, most testators seemed convinced by the end of the century that the mass was not only for themselves but also for others, and that they were required to look beyond their own "self" in order to reap the full benefits of the salvation offered by the church. Second, these requests also disclose the fact that, in spite of all other gestures, the "self" always came first in terms of the number of masses requested. Third, these mass intentions reveal a network of responsibilities and obligations that made the living accountable for the fate of the dead. This could be as much of a burden as a comfort, however, and in many ways reflected that already familiar dialectic between confidence and anxiety that was so much a part of Spanish attitudes toward death and the afterlife.

Coping with the inflation of masses

It was one thing to request masses in Madrid and quite another actually to have them said. First, executors did not always fulfill their duties. Sermon *exempla* and devotional treatises contained warnings about lax executors whose dereliction caused them to end up in hell or made them spend extra time in purgatory.[89] We also know that some dioceses threatened negligent testators with excommunication[90] and that some Spanish synods sought to correct this problem.[91] Venegas thought this negligence was rampant in Spanish society and spoke out against it:

Executors and heirs can seldom be counted upon to fulfill a testator's requests, and those that they actually carry out are performed poorly and tardily . . . or

---

[89] Orozco, *Victoria de la muerte*, pp. 180–81, cites an ancient *exemplum* from St. Gregory's *Dialogues* (sixth century). See also Juan Garcia Polanco, "Memoria de las misas que en sus testamentos y por las animas del purgatorio y por otros negocios gravísimos o devociones particulares se dicen" (1625) BNM ms. 18728, n. 9, fol. 44v.

[90] L. Gomez Nieto, *Ritos funerarios*, p. 100.

[91] *Constituciones sinodales del obispado de Segovia, del Consejo de Su Majestad y electo Arçobispo de Çaragoza en el año 1586* (1587), fol. 75.

not exactly in the form and manner the testator would have wanted. And the ears of the heirs grow deaf to the pleas of the testator, who, plagued with torments, cries out from purgatory with doleful laments, *Miserere mei*, have mercy on me.[92]

When it came to pious bequests, good intentions were not enough. For the punishment in purgatory to be lessened, the masses had to be actually said. Alonso de Orozco saw no room for mercy or leniency on the deity's part when it came to pious bequests. His God was not only a stern judge but also the most exacting accountant: Even though heirs and executors who neglected their duties would be duly punished, the wretched testator's time in purgatory would *not* be reduced.[93] It was a frightful formula: No masses, no mercy for anyone.

As if this were not enough, the clergy, too, could fail to deliver their services. Throughout the sixteenth century, as mass requests continually increased, the clergy in Madrid found themselves hard pressed to fulfill their duties. Even as early as 1528, long before mass requests became inflated, there were signs of trouble. A priest, Hernando de la Parra, requested fifty masses for his father at San Ginés but was cautious enough to add: "I ask for these masses in good will, but I do not demand that they all be said, because they [the priests at San Ginés] are overburdened with testamentary requests." One reason he was so accommodating may have been that he himself was overburdened, since he bequeathed some of his own unfulfilled mass responsibilities to other priests.[94]

It seems clear, then, that the parish clergy in Madrid took on many more masses than they could hope to say and that some testators knew that their requests could not be completely fulfilled. This situation was made worse by the inflation in the economy. As the cost of living increased, the masses set up earlier at lower prices could no longer support the clergy. Consequently, it is hardly surprising to find that in 1596, when mass requests were reaching ever higher numbers, some testators paid a higher price for masses than that which was required, creating, as it were, a black market in masses. In one such case, the carpenter Pedro de Torres revealed the mechanism of the inflationary spiral by saying:

[92] Venegas, *Agonía*, p. 132.   [93] Orozco, *Victoria de la muerte*, p. 181.
[94] AHPM 55.728 (1528).

I want to pay five *reales* for each mass, so that they will have a more solid perpetuity, and be said with greater care and punctuality . . . and I do not want this to be considered a simple alm. . . . I want it to carry a greater weight as a salary for the priest.[95]

Here we see the economy of the marketplace invading the world of pious bequests: You get what you pay for. Apparently, one could not hope to please the priests with only 2 *reales* per mass, which was the official price. Pedro knew that his higher fee would actually "carry a greater weight" (*mas fuerza*) with the priests, and provide the proper incentive for them as a "salary," that is, a decent wage rather than a paltry *limosna*, or alm. Conversely, he feared that if he paid the normal fee for his masses, the priest would be forced to take on more liturgies in order to make ends meet, and his masses might go unsaid.

This was nothing new, however. Negligent priests had long been making life and death difficult for the laity. In the early part of the century, cases of derelict priests often came to the attention of the Inquisition. One such case from Guadalajara, not far to the east of Madrid, dragged on for twelve years (1521–33). It involved a certain Alonso Hernandez de la Fuente, a parish priest who was accused of all sorts of misbehavior: not saying his prayers, saying mass without devotion, snapping his fingers during the liturgy, wiping his nose on the altarcloths, and making a ring for a woman friend from a silver crucifix he had melted down. One accuser leveled the following charge, which, like all the others, was denied by Father Alonso: "I do not regard him as a good Christian, for he does not say his masses for the dead, and he usurps the money that is given to him for the performance of all of the church's obligations." Though he was found guilty, Father Alonso was given a very light sentence: to fast and to recite seven penitential psalms in public. If his sentence is any indication of the punishment meted out for such infractions, then it should not seem surprising that the problem of unfulfilled mass requests continued to worsen.[96]

The situation had already reached a crisis point by the mid-1560s

---

95 AHPM 1410.679 (1596).

96 AHN, Inquisición, Toledo, Legajo 225, n. 11. My own survey of lists of trials for the Toledan tribunal suggested to me that the number of cases of clerical abuse was relatively low until the 1570s. From that time on, however, they begin to appear in the ledgers with increasing frequency.

when the reforming spirit of the Council of Trent began to take hold at several diocesan councils. The decrees of these local councils suggest that the system of pious bequests seems to have fallen into disarray, not only in Madrid but in all of Spain. In the second half of the sixteenth century, inflation hit the clergy hard, for it devalued their income. Many priests fell behind or cut corners with their mass obligations at the same time that they began to accept more pious bequests.[97]

In the diocese of Santiago, the Council of Salamanca (1565) had to issue a strong statement reminding the clergy to fulfill their obligations.[98] At the same time, this council also called for restraint on the part of the clergy, who apparently were taking on too many masses. As the council put it, this practice debased the value of the mass:

It would be most useful to find some remedy so that priests would stop saying mass so frequently, because this great ministry has become corrupted . . . and as a result of these customs, little fruit can be drawn from the mass. It seems likely, therefore, that many of these priests have never approached the mass with the appropriate preparation.[99]

The Council of Valencia, which also met during 1565, took up this issue, referring more directly to the problem of unfulfilled testamentary requests, ordering all priests to perform their duties, so that "the pious wishes of the testators may be carried out, and their souls not be deprived of the suffrages owed to them." This council also ordered all pastors to report to the proper church officials the exact number of testamentary masses that had not yet been said by the end of the year, so that some solution could be found for such a problem.[100]

That same year, the Council of Granada set out to correct similar abuses. In their decree concerning pious bequests, the council fathers offered some perceptive observations about this phenomenon:

[97] Evidence of the widespread nature of this problem is beginning to surface. Lorenzo Pinar has uncovered a similar situation, *Zamora*, p. 78, and so has Nalle, *God in La Mancha*, p. 187.

[98] Tejada, vol. 5, p. 317: "Envie con frecuencia el obispo cartas enciclicas en que exhorte a los clerigos, curas y habitantes de los pueblos a que cumplan sus oficios con diligencia, y en cada pueblo ponga hombres sobresalientes en virtud, que hagan las veces de atalayas, y le avisen con cautela de lo que necesite correccion."

[99] Ibid., p. 317.   [100] Ibid., p. 301.

In the churches, monasteries, and pious institutions of these kingdoms there are many mass bequests, divine offices, and other pious works, many of which are never fulfilled for several reasons: because they were instituted very long ago; or because of negligence and carelessness on the part of those who ought to fulfill them; or because so many have been requested and accepted, that it is utterly impossible to fulfill them satisfactorily; or because the funds provided for them are so meager, that they do not seem sufficient for all the care they require. And this common, widespread practice is a very serious problem for this kingdom, since it leads to great disorder, and through it the donations and foundations of many testators are grievously harmed and defrauded.[101]

Although there is no such direct testimony to corruption in Madrid at this time, there is little reason to suspect that the situation could have been much different, especially if one takes into account the population change effected by the arrival of the royal court in 1561 and the subsequent increase in mass requests. Moreover, there is some evidence that this problem was still a great concern within Madrid's diocese almost two decades later.

In 1582, the Council of Toledo devoted a great deal of attention to unfulfilled mass requests. Apparently, the situation was not much different from that described in 1565 by the Council of Granada. First, the Council of Toledo declared that the fulfillment of mass requests was in disarray and ordered an immediate correction of all abuses. Priests were no longer to be allowed to farm out their duties to others; instead, they were under obligation to say their own masses.[102] One Madrid will written by a priest proves that this was a common practice: Among the many debts owed to Father Juan de Madrid, there were two from other priests who had not yet paid him for masses that he had said in their place.[103]

In addition to complaining about chaplaincies, this council also bemoaned the fact that "there are many masses to be said, and no one to say them, so that the requests of testators are not being fulfilled."[104]

[101] Ibid., p. 385.
[102] Ibid., p. 421: "Porque en esta dicha iglesia ay muchas capellanias muy pingües y sacristanias que tienen residencia de choro por constitucion de sus fundadores, se manda que no se pueda servir por substitutos."
[103] AHPM 107, s.f. (1550).
[104] Tejada, vol. 5, pp. 428, 458. In Canon X of this council, the fathers made clear their

The cause of all this, according to the council fathers, seemed to be financial:

It has caused these fathers enormous grief to learn that in some churches a great number of masses are postponed or reassigned to a later time . . . due to the smallness of the alms in relation to the current expensive cost of living.[105]

Although it seemed logical to suggest that these existing requests be reduced, the council refused to consider such a solution. Instead, the council commanded that all testamentary mass requests be fulfilled without delay. To prevent the continuation of this inflationary problem, it also ordered all bishops within the diocese to hold local synods, in keeping with the spirit of the Council of Trent, and to settle upon new, adequate mass prices according to regional needs and customs. The seriousness of this problem is indicated by the fact that the council called for "eternal damnation" on anyone who failed to comply.[106]

What these conciliar documents demonstrate is that the mass requests in Madrid wills were perhaps more of an ideal than a reality – a distant target beyond reach. Certainly, if the abuses were as common as the councils seem to indicate, most testators would have been aware of them and would have therefore known that their pious bequests could go unfulfilled. In other words, if everyone knew that most priests were incapable of actually saying all the masses they took on, then everyone must have also suspected that only a fraction of their entire request would ever be realized. And this is in fact what would be openly admitted in the seventeenth century, as mass requests continued rising. For

---

displeasure with this state of affairs: "Es una iniquidad no cumplir las piadosas voluntades de los testadores; pues es un deber, no solo de caridad, sino de justicia, ejecutar y cumplir en los tiempos prescritos las preces y legados sacros dejados por los fieles difuntos."

[105] Tejada, vol. 5, p. 458. This problem seemed endemic in all of Spain and even in its overseas empire. In that same year, 1585, another council was considering the same problem across the ocean in Mexico. See Tejada, vol. 5, p. 598.

[106] Tejada, vol. 5, pp. 458–9: "Y queriendo el santo sinodo poner remedio a este mal, y quitar la ocasion de que los maldicientes vituperen nuestro ministerio, quiere que a la mayor brevedad se celebren sinodos diocesanos; y manda estrechamente a los obispos, y hasta los conmina con la maldicion eterna, que en ellos, propuesta toda tardanza, y con sujecion al sagrado concilio Tridentino, y teniendo en consideracion los tiempos, lugares, frutos y cargas, si es que con alguna estan grabados los beneficios, decreten por constitucion general, que limosna debe asignarse a cada misa."

instance, in Oviedo in 1606 a reduction in masses took place that was keyed to the monetary value of the pious bequests: For every 10,000 *maravedis* bequeathed for masses, priests were now to say one anniversary mass with vigil and matins, regardless of the original number of masses funded by that income.[107]

In the long run, testators and their heirs did not have much control over pious bequests. How could anyone supervise the clergy or somehow ensure that masses would be said, especially perpetual masses, which were supposed to be said "forever and ever"? One way to ensure compliance with one's will, especially in the case of perpetual masses, was to have some relative act as chaplain. Another was to make sure that the priest received adequate or better than average compensation for his services. One could also take legal action against priests who failed to say masses, but very few testators seem to have resorted to this remedy.[108]

Because there were no adequate or fully accessible safeguards, it seems that most testators could not really do too much to force the clergy to say as many masses as they actually requested. Is it possible, then, that the inflation in mass requests could be directly related to this problem? Could it be that the ever increasing number of masses requested by Madrileños resulted from shrinking expectations about what could really be accomplished? After all, even as early as the 1520s some testators could request a certain number of masses, knowing that they would not all be said.[109] Could it be that testators requested higher, unrealistic numbers so that some lower number might actually be said? Let us consider, for instance, a hypothetical example: some testator who wanted 200 masses but requested 500, knowing full well that it would take an inflated request to obtain his desired number. Is it possible that such practices were partially (or greatly) responsible for the inflation in mass requests throughout the century?

Perhaps, but it would be immensely difficult to prove. If this were

[107] Lopez Lopez, *Comportamientos religiosos*, pp. 138–43. This reduction failed to have the desired effect, for mass foundations continued to fall into disarray throughout the seventeenth century. A second reduction had to be ordered in 1689–90.

[108] Only one will in the entire sample mentions a *pleito* against priests who were not fulfilling their obligations, but it is by no means typical. The testator was himself a lawyer, and the church involved was in Salamanca, not Madrid: AHPM 1403.770 (1592).

[109] AHPM 55.728 (1528).

true, it would not be revealed but would be cloaked by the wills. Moreover, the only other evidence that could be summoned obliquely to confirm these suspicions no longer exists. This other possibility would be the parish records of Madrid churches, where one could compare the actual number of masses said against the number requested. Tragically, most of these archives were deliberately set ablaze in the 1930s as an iconoclastic gesture. The surviving records are far too meager and fragmentary and not at all adequate for the types of statistical searches that would be needed in this case. Consequently, this explanation remains more in the realm of conjecture than of demonstration. A more definite conclusion about the causes of the inflationary spiral in pious bequests will not be reached until additional research is carried out in other locations with undamaged church archives. In the meantime, however, there can be no doubt about this inflation, the abuses it engendered, and the measures taken by the church to correct them. Even without conclusive proof of a cause, these facts are by no means incomprehensible or insignificant.

The inflationary spiral in pious bequests discloses a mounting tension among sixteenth-century Madrileños and some uneasiness in the face of death. This anxiety was fueled to a large extent by ambivalence over the redemptive value of postmortem liturgies. On the one hand, many Madrileños confidently seized on the mass as an antidote to purgatory, but on the other hand, they seemed somewhat uncertain about its purchasing power (much like the coin of the realm). As the number of masses requested grew larger and larger, the value of each individual mass became smaller and smaller. In this way, the economy of salvation reflected the sense of confusion engendered by the larger crisis in the material economy of Spain.

Pious bequests and the Tridentine reform

The disparity between the number of masses requested and the number actually said by the clergy was not the only abuse that caught the attention of church reformers in the sixteenth century. One of the more remarkable changes wrought in popular piety by the reforms of the Council of Trent was the gradual extirpation of devotions that were deemed "superstitious," most notably the *treintanarios revelados,* and those other specific mass cycles known by name, such as the "Misas del

Conde," the "Misas de San Amador," the "Masses of the Five Wounds," and others (see Table 5.3).[110]

The abruptness of certain changes is difficult to miss when one glances at the figures. Whereas more than a third of all testators requested some kind of *treintanario* (a set of thirty masses to be said on specific days) before 1550, hardly any at all made such a request after 1569. The *Misas del Conde*, which were requested by more than a quarter of all testators (26%) in the 1520s, fail to show up in any testament after 1550. Similarly, the *Misas de San Amador*, which were quite popular in the first half of the century, being requested by nearly a third (31%) of the wills in 1540–9, suddenly stop being mentioned in the 1560s, dipping to a mere trace (2 to 3%) in the final three decades of 1570–99. The ancient and ever popular *novenario* (a set of nine masses on nine consecutive days)[111] does not disappear but becomes less favored over the century, shrinking in stages, from 91 percent in the 1520s to 57 percent in the 1550s, and from 31 percent in the 1570s, to 21 percent in the 1590s.

It would seem, then, that Madrileños traded one kind of numerical obsession for another, changing their pious bequests from sets of specific numbers of masses to ever higher and higher unspecific numbers. But there is much more at work here than a preoccupation with numbers. These changes are due, for the most part, to the ecclesiastical reforms that accompanied the Council of Trent (1547–63). In fact, this phenomenon proves that in some instances popular devotions could actually be molded from above by the elite, confirming the assumption of the council fathers themselves, who wanted to supplant the superstitions of the people with their own version of true Christian piety.

Most of these so-called superstitious mass series consisted of complex, detailed arrangements and promised specific results in return for observance of their special instructions. On one level, they were supposed to work very much like a magical incantation: If the proper words,

---

[110] L. Gomez Nieto, *Ritos funerarios*, p. 92, contains a much longer list, possibly because of mass cycles requested in the second half of the fifteenth century.

[111] The custom of having a nine-day mourning period accompanied by food offerings and feasts dates back to pre-Christian times. Though condemned by St. Augustine in the fourth century, it was adopted by Christians in the West. See Fredrick Paxton, *Christianizing Death: The Creation of a Ritual Process in Early Medieval Europe* (Ithaca NY, 1990), pp. 23, 26.

gestures, and material elements were mixed in the required order, then some specific end would be achieved. These mass cycles promised much and demanded a great deal of attention. Generally, they specified which masses ought to be said, on which day, with which prayers, and with how many candles. Take, for instance, the instructions for the *Misas de San Amador,* which were included in the Valencia missal (1492) and the Zaragoza missal (1498), and which promised to be "extremely beneficious to the souls in purgatory." In this formulation, the various elements are to be mixed in the proper quantities and order, much like some recipe or formula: If one desires to free a soul from purgatory, this is what one must have the priest perform:

1. One mass, first Sunday in Advent, seven candles.
2. One mass, Christmas, seven candles.
3. One mass, Epiphany, seven candles.
4. One mass, Easter, three candles.
5. One mass, Ascension of Christ, three candles.
6. One mass, Pentecost, seven candles.
7. One mass, Assumption of Mary, seven candles.
8. Seven masses of the Holy Spirit, seven candles each.
9. Three masses of the Holy Trinity, three candles each.
10. Five masses of the Five Wounds, five candles each.
11. Three masses of the Holy Archangels, three candles each.
12. One mass of the Holy Apostles, twelve candles.
13. One mass of the Holy Martyrs, twelve candles.
14. One mass of the Holy Confessors, five candles.
15. One mass of the Holy Virgins, three candles.
16. One mass, feast of All Saints, three candles.
17. Three requiem masses, three candles each.[112]

Whereas this mass cycle seemed preoccupied with feasts and candles, the so-called Masses of the Five Wounds focused attention on specific

[112] José Luis Gonzalez Novalín, "Misas supersticiosas y misas votivas en la piedad popular del tiempo de la reforma," in *Miscelania José Zunzuneguí* (Vitoria, 1975), vol. 2, p. 293. This formula is different from that recorded by Juan Garcia de Polanco in his manuscript, "Memoria de las misas que en sus testamentos y por las animas del purgatorio y por otros negocios gravísimos o devociones particulares se dicen" (1625) BNM ms. 18728, n. 9. These mass cycles developed substantial local variations.

prayers, going so far as to indicate which psalms should be recited on which days.[113]

Such complex, exact prescriptions had been common in all of Christian Europe throughout the Middle Ages. One of the most widespread and revered mass cycles was that known as the Masses of St. Gregory, or Gregorian Masses, attributed to none other than Pope Gregory I, the Great. As related in his *Dialogues,* the efficacy of this particular cycle had been revealed to St. Gregory by an angel. Because of its ostensibly unimpeachable authority, church reformers did not consider this to be a superstitious cycle, so it remained immensely popular well into the eighteenth century. Curiously enough, however, the Gregorian Masses were not requested by any Madrid testators.[114]

These "revealed" cycles proliferated throughout Europe in the Middle Ages. Because each diocese usually had its own missal and its own minor variations on liturgical celebrations, the cycles varied from place to place. With the advent of printing in the mid–fifteenth century, the publication of missals *secundum usum* (according to the practice) of individual dioceses further intensified local variations in these mass cycles.[115] The greatest difference among these various local missals was not in the order of the liturgy itself or in its prayers but, rather, in the long series of votive mass cycles intended for specific purposes. The possibilities for variation were as innumerable as the ills that can plague the human race. There were masses for specific illnesses, masses for plagues, masses for rebellious children, masses to ward off evil thoughts, masses against lust, and even masses to gain back something that had

---

[113] The cycle of the Five Wounds required five masses on five consecutive days, each in honor of a different wound of Jesus. The closing psalms, in order, from day one to day five were 21, 34, 54, 68, and 109. Once the cycle was concluded, it was deemed advisable also to add a Mass of the Resurrection. See: Gonzalez Novalín, "Misas supersticiosas," pp. 23–6.

[114] *Dialogues* 4.57 (Migne, *Patrologia Latina* 77:416–21) tells how a monk was freed from purgatory by thirty masses on thirty consecutive days. For more on this cycle consult: Gonzalez Novalín, "Misas supersticiosas," pp. 21–3; A. C. Rush, *Death and Burial in Christian Antiquity* (Washington DC, 1941); and T. Maertens and L. Heuschen, *Doctrine et pastorale de la liturgie de la mort* (Bruges, 1957).

[115] A. Odriozola describes the late fifteenth and early sixteenth centuries in Spain as a period in which the liturgy fell into confusion and "near anarchy." See his article "Liturgia: Libros liturgicos impresos," in *Diccionario de historia eclesiastica de España,* 4 vols., plus supplement (Madrid, 1972), vol. 2, pp. 1326–30.

been stolen. Many cycles focused on death and the afterlife, with a certain degree of specialization, almost as if to cover every possibility. There were even special mass cycles for those who had lost the power of speech and could not make a deathbed confession and "for those who see the end approaching due to old age, plague, or bad weather, or any other reason." A missal from Plasencia contained a mass cycle that would have pleased Charles V. It was "for those who celebrate their own funeral before they die."[116]

Criticism of mass cycles was sporadic in the Spanish kingdoms. In 1497, the Synod of the Canary Islands condemned many practices connected with these cycles (such as the lighting of specific numbers of candles) and ordered all priests to stop saying such masses under pain of excommunication.[117] More stringent criticism came from Erasmian humanists in the early sixteenth century. Pedro Ciruelo devoted much attention to this problem in his *Condemnation of Superstition and Sorcery* (1530), lashing out against those who placed faith in "vain ceremonies" such as those included in the formularies for *treintanarios . . . las misas del Conde y las misas de Sant Amador.* It did not matter how many masses were said, he argued, or how, or when, or with how many candles. To place faith in these gestures was "superstition, and a kind of idolatry and sorcery." Worst of all, it was the work of the devil. "When a good Christian writes a will," he concluded, "he should not worry as much about counting the number of masses to be said for him, as he should about the devotion with which they are to be said, whether they be many or few."[118] Alfonso de Valdés attacked these beliefs in a more humorous

---

[116] José Luis Gonzalez Novalín, "Las misas 'artificiosamente ordenadas' en los misales y escritos renascentistas," in *Doce consideraciones sobre el mundo hispano-italiano en tiempos de Alfonso y Juan de Valdés. Coloquio interdisciplinar, Bologna, Abril 1976,* ed. by Francisco Ramos Ortega (Rome, 1979), pp. 283, 289–90.

[117] "Constituciones sinodales de la diócesis de Canarias (1497)," in *El Museo Canario* 15 (1945): 112–31. This synod condemned those who "con simpleza demandan que les sean dichas unas misas que dicen de Santo Amador e otras que llaman del Conde y otras de Sant Vicente, con cinco candelas, e otras con siete e otras con nueve, creyendo que las tales misas no tendran eficacia para lo que desean si no se dijesen con tal numero, con otras supersticiones asi en los colores de las candelas como en el estar juntas o fechas cruz, e otras vanidades . . ."

[118] Pedro Ciruelo, *Reprobación de las supersticiones y hechicerias* (1530), ed. Francisco Tolsada (Madrid, 1952), pp. 127–33. "Maestro Ciruelo," as he is more commonly known, had studied at Salamanca and Paris. He was not only a philosopher and

vein in his *Dialogue Between Mercury and Charon* (1530), in which he ridiculed those who thought they could escape purgatory through certain prayers and liturgies.[119]

At the Council of Trent, these forms of popular devotion were carefully scrutinized. Among the first to call attention to this problem was Bishop Bartolomé De los Martires of Portugal, who wrote a report on liturgical abuses and pleaded: "We must prohibit those so-called Masses of Saint Amador, because of their superfluous ceremonies."[120] Near the closing stages of the council, in July 1562, a commission of seven bishops was formed to study liturgical abuses and propose remedies. Their report on numbered mass cycles was very cautious.[121] Instead of condemning these practices outright, as the Erasmians and Bishop De los Martires had done, the commission sought to walk a tightrope:

It seems an abuse that some votive masses are celebrated with a certain specific number of candles. . . . But one must be very careful in suppressing them because of the devotion that many have in them. It would be best not to focus attention on the number of those masses but, rather, to insist that the masses be said for the living and the dead with the proper devotion.[122]

Apparently, the recommendation of this commission was taken to heart, because reforms were instituted in a roundabout way, without a

theologian but also a mathematician. His *Reprobación* enjoyed enormous success, and at le·st ten editions between 1530 and 1557. Another contemporary treatise on this subject was Martín de Castanega's *Tratado de las supersticiones, hechicerias y varios conjors y abusiones y de la posibilidad y remedio dellos* (Logroño, 1529). For more on this subject, see Menendez Pelayo, *Heterodoxos*, V, pp. 352 ff.

119 Alfonso de Valdés, *Dialogo de Mercurio y Carón* (Madrid, 1954), pp. 53, 197. In this dialogue, Valdés has one character rail against the missals and books of hours that contained "muchas oraciones por idiotas y ignorantemente ordenadas . . . en que se hallaba no poca supersticion y aun idolatria tan manifesta que apenas podia leerlas sin llorar."

120 CT 13.1, 544.

121 CT 8, 720–724 contains the list of abuses presented to the council on 25 August 1562: "Compendium abusuum circa sacrificium missae." CT 8, 916–21 contains the deliberations on this report. The final decree of session XXII (17 September), the "Decretum de observandis et evitandis in coelebratione missarum," is in CT 8, 962–3. A good synthesis of the liturgical reforms of Trent can be found in: E. Cattaneo, *Introduzione alla storia della liturgia occidentale* (Milan, 1969), pp. 308–17.

122 CT 8, 917.

blanket condemnation of *all* numbered mass cycles. Distinguishing between licit and "superstitious" liturgies, the council pronounced the following in its Decree concerning the things to be observed and avoided in the celebration of the mass":

Finally, that no room may be given to superstition, they [the local ordinaries] shall by ordinance and prescribed penalties provide that priests do not . . . make use of rites or ceremonies and prayers in the celebration of masses other than those that have been approved by the Church and have been received through frequent and praiseworthy usage. They shall completely banish from the Church the practice of any fixed number of masses and candles, which has its origin in superstitious worship rather than in true religion.[123]

The work of this commission had a much greater effect on the preparation of the new breviary (1568) and missal (1570) that were later published by Pope Pius V. The new Roman missal, which standardized worship more rigidly by displacing all local *secundum usum* missals, excluded many numerically minded mass cycles. A few years later in 1588, Pope Sixtus V founded the Congregation of Rites, which had the reform and correction of liturgical books as its primary objective. In addition, many of the local missals were included in the *Index of Forbidden Books* precisely because they contained "superstitious" rubrics.

Because the Council of Trent left the actual work of reforming to local churches, it became the duty of local synods to determine which liturgies were legitimate and which were superstitious.[124] In Spain and its colonies, the *Misas de San Amador* and *Misas del Conde* were singled out as superstitious, just as had been done earlier in 1497 by the Synod of the Canary Islands.[125] In some dioceses, such as Zaragoza, special

---

[123] *Canons and Decrees of the Council of Trent*, Session 22, chap. 9, trans. H. J. Schroeder, O.P. (Rockford IL, 1978), p. 151.

[124] *Canons and Decrees*, Schroeder, p. 152, 22nd session.

[125] The Council of Valencia (1565) argued that the prescription for specific numbers of candles "smelled of superstition" (Tejada, vol. 5, p. 288). The First Provincial Council of Mexico (1555) anticipated the reforms of Trent by repeating verbatim the prohibitions of the Canary Islands (1497) but apparently failed to enforce its pronouncements. Thirty years later, at the Council of 1585, the same condemnations had to be issued again (Tejada, vol. 5, pp. 138, 608).

"masters of ceremonies" were appointed to oversee the enforcement of liturgical reforms.[126]

Madrid's wills conclusively prove how effective these reforms really were. Without having to refer to any local synod or ordinance, it becomes immediately evident in the wills that the trentals are wiped out: first, the *Misas del Conde* suddenly disappear in the 1550s, as the Council of Trent was meeting, and then the *Misas de San Amador* vanish in the 1560s, after the pronouncement of Tridentine reforms. In the case of the Conde Masses, the reforms were completely successful; not one single request appears after 1549. The Amador Masses were also successfully curtailed but not as completely. In the 1560s, this mass cycle was requested by only four testators in our sample (9%), a great decline from the 20 percent figure in the previous decade. In the following decades, 1570–99, this cycle continued to be requested sporadically but never by more than one or two renegade testators. It is quite possible that these requests were made by testators who were not aware of the new reforms and that they were simply inscribed by an indulgent notary but never actually fulfilled.[127]

It is no accident that as these "superstitious" mass cycles disappear from the wills of Madrileños, a new devotion also makes its appearance, the *Misa del Anima*, or Mass for the Soul.[128] Suddenly, beginning in the 1570s, just after the Tridentine reforms began to be implemented, this mass appears in 13 percent of the wills. In the 1580s, it was requested by more than half of all testators (55%). By the end of the century, it could be found in nearly two-thirds (62%) of the wills.

The *Misa del Anima* was a special, approved liturgy that could be said to gain the release of souls from purgatory at specific, indulgenced altars. As many of the notaries inscribed the request, this was a mass to

---

126 Tejada, vol. 5, p. 357.

127 Trentals also disappear from the wills in Cuenca between 1575 and 1585, though a few requests for blocks of thirty masses can be found after that. Nalle, *God in La Mancha*, pp. 190–1. In contrast, the Gregorian trental began to gain popularity in Siena. Cohn, *Death and Property*, p. 167.

128 Knowledge about this new type of suffrage was disseminated by the clergy and by the death literature that began to proliferate in the latter part of the sixteenth century. For example, Medina's *Libro de la Verdad*, III, p. 178, was one of the first (1555) to advise its readers to request this type of mass.

be said "at that altar where the souls are rescued from purgatory" (*en el altar donde se sacan animas del purgatorio*). The result promised by this new Tridentine liturgy – based, of course, on traditional principles – was not much different from that of the "superstitious" mass cycles. The big difference, as perceived by theologians and reforming ecclesiastics, was in method rather than objective. This was a liturgy that did not claim effectiveness through the observance of certain magically inclined or numerically oriented gestures but, rather, through the simple redemptive force inherent in the mass itself and through the "power of the keys" granted to Peter and his successors.

The replacement of the Conde and Amador cycles with the Mass for the Soul was an attempt on the part of the church elites to bridge a gap they perceived between popular religion, which had lapsed into "superstition," and orthodox Christian teaching. The wills from Madrid indicate that this was a very successful accommodation, effected practically overnight without much resistance. As the "superstitious" cycles disappear, the acceptable substitute takes over. One reason for such a triumph is the fact that the *objectives* of popular piety were not changed but merely redirected. When one considers the abruptness of the change, it seems as if Madrileños did not care too much for the mass cycles themselves or were convinced of their efficacy. What apparently mattered most was the *promise* of redemption guaranteed by the church, not the method through which the promise was effected.

This phenomenon should not be mistakenly interpreted as sheer docility on the part of the laity or as an indication of their readiness to accept the dictates by the clergy, as if the process of reform were a downward cascade, flowing irresistibly from on high. The process revealed by Madrid wills is more complex, and it is more accurately represented by the metaphor of the tidal estuary, where salt and fresh water flow in from two directions to mix. One must never forget that the clergy, even the bishops, could not distance themselves completely from "popular" religion and that their efforts at reform were never totally alienated from the matrix of beliefs that they shared with the laity.

The liturgical reforms effected in the 1560s were as much an accommodation to so-called popular piety as a repudiation of superstition. Certain gestures were changed, but nothing of substance was changed. No one denied the redemptive power of the mass or even the existence of purgatory, as Protestants had done elsewhere. The wills from Madrid prove convincingly that the traditional system of salvation was not changed, that the basic beliefs remained the same, and that so-called popular piety remained interested in the same objectives.[129] If nothing else, the liturgical reforms of the 1560s seem to have *intensified* popular interest in postmortem devotions by simplifying the liturgical suffrage system and by redirecting public attention to the purported redemptive efficacy of the mass. This was not so much a case of elites versus the common people, or of "official" versus "popular" religion, as of the elites reinvigorating the piety they shared with the common people.

---

[129] What James Banker has said of late medieval "popular" piety in Italy may also be said of Spain: "It was not pagan or heretical, but a lay culture concerned with achieving social esteem at death and remembrance thereafter within a general Christian framework." *Death and the Community*, p. 8.

6

~~~~~~

Aiding the needy, aiding oneself

Most Madrileños seemed to conceive of the road to heaven as literally paved with good intentions and of heaven's gate as flanked by the twin pillars of masses and alms. In the sixteenth century, pious bequests were not limited to liturgies; they also extended to almsgiving.

Death and charity

Throughout the Middle Ages it had been commonly believed that charity was a redemptive act. In some pre-Tridentine Spanish missals from the late fifteenth and early sixteenth century, for example, there was a special liturgy *pro benefactoribus*, in which the collect prayer spoke of charity as a "second baptism" that wiped out sins.[1] Although the theological soundness of such an expression was questionable, this prayer provides us with a good indication of what many medieval Christians were taught to believe about charity. In brief, it was not uncommon to think that one could literally buy one's way into heaven – or at least improve one's chances of ever getting there – through almsgiving.[2]

---

[1] "Deus qui post baptismi sacramentum secundam abolitionem peccatorum elemosinis indidisti . . . fac . . . proemio beatos quos fecisti pietate devotos ut recipiant pro parvis magna, pro terrenis coelestia, pro temporalibus sempiterna . . ." Cited by José Luis Gonzalez Novalín, "Misas supersticiosas y misas votivas en la piedad popular del tiempo de la reforma," in *Miscelanea José Zunzunegui* (Vitoria, 1975), vol. 2, p. 9.

[2] M. del Arbol Navarro discusses the question of possible Islamic influence on funerary almsgiving and in the process provides a summary of such customs in Spain. *Spanisches funeralbrauchtum*, pp. 115–46.

Many medieval testators from northern Castile explicitly stated that they wanted alms to be distributed "for the cure of my soul," or "to evade the gates of hell," or even, as some put it, "to extinguish the flames of the fires of hell." Some scholars who have closely analyzed these medieval Castilian wills have observed that the purpose of many of them was not to feed or clothe the poor but to assure the testators' salvation.[3]

This attitude was further reinforced in the mid–sixteenth century by the Council of Trent, which emphasized "the great necessity of alms-deeds."[4] According to the Catechism of the Council of Trent, the instrument through which all the Catholic faithful of Europe were to be instructed, almsgiving was an act that "redeemed our offenses against man"[5] and that served as "a medicine suited to heal the wounds of the soul."[6]

If charity helped to purify the soul, what better occasion to practice almsgiving than at one's death, when the effects of one's generosity could extend directly into the afterlife? Before the Protestant Reformation called into question the salvific value of all human acts, Christian Europe as a whole had a long-standing tradition of deathbed almsgiving,

---

[3] Luciano Serrano, ed., *Fuentes para la historia de Castilla*, 3 vols. (Valladolid, 1906–10), vol. 3, pp. 108–10, 189–90. I am indebted to Teofilo F. Ruiz for allowing me to read and cite from his unpublished paper, "Feeding and Clothing the Poor: Private Charity and Social Distinction in Northern Castile Before the Black Death." See also Joel T. Rosenthal, *The Purchase of Paradise: Gift Giving and the Aristocracy, 1307–1485* (London, 1972), esp. pp. 11–15.

[4] Catechism of the Council of Trent, Part III, chap. 8, quest. 16 ("What is to be thought of alms?"). In this question, the catechism taught that "God will abhor and consign to everlasting fire those who shall have omitted or neglected the offices of charity, but will invite in the language of praise, and introduce into their heavenly country, those who shall have acted kindly towards the poor."

[5] Catechism of the Council of Trent, Part IV, chap. 8, quest. 9 ("That prayer may be fervent and efficacious, fasting and almsgiving must be added"). Along with prayer and fasting, almsgiving was absolutely necessary for salvation: "This triple remedy was therefore divinely ordained to aid man towards the attainment of salvation; for whereas by sin we offend God, wrong our neighbor, or injure ourselves, we appease the wrath of God by holy prayer; redeem our offenses against man by almsdeeds; by fasting, wash away the defilements of our past life."

[6] Catechism of the Council of Trent, Part IV, chap. 15, quest. 23 ("What are the chief remedies to heal the wounds of the soul?").

and Spain was no exception.[7] When the Council of Trent reaffirmed the redemptive value of charity over and against the Protestant challenge, the attitudes already prevalent in Spain were further intensified.

In medieval and early modern Spain, charitable bequests were an integral part of all wills. By law, all testators were obliged to leave at least a token amount to certain established municipal charities. These *mandas forzosas*, or mandatory gifts, never required a great expenditure. Sixteenth-century Madrileños seldom mentioned the exact amount, merely stating that the *mandas forzosas* should be paid, but occasionally some testator specified the sum. In all these cases, the gifts did not amount to much. In the 1530s, two or three charities would each be given somewhere between 3 to 5 *maravedis*. By the 1560s and 1570s, inflation had raised the sum to as much as 1 *real* for each charity but usually less, about half a *real*. Two decades later, in the 1590s, it had still not risen much higher. These charities, which were selected by urban governments, would be routinely notified of all the pertinent deaths in any given community so that they could send some representative to collect their alms at the home of the deceased.[8] The recipients of the alms varied but were hardly ever specified. The few ever mentioned in Madrid wills were those institutions that aided poor people and orphans, or that paid ransom for the redemption of captives in North Africa.

In the true sense of the word, these token contributions were far from charitable because they were not freely given. However, in spite of the fact that these small sums were taken from every estate by law, as a death tax of sorts, they were still technically considered as alms. This was a formalized, compulsory form of charity that served several practical

---

[7] Among the many studies available on medieval poverty, the following provide excellent summaries and bibliographies: Michel Mollat, *Les pauvres au Moyen Age* (Paris, 1978); *Etudes sur l'histoire de la pauvreté (Moyen Age – XIVe siècle)*, ed. Michel Mollat, 2 vols. (Paris, 1974); Carmen Lopez Alonso, *Los rostros, la realidad de la pobreza en la sociedad castellana medieval (siglos XIII–XV)* (Madrid, 1983); and her more recent *La pobreza en la España medieval. Estudio historico-social* (Madrid, 1986); Linda Martz, *Poverty and Welfare in Hapsburg Spain* (Cambridge, 1984); *A pobreza e a assistencia aos pobres na peninsula Iberica durante a Idade Media. Actas das Ias jornadas luso-espanholas de historia medieval*, 2 vols. (Lisbon, 1973).

[8] Most wills state that the proper charities should come to the testator's house to beg for their alms. One of many possible examples was Maria Gomez, the widow of a farm laborer, whose will simply read: "A las mandas forzosas, un real, que lo ruegen a mi casa." AHPM 542.433 (1568).

purposes, some aimed at this world, others at the hereafter. Aside from the most obvious function of contributing to poor relief, the *mandas forzosas* also provided every testator with certain spiritual benefits. As an act of charity, they obtained merit for the testator, thereby lessening punishment in purgatory. Moreover, this gesture entitled the testator to ask for the prayers of those receiving the alms. Quite often, one finds wills in which the testator insists that the beneficiaries of the *mandas* be asked to "pray to God for me."[9] As was the case with the orphans and poor people who were asked to form part of the funeral cortege, this was not necessarily an altruistic gesture, since it made the needy indebted to the deceased, reminded them of their lower status, and forced them to labor as intercessors.

Altruism and genuine philanthropy had never been the primary objective of deathbed charity in Spain. Throughout the Middle Ages, civil law continually sought to regulate testamentary almsgiving, restricting it in forms that helped maintain the status quo of a rigidly hierarchical, martial, and nobiliary society.[10] Although the law forced all testators to contribute at least a token sum to charity, it also prohibited them from being *too* charitable. Guided by the dictum "charity begins at home," Castilian legal codes in the Middle Ages attempted to protect the families of testators, especially the children and grandchildren, from those who would willingly hand over entire estates to charity in exchange for an assurance of salvation.

The *Ordenamiento de Najera* (1135) made it clear that those who had children or relatives could not donate more than one-fifth of their estate "to their soul," and in 1255 this law was confirmed by a *Fuero Real.*[11] The great legal code of Alfonso X, the *Siete Partidas,* further refined this prohibition, establishing priorities in the ways in which this *quinto,* or fifth, of the estate could be distributed. According to this law, charitable bequests were to follow certain guidelines:

1. Christians were to be helped before non-Christians.
2. Christian captives held by Moslems should receive the greatest attention.

---

[9] AHPM 1410.669 is but one such example.
[10] Teofilo F. Ruiz, "Feeding and Clothing the Poor," p. 9.
[11] "Obras pias y testamentos," *Enciclopedia Universal Ilustrada,* 70 vols. (Madrid, 1928–30), vol. 61, p. 119.

3. Persons imprisoned for debts should be next in line.
4. The appropriate time for almsgiving should be carefully chosen.
5. Contributions should never be excessive or directed solely to one person but should be scattered among many recipients.
6. Relatives should be helped before nonrelatives.
7. The aged should be helped before the young.
8. The sick and handicapped should be helped before the healthy.
9. Nobles or rich people who have fallen into hard times should be helped before those who have always been poor.[12]

In addition to being asked to keep these priorities in mind, Spanish testators were also encouraged to bestow gifts on churches and monasteries and to consider these gifts as alms. Because many testators in medieval and early modern Spain thought that they could fulfill their almsgiving obligations in this way, the amount of aid available to the needy was further restricted.[13]

The structures of almsgiving

Sixteenth-century Madrileños practiced their deathbed charity within the boundaries established by medieval tradition and confirmed by the Council of Trent, thus creating a system of almsgiving with a very limited, closely defined structure. In this system, masses and alms may have been the twin pillars that flanked heaven's gate, but they were somewhat uneven. Whereas nearly everyone invested much in requests for masses, only a moderate percentage of testators ever left bequests for alms beyond the *mandas forzosas*.

This discrepancy may be explained in part by a practical consideration. In many ways, charity was a privilege restricted to the affluent. Whereas nearly everyone who was in a position to write a will could afford at least a minimum of nine masses, not everyone could afford to be charitable beyond the family circle. The *Siete Partidas* had made it clear, after all, that charity literally began at home and that one must attend to the needs of relatives before turning to strangers. To give alms

---

[12] Partida I, 23.7–10, in: *Los códigos españoles concordados y anotados,* ed. M. Rivadeneyra, 12 vols. (Madrid, 1847–51), vol. 2, pp. 310–12.

[13] This, too, was a common medieval practice throughout Europe. See Rosenthal, *Purchase of Paradise,* p. 9.

to nonrelatives with a clear conscience, testators first had to make sure that their families wanted for nothing. In sixteenth-century Madrid, even more than in affluent modern societies, relatively few people considered themselves so fortunate. In the spiritual marketplace, as in the material economy, the wealthy could always afford more: greater numbers of masses and larger charitable bequests. Those who could afford to do so extended their almsgiving beyond the family circle, gaining an even greater merit for their charity. Most others could look no further than the *mandas forzosas,* which technically counted as alms, and the claims of their children, spouses, nephews, nieces, cousins, grandchildren, and in-laws, which lay in a gray area between meritorious almsgiving and the simple redistribution of property.

Madrid wills seem to indicate a gradual, yet noticeable increase in almsgiving as the sixteenth century progressed (see Table 6.1). In the 1520s, for instance, only one-tenth of all testators (10%) contributed to charity beyond the *mandas forzosas.* By the 1590s, in contrast, more than one-third (36%) made similar bequests. This increase may be explained in part but not completely by the influx of the privileged into Madrid after 1561. Between the 1520s and 1540s, before Madrid became a capital city, the increase in almsgiving was already significant, rising from 10 percent in the 1520s to 24 percent in the 1540s. This fourteen-point difference is a higher rate of increase than that which occurred between the 1560s and 1590s, when nobles and courtiers flocked to Madrid. In these later decades, the percentages increased by only eight points, from 28 percent in the 1560s to 36 percent in the 1590s.

This increase in almsgiving seems to be a genuine change in customs. It is not only the number of contributors to charity that increases but also the number of contributions made by each of them. To cite but one brief, revealing example: In the 1520s, only five testators made one charitable bequest each; by the 1590s, in contrast, twenty-one testators made thirty-nine bequests, nearly two bequests per will, or double the figure for the 1520s.

What could have caused this change, and what is its significance? Is the influx of the rich and powerful into Madrid responsible for the increase in almsgiving? Because many of the earlier wills (especially those from 1520 to 1550) do not specify the status or profession of the testators, it is difficult to compare the social profiles of almsgivers before and after the court moved to Madrid in 1561 (see Table 6.2). Nonethe-

237

Table 6.1. *Charitable bequests in Madrid wills, 1520–99*

	Number of Testators by decade							
	1520's	1530's	1540's	1550's	1560's	1570's	1580's	1590's
Number of Wills Sampled	50	51	50	48	50	76	54	57
Number of testators making bequests	5	7	12	8	14	26	19	21
Total number of bequests made	5	7	17	9	23	57	31	39
Bequest Intentions								
Feeding the poor	2	1	1	0	2	1	0	1
Clothing the poor	0	0	0	1	1	2	0	0
Alms for the poor	1	6	5	4	2	5	3	6
Dowries for orphan girls	0	0	0	0	1	5	4	3
Alms for charity children	0	0	0	0	0	2	0	1
Release of debtors from prison	0	0	0	0	0	3	1	2
Contribution to specific church	1	0	2	2	2	2	0	3
Contribution to monastery or convent	0	0	1	2	5	12	9	6
Contribution to Jesuit school	0	0	0	0	2	3	1	1
Contributions to hospitals	1	0	6	1	6	12	9	10
Contribution to confraternities	1	0	6	1	6	12	9	10
Contribution to universities	0	0	1	0	1	3	3	2
Promotion of canonization process	0	0	0	0	0	0	0	1
Redemption of hostages	0	0	1	0	0	2	1	0
Alms For The Poor In Funerals								
Number of poor people: 2	0	0	1	2	0	0	0	0
4	0	3	1	12	4	7	3	0
6	1	1	7	10	10	24	3	5
8	1	1	3	2	4	5	13	8
10	0	0	0	0	0	2	0	5
12	0	1	3	0	2	7	6	4
13+	0	0	0	1	1	1	1	0
Charity Children	0	0	0	5	24	41	29	24

Table 6.2. *Professional or social status of testators making charitable bequests,*
1520–99

	1520's	1530's	1540's	1550's	1560's	1570's	1580's	1590's
Number of Wills sampled	50	51	50	48	50	76	54	57
No. of testators making bequests	5	7	12	8	14	26	19	21

PROFESSION OR STATUS

Nobility	0	1	0	2	2	2	0	4
Attendants at Royal Court	0	0	4	0	3	9	4	6
Civil Administrators	0	0	0	0	1	1	1	0
Lawyers	0	0	0	0	0	2	0	0
Barber/Surgeons	0	0	1	0	0	0	0	1
Priest	0	0	0	2	0	1	4	0
Merchants	0	0	0	1	0	2	2	0
Artisans	0	0	1	1	3	0	1	4
Servants	0	1	0	0	0	0	1	0
Prostitutes	0	1	0	0	0	0	0	0
Unspecified	5	4	6	2	5	9	6	6

less, it seems that some other explanation is needed beyond that of demographic change in Madrid. From the information that *is* available, the following observations can be made.

First, although it is true that nobles and courtiers made up a good percentage of the testators making charitable bequests in the latter third of the century, it is also true that there were testators in the same positions making charitable bequests in the 1530s and 1540s. When the alms of these ostensibly wealthier testators are compared, it becomes evident that the bequests from the 1530s and 1540s are fewer in number and smaller in quantity.

Second, we cannot assume that only nobles and courtiers could afford to be charitable. Throughout the entire century, one can also find artisans, merchants, and cooks – and their widows – leaving alms beyond those required by law. When the bequests of these ostensibly poorer testators are compared, it seems that almsgiving in the latter part of the century was more widespread and more generous than in the first half.

What this evidence seems to indicate is that the increase in almsgiving was not simply a case of more rich people moving to Madrid who could make larger contributions (although this surely had some effect) but also of an increased popularity in testamentary charity, a genuine change in attitude. To some extent, this change reflects the efficacy of the Tridentine reform and its reinvigorated theology of almsgiving.

The distribution of bequests

Because Madrid was not an exceptionally large city throughout most of the sixteenth century, the actual number of institutions that could receive charitable bequests was not very sizeable. Throughout the century, Madrileños continued to list the same institutions as recipients of their charity. As the city began to grow after 1561, a few new beneficiaries began to appear in Madrid wills, but for the most part the patterns of distribution remained fairly constant.

For instance, consider the breakdown between gifts to ecclesiastical institutions or causes (churches, monasteries, convents, and canonization promotions) and gifts to beneficent institutions (hospitals, orphanages, poor houses). Throughout the century, Madrileños contributed more liberally to beneficent institutions than to ecclesiastical foundations (see Table 6.3). The actual distribution of gifts varied from decade to decade but without any significant change in pattern. Without exception, ecclesiastical institutions always received less than half of all charitable bequests.

Among beneficent institutions, hospitals received the largest number of bequests. Feeding and clothing the poor or giving alms to the poor

Table 6.3. *Distribution of charitable bequests: Number and percentage of testators by decade*

Decade	Total number of bequests	Ecclesiastical	Beneficent
1520s	5	1 = 20%	4 = 80%
1530s	7	0 = 0%	7 = 100%
1540s	17	3 = 18%	14 = 82%
1550s	9	4 = 44%	5 = 56%
1560s	23	7 = 30%	16 = 70%
1570s	57	14 = 24%	43 = 76%
1580s	31	13 = 42%	18 = 58%
1590s	39	11 = 28%	28 = 72%

remained fairly constant throughout the century. Beginning in the 1560s and 1570s, during the time when the reforms of Trent began to be instituted, two new bequests appeared in Madrid wills: alms to help release debtors from prison and alms to provide dowries for orphan girls. All of this was in addition to established patterns of helping the needy through the funeral itself, by asking for the participation of orphans and poor people in the cortege.

Among ecclesiastical institutions, monasteries and convents led the list of beneficiaries. Contributions to confraternities, schools, and canonization proceedings remained far behind. The only noticeable change is the sudden appearance of the Jesuit school in Madrid, which began to receive bequests immediately after its founding in the 1560s and even outstripped the University of Alcalá and other well-established institutions.

In the early part of the century, charitable bequests in Madrid were goods rather than currency, reflecting the nearly rural character of the city's economy. In 1528, for example, Elvira Dengorte, a widow, asked that all her linen and clothing be distributed among the poor, and Pedro de Rojas gave someone permission to drink as much of his wine as possible. The following year Juana Lopez bequeathed her best cow to the church of San Juan.[14] In the 1540s, it was still a common practice to make these kinds of gifts: Inés Fernandez gave a chalice, paten, and ciborium for the altar of the Court Hospital chapel, and a bed with one change of linen to the hospital itself.[15] Five years later, Maria Mendez left detailed instructions about the bed and linens she wished to bequeath to another Madrid hospital.[16]

Although such charity was generally replaced by specific sums of money in the 1550s, a few testators continued to ask for the older, traditional bequests. In 1564, Bartolomé Martinez requested that all the poor of Carabanchel, then a village near Madrid, be fed on the feasts of Christmas, Easter, and Pentecost. To do this, he asked that two fanegas of wheat be used, stipulating that the bread was to be distributed "ac-

[14] Elvira Dengorte, AHPM 55.748; Pedro de Rojas, AHPM 55.757; Juan Lopez, AHPM 55.805.

[15] AHPM 136.470 (1540).

[16] AHPM 73.405 (1545). "Una cama para los pobres, que tenga un pergón y un colchón de los de mis casa, y dos sabanas de estopa, y una frazada y dos almohadas con su lana."

cording to the rank and poverty of each person." In addition, he also demanded that three poor people each be given a change of clothing.[17] In 1594, Francisco de Zamora, one of the king's physicians, divided his library between two institutions, giving all of his theology books to the Discalced Carmelites and all of his medical books to one of the colleges of the University of Alcalá.[18] Some testators combined the older traditions with monetary contributions. In addition to listing several exact sums to be given to certain institutions, Beatriz de Valderas, for instance, asked that four of her shawls be given to four poor women. Inez Manrique bequeathed 500 *reales* for the needy and also asked that three poor people (one man, one woman, and one child) be clothed on Christmas. Similarly, Francisco de Manta left 1,000 *maravedis* for the poor and also requested that one of his servants be provided with writing lessons.[19]

The vast majority of all charitable bequests were made in currency, but the amounts and intentions varied immensely. Some testators selected the recipients and decided on very precise gifts, suggesting some degree of concern. Diego de Herrera, for instance, bequeathed 26 *reales* to feed one poor person for an entire year (at the minimum subsistence rate of 0.5 *real* per week).[20] Juan de Salcedo, a royal librarian, left a much more generous gift of 400 *ducados* to be divided equally between four orphan girls.[21] Francisco de Rojas and his wife carefully stipulated that they wanted five poor people (three women and two men) to receive 5,000 *maravedis* each and insisted that these people had to be "the neediest that could be found wherever we happen to die."[22] Francisco de Berestegui, a Knight of Santiago, left detailed instructions explaining how 10,000 *maravedis* were to be given every year "forevermore" to a poor girl in his native Palencia.[23] Isabel Gutierrez, the wife of a merchant, made even more complex arrangements to ensure that the poor of

---

[17] AHPM 314.308 (1564).   [18] AHPM 626.539 (1594).

[19] Beatriz de Valderas, AHPM 457.1227; Inés Manrique, AHPM 286.426 (1579); Francisco de Manta, AHPM 105, s.f.(1540).

[20] AHPM 139.375 (1544).   [21] AHPM 412.464 (1577).   [22] AHPM 136.216 (1540).

[23] AHPM 542.504 (1568). The poor girl was to be chosen by his direct heir, in conjunction with the priors of the Dominican and Franciscan houses, and announced every Easter Sunday. In addition to the yearly sum, this girl was to be given a dowry "para ayudarla casar."

San Miguel parish would be fed nine days a year, "forever and ever," during the nine feasts of Mary.[24]

Some testators took these charitable bequests seriously and made generous gifts. The wife of one silversmith left 50 *ducados* to be divided equally between five poor parishioners of San Ginés.[25] Another silversmith's wife bequeathed over 180 *ducados* to sixteen different charities.[26] The widow of Hernando Pizarro distributed more than 100 *ducados* to charity, including gifts of 200 *reales* to each of three hospitals and one orphanage.[27] Gregorio de Oviedo, who referred to himself as "an unworthy priest," made twenty-two bequests totaling more than 181,140 *maravedis* (5,327 *reales* or 484 *ducados*). Isabel de Rojas topped Father Gregorio and almost every other testator in our sample by making twenty bequests totaling more than 1,200 *ducados!*[28] Those who were very wealthy could afford to make grand gestures. A good example was Antonio Josepfe, Viscount of Milan, who used his entire estate to establish the Italian Hospital in Madrid.[29]

Not all testators were as careful or generous. Some who cared much more for their own souls than for the poor made gifts that were no more than impractical token gestures. Benito de Carabanchal, a man who requested ninety-three masses for himself and his parents, left a paltry 5 *reales* to the church of San Pedro. Juan Ortiz spent more than 70 *reales* on masses but bequeathed only 8 *reales* to San Francisco. Alonso Ramirez proudly listed gifts of 1 *ducado* for the Anton Martín hospital and 1 *ducado* for the *Arrepentidas* (reformed prostitutes): meager sums, especially when compared to the more than 300 *reales* he spent for masses. Guillén Corvera, an artisan, requested more than 100 masses for himself and his relatives but left no more than 2 *ducados* each for his con-

[24] AHPM 586.500 (1587). Doña Isabel arranged for a certain piece of land to be used to grow wheat "para que siempre se gaste y distribuya perpetuamente para siempre jamas en el dar de pan a los pobres por los dias de Nuestra Señora que son nueve fiestas." To remind the priests of San Miguel of their duty, she also arranged for them to collect twenty fanegas of wheat initially, as soon as she died, and one fanega of wheat afterward, each of these nine times a year.

[25] AHPM 147.215 (1552).   [26] AHPM 457.1227 (1573).

[27] AHPM 1810.734 (1598).

[28] Gregorio de Oviedo, AHPM 457.1219 (1573); Isabel de Rojas, AHPM 412.388 (1579).

[29] AHPM 1412.737 (1597).

fraternity and the Anton Martín hospital.[30] No other testator was more parsimonious than Father Blas Nuñez, a priest who spent more than 700 *reales* on masses for himself but bequeathed only 1 *real* to a hospital.[31]

In most of these wills it is hard to discern genuinely disinterested charity or altruism. Many of these gifts, from the largest to the smallest, served multiple purposes and stood squarely in a gray area halfway between charity and self-interest. First, many gifts that were considered *limosna* were aimed solely at ecclesiastical foundations. In this way, much of what was called "charity" did not directly help the poor. To aid the church and to contribute to the promotion of the sacred was no different from giving money to the poor. Hence, it is possible to find testators such as Inés Fernandez, who could list her *limosna* as one bed for the royal hospital and a new set of sacred vessels for the altar of the royal chapel. In the same way, Mariana de Villanueva could not distinguish between helping the needy and contributing to the church. Although she bequeathed 60 *reales* to two hospitals to help the poor, she also contributed the same amount to purchase a new vestment for the image of Our Lady of the Remedies at the monastery of La Merced and an additional 30 *reales* for the shrine of Our Lady of Atocha.[32]

Moreover, because church teaching and popular piety reinforced the idea that charity was a mandatory gesture, something everyone must practice in order to escape damnation and punishment, it is not surprising that some testators practiced a grudging sort of philanthropy. Fernan Perez de Lujan, a Knight of Santiago, made no effort at all to seem unselfish: "Since today . . . I am *obligated* [my emphasis] to give a bed with linens for the poor, I hereby request that my executors give 4,000 *maravedis* for this purpose, as they deem best."[33] Charity, then, could be something one owed, an obligation, not a gift freely given.

If charity was often viewed as a duty or a contractual gesture of sorts, then it was not unreasonable to think of alms as a debt. Consequently, it

---

[30] AHPM 1404.275 (1593). With its gift of 2 *ducados*, the hospital could have purchased only *one* of the following items: forty small (two-ounce) candles; or thirty-one pounds of mutton; or five *arrobas* of wine; or slightly over one *fanega* of wheat.

[31] Benito de Carabanchal, AHPM 73, 78 (1542); Juan de Ortiz, AHPM 144.475 (1549); Alonso Ramirez, AHPM 746.21 (1579); Blas Nuñez, AHPM 571.13 (1581).

[32] Inés Fernandez, AHPM 136.470 (1540); Maria de Villanueva, AHPM 567.1950 (1579).

[33] AHPM 107, s.f. (1549).

is not surprising to find some testators who could not distinguish between alms and the debts they owed to others. Every will was supposed to include a section in which one's debts were detailed in order to clear the soul's path to salvation. In some wills, however, the list of debts to be paid merges with the list of alms to be given, and the two become so intertwined as to be indistinguishable. Juan Lopez de Garavato, for example, listed his gifts to charity alongside the money he owed to some of his neighbors, and simply asked his executors "to pay what I owe . . . lest my soul suffer for it."[34]

Miguel de Jéronimo, a silversmith, blurred the lines between debts and charity even further. Because he did not have enough money to pay back his creditors, he boldly stated in his will, he wanted to substitute this debt with a contribution of 100 *reales* for the poor. Apparently, he had no trouble thinking that the merits of this action and his debts were interchangeable.[35] Whether his creditors shared his view is another question. The merchant Gomez Guerrero actually considered alms to serve as an expiation for his debts. After requesting that 30 *reales* be given to three hospitals, he frankly admitted that he wanted these alms to cover whatever debts he might have still owed but forgotten.[36]

The true outlines of charity seemed even more blurred from another perspective. Quite often, testators took to heart the dictum that charity begins at home, listing as alms those gifts that they bequeathed to their relatives. Juan de Salcedo had no qualms about calling a *limosna* those funds he set aside as a dowry for an illegitimate daughter. Diego de Ortega, a court official, counted as alms the 150 *ducados* bequeathed to three of his nieces. Inés de Rivadeneyra set up a fund to pay 3,000 *maravedis* a year to two of her sisters and one cousin, all of whom were nuns, and included this gift among her alms. Gregorio de Oviedo also listed as alms the 100 *ducados* with which one of his nephews, a priest, was to be paid for saying certain masses.[37]

Strictly speaking, Father Gregorio was fully entitled to count his 100 *ducados* as *limosna* because masses were technically said in exchange for alms, not for a fee. This brings us to yet another further blurring of the

---

[34] AHPM 55.894 (1530).
[35] AHPM 61.451 (1563).   [36] AHPM 390.609 (1584).
[37] Juan de Salcedo, AHPM 566.30 (1579); Diego Ortega, AHPM 800.1168 (1581); Inés de Rivadeneyra, AHPM 586.500 (1587); Gregorio de Oviedo, AHPM 457.1219 (1573).

line between charity and self-interest. Because alms placed the recipient in debt to the giver, testators could always demand spiritual favors from those on whom they bestowed their charity. To a considerable extent, almsgiving was an exchange of services in which both parties enjoyed some benefits. The needy, of course, received some immediate material assistance. The benefactors received an intangible but no less significant set of blessings in return: the intercessory prayers of those who had been helped and the merits accrued in heaven by all charitable gestures.

The vast majority of all wills demonstrated a keen interest in seeing some return on their almsgiving. Practically all testators who made charitable bequests also pointed out carefully that the recipients of their gifts should pray to God for the testators' souls. Hardly a bequest fails to be accompanied by the proviso *que ruegen a Dios por mi anima*. Felipe Marichal, a Flemish servant of King Philip II, knew his rights as a benefactor. When he left 100 *ducados* to free poor and honest debtors from prison, he stipulated "that their consciences be charged, because this is an alm and a meritorious work."[38] Francisco de Guara also knew what he deserved as a charitable Catholic. "I bequeath 100 *ducados* to the poor beggars of this parish," he said, "for the better healing and cleansing of my conscience . . . so I may enjoy all the graces, indulgences, and privileges that are granted in return for this by the Apostolic See."[39]

Because all alms given to the church were as meritorious as those given to the needy and all served as an exchange for spiritual benefits, testators often made bequests that aimed specifically to gain these favors, especially in regard to masses. When Gregorio de Oviedo listed each of the twenty-two charities to which he gave alms, he made sure to repeat the same phrase at the end of each listing, "that they may say masses for my soul."[40] Catalina Sanchez gave 100 *ducados* to the monastery of La Merced, "so that the monks may be obliged to say four high masses for my soul every year."[41]

This desire to exchange alms for masses was most intense among those testators who made gifts to the Jesuit school. Because the Society of Jesus prohibited its priests from taking on the responsibility of saying masses for the dead, so that they could devote their undivided attention

---

[38] AHPM 1407.105 (1595).   [39] AHPM 457.1072 (1573).
[40] AHPM 457.1219 (1573).   [41] AHPM 586.229v (1587).

to preaching and teaching, the Jesuits in Madrid were under no obligation to say masses for anyone. Still, the contributions poured in. Undeterred by the rules of the Society, testator after testator made bequests, and then pleaded for the "special" favor of masses. Maria de Gribaja, for instance, left 200 *ducados* to the Jesuit fathers, "without obliging them" to say masses but still asked "that they may say at least some masses for me." Beatriz de Valderas, perhaps encouraged by the same notary, made exactly the same request "without obligation" in exchange for her 40 *ducados*.[42] Francisca de Jara, whose own brother was a Jesuit, made the most eloquent plea:

I bequeath one hundred reales to the school of the Society of Jesus, and I ask, for the love of Our Lord, that the rector and fathers of this school, without any obligation whatsoever, may say some masses for me, and apply to me the indulgenced graces that some of them have, and I ask all this because of the great love and devotion I have for them.[43]

In this way, the charitable bequests of many testators betrayed a certain dimension of self-interest. As had been the case throughout the Middle Ages in Castile, much of charitable giving was aimed at gaining spiritual favors or at communicating a message to the poor about their own dependence and lack of self-worth.[44] Many of the bequests made by sixteenth-century Madrileños openly asked for prayers and intercession in return from the poor or sought in some way to confirm and display the social status of the benefactor. Madrileños believed in the salvific power of almsgiving, but in death as in life they assigned a very broad meaning to the term "charity," and sought to derive as much personal gain as possible – in this world as well as the next – from each *real* bequeathed as *limosna* in their wills.

[42] Maria de Gribaja, AHPM 457.1160 (1573); Beatriz de Valderas, AHPM 457.1227 (1573).
[43] AHPM 457.1198 (1573).   [44] Ruiz, "Feeding and Clothing the Poor," p. 35.

Conclusion

In one scene from *Don Quixote*, Sancho Panza becomes trapped in a cave and begins to shout for help. When Don Quixote finally stumbles upon the cave and hears Sancho's desperate cries for help, he immediately thinks he is hearing the voice of a dead person. "If you are a suffering soul, tell me what you want me to do for you," says Don Quixote, "for since it is my purpose to aid and favor the needy in this world, I shall also assist and relieve the needy in the other world who cannot help themselves." When he dimly recognizes Sancho's voice, his offers of otherworldly assistance intensify and become more specific. In the process of explaining what he can do for the dead Sancho, Cervantes's mad knight succinctly summarizes the attitudes and behavior analyzed in this book:

If you are Sancho Panza and you have died, and, if by the mercy of God you have not been taken away by the devils, and are now in purgatory, there are plenty of suffrages offered by our holy mother the Roman Catholic Church that can rescue you from your present torment, and I shall obtain these from her, with whatever is available from my estate.[45]

It is no trivial matter that in Cervantes's *Don Quixote* the hero of the novel should proclaim "I am . . . he who professes to aid and succor both the living and the dead in their needs," and that he should pledge to mortgage his entire estate to rescue a single soul from purgatory. Like Don Quixote, sixteenth-century Madrileños were willing to spend

---

[45] Cervantes, *Don Quixote*, Bk. II, chap. 60 (Barcelona, 1975), p. 918. A similar statement is made earlier by Don Quixote to someone else: Bk. II, chap. 48, p. 862.

abundant time and money on the dead, and in such a fashion as to make this-worldly concerns nearly indistinguishable from other-worldly concerns. Two indisputable facts emerge from the testamentary discourse: that Madrileños had devised clearly defined and complex strategies for dealing with death and that they conceived of death and the hereafter as intricately bound to earthly life. The vast majority of the testators studied here thought there was much they *could* and *should* do for themselves and for others in the afterlife, and they envisaged post-earthly existence as intermeshed with the social realities of their world. The *aquí* (here) and the *mas allá* (hereafter) were not far from each other in a double sense: What one did in this world could have a direct impact on the other world, and, at the same time, what impressed God also impressed one's neighbor. Consequently, commerce between the living and the dead could not be much different from commerce in the earthly marketplace, and inflation in the monetary economy could also mean inflation in the economy of salvation. Also, because they understood the Heavenly Court where they would be judged as being similar to the earthly court that was so near to them, it stands to reason, then, that their attitudes and behavior toward death should have somehow been affected by the increased presence of the king and his court after 1561.

It has been said that the history of death rites reveals the sheer intricacy of how ritual and society define each other.[46] The history of funeral customs and postmortem devotions gleaned from Madrid's wills reveals a mentality that was simultaneously interested in salvation in the hereafter and in status and rank in this world. At century's end, the grim reaper could still be portrayed as the great leveler, relentlessly mowing down the great and the small. "In death we are all one," said Rebolledos in 1600, "it treads us all down equally."[47] But death was no great leveler in sixteenth-century Madrid, at least not in regard to what Madrileños thought they could do for the dead. In myriad ways, death ritual was an extension of the status quo: The more you had to spend, the better your funeral and your pious bequests and the quicker your release from purgatory. Because funerals and suffrages depended on the economic capacity of the testators, the ever growing cult of the dead in sixteenth-century Madrid was a phenomenon activated by the amount of money

[46] Strocchia, *Death and Ritual*, p. 238. [47] Rebolledos, *Oraciones fúnebres*, fol. 12.

available at the time.[48] There can be no doubt whatsoever that in sixteenth-century Madrid, death ritual expressed socioeconomic realities and salvation was intimately connected with property.[49]

This interweaving of the sacred and the profane should not be mistaken for a lack of sincerity or as a masking over of materialistic concerns. In the sixteenth century, it was the Protestants north of the Pyrenees who conceived of "material" and "spiritual" as polarities; Spanish Catholics, as a rule, saw the two spheres as intimately related, and they were not inclined toward polarization in their ritual life. On the contrary, their piety sought to blur the lines between the this-worldly and the other-worldly, to sacralize the mundane. To say, as one recent study of death rites in Zamora has, that "these rituals disclose a world of material concerns or of prestige covered by a veneer of spirituality," is to engage in a perilous kind of reductionism.[50] The social and economic dimension of death rites in Madrid was no veneer, no thin transparent coating over a more substantial item, no epiphenomenon, no disguise for some deeper socioeconomic processes.[51] On the contrary, the "materialism" of these death rites was their very structure, and it was also part of their essence. Not to grasp this is to misconstrue the ethos of early modern Spanish Catholicism. Myth and ritual, belief and piety were inseparable from the existing social structures that defined them, but their ultimate goal was to find transcendence through the things of this

---

[48] A similar observation has been made about death rites in Valladolid by Maximo Garcia Fernández, "Vida y muerte en Valladolid. Un estudio de religiosidad popular y mentalidad colectiva: los testamentos," in *Religiosidad popular*, vol. 2, pp. 232–3, 240.

[49] Sara Nalle makes the same observation about Cuenca in the sixteenth and seventeenth centuries: "Salvation was a matter of property. The poor might take comfort in the teaching of the Gospel, but the rich knew that the way to heaven was paved with suffrages." *God in La Mancha*, p. 182.

[50] Lorenzo Pinar, *Zamora*, p. 92. Against such a notion of religion stands the observation of Edmund Leach: "Most people in most societies have only the haziest ideas about the distinction between sacred and profane or between rational and nonrational; it is a scholastic illusion to suppose that human actions are everywhere ordered according to such discriminations." *International Encyclopedia of the Social Sciences*, "Ritual," vol. 13, p. 526.

[51] Victor Turner understood the transcendent dimension of all ritual to be its central meaning and cautioned, "We have to put ourselves in some way inside religious processes to obtain knowledge of them." *Revelation and Divination Among the Ndembu* (Ithaca NY, 1967), pp. 31–2.

world. Though there were probably some Madrileños for whom this transcendence was lacking, there were many others for whom it seemed abundant.

Paradox was central to this religious mentality. So was the notion of hierarchy. Matter and spirit were deeply interconnected – as were heaven and earth – but more in an emotional than rational sense. Ultimately, the two spheres were simultaneously compatible but unequal, and it was the spiritual realm that was considered ontologically superior. The ultimate promise of redemption held out to sixteenth-century Madrilenos was one in which a highly spiritualized material body would inhabit heaven for eternity. Though most of these sixteenth-century testators seemed certain that death would take them straight from Madrid to purgatory, they showed themselves eager for heaven: eager not only in the sense of longing but also of action, as people who worked hard to gain a highly desired place in paradise, at the Heavenly Court. In Castilian Spanish one could say that these Madrileños were *empeñados al cielo,* a rough equivalent of "eager for heaven," a phrase that conveys a double meaning and brings us naturally closer to the attitudes we are studying here, for it speaks simultaneously of emotional and financial investments. *Empeñar* is not only to persist but also to pawn. Our Madrileños were not only bent on heaven but also in hock to heaven: They hoped their souls would be redeemed by their efforts. Though few, if any, of the testators studied here hoped to go directly to paradise, most of them literally pawned part of their earthly fortune in exchange for a briefer passage through purgatory.

BOOK TWO

The king's dissolving body
Philip II and the royal paradigm of death

When we leave the world and are put underground, the prince
follows as narrow a path as the common laborer and the Pope's
body takes up no more earth than that of the sacristan, though one
be a loftier person than the other; for when we enter into the grave
we squeeze and compress ourselves, or rather we are squeezed and
made smaller, whether we like it or not.

– Sancho Panza[1]

[1] *Don Quixote,* Bk II, chap. 33 (Barcelona, 1975), p. 772.

King Philip and his palace of death

In 1595, three years before the death of Philip II, William Shakespeare staged the first performance of his political play *The Tragedy of King Richard II*. It matters little to us now that Spain and England were the bitterest of enemies at the time, a scant seven years after the debacle of the Armada. What Shakespeare said then about the death of kings had the ring of universal truth and could have been applied to Queen Elizabeth as much as to Philip II or any other monarch:

> For God's sake, let us sit upon the ground
> And tell sad stories of the death of kings . . .
> for within the hollow crown
> That rounds the mortal temples of a king
> Keeps Death his court, and there the antic sits,
> Scoffing his state and grinning at his pomp
> Allowing him a breath, a little scene,
> To monarchize, be fear'd and kill with looks,
> Infusing him with self and vain conceit,
> As if this flesh which walls about our life
> Were brass impregnable, and humour'd thus
> Comes at the last and with a little pin
> Bores through his castle wall, and farewell king![2]

[2] William Shakespeare, *Richard II* (III, 2).

El Greco, *The Dream of Philip II*, 1578–80. Also known as *The Adoration of the Holy Name of Jesus* and *Allegory of the Holy League*.

Although Philip II disliked this painting, it reveals much about his character. El Greco here depicts the Spanish monarch kneeling before the presence of Christ, accompanied by other members of the Holy League formed to fight against Turkish expansionism. Philip is here engrossed in prayer before the divine, poised between heaven and hell. Purgatory is depicted as a bridge to the afterlife, directly above the jaws of hell.

Pondering the death of kings

There is something uniquely tragic about the death of kings, especially those who are powerful or have reigned a long time. When kings die, everyone is reminded of the universality of death and the ultimate feebleness of all human power. The death of a king teaches a lesson in mortality: By meditating upon the demise of kings, every individual can realize the awful truth that death is the ultimate victor over all human effort and ambition. As another English poet phrased it in the eighteenth century:

> The boast of heraldry, the pomp of pow'r,
> And all that beauty, all that wealth e'er gave
> Await alike th'inevitable hour.
> The paths of glory lead but to the grave.[3]

Though many of Philip's contemporaries did not necessarily sit upon the ground, as Shakespeare advised, to tell sad stories about his passing, they certainly took a profound interest in the details of his death. Some undoubtedly sat upon comfortable chairs to write the story, while others labored in printing shops to publish detailed meditations upon the event. Just as Philip's mother's corpse had brought Francis Borgia face to face with death, Philip's dissolving flesh now compelled his subjects to ponder their own mortality.

What is most remarkable about the death of Philip II is not the event itself, as gruesome and pathetic as it is, but the amount of attention it received from contemporaries. Even more significant than the *amount* is the *kind* of attention paid to it in numerous treatises published in Spain and the rest of Western Europe. It might be fair to say that the death of no other monarch or public figure in early modern European history ever attracted as much attention as that of Philip II. The obvious question to ask, then, is why this should have happened.

The death of Philip quickly assumed a mythic quality: Although it was a portentous historical event and was celebrated as such, it soon began to be viewed as a phenomenon that pointed beyond itself toward larger questions dealing with attitudes toward mortality and the royal person.

---

[3] Thomas Gray, "Elegy Written in a Country Church Yard," *The Norton Anthology of Poetry*, Shorter Edition, ed. Arthur M. Eastman (New York, 1970), p. 208.

In brief, the story of the king's death became more than a narrative: It became a lesson in death and the art of dying and a convenient vehicle for religious and monarchical propaganda. The fact that so many unpleasant and humiliating details should have been made public immediately after the monarch's death says something in and of itself. What possible good could the monarchy derive from having the public know, for instance, that Philip II practically rotted away in his own excrement? Or to meditate upon other graphic horrors, as summarized in a funeral sermon:

Oh, what kind of lesson has this recent one been for all mortals: to see such a great monarch dying for so many days and weeks, lingering, suffering, agonizing, gushing forth pus through all the holes that burst open in his body, in that cleanest, most fastidious, and most esteemed body?[4]

There is more at work here than curiosity about the royal person or morbid interest. We know so much about the details of Philip's final agony because it served several important functions, not the least of which was the promotion of certain attitudes toward death, religion, and the monarchy.

But to understand these attitudes one must begin at the place where Philip ended, at the Escorial, his unique monument to the correlation of death with architecture, sacrament, and kingship.

The Escorial as message

On the night of 30 August 1595, in the very center of the Iberian peninsula, at the foot of the rocky Sierra de Guadarrama, about thirty miles northwest of Madrid, a wondrous spectacle unfolded before the eyes of all those who were present at the royal court of the ailing King Philip II. The enormous, imposing building of San Lorenzo del Escorial, which had been under construction for thirty-two years and which some contemporaries were already hailing as the "eighth wonder of the world," was readied for consecration on the feast day of its patron,

---

[4] The royal preacher Alonso Cabrera, funeral sermon preached at the monastery church of San Domingo, Madrid, 31 October 1598, in *Sermones funerales en las honras del Rey Nuestro Señor don Felipe Segundo*, recogidos por Juan Iñiguez de Lequerica (Madrid, 1601), BNM 2-57997.

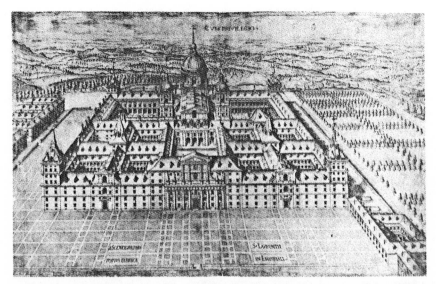

Bird's Eye View of the Escorial. Drawing by Juan de Herrera, engraving by Pedro Perret, 1587. Reproduced in Luis Cervera Vera, *Las estampas y el sumario de El Escorial por Juan de Herrera* (Madrid, 1954).

Saint Lawrence. Six thousand pottery oil lamps were carefully arranged along the entire façade of the edifice, on every ledge, window, and gable, around its great central dome, up in all the towers and steeples, even on every one of the decorative spires and balls that crown its higher reaches. Though most of the workmen who installed these lights were "as full of wine as the lamps were full of oil,"[5] no one was injured, and the celebration got under way quickly and flawlessly at dusk. In the dark night, the Escorial glowed with an ethereal splendor. To one observer, Fray José de Siguenza, the very stones seemed luminous. For him, this was an apocalyptic moment, a hierophany, an irruption of the sacred. "It did not seem to be an earthly thing," he said. "Anyone who saw it would have to swear that it looked very much like the holy city of Jerusalem which the Apostle saw descending from heaven."[6]

[5] Fray José de Siguenza, *Fundación del monasterio de El Escorial* [1602] (Madrid, 1963), p. 145.

[6] Ibid. According to the now classic interpretation of Mircea Eliade, Siguenza was merely giving voice to one of the central assumptions of European and Asian religion:

The king's dissolving body

King Philip II had carefully planned the building of this complex structure to serve multiple interrelated functions. It was a royal residence and retreat, as well as a holy shrine that contained over 7,500 relics, a monastery, and a place of learning. Philip not only assembled a great library at the Escorial but also established a school for the training of clergy and even provided these clerics with their own hospital and botanical gardens. Above all, however, the Escorial was a necropolis, a mausoleum for the Hapsburg dynasty, and its many functions revolved around a central focus: death. The place was dedicated primarily to serving the material and spiritual needs of the dead Hapsburg kings and their immediate families according to Roman Catholic belief and practice.

King Philip had invested much of himself in this building, taking a keen interest in even the smallest details of its design. He had been most keenly interested in its mortuary function and in the assembling together of his dynasty's corpses, which, very much like the stones quarried from various regions of the Iberian peninsula for use in the building's construction, were ceremoniously hauled to that geographical and symbolic center from distant, scattered graves: from Valladolid, Tordesillas, Granada, Mérida, Yuste, and Madrid.[7] These translations were in fact elaborate funeral corteges composed of honor guards, clerics, nobles, and servants. At every stage of these long journeys, the corteges would stop at churches for requiem masses.[8] Philip was on intimate terms with death, and these corpses proved it. Eleven corpses were taken there in 1573–4, each one of them an intimate loss. By the time Philip wrote his will in 1594, the number had grown, and he could ask to be buried with sixteen members of his immediate family: his father and mother, three of his wives, five of his children, three brothers, two aunts, and one nephew.[9] His preoccupation with these corpses became legend. He

"In the great oriental civilizations – from Mesopotamia and Egypt to China and India – the temple received a new and important valorization. It is not only an *imago mundi;* it is also interpreted as the earthly reproduction of a transcendent model. Judaism inherited this ancient oriental conception of the temple as a copy of a celestial work of architecture." *The Sacred and the Profane: The Nature of Religion* (New York, 1959), pp. 58, 145.

[7] Siguenza, *Escorial*, pp. 47–53; Varela, *Muerte del rey*, pp. 27–9. Varela counts eighteen corpses by 1586.

[8] Ludwig Pfandl, *Philippe II*, tr. by M. E. Lepointe (Paris, 1942), pp. 488 ff.

[9] *Testamento de Felipe II*, facsimile edition (Madrid, 1982), pp. 4–5.

asked for accounts of their translations, gave instructions, and passed comments on the details.[10] When told in a report that the corpses from the royal chapel at Granada needed new coffins, he gave his opinion on the margin.[11] He also gave instructions regarding what should be inscribed on his father's coffin, and how many more masses should be said for his deceased wife, Elizabeth of Valois.[12] So keen was his interest that many of the people involved in the translation of the corpses felt him to be looking over their shoulder. Rumors spread that he had gone to Yuste secretly to observe the removal of his father's remains and that he had followed the cortege to Talavera and Casarrubios. No one ever saw him, but many reported that they had felt his presence.[13]

It is a testament to King Philip's abilities as a statesman, armchair architect, and lay theologian that the symbolic dimensions of his monumental retreat have often overshadowed the functional dimensions. The architecture of the Escorial and its "message" have been under constant scrutiny since the sixteenth century, down to the present.[14] Though few visitors to the Escorial have ever experienced anything close to Siguenza's vision at the dedication ceremony, most would agree that the Escorial is a structure that invites interpretation, a message waiting to be decoded.[15] A mere two months after Philip's death, it was extolled

---

[10] IVDJ, Envio 61-II, fols. 44-46, 57, 59, 64, 110.

[11] IVDJ, Envio 61-II, fol. 167: "Conforme a esto se responde que me parece lo mejor."

[12] On Charles V: IVDJ, Envio 61-II, fol. 64; On Elizabeth: IVDJ, Envio 100, fol. 81.

[13] Ms., Real Academia de la Historia, Madrid, 9-5558: "Relación muy verdadera de la jornada que el muy Ilustre y Reverendo Señor don Francisco Delgado, Arçobispo de Sanctiago, hizo por mandado de la S.C.R.M. del Rey don Philippe nuestro señor, Segundo de este nombre, en la traslación de los cuerpos reales."

[14] Most recently, in 1986, during the four-hundredth anniversary of the completion of the Escorial, several public exhibits were mounted in Spain by the Ministry of Fine Arts, some of which focused attention on the symbolic dimensions of the building. The various catalogs for these exhibits were published separately, with scholarly articles included. Unfortunately, the catalogs were issued without much concern for bibliographical clarity. All catalogs are entitled *Quarto Centenario del Monasterio de El Escorial*, but each has its own subtitle (without an individual volume number). To make matters worse, no credit is given to the individual editors of each volume. The two catalogs most intensely concerned with the symbolic dimensions of the Escorial are *Iglesia y Monarquía. La Liturgia*, and *Las Casas Reales. El Palacio* (Madrid, 1986).

[15] Saturnino Alvarez Turienzo has collected and analyzed the most significant interpretive texts published in Spain during the past four centuries in *El Escorial en las letras españolas* (Madrid, 1985).

as a *memento mori* in stone and a call to repentance for the whole world.[16] One generation after Siguenza's time, in 1638 a Spanish poet proclaimed it "this Orpheus in stone."[17] In 1623, an English visitor seemed as awed by its symbolic content as by its architectural grandeur:

I was yesterday at the Escurial to see the Monastery of Saint Lawrence, the eighth wonder of the world; and truly considering the site of the place, the state of the thing, and the symmetry of the structure, with divers other rarities, it may be call'd so; for what I have seen in Italy and other places, are but baubles to it. It is built amongst a company of raggy, barren hills . . . of free-stone and marble, and that with such solidity and moderate height, that surely Philip the Second's chief design was to make a sacrifice of it to eternity, and to contest with the Meteors and Time itself. . . . By this mighty Monument it may be inferr'd that Philip the Second, though he was a little man, yet had the vast, gigantic thoughts in him to leave such a huge pile for posterity to gaze upon and admire his memory.[18]

In our own century, the philosopher Miguel de Unamuno observed that it is impossible *not* to read meaning into the Escorial and *not* to seek within it whatever one conceives to be the shadow of Philip II.[19] Whereas Unamuno placed this hermeneutical imperative within the mind of the visitor, José Ortega y Gasset saw it as embedded in the very fabric of the building itself, which, according to him, was a monument to the darker side of the Spanish character: "We apprehend here better than anywhere else the Spanish essence, that subterranean spring from which

[16] Sermon of Lorenzo de Ayalá, at the monastery of San Benito el Real of Valladolid, 15 November 1598, *Sermones funerales*, fols. 103v–104r.

[17] Gabriel Bocángel, *Escuriale* (Madrid, 1638), p. 4. Cited in Saturnino Alvarez Turienzo, *El Escorial en las letras españolas* (Madrid, 1985), p. 126.

[18] James Howell, *Epistolae* (London, 1665), vol. I, p. 162. Cited in Ludwig Pfandl, *Cultura y costumbres del pueblo español de los siglos XVI y XVII*, first Spanish edition (Barcelona, 1929), pp. 317–18.

[19] Miguel de Unamuno, *Andanzas y visiones españolas*, in *Obras*, vol. I (Madrid, 1966), p. 392: "Lo cierto es que apenas hay quien se llegue a visitar El Escorial con ánimo desprevenido y sereno, a recibir la impresión de una obra de arte, a gozar con el goce más refinado y más raro cual es la contemplación del desnudo arquitectonico. Casi todos los que van a ver El Escorial se llegan con anteojeras, con prejuicios políticos o religiosos. . . . Van a buscar la sombra de Felipe II mal conocido también y peor comprendido, y si no la encuentran, se la fingen."

has bubbled up the history of Europe's most abnormal people."[20] A recent study has identified some of the central themes suggested through the centuries: the Escorial as a symbol of the Tridentine Catholic Reformation; the Escorial as monument to the military might of Spain; the Escorial as the new Temple of Solomon; the Escorial as the expression of a sacralized monarchy.[21] Many of these attempts to "decode" the Escorial have separated its functional and symbolic aspects, investing its architecture with an iconographical quality of its own, assuming that its visual forms correspond more directly to hidden symbolism in theology, philosophy, or psychology than to functional design.[22] One recent manifestation of this tendency has been the attempt by René Taylor to prove that the Escorial was intentionally designed to convey the secret messages of the occult hermetic tradition.[23] At the other end of the spectrum, George Kubler has proposed a separation of architecture and symbol, arguing that the Escorial cannot be "explained" by the supposition that its visual forms necessarily correspond to identifiable abstract ideas or psychological states.[24] Though all experts would agree that the Escorial has many messages and that no single function can be

---

[20] "A quién dedicó Felipe II esta enorme profesión de fe, que es, después de San Pedro, en Roma, el credo que pesa más sobre la tierra europea? . . . El Dios de Felipe II, o, lo que es lo mismo, su ideal, tiene en el Monasterio un comentario voluminoso. Que expresa la masa enorme de este edificio? Si todo monumento es un esfuerzo consagrado a la expresión de un ideal, que ideal se afirma y hieratiza en este fastuoso sacrificio de esfuerzo?" (*El Espectador*, VI), "Meditación del Escorial," in *Obras Completas* (Madrid, 1954), vol. II, pp. 553–7.

[21] Cornelia von der Osten Sacken, *San Lorenzo el Real de el Escorial. Studien zur baugeschichte und ikonologie* (Mittenwand-München, 1979). Another recent study concerned with the artistic and symbolic dimensions of the Escorial is Maria Calì, *Da Michelangelo all'Escorial. Momenti del dibattito religioso nell'arte del Cinquecento* (Turin, 1980).

[22] A recent discussion of hidden symbolism in a different context can shed light on past approaches to the Escorial as an architectural icon. See Keith Moxey, "Interpreting Pieter Aertsen: The Problem of 'Hidden Symbolism'," *Nederlands Kunsthistorisch Jaerboek* 40 (1989): 29–39.

[23] René Taylor, "Architecture and Magic: Considerations on the Idea of the Escorial," in *Essays in the History of Architecture Presented to Rudolf Wittkower* (New York, 1967), pp. 81–109.

[24] George Kubler, *Building the Escorial* (Princeton, 1982), p. 125. "The visual forms correspond less to individual psychology than to collective traditions in architectural design."

isolated as the *key* to its symbolic structure, there is no denying the centrality of death in its functional and symbolic plan.

Death's dominant role in the symbolic structure of the Escorial is a reflection of its significance in the Spanish mentality of Philip's age, for the symbolic forms by which kings justify themselves are also the central symbols of their society. Kings are the center of the order of symbols, values, and beliefs that govern a society.[25] Social scientists have established that the most important aspects of kingship, stressed by different cultures in different ways, are the king's centrality and his role as a symbol of totality.[26] Power and symbolism are symbiotically related, for the concept of central authority that is the very foundation of kingship is a cultural construct.[27] Consequently, the political functions of kings are inseparable from their symbolic functions. They rule by virtue of their intimate connection to the symbolism of the "center," as symbols of total order, meaning, and power. Their ability to coerce obedience by the sword rests on their capacity to perform the symbolic function of representing power itself and the very existence of the kingdom, to evince that they represent the creation and maintenance of order, security, and prosperity.[28]

Symbolic power was imparted to the Escorial not only by the centrality of kingship but also by the myth and ritual that it embodied. The Escorial was above all else a sacred shrine and was consciously designed as such by Philip. It was a temple, an edifice where God dwelt; a basilica, a church erected over a martyr's tomb; a reliquary, a collection of the remains of saints; a mausoleum, a burial place for the ruling dynasty; a

---

[25] Edward Sills, "Center and Periphery," p. 3: "There is a central zone in the structure of society. Membership in the society . . . is constituted by relationship to this central zone. . . . The center is also a phenomenon of the realm of action. It is a structure of activities, of roles and persons, within the network of institutions. It is in these roles that the values and beliefs which are central are embodied and propounded."

[26] Cristiano Grottanelli, "Kingship: an Overview," *The Encyclopedia of Religion*, ed. Mircea Eliade (New York, 1987), vol. 8, p. 313.

[27] Clifford Geertz, "Centers, kings, and charisma," *Rites of Power: Symbolism, Ritual, and Politics Since the Middle Ages*, ed. Sean Wilentz (Philadelphia, 1985), p. 30: "Political authority still requires a cultural frame in which to define itself and advance its claims."

[28] Ray, *Myth, Ritual, and Kingship in Buganda*, p. 11; John Beattie, "Kingship," *International Encyclopedia of the Social Sciences*, vol. 8, p. 388.

palace, a home for the king and his court; and it was a great place for a king to die. It was a shrine to God and king. Its intimate dual connection to death ritual and to the myth of the sacrality of kingship were deliberately and carefully constructed. So profound and so multidimensional was the intended ritual symbolism of the Escorial that it shatters some of the paradigms established by anthropologists who have studied royal shrines. It has been contended, for instance, that because royal shrines are "openings" to the spiritual world, they normally remain separate from the political capital. The Escorial follows this paradigm to some extent but not completely. It was not in Madrid, but it was near it. A concomitant anthropological paradigm is that in the royal shrines it is ritual, not politics that prevails.[29] Not so at the Escorial, for when the king was in residence, the politics came with him.

Social scientists have long known and argued that royal rites are not "mere" ceremonial trappings but primary components in the symbolics of power. Rites of passage, especially rites surrounding a dead or dying king, are not only ceremonies. They are also instruments of power. It was an awareness of this that inspired the writing of what are arguably the two most influential studies of the symbolics of royal power, leading Sir James Frazer to devote twelve volumes worth of attention to the anthropological significance of the rites surrounding the king's body and prompting Ernst Kantorowicz to analyze the "political theology" of the king's two bodies.[30] It is a similar awareness that has led me to the Escorial and the king's dissolving body. Given that kings *symbolize* as much as they rule and that they are acknowledged to represent ultimate values, there is no denying the significance of Philip's choice of symbols in the Escorial. Moreover, when one considers that the Escorial was no inchoate expression, that Philip himself and many others in his day were acutely aware of the symbolic dimension of the building and of the centrality of death within its symbolic structure, one must conclude that the Escorial and the dying king within it were a summation of Spanish attitudes toward death and the afterlife.

---

[29] Ray, *Myth, Ritual, and Kingship*, p. 158, debating some of the assertions made by Jonathan Z. Smith in *To Take Place* (Chicago, 1987), p. 109.

[30] James G. Frazer, *The Golden Bough*, 12 vols. (London, 1911–15); Ernst Kantorowicz, *The King's Two Bodies* (Princeton, 1957). See Ray, *Myth, Ritual, and Kingship*, p. 105.

Death most horrendous, death most felicitous

When King Philip II first contemplated building the Escorial as his dying place and family pantheon, he also envisioned it as a site where he could assemble one of the world's largest relic collections and give himself ready access to the bones of dead saints. As soon as plans for this edifice began to be drawn up in 1563, Philip began searching for these holy treasures throughout Spain and Europe. In 1564 he received the first, a tooth of Saint Lawrence, from a monastery in Montpellier. Over the next four decades Philip importuned several popes, bishops, and secular rulers to send him relics for the Escorial, and these gifts streamed in steadily, translated from near and far, until their number reached well over 7,000. The king wanted to leave no stone unturned, and he pursued his search with fervor. Bishops received inquiries from Philip in which he asked them not only to send him some relics but also to send reports about them. What were the relics in their diocese? What was their condition? Were they suitably enshrined? Was sufficient devotion being shown to them? When the Bishop of Orense sent Philip some relics, he also sent him the required report. The king read it, thanked the bishop in a letter, and told him he was glad to see that the relics of Orense were "well kept and venerated."[31]

The grand designs of Philip for his relic collection – and his fondest desires – are revealed by one plan that never materialized: the translation of the body of St. James the Apostle, Spain's preeminent relic, from Santiago de Compostela to the Escorial. In his initial inquiry into this possibility, Philip cited several reasons for wanting to change the location of what was arguably Europe's most revered pilgrimage shrine, including the fear of depredations at the hands of iconoclastic English pirates or French Hugenots. His argument primarily hinged on the issue of monarchical centralization. Philip favored having St. James at the geographical center and argued that the Escorial would be a much easier site to reach by all pilgrims because more roads led to the heart of Spain than to rustic, distant Galicia. Philip also favored collapsing yet another dimension of sacrality into the symbolic center and argued that the Escorial was a more fitting place for the national patron saint, not only because of the superiority of the edifice itself, which he deemed on a par

---

[31] IVDJ, Envio 61-II, fols. 286–290.

with St. Peter's basilica in Rome, but also because of its intimate connection with the court. Moreover, he continued, it would be best for
Spain to have its king and its patron in continuous proximity to one
another. Philip lamented that as long as St. James remained in Galicia,
each king could visit him only once in a lifetime, and that was not good
for the saint or the monarchy or the realm. The king never pursued this
translation vigorously, perhaps because of the frank reply sent to him
from Galicia, which could have made him realize that the traditional
custodians of this relic guarded their privileges (*fueros*) jealously, and
were not about to relinquish them without a fight.[32]

Some relics were obtained with ease, as were those collected by Philip's diplomats in northern Italy. Others were harder to obtain. When
Philip requested a large relic of St. Lawrence from the church of St.
John Lateran in Rome, his envoy ran into stiff opposition and even had
to appeal to the pope.[33] By far the largest and most dramatic translation
took place in 1597–8, when four sizable crates full of relics made their
way from Cologne to the Escorial.[34] These were relics supposedly rescued from the iconoclastic ravages of Protestant heretics in Germany
and the Low Countries – relics saved from those who "waged bloody
warfare against God's saints," as one chronicler put it. Philip especially
prized this sacred cache not only because of the great number of significant relics but also because of the symbolism inherent in their deliver-
ance. This rescue touched him deeply, for it was a token of his piety and
of his efforts to combat Protestantism. It is meaningful that one of his
favorite pieces in this collection was not a saint's relic but a miraculous
host that had reportedly bled when stomped upon by a Dutch Calvinist
iconoclast.[35]

---

[32] IVDJ, Envio 61-II, fols. 197–8.

[33] Northern Italy: IVDJ, Envio 61-II, fol. 72; Rome: IVDJ, Envio 61-II, fol. 144. Philip
obtained his relic of St. Lawrence and compensated the canons of St. John Lateran
with two silver statues worth 2,000 *ducados*.

[34] "Relatio Notarii super transportatione, consignatione, et depositione ss. Reliquiarum
ad manus Catholicae Maiestatis Serenissimi Hispaniarum Regis Phillippi II," a
manuscript account by Roland Weierstras, Notary Apostolic, has been edited and
published by Juan Manuel del Estal, O.S.A. in *Monasterio de San Lorenzo el Real*
(Escorial, 1964), "Curioso memorial del mayor traslado de reliquias de Alemania al
Escorial (1597–98)," pp. 403–49.

[35] Fray José de Sigüenza, *Fundación del monasterio de El Escorial* (Madrid, 1963), p. 165.
For a detailed account of Philip's relic collection, see Juan Manuel del Estal, "Felipe

This translation of relics made its way up the Rhine in December 1597. It faced danger from natural obstacles and from Protestants. In Frankfurt, for instance, it was greeted by a hostile crowd of about 3,000 Calvinists who opposed its passage through the city.[36] Once safely out of hostile territory, the translation crossed the Alps to Milan, moved on down to the coast at Genoa, and across the sea on board a ship to Barcelona, being greeted everywhere with elaborate liturgical spectacles. On 8 May 1598, the relics arrived in Madrid, where they occasioned similar festivities after being privately received and "adored with great reverence and joy" by the monarch and his heir to the throne. King Philip was thrilled beyond description. Gravely ill and tormented by gout, he sought solace in these "flowers of heaven."[37] He continually asked for them to be pressed against his eyes, mouth, head, and hands, driving his *relicario*, Fray Martin de Villanueva, to distraction. Philip became obsessed with them and was driven nearly mad. He repeatedly asked for the certificates of authenticity to be read to him, as well as other documents related to the translation. He guarded the relics jealously, carefully watching for any particles that would fall off, lest they be surreptitiously taken away. "He did not think them safe anywhere," said a chronicler, "he suspected and distrusted everyone." Philip had the collection inventoried several times in Madrid and asked for the lists to be read to him. His health worsening, Philip dispatched the relics to the Escorial on 11 June 1598. They were received with elaborate rituals by the Hieronymite monks, who sent Philip a detailed description of the event. When Philip heard that poems had been written in honor of the occasion, he asked that these all be sent to him and that they be read slowly. This amazed those around Philip and confirmed for them the intensity of his obsession, for, as many of them knew, "he had no great love for poetry."[38]

By this time, Philip II had good reason to be alarmed at the deteriorating state of his health and to fear that his days were numbered. Throughout the spring of 1598, the king's ailments, already an impediment to him and the court, steadily became an unbearable burden. For the past two years Philip's mobility had been seriously hampered by the

II y su archivo hagiográfico de El Escorial," *Hispania Sacra* 23 (1970): 193–333. The bleeding host is described on p. 287.
[36] Weierstras, "Relatio Notarii," p. 416.   [37] Siguenza, *Fundación*, p. 167.
[38] Siguenza, *Fundación*, p. 169.

pain in his hands and feet. He was barely able to stand or walk unassisted and could not even sign documents with his hands.[39] Now, on top of this gout and arthritis, dropsy set in, combined with an unrelenting fever. An infection also apparently caused his skin to erupt into frightful boils and ulcers. Diego de Yepes reports that by April Philip could no longer stand on his own two feet at all. When the time came in May for the monarch's usual trip to his beloved retreat at nearby Aranjuez, he was forced to remain in Madrid. As his condition further deteriorated in June, Philip decided it was time to set out for his final journey to the Escorial, the place he had so carefully planned as the best possible setting for his death.[40]

Despite protests from all his physicians and many of his advisors, Philip departed from Madrid for the last time on Tuesday, 30 June 1598. One of his physicians observed that Philip knew that he was taking his body to be buried.[41] The Hieronymite chronicler Fray José de Siguenza remarked that the king had decided to "go home" to his grave.[42] He was gingerly carried out in the special chair designed for him by Jean Lhermite that was borne on the shoulders of two servants at

[39] Philip found it necessary to mention his inability to sign documents in the final codicil to his will, written in August 1597, to ensure that the seal he had been using would be accepted: "Digo y declaro que porque con mis indispusiciones y impedimentos de la gota, no se tardasse el despacho de los necocios . . . he usado por beneficio comun, de firmar y señalar con estampa, quando no he podido de mi mano." *Testamento de Felipe II*, facsimile edition, with transcription by José Luis de la Peña 39 (Madrid, 1982), p. 93.

[40] Diego de Yepes, *Relación de algunas particularidades que pasaron en los vecinos dias de la enfermedad de que murió nuestro Catolico Rey Don Phelipe II*, BNM 1504 F154, fol. 56. All citations refer to this manuscript version. A printed version is available in an appendix to Luis Cabrera de Cordoba, *Felipe II, Rey de España*, 4 vols. (Madrid, 1877), vol. 4, pp. 384–90. I have chosen to rely on the manuscript because of minor discrepancies in transcription.

[41] Cristobal Perez de Herrera, *Elogio a las esclarecidas virtudes del Rey Nuestro Señor Don Felipe II, que está en el cielo y de su exemplar y cristianisima muerte* (Valladolid, 1604), included as an appendix to Luis Cabrera de Cordoba, *Felipe II, Rey de España*, 4 vols. (Madrid, 1877), vol. 4, p. 374: "Pues dixo su Majestad cuando partió de Madrid, muy apercebido y prevenido para irse a morir a su Real Casa de San Lorenzo, que ninguno le podia llevar su cuerpo mas honradamente que el mismo."

[42] Siguenza, *Fundación*, p. 171: "Aunque se estaba flaco y gastado de las continuas dolencias y mal convalecido, determinose de partir para su casa de San Lorenzo, o por decirlo mejor, para su gloriosa sepultura."

a snail's pace over the smoothest possible terrain.[43] A journey that had once taken the king only five or six hours on horseback in better days now turned into an agonizingly slow and painful six-day pilgrimage. The king's party did not arrive at La Fresneda, within sight of the Escorial, until Sunday, 5 July. Early the next morning, Philip II was met at La Fresneda by his son, the future Philip III, and his daughter, the Infanta, Isabel Clara Eugenia. By late afternoon of 6 July, the royal family finally made its entrance to the Escorial. The king seemed ebullient, even though he was almost entirely prone in his special chair. To show how good he was feeling and how much his gout had improved merely by coming to the Escorial, he took a book in his hands and paged through it vigorously. José de Siguenza observed that because this was the last time the monks of San Lorenzo welcomed their founder and benefactor, the event "could not be remembered without tears."[44]

On Wednesday, 8 July, Philip was carried about in his special chair for a farewell tour of his very own "eighth wonder of the world."[45] Given Philip's condition, it could be only a limited inspection. The king spent a good deal of time admiring the newly arrived relics and their reliquaries, giving specific orders as to how they should be arranged and displayed. Although he was so entranced by the relics that he found it difficult to tear himself away from them, he ordered himself to be taken to the library before retiring for the day. According to Siguenza, he was very pleased with what he saw.[46]

Over the next few days, Philip busied himself with the arrangement of the relic collection, even though his health continued to deteriorate. Confined to his special chair, sitting or partly prone, feverish and pain-ridden, the king still directed a limited amount of business. It seemed clear to all that little time remained for Philip and that in spite of his continued involvement in affairs near and far, this was not a joyous

---

[43] Jehan Lhermite, *Le Passetemps* (1602 manuscript) ed. by Ch. Ruelens, 2 vols. (Antwerp, 1890–1896; reprinted in Geneva, 1971), vol. 2, pp. 112–13. A drawing of this special chair, from Lhermite's original manuscript, is included in vol. 1, p. 256.

[44] Siguenza, *Fundación*, pp. 171–2.

[45] Ibid., p. 172. Baltasar Porreño, *Dichos y Hechos del Rey Don Felipe II*, 1628 (Madrid, 1942), pp. 91, 186, is but one of many contemporaries who felt justified in not only comparing the Escorial to the seven wonders of the ancient world but also boasting that it surpassed them in every respect.

[46] Siguenza, *Fundación*, p. 172.

homecoming. Some saw Philip's sad perambulations as a rehearsal for his funeral. "Since he was forced to move about in his chair, it was as if he had to see himself carried to the grave every day."[47]

On 22 July Philip was carried to his bed for the last time. Around midnight, he developed a high fever that signaled the beginning of a long, agonizing demise. What followed was truly horrifying and made such an impression on all who witnessed it that even the smallest details were recorded and given symbolic significance. The king who ruled over an empire on which the sun never set, who was considered the most powerful man on earth by those around him, now lay helpless in his bed, assailed by a "terrifying horde of miseries."[48] One of the principal chroniclers of this event went as far as to claim that Philip experienced pain in every single part of his body, even though Galen had argued that this was impossible.[49]

For the next fifty-three days Philip was forced to lie flat on his back, unable to move and unable to be moved or touched without pain. Even the weight of the sheets caused him distress. The gout and arthritis that had plagued him for the past few years continued to torment him and may have even intensified. The dreaded *tercianas* fever caused him to alternate between hot flashes and chills. The sores on his hands and feet also worsened and had to be lanced. He developed a festering abscess above his right knee that also had to be lanced without the aid of any anesthetic on 6 August. This open wound would not drain properly and had to be squeezed, yielding two basins full of pus each day. Philip's chronic dropsy caused his abdomen and joints to swell with fluid. Bed sores erupted all along his backside as the ordeal progressed and he remained immobile. Although at times he lapsed into a fitful sleep or seemed barely conscious, he was troubled by insomnia and never fully escaped from the horror of his condition.[50]

---

[47] Ibid., p. 173.

[48] Ibid., p. 174. "Comenzó ahora como de nuevo a acometerle una espantable escuadra de miserias, aunque alguna de ellas bastara a acabar con la vida, ninguna ni todas juntas pudieron mellarle la paciencia."

[49] Luis Cervera de la Torre, *Testimonio Autentico y Verdadero de las cosas notables que pasaron en la dichosa muerte del Rey Nuestro Senor Don Felipe Segundo* (Valencia, 1599), p. 10.

[50] Lhermite, *Passetemps*, vol. 2, pp. 114–19. Of all the chroniclers, Lhermite provides the most compact summary and the most sensible chronology. Although he was an eyewitness, he was prevented from entering the king's chamber from 15 August to 30

According to all eyewitnesses, the worst torment of all was the diarrhea that developed about halfway into this final illness. Because the pain caused by being touched or moved was too great for Philip to bear, "it seemed best not to clean the ordure that he produced, and not even to change the linens, so many times the bed remained fouled, creating an awful stench."[51] Eventually a hole was cut into the mattress to help relieve this problem, but it was only a partial remedy. Philip continued to waste away, wallowing in his own filth, tormented by the smell and the degradation of it all. According to one account, he was also plagued by lice.[52] "It was as if he were already buried alive," commented Siguenza. "Considering the fastidiousness, care, and cleanliness that he always had in all things, so that it was even difficult for him to tolerate a mark on the wall, or a spot on the floor, or any dust, or a spider web . . . it was pitiful to see him in such a loathsome condition."[53] Cervera de la Torre lists the "torment of the nose" as one of the worst suffered by Philip, adding that monarchs suffer much more than other mortals because of their upbringing. "Royal persons are much more afflicted and easily tormented. Since they are reared with such great care and delicacy, their senses are more refined and perceptive."[54]

Throughout all of this Philip displayed an exemplary composure. According to all of the eyewitness reports, he never once cried out in pain or expressed any bitterness about his condition. Diego de Yepes, his confessor, praised him for never once mistreating his servants during this difficult time and for even going so far as to look after their welfare, ordering them to rest or get some sleep if they needed it.[55] In spite of his debased physical condition, the king still acted with pride and magna-

August, while he attended to the needs of a close friend from the Netherlands who had fallen ill and was also dying (pp. 138–9).

[51] Cervera de la Torre, *Testimonio*, p. 19.

[52] "A briefe and true Declaration of the Sicnesse, last Wordes, and Death of the King of Spaine, Philip, the Second of that Name. . . . Written from Madrill, in a Spanish Letter, and translated into English according to the true Copie" (London, 1599). Reprinted in the various editions of *The Harleian Miscellany*, vol. II, pp. 377–9. I have consulted the 1744 London edition.

[53] Siguenza, *Fundación*, p. 177. A similar observation was made by Agustin Davila, O. P., in his funeral sermon for King Philip at Valladolid, published first in Seville (1599), and then in the collection of 1601, *Sermones funerales*, fol. 87r.

[54] Cervera de la Torre, *Testamento*, p. 31.

[55] Diego de Yepes, *Relación*, fol. 58v.; Siguenza, *Fundación*, p. 179.

nimity and even conducted some official business. In the midst of all this, for instance, Philip arranged for the consecration ceremony of Garcia de Loaysa Girón as Archbishop of Toledo. On 16 August the new archbishop was consecrated by the papal legate Camilo Gaetano in the basilica at the Escorial as Philip watched from his bed, which was especially positioned to offer a view of the high altar.[56] "It seemed he wanted to be king and lord over death itself . . . thus he dealt with great affairs of state and the governance of his kingdoms at the same time that he planned his own death and burial, as if there were no difference between these tasks, being equally serene in one as in the other."[57]

Even more important, he showed remarkable patience and faith in God, repeating pious expressions over and over, such as: "Holy God, you alone are Lord," "Grant me, oh Lord, a good death through your Son's holiest death,"[58] and "Oh Lord, forgive my sins."[59] He recited appropriate scripture passages, such as the words of Jesus during His agony in the garden, "Father, not my will, but thine be done,"[60] or the plaint of the psalmist, "As a hart longs for flowing springs, so does my soul long for you, oh Lord."[61] When those around him begged him to rest from praying, the king only insisted in praying even more. "This is no time to stop praying," he said, "but rather to watch and be alert, lest death catch me sleeping."[62] Much would be made of this later, when chroniclers of the event sought to draw moral lessons from the king's demeanor.[63]

---

[56] After the archbishop's consecration, Philip obtained a special papal pardon from legate Gaetano. Perez de Herrera, *Elogio*, in Cabrera, *Felipe II*, vol. 4, p. 377.

[57] Siguenza, *Fundación*, p. 188.

[58] Perez de Herrera, *Elogio*, in Cabrera de Cordoba, *Felipe II*, vol. 4, p. 375.

[59] Yepes, *Relación*, fol. 58v.

[60] Cervera de la Torre, *Testimonio*, p. 56. (Luke 22:39). Philip received great consolation, it seems, from having the various passion narratives read to him repeatedly during his worst moments and always expressed special interest in dwelling on this particular passage. He was also fond of having the meditations of Louis de Blois (Ludovicus Blosius) on the agony in the garden read to him from a Spanish translation of one of his works, *La Tabla Espiritual*, fol. 187v.

[61] Siguenza, *Fundación*, p. 181. (Psalm 42:1).

[62] Perez de Herrera, *Elogio*, in Cabrera de Cordoba, *Felipe II*, vol. 4, p. 378. On this occasion, Philip was alluding to Jesus's admonition in Luke 12:35, "Blessed are those servants whom the master finds awake when he comes."

[63] Baltasar Porreño, *Dichos y Hechos*, p. 21: "La gravedad, severidad, mesura y compos-

The king's dissolving body

When Philip's physicians could no longer offer him any hope for recovery toward the end of August, a majority agreed it would be good for him to receive the last rites, though some dissented, thinking the news might weaken his will to keep up the struggle.[64] Contrary to some of the dissenting doctors' opinions, Philip was glad to hear the news when he was finally informed and asked Diego de Yepes to hear his confession.[65] Though he had availed himself of this sacrament several times during this final illness, this time he took three days to complete his confession, dwelling scrupulously, it appears, on the many details of his entire life.[66]

In keeping with his predilection for thoroughness and attention to detail, Philip ordered that the sacrament of extreme unction be thoroughly explained to him before he received it. He ordered Don Fernando de Toledo to inquire from the newly consecrated Archbishop of Toledo just exactly where and in how many places his body would be anointed, and he asked Diego de Yepes to read the entire service to him one time before actually administering the sacrament. Yepes complied, of course, but underestimated the king's intense devotion to detail. When the time came for the real service to be performed on the night of 1 September, Yepes suggested that it was not necessary to read the very lengthy opening prayer again, since it had already been done once. Philip balked at the suggestion. "No," he said, "say the prayer

tura que tanto guardó en vida, que fue virtud singularisima y propria suya entre los reyes y principes del mundo, esa misma tuvo en la muerte . . . y asi murió como un varon santo, que morir tan sereno, condición de justo es."

[64] Siguenza, *Fundación*, p. 180.

[65] Alonso Cabrera added some details in his funeral sermon for King Philip. According to him, someone lied to Philip, saying the doctors had given him another two years to live. The king did not respond. Instead he said, "Quando me muera dadle aquella imagen de Nuestra Señora a la Infanta, que era de mi madre, y la he traido conmigo cincuenta y seis años." Sermon at San Domingo, Madrid, 31 October 1598, *Sermones funerales*, fol. 64v.

[66] Yepes, *Relación*, fol. 56v. Father Yepes was ordered by the king to conduct a very careful examination of conscience: "Al punto de termino de confesarse generalmente mandandome que en esto le ayudase con mucho cuydado y iciese un riguroso interrogatorio, como lo yze." Philip's meticulous attention to detail in this confession seems even more intense in light of the plenary pardon he had already received from Pope Clement VIII through his legate Camilo Gaetano on 16 August (Lhermite, *Passetemps*, vol. 2, pp. 135–7; Siguenza, *Fundación*, p. 186).

again, because it is a very good one." In spite of the pain it would cause him, he asked that his hands be washed and his nails trimmed, so he could more reverently receive the sacrament.

Contrary to an established tradition that prohibited kings from witnessing death or any event related to the dying process, he also requested that young Philip, his son and heir to the throne, be present to witness the ceremony. According to Siguenza, the Spanish monarchs had long been shielded from such events as much as possible, "as if this would ensure their being able to escape from the hands of death." The king who built the Escorial as a monument to death and continuity within the royal family thought this was a "great error," and sought to teach his son a thorough lesson on the inevitability of death by actively involving him in the process of dying. Philip II regretted having gone through life without ever witnessing the last rites and apparently also regretted not being present at his own father's exemplary death, and he wanted to spare his son the same deprivation.[67] This intense involvement of the young Philip III in his father's gruesome death would later have a tremendous effect on the future monarch.[68]

Philip II was administered the last rites by the new Primate of Spain, Garcia de Loaysa Girón, who seems to have faltered a few times during the ceremony, overcome by emotion. The event was witnessed "with great serenity" by the prince, as well as by some of the king's attendants, the three confessors of the royal family (of the king, the prince, and the Infanta), Fray Gaspar de Cordoba, prior of the Escorial, and four other monks chosen by Philip II. After the ceremony, he asked to be left alone with his son. Philip III later revealed what his father had said to him at that moment: "I wanted you to be present during this event so that you could see how kingdoms and everything in this world come to an end." The dying king also advised the prince to concern himself with the cause of true religion and to defend the Catholic faith and govern justly, so that when it came time for him too to die, he could do so with a clear conscience. After this lesson in mortality, the prince received some specific advice about the way in which a king should govern.[69]

---

[67] Yepes, *Relación*, fol. 57v. Siguenza, *Fundación*, p. 186.
[68] David Lagomarsino, "Hapsburg Way of Death," unpublished paper, pp. 15–16, 20.
[69] Siguenza, *Fundación*, p. 187.

Now fully prepared for death, the king began to withdraw into an inner world, "to look into his soul and contemplate the moment of parting, as one who had already divorced himself from the world."[70] Diego de Yepes reports that Philip seemed very happy when he called on the king the next morning, following the ceremony. According to Yepes, the king said "he had never in his life felt more consoled than after receiving that holy sacrament." Yepes also adds that during the next eleven days that remained, the king conducted no official business and instead concerned himself exclusively with spiritual matters, having people read to him from devotional books or comfort him with uplifting advice.[71] Philip ordered that from that day forward at least two priests be with him at all times. In addition to having mass said daily in his chamber, he was able to see the high altar of the basilica from his bed, and he watched all the masses being said there.[72]

A carefully orchestrated and obviously mimetic ritual now began to unfold in Philip's chamber. Years before, when the Emperor Charles V had died at Yuste, he had carefully arranged for his own funeral. A legend arose that Charles had even participated in a funeral ceremony while still alive.[73] More important, he left behind certain instructions for his son Philip regarding his death and burial, not the least of which, of course, was the order to have a proper mausoleum built for the Hapsburg dynasty, now so grandly accomplished with the building of the Escorial. Philip II had obviously taken his father's wishes seriously, and as the moment of his own death neared, he began to act much as his father had done and also apparently as he thought his father Charles had wanted him to. Twenty-three days into his final illness, a month before he died, Philip ordered some of the monks, "in secret," to go down into

---

[70] Ibid., p. 188.

[71] Yepes, *Relación*, fol. 58. Siguenza quotes directly from Yepes, word for word, in *Fundación*, p. 187.

[72] Lhermite, *Passetemps*, vol. 2, p. 141.

[73] A complete bibliography of the literature dealing with the death of Charles V at Yuste would fill several pages. Among the most important works to consult are Francisco Gonzalez de Andia, Marques de Valparaiso, *El Perfecto Desengaño*, 1638 (Madrid, 1983); Louis P. Gachard, *Sur le sejour de Charles Quint au Monastere de Yuste* (Brussels, 1844); François Mignet, *Charles Quint, son abdication, son sejour et sa mort au monastere de Yuste* (Paris, 1854–56); and William Stirling-Maxwell, *The Cloister Life of the Emperor Charles V* (London, 1853).

the burial crypt, open the casket of his father, and carefully note all the details about its measurements and the way in which the emperor's remains were dressed, so that when the time came, "they could also dress him in the same manner."[74] Once the monks reported on their findings, he ordered Cristobal de Mora to bury him in a simple gown, to wrap him in a winding sheet, and to hang a plain wooden cross around his neck.

The king's interest in imitating the death of Charles V is also revealed in another way. Philip had always had in his possession a chest bequeathed by his father that was to be used specifically at the moment of death. In 1591, perhaps as Philip thought his own end might be near, he showed this box to one of his secretaries, Juan Ruiz de Velasco, and asked him to open it. What the secretary found inside were two candles from the shrine of Our Lady of Montserrat and a small crucifix.[75] Philip said to his secretary at that time: "Remember this well, for I will ask for it again someday. These candles and this crucifix belonged to my father, the Emperor, and he died with them, holding the crucifix in his hands. I plan to die the same way."[76] Four days before Philip's death, on 9 September, this same secretary had to perform the task of bringing out the chest when Philip called for it. In addition to the candles and the crucifix, the box was now reported to contain two whips, one well used and still stained with blood. Philip said they were his father's "disciplines" at Yuste, which he had often used in the presence of the monks. Philip ordered his father's crucifix to be hung where he could see it, inside the bed curtains, and asked Fernando de Toledo to keep the candles near at hand. Showing a marked interest in the symbolic value of ritual continuity within the royal family, Philip also asked his son to place these items back in the same box after he had died, so that the prince could also use them when his own inevitable moment arrived.[77]

[74] Siguenza, *Fundación*, p. 188.

[75] It was generally believed that these kinds of candles made at Montserrat with a likeness of that shrine's famous Marian image warded off the devils who gathered at the deathbed: "parece que solamente de la figura de Nuestra Señora tienen gran temor los demonios." *Libro de la historia y milagros, hechos a la invocación de Nuestra Señora de Montserrate* (Barcelona, 1594). The practice of dying with a candle in one's hand was also associated with one Biblical text (Luke 12.35): "Let your loins be girded and your lamps burning."

[76] Siguenza, *Fundación*, p. 189. Also: Yepes, *Relación*, fol. 58v.

[77] Siguenza, *Fundación*, p. 189.

About this same time (the eyewitness reports give no indication of the exact date), Philip also ordered that a coffin be built and brought to his room. He provided specific instructions for the construction of the coffin. He had already set aside the wood for it some time before from the remains of a Portuguese shipwreck that had been built from a particularly durable East Indian wood (appropriately enough, called a "tree of paradise"). The ship itself also had an appropriate name, *Cinco Chagas* (five wounds), which alluded to the passion and death of Christ. Philip had the keel from this ship brought to the Escorial from Lisbon at a great expense, since it was very large and heavy, and he carefully allotted part of the wood for the large crucifix over the main altar in the basilica under which he was to be buried, and another part for a smaller crucifix over the altar next to the door leading to the main cloister. He may have overestimated how much was needed for his coffin, for after it was built, a large piece remained unused, which the monks placed near the entrance to the monastery, to be used as a bench by the poor people who came begging.[78] Philip also ordered that the coffin be fitted with an inner lining of lead that could be securely sealed, to "prevent any bad odors from escaping," and asked for the interior to be covered with white silk and the exterior with black silk, trimmed in gold.

During his final days, Philip leaned heavily on his confessor and other spiritual advisors. Time after time he asked if the hour of his death had arrived and begged to be warned of its approach so that he could be truly ready. Two days before his death, Philip gave a document to Father Yepes that was to be passed on to the prince. It contained advice on how best to live and govern as a monarch and was supposedly modeled after the deathbed advice given by King Louis IX (St. Louis) of France to his son. Philip thus continued to pattern his own death according to models set by previous monarchs whom he regarded as holy.[79] This document was full of admonitions strictly in line with Catholic theology and piety:

[78] Ibid., pp. 189–90. The symbolic coincidences related to all of this are enough to send Siguenza into a paroxysm of devotional enthusiasm: "Quien considere tantas circunstancias del arbol, de su nombre, de la tierra, del oficio, y del fin, podra sin miedo decir que son cosa mas que acaso."

[79] Yepes, *Relación*, fol. 59. The confessor comments that Philip asked for this to be done "pareciendole que no podia el añadir a lo que este santo Rey con su espiritu de Dios abia aconsejado en aquel articulo." This document was read to Philip III by Yepes on the day of his father's funeral.

"Never allow yourself to fall into mortal sin. You should be willing to suffer any kind of torment rather than damage your soul with such a stain. . . . Confess your sins often. . . . Find yourself a good confessor. . . . Attend the Divine Office devoutly. . . . Listen to sermons from good preachers who condemn vices and express zeal for the honor and service of God. Try also to obtain pardons and indulgences. Love all that is good, despise what is evil." At the end, Philip reminded the prince: "I ask you to swear, my son, that if God sees fit to take me from this present life during this illness, you make sure that masses and sacrifices be offered for my soul throughout the entire realm."[80]

After he received the last rites, Philip took communion twice. But by 12 September he was so weak and wasted that his chaplains would not allow him to take communion, fearing he would not be able to digest the consecrated host. Philip was heartbroken to hear he could not partake of the sacrament and appealed to his physicians, but the doctors agreed with the priests, and the king was denied his wish. This was yet another form of torture for Philip, who throughout his life had shown ardent devotion to the Eucharist, even to the point of kneeling in public whenever he encountered the *viaticum* being taken to some dying person. In 1596, crippled with gout, Philip had run into one of these eucharistic processions. Wishing to express his devotion but unable to move, he made his son, the future Philip III, get out of the royal carriage, kneel, and join the procession. So it was that out of devotion to the eucharist that the prince walked through the streets of Madrid bareheaded (both were signs of abject humility for a royal personage), holding a candle behind the *viaticum* all the way into a dying commoner's room, and knelt at his bedside with no pillow under his knees (another gesture of humility). When the prince returned to the carriage, his father praised him, saying he would have done the same thing if his legs had been better.[81] Now the *viaticum* was denied to the king.

When the monks of the Escorial heard the news that Philip was fading fast, they flocked to prayer, "aiding him with their tears and prayers and other devotions proper to the hour." The Archbishop of Toledo entered Philip's chamber to comfort him personally during his final hours.

[80] Appendix to Cabrera de Cordoba, *Felipe II*, vol. 4, p. 392.
[81] Varela, *Muerte del rey*, p. 75, citing Jerónimo de Sepulveda, *Documentos para la historia del monasterio de San Lorenzo del Escorial* (Madrid, 1924, 1964–5), vol. 4, p. 183.

Among other things, the archbishop asked Philip to make a profession of faith, as an obedient son of the Church, testifying to his adherence to "the Catholic Faith, the Roman Church, and the Supreme Pontiff." Philip complied gladly and asked the archbishop to read to him the passion story from John's gospel. Father Yepes also spoke to him for some time after the archbishop had finished his reading, for Philip did not want all of this to stop while he was conscious. "Fathers, tell me more," he would say. Near midnight on 12 September, as those around him realized that little time remained, Philip seems to have gained some sense of his own condition. Whereas before he asked to be told if death was near, now he gave the impression that he knew when the hour would come. Fernando de Toledo, who had been entrusted with the box containing the candles and the crucifix of Charles V, tried to give the box to Philip at midnight. "Hold on to it," said the king, "for the hour has not yet arrived."[82]

In all the eyewitness accounts of Philip's passing, the moment of death itself is somewhat anticlimactic, but all the chroniclers want to make it clear that the *transito,* or crossing over from this world to the next, is something that should be experienced while fully conscious. Philip wanted to know exactly what was happening and when it was happening. He had often prayed throughout his long final illness that God grant him a lucid mind at the final moment, and he had also asked all those around him and at the monastery to pray for the same thing.[83] It was important to Philip, as accepted teaching advised, not to have to dwell on his corporeal existence during that moment, not to be distracted by pain, or to be in some foggy oblivion, but to be able to clearly "contemplate the divine mercy of God, embrace Him, and deal with his salvation." Siguenza claims that Philip was granted his prayer and that he was freed from pain for the last day and a half.[84]

At three in the morning of 13 September, Fernando de Toledo offered Charles V's box to Philip once again. This time, Philip lifted his eyes and said, laughing, "Give it to me, for the hour has come." Siguenza draws a lesson from this rather unusual response. "That is no time for laughter," he says. Those who have sought only the pleasures of this world are normally sad at such a moment, not happy. "But for those

[82] Siguenza, *Fundación,* pp. 191–2. [83] Yepes, *Relación,* fol. 59.
[84] Siguenza, *Fundación,* p. 192.

fortunate souls that used the things of this world, and carried out their duties and enjoyed their earthly dignities with no real attachment, this is the moment when their true happiness begins, and they can laugh."[85] Philip held the crucifix and one candle, as his father had done, and then lapsed into unconsciousness.

Shortly thereafter, the king suffered a violent seizure that greatly alarmed all who were in his chamber; when it subsided, some thought that he had finally died and wanted to cover his face. Suddenly, and much to everyone's surprise, the king opened his eyes and stared alertly. Noticing immediately that Fernando de Toledo had removed the crucifix and candle from his hands, he took them back, and "with great tenderness and devotion kissed the crucifix that he had in one hand many times, and also did the same with the image of Our Lady of Montserrat imprinted on the one candle that he held in his other hand." As the king clutched his father's crucifix, "tenderly" smothering Christ's feet with kisses, the prior of the Escorial read a special prayer for Philip's soul from the Roman missal, which made Philip even happier.[86]

The king's last words, which he apparently spoke with some difficulty, testified that he was dying "as a Catholic, in the faith and obedience of the holy Roman Church." He died holding the crucifix and candle his father had also used at the same moment, one in each hand, "kissing his crucifix thousands of times," with a relic of Saint Alban displayed before him on the bed, "for its indulgences." He drifted away slowly and peacefully, "and with two or three gasps his holy soul departed to enjoy the sovereign Kingdom, as is proven by so many signs." Philip died at sunrise on the morning of 13 September, "in the same house and temple

---

[85] Ibid.

[86] Yepes, *Relación*, fol. 59v places the event earlier, at about two or three hours before Philip's death. Siguenza, *Fundación*, p. 192, says this took place one and a half hours before the king died. Both interpret the paroxysm as some kind of spiritual rapture rather than a violent physical reaction. Cervera de la Torre, *Testimonio*, p. 125–8, who edited the reports of many eyewitnesses, claims this happened two hours before Philip died. His description of Philip's devotion to the articles left behind for this purpose by his father is the most detailed. He says Philip was aided by three men: Enrique de Guzmán helped with the candle, Fernando de Toledo with the crucifix, and Francisco de Ribera with the relic. As to the way in which the king kissed the crucifix, Cervera de la Torre says: "Y daba grandisimas muestras del deseo ardiente que tenia por morir besando los pies del santo crucifixo, que se los metía dentro de la boca, con grandisima ternura y edificación de todos."

of San Lorenzo that he had built, and almost directly over his own grave
. . . as dawn broke in the east and the sun's rays brought in the light of
Sunday, the day of light and the day of the Lord, and as the boys of the
seminary sang the morning mass, the final one of his life, and the first
one of his death."[87]

[87] Siguenza, *Fundación*, p. 193. The fact that Philip died as the seminary boys were
singing is not without significance. It was commonly believed that the prayers of
children on behalf of the dead were especially efficacious. Venegas *Agonía*, p. 140:
"Ademas de los clerigos y otros circumstantes, que rezarán en el tiempo del transito,
harán a todos los niños que estuvieren en casa, o fueren llamados de vecinos, que
también ellos se pongan en oración, porque es muy acepta a Dios aquella inocencia
bautismal que tienen; que aunque por no tener el uso de la razón no hacen obras de
merecer, es cosa congruente por la imensa bondad de Dios, que oye la plegaria de
aquellos niños por el estado de gracia en que están."

2

The king's many requiems

Because a king needs to embody the ultimate values of his realm, yet also be above his subjects, his funerary ritual is simultaneously a participation in the ritual life of the people and a mark of distinction. Like virtually all Spaniards, Philip was buried according to the rites of the Roman Catholic Church, but unlike most Spaniards, he was buried directly beneath the room in which he died and had the benefits of multiple funerals elsewhere. In significant ways, Philip reified the death paradigms found in Madrid testaments. At the same time, however, he went beyond these to establish paradigms of his own. To better understand this two-way interrelation of attitudes and gestures, let us briefly look at Philip's testament and burial and at the ceremonies throughout Spain that marked his passing.

Philip's testament

As the *Ars Moriendi* advised, in 1594 Philip wrote a will before his final illness and added some codicils later. As could be expected, Philip showed a marked concern for the details of his funeral arrangements and pious bequests. His requests are much like those of Madrid's testators but with one significant difference: Philip could ask for so much more. In some ways, his was the ideal testament, for he was able to tap the salvific resources of the church to their fullest. Take, for instance, the invocation of the saints. Though he offered his body to the earth and his soul to God, professed his faith in the Roman Catholic Church, begged for forgiveness, and implored the saints in heaven for assistance like any

other sinner, Philip addressed so many intercessors that his list of advocates nearly matches name for name the *total* list of those invoked by all
Madrid testators.[1]

When it came to suffrages, the king pulled out all the stops, consign-
ing the Hieronymite fathers of the Escorial to perpetual labor and laying
heavy responsibilities on other clerics elsewhere. To begin with, Philip
wanted masses to be said for his soul by all the priests of the Escorial for
the first nine days after his death: a *novenario* truly fit for a king. In
addition, he requested that in the shortest amount of time possible (*lo
mas presto que ser pueda*), 30,000 masses be said for his soul at whichever
observant Franciscan monastery could do so with the greatest devotion
(to be chosen by his executors). These 30,000 were to be divided into
thirds: 10,000 requiem masses, 10,000 masses of the Passion of Christ,
and 10,000 masses of Our Lady. For the souls in purgatory, Philip
requested an additional 2,000 masses and at the end of each of them,
special prayers for his own soul.[2]

In a codicil, Philip requested even more. At the Escorial, at the altar
directly above the royal mausoleum, one high mass was to be said for his
soul every single day until Christ's second coming. Also daily, the Hieronymites of the Escorial were to add a prayer for his soul to their
canonical hours. Two perpetual anniversary masses were to be said for
him as well: one on his birth date and one on his death date. The same
dual anniversary masses were to be said for each of the following: his
parents, Charles and Isabel, and his wife Queen Ana, the mother of the
heir to the throne, Philip III. A single anniversary mass was to be said on
the death dates of eight other relatives, including those of his three other
wives and his ill-fated son Don Carlos. This was all in addition to many
other masses that had already been established and had been punctually
said ever since the royal corpses had come to the Escorial in 1574. The

---

[1] *Testamento de Felipe II*, pp. 2–3. In addition to Mary, Philip invoked the following
saints, by category: (1) Angels: Michael, Gabriel, his guardian angel, and all the angels
in heaven; (2) New Testament saints: John the Baptist, Peter and Paul, James (patron
of all Spain), Andrew, John the Evangelist, Philip (his name saint), Mary Magdalene,
(patroness of repentant sinners) and Anne (apocryphal); (3) Patristic era patron saints:
Lawrence and Jerome (both significant for the Escorial), and George (patron of
Catalonia); (4) Monastic leaders: Benedict, Bernard, Dominic, Francis; (5) Local
saint: Diego de Alcalá.

[2] *Testamento de Felipe II*, pp. 6–7.

total was staggering: Siguenza's accounting put the number at 7,300 masses per year – and this figure did not include the anniversary liturgies! On top of all this, Philip also requested that two monks always be at prayer around the clock in perpetual adoration of the Blessed Sacrament at the basilica of the Escorial, "forever and ever," interceding for his soul and the souls of the royal family. "Altogether it makes for a most weighty load," winced Siguenza, observing that only the most highly dedicated, self-renouncing men would dare join the Hieronymites at the Escorial.[3]

Philip also left more to charity than almost anyone else could, especially if one counts the foundation of the Escorial and numerous other bequests not mentioned in the will. Nonetheless, the charitable bequests in his will do not seem to be a fair reflection of his vast fortune. His choices conformed to accepted patterns: clothing for 100 poor people; 10,000 *ducados* for the dowries of poor girls, with preference for the daughters of his servants; 30,000 *ducados* for the redemption of captives, with preference for Spanish soldiers; and 2,000 *ducados* each to the shrines of Santiago and Montserrat for the purchase of silver lamps.[4]

Philip asked for a papal jubilee and plenary indulgence for all his masses and works of charity "so they be more acceptable to God and of greater usefulness toward the salvation of my soul." The pope obliged. Philip also asked for and was granted a papal jubilee for the feasts of St. Philip and St. James celebrated at the Escorial.[5]

Philip's burial

As soon as the king died, his corpse was dressed in a simple tunic, wrapped in a winding sheet, and placed in a lead casket. Soldered shut, this was then placed inside the wooden coffin that had been made from the Portuguese shipwreck, all according to Philip's meticulous deathbed instructions. A simple wooden cross hung from Philip's neck on a rope, the only adornment on the man who owned the globe's richest treasures.[6]

---

[3] Siguenza, *Fundación*, pp. 196–97. The codicil outlined by Siguenza has not been included in *Testamento de Felipe II.*

[4] Ibid., pp. 8–9. [5] Ibid., pp. 10–11.

[6] Siguenza, *Fundación*, p. 194. Lhermite, *Passetemps*, II, p. 145, adds that two whips made from cords were placed on either side of the body.

The Hieronymites began their liturgical duties immediately, saying masses for his soul at every altar of the Escorial. A solemn requiem mass was said by the prior at the high altar at nine in the morning, while Philip's body still lay in his chambers, which was followed by prayers (*responsos*) and an afternoon vigil with more *responsos*. At six in the afternoon his corpse was taken into the basilica's sacristy by a small band of candle-carrying Hieronymites who solemnly intoned *De profundis* and other mournful psalms. Philip's coffin was so heavy that it took several men a long time to lift it off the floor of his chamber and ferry it the short distance to the sacristy, where they laid it on a carpet-covered table, under a brocade canopy. A vigil was then held there throughout the night.[7]

On the following day, 14 September, the coffin was taken from the sacristy in a solemn procession to the main cloister of the Escorial and around its perimeter to a door on the south wall of the basilica, into the temple, and up to a catafalque that had been erected beneath the dome. The new king Philip III took part in this funeral cortege, along with the entire Hieronymite community and all others who were present at court. The king and his attendants were dressed in the customary mourning robes (*loba con cola larga, capirote y caperuza*), which were long and hooded. Every participant carried a candle. It was a slow and arduous procession, with numerous *posas* and *responsos*, for many weeping Hieronymites and *caballeros* had to take turns carrying Philip's heavy coffin.[8] A two-hour high requiem mass was then said for the king by the Archbishop of Toledo, who was so overcome with weeping that he had difficulty getting through the opening prayer. Afterward, another solemn procession carried the king's remains to the burial vault that lay directly beneath the high altar of the basilica. Philip III followed the coffin all the way into the vault where he and his descendants were also to be buried and saw how his father's coffin was placed next to his mother's.[9]

---

[7] According to Lhermite, *Passetemps*, II, p. 149, the carpet used here was the one used twice a year for Charles V's anniversary masses.

[8] Lhermite, *Passetemps* II, p. 151, Cervera de la Torre, pp. 149–51, lists twenty-three grandees and titled nobles who carried the king's coffin.

[9] Cervera de la Torre, p. 152, said of Philip II's location, "Y viene a estar el cuerpo debaxo de las gradas del altar mayor, donde el sacerdote pone los pies quando dize la Confession de la Missa." The burial crypt was at this time unadorned. According to Lhermite, *Passetemps*, II, pp. 152–3, it was simply painted white, and the coffins were

On Tuesday 15 September, Rodrigo Vazquez de Arce, president of the Royal Council, opened Philip II's will and read it to Philip III, the royal family, the members of the court, the prior of the Escorial, and some Hieronymites. Philip III retired to Madrid on the 16 September to begin a mourning period at the royal apartment that Philip II had built at the Hieronymite monastery of San Jerónimo el Real. As the dead king had requested in his will, each day for the next nine, every priest at the Escorial said a mass for his soul.[10]

With the death of the king, the entire realm went into mourning. A proclamation issued by Philip III ordered every citizen to don mourning garb and to refrain from lighthearted activities upon pain of imprisonment.[11] Civic officials throughout the realm purchased gowns for themselves and draperies for public buildings at government expense. In Seville, so much black fabric was sold that it began to fetch black market prices. Poor people who could not afford the appropriate garb were arrested and thrown into prison. Apparently, the number of arrests was so high that Philip III had to modify the requirements, allowing the poor simply to wear unadorned hats.[12]

Philip's exequies

A single funeral ceremony held in the privacy of the Escorial was not sufficient for the monarch. Public rites also had to be observed in the capital and throughout the realm. These ceremonies, which were called royal exequies (*exequias reales*) or funerary honors (*honras fúnebres*) were not burial rites in the strict meaning of the term. Yet, they were much more than memorial services, that is, solemn acts of remembrance for a deceased person in which the corpse is not present and in which no burial takes place. Though the royal corpse was not present, these royal exequies were quasi-funeral rituals with requiem masses. They recapitu-

---

deposited in niches along one wall. The only decorations were two crosses on which hung some whips "en signe et remonstrance de lieu de penitence et contrition."

[10] Siguenza, *Fundación*, p. 196.

[11] Francisco Jerónimo Collado, *Descripción del Túmulo y relación de las exequias que hizo la ciudad de Sevilla en la muerte del Rey don Felipe II* (1598), in *Sociedad de Bibliófilos Andaluces*, series 2, vol. 22 (Seville, 1869), p. 2.

[12] Francisco de Ariño, *Sucesos de Sevilla de 1592 á 1604, Sociedad de Bibliófilos Andaluces*, series 1 (Seville, 1873).

lated and symbolized Philip's burial at the Escorial on a local level throughout Iberia, and even around the globe, from Brussels and Naples to Mexico and Manila. They were rites of passage for the Spanish empire. Though the king had been buried in his palace of death at its center, he still needed to be laid to rest symbolically by his subjects throughout the periphery.[13]

Charles V had injected much of Burgundian court ritual into the Spanish monarchy, and a significant element of this Burgundian heritage was the celebration of royal exequies.[14] *Honras fúnebres* had been observed throughout the Iberian kingdoms in medieval times, but it was Charles's fondness for certain kinds of symbolic splendor that set the tone for generations to come.[15] One of the most salient features of the royal exequies for Charles and his Hapsburg successors was the creation of lavish ephemeral decorations for the major churches where exequies would be held.[16] Black draperies were hung throughout the entire church, usually in such a manner as to conceal the edifice and transform its appearance. The exterior entrance, the nave, and the transept were covered in somber black and festooned with symbolic regalia: shields, flags, emblems, and a peculiar genre of verbal/pictorial epigrams known as hieroglyphs.[17] The nave was turned into a narrow aisle, with seating

[13] A sentiment clearly voiced by Agustín Davila, O.P., in his funeral sermon for Philip II at Valladolid, 1598: *Sermones funerales*, fol. 69r-v.

[14] On the emperor's role in the creation of ceremonial, see Ludwig Pfandl, *Philippe II*, tr. M. E. Lepointe (Paris, 1942), pp. 116 ff.; and Julián Gallego, *Vision et symboles dans la peinture Espagnole du siècle d'or* (Paris, 1968), pp. 120ff. On Burgundian ceremonial, see O. von Cartellieri, *The Court of Burgundy* (London, 1929), and R. Vaughan, *Philip the Good* (New York, 1970), and *Valois Burgundy* (London, 1974). On late medieval Burgundian funeral rites, see L. Lemaire, "La mort de Philippe le Bon," *Revue du Nord* 1 (1910): 321–6; and the manuscript account of Philip the Good's exequies, ed. E. Lory, under the title *Les obsèques de Philippe le Bon* (Dijon, 1869).

[15] For an overview of Hapsburg ceremonies, see Christina Hofmann, *Das Spanische Hofzeremoniell von 1500–1700* (Frankfurt am Main, 1985).

[16] The apogee of these celebrations in the seventeenth century has been examined in great detail by Steven N. Orso, *Art and Death at the Spanish Court: The Royal Exequies for Philip IV* (Columbia MO, 1989). Orso deals briefly with the development of these rites in Spain, esp. pp. 6–26.

[17] The appearance of emblems and hieroglyphs in Spanish royal exequies coincides with the publication of Andrea Alciato's *Emblematum libellis* (1531), translated into Castilian Spanish in 1549. Sebastián de Horozco further developed and publicized these encoded signs in his *Emblemas morales* (Segovia, 1589). See Varela, *Muerte del rey,*

along the sides. In some cases, the side chapels were totally hidden; in others, they were used for seating. The impermanent nature of such costly decorations pointed to the fleeting character of life itself; the constriction of the nave denoted the narrowness of the true path of life and its likeness to a pilgrimage, a journey, or a passage (*tránsito*) to the hereafter. That was but the overall effect. The entire display was a barrage of the most complex and tightly encoded sort of symbolic minutiae, a semiotic extravaganza that begged interpretation and required decoding manuals.[18] These displays sought to teach thousands of lessons at once and at many different levels.

But there was no mistaking the chief symbol within this riot of symbols, for the narrowness of the nave and arrangement of the seating led everyone's eye straight to the catafalque at the transept, the *túmulo*, an elaborate columned and arched structure of immense proportions, bedecked with emblems and thousands of candles, in which the royal insignia rested on a sepulchral slab (*tumba*) during the requiem mass. When fully lit, the catafalque was an awesome sight: The light could be blinding, the heat and smoke overwhelming. The symbolism was as thick as the smoke, but one message was clear: The catafalque, the *tumba*, and the royal insignia represented the king's real body at the Escorial.[19] The symbolism of the candles could also be easily discerned. Because light is the most ephemeral element, it stood for the soul. Additionally, the contrast between brilliance of the catafalque and the darkness of the church stood for the triumph of life over death.[20] These symbols could refer at once to the king and to every human being. One funeral sermon, for instance, declared that the catafalque and the crown

---

p. 53; and Aquilino Sánchez Perez, *La literatura emblemática española (Siglos XVI y XVII)* (Madrid, 1977).

[18] Gallego, *Vision et symboles*, pp. 134 ff. Such manuals began to be published regularly in the seventeenth century, as the royal exequies became more rigidly codified. See Steven Orso's bibliography in *Art and Death*, pp. 201–8. Two examples: *Relación de las Honras del Rey Felipe Tercero que está en el cielo, y la solene entrada en Madrid del Rey Felipe Quarto, que Dios guarde* (Madrid, 1621); for Philip IV: Pedro Rodriguez de Monforte, *Descripción de las honras que se hicieron a la Catholica Magestad de Don Phelippe quarto Rey de las Españas y del nuevo mundo en el Real Convento de la Encarnación* (Madrid, 1666)

[19] Martín de Castro, funeral sermon for Philip II at the Royal Chapel of Granada, 1598: *Sermones funerales*, fol. 231 r.

[20] Ibid., fols. 231r–v.

Catafalque of the Emperor Charles V at San Benito El Real, Valladolid 1559. From Juan Cristóbal Calvete de Estrella, *El Tumulo Imperial adornado de Historias y Letreros, Epitaphios en prosa y verso* (Valladolid, 1559).

resting on its pillow were symbols of God's justice and of the sentence of death He had passed on all of humanity for Adam's disobedience.[21] On a more mundane level, many could also not help but notice that whereas they were limited to a dozen candles at their funerals by sumptuary laws (or at most two dozen if they were nobles), the monarch could have dozens upon dozens.

The Burgundians had employed these *chapelles ardentes,* or flaming chapels, in their royal funerals, and at the time of Charles V's exequies they had been widely used, even in Spain.[22] It was at the time of Philip II's exequies, however, that the Spanish adopted the catafalque with a zeal all their own.[23] Philip II's exequies bristled with catafalques: Nearly all the printed funeral sermons made some reference to the local *túmulo* and interpreted its symbolism. In Valladolid alone, Philip's birthplace, at least three were erected.[24] Among the most magnificent was that in the cathedral of Seville, which sought to imitate the Escorial, down to the color of its stones. This monument was as high as the nave itself and was massively broad, with two lateral galleries that crossed the transept from end to end. Illumined by 2,320 candles of various sizes, bedecked with emblematic art, and topped off by a phoenix, it was a veritable triumph of ephemeral art.[25] Two of Spain's most illustrious authors even commented on it. Lope de Vega pondered: "What was this immense structure to a king who governed the world, and whom earth could not

---

[21] Luis Montesino, funeral sermon at the collegial church of Sts. Justo y Pastor, Alcalá de Henares, 1598: *Sermones funerales,* fol. 115v.

[22] There were several other names used for the catafalque in Spain: *catafalco, capelardente, pira, mausoleo, monumento,* and *máquina.* Varela, *Muerte del rey,* p. 112, and fig. 11 for illustrations of the 1558 catafalques for Charles V at Brussels and Valladolid.

[23] Julián Gallego, *Vision et symboles,* p. 131, says that death was "une des principales sources des fêtes et célébrations espagnoles," and that catafalques dwarfed all other forms of ceremonial art in terms of scale and significance. Philip II had already held exequies in Madrid for his son Don Carlos, and his wives Elizabeth of Valois and Anne of Austria. See Dalmiro de la Valgoma y Díaz Varela, "Honras fúnebres regias en tiempo de Felipe II," in *El Escorial 1563–1963* (Madrid, 1963), vol. I, pp. 359–98.

[24] *Sermones funerales;* At Valladolid: at an unidentified church, fols. 69r–v; at San Benito el Real, fol. 92r; and at the university, fols. 259r, 265r. Among other catafalques mentioned: Baeza, fol. 9r.; Alcalá, fol. 115v; Barcelona, fol. 131r; Logroño, fol. 206r; Granada, fols. 231r–v.

[25] Collado, *Descripción del túmulo,* esp. pp. 20–21; 216–17; 222–3; Ariño, *Sucesos de Sevilla,* pp. 103–5, plus appendixes with documents pertaining to the construction of the catafalque, pp. 121–292.

contain, and now fits into a small box at the Escorial, and has room to spare?"[26] Cervantes was filled with awe and suggested that Philip II would gladly leave heaven just to see it. "It is a shame," he added, "that this shall not last a century."[27]

As in all things Spanish at this time, there was a hierarchy among exequies, and the most notable of all was that in which the new king took part. Beginning with the death of Philip II, this ritual unfolded for the Hapsburgs at the monastery church of San Jerónimo el Real on the eastern rim of Madrid. This Hieronymite monastery had been a place of retreat for Philip II, a small reflection of the Escorial.[28] Its prominence among Madrid's churches was undeniable; under Philip IV, it evolved into the splendid Palacio del Buen Retiro.[29] It was there that Philip III went into seclusion to observe a mourning period – and to allow time for the construction of the catafalque and the decoration of the church.

On 18 to 19 October 1598, funeral honors were celebrated for Philip II at San Jerónimo.[30] A sumptuous catafalque had been constructed,

[26] Lope de Vega, "El amante agradecido," *Obras de Lope de Vega*, Real Academia Española (Madrid, 1917), vol. 3, pp. 118–120.

[27] "Al Túmulo de Felipe II," *Obras Completas de Miguel de Cervantes Saavedra*, Real Academia Española (Madrid, 1923), vol. 7, p. 253: "Voto a Dios que me espanta esta grandeza/ y que diera un doblón por describilla,/ a quién no le espanta y maravilla/ esta maquina insigne, esta belleza?/ . . . es mancilla/ que esto no dure un siglo."

[28] On the history of this institution see Baltasar Cuartero y Huerta, *El monasterio de San Jerónimo el Real: Protección y dádivas de los Reyes de España a dicho Monasterio* (Madrid, 1966); and Aurea de la Morena, "El Monasterio de San Jerónimo el Real, de Madrid," *Anales del Instituto de Estudios Madrileños* 10 (1974): 47–78. On the relation between the monarchy and the Hieronymite order see Jonathan Brown, *Images and Ideas in Seventeenth-Century Spanish Painting* (Princeton, 1978), pp. 112–27.

[29] Jonathan Brown and John Elliott, *A Palace for a King: The Buen Retiro and the Court of Philip IV* (New Haven/London, 1980). Ironically, Philip IV had his exequies at the convent church of La Encarnación.

[30] I have relied chiefly on the account published by Juan Iñiguez de Lequerica with the *Sermones funerales*, fols. 5v–7v: "Relación de la forma en que se hizieron las honras del Rey don Felipe Nuestro Señor, Segundo de ese nombre, difunto que se en gloria, en el Monasterio de San Jerónimo el Real de Madrid, el 18 de Octubre de 1598." I have also used Lhermite, *Passetemps*, II, pp. 158–166. I did not consult two manuscripts that came to my attention only as this book was going to press in 1994: "Naçimiento y successos (Por mayor) Del Rey Don Phelipe Segundo nuestro señor, y su testamento, muerte, y honras," London, British Library, Ms. Add. 10,236, fols. 27–45; and "Relaçión de lo que paso a loas honrras que su magestad mando hazer en San

rising to the summit of the transept, topped off with a giant crown. It was square, with twelve columns, golden molding, nearly 1,000 twelve-ounce candles, four large tapers, and twenty-four torches; additional candles throughout the church brought the total number of lights to 2,500! The sides of the altar were draped in gold and black cloth, the rest of the church in black damask and velvet. In the center of the lowest level of the *túmulo* stood a pall-covered sepulcher (*tumba*); atop it, the royal insignia rested on a pillow: a crown, a scepter, a sword, and a collar of the Order of the Golden Fleece.[31] The same black and gold cloth was used for the pall on the *tumba* as for the vestments of the chief celebrant, the Archbishop of Toledo. This was a detail carefully planned by Philip II, who had chosen the fabric for this occasion before his death.[32]

On 18 October, a Sunday, Philip III left San Jerónimo in a curtained carriage at 2:00 P.M. Hiding thus from the public's eye, he traveled a short distance to pick up his sister at the convent of the Descalzas Reales, where she was spending her mourning period. This was only the second time the new king had ventured in seclusion from his retreat since having arrived there the previous month. While the king was on this errand, the candles were lit at San Jerónimo and the church began to fill with notables who processed in and were seated according to rank: bishops in the chancel, to the left of the high altar; grandees, ambassadors, and the king's *mayordomos* and chaplains in the transept, closest to the catafalque; and all of the king's councils along both sides of the nave. Ladies were relegated to the side chapels. The highest places were reserved for the Archbishop of Toledo and the royal family. The prince and other royals – the last to enter before the king – had their own custom-built oratory in the transept. The king had his own oratory there as well, with an unobstructed view of the catafalque and the high altar.[33]

Geronimo de Madrid por el rey nuestro señor su padre queaya gloria, domingo 17 de octubre de 1598," BNM, Ms. 18,718.

[31] The Order of the Golden Fleece was of Burgundian origin, and this collar was a favorite of Charles V and Philip II. For more on this collar and its symbolism, see Earl E. Rosenthal, "The Invention of the Columnar Device of Emperor Charles V at the Court of Burgundy in Flanders in 1516," *Journal of the Warburg and Courtauld Institutes* 36 (1973): 198–230.

[32] *Sermones funerales*, fol. 5v, 6r, 7v.

[33] Cervera de la Torre lists some of the grandees and other notables in attendance,

Catafalque of King Philip II at San Jerónimo El Real, Madrid 1598 (frontal view).
Drawing from Jean Lhermite's manuscript, *Le Passetemps,* early 1600s, published at
Antwerp 1890–6.

When the king arrived at San Jerónimo, he entered from the monastery cloister through a side door to the church, wearing his long mourning robe, his head and face hidden by its large drooping hood. Accompanied by a retinue of grandees, nobles, and *mayordomos*, the king made his way around the back of the catafalque to his private, curtained oratory in the transept from which he could observe the rites and not be seen by anyone. Throughout this three-hour funeral vespers service, Philip remained hidden from all.[34]

On the following day, services began at 6:00 A.M. with matins and lauds. The Bishop of Guadix then celebrated a pontifical mass of Our Lady in white vestments. He was followed by the Bishop of Ciudad Rodrigo, who said a pontifical mass of the Holy Spirit in red vestments. Afterward, the notables began to assemble for the main event: a high requiem mass by the Archbishop of Toledo in the somber vestments designed by Philip II. The same order of procession was observed as the day before. Again, Philip III was the last to enter, unseen, as soon as the new set of 2,500 candles on the catafalque and in the church were lit. At the offertory, Philip III emerged from hiding for the first and last time, to hand a gold doubloon to a deacon, who then passed it on to the Archbishop of Toledo. The archbishop closed the mass with a rite of absolution in which he wafted incense and sprinkled holy water on the royal insignia in the catafalque while *responsas* were sung. By the time the participants began to file out in the proper order, it was already 2:00 in the afternoon.[35] Philip II had just been laid to rest in Madrid. Now the rest of his empire had to do the same, city by city.

Outside Madrid, however, exequies could become ritual disasters. In Seville, a dispute about rank and mourning draperies involving the city council, the Inquisition, and the *Real Audiencia* led to the abrupt cancellation of the requiem mass on 26 November, as the Gospel was about to be read, and resulted in the imprisonment of the *Alcalde Mayor* and some of the city's highest officials. The 6,144 candles being held by clerics and the 2,320 on the catafalque were snuffed out, and while the

pp. 154–6. An illustration of the seating arrangement at another royal exequy at San Jerónimo, shown in Fig. 16 of Varela, *Muerte del rey*, fits the description in the *Sermones funebres*.

34 Lhermite, *Passetemps*, II, pp. 161–2. The oratory is described by Steven Orso, *Art and Death*, p. 20.

35 *Sermones funerales*, fols. 7r-v; Lhermite, *Passetemps*, II, pp. 164–6.

case was being settled in court, the ceremonies were put on hold. It took a royal order from Philip III to force the city to hold the exequies on New Year's Eve – without the disputed draperies.[36]

Dead king, king installed

"Rey muerto, rey puesto," asserts an ancient Castilian proverb, meaning that as soon as one king dies, another succeeds him.[37] Out with the old, in with the new: The king's body may dissolve, but the monarchy endures. The exequies celebrated at San Jerónimo, and to a lesser degree those celebrated elsewhere, were also a rite of succession. Inasmuch as the royal paradigm of death was intimately tied to the question of the stability and sacredness of the monarchy, a few comments are in order about the peculiarities of royal succession in Spain.

Though Philip II was monarch of all the various Iberian kingdoms at the time of his death, he was not the ruler of a nation state in the modern sense. Quite the contrary, he governed an immense patchwork of realms assembled principally through dynastic intermarriage and conquest. Though the tenuousness of his rule was most painfully evident in places outside Iberia, such as the Netherlands, it was not much firmer even within the confines of the peninsula.[38] He may have had a single symbolic crown resting within the catafalque at San Jerónimo, but in actual fact he had an array of crowns, some of which were themselves cumulative agglutinations: the crown of Castile and León (containing also Galicia, Asturias, Extremadura, Andalusia, and Granada), the crown of Aragón (containing also Valencia and Catalonia), the crown of Navarre (including the Basque lands), and the crown of Portugal (acquired with some resistance in 1580). Philip's Iberian kingdoms were an ethnic collage where racial and regional prejudices ran deep. Moreover, they shared no sole primordial allegiance, no unified code of law, no single

---

[36] Ariño, *Suceşos de Sevilla,* pp. 102–5. This volume also contains numerous legal documents related to this fiasco, pp. 297–526.

[37] Nieto Soria, *Poder Real,* p. 240, citing Eleanor O'Kane, *Refranes y frases proverbiales españolas de la Edad Media* (Madrid, 1959).

[38] As the revolts of Portugal and Catalonia would prove in 1640. See John H. Elliott, *The Revolt of the Catalans: A Study in the Decline of Spain, 1598–1640* (Cambridge, 1963), esp. pp. 1–21; and *The Count-Duke of Olivares: The Statesman in an Age of Decline* (New Haven/London, 1986), esp. pp. 191–202, 244–77.

coinage, no common language, and no single tradition of political rights. Moreover, Philip's sovereignty was limited, checked as it was at almost every turn by a tangled web of local and corporate privileges (*fueros*).

In Spain, then, it was the person of the king that held the realm together rather than a singular constitutional framework or an abstract concept of monarchy. Because of this, the monarch's death was a perilous moment. As his body dissolved, so could his rule. Each of his Iberian kingdoms, of course, had similar enough traditions of succession to ensure agreement upon dynastic continuity, but, as will be seen more clearly in the final chapter of this second book, Philip had no single ancient myth, no common symbolic tradition, and no unified rite of succession he could rely on to keep centrifugal forces at bay. Because the potential for disaster lurked at the moment of succession, Philip relied on his own peculiar religious intuition – as he had done with the building of the Escorial – and enhanced the monarchy's centripetal force through the orchestration of myth, ritual, and symbol. And he did so by blending Roman Catholic liturgical forms, Burgundian court ritual, and Castilian traditions of royal succession.

In medieval Castile, the beginning of the king's reign dated from the death of his predecessor, and there was no constitutional significance attached to the burial of the dead king or to the acclamation of the new. As a rule, Castilian kings had no coronation ceremony. This is not to say that ritual played no role. A critical point in the succession process was the ritual swearing in (*juramento*) of the heir apparent, who was chosen by the king from among his children and who from that point forward would be known as "the sworn prince" (*príncipe jurado*). Upon the king's death, the sworn prince would succeed him automatically. Nonetheless, accession rituals at this liminal time of transition seem to have been viewed as an efficient cause of kingship. Public ceremony served to confirm a myth about Castilian kingship: the notion that the monarchs were theoretically elected by the nobility and acclaimed by the people.[39] Since 1366 this election/acclamation had been ritually accomplished throughout Castile by means of a ceremony known as the *levantamiento*

[39] Angus Mackay, "Ritual and Propaganda in Fifteenth-Century Castile," *Past and Present* 107 (1985): 19–20. See also: Pedro Longas, "La coronación liturgica del rey en la Edad Media," *Anuario de Historia del Derecho Español* 23 (1953): 371–81; and Luis G. Valdevellano, *Curso de historia de las instituciones españolas: De los órigines al final de la edad media* (Madrid, 1968), p. 431.

del pendón, or raising of the standard, which was usually celebrated in the major cities of the realm.[40] The exact rubrics of the ritual varied from place to place, but its function everywhere was similar: This ceremony combined funeral honors for the dead king with the acclamation of his successor. To be more specific, let us look at one such event: the raising of the standard at Avila upon the death of Henry IV. The ritual began with a mourning procession consisting of representatives of the city's oligarchy, which involved ritual crying (*llantos*) and the symbolic break-ing of the dead king's shields at strategic places within the city. This was followed by a requiem mass in the cathedral. At the end of the mass, a black standard (*pendón*) that stood for the dead king was torn as one final mourning cry marked his passing. The oligarchs who had formed the procession then changed from their mourning garb and re-entered the church with gold shields and a red banner. The standard bearer raised the new king's *pendón* and proclaimed: "Castile, Castile for the most high and illustrious lady, our lady Queen Doña Isabella!", and "Castile, Castile for the most high and most powerful lord, our lord King Don Ferdinand, her lawful husband!" This pronouncement was then ac-claimed by the congregation: "Amen! Amen!" The same oligarchs who had processed into the church made their way back through the city, raising the standard and repeating the acclamation at strategic locations. This ritual completed, the city sent representatives to Isabella at Segovia to swear their allegiance through the kissing of her hands (*besamanos*).[41] It seems, then, that a monarch remained somehow "imperfect" until acclaimed in public ceremonies.

One significant change from this medieval Castilian tradition in Philip II's exequies was the separation of the funeral honors from the acclama-tion ritual. Even more significant was the inversion of their chronology. Whereas the earlier tradition had been to hold the acclamation *after* the funeral honors, the raising of the standard for Philip III took place in Madrid on 10 October 1598, a week *before* the royal exequies at San

[40] Varela, *Muerte del rey*, p. 61.
[41] Angus Mackay, "Ritual and Propaganda," p. 24. The event is reconstructed from "Honras por Enrique IV y proclamación de Isabel la Cátolica en la ciudad de Avila," *Boletín de la Real Academia de la Historia* 63 (1913): 417–34. For comparison with another locality's celebration, see Juan Torres Fontes, *Estampas de la vida en Murcia en el reinado de los Reyes Cátolicos* (Murcia, 1961), pt. 6, pp. 21–6.

Jerónimo.[42] This was the first occasion in which the new king had left his retreat, traveling across the city to the Alcazar in his curtained coach. As in the exequies, Philip III remained concealed from the public, even as he was acclaimed by a crowd outside the palace. "He saw everything, and no one saw him," said one account of this ceremony.[43]

Acclaiming the new Philip before the old one had fully departed meant, of course, that the question of succession had been tidied up in a state of liminality, when *potential* is more easily turned into *fact* by ritual. In other words, Philip III gained ritual recognition as king while his father was still symbolically present, hovering over Madrid, as it were, waiting for his funeral honors. This enhanced the acclamation by making it ritually impossible to question the king's status once his father was "fully" dead. This calculated attempt to extract as much symbolic and ritual advantage from liminality may also go a long way toward explaining why Philip III remained concealed when he participated in the acclamation and the funeral honors, and why he did not reveal himself to the citizens of Madrid in a grand entrance ceremony until 8 November.[44] In a culture where symbol and ritual were the language of power, these gestures spoke volumes about questions that surrounded the nature and character of the monarchy. And, as we shall soon see, these were not academic questions at the time of Philip II's death.

[42] Lhermite, *Passetemps*, II, p. 158. This varied according to location, but Madrid's symbolic centrality enhances the significance of the gesture. The raising of the standard in Seville took place *after* the exequies and was quite different from that of Madrid. Ariño, *Sucesos de Sevilla*, pp. 108–9.

[43] Varela, *Muerte del rey*, p. 61, quoting from "Libro de noticias particulares," Archivo de la Villa de Madrid, Secretaría, 4-122-15.

[44] Lhermite, *Passetemps* II, p. 170. After the exequies, Philip III left Madrid for the Escorial, Segovia, Balsaín, and El Pardo, where he gave himself over to the royal pastime of the hunt.

3

Drawing lessons
from the king's death

Immediately following the death of Philip and for some time afterward, many accounts of his death were published; some of them were officially commissioned, and others were published through private initiative. Derived mostly from eyewitness reports, there is very little disagreement or contradiction among them. Though all these accounts aimed to portray Philip in the best possible light, their attention to grossly unpleasant details indicates a certain commitment to historical accuracy in their narrative. What matters most for our purposes here, however, is not so much the accuracy of their narratives as their passionate, mythopoeic interpretation of the events and their unified sense of purpose.

Eyewitnesses and interpreters

To better understand the content of these various treatises, let us reconstruct the publishing history of this peculiar body of literature. Because we are dealing here with a very specialized, narrow corpus of works, it might be best to try to establish that this is no obscurantist enterprise. Some of these works are very well known and have been reprinted in numerous editions down to our own century. Others are far from famous, but their publishing history, limited as it may be, shows that they enjoyed some popularity and that the subject of Philip's death received substantial attention even long after the event.

The first attempt to glorify the death of Philip came from the titular leader of the Catholic Church in Spain. Within a week of Philip's death, on 20 September 1598, the Archbishop of Toledo, himself an eyewitness and participant in the drama, commissioned an investigation of the event so that a full account could be published. Special powers were given to one of Philip's chaplains, Antonio Cervera de la Torre, to question the other eyewitnesses and prepare a special report. Armed with a questionnaire and the power to excommunicate anyone who refused to cooperate, Cervera de la Torre interviewed twelve of those who had been present at the scene. By February 1599, his digest of all these reports was ready for publication and came off the press of Pedro Mey in Valencia under the title *A True and authentic testimony of the remarkable events that took place during the felicitous death of our King and Lord, Don Phelipe II.*[1] In his preface, the archbishop wasted few words in getting to the point: "In this work will be found an example to be followed in the most admirable patience, faith, and Christian prudence, not only by kings and princes, but also by everyone; so that by imitating the footsteps of such a good and holy King, all may attain the Heavenly glory that we so fervently believe he, our good King and Lord, is now enjoying."

Cervera de la Torre also manifested the same purpose in his own dedicatory letter to the new King Philip III. There was much to be learned from the death of Philip II, he said. Because the former monarch had ruled his subjects with such fairness and justice, it was only to be expected that even after death he could still "persuade them to hold this world in low esteem, and teach them patience in adversity . . . and serve as an example of many other virtues." In his death Philip II embodied so many good Catholic qualities that it was only fitting to tell the story in detail. "It is nothing new to write about the exemplary deaths of kings and princes," Cervera de la Torre reminded his readers. It was common knowledge that the "good deaths" of kings needed to be publicized "so that they could be imitated by their children and grandchildren, and that their praises be sung by all the people."[2]

---

[1] *Testimonio autentico, y verdadero de las cosas notables que pasaron en la dichosa muerte del Rey Nuestro Señor Don Phelipe Segundo,* autor, su Capellan el Licenciado Cervera de la Torre, de la Orden de Calatrava, natural de Ciudad Real (Valencia, 1599). A second edition was also published in Madrid the following year, in 1600. All citations here refer to the Valencia edition.

[2] *Testimonio,* prefatory letter to King Philip III, n.p. Cervera de la Torre cites some Biblical passages to prove his point (Ecclesiasticus 44, "laudemus viros gloriosos et parentes"; Heb. 13:17, "Obey your leaders and submit to them; for they are keeping

Cervera de la Torre's *Testimonio* was a timely lesson in the art of dying as much as an exhaustive account of the details of Philip II's death, and it seems to have whetted the public's appetite for the subject, not only in Spain but also abroad. The appearance of a Latin translation, published at Freiburg-im-Breisgau in 1609, indicates that there was continued interest in the subject a full decade after the event, at least in some learned circles outside of Spain. By 1609, other accounts had appeared, all equally intent upon drawing lessons from the event.

In the final months of 1598, as we have seen, funeral services were held for Philip II throughout the realm; shortly afterward, accounts of a few of these were published.[3] In 1601 a larger collection was published by Juan Iñiguez de Lequerica that contained fourteen sermons preached in major cities throughout the Iberian kingdoms, as well as a description of the funeral services held for Philip at San Jerónimo in Madrid.[4] When originally preached, these sermons had been the first public proclamation and interpretation of the details of Philip's death. Though it is likely that Cervera de la Torre used manuscript versions of some of these sermons, it cannot be proven. At any rate, their significance rests not so much on their narrative detail as on their interpretation of the death of Philip. The editor hoped this book would glorify the dead king, serve as an *Ars Moriendi,* and also provide models for other sermons.

watch over your souls," in a rather free translation that stretches the meaning of the original text beyond recognition; and Rev. 14.13, "Blessed are the dead who die in the Lord.") He also cites previous examples of authors who publicized "good deaths": St. Gregory the Great on the death of St. Herminigildo, a Spanish Visigoth prince and martyr; St. Ambrose on the Emperors Valentian and Theodosius; Juan de Mariana, S. J., *Historiae de rebus Hispaniae* (Toledo, 1592) on King Recared, another Spanish Visigoth king; and finally Pope Gregory XIV on St. Charles Borromeo.

[3] The first to appear in 1599 were from in or near the capital city: Aguilar de Terrones preached at San Jerónimo in Madrid, Alonso Cabrera at San Domingo in Madrid, and Luis Montesino at Alcalá. I was not able to locate these early printings, mentioned in *Bibliografía Madrileña,* ed. Cristobal Perez Pastor, 4 vols. (Madrid, 1891), vol. I, n. 657. That same year, another printing made available the sermons of Terrones and Cabrera (just mentioned), as well as those of Francisco Davila (Belmonte) and Juan Bernal (who was not included in the 1601 collection): *Sermones predicados a las honras del Rey Nuestro Señor Don Philipo Segundo este año de 1598* (Seville, 1599), British Library 4423.g.1 (1–4). In 1600, a collection of Portuguese sermons appeared: *Relaçao das exequias d'el Rey Dom Filippe nosso senhor, primeiro deste nome dos Reys de Portugal, com alguns sermones que neste reyno se fizerâo* (Lisbon, 1600), British Library 10632.a.41.

[4] *Sermones funerales en las honras del Rey Nuestro Señor don Felipe Segundo* (Madrid, 1601).

In his history of the Escorial (1602), Fray José de Siguenza dwelt on Philip's death at length. Although he was an eyewitness himself, he claims to have used Cervera de la Torre's *Testimonio* as his principal source for details.[5] Never one to be at a loss for words, Fray Siguenza actually added much of his own in the way of narrative as well as interpretation, and his account remains one of our principal sources of information about the death of Philip II and the ways in which it was perceived by his contemporaries.

Another eyewitness to the death of Philip II, one of his physicians, Cristobal Perez de Herrera, published his own account in 1604. He states in the preface that he was urged to do this by many acquaintances and others in high places, but because he was not among the twelve witnesses interviewed by Cervera de la Torre it may well be that he was at least partly motivated by a desire to rectify this omission.[6] Certainly, Perez de Herrera had no wish to contradict previous accounts. He even had little desire to add any new facts. His purpose was to interpret the event and praise Philip II. Consequently, the larger part of this treatise is not devoted to the details of the king's death but to his virtues in life. As was common at the time, the author chose a title that said it all: *Eulogy to the illustrious virtues of the King Our Lord, Don Phelipe II, who is in heaven, and to his most Christian, exemplary death.*[7] Perez de Herrera also in-

---

[5] Fray José de Siguenza, *Fundación del monasterio de El Escorial* (Madrid, 1963), p. 172.

[6] Cervera de la Torre omitted several known eyewitnesses from his investigation, and some of them later wrote their own accounts, including Fray José de Siguenza and Jehan Lhermite. The complete list of witnesses provided by Cervera de la Torre is as follows (*Testimonio*, list of witnesses, n.p.): Dr. Andrés Camudio de Alfaro, Proto-medico general, y medico de la camara de Su Majestad; Don Antonio de Toledo, Cazador mayor del Rey, y gentilhombre de su camara; Dr. García de Oñate, medico de la camara de Su Majestad; Dr. Juan Gómez de Sanabria, medico de la camara de Su Majestad; Don Henrique de Guzmán, gentilhombre de la camara de Su Majestad; Juan Ruyz de Velasco, de la camara de Su Majestad, y secretario de la Reyna; Don Francisco de Ribera, de la camara de Su Majestad; Fray Diego de Yepes, de la Orden de San Gerónimo, confesor de Su Majestad; Fray García de Santa Maria, Prior del Sacro y Real Convento de San Lorenzo; Juan de Guzmán, sumilier de la cortina del Rey, y limosnero de la Reyna; Don Hernando de Toledo, gentilhombre de la camara de Su Majestad; Don Pedro de Castro y Bobadilla, gentilhombre de la camara de Su Majestad.

[7] Cristobal Perez de Herrera, *Elogio a las esclarecidas virtudes del Rey Nuestro Señor Don Felipe II, que está en el cielo, y de su exemplar y cristianisima muerte* (Valladolid, 1604), published as an appendix to Luis Cabrera de Cordoba's *Felipe Segundo Rey de España, 4*

cluded as an appendix to his own treatise the narrative eyewitness account of Fray Diego de Yepes, Philip II's confessor, who was one of those interviewed by Cervera de la Torre. Father Yepes's account, as can be expected, added some minor details to the general narrative and lent an added air of authority to the *Eulogy*, but it did not reveal anything substantially new.[8]

Diego de Yepes's narrative seems to have been much more popular and influential in its own day than any of the others. It certainly received more attention abroad. Oddly enough, it appears to have been published in French and German translations at least five years before it appeared in Spain. The first Castilian Spanish edition I could track down was that provided in Perez de Herrera's *Eulogy*.[9] Two other Castilian editions appeared after this: one in Milan in 1607, along with an Italian translation, and another the following year in Barcelona.[10]

Two decades later, Baltasar Porreño published a slim volume in praise of the wisdom and virtue of Philip II in which he often referred to

vols. (Madrid, 1877), vol. 4, p. 337. Perez de Herrera claims he began to write this document while Philip II was dying and that he presented a finished manuscript to Philip III a few days after his father's death while the young king was still mourning at San Jerónimo in Madrid.

[8] Diego de Yepes, *Relación de algunas particularidades que pasaron en los vecinos dias de la enfermedad de que murió nuestro Catolico Rey Don Phelipe II*. Apparently, Fray Diego had written his own version of the events surrounding Philip's death, independently of Cervera de la Torre's investigation. Several manuscripts of this *Relación* are extant. I have consulted Ms. 1504 F154 at the Biblioteca Nacional, Madrid, which differs only slightly from the one published by Perez de Herrera.

[9] Two French editions appeared at about the same time: *Translat de la relation faicte en langue Espagnole par le reverend confesseur de le Roy Philippe II, de la forme de la derniere maladie et mort de sa dicte Maisté* (Antwerp, 1599); and *Discours de la maladie et trespas de Phillipe II, roy de Espagne* (Lyon, 1599). These were complemented by a German translation: *Christlich gottselig Absterben, Weylandt des durchleugstigen grossmechstigste Fürst und herrn Phillip II, könig von Spanien* (Augsburg, 1599). These translations probably used manuscript versions of Yepes's account. Although it is possible that they could have used a printed version, I have not been able to verify the existence of any Spanish publication prior to 1604.

[10] The Castilian edition was published along with an "Index of the memorable events of the life of King Philip II" compiled by Diego Ruiz de Ledesma, who referred to himself as "criado del Rey Nuestro Señor" (Milan, 1607). The Italian translation also included the "Index" of Ruiz de Ledesma: *Breve relatione della cristianissima et essemplar morte del catolico e prudentissimo re di Spagna et del mondo nuovo Don Filipo II, di don Diego de Yepes* (Milan, 1607).

the death of the king as the most convincing proof of his great qualities. Porreño's work was highly derivative yet somewhat innovative: Although he depended exclusively on previous published accounts, at times he took the liberty of embellishing the facts. This work, entitled *The Maxims and Deeds of the King Don Felipe II,* may well have done more to perpetuate the myth of Philip's good death than any of the eyewitness accounts on which it drew. Porreño's *Maxims and Deeds* not only passed on the tradition of Philip's death as an *Ars Moriendi* to new generations, but it did so in a compact, topical manner, through eighteen chapters devoted to separate specific virtues. Because Porreño wove together the many virtues of Philip in life and death into one continuous whole, trying to prove that a good death does indeed indicate a good life (and that a good life will end in a good death), he may have driven home his lessons much more effectively than his predecessors, who dwelt almost exclusively on the death scene. This work remained popular at home and abroad for several generations.[11]

At the fringes of this list of eyewitnesses and interpreters stand some works that are difficult to categorize. One eyewitness account penned in the early 1600s did not have much influence at the time but has come to be regarded as a primary source of information by modern scholars. Jehan Lhermite's *Passetemps*, composed in 1602, languished in a Belgian archive until it was published in the late nineteenth century.[12] Another report, written by a certain Juan de Sandoval, remained unpublished and now, unfortunately, appears to be lost.[13] A third report, an anony-

---

[11] Baltasar Porreño, *Dichos y Hechos del Rey Don Felipe II* (Madrid, 1942). First edition: Cuenca, 1628. Subsequent editions: Madrid, 1639; Seville, 1639; Madrid, 1663; Brussels, 1666; Madrid, 1748; Madrid, 1863. French translation: Cologne, 1671.

[12] Jehan Lhermite, *Passetemps*, 2 vols. (Antwerp, 1890–96), reprinted (Geneva, 1971). Lhermite was present for part of Philip's deathbed ordeal and no doubt witnessed many of the events, but his narrative closely resembles Cervera de la Torre's *Testimonio* in many places.

[13] A copy of this manuscript was listed in the catalogue of the Biblioteca Nacional in Madrid until 1984 (9405 Cc 46, fol. 156 ff.). The catalogue entry did not in any way indicate the date of composition or whether this was an original document or a copy. Unfortunately, by trying to find out more about this manuscript, I unwittingly caused a bibliographic catastrophe. Either because of theft or a cataloguing error, the document could not be found in the location mentioned by the catalogue. When I brought this to the attention of an archivist, she carelessly responded by tearing up the catalogue card and saying, "If it's not here, I'll have to destroy this record." Despite

mous letter from Spain translated into English and printed in London in
1599, had a long publication history.[14] This brief account, which added
some minor details not available in any other eyewitness reports, such as
the claim that Philip was infested with lice on his deathbed, or that he
asked for a crowned skull to be placed near him, was ironically used to
promote the myth of the "Black Legend," as proof of the Spanish
monarch's wickedness. According to the English publishers of an
eighteenth-century edition, the event of Philip's death proved exactly
the opposite of what all the Spanish chroniclers had tried so hard to get
across:

This is the King of Spain, whose Cruelties in the Indies and the Netherlands
have recorded him among the most bloody Tyrants, and his continual Attempts
to poison, assassinate, or dethrone Queen Elisabeth, and to invade and conquer
England, have rendered his Name odious to every true Englishman: And whose
universal Character is a Compound of Pride, Ambition, Injustice, Oppression,
Treachery, and Bloodshed: For all which, by the short Account following, you
will perceive, that God called him to Judgment; and, by the Plague of Lice,
declared his Detestation of that sinful Prince, before he departed this Life. Yet,
in this same Account, it is remarkable, that he was arrived to that State of
hypocritical Insensibility, and Delusion, that he thought all his Barbarities,
Treachery, and Treasons were doing God's Service, and that himself was ready
to depart this Life in the Favour of God.[15]

my protests, this entry was not reinserted into the catalogue. Consequently, there is
no longer any official listing of this manuscript in the Biblioteca Nacional.

[14] *A briefe and true declaration of the sicknesse, last wordes, and death of the Kinge of Spaine
Philip the Second of that name, who died in his Abbey of S. Laurance at Escuriall, seven
Miles from Madrill, the Thirteenth of September, 1598. Written from Madrill in a Spanish
letter, and translated into English according to the true Copie* (London, 1599). Reprinted in
the various editions of *The Harleian Miscellany: or, a Collection of Scarce, Curious, and
Entertaining Pamphlets and Tracts* (London, 1744, 1751, 1809). I have consulted the
1744 edition, vol. II, pp. 377–9. For more on English attitudes toward Philip II,
consult William S. Maltby, *The Black Legend in England* (Durham NC, 1971), and
Henry Kamen and Joseph Perez, *La Imagen Internacional de la España de Felipe II*
(Valladolid, 1980).

[15] *Harleian Miscellany* (1744), vol. II, p. 377. The tone of the letter itself is quite reverent
and sympathetic.

This interpretation died a slower death than Philip II himself, for it was again hauled into service in the United States in 1898 as part of the propaganda campaign surrounding the Spanish–American War.[16]

There was no neutral ground for accounts of Philip's death. Those who put time and effort into writing and publishing accounts of the event did so for polemical purposes: either to show that Philip died an exemplary death or to prove that he was justly punished by God. Either way, lessons were drawn from the event. Little doubt can remain, then, that an interest in the death of Philip II continued long after the event, both at home and abroad, or that much of what was written about it had a decidedly didactic or polemical edge. Altogether, about half a dozen different publications dealing with his death appeared in Spain (not counting individually published funeral sermons), some being published ten years after the event, others being reissued repeatedly. Abroad, translations became available in Latin, French, German, Italian, English, and Dutch.[17] But what, specifically, were the lessons drawn from the event of Philip II's death in all these different accounts, and what kind of significance can we attribute to them?

Philip as a heuristic device

Among the most poignant of lessons to be drawn by the passing of any monarch is that which teaches the universality of death: the awful truth that all humans are mortal and that no one can hope to live forever, no matter how exalted or powerful one might be. There is something inherent in the concept of a monarchy itself that makes kings appear exempt

---

[16] James C. Fernald, *The Spaniard in History* (New York, 1898), pp. 102–3: "It is impossible not to feel a grim satisfaction that this royal monster of perfidy, ingratitude, tyranny, cruelty, and lust at last met with the fate of Herod Agrippa: 'He was eaten by worms and gave up the ghost' (Acts 12.23). . . . The manner of his death is an emblem of the irredeemable corruption to which he had reduced his kingdom, which has resisted alike the surgery of war and the medication of statesmanship for four hundred years."

[17] The Dutch work did not deal with Philip II's death per se but was a translation of his deathbed advice to Philip III. *Cort warachtich verhael vande siecte, leste woorden ende doot van . . . Philips de tweede . . . gescreven in Spaensch ende overgeset in Duyts, door een liebhavver den selven taels* (Antwerp, 1598).

from common universal attributes. The monarch, by virtue of the fact that he reigns supreme over his fellow human beings, enjoys privileges that are denied to everyone else. The more powerful a monarch is, the higher the expectations are bound to be about his special status as a human being above all others. Medieval political theology was often constructed in the language of symbol, analogy, and metaphor. Within this symbolic structure, the body played a key role, principally because of its function as a complex organism.[18] If the state itself was viewed as a body, it followed that the king was viewed as its head or soul.[19] It was a powerful metaphor that conveyed many a truism, but, as is the case with metaphorical language, the analogy could be taken only so far. And it was at the very limits of the analogy that the deepest meanings were sought. What did it mean for the body politic to survive the death of its head, the king? In Philip's Spain, as in all other monarchical societies, the death of the king was a threat to stability and order and a powerful reminder of the finality of all things human, yet it also offered a paradoxical opportunity for hope. The death of the king and the survival of the state pointed to redemption and continuity within a world of flux and decay.[20] It was only natural, then, that those who wrote about Philip's death should have tried to universalize the experience and to draw lessons from the king's death.

The death of kings symbolized in a very powerful way the universality of death and pointed to the death of each human individual: Those who enjoyed every possible privilege and exemption and those upon whom

[18] Mary Douglas, *Purity and Danger* (London, 1966), p. 115, observes: "The human body is a complete structure. The functions of its different parts and their relation afford a source of symbols for other complex structures."

[19] Castilian kings themselves embraced the metaphor. "Emperadores et reyes son menzamiento et cabeza de los otros . . . alma e cabeza, et ellos los membros." *Las Siete Partidas del Rey Don Alfonso el Sabio, cotejadas con varios codices antiguos* (Madrid, 1807), p. 3. Philip's funeral sermons were filled with similar statements. Two examples: Martín de Castro, at the Royal Chapel in Granada, and Francisco de Avila, at Belmonte. *Sermones funerales*, fols. 232r, 245r.

[20] The classic interpretation of this problem is Ernst Kantorowicz's *The King's Two Bodies: A Study in Medieval Political Theology* (Princeton, 1957). Although this monumental work concentrates on France and England, it provides an indispensable analysis of the problem of transition. Similarly, Ralph E. Giesey's *The Royal Funeral Ceremony in Renaissance France* (Geneva, 1960) also has insights to offer on this question, especially pp. 177–92.

everyone else depended for guidance and protection would never be spared by the Grim Reaper. If kings died, no one could hope for a reprieve.[21] This was an ancient sentiment, voiced repeatedly through the centuries. Shakespeare was not the first poet to contemplate "sad stories of the death of kings," nor was Perez de Herrera the first to observe that

What we ought principally to learn from the death of such a great king as His Majesty [Philip II] is the lesson that one day we will all suffer the same fate. If death did not spare him, and even dared to bring down such a Majesty, then it is very clear that we are all in a precarious position, and that we have to see ourselves fading and dying with each passing hour, wearing out, much like flowing water that cannot turn back.[22]

The image of death reaching with its scythe for emperors, kings, popes, bishops, and all the mighty as well as all the lowly was the central motif of the Dance of Death in the Middle Ages.[23] This lesson was as popular in Spain as in the rest of Europe well into the sixteenth century and was used more than once in Philip's funeral sermons.[24] The death of the mighty was not a theme specifically restricted to the Dance of Death; it could also appear in moral treatises of a more general nature or in songs and plays.[25] For example, Sebastián de Horozco's musical

[21] "Assi la muerte de un hombre ordinario haze os callar, mas la de un Principe que cae de tan alto a la sepultura, espanta y amedrenta." Aguilar de Terrones, sermon preached at the Royal Chapel, Madrid, at the funeral honors for the Infanta Catalina, 20 December 1597, *Sermones funerales*, fol. 280v.

[22] Perez de Herrera, *Elogio*, p. 372. For much earlier examples of this sentiment, see *The Oxford Book of Death*, ed. D. J. Enright (New York, 1983), pp. 9–10; and *Death in Literature*, ed. Robert F. Weir (New York, 1980), pp. 6–10.

[23] Leonard P. Kurtz, *The Dance of Death and the Macabre Spirit in European Literature* (New York, 1934; Geneva, 1975), esp. pp. 147–53. Also Jean Batany, "Les 'Danses Macabres': Une Image en Negatif du Fonctionalisme Social" in *Dies Illa: Death in the Middle Ages*, Proceedings of the 1983 Manchester Colloquium, ed. Jane H. M. Taylor (Liverpool, 1984).

[24] For example: "Quando menos que triunfa de los monarcas, derrueca los tronos Reales, burla de los cetros y coronas, no haze cuenta de las mitras, baculos, y tiaras, tenemos más justa razón de tenerle miedo," Agustín Salucio, at Cordoba, 1598, *Sermones funerales*, fol. 174v. Similar remarks were made by Francisco Sobrino in his sermon at the University of Valladolid, fol. 263 v.

[25] For a detailed description of this literary tradition, see Joel Saugnieux, *Les danses macabres de France et d'Espagne et leurs prolongements litteraires* (Lyon, 1971), esp.

composition "The Dialogue of Death with All Ages and Stations" (1580) contained the following meditation:

> Popes and Cardinals,
> Emperors and Kings,
> will be the same in this
> as those who tend cattle;
> and like tributary streams
> that all flow into the sea,
> thus do they all end up in me,
> with their good or with their evil.[26]

Theatrical productions that featured the Dance of Death were popular enough to receive Cervantes's attention in *Don Quixote*, in that scene where the hero and his page encounter a troupe of actors traversing the roads in costume, hurrying from one performance to the next of their morality play, *Las Cortes de la Muerte* (*The Courts of Death*). It is a scene at once eerie and comic. An actor dressed as Death is driving a wagon filled with other characters that represent certain social types. Don Quixote pays most attention to the actor dressed as an emperor with a gold crown on his head.[27] A graphic representation of this theme can be found in a crude Spanish woodcut from a 1595 book on the theological virtues that depicted the figure of Death aiming an arrow directly against a pope and a king. The bearded king in this illustration bears some resemblance to Philip and his father, the Emperor Charles.[28]

In the case of Philip II, the lesson in mortality seemed to achieve a special poignancy. Not without reason, Philip was regarded by his subjects and by some of his enemies as the most powerful monarch who had

---

pp. 57–87. For its place in Spanish literature, see Eduardo Camacho Guizado, *La elegía funeral en la poesía Española* (Madrid, 1969), pp. 92–112.

[26] Sebastian de Horozco, "Coloquio de la muerte con todas las edades y estaciones," published in the *Cancionero de la Sociedad de Historia de Sevilla* (Seville, 1874).

[27] *Don Quixote*, Book II, ch. 11 (Barcelona, 1975), pp. 610–16.

[28] "Alegoría de la muerte," illustration in Pedro Sanchez, *Triangulo de Virtudes Theologicas y Quadrangulo de Virtudes Cardinales* (Toledo, 1595). Reproduced in Blanca Garcia Vega, *El Grabado del Libro Español, Siglos XV, XVI, XVIII*, 2 vols. (Valladolid, 1984), vol. I, plate 398. Similar illustrations depicting "la muerte arrastrando a un rey" and "el rey vencido por la muerte" also appeared in *Statutos del Studio General y Universidad de Valladolid* (Valladolid, 1581). These illustrations are listed by Garcia Vega in her catalogue (*El Grabado*, nos. 871, 873) but are not reproduced.

Death Takes Aim Against the High and Mighty. From Pedro Sanchez, *Triangulo de Virtudes Theologicas y Quadrangulo de Virtudes Cardinales* (Toledo, 1595). Reproduced in Blanca Garcia Vega, *El grabado del libro español, siglos* XV, XVI, XVII, 2 vols. (Valladolid, 1984), Vol. 1, plate 398.

ever lived.[29] He ruled a global empire over which the sun never set. He was lord of all the Iberian kingdoms, including Portugal, as well as of scattered territories throughout Europe, from the Low Countries in the North to Sicily in the South, and of all the lands of the New World, and even of some in Asia, not the least of which were the islands named after him, the Philippines. At no previous time in human history had any single individual nominally ruled over such a vast empire and so many different kinds of people. Cristobal Perez de Herrera was but one of many who saw a special lesson in mortality through the death of Philip II:

Oh brave and inexhorable death! Is there anyone that does not admire your boldness? anyone who is not terrified by your bravery or who does not fear your cruel, ferocious blow? You humble everything, you subdue and conquer all: As

[29] Geoffrey Parker, *Philip II* (Boston, 1978), pp. 159ff.

a quick and furious bolt of lightning, you strike against the highest point and destroy that which is strongest. Is it possible that so much majesty did not trouble or detain you? Did not such sublime and admirable greatness restrain your impudence? Did not such superb courage and equanimity arrest and undo your arrogant pride? Will you not shed your dangerous, irreparable rage? Imagine, turning such a powerful monarch into a poor wretch! Imagine, changing someone who was so feared and respected into a lowly and contemptible man! Thus do you humble the exalted.[30]

In a more general sense, the death of Philip II could be turned into a heuristic device because of certain elitist attitudes toward social organization and the transmission of values. As one sermon put it: "The nobles have a passion for imitating the grandees, and the grandees have a passion for imitating the king."[31] Hierarchical notions of power and influence that placed ultimate responsibility for social behavior on the person of the monarch played an important role in the interpretation of Philip II's death.[32] Cervera de la Torre, for one, was convinced of the mimetic susceptibility of subjects before their king and explained the phenomenon in neoplatonic terms, according to a hierarchy of lights: "Those examples which shine brightest and have the greatest impact are those set by great, distinguished people and kings, who, like lights set into lamps, illumine all others." Because the example set by monarchs is the most valuable, he argued, God often tries those in power with all sorts of calamities. After all, he concluded, was not the example set by Jesus himself, the Heavenly King, proof of the truism that the best guide for human behavior is the imitation of the powerful?[33]

Such notions were taken for granted by those who chronicled the

[30] Perez de Herrera, *Elogio*, p. 364. Luis Montesino said in his funeral sermon at Alcalá that Philip's death was the ultimate *exemplum:* What else could one do but prepare for death after seeing the king "encerrado en un estrecho ataud, y ayer mandava el mundo, y no cabía en el su grandeza y magestad." *Sermones funerales,* fol. 113r.

[31] Agustín Salucio, at Cordoba, 1598, *Sermones funerales,* fol. 179r.

[32] For a discussion of the royal court as an "exemplary center," see J. H. Elliott, "The Court of the Spanish Habsburgs: A Peculiar Institution?" in *Politics and Culture in Early Modern Europe: Essays in Honor of H. G. Koenigsberger,* ed. P. Mack and M. C. Jacob (Cambridge UK, 1987), p. 9.

[33] Cervera de la Torre, *Testimonio,* "Al Lector," n.p. Cristobal Perez de Herrera opens his narrative with a discussion of the divine right of kings, arguing that since they rule in God's place they must be obeyed, respected, and imitated: *Elogio,* pp. 336, 338.

details of Philip's death. Consequently, every act of Philip's on his deathbed, every single response to his suffering became a lesson in itself, a practical chapter in a very vivid *Ars Moriendi*. As one preacher said in a funeral sermon: "He was in that deathbed for fifty-three days, and as he had been an example of good living for other kings, now he became a master of good dying."[34] This prescriptive dimension pervades all the accounts including that of Jehan Lhermite. In explaining why it is that he has translated Philip's deathbed confession into French for his readers, Lhermite said:

I have done this . . . so that we may all be more easily helped in our time of need. When the time comes for our Merciful God to call us to himself, and we find ourselves in a situation similar to that of our good King and Lord [Philip], we should by all means imitate him, so that we may come to enjoy, along with him, the repose and bliss of Heaven.[35]

Fray José de Siguenza went even further, openly referring to Philip as "saintly" and saying that his good death was a better example than that provided by many other holy people:

From now on we will have a primer to teach us the art of dying well simply by reading what this saintly King said and did in his final illness and death. All will be able to depend on this greatest of teachers, who has shown us much more than many holy saints.[36]

Against the background of the Protestant Reformation, Philip's death could also assume a sharp polemical edge. More than an *Ars Moriendi*, his death became an *Ars Confutandi*. One funeral sermon said it all:

His death can stand as normative, and as a lesson in dying well, and can also be used to confute all heretics and pagans: I believe that if they could but see this death, it would be enough to soften and convert them – that is, if they were not as stubborn as demons. For they might see here that only in the Roman Catholic Church can one die a good Christian death.[37]

---

[34] Agustín Davila, O.P., at Valladolid, 1598, *Sermones funerales*, fol. 87r.

[35] Lhermite, *Passetemps*, vol. 2, p. 131. This passage indicates that Lhermite intended to publish his manuscript. These sentiments were voiced repeatedly in the funeral sermons. One example: Luis Montesino, at Alcalá, 1598, *Sermones funerales*, fol. 127r.

[36] Siguenza, *Fundación*, p. 180.

[37] Alonso Cabrera, royal preacher, at the church of San Domingo, Madrid, 1598, *Sermones funerales*, fol. 67v.

Let us now examine the details of Philip's death to see what kinds of lessons were drawn from it and how these lessons reflected specific Roman Catholic values.

King of pain

We have already seen how the *Ars Moriendi* tradition emphasized the importance of the moment of death for the salvation of the individual and how this was expressed in the maxim *salus hominis in fine consistet.* This stress on the final moment (or series of moments, broadly considered as a single event) as the pivot of one's salvific status was a natural development of the central assumptions of Roman Catholic soteriology. In the case of Philip, his "good death" became a lesson in the value of such Catholic teachings.[38]

The way in which Philip approached death, according to those who chronicled his passing, was fully in keeping with this attitude and provided a timely example of the way in which all good Catholic Christians should constantly prepare for death. Cervera de la Torre, for instance, saw Philip's readiness for death as a clear indication of holiness, and he left no doubt that the king's training had assured him entrance into heaven:

The peace and great serenity with which His Majesty passed on from this present life . . . strongly assure us that he . . . went straight to heaven from his deathbed. And we should feel certain that such a life and such a death prove that we can regard His Majesty as a saint, since he behaved so correctly, *and knew how to die so well, as if he had done it many times before. Because he trained for dying, and very much wanted to act correctly at the moment of death, he could not err at this point, and is now enjoying the heavenly glory he so much wanted to attain* [emphasis added].[39]

Through his behavior Philip thus proved a good Catholic truism: that one is indeed responsible for one's behavior and can do much to im-

---

[38] Venegas, *Agonía*, p. 254. Alonso Cabrera, royal preacher, stressed this point to those who had gathered for Philip's funeral honors at San Domingo in Madrid: "No prediques alguno por dichoso y bienaventurado en vida, hasta ver que aya fenecido con buena muerte: dexale que pase toda la carrera, que al fin se canta la gloria." *Sermones funerales*, fol. 63v.

[39] Cervera de la Torre, *Testimonio*, p. 130.

prove it. As in any other human enterprise, discipline and exercise pay off when one is tested. The lesson to be learned here is elementary, yet crucial. In a belief system that upholds the concept of free will and human responsibility for sin and considers the individual's behavior at the moment of death the final determining factor for one's assignment to a place in the hereafter, it becomes necessary to practice for the inevitable moment of death in order to ensure salvation.

Since early Christian times, it was generally believed that a good life would end in a good death, or conversely, that a good, holy death indicated the completion of a good, holy life. This attitude may have had its roots in the pagan classical past, as expressed in Ovid's dictum, *"exitus acta probat,"* but it acquired a certain soteriological character among Christians.[40] Within this framework of assumptions, there were signs to be read: One's death gave an indication of the status of one's soul immediately following death. It was commonly believed that those who entered heaven showed no dread or hesitation and even expressed an eagerness to die.[41] This was most obvious in the case of genuine martyrs, such as St. Stephen, who claimed to see the heavens opening to him as he was being stoned to death (Acts 7: 54), or Ignatius of Antioch, who could not wait to feel himself devoured by wild beasts in the arena.[42] The traditional account of the martyrdom of St. Lawrence, the patron of the Escorial, played with this theme in a macabre way, almost on the verge of giddiness. According to tradition, St. Lawrence said to his tormentors, as he was being roasted alive on a grill: "This side is now done, please turn me over."[43]

---

[40] Perez de Herrera, who delights in quoting classical authors as much as the Bible or the Fathers, cites this saying from Ovid's "De Arte Amandi," *Elogio*, p. 363.

[41] Alonso de Orozco, one of Philip's favorite chaplains, had stressed this point in his *Victoria de la muerte*, pp. 63–4, 115, 247. Popular belief also had it, however, that kings, nobles, and the wealthy did not as a rule suffer long, agonizing deaths. This made Philip's composure all the more astounding, according to Aguilar de Terrones in his sermon at San Jerónimo: *Sermones funerales*, fol. 33v.

[42] Ignatius of Antioch, "Letter to the Romans"; "The Martyrdom of Polycarp" in *Sources Chretiennes*, ed. H. de Lubac and J. Danielou (Paris, 1946), vol. 10, pp. 131–7; 242–75. For an overview of this subject, consult Hippolyte Delehaye, *Les passions des martyrs et les genres litteraires* (Brussels, 1921).

[43] *The Oxford Dictionary of the Christian Church*, ed. F. L. Cross (Oxford, 1957), p. 790. The symbolism of St. Lawrence's griddle did not escape notice at the Escorial. Some of the tools used in its construction had this symbol imprinted on them. Even more

Conversely, those who feared the torments of purgatory or hell and shrank back from death showed that they were unprepared for the final moment of truth. A "bad death" indicated that one's soul was stained and that there was little hope for one's salvation.[44] Philip's death was promoted as a "good death" in Spain because it served to prove all of his best qualities as a Catholic monarch. In all the accounts of his death, there is little extraneous detail. Every action is interpreted as conclusive proof of the constancy of Philip's traits. The lesson here is that a good life leads to a good death: As a man lives, so does he die.

The great dignity and seriousness with which he maintained his composure during his life, which was his most singular virtue, and which he alone possessed among the kings and princes of this world, is the same that he maintained in death. And so he died like a saint, because it is a trait of the just to die so calmly.[45]

Calmness in the face of death was one of the more important signs of a good death. Philip had certainly showed this, not only in his own case but also on those other numerous occasions in which his loved ones had died. "He witnessed the deaths of almost all those whom he loved dearly," wrote Porreño. He suffered the loss of his parents, four wives, several children, and many other relatives, as well as of numerous trusted ministers and servants, and yet maintained such a great composure that he "astounded the whole world." In addition, Philip serenely directed the details of his own burial and took great delight in discussing

---

significant, the plan of the building itself closely resembles the symbol of its patron saint. Could Philip's contemporaries have seen some symbolic irony in the fact that the king suffered mightily in his bed but could not turn over?

[44] Venegas, *Agonía*, p. 122, citing St. Cyprian's *Sermone de mortalitate:* "Quién es el que se acongoja por salir de esta vida sin el que está dudoso en la fé y vacio de esperanza? De aquél es temer la muerte que no quiere la compañia de Cristo, y de aquél es rehusar tal compañia que no cree que ha de reinar con Cristo." Luis de Rebolledo voiced the same opinion in *Oraciones fúnebres*, fol. 315: "Si viene la muerte de vida viciosa, será muerte desastrada."

[45] Porreño, *Dichos y Hechos*, p. 21. Cervera de la Torre had voiced similar sentiments in 1599: "Pues lo es muy grande aver tenido un Principe tan Catholico y tan Christiano. . . . Estas gran virtudes las descrubrio por todo el discurso de su vida . . . y por toda su vida fue perfeccionando con gran cuydado y diligencia, *encaminandolo todo para su fin y muerte*, como quien tan bien sabía *quan necesario es para tener buena muerte el discurso de la buena vida pasada* [emphasis added]" (*Testimonio*, p. 2).

the topic of death.[46] Could one ask for any greater calm than this from anyone?[47]

Fray José de Siguenza saw in Philip's serenity a sure sign of the king's confidence in salvation and of his entry into heaven. In his account, Philip's involvement in the details of his own burial is offered as proof that Philip knew he was on his way to heaven, as a "sign of the certainty with which he departed for his true fatherland."[48]

An underlying assumption of the concept of a "good death," of course, is the notion that the actions of the dying person actually have some salvific effect. In the case of Philip, as in the *Ars Moriendi* tradition, the moment of death is seen as a test.[49] The many temptations faced during life are concentrated into one moment when life hangs in the balance. Because sin is the measuring rod of damnation, resistance to temptation during this critical period is essential. Among the numerous invitations to sin that troubled the dying person, none was considered more dangerous than spiritual despair. Impatience in the face of spiritual and physical suffering could cause an individual to lose faith in God's goodness and therefore also lose any chance of divine forgiveness.[50] Consequently, much attention was paid to the role of suffering in the salvific process and even more to the virtue of patience, which kept sin at bay.

The redemptive value of suffering – especially patient suffering – had no better model than Christ Himself, of course. Some theologians fo-

---

[46] Details of Philip's obsession with his own funeral began to be made public immediately after his death in the funeral sermons. One especially revealing summary was that of Aguilar de Terrones, royal preacher, at the exequies in San Jerónimo, Madrid, 19 October 1598: "Tuvo imperio sobre la muerte, no siendo acometido, y sobre faltado de ella, sino llamandola, teniendola, y deteniendola, y trayendola por la mano, al dia, y a la hora que fué su sazón. . . . Pondero el gusto con que murió: 'Dadme el ataud, preparense los balsamos, mostradme mi mortaja, aforrese de esto, sueldese con lo otro, ponganme de tal suerte, saquenme por aquí, entrenme por aculla,' saboreandose, y entreteniendose con ello, como cosa de gusto."

[47] Porreño, *Dichos y Hechos*, p. 44.

[48] Siguenza, *Fundación*, p. 189. Such sentiments were commonplace in *Ars Moriendi* literature: Venegas, *Agonía*, pp. 121-2, spoke of life as exile and of death as "*un caminar a la patria.*"

[49] Venegas, *Agonía*, p. 140: "No recibirá la corona de gloria sino el que en la pelea espiritual contiende varonilmente contra todos sus adversarios."

[50] Venegas, *Agonía*, p. 145.

cused on Christ's passion as the central act of salvation, almost to the exclusion of other considerations, and turned suffering into a soteriological necessity for all Christians.[51] Cervera de la Torre, for one, picked up on this theme and applied it to the case of Philip. According to him, the greatest merit of Christ's salvific act was concentrated in His physical suffering, not in His preaching or miracles. "The remedy for our salvation," he said, "does not consist so much in the imitation of the other virtues of the Son of God, as in the emulation of his passion and of the way he bore his pain, because it was from the cross, where he suffered so much, that he began to reign."[52] Under this salvific scheme, suffering becomes the supreme redemptive act, not just on the part of Christ but also on the part of every individual who is called to imitate the Savior. In this soteriological model the triumph of Christ over sin is achieved through submission to pain and death, and it is also assumed that the benefits of this act cannot be fully enjoyed by anyone without some sort of mimetic participation.[53]

Such notions of the redemptive value of mimetic suffering played a large role in the interpretation of Philip's death. In many ways, Philip's actions simultaneously reflected and validated these commonplace expectations. Moreover, because Philip was a monarch his suffering also corresponded to the principle of Christomimesis, that medieval notion wherein the king was seen as a reflection of Christ Himself.[54] This analogical principle conveyed meaning on various symbolic levels, but here it was taken to new heights and given an added soteriological dimension.[55] Philip himself consciously depended on these notions and,

---

[51] Orozco, *Victoria de la muerte*, p. 83, spoke of suffering as Christ's weapons, and added: "Con estas armas venció El padeciendo, y con las mismas hemos nosotros de gozar de la victoria que El nos ganó."

[52] Cervera de la Torre, *Testimonio*, p. 3, cites numerous authorities on the value of suffering, including Aristotle (*Nicomachean Ethics*) and Thomas Aquinas (*Summa Theologica*), as well as St. Ambrose and St. Paul (*II Tim, 2*). His conclusion is that "mucho mas dificultoso es ser yunque que martillo, ser paciente, que agente."

[53] This teaching is explained in the Catechism of the Council of Trent, Part II, Chap. 1, quest. 47–9. Venegas also developed this model of "conformation" in his *Agonía*, pp. 234–40. See also Orozco, *Victoria de la muerte*, pp. 83, 152.

[54] Sergio Bertelli, *Il corpo del re: sacralità del potere nell'Europa medievale e moderna* (Florence, 1990), esp. pp. 129–37.

[55] Lorenzo de Ayala preached on this theme in his funeral sermon at the monastery church of San Benito el Real of Valladolid, 1598: "Que una cosa era ser Rey de tantos

as we shall soon see, tried very hard to imitate the patience and resignation of Christ while he was suffering. This salvific model contrasted sharply with Protestant soteriology, which taught salvation by faith rather than works, and which concentrated on imputed rather than earned merit. One does not have to look far to find a polemical, didactic edge to the many descriptions of Philip's patience in the face of suffering. His patience was more than an example; it was a lesson in Catholic soteriology.

Suffering alone, however, did not guarantee salvation. Only the right kind of attitude in the face of suffering could save the dying person. In this respect, Philip proved to have what was needed according to all accounts: patience. Much was made of the fact that Philip bore his sufferings without complaint, like Christ, and that he never showed signs of despair while he was "crucified" to his bed for fifty-three agonizing days.[56] Courage and fortitude were requisite qualities for any good monarch, but in this case Philip is portrayed as someone who exceeded these requirements. His resignation to suffering was not passive but active; he not only refrained from complaining but also praised God and prayed throughout his ordeal. "He endured his illnesses and torments with the greatest possible patience," said his confessor. Not once did he complain or lose his temper, despite his horrible condition. Instead of cursing, he comforted those around him. The words he uttered most often were: "Lord, please forgive my sins."[57]

Philip's concern with sinfulness in the face of suffering was very much in keeping with accepted soteriological notions. Pain and death were, after all, the punishment inflicted on the human race for sin. Suffering was believed to cleanse the soul in this life and to diminish future punishments in purgatory when it was accepted willingly.[58]

Reynos, y otra ser Virrey y Lugarteniente de Christo: ser un Vicechristo en sufrir azotes y tribulaciones, y que por este camino assegurava el partido de su salvación y reyno eterno." *Sermones funerales*, fol. 108r.

[56] Alonso Cabrera, royal preacher, at San Domingo, Madrid, *Sermones funerales*, fol. 61v. Cabrera also called Philip "nuestro segundo Job," and another preacher said he was better than Job for not complaining at all. Agustín Salucio, at Cordoba, fol. 174v.

[57] Yepes, *Relación*, fol. 58v.

[58] Venegas, *Agonía*, p. 146. Martín de Castro asserted in his sermon at the Royal Chapel of Granada that Philip had been purified by his awful death, *Sermones funerales*, fols. 239r, 257r. Francisco Sobrino agreed in his sermon at the University of Valladolid, fols. 269r-v.

The one event singled out by most accounts as the toughest test of Philip's patience was the time his abscess was lanced. All eyewitnesses seemed amazed by the king's behavior: Instead of crying out in pain, he remained silent through the whole procedure. Father Yepes reports that the only sound in the room was his own voice, repeating the words uttered by Jesus the night before his passion over and over (Mt. 26:36): "My Father, if it be possible, let this cup pass from me; nevertheless, not as I will, but as thou wilt."[59] Baltasar Porreño offered a slight, yet revealing embellishment later by adding that when the king was asked if he was in pain after this ordeal, he replied: "My sins hurt me more and make me feel worse than this."[60]

In one respect, Philip's "good death" deviated slightly from the model proposed by the *Ars Moriendi*. In the more traditional examples of this genre, such as Venegas's *Agonía*, the devil constantly hovers over the dying person.[61] He is ever present as the agent of temptation, trying to ensnare the soul through five sins to which it is especially vulnerable at this time: faithlessness, despair, impatience, pride, and worldliness.[62] Kings, princes, and great lords faced additional temptations because the power that they had exercised laid them open to greater accountability in the eyes of God. This meant that their consciences had more to be troubled about than those of others.[63] Although according to all accounts Philip was able to conquer these temptations, the devil was conspicuously absent from the scene. Philip was tempted by legions of specific ailments instead of demons. Even Father Siguenza, who often blamed the devil for many adverse situations, refrained from bringing him into this struggle.[64] We might assume that the role of the devil was

---

[59] Yepes, *Relación*, fol. 57. Philip asked Father Yepes to kneel behind his bed and read Matthew's passion narrative. When the surgery was completed, Philip asked all who were in the room, including the surgeons, to kneel and offer thanks to God. Yepes comments: "Y no se yo que ningun religioso ni hermitaño aya tomado tal entretenimiento para semejante acto." See also Siguenza, *Fundación*, p. 176. This event was reported in practically every funeral sermon of 1598.

[60] Porreño, *Dichos y Hechos*, p. 60.

[61] Venegas, *Agonía*, pp. 142–90.

[62] See my article, "Ars Moriendi," *Westminster Dictionary of Christian Spirituality* (Philadelphia, 1983), p. 21; and Roger Chartier, "Les Arts de Mourir, 1450–1600" *Annales, E.S.C.* 31 (1976):51–76.

[63] Venegas, *Agonía*, p. 178.

[64] For examples of the devil's work according to Siguenza, see *Fundación*, pp. 19, 40, 50.

taken into account at least implicitly, but because he is conspicuously absent, we must conclude that there was some reason for his non-appearance.

First, one must consider that Philip's death was an historical event of great significance. Anything written about it, even if intended as an *Ars Moriendi* of sorts, did not have to conform slavishly to medieval models. *Ars Moriendi* texts were practical manuals that dealt with death as a universal problem, and as such they had to generalize. To some extent, they also resorted to abstraction and symbolism. The figure of the devil was a very useful convention that helped to get across the problem of temptation in a general way within the confines of accepted belief. In contrast, Philip's case was a particular event from which lessons were drawn. Instead of attempting to generalize, as the *Ars Moriendi* did, all the accounts of Philip's death tried to interpret a specific experience. The various authors did not have to look very far for an agent of suffering and temptation: One of their principal tasks was to explain the meaning of Philip's physical agony.

Without the devil, Philip's patience in the face of suffering becomes a very practical model, a paradigm, and a vivid lesson. The merit of Philip's constancy and faithfulness becomes all the more exemplary when it is highlighted against the backdrop of very physical, excruciatingly painful temptations. The accounts of Philip's gruesome death focus on the details of his final humiliation precisely for this reason, so that the readers could fully identify with the magnitude of his suffering and the merit of his patience.

By promoting Philip's death as "good" within this framework of belief, little or no room was left for any other interpretations. If such suffering and patience were indeed the mark of a blessed end and a sign of salvation, then it would be impossible to view Philip's death in the way in which Protestants saw it – as divine retribution for wickedness and delusion.[65] Faced with the horror of an experience that could have easily been interpreted as a punishment rather than a blessing, Philip's chroniclers chose to accentuate precisely those aspects of Catholic belief and practice that made his death seem exemplary.

[65] *Harleian Miscellany* (1744), vol. II, p. 377. Alonso Cabrera seemed to have anticipated such charges in his funeral sermon at San Domingo in Madrid: "Que quando toda su vida huviera sido perdida y desbaratada, bastara a honestarla esta buena muerte." *Sermones funerales*, fol. 64r.

4

~~~~~~

Defending the faith through ritual

The death of Philip II was also promoted as exemplary within another context, because of the way in which he availed himself of the proper devotional aids according to Catholic belief and ritual at a time when such piety was being seriously challenged elsewhere.

The didactic quality of Philip's final gestures

Throughout his life, Philip had regarded himself as the supreme defender of the Catholic faith in Europe. He had devoted himself to the struggle against Protestantism and had committed the resources of all his dominions to fight against heretics everywhere. Under his leadership, even more than under his father's, Spain assumed a leading role in the defense of Catholicism.[1] In keeping with the dictum "as one lives, so shall one die," Philip continued to devote himself to the defense of Catholicism on his deathbed and even intensified his efforts in a grandly symbolic manner. Those around him who shared his outlook, convinced as they were that they lived in the most Catholic kingdom on earth, interpreted Philip's deathbed devotions against the backdrop of confessional turmoil, as proofs of the ultimate superiority of Catholicism.[2]

---

[1] Ricardo Garcia Villoslada has provided a thorough overview of Philip's involvement in the defense of Catholicism: *Historia de la Iglesia en España* (Madrid, 1980), vol. III, part 2, pp. 3–105 ("Felipe II y la Contrareforma Catolica").

[2] Luis Montesino spelled it out clearly in his funeral sermon at Alcalá, 1598, saying that God had afflicted Philip with such a painful death "para que con su devoción y

Catholic piety, as reflected in the *Ars Moriendi* tradition, had long advised the dying person to seek comfort through the material intervention of sacraments, holy water, images, and relics. Participation in the sacraments of penance, communion, and extreme unction were deemed an absolute necessity. Religious images, crucifixes, and relics were also promoted as aids in meditation and prayer.

Such practices were firmly grounded in Roman Catholic teachings about the nature of worship: They affirmed the notion that natural means were capable of conveying supernatural benefits. In other words, these practices took for granted a certain metaphysical outlook. Catholic metaphysics interpreted reality to be composed of two distinct spheres of existence: the spiritual and the material. More important, these spheres were considered to be compatible. Although spirit and matter were certainly dissimilar, they were not totally opposed: Nature and grace, spirit and matter were dynamic dialectical partners, not enemies. As Thomas Aquinas summarized it in his great dictum, it was believed that "grace does not destroy nature but, rather, perfects it."[3]

Nothing could be further from Protestant metaphysical assumptions, especially as formulated in the Reformed tradition. Following instead the obverse dictum first formulated by Zwingli, that "the more you give to the material, the more you take away from the spiritual," Reformed Protestants severely restricted the relation between the material and spiritual spheres.[4] For many Protestants, and above all for Calvinists, this was not some purely intellectual objection but, rather, a call to battle against the Catholic Church and its rituals.[5]

It is against the backdrop of the Protestant rejection of Catholic worship, particularly as expressed by Calvinist iconoclasts in the Netherlands, where Philip had so desperately tried to combat "heresy," that the interpretation of Philip's deathbed devotions must be understood. Philip

reverencia a las cosas del culto divino, y con su Christianidad quedasen los Hereges de nuestros tiempos confussos, y aun confudidos." *Sermones funerales*, fol. 124v.

[3] Thomas Aquinas, *Summa Theologica*, 1a, 95.4, ad 1.

[4] "Quantum sensui tribueris, tantum spiritui detraxeris," *Huldreich Zwinglis Sämtliche Werke*, ed. E. Egli, W. Köhler, F. Blanke et al. (Berlin/Zurich, 1905), vol. 8, pp. 194–5.

[5] For a more detailed analysis of this problem, see my *War Against the Idols: The Reformation of Worship from Erasmus to Calvin* (New York, 1986), esp. chaps. 3 and 6.

had paid close attention to the iconoclastic ravages of Dutch Calvinists. As one funeral sermon phrased it, the king had "wept tears of blood in his heart upon seeing the profaning of temples, the scorning of sacraments, the breaking of images, and the mocking of the Roman Church."[6] Philip's zealous concern for the ritual objects threatened in the North had even prompted him to bring that final collection of relics to the Escorial from Cologne. (And these relics played a very important role in his death, as we shall soon see.) In fact, the Escorial itself, which was an integral part of Philip's death, was perceived as one grand symbolic gesture against Protestantism:

At the same time that other princes were destroying churches, attacking religion, laughing at images, mocking the relics of the saints and everything that was good and pious in the Church, here [at the Escorial] was begun the work of eternalizing and ennobling such things, all under the watchful eye of a king who *did all this as a great contradiction* [emphasis added].[7]

In addition to defending Catholic ritual, Philip also demonstrated through his death the value of other Catholic virtues, not the least of which was the notion that one is ultimately responsible for one's salvation through one's own efforts. The notion of justification through earned merit, which Martin Luther and all the magisterial Reformers had dismissed as "works righteousness," and replaced with the concept of justification by faith alone, was wholeheartedly accepted by Philip and all those who wrote about his death. According to Catholic teaching, one's virtues, as developed over a lifetime of effort aided by grace, determined one's salvation. In the case of Philip, there was little doubt in the mind of his chroniclers that he had *merited* his salvation:

It is good for us to learn from Your Majesty the great power of virtue. What advantage could you have gained from your greatness and your regal majesty? Of what value would it have been for you to be lord of almost the whole world, as you were? How would it have helped you to be feared, obeyed, and respected, if in the crossing over at death you had been lacking the aid of your patrons, that is, the virtues and all the good works that escorted your soul?[8]

---

[6] Juan Lopez Salmerón, at Logroño, 1598, *Sermones funerales*, fol. 215r.
[7] Siguenza, *Fundación*, p. 19.   [8] Perez de Herrera, *Elogio*, pp. 363–4.

Within this framework of expectations, then, the devotions practiced by Philip on his deathbed assumed an especially powerful didactic quality. If one could indeed *do* something to aid one's salvation at the moment of death and avail oneself of all sorts of material devotional aids, then it only made sense to publicize the way in which Philip confirmed the truth of Catholic teaching and piety through his final deeds.

Let us now examine each of the devotions employed by Philip and determine how were these actions were interpreted.

Philip's devotional readings

Because the death of Philip II was promoted as an *Ars Moriendi* of sorts, as an example and lesson, it stands to reason that it should confirm and reify the paradigms of that genre itself. It was thus taken for granted in all accounts of his death, as in all of the *Ars Moriendi*, that he needed instruction, that some pattern had to be provided to guide him through this most difficult moment. It is interesting that although Philip availed himself of devotional readings on his deathbed, he did not use any of the popular Spanish *Ars Moriendi* manuals. To some extent, the king's devotional reading was of a less instructional nature. We may safely assume that because he had a personal confessor at his disposal, as well as many other clerics, including the entire Hieronymite community at the Escorial, Philip did not need to be instructed in the same way as other mortals. Consequently, most of his reading was of a more meditative nature.

This does not mean, of course, that Philip deviated from the pattern provided in *Ars Moriendi* literature; in these books themselves, the dying person is often advised to make use of devotional readings. Under the guidance of his confessor, Diego de Yepes, and the assistance of his other chaplains, chamberlains, and family members, Philip prepared for death by immersing himself in a circumscribed number of Biblical texts and some meditative works by two spiritual writers.[9]

Philip was greatly comforted during some of his most difficult moments by readings from Scripture, particularly the Psalms and the Gos-

---

[9] A fact mentioned by nearly all the funeral sermons, including that of Alonso Cabrera, which was first published in 1599. *Sermones funerales*, fol. 66v.

pels. Philip was fond of Psalms that expressed affection for God or that proclaimed a sense of resignation to His will. He often repeated the words of Psalm 42 throughout his ordeal: "As a hart longs for flowing streams, so longs my soul for you, oh God."[10] His favorite readings from the Gospels fell into two categories. First, he liked to meditate on those passages that emphasized forgiveness, such as the stories of Mary Magdalene, the thief on the cross, and the parable of the prodigal son. Second, he also showed great interest in the passion narratives, particularly that of Matthew's Gospel.[11] These readings helped Philip endure his pain and face his death and impending judgment by focusing his attention on the mercy of God and the redemptive value of suffering. Such devotion was interpreted as an auspicious indication of his spiritual sincerity. As one observer put it: "This hunger and thirst that His Majesty had for the Word of God was one of the signs of his predestination."[12]

The dying king also found consolation in other texts. This additional reading was limited to two authors: the great Spanish mystic Luis de Granada[13] and the Flemish Benedictine François Louis de Blois (more commonly known as Ludovicus Blosius).[14] This may seem a bit peculiar, especially when one considers the vast corpus of spiritual literature from which the king could have selected his authors. Given that Philip's Spain was a land overrun by mystics and spiritual writers, one would expect a more extensive and representative list of readings, but ultimately it is difficult to tell from the available sources how or why such choices were made.

---

[10] Cervera de la Torre, *Testimonio*, pp. 49, 59.

[11] Ibid., pp. 49, 59–61. Also Lhermite, *Passetemps*, vol. II, pp. 125, 126–7.

[12] Cervera de la Torre, *Testimonio*, p. 47.

[13] Luis de Granada (1504–88), a Dominican friar, was born to a very poor family but eventually became one of the most influential spiritual writers of the Golden Age in Spain. He was a great preacher and also a reformer within his order. A constant theme in his many writings is that of love as the key to spiritual perfection. For more, consult J. Cuervo, *Biografía de Fray Luis de Granada* (Madrid, 1895); M. Llaneza, *Bibliografía de Fray Luis de Granada*, 4 vols. (Salamanca, 1926–28).

[14] Blosius (1506–66), abbot of Liesses, came from the lesser nobility of Flanders and, as a boy, served for some time as a page in the court of Charles V. For more on his life and works consult G. de Blois, *A Benedictine of the Sixteenth Century: Blosius*, trans. Lady Lovat (London, 1878). Blosius' *Works* are available in the English translation of B. A. Wilberforce (London, 1876).

Something that can be easily determined is the fact that Philip preferred Blosius to Luis de Granada. The Spanish mystic receives only the briefest mention in one account, and so little is said about him that it is impossible for us to know which of his works were used by Philip.[15] In contrast, much attention is paid to Blosius, whose work is not only praised but also quoted at length in many accounts. Philip was introduced to Blosius by his daughter, Isabel Clara Eugenia, who first read to him some passages chosen by Father Yepes.[16] Cervera de la Torre devotes almost twenty pages to Blosius and quotes him at considerable length, stating plainly that he is doing this for a simple reason: to allow others to experience the same comfort that the king derived from his readings.

The passages quoted by Cervera de la Torre give us a good indication of the themes that interested Philip. Much of Blosius's work focuses on the surrender of the human self to God, as something to be achieved through a total conformity of wills. Many of the passages read to Philip revolved around this general theme.[17]

These readings also focused on the theme of God's mercy, especially as revealed in the redemptive suffering of Jesus Christ. Cervera de la Torre quotes passages from Blosius that pay close attention to the passion of Jesus as the means through which each individual obtains forgiveness for sins. Philip was especially fond of such meditations and often repeated these words three times in a row, along with Father Yepes:

Oh my most certain hope, forgive me. I beseech you, save me through your holy name. Oh sweet Jesus. I offer up for the remission of all my sins, that amazing love with which you, God of eternal majesty, did not refrain from becoming a suffering man for us. . . . I offer you that sorrow, that bloody perspiration, those anxieties you endured. . . . I offer you every single drop of your red blood. . . . I thank you and I call on your infinite mercy, so that you may purify me through these merits, and make me pleasing to you, and bring me to eternal life.[18]

Blosius also focused on the redemptive value of human suffering, both in this life and the next. Again, what we find here is a strong

---

[15] Cervera de la Torre, *Testimonio*, p. 89.   [16] Yepes, *Relación*, fol. 56v.
[17] Cervera de la Torre, *Testimonio*, pp. 51, 57, 58.
[18] Ibid., pp. 63–6. This is only part of a very long meditation in which Blosius mentions every conceivable sorrow endured by Jesus in His passion.

affirmation of Catholic soteriology, especially of the concept of purgation through suffering. Cervera de la Torre quotes lengthy passages from Blosius that discuss the way in which the faithful willingly undergo great torments in purgatory.[19] In addition, many passages also promote the idea that suffering in this life is to be viewed as something good, because it restrains one from sinning and also lessens one's punishments in the afterlife. Philip apparently took great comfort from one passage that argued that those who suffer much in this life are truly blessed. As Blosius put it: "God allows those whom he loves to suffer much, because without sorrows, anxieties and fears, they could easily seek to vainly please themselves, and thus preoccupied, fall from Grace."[20]

Philip also meditated on passages from Blosius that spoke of death as a transition to a better state of existence or even as something to be fervently desired. Why wish to remain in this life, asked Blosius in one such passage, where the danger of sin is ever present and the threat of damnation always near? Why wish to remain trapped in a corruptible body, in bondage to a recalcitrant, damaged will? For Blosius, the proper end of human existence was conformity to the will of God, but this was an end that could never be reached fully in this life, where temptations never ceased. Philip was read passages in which Blosius argued that it would be much easier to come to know God and conform to his will once one was freed from one's body.[21]

It is not difficult to see how such meditations could have helped Philip interpret his own innumerable physical torments as something beneficial. Likewise, it does not take much effort to grasp the significance of Philip's fascination with these readings or the meaning of the chroniclers' tedious attention to their content. Blosius helped set Philip's eyes on the afterlife and also helped make Philip's suffering easier to bear by placing it in the context of salvation. Through his intense and repetitive use of such literature, Philip not only affirmed the theological merit of the message contained in such readings but also provided an admirable example to be followed in the art of dying.[22]

---

[19] Ibid., pp. 52–3. [20] Ibid., pp. 56–7. [21] Ibid., pp. 52–3.

[22] Cervera de la Torre (*Testimonio*, p. 72) made sure this lesson got across clearly by saying: "Pero para que sea provechosa esta lección, ha de ser . . . no de prisa, sino con espacio y consideración, como su Magestad que Dios tiene, lo hazía, que como se diría no se contentava con esto, pero aun yva repitiendo lo que su Confesor le leía; y esto para que acabado de leer, no se cayga de la memoria, sino a la manera del Buey,

Prayer, images, and crucifixes

According to all witnesses, Philip prayed ceaselessly throughout his final ordeal. This itself was meritorious and noteworthy but hardly remarkable. One would expect as much from any dying Catholic who took his religion as seriously as Philip. If he had prayed four to five hours daily before he became ill, as some testified, then one would only assume that such devotion would intensify as death approached.[23] What is most remarkable about Philip's deathbed prayer is the way in which so much of it was linked to the use of religious images (especially crucifixes) as a focus of devotion.

Anyone who visits Philip's chamber at the Escorial today will see an austere, sparsely decorated room. This was not the case during the king's final days in August and September 1598, when there was "hardly one small empty space that did not contain a devout image of some saint, or a crucifix," on which the king kept his eyes constantly fixed.[24] Most of these objects were not permanent fixtures of the royal chamber but had been brought in especially for the purpose of aiding the king's death. José de Siguenza reports that Philip had "crucifixes and images on every side of his bed and on every wall."[25] Another eyewitness, Juan Ruiz de Velasco, was placed in charge of a portable oratory that he would open for display daily, after the king's dinner (while Philip could still eat). This heavily indulgenced oratory, which accompanied Philip on all his voyages, contained some silver, bas-relief representations of the Virgin Mary and a crucifix.[26] Philip would pray before these images "with great devotion, and sometimes with tears."[27]

que lo que esta alla dentro del pecho lo buelve a sacar a fuera para volverlo a rumiar; como lo hazía la Virgen Sacratissima . . . que conservaba todo lo que oía, y lo rumiaba y confería en su corazón."

[23] Ibid., p. 87. Philip's daily prayer habits are also described by Lhermite, *Passetemps*, II, p. 130.

[24] Lhermite, *Passetemps*, II, p. 130.   [25] Siguenza, *Fundación*, p. 184.

[26] Lhermite, *Passetemps*, II, p. 130. Philip paid close attention to the final distribution of crosses and images to his immediate family in the codicil to his will written in August 1597, a year before his death, even to the point of telling his son where to hang a certain image of Christ. Among the items listed in this codicil, a portable oratory willed to Isabel Clara Eugenia might be the same one used by Philip in his final days. For detailed descriptions of these items, see *Testamento de Felipe II*, Edicion Facsimil (Madrid, 1982), pp. 85–91.

[27] Cervera de la Torre, *Testimonio*, p. 86.

In keeping with the intense concentration on Christ's redemptive suffering in the king's devotional reading, special attention was paid, above all, to images of the crucified Savior. We are told that Philip ordered crucifixes to be hung everywhere around his bed "so he could pray to them whichever way he faced."[28] Toward the final days of Philip's agony, when he asked that his father's crucifix be taken out of its special chest and hung directly before him, inside the bed curtains, the king focused most of his attention on this object. One witness reported that he often came into Philip's chamber during those last days and found the king gazing intently upon his father's crucifix. In his final hours, Philip would clutch it, as Charles V had done, and kiss it repeatedly, "with such great expressions of contrition and love that it seemed as if he wanted to swallow it."[29] One of the funeral sermons put it differently, but the meaning was the same: "It seemed he wanted to bring it into his soul."[30]

Through these fervent devotions Philip displayed his belief in the power of images and confirmed their rightful place in worship. Unlike the Protestant iconoclasts, who did not accept any artistic representation as capable of conveying spiritual benefits, Philip and those around him concretely affirmed the transcendental capacity of images. This was the lesson to be learned here: Images could be used as points of contact with a higher reality and were most helpful for a dying person who was just about to cross over into that other realm.

Jehan Lhermite said that when Philip gazed upon the images, "his spirit was elevated to heaven."[31] Fray José de Siguenza spelled out the lesson in greater detail, giving a full account of the epistemological value of the images for the dying king:

He had images and crucifixes all around his bed, and also on all the walls, to refresh his memory, and to prevent external circumstances or his own bodily ills from distracting him, so that those signs could enter naturally into his eyes, and

---

[28] Ibid., p. 30.

[29] Ibid. To further prove the intensity of this devotion, Cervera de la Torre indicates that half of all the memorial masses ordered by Philip were devoted to the Holy Cross. Venegas had advised embracing a cross while dying. *Agonía*, p. 171.

[30] Alonso Cabrera, at San Domingo, Madrid, *Sermones funerales*, fol. 67r.

[31] Lhermite, *Passetemps*, II, p. 130.

through them to his heart, and he thus would not lose something so important from his sight.[32]

Aside from serving these functions, Philip's images also brought the presence of the divine directly into the room. Philip, like many of his contemporaries, regarded the images as much more than passive agents of a heavenly reality. For Philip, the images were active points of contact with the realities they signified: They somehow ensured the presence of the holy.

At times, it seemed as if Philip believed that the images participated actively in everything that happened in his chamber. This is dramatically disclosed in one anecdote told by Jehan Lhermite. As Philip lay dying, he ordered Lhermite to fetch him his chamber pot one day, so he could relieve his bladder. Before performing this bodily function, however, he commanded Lhermite to cover up a "very devout image" of the suffering Christ and another image of the Virgin Mary that were near his bed, within the line of vision.[33] Lhermite relates this story in order to prove the king's exceptional reverence for images, and also teach a lesson. By doing so, he reveals much about Catholic attitudes toward the function of images. When Philip ordered these images covered, he showed that he regarded them as capable of experiencing the events around them. To him they were silent, supernatural witnesses and companions. Those who promoted the king's behavior as exemplary shared in this attitude and wanted to affirm its value.

Relics

Philip's devotion to images, intense as it was, pales in comparison to his love for relics. No single aspect of his deathbed devotions showed his wholesale acceptance of Catholic piety more transparently than his reliance on the power of the nearly 8,000 relics he had collected at the

---

[32] Siguenza, *Fundación*, p. 184. This explanation of the function of images is fully in agreement with that provided in medieval theology and the Catechism of Trent, Part III, chap. 2, quest. 24. For more on this point consult Johannes Kollwitz, "Bild und Bildertheologie im Mittelalter," in *Das Gottebild im Abendland* (Witten/Berlin, 1959), esp. pp. 125–8.

[33] Lhermite, *Passetemps*, vol. 2, p. 124.

Escorial. No other devotion seemed to prove more convincingly for his chroniclers and eulogizers the king's role as protector of the faith.

All the major chroniclers of Philip's death agree that the king provided a "singular example" of his faith in "divine things" by availing himself of the spiritual and physical power of the relics with which he had so carefully surrounded himself.[34] "From the time he fell ill until the day he died," reported Father Yepes, "during every single day, the relics of the many saints to whom he was devoted were brought to him, and he adored and kissed them with great reverence."[35]

These daily rituals were punctuated with some especially significant devotions. Two days before Philip's knee was lanced, for instance, he asked that some specific relics be brought to him "with full ecclesiastical solemnity." The order was carried out by his confessor, Diego de Yepes, his son's confessor, Gaspar de Cordoba, and the prior of the Escorial, Garcia de Santa Maria. Attired in surplices and stoles, the three priests entered the king's chamber, each carrying one relic, and each prepared to provide the king with a "spiritual chat."[36] The relics requested by Philip were no doubt intended to serve the specific purpose of aiding him through the upcoming ordeal and all its possible consequences. It is relatively easy to discern the reasons for the king's choices in the case of two of these relics.

First, he asked for "the entire knee of the glorious martyr Saint Sebastian, with all its bone and skin." Since Philip was about to subject his own knee to the surgeon's knife, this would seem an obviously appropriate choice.[37] Second, he requested a rib of St. Alban that had been sent to him as a gift by Pope Clement VIII; the rib carried a special plenary indulgence for Philip at the point of death and yet another special indulgence that would ensure the release of his soul from purgatory. Because Philip was now dangerously close to death and was about to be placed in greater risk, this choice also seemed most appropriate.[38]

---

[34] Siguenza, *Fundación*, p. 181. His devotion to relics is mentioned in practically every funeral sermon.

[35] Yepes, *Relación*, fol. 57.

[36] Siguenza, *Fundación*, p. 181.

[37] Ibid.

[38] Ibid. The special indulgences are described by Siguenza as follows: "Una indulgencia plenaria para el punto de su muerte, y otra muy singular, que no me acuerdo haberse concedido a otro: que cualquier sacerdote que dijere por el misa en esta su casa, en cualquier altar y cuantas veces quisiere, saque su anima del Purgatorio."

The third choice is more difficult to fathom: the arm of Saint Vincent Ferrer.[39]

Each priest displayed his relic in turn, intoned the appropriate prayers for each saint, and provided Philip with a brief talk. Philip responded with wild enthusiasm:

He kissed these relics with his lips and eyes, and asked that his swollen knee be touched with them. When the priests said their farewell, he remained joyful and fearless, fully prepared for the martyrdom that awaited him. He obtained such comfort from the presence and touch of these holy relics, that from that day on, throughout the rest of his illness, not one day passed in which Fray Martín de Villanueva (who was in charge of them) did not assemble a vast quantity of relics on an altar before him. He [Philip] ordered these relics be brought to him so he could kiss and adore them, and have them placed over his lesions.[40]

Martín de Villanueva was kept very busy by the king, whose desire to have as many relics brought to him as possible was nearly inexhaustible and whose knowledge about them may have been better than the friar's. Every day, Fray Martín had to display a vast array of relics before Philip and bring them one by one to be kissed by the king. On at least one occasion, Fray Martín lost track of what he was doing and started to put away the relics before he had brought them all to Philip's bedside. The king, who had been carefully keeping count, reprimanded him and ordered him "to bring over the relic of that saint he had forgotten, because he had not yet had a chance to kiss it."[41]

Philip's devotion to relics was assigned a special significance by those who commented upon his behavior. Here, again, we can see revealed the didactic and polemical edge of the interpreters' designs. As with other aspects of Philip's deathbed behavior, this particular devotion was highlighted against the backdrop of the Protestant Reformation. Philip was portrayed as the supreme defender of the faith, and every detail of his behavior was promoted as exemplary Catholic conduct. "We can draw a very useful lesson from this," said Cervera de la Torre, "because when

---

[39] Aside from the fact that Vincent Ferrer was a popular Spanish saint, Philip may have been influenced in this choice by the saint's reputation as the "angel of judgment." Vincent Ferrer had achieved fame principally as a preacher who focused on the apocalypse and the Last Judgment. See Francis Oakley, *The Western Church in the Later Middle Ages* (Ithaca/London, 1979), pp. 261–270.

[40] Siguenza, *Fundación*, p. 181.   [41] Ibid., p. 182.

the people see their monarchs venerating relics in such a way, they will also show great respect and reverence toward them."[42]

But Philip did more than provide an example for his own subjects. At no other point in the various accounts of Philip's death does the polemical edge seem sharper. These devotions were not only described in detail but were also contrasted with Protestant piety.[43] Siguenza, for example, turned Philip's behavior into an international confessional statement:

It will be very good to remember all these things, because they will be of great use to those who follow us, and will help them to be free from vice: they will know that during our own miserable age, when many foreign princes who would like to call themselves Christians hardly had any faith or piety, there was a king in Spain who showed such great affection to all the sacraments of the Church and to the relics of the saints, in life as well as in death.[44]

Baltasar Porreño drew the broader outlines of Philip's symbolic gestures even more dramatically:

So great was his devotion to relics and churches that in order to offer them the highest reverence he built the magnificent temple of San Lorenzo el Real, which merits the first place among the Seven Wonders of the World. He began to build this great temple and house of God when the enemies of Christ, showing contempt for the Catholic Church and all holy relics, would burn and destroy temples, desecrate churches, abuse images, destroy sanctuaries, silence praises to God, and remove the Holy Sacrament from the altar.[45]

Holy water

Philip displayed equal intensity in his devotion to holy water. Here, once more, we can see the king seeking spiritual power through the mediation of sanctified matter. All witnesses agree that Philip continually asked for holy water to be sprinkled on his face and body and that he would not go

---

[42] Cervera de la Torre, *Testimonio*, p. 41. Such an observation is based on a general principle, clearly stated by the same author: "De la misma suerte la gente no cae en la cuenta de lo que deben a las cosas sagradas, hasta que ven la reverencia que les hazen las cabezas, y luego ellos se esmeran en esta veneracion."

[43] As in Lorenzo de Ayala's sermon at San Benito el Real, Valladolid, *Sermones funerales*, fol. 98v.

[44] Siguenza, *Fundación*, p. 182.   [45] Porreño, *Dichos y Hechos*, pp. 71–2.

to sleep without first crossing himself with holy water. This was another important lesson in Catholic soteriology. According to Cervera de la Torre and Siguenza, the king was aware of the church's teaching on the power of holy water to wash away venial sins. "His majesty so abhorred venial sins, that he would constantly sprinkle and cross himself with holy water, to correct the damage incurred by these sins."[46]

Acts of charity

Philip distinguished himself at death in yet another exemplary manner, through numerous acts of charity. This, too, had a soteriological value because almsgiving was considered a redemptive act. Traditional *Ars Moriendi* literature had promoted the practice of deathbed philanthropy as especially meritorious. This was part and parcel of traditional Catholic teaching, especially as reaffirmed by the Council of Trent, which placed responsibility for salvation on the individual's free will and granted merit for acts of charity. The Catechism of Trent stated this plainly: "We redeem our offences against others by almsdeeds."[47]

As king, Philip had an even greater need to practice charity than other mortals. Having so much of the wealth of his kingdoms at his disposal, he also had the added responsibility of answering to God for the welfare of his people. Philip's final acts of charity were thus also seen as a royal function imbued with deeply soteriological overtones. In distributing so much of his wealth for charitable purposes, Philip was not only fulfilling his duties as a good king; he was also practicing a redeeming Christian virtue and setting an example for others to follow.[48]

Philip's final bequests reveal much about Catholic attitudes toward charity. José de Siguenza says that "as far as piety and almsgiving were

[46] Cervera de la Torre, *Testimonio*, p. 46. Also Siguenza, *Fundación*, p. 182, and Lhermite, *Passetemps*, p. 125: "La devotion que sa majeste avoit avec l'eau beniste n'estoit veritablement moindre que celle que dict avons des sainctes reliques."

[47] Catechism of Trent, Part IV, chap. 8, quest. 9. According to this catechism, every sin always had a triple effect because it offended God, damaged one's neighbor, and polluted one's self. Every sin, then, had a triple remedy: (1) Prayer appeased God's wrath; (2) Almsgiving redeemed offenses against one's neighbor; (3) Fasting washed away personal defilement. Jehan Lhermite apparently knew his catechism well, for he cites this lesson on almsgiving directly when he speaks of Philip's charity (*Passetemps*, II, p. 128).

[48] Aguilar de Terrones, sermon at San Jerónimo, Madrid, *Sermones funerales*, fol. 27v.

concerned, he [Philip] could hardly ever say 'no.' "[49] The terms used by Siguenza, *piedad* and *limosna*, seem to fall into the same category here, even though they refer to two different types of acts. *Limosna* refers specifically to acts of public relief, such as aid to the needy. *Piedad*, in this instance, refers specifically to donations to ecclesiastical institutions, such as shrines, convents, and churches. Though these two kinds of donations had an obviously different impact upon society, they were considered to be equally meritorious on a soteriological level. Charity was not restricted to the area of public relief but also extended into the realm of devotion.

Judging from the list of Philip's last charitable donations, in which acts of *piedad* outnumber those of *limosna*, it would seem that a greater value was placed on devotional contributions. Whether or not Philip actually distributed more money to ecclesiastical causes than to the poor is uncertain. We are simply told that he "gave alms to marry orphan girls and help widows," disbursed 20,000 *ducados* "for charity" through the Archbishop of Toledo, apportioned some extra funds for the poor who came begging at the Escorial, and lavished "much more" on some unspecified recipients, but no detailed accounting is made of these contributions.[50]

In contrast, Philip's devotional gifts are carefully recorded. We are told that Philip donated 20,000 *ducados* for a retable at the shrine of Our Lady of Guadalupe (the same amount allotted for charity in Toledo); that he gave 10,000 *ducados* to the shrine of Our Lady of Montserrat, 5,000 *ducados* to the Dominican friars of Valencia; 3,000 *ducados* to the monastery of San Benito el Real in Valladolid; and 6,000 *ducados* to the promotion of the canonization of Raymundo de Penyafort (finally canonized in 1601). In addition, an unspecified amount was spent for the foundation of an Augustinian monastery in Huesca. "Other similar gifts," including donations for masses to be said at certain unspecified locations, are also mentioned, but no details are provided.[51] This list does not take into account the vast sums lavished on the Escorial itself or on the almost innumerable masses to be said there for Philip and the entire Hapsburg dynasty.

[49] Siguenza, *Fundación*, p. 184.   [50] Cervera de la Torre, *Testimonio*, p. 73.

[51] Ibid. See also: Siguenza, *Fundación*, p. 184; Lhermite, *Passetemps*, II, p. 129. All these donations were supplemental to those already ordered in Philip's will. For a detailed listing of these see *Testamento de Felipe II*, pp. 7–11.

Church patronage

This particular emphasis on ecclesiastical donations as acts of charity pointed to another specific lesson that the interpreters of Philip's death wanted to promote. Through his support of the church, Philip performed the role of supreme protector and benefactor of Catholicism and also fulfilled a family tradition. "The very Catholic kings of Spain have always been very pious and generous towards the needy, and especially towards churches and monasteries," said Cervera de la Torre. Philip's interest in church building was thus promoted as the culmination of a long legacy.[52] Baltasar Porreño launched into a hyperbolic acclamation when he considered this point, and he made it clear that Philip's church building needed to be seen as a heroic response to the rejection of Catholic piety elsewhere and as the greatest architectural triumph in all of history:

He devoted his whole life to rebuilding ruined churches and to purifying violated temples. . . . Who else in the whole world has made a greater effort to build churches? Certainly, just by constructing a single one at the site of the Escorial, he eclipsed the temple of Diana in Ephesus, the house of the sun, the walls of Babylon, the Colossus of Rhodes, the pyramids of Egypt, and all the wonders of the world.[53]

Cervera de la Torre spent considerable time dwelling on this lesson, not only to prove the point that at his death Philip had acted in the most exemplary manner but also to claim that he had exceeded all other monarchs, Spanish or foreign, in this virtue. Cervera de la Torre went as far as to say that the generosity of the Spanish monarchs toward the church had been foretold by Isaiah (60:9): "For the coastlands shall wait for me . . . to bring your sons from far, their silver and gold with them." Did not the fact that the first shipment of gold from the New World was used to decorate the cathedral of Toledo prove that God had chosen the Spanish fleet to serve a special purpose? Did not Spain's privileged position grant its monarchy a special sign of distinction and divine favor? Did not Philip's actions show, beyond a shadow of a doubt, that the holy

---

[52] Cervera de la Torre, *Testimonio,* p. 75. This claim is supported by a long, nine-page list of royal involvement in the foundation of churches and monasteries.

[53] Porreño, *Dichos y Hechos,* p. 91.

intentions of the Spanish crown were no more than a direct manifestation of the divine will? This was particularly evident, Cervera de la Torre thought, when one contrasted Philip's behavior with that of his contemporaries:

At the very same time that Henry VIII sacked and burned more than ten thousand churches in England, and at the same time that the French looted and torched their temples, His Majesty, who rests now with God, showed himself to be most generous and magnanimous. He founded and built the holy, royal monastery of San Lorenzo . . . and filled this house with the greatest gems and riches ever seen. It is now the greatest sanctuary and reliquary in the world. In that holy house, so pleasing to God, the divine services celebrated by the priests and monks, which are so devout and punctual, provide a great model of piety and virtue for the whole world.[54]

So it was that the Escorial, a building complex devoted primarily to the cult of the dead, came to be promoted as the ultimate symbol of Catholic piety in an age of religious turmoil. From a strictly Spanish perspective, as manifested in the works of Siguenza, Cervera de la Torre, Porreño and others, the building of the Escorial could not be fully separated from the exemplary death of Philip II. The Escorial was but the culmination of a holy tradition of royal church patronage, a legacy that had immense soteriological value and which Philip intensified on his deathbed. The event of Philip's death and the specially prepared location for the event served as symbols for the truth of the Catholic faith and, perhaps more significantly, for the special role the Spanish monarchy served in the master plan of divine providence.

Philip's ultimate devotional aid

In many ways, and at various levels of meaning, the Escorial was a functional theological lesson: a liturgical machine[55] that affirmed Ro-

---

[54] Cervera de la Torre, *Testimonio*, p. 85.

[55] Many Spanish poems written in honor of the Escorial address it as a *maquina* (a construction) (*grave maquina, fastuosa maquina, maquina maravillosa*). Alvarez Turienzo has identified numerous such references, especially from the baroque period, in *El Escorial en las letras españolas*, p. 72. Though *maquina* did not have a mechanical meaning at the time, I have used it in this sense because it adequately describes the building's function.

man Catholic teaching on the relationship between spiritual and material realities, between the seen and the unseen, between this world and the next. "Oh sacred, awe-inspiring place, divine sanctuary worthy of the greatest reverence and adoration," said one of Philip's funeral preachers. "What we have here is no less than a house of God, and a door to heaven."[56] The consecration ritual highlighted in a very literal sense, through thousands of glowing oil lamps and through special prayers, the most basic symbolism of the building, that is, its function as a sacred space, a nexus between heaven and earth. The nighttime light show was a spectacular display for the physical senses as well as a celebration of the completion of the building, but it was also much more. It was a lesson on the connection between the visible and the invisible, the temporal and eternal, the sacred and the profane.[57]

Fray José de Siguenza, the Hieronymite monk who chronicled the building of the Escorial and compared the edifice to the heavenly Jerusalem, thought it useful to describe the consecration ceremony in great detail, counting nearly every drop of holy water that was sprinkled, for he believed that these rituals raised the ontological status of the building's material objects to a higher level. Citing Thomas Aquinas, Siguenza argued, "It is accepted by the Church, and confirmed by the most learned and holy doctors, that these stones from which altars and churches or any other material things are constructed receive unto themselves, through consecration, a special spiritual virtue, with which they rise above their earthly and material existence to a divine order."[58]

The symbolism of the lighting ceremony derived its meaning from this liturgical theology. In the same way that the thousands of burning lamps made the physical reality of the Escorial visible in the gloom of night, the ceremonies the next day made visible the spiritual dimension of the sacred spaces within the building. For Siguenza, the repetitive gestures of the clergy who consecrated Philip's building were not to be seen as a human activity but as a divine reality: "If one looks within the

---

[56] Alonso Cabrera, at San Domingo, Madrid, *Sermones funerales*, fol. 58r.

[57] Mircea Eliade in *The Sacred and Profane* (p. 63) has observed: "The irruption of the sacred does not only project a fixed point into the formless fluidity of profane space, a center into chaos; it also effects a break in plane, that is, it opens communication between the cosmic planes [between earth and heaven] and makes possible ontological passage from one mode of being to another."

[58] Siguenza, *Fundación*, p. 141, citing the *Summa Theologica* (3p., q. 83, art. 3).

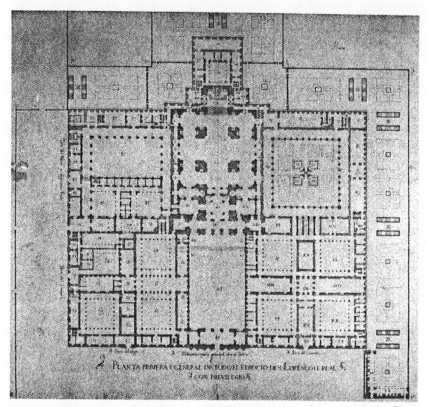

Floor Plan of the Escorial. Drawing by Juan de Herrera, engraving by Pedro Peret, 1587. Reproduced in Luis Cervera Vera, *Las estampas y el sumario de El Escorial por Juan de Herrera* (Madrid, 1954).

ceremonies, to what is inside, to what they represent, to what they seek to accomplish, then one would see there can be nothing that is more heavenly or divine."[59] It is precisely this sacramental dimension that Philip II sought to capture most powerfully through the Escorial itself.

The Escorial was planned according to spiritual blueprints as much as

[59] Ibid., pp. 141–153. According to Siguenza, Jesus Christ Himself is present through the person of the priest who officiates at any church ceremony, and through His divine power "the inanimate stones become able, after consecration, to awaken in us a special devotion and reverence for heavenly things."

material ones. It is possible to speak of an invisible architecture that made the material form follow a spiritual function and to refer to the liturgical infrastructure as the framework that held together the many disparate parts of a gigantic whole. As one scholar has observed, it is a basilica that was built as much out of prayer as out of stone, a visible symbol in which a perpetual liturgy for the dead rose to God.[60]

Viewed strictly from the vantage point of its functional purpose as a house of the dead, the Escorial can be seen as a monument to the continuity of the Hapsburg dynasty in Spain: a living monument with a profoundly sacral dimension.[61] It was not only a place for burial but also a repository for the relics of thousands of saints and a perpetual prayer machine for the souls of the dead. It was a nexus between the living and the dead because it was also a palace; and it was also a connecting point between this world and the next for all the monarchs who inhabited it, whether living or dead. The presence of an entire dynasty within one ritual shrine that also served as a palace enhanced the monarchy's claim on time itself. The living king was not just a man whose body would one day dissolve; he was the temporal embodiment of an eternal monarchy – one point in an ostensibly indissoluble continuum. The supreme function of the Escorial was to assert the coincidence of opposites through ritual: not just between the visible and invisible, or the sacred and the profane, but between the temporal character of the kingship embodied by the monarch who resided there and its eternal nature embodied in the royal corpses that lay in such close proximity to the body of Christ (the Eucharist) and the bodies of the saints (the relics).[62]

Some of Philip II's contemporaries understood this function clearly. Two of the chroniclers who published accounts of the death of Philip referred to the Escorial as the King's cocoon, though each employed the metaphor in a different sense, complementing through their images the full meaning of a sense of continuity and rebirth. To one, the Escorial was a cocoon for the rebirth of the king in a personal, spiritual sense: Philip, much as a silkworm, had spun his own cocoon in the Escorial so

---

[60] Louis Bertrand, *Philippe II à L'Escorial* (Paris, 1929), p. 67.

[61] Some of the larger funerary themes of the Escorial have been highlighted by Maria Leticia Sánchez, "El sentido de la muerte en El Escorial," *IV Centenario de monasterio de El Escorial. Las casas reales, el palacio* (Madrid, 1986), pp. 69–78.

[62] Benjamin Ray has made the same observation about some East African royal shrines. *Myth, Ritual, and Kingship in Buganda*, pp. 20, 158–9.

he would have a place in which to cross over into a new life in the hereafter.[63] To the other chronicler, the Escorial was a cocoon for the rebirth of the monarchy itself in a material sense: The Escorial was the place where a dying king could enter and a new, youthful successor emerge.[64]

In a similar vein, Philip was compared to the mythical phoenix, the bird that was consumed in flames but rose to new life from its ashes. Aguilar de Terrones, preaching at the funeral exequies at San Jerónimo in Madrid, in the presence of Philip III, launched his sermon into a metaphorical flight: Philip II was a phoenix, who, knowing that his death was near retired to his nest on a sacred mountain, the Escorial. What made the Escorial sacred was the fact that it was an affront to the Protestant heretics, a sacrifice acceptable to God when His temples were being desecrated elsewhere. God had sent down fire to this nest as a sign of His approval: first, in a lightning storm that had struck the building and charred a tower; then, as if to confirm the symbolic meaning of St. Lawrence's grill, in the illness that consumed Philip, bringing him to his phoenix-like death and transit to eternal life.[65] Phoenix imagery was prevalent at the exequies in Seville, not just in the sermon by Juan Bernal but on the Escorial-like catafalque, which was topped off with a large statue of the mythical bird.[66]

The celebration of the sacrament of the Eucharist was the fulcrum of the Escorial, physically and spiritually. The visible center of the edifice is the dome of the basilica, where the royal dead were buried amidst 7,500 relics and where innumerable masses were offered up on behalf of their souls.[67] Although the entire plan for the Escorial was attained only "gradually and by accretion rather than by instantaneous foresight," as

[63] Cabrera de Cordoba, p. 379. He also compares the Escorial to a phoenix's nest.

[64] Porreño, p. 18. A metaphor first used by Aguilar de Terrones in his funeral sermon for Philip, *Sermones funerales*, fol. 37v.

[65] *Sermones funerales*, fol. 37r: "Sobre estas parrillas se recogió el buen Rey, quando se vió cercano a la muerte, y cercado de reliquias de Santos olorosas, començo a arder con fuego de dolores, y tornarse en ceniza la santa fenix."

[66] On the catafalque: Collado, *Túmulo*, pp. 118–19; the sermon: Ariño, *Suçesos de Sevilla*, appendix, pp. 548–49.

[67] Louis Bertrand, *Philppe II à l'Escorial* (Paris, 1929), p. 66. "A l'Escorial, le temple est le centre de l'edifice. Comme une couronne imperiale, la coupole domine toute le batisse."

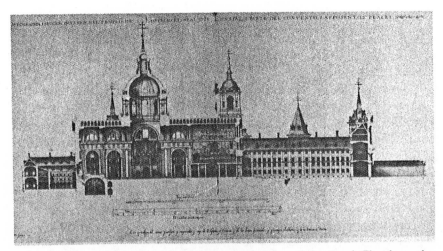

Cross-section of the Escorial, Showing the Interior of the Royal Chambers, the Basilica, and the Royal Tombs. Reproduced in Luis Cervera Vera, *Las estampas y el sumario de El Escorial por Juan de Herrera* (Madrid, 1954).

George Kubler has indicated, the initial and constant requirement guiding its construction was Philip's desire to erect a dynastic necropolis and temple.[68]

Though novel in its size and complexity, the Escorial was firmly rooted in ancient and medieval traditions, some common to most of Western Europe, others peculiarly Spanish in character. The imperial palace complexes at Spoleto, Constantinople, Ravenna, and Aachen could all have served as models. The dynastic burial sites of Westminster in England and St. Denis in France also drew upon and further continued the ancient tradition of combining palace, church, and necropolis. Throughout the *Reconquista*, the monarchs of the medieval Iberian kingdoms usually constructed palaces in which a monastery and burial grounds were combined, such as at Oviedo (Asturias, ninth century), Santa Maria la Real de las Huelgas de Burgos (Old Castille, 1187), Santa Creus (Catalonia, 1280), Poblet (Catalonia, 1380), San Juan de Toledo (New Castille, fifteenth century).[69] The novelty of the

[68] George Kubler, *Building the Escorial* (Princeton, 1982), p. 44.
[69] See R. Arco, *Sepulcros de la casa real de Castilla* (Madrid, 1954).

Escorial, then, was its attempt to encompass and centralize an entire tradition.[70]

The most peculiar feature of the Iberian palace/monasteries continued at the Escorial was the proximity of the royal chambers to the chapel, sacristy, and choir.[71] The location of the royal chambers and the royal mausoleum at the Escorial carried this medieval Spanish tradition further, placing the monarchs as close to the eucharistic tabernacle as possible. As can be clearly seen in the plans for the building, the royal mausoleum and the temporary burial chambers (*pudrideros*) are located directly beneath the main altar of the basilica. The private royal chambers for king and queen are directly behind and around the altar and thus nearly adjacent to the mausoleum itself. Philip II and his architects planned carefully and deliberately so that the king could sleep almost directly above his own grave as well as that of his parents and descendants and could also see the main altar from his bed through an open door.[72]

In physical and spiritual terms, function and symbolism coincide: The axis between sacrament and kingship is clearly visible. Within this *sanctum sanctorum* only priests and monarchs (and their assistants) are allowed. Within this sacred space, the power of the *rex/sacerdos* (king/priest) is celebrated for the glory of God as well as for the glory of the dynastic ruling house. Through this intimate arrangement of space, the palace and the church become as one in a daring "mystical embrace,"[73]

---

[70] Fernando Chueca, *Casas Reales en Monasterios y Conventos Españoles* (Madrid, 1966), pp. 13–14, 151.

[71] Chueca, p. 181. "No se trata aquí solamente de la comodidad . . . sino de algo mas elevado: de la expresión arquitectonica, de una función representativa, de la manifestación de una jerarquía y de una visión teocentrica de la politica."

[72] This was widely proclaimed, as attested to by Aguilar de Terrone's funeral sermon at San Jerónimo: "Donde edificó nuestro monarca el Palacio querido? Donde tuvo su dormitorio, sino pared en medio del altar mayor del octavo milagro del mundo, que dedicó a San Lorenzo? Desde allí, puesto en necesidades suyas y de la Iglesia, bolvía su cara a la pared, como Ezechias, a invocar a Dios." *Sermones funerales*, fol. 27v.

[73] Chueca, p. 202, adds: "El grado de unión, de unción, de religación entre el altar, el tabernaculo y la camara regia, entendida como ultimo y hermetico habitaculo del monarca, es algo que estremece, es algo que confunde con solo mirar los planos del Monasterio, si estos planos se miran no como simple proyección de un cuerpo arquitectonico, sino como revelación de una idea. En ese caso los planos se nos harán eloquentes, no solo serán idea de una arquitectura, sino más bien arquitectura de una idea."

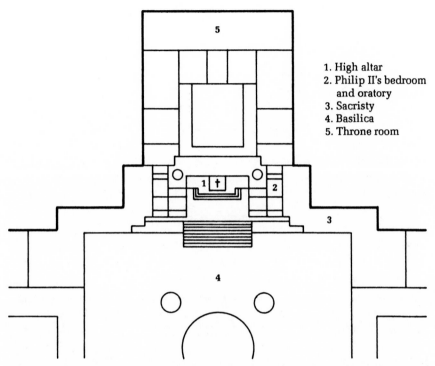

1. High altar
2. Philip II's bedroom
   and oratory
3. Sacristy
4. Basilica
5. Throne room

(A) Floor plan showing the relation of the royal chambers to the basilica at the Escorial

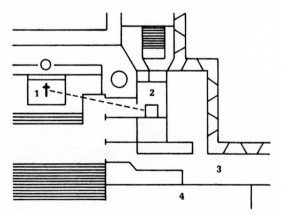

(B) Detail of Philip II's chambers at the Escorial, showing the sight line from his deathbed to the high altar

an embrace that clearly proclaims that particular sacred space as an *axis mundi*, the center where passage is possible from one cosmic region to another, from heaven to earth and the underworld and, vice versa, from the underworld to earth and heaven.[74]

Moreover, the architectural arrangement of the royal chambers not only joins king and priest but also the living and the dead in a sacramental embrace. Within this carefully delineated sacred space, the body of Christ, offered in the sacrifice of the mass for the benefit of the living and the dead, is placed in physical proximity to the bodies of the Hapsburg monarchs, living and dead.[75] The proximity of Christ to the Hapsburgs serves as testimony not only to the physical presence of the two central realities of the Spanish church/state, God and king, but also to the historical continuity of a nation itself under the aegis of the divine. This architectural arrangement further glorifies the interdependency of the political and sacred realms by also affirming an eschatological dimension to kingship. The assemblage of the Hapsburgs, living and dead, in such close proximity to one another and to Christ is a powerful confirmation of the *communio sanctorum*, a show of confidence in that very sacramental soteriology of the Catholic Church that the Protestant heretics had dared to renounce and that the Spanish Hapsburgs had committed themselves to defend. The presence of thousands of relics, many of them rescued from the hands of Protestant iconoclasts in Germany and the Netherlands, further reinforced the visible presence of the *communio sanctorum*.[76]

In the architectural "embrace" of the basilica and royal chambers, then, the intercessory power of the church is highlighted, and the notion of the divine-right monarchy is further consolidated through ritual sym-

---

[74] See Eliade, *Sacred and Profane*, p. 37. For a more detailed discussion of the symbolism of the "center," or "axis mundi," see Eliade's *Images and Symbols. Studies in Religious Symbolism* (New York, 1969), pp. 27–56.

[75] This is the way Charles V wanted his own body to be buried: "Que la mitad de mi cuerpo hasta los pechos esté debaxo del dicho altar y la otra mitad de los pechos a la cabeça salga fuera dél, de manera que cualquier sacerdote que dixare missa, ponga los pies sobre mi pecho y cabeça." *Testamento de Carlos V*, facsimile edition (Madrid, 1982), Codicil, pp. 109–110.

[76] Philip's effort to rescue and protect relics is carefully outlined by Juan Manuel del Estal, "Felipe II y su archivo hagiografico de El Escorial," *Hispania Sacra*, XXIII (1970): 1–96.

bol. To heighten the symbolic intensity of the whole and to drive home this message within the basilica itself, Philip also commissioned an imposing set of effigies from Pompeo Leoni, which were erected at each side of the main altar. On one side, Charles V and his wives kneel in perpetual adoration of the eucharist. Directly across, Philip and the three wives buried with him do the same. The Spanish monarchs may not have had a second body at their funerals, as did the French, but they had instead enduring effigies that proclaimed the sacredness of the Hapsburgs within what was intended to be the most sacred spot on Spanish soil. It was to this carefully constructed "cocoon" that Philip II came to undergo his *transito,* to show to the world as much as to God the depth and fervor of his piety and the sincerity of his passion for the best possible death.

5

Death, the Spanish monarchy, and the myth of sacredness

If so much attention was paid to the individual's preparation for death, one would naturally expect a greater scrutiny of the moment of death itself. In the case of Philip II this is certainly true. For his chroniclers, the entire worth of his person, his value as a king and a good Catholic, shine most brightly at the very last moment, as he crosses over from this life to the next. At that crucial point when Philip finally dies, all his virtues are proven true. It should come as no surprise, then, that in all the accounts of Philip's death, the final moment of transition assumes an unmistakably catechetical character, at times even stronger than that of his preparation for death. This final lesson becomes not only a summary of all lessons in the art of dying but also a compendium of the most important teachings of the Roman Catholic Church.

Death as the ultimate testimony

Up to the very end, Philip showed himself to be a perfect model of obedience to the church and its teachings. Professing total submission to the ecclesiastical system, he said the following to his confessor shortly before dying: "Father, you stand here in the place of God, and I promise to do whatever you say is best for my salvation, so it is up to you to tell me what to do because I am ready to do it all."[1]

---

[1] Yepes, *Relación*, fol. 57v. According to Perez de Herrera, Philip made forty full confessions to Father Yepes during his final illness: *Elogio*, p. 379. Philip's total submission to his confessor was mentioned in many of the 1598 funeral sermons.

In keeping with such submissiveness, Philip made one final public profession of faith in which he confessed his faults and affirmed his loyalty to the church. According to Lhermite, this final public prayer was largely taken from the writings of Blosius by Father Yepes, who helped the king recite it.[2] This profession of faith contained all the requisite standard petitions and declarations. Calling himself a "vile sinner," Philip begged God to forgive him and also asked pardon from all those whom he had offended throughout his life. Expressing confidence in God's redemptive love, he exclaimed that he would seek refuge in Christ's passion and offer it up to the Trinity for those merits that he still lacked and for the "full satisfaction" of all his sins. After reciting the creed, Philip uttered some words similar to those commonly found in most Spanish wills:

I declare before God and his celestial court that I desire to end my life in that Faith in which every obedient son of the Holy Mother Church ought to die. I declare that I believe everything that the Holy Mother, the Catholic Church holds true, and all that which true Catholics and followers of Christ ought to believe.[3]

This declaration was followed by a cautionary clause in which Philip denied responsibility for any statements he might make or thoughts he might have under duress from that point forward, whether incited by "the temptation of the devil" or some effect of his illness. Then he closed with the following statement: "I am gladdened, and I thank my Creator and most merciful Redeemer, in whose ineffable mercy I trust, as I die in the holy Christian Faith, and into Whose most holy hands I commend my soul and body, now and at the hour of my death."[4]

By showing remarkable calmness when faced with the immediate prospect of divine judgment at death, Philip proved, more than by almost any other act, that he was indeed dying a good death. We are told that Philip showed no fear when told of "the great abyss of God's justice," and that he carefully considered all his past responsibilities with serenity. "He approached his death as if he were going to take a nap," said one eulogist.[5] Even when confronted with the consequences of so many actions he had taken, so many people he had governed, and "so

[2] Lhermite, *Passetemps*, II, p. 131.   [3] Cervera de la Torre, *Testimonio*, pp. 92–93.
[4] Ibid., p. 93.   [5] Agustín Davila, O. P., at Valladolid, *Sermones funerales*, fol. 87v.

349

much blood which had been shed," Philip valiantly resisted the temptation to despair. The picture that emerges is one of Philip calmly considering his past life as one in which he had often been wronged rather than as one in which he had committed much evil.[6] The king's greatest concern, it appears, was his wish to be lucid at the moment of death, so he could commend his soul to God "with the same words that His Son uttered when he expired on the cross."[7]

At the moment of death itself, we are told, he seemed most tranquil. Cervera de la Torre remarked that the look on Philip's face was very peaceful and that it encouraged all those present to believe that the king had gone straight to heaven from his bed.[8] The message conveyed here was fairly straightforward: Those who entrusted themselves wholeheartedly to the salvational system of the church, as Philip did, would have no need to fear death and the afterlife.

Philip, of course, was in a privileged position. Although he suffered much in his final illness, he had at his disposal the full resources of the church. Few other mortals could avail themselves of the same kind of ecclesiastical support as the king of Spain. Philip relied for help on his confessor, his chaplains, the monks of the Escorial, and the Archbishop of Toledo. In addition, he also received special attention from Clement VIII, the supreme pontiff at Rome. If he died with a peaceful look on his face, fully confident in God's forgiveness, it was largely due to his reliance on a system of salvation that had given him the fullest possible attention.

Philip received a special visit from the papal nuncio about three weeks before his death. Camilo Gaetano, who in addition to serving as the pope's representative in Spain also held the title of Patriarch of Alexandria, spent several hours consoling Philip. He talked to the king and prayed with him. Philip asked the nuncio for a papal blessing and a plenary absolution, "with the intention of receiving all the blessings, indulgences, and spiritual fruits that one can obtain from His Holiness under such conditions." Gaetano had not been instructed to do this by the pope, but he granted Philip his wish and assured him that the pope would later ratify these actions retroactively. Philip received this plenary absolution "with a smiling face and a fearless spirit." (Notice here again

[6] Porreño, *Dichos y Hechos*, pp. 183–4.   [7] Yepes, *Relación*, fol. 59.
[8] Cervera de la Torre, *Testimonio*, p. 130; also Perez de Herrera, *Elogio*, p. 377.

how the king's facial expressions are used to indicate the positive effect of such ministrations.) Confirmation of the pope's approval for the nuncio's actions arrived at the Escorial before Philip died, further easing his mind and preparing him for a peaceful departure, "and so he went to enjoy God in heaven, after having loved and served Him for so long on earth."[9]

A few weeks after Philip died, on 9 October 1598, Pope Clement VIII eulogized the Spanish king before the College of Cardinals. In this eulogy, Clement reaffirmed what already seemed to be the general consensus on Philip. He said he was greatly comforted by the reports he had received about Philip's death, especially by descriptions of his peaceful demeanor, which encouraged him to have "a firm hope that he was in heaven, enjoying the eternal reward he had earned through his lifetime service to the Divine Majesty."[10] In death, as much as in life, Philip and Pope Clement had a reciprocal need for each other's assistance. From Philip's perspective, the support of the pope was crucial at all times. Although the king was often at odds with the papacy concerning matters of ecclesiastical and civil policy, he desperately wanted to remain faithful to the church and the pope.[11] In Philip's mental world, there was no such thing as purely secular power: His was a sacred Catholic kingship, and as such it needed the approval and blessing of the supreme pontiff in Rome. At the moment of death, Philip prevailed upon the pope through his nuncio to grant him a very special absolution, and he received it. According to all accounts this privilege was a great comfort to Philip.

From Pope Clement's perspective, the church needed the support of princes such as Philip. In his eulogy, Clement made it clear that Philip had earned his way to heaven through his tireless support of the church:

Because he wanted to subject the vassals of other kingdoms to the Catholic Faith, and to obedience to this Holy See, he pledged his entire royal patrimony,

---

9 Cervera de la Torre, *Testimonio*, pp. 104–6. The text of the nuncio's report is also cited in full by Lhermite, *Passetemps*, II, pp. 135–7.

10 Cervera de la Torre, *Testimonio*, p. 134. This eulogy was publicized in some funeral sermons, such as that of Francisco Sobrino at Valladolid, *Sermones funerales*, fol. 274r.

11 For a detailed account of Philip's relations with the papacy, see Ricardo Garcia-Villoslada, "El Rey Catolico y los papas," in *Historia de la Iglesia en España*, ed. R. Garcia-Villoslada, vol. III, part 2, pp. 33–78. Also G. Catalano, *Controversie giurisdizionali tra Chiesa e Stato nell'età di Gregorio XIII e Fillipo II* (Palermo, 1955).

and expended on this effort the great treasures which were brought to him from the Indies, as well as those he collected from his Spanish kingdoms in all the years that he reigned. Consequently, it is possible to say that the entire life of this king was a continual struggle against the enemies of our holy Faith. When it comes to matters of piety and zeal, I can say that no one can compare with his Majesty, except for those saints who are enjoying heavenly bliss forever.[12]

Clement was grateful for Philip's support, and Philip in turn was most grateful for the pope's final blessing. Even in death, it was impossible to untangle the symbiotic relationship that had developed between the Spanish crown and the papacy. Philip's request for a special absolution shows not only that he believed in the special powers of the pope but that he also knew that the pope owed much to him. Clement's eulogy shows that the pope was well aware of the special role played by the Spanish monarchy in the promotion of Catholicism throughout the world and that he fervently hoped Philip's death would not mean the end of this support. Speaking of Philip III and his accession to the throne, Clement said he hoped "not so much for a succession, as for a resurrection,"[13] meaning, of course, that he expected the policies of the Spanish crown toward the papacy to remain unchanged after the death of Philip II.

God and the Spanish monarchy

The pope's wish for a "resurrection" of Philip II in the person of his son Philip III was also shared by many Spaniards. After many decades of prosperity and success, Spain had begun to experience some ominous setbacks in the closing years of the sixteenth century. Drought, plague, and military defeats had filled some citizens with a sense of foreboding about the future. Now, with the death of the monarch who had embodied the myth of Spanish invulnerability, there was even greater reason for apprehension. The alarm can be felt in some of the funeral sermons. Some of them mentioned that Philip's death had been presaged by a nine-month drought in Castile and by pestilence.[14] Others dwelt on recent eclipses as ominous signs.[15] One alluded to the fact that the

[12] Cervera de la Torre, *Testimonio,* p. 134.   [13] Ibid.
[14] Lorenzo de Ayala, at Valladolid, and Manuel Sarmiento, at the University of Salamanca. *Sermones funerales,* fols. 93r, 220r.
[15] Juan Lopez Salmeron, at Logroño; Manuel Sarmiento, at Salamanca; and Francisco Sobrino, at the University of Valladolid. *Sermones funerales,* fols. 210r-v, 220r, 273v.

king's death had coincided with the beginning of autumn and the approach of barrenness and darkness.[16] And one went as far as to exclaim in a shrill tone that nature itself had ceased functioning properly because it knew that the death of Philip was the greatest ill (*el mayor daño*) to befall Spain since the time of Noah![17] To allay their fears, many began to focus on the strength and purpose of the crown. Cervera de la Torre spoke for many of his contemporaries when he nervously boasted:

It is the special privilege of Spain to extend its jurisdiction over all peoples and nations, uniting them in the Holy Catholic Faith; and as long as this Faith endures in our monarchy, its empire will continue to expand and flourish, to cover everything here beneath the moon.[18]

The death of Philip II, though lamentable and frightful, was interpreted by Spanish propagandists as a triumph. In their eyes, Philip had died a good, holy death, as had most of his ancestors. Philip's death was but one more in a long line of exemplary deaths that proved beyond a doubt that Spain was especially blessed and charged with a divine purpose in the world. Cervera de la Torre patiently listed all the kings who died exemplary deaths in the history of the various Iberian kingdoms, filling five pages with their names. In Castile alone, he counted fifty-two kings, none of whom had ever died unprepared or unrepentant. It was truly remarkable to observe, he said, how many good deaths one could find in the history of the Spanish monarchy and how difficult it was to find cases of tyrants or heretics who had died unworthily. There was no doubt in his mind that no other royal line in Europe could even come close to this record:

If one carefully ponders this, and compares the Catholic monarchs of Spain to foreign kings, or to those who had little faith, or to those who destroyed churches and lacked piety and devotion, one will discover that their sorrowful and wretched deaths were caused by their sins. From this one may conclude

---

[16] Juan Lopez Salmeron, at Logroño, *Sermones funerales*, fol. 212v.

[17] Lorenzo de Ayala, at Valladolid, *Sermones funerales*, fol. 93r.

[18] Cervera de la Torre, *Testimonio*, p. 98. See Fray Juan de Salazar, *Politica Española*, first published in 1619 (Madrid, 1945), especially the introduction to the modern edition by Miguel Herrero Garcia. Also by Herrero Garcia, *Ideas de los españoles en el siglo XVII*, 2nd ed. (Madrid, 1966).

that the many good, pious and holy deaths which the kings of Spain have always enjoyed have been the result of their great faith and devotion.[19]

This account, as most historians would immediately notice, is a rather curious distortion of the history of medieval Spanish kingship.[20] Whether or not Cervera de la Torre had his facts straight is irrelevant at this point. What matters are the reasons for his interpretation of history and his understanding of the role of the "good death" of monarchs. It is precisely here, in dealing with this issue, that Cervera de la Torre reveals why he thought it was so important to interpret Philip's death and promote it as a model. Here we can see his plan reduced to a simple theorem: A good death means holiness; a holy monarchy means a chosen people. In this scheme of things, Philip's holy death proved that he had done God's work and that his kingdom was the chosen instrument of God's will.

This notion of chosenness and of the special role played in God's plan by the Spanish monarchy was perhaps the most important point to be promoted by those who chronicled Philip's death. There were many lessons to be drawn from all the lugubrious details of the king's demise, but one lesson seems to stand above all others in terms of political significance: By dying well Philip proved that he was a good Catholic, and by proving that he was a good Catholic, he proved once again that the True Faith had always been professed by the Spanish monarchy. Those who interpreted Philip's death, then, were interested in doing more than promoting his example as an *Ars Moriendi*. Some also wanted to advance a certain notion of sacred kingship and to affirm a particular sense of nationalistic and religious chauvinism:

[19] On pp. 143, 148, *Testimonio*, Cervera de la Torre provides a long list of kings and rulers who have suffered horrible deaths as a result of their impiety. Although many on the list are pagan Roman emperors, most are Byzantine Christian emperors. It is an impressive catalogue of misfortunes: emperors who are driven mad, or are killed by their own children, or are struck by lightning. These wretched deaths are compared with those of Spanish monarchs: "Ninguno murió su muerte, sino todas violentas, porque perdieron la Fé, la verguenza a Dios, y a la Yglesia. . . . De donde se infiere que a los Reyes Catholicos de España da Dios exemplares muertes, por su gran Fé, religión, y respeto a las Yglesias."

[20] For a quite different interpretation, see Teofilo F. Ruiz, "Unsacred Monarchy: The Kings of Castille in the Late Middle Ages," in Sean Wilentz, ed., *Rites of Power: Symbolism, Ritual, and Politics Since the Middle Ages* (Philadelphia, 1985), pp. 111, 132.

No other nation or people, from Adam on down, has been able to bring together under one Faith and one religion such a great diversity of other nations and races, or languages and customs, as have the kings of Spain. All of this is due to their great piety and their Catholic Faith, which has endured for such a long time. One cannot find a similar example in Greek or Roman history, nor in any other foreign language. No other monarchy has persevered as much, no other line of succession is as unbroken, no other kings have lasted as long as the kings of Spain.[21]

So it is that the death of Philip served as a lesson in the sacredness, orthodoxy, and prestige of the Spanish monarchy. At a time when the kingdom seemed most vulnerable, immediately after the death of such a strong and long-lived monarch, it must have been very reassuring to ponder such lessons. The attempt to interpret the death of Philip as a "good" event rather than a tragedy can be better understood if one takes into account the trauma of succession. As Cervantes put it, what made Philip's virtue shine most brightly was the fact that he was "good in life, good in death, and good in his successor."[22] Almost all the accounts of Philip II's death are dedicated to his son and heir to the throne, Philip III. They therefore look forward as much as they do backward. Some of the sermons focus on the new king, shouting a warning to all heretics, infidels, and enemies of the church: Do not rejoice over the death of Philip II, for his son will prove an even mightier scourge![23] By dwelling on the many good qualities so intensely exemplified by Philip II on his deathbed, these treatises hoped not only to praise the dead king or provide an example for all to follow but also expected to prove that there was something extraordinary about the royal person.

Philip II had been an exceptional monarch. To allay the fear that his successor might not be equally majestic, it was necessary to imbue the office of the monarchy itself with exceptional characteristics that ensured some sense of invulnerability. If Philip II died a good death, then, it was not entirely due to personal traits but also to special favors from

[21] Cervera de la Torre, *Testimonio*, p. 95. Martín de Castro, in his sermon at the Royal Chapel of Granada, proclaimed that Spain had always had the noblest and holiest kings in all of Christendom, and that among these Philip had been the very best. *Sermones funerales*, fol. 240r.

[22] Cervantes, "A la muerte del Rey Don Felipe II," *Obras* (1923), vol. 7, p. 253.

[23] Juan Lopez Salmerón, at Logroño; Martín de Castro, at Granada. *Sermones funerales*, fols. 209v, 244r.

God. There was something unique about the constancy of the Spanish monarchy; because of divine election, their orthodoxy was almost guaranteed. Furthermore, it was through the faithfulness of the monarchy that the nation as a whole was blessed. "Whence comes all of Spain's glory?" asked one of the funeral sermons. "From its Catholic kings," came the reply.[24] If Philip II and all his ancestors had died good deaths, it was an indication that Philip III would also enjoy the same privilege. To desire a good death for the new monarch might seem a bit odd, but it was actually a sincere way of wishing that he would prove himself a good king and a worthy successor to his father.[25]

So it is that by focusing on death, these writers paradoxically expressed their faith in the continuity of life and the perseverance of the monarchy. By highlighting what was good about Philip's death within a certain theological framework, these interpreters promoted the idea of sacred kingship and of Spain's privileged place in the world as the supreme defender of Catholic orthodoxy.

Lest it all sound too much like Calvinist notions of predestination, let us keep in mind that some ambivalence is expressed about this notion of divine election and about the sacred character of the monarchy. Although confidence is shown about the future, it is tempered by a significant conditional clause. All of Philip's accomplishments and all of Spain's glory had hinged on the king's religious devotion, and the dying king himself had made this clear to his son and heir, admonishing him to fend off all attacks on the faith in order to preserve his kingdom.[26] The continued progress of Spain toward glory and world domination hung on the condition that future kings exercise their piety correctly. Only "as long as the faith endures in our monarchy," says Cervera de la Torre, will Spain be able to enjoy its special privileges.[27]

This brings us to a final set of considerations about the death of Philip II and its interpretations. The death of Philip was promoted as exempla-

---

[24] Juan Lopez Salmerón, at Logroño, *Sermones funerales*, fol. 212r–214v, also added: "O gloriosa España, numerosa de gente, poderosa de armas, maestra de guerras, rica de perlas y de oro, abundante de vituallas, copiosa de todas las cosas, mas copiosisima de devocion, de santidad, de Religion y Fe."

[25] For an example of such wishes, see Perez de Herrera, *Elogio*, pp. 335, 338.

[26] Martín de Castro, at Granada, *Sermones funerales*, fol. 236r-v: "La Religion y Christiandad hizo a nuestro gran Monarca vencedor de todos sus enemigos."

[27] Cervera de la Torre, *Testimonio*, p. 98.

ry for two complementary reasons: to serve as an *Ars Moriendi*, as a model of true faith and piety; and also to serve as a testimony of the sacredness of the person of the king. Although the sacredness of Philip as a monarch seems at times to be taken for granted, and some inclination is manifested toward notions of divine election and the inevitability of his sacredness and the prosperity of his kingdom, there is no overriding concept of predestination behind these ideas. The sacredness of Philip, according to these interpretations, is due more to his *actions*, through which he proves that divine favor rests on him, than to some conception of his royal person as sacred in and of itself.[28]

Though the sacred character of the Spanish monarchy was taken as being axiomatic, it was not the same kind of conception of divine kingship accepted elsewhere in Europe.[29] Despite his Burgundian and Hapsburg ancestry, Philip had assumed a kingship that was still thoroughly Spanish – and especially Castilian – in its sacral dimension. Throughout the Middle Ages Castile had developed a rich symbolic tradition of royal sacredness that drew upon wider European notions of kingship but differed from them in significant ways.[30] Castilian kings had never considered their office to be sacred in the same way as had the French or the English, even though they believed that their responsibilities had been entrusted to them directly by God. Birth, coronation, death, and burial were not associated with the same ceremonies in medieval Castile as elsewhere. In the various Iberian kingdoms inherited by Philip, there was not a saintly founder of the dynasty or a saintly

[28] This conception of kingship had ancient roots in Spain, as indicated by the Visigothic maxim: "Rex eris si recte facias, et si non facias, non eris." See Sergio Bertelli, *Corpo di re*, p. 208. It also ran strong among the Aragonese, who swore fealty to their king conditionally, "Y si no, no." See Ralph Giesey, *If Not, Not: The Oath of the Aragonese and the Legendary Laws of Sobrarbe* (Princeton, 1968).

[29] J. H. Elliott, "Power and Propaganda in the Spain of Philip IV," in *Rites of Power: Symbolism, Ritual, and Politics Since the Middle Ages*, ed. Sean Wilentz (Philadelphia, 1985), p. 148.

[30] Nieto Soria, *Poder real*, pp. 51 ff., eloquently argues that medieval Castile developed its own notion of sacred kingship and outlines the following typology for the imagery employed: (1) theocentric (relating the monarchy to God); (2) sacralizing (investing the monarchy with sacred powers); (3) moralizing (exalting the virtues of the monarchy); and (4) organic (explaining the relation between the monarchy and society through body metaphors). This typology is confirmed on all accounts in the case of Philip II.

blood connection to sanctify the royal family.[31] More significantly, no Iberian king had ever professed to have the healing powers claimed by the French monarchy.[32] Unlike the French and English kings who, according to the classic formulation, enjoyed the privilege of having two bodies, one mortal (their personal self) and one immortal and sacred (that of their office), the Spanish monarchs had but one body.[33]

In France and England, effigies of dead kings were used in funeral rituals as a means of easing the transition of power. The effigy, a *persona ficta*, represented another *persona ficta*, the monarch's *dignitas*.[34] No such tradition had evolved in Spain. In Castile, particularly, there was a strong tendency to view the king's *dignitas* as conditional: A *tyrano* (tyrant), a *rey yndoto* (an unskilled or unlearned king), or a *rey ynabil* (an inept king) could risk deposition and plunge the realm into conflict. One salient example was Philip II's ancestor, King Henry IV of Castile "the Impotent" (1454–74). This half brother of Queen Isabella lost the support of some nobles and precipitated a civil war. Accused of gross incompetence and homosexuality, he was ritually deposed in 1465 in an elaborate public ceremony at Avila.[35] A wooden effigy was used, attired in mourning clothes and fitted with the royal insignia of the crown, scepter, and sword. The archbishop initiated the deposition ritual by removing the crown. He was followed by grandees and nobles who then removed the other royal insignia, threw the effigy down from its throne, and kicked it off the platform shouting, "To the ground, sodomite!"[36]

[31] For an incisive analysis of medieval Castilian kingship, see Teofilo F. Ruiz, "Unsacred Monarchy," esp. p. 114.

[32] Marc Bloch, *Les rois thaumaturges* (Paris, 1961), p. 155.

[33] Ernst Kantorowicz, *The King's Two Bodies: A Study in Medieval Political Theology* (Princeton, 1957). Teofilo Ruiz comments: "Those who ruled and those who wanted to rule had, more often than not, one body instead of two." Ruiz, "Unsacred Monarchy," p. 131.

[34] Kantorowicz, *Two Bodies*, p. 420. See also Ralph E. Giesey, *Royal Funeral Ceremony in Renaissance France* (Geneva, 1960).

[35] Detailed in Mackay, "Ritual and Propaganda," esp. pp. 8–11, 39–42. On the grievances against King Henry, see William D. Phillips, *Enrique IV and the Crisis of Fifteenth-Century Castile, 1425–1480* (Cambridge MA, 1978).

[36] The primary sources for this event are: "Coplas de Mingo Revulgo" (15th c. poem), ed. Marcella Ciceri, *Cultura neolatina* 37 (1977): 75–149, 189–266; Alonso de Palencia, *Crónica de Enrique IV*, ed. A. Paz y Mélia, 3 vols. (Madrid, 1973–75); and Diego

So entrenched seemed the notion of the conditionality of the king's *dignitas* in Castile that although effigies were shunned for funerals, they could be used in a deposition.

The privileged position of Spain in the world may have been believed to depend on the faith of its monarchy, but ultimately this privilege did not rest on some abstract characteristic of the kingly office but on the free will of each individual king, aided, of course, by the grace of God. It was up to the monarch to *act* correctly, to rule justly and defend the faith in order for the divine favor to be showered on his nation.[37]

With Philip II, the Spanish monarchy assumed an overtly religious character. Under his successors, Philip III and Philip IV, this quality was further intensified. In the seventeenth century, most of the king's public appearances were at religious functions of one sort or another. It became increasingly evident that the *rey catolico* took very seriously his role as the supreme defender of orthodoxy and true piety, at least in a ceremonial sense, and that few were willing to dismiss the idea that the divine favor that had made Spain the greatest nation in the world rested on his fulfillment of certain religious and moral obligations.[38] Cristobal Perez de Herrera made this clear when he said the following:

The main reason that our lord the king [Philip II] died feeling so consoled is the same reason for which all of us his servants and vassals feel so comforted, and this is in seeing that although we lost such a great and powerful Philip, we have gained another one who resembles him as much in all other respects as he does in his name; and that as a sapling planted, nurtured, and cultivated by his own hand, as a shoot and branch from the same tree, he continues to produce the same marvelous fruit, as we can all see. We trust in God Our Lord, that this will continue to be so, and that his kingdoms will still be protected and favored by the closeness and shade of his greatness and generosity, and that they will grow

---

Enríquez del Castillo, *Crónica del Rey Don Enrique el Cuarto de este nombre, Biblioteca de Autores Españoles*, vol. 70 (Madrid, 1953).

[37] Juan Lopez Salmerón, at Logroño, *Sermones funerales*, fol. 207v: "Donde menos foragidos, vandoleros, ladrones, salteadores, y facinorosos que en nuestra España, por el govierno, por la virtud, por la santidad, por la justicia de un tan gran Rey."

[38] J. H. Elliott, "The Court of the Spanish Habsburgs: A Peculiar Institution?" in *Politics and Culture in Early Modern Europe: Essays in Honor of H. G. Koenigsberger*, ed. Phyllis Mack and Margaret C. Jacob (Cambridge UK, 1987), p. 10.

more and more each day, sustained and refreshed by the fruits of the exceptional virtues that will blossom in his Majesty.[39]

After the death of Philip II, Spanish commentators seem to have felt a continuing need to focus on the piety of their monarchs, as if they desperately wanted to show that the king's zeal for religion was genuine. Hyperbole and exaggeration were already in full bloom at the royal exequies: One sermon went so far as to say that because Philip had saved the church from being thrown into darkness by the Protestant heretics, he had become the fourth most important person in revelation history, right behind Noah, Moses, and Christ![40] This mantle passed on to his son, as is confirmed by the observations of a French courtier who traveled throughout Spain in 1603–4. Aware of Philip III's weakness, he was all the more impressed by his reputation as a devout man. The same monarch who had virtually handed over the task of governing to the Duke of Lerma and who spent so much time hunting also attended mass daily and prayed for about three hours each day. Not only that, his subjects spoke of him as a "great Christian" and a "holy angel from heaven," and addressed him as "Your Sacred Majesty."[41] These constant references to the sacred ties that bound God and the Spanish monarch served a dual purpose. To the world outside Spain, they helped to advance the idea of the Spanish king as the most Catholic of all monarchs. Within Spain and its dominions, they were an indispensable means of promoting political and social harmony. The bond between king and church, which was perhaps the strongest stabilizing element in a politically and linguistically fragmented peninsula, not only helped produce religious uniformity but also further legitimized the claims of the monarchy.[42]

The death of Philip II created an opportunity for mythmaking at a time when the monarchy was in urgent need of myths. The many interpretations of Philip's death can be seen as part of an attempt to clarify and enhance a peculiar concept of royal *sacredness*.[43] It has been argued

[39] Perez de Herrera, *Elogio*, p. 397.

[40] Lorenzo de Ayala, at Valladolid, *Sermones funerales*, fol. 112r.

[41] J. García Mercadal, *Viajes de extranjeros por España y Portugal*, 2 vols. (Madrid, 1959), vol. II, pp. 94–5; José Maria Diez Borque, *La vida Española en el Siglo de Oro según los extranjeros* (Barcelona, 1990), p. 152.

[42] Elliott, "Power and Propaganda," p. 152.

[43] Social scientists have devoted much attention to the sacrality of kingship throughout

that the Spanish monarchy developed no myths with which to surround its sacred character.[44] If one thinks strictly in terms of myths such as those employed by the French and English monarchs, especially the myth of healing powers, it might seem as if the Spanish kings did really lack a sacral dimension. If, however, one is willing to accept the proposition "all kings are 'divine' but some kingships are more divine than others,"[45] then one might begin to suspect that there can be forms of royal sacredness other than those proposed by the French and English models, and one might also come to see that the Spanish monarchy did indeed have a sacred character and a rich mythology of kingship.[46] Within such a framework, it then also becomes possible to argue that this sacred dimension, as expressed in the myth of the "good death" of the monarch, began to be promoted most vigorously when Philip II died.

According to prevailing medieval Spanish notions of kingship developed during the *Reconquista*, the legitimacy of a monarch ultimately rested on his deeds more than on any other consideration. Although Cervera de la Torre offered a placid and gentle history of the Spanish monarchy, the truth is that ferocity often guaranteed succession to the throne much more firmly than did other qualities.[47] In Spain, therefore, the legitimacy and sacredness of the king depended on his actions rather than on some abstract power inherent in the office itself.

By the sixteenth century, Spanish kings no longer needed to display the same kind of ferocity, but they still had to live up to certain standards of valor, fairness, and piety. Under this scheme of things, it only made sense to try to prove a king's sacred character through his accomplish-

the world. E. E. Evans-Pritchard argued that "everywhere and at all times" the king "must be in society and yet stand outside it, and this is only possible if his office is raised to a mystical plane." Frazer Lecture (1948), "The Divine Kingship of the Shilluk of the Nilotic Sudan," *Social Anthropology and Other Essays* (New York, 1962), p. 210. For more on sacred kingship, see Edward Shils and Michael Young, "The Meaning of the Coronation," in Shils, *Center and Periphery*, pp. 135–52; and Ray, *Myth, Ritual, and Kingship*, esp. pp. 201–6.
44 Ruiz, "Unsacred Monarchy," p. 128.
45 John Beattie, "Kingship," *International Encyclopedia of the Social Sciences*, vol. 8, p. 388.
46 This is the central thesis of Nieto Soria, *Poder real*. See also Denis Menjot, "Les funérailles des souverains castillans du Bas Moyen Age racontées par les chroniqueurs: une image de la souveraineté," *Annales de la Faculté des Lettres et Sciences Humaines de Nice* 39 (1985): 3–43.
47 Ruiz, "Unsacred Monarchy," p. 132.

ments. If, as was also commonly believed, a good death was the best possible indication of a good life for all mortals (*exitus acta probat*), then all the more so for a Spanish king. Charles V had prepared the way for the enhancement of this notion through his dramatic preparation for death at the monastery of Yuste. Now, with Philip II and his palace of death, the Escorial, the stage was set for a monumental sort of myth-making and for the promotion of an additional "master fiction" through which the monarchy expressed its power.[48]

The mythopoesis began to take shape as early as the funeral sermons. At the central exequies in the church of San Jerónimo, the royal preacher Aguilar de Terrones linked the survival of the monarchy to its sacredness and to the virtues embodied in Philip II and his son (who was but a few yards across the transept from the pulpit, concealed in the royal oratory). Kings are sacred, he exclaimed, for they are "God in human form." Injecting a note of caution after such an extreme statement, he continued: Surely, they are fully human, but if they are pious and just they can become godlike. "And after adoring God," he concluded, "we ought next to adore our good King, for whom all things remain alive after death."[49] This survival he spoke about hinged on virtue. Though the king had died, there was no need to fear: His virtue was not only alive but undiminished in the royal person of Philip III. In fact, nothing proved the sacredness of the king more clearly than his successor, for the greatest legacy of any king was a virtuous heir.[50] Another royal preacher, Alonso Cabrera, also emphasized the sacredness of the monarchy at the exequies held in the monastery church of San Domingo. Earthly kings, though mortal, were "God's viceroys" on earth, and they shared in His dignity. And this did not apply exclusively to the ancient Jewish kings. On the contrary, God's presence was still very evident in recent Spanish kings. Having said this, Cabrera then went on to invest

---

[48] Clifford Geertz has argued that all polities are governed by "master fictions" as well as by the threat of official or sanctioned force. See "Centers, Kings, and Charisma: Reflections on the Symbolics of Power," in *Rites of Power*, ed. S. Wilentz, esp. p. 15.

[49] Aguilar de Terrones, *Sermones funerales*, fols. 39r-v: "El rey es un Dios en carne humana." "El rey es hombre, pero si es religioso y justiciero, Dios se torna." He attributes these statements to Seneca.

[50] Aguilar de Terrones, *Sermones funerales*, fols. 35v-36v: "No nos ha quitado la muerte sus virtudes: todas, sin faltar ninguna, las tenemos vivas, y las poseemos tan enteras y tan vivas para nosotros, como oy ha veynte años."

the Hapsburg lineage with a mantle of biblical sacredness, comparing Charles V to King David and Philip II to Solomon.[51] At Seville, Juan Bernal compared Charles V to David, Philip II to Ezekiel, and Philip III to Josiah.[52]

Two other preachers who spoke of the monarchy as sacred also went so far as to pin its very survival on the paradigm of the good royal death. Martín de Castro, preaching directly above the burial crypt of the Catholic Kings Ferdinand and Isabella, said that the climactic point of Philip II's death had been the moment when he passed on to his son the box that contained Charles V's ritual death paraphernalia. At that instant, said Castro, Philip II revealed to Philip III the instruments with which Spanish monarchs could conquer God and heaven.[53] At the University of Salamanca, Manuel Sarmiento likewise focused on the death box of Charles V. For him, this box was the preeminent symbol of royal power. It was at the instant that Philip II handed this box over to his son that the kingship had been passed on. Whereas other kings passed on their rulership with rings, crowns, and other such symbols, said Sarmiento, Philip II transferred his power through ritual objects associated with death.[54]

Terrones, Cabrera, Castro, and Sarmiento had grasped one key meaning of the symbolic messages conveyed by recent events: They knew that Philip had not only reified a paradigm through his death but had also given it new dimensions. But these preachers did more than read symbols; they interpreted them for an audience. By making their insights public, they shared in the mythopoeic process, revealing to others what may only have been dimly understood: that the sacredness of the Spanish depended on deeds rather than on some special ontological status and that these deeds in turn were intimately and dynamically related to Spanish attitudes toward death and the afterlife.

[51] Alonso Cabrera, *Sermones funerales*, fols. 52r-54v. Cabrera thought that Philip's Solomonic identity was proven by the Escorial, which was a superior reflection of Solomon's Temple in Jerusalem. At Valladolid, Lorenzo de Ayala also compared Charles V to David and Philip II to Solomon: fols. 98r-v.

[52] Bernal, "Sermon," appendix to Ariño, *Suçesos de Sevilla*, pp. 552–3.

[53] Martín de Castro, at Royal Chapel, Granada, *Sermones funerales*, fol. 240r: "Para darle entender que aquella era la principal herencia que le dejava . . . que con aquellas disciplinas avian sus avuelos conquistado a Dios, y con las mesmas, ya que quedava Rey en la tierra, avia de conquistar el Reyno de los cielos."

[54] Manuel Sarmiento, *Sermones funerales*, fol. 227v.

From the perspective of the late twentieth century, it may seem odd, even bizarre, that so many of Philip's eulogists and propagandists should have seized on the paradigm of the good royal death as a means of enhancing the monarchy. And it is precisely by perceiving this "oddness" that we gain perspective on the Spanish mentality at the cusp of the Baroque age. Structures of power and structures of meaning were dynamically interrelated in Philip's Spain. The myths, symbols, and rituals surrounding the monarch were not only expressions of ultimate values; they were also the negative or mirror images of ultimate fears. Paradigms, like ritual, speak in the subjunctive mood: They suggest how things *should* be. They also offer the comforting reassurance of perfection and stability within an imperfect world of flux and decay.

Dark clouds hung low over Philip's exequies, and some seemed more aware of them than others. Yet, one does not have to strain to find men who betrayed their nervousness about the succession to the monarchy and expressed their fears about a declining Spain. Simply by choosing to dwell on the paradigmatic "good" death, these eulogists and propagandists necessarily exposed its mirror image, the "bad" death. The louder that some of these men preached about the paradigm, the more they betrayed their culture's anxieties. One particularly nervous sermon, that of Martín Castro at Granada, took a dizzying plunge immediately after having praised the king's sacred virtues to the skies. Philip had been the holiest king ever to have ruled in Christendom, Castro proclaimed. He was so good and so holy, in fact, that his death could only be explained as a punishment for the sins of his people. If Philip's subjects had been holier, if they had fasted more and done more public penance and arranged more processions for Philip's health, then he would still be alive. Castro's descent continued: Did anyone in Granada do any of this for Philip? No, of course not. They and all of Philip's subjects were responsible for his death. Hitting bottom, Castro articulated his deepest anxieties and those of his culture: "Pray God this punishment is not the beginning of greater punishments to come!" Utter destruction, he warned, lurked at the horizon.[55]

Looking beyond Spain to the Europe where Philip's hated Protestants lived, the myth of the "good death" of Spanish monarchs assumed a decidedly polemical dimension. This was a very Tridentine myth, an

[55] Martín de Castro, *Sermones funerales*, fol. 241r.

expression of the ethos of the Catholic Reformation. Because the Spanish monarch was *el rey catolico,* the amplification of the sacredness of his character was essential to the religious cause he championed. Furthermore, because the sacredness of the monarch ultimately depended on the exercise of his free will, the myth itself served as a powerful affirmation of Catholic soteriology and a negation of the central Protestant teaching of salvation through faith alone. Granted, ill-defined notions of divine election clung to the Spanish monarchy, but this presumption was always ultimately tempered by the harsh reality of the king's personal responsibility. Ultimately, the king had to prove his sacredness by being a good Catholic Christian, and the final and most convincing proof came at death.

Conclusion

Charles V certainly bears responsibility for developing certain paradigms in regard to death and the monarchy, but it was his son Philip II who created and firmly established the full-blown myth of the "good" royal death in Spain. And he did this principally by constructing an exemplary ritual center at the Escorial, that multilayered symbolic expression of the connection between death and the sacred character of the Spanish monarchy. At the end of the sixteenth century, the kings of Spain had no *official* throne, no scepter, and no crown, despite the fact that these insignia had been used in medieval Castile as symbols of royal dignity.[56] Unlike their French and English counterparts, they also had no coronation ceremonies and no annointings and could not lay any real claim to healing powers.[57] Thanks to Philip II, though, they now had an incomparable monument to death in which they could live, rule, pray, and die and in which they could confirm their roles as *rex et sacerdos* largely through mortuary symbols.

It is not difficult to imagine how the myth of the "good death," promoted so vigorously through the case of Philip II, could become a crushing burden for those who followed after him, and how it could also become a convenient, yet pathetic, explanation for the subsequent decline of Spain. If the welfare of the nation depended on the monarch's

[56] Percy Ernst Schramm, *Herzschaftszeichen und Staatsymbolik* (Stuttgart, 1956), vol. 3, pp. 1025–31.

[57] Nieto Soria, *Poder real*, discusses the ways in which these ceremonies and attributes, though lacking, were reflected in the Castilian monarchy, esp. pp. 61–5, 67–71.

faithfulness to his sacred duties, any reverse in fortunes could be blamed on the king. Little surprise, then, that as God's favorite empire began to deteriorate, Philip III died with a monstrously tortured conscience, or that Philip IV, who completed the royal pantheon at the Escorial, should have said early in his reign, "I consider that God is angry with me and my kingdoms for our sins, and in particular for mine."[58]

The recent interest shown by historians in political symbols and acts of persuasion has led some of them to interpret royal functions and myths as metaphors upon which are inscribed the assumptions that "either legitimize a political order or hasten its disintegration."[59] In the case of the death of Philip II, with the promotion of the myth of the "good death," we confront one instance in which it is difficult to distinguish between the processes of legitimation and disintegration. Such ambiguity perhaps made it an appropriate myth for the seventeenth century, that troubled age when an enfeebled Spanish monarchy conceived of its destiny largely in terms of the resplendent examples of its dead forefathers, in the shadow of the Escorial.

Because kings embody the ultimate values of their kingdoms – because they are the *center* of their realms – the Hapsburg paradigm of the good royal death discloses some of the most fundamental building blocks of the sixteenth-century Spanish mentality. This is not to say that the king or the elites who labored to enhance his power drew the blueprints, trucked in the building blocks, and then forced the nonelites to assemble them according to plan. On the contrary, what I hope to have shown here is the way in which structures of meaning and structures of power are dynamically interrelated, how the mythopoeic process surrounding Philip's death *both* expressed and shaped the collective mentality. Américo Castro once observed that Philip II "viewed Spain as a vast monastic institution in which all his subjects ought to prepare themselves to ascend to heaven, submissively and methodically, guarded over by the rigorous and meticulous vigilance of their king."[60] Although this

---

[58] Letter of King Philip IV, Archivo Historico Nacional, Madrid, libro 857, fol. 182. Quoted in J. H. Elliott, "Self-Perception and Decline in Early Seventeenth-Century Spain," *Past and Present*, 74 (1977): 47.

[59] Wilentz, introduction to *Rites of Power*, pp. 3–4.

[60] Américo Castro, "Por qué no quisieron los Españoles a Felipe II," *España en su historia*, app. 3, p. 649.

insight rings true, it ought to be understood in the dynamic sense proposed here. Philip partook of his culture as much as he shaped it, or tried to shape it. If he wished to turn the mentality of his realm toward the pursuit of heaven, it was only because the desire for that pursuit was already there among his subjects.

BOOK THREE

The saint's heavenly corpse
Teresa of Avila
and the ultimate paradigm of death

"So tell me now," replied Sancho, "which is greater: to raise someone from the dead, or to slay a giant?"

"The answer is obvious," Don Quixote responded, "it is greater to resurrect a dead man."

"Now I have you," said Sancho, "thus it is that those who quicken the dead, restore sight to the blind, heal the lame and cure the sick shall have the greater fame; it is they who have graves festooned with burning lamps, it is they whose chapels are overflowing with devout people who kneel to adore their relics; greater renown have they in this and in following centuries than has ever been had by all the worldly emperors and knights errant that ever existed."

"I also assent to this truth," responded Don Quixote.

"Thus it is that this fame, these favors, these prerogatives, as they are called, are enjoyed by the bodies and the relics of the saints," Sancho responded, "for with the approval and support of our Holy Mother Church, they have lamps, candles, shrouds, crutches, paintings, locks of hair, and legs with which they increase devotion and extend their Christian reputation. Kings bear the bodies of the saints or their relics on their backs, kiss fragments of their bones, and use them to adorn and enrich their chapels and their favorite altars."

"What is it you want me to make of all that you have told me?" said Don Quixote.

"What I mean," said Sancho, "is that we should aim to become saints, so we may more readily attain the fame we are seeking."[1]

---

[1] *Don Quixote*, Bk. II, ch. 8 (Barcelona, 1975), pp. 596–97. The crutches, eyes, legs, and locks of hair that surround the graves of saints are, of course, *ex votos*, or thank offerings, left behind at shrines.

I

~~~~~~

From Alba to heaven
Death and the saint

At the summit of the Catholic society of Philip II stood the figure of the saint, not of the monarch. Though the king was himself the apex of civil power, bedecked with symbols of sacrality, he could never fully extend his dominion beyond the earthly realm and would never command the same veneration as the saints. No matter how exalted the monarch's paradigm might be, it could never be ultimate. A case in point is Philip II himself. Despite all the mythmaking unleashed after his death, he could not be universally revered a generation later. In 1628, Francisco de Quevedo revealed something that none of Philip's eulogists had even hinted at. According to Quevedo, it was commonly believed by the religious order of the Carmelites that St. Teresa of Avila, one of their own, had gained Philip's release from purgatory in eight days. Never mind the monarch's "good death," the thousands of masses, the funeral honors and prayers: It was the intercession of a single saint that had rescued Philip. And the reasoning behind this belief betrayed even more about the relative fragility of the royal paradigm when compared to a saintly one. Teresa's rescue of Philip was the clearest possible indication of her intercessory prowess, for it amounted to a nearly impossible feat. Philip was an easily recognizable hard case, for, as Quevedo put it, anyone could easily discern "that he deserved a long stay in purgatory."[2]

---

[2] "Porque no fuera largo desmán de la imaginación arremeterse a pensar que había de tener largo purgatorio." Francisco de Quevedo, *Su espada por Santiago* (1628), *Biblioteca de Autores Españoles*, vol. 48, p. 438. For a discussion of this see Américo Castro, *España en su historia* (Buenos Aires, 1948), p. 181.

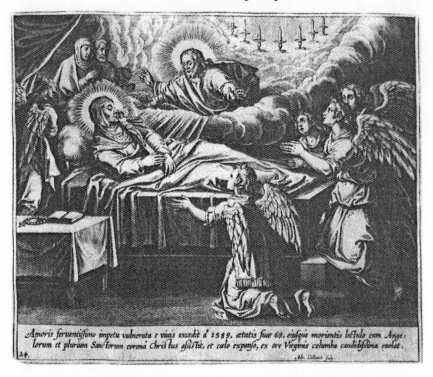

The Death of Saint Teresa. From Adriaen Collaert, *Vita b. Virginis Teresiae a Iesu ordinis Carmelitarum excalceatorum piae restauratricis* (Antwerp, 1613), plate 24. Reproduced in Irving Lavin, *Bernini and the Unity of the Visual Arts* (New York/Oxford, 1980), plate 236.

Saints and the collective mentality

In a society such as that of sixteenth-century Spain, where all ultimate values were officially and self-consciously framed in religious terms, against the backdrop of a higher transcendent reality, and where the monarchy was not imbued with overtly divine qualities, the supreme place of honor could be reserved for only those men and women who had most perfectly lived out the religious ideals of that society. At the moment of truth, even pious monarchs would find that their exalted position was confined to earth. When it came to death, the king was but another meek supplicant before the throne of heaven. During his final desperate hours, King Philip II – arguably the most powerful monarch on earth – found himself embracing the relics of the saints and humbly beseeching their aid. In the realm of heaven, where ultimate power re-sided, it was the saints who stood near God, the Lord of the universe. It was the saints who could intercede for the human race, acting as advo-cates in the highest court of all. As one of St. Teresa's confessors once wrote, the saints were so close to God as to be inseparable from Him: "The blessed are in eternity transformed into God Himself, enjoying His divinity." Because God was omnipotent and ubiquitous, the saints too could be invoked everywhere for every need.[3]

Moreover, when it came to the pursuit of heaven, saints were the most eminent archetypes of success; in death, as in life, the saint was the ultimate exemplar. In the theology of the Roman Catholic Church and in popular belief holiness and sainthood were defined by behavior. Only those who had molded their will to God's – with the aid of His grace – and had acted according to His commands could be considered saints. In brief, a saint was a man or woman who had *earned* a place in heaven after death through virtuous behavior on earth. If one craved to gain heaven, then one had better live like a saint and die like a saint. Anything less than that would only earn one a stint in purgatory, or worse, a descent to the eternal flames of hell.

Consequently, the death of the saint assumed a central place in the mentality of a Catholic society such as sixteenth-century Spain. It was an event or series of events that disclosed some of the deepest beliefs and attitudes of that society.[4] For, if it is true that death ritual is "not so much a question of dealing with a corpse as of reaffirming the secular and spiritual order by means of a corpse,"[5] it is also certainly true that the death of the saint offered unique prospects for the affirmation of

[3] Jerónimo Gracián de la Madre de Dios, "Dialogos del tránsito de la Madre Teresa de Jesús," (1584) in *Fuentes historicas sobre la muerte y cuerpo de la Santa Teresa de Jesús (1582–1596)*, ed. by J. L. Astigarraga, E. Pacho, and O. Rodriguez (Rome, 1982), p. 122. Alejo Venegas had said the same thing in his *Agonía*, p. 279: "La anima glorificada se convierte en Dios por participación."

[4] What Jacques Le Goff has said about sainthood and the medieval mentality also applies here: "L'hagiographie met en lumière des structures mentales de base: la perméabilité entre le monde sensible et le monde surnaturel, l'identité de nature entre le corporel et le psychique." *Faire de l'histoire*, ed. J. Le Goff, "Les Mentalités," Pt. 3, p. 86.

[5] R. C. Finucane, "Sacred Corpse, Profane Carrion: Social Ideals and Death Rituals in the Later Middle Ages," in *Mirrors of Mortality: Studies in the Social History of Death*, ed. Joachim Whaley (London, 1981; New York, 1982), pp. 40–1.

attitudes and the molding of mentalities. We have already seen the ways in which the death of the king as a paradigm or model – the apex of secular power – could be manipulated and made to represent certain ideals in late sixteenth-century Spain. Now it is the death of a saint that we analyze as a paradigm or model – the apex of spiritual power – in order to better understand the mentality of the age of Philip II and the ways in which the dead could be further used to reinvigorate existing ideals and foster new attitudes. The saint in question is the one who had supposedly rescued Philip from purgatory in eight days, the Carmelite nun and reformer Teresa de Ahumada y Cepeda, better known as Teresa de Jesús, or Teresa of Avila (1515–82).

In attempting to peer into "the macrocosmic imagination through the observation of a microcosmic image," I am following an ancient tradition in hagiography and a more recent development in the study of sainthood in its social context.[6] In brief, I am echoing what Donald Weinstein and Rudolph Bell said at the outset of their pathfinding study, *Saints and Society:* "We study saints in order to understand piety; we study piety in order to understand society, for it is one of our basic premises that the pursuit as well as the perception of holiness mirrored social values and concerns."[7] Though saints are an elite minority and are by definition exceptional human beings, they can still be seen as representative of the values of their society in a way not much different from the photographic process whereby a picture is developed from a negative image.[8] William Christian, Jr., has eloquently defended this notion: "What people hear the saints say, or the way they see the saints, reveals their deepest preoccupations. The changing faces of divine figures over the last six hundred years lead us to changes in the societies that meet them."[9]

[6] This is how Charles W. Jones explained his aim in *Saint Nicholas of Myra, Bari, and Manhattan: Biography of a Legend* (Chicago, 1978). Another work that treats the saint as a type that mirrors the values of society is John M. Mecklin's *The Passing of the Saint: A Study of a Culture Type* (Chicago, 1941).

[7] Donald Weinstein and Rudolph M. Bell, *Saints and Society. The Two Worlds of Western Christendom, 1000–1700* (Chicago, 1982), p. 6.

[8] Inspired by Peter Brown's mention of Ortega y Gasset's dictum (*Cult of the Saints,* p. 91), "The virtues which count most for us are those we do not possess," Weinstein and Bell (*Saints and Society,* p. 8) said: "Our premise here is that a society's heroes reflect through antithesis and projection, its real condition and its longings."

[9] William A. Christian, Jr., *Apparitions in Late Medieval and Renaissance Spain* (Princeton, 1981), p. 4.

Death and the saint

There is no denying that throughout the patristic and medieval eras the lives of the saints served a crucial role in the formation of Christian piety, as an indispensable complement to dogmatic theology.[10] Hagiography, that genre of literature that sought to extol the virtues of the saints and to enkindle devotion to them, became a narrative form of theology, a way of illustrating and proving the truth of the Christian message. Hagiographic accounts are inevitably linked to faith rather than to history, and they are wholly dedicated to the promotion of the miraculous.[11] Consequently, although hagiography has often been of great use to the faithful, it has also been questioned, dismissed, and ridiculed by nonbelievers. Yet, in spite of its subjective dimension – or one might say *because* of it – hagiography can offer abundant information to the historian of mentalities.[12] As long as one distinguishes between the saint as a historical person and the saint as a construct, between the events of the saint's life as they may have actually occurred and the narration of these events as the creation of other people's collective perceptions and expectations, hagiographic material can shed abundant light on the attitudes of the society that produced it.[13] Although hagiographers are overwhelmingly from the *clergy* (especially in the case of St.

[10] I have depended on the following introductions to the field of hagiography. René Aigrain, *L'Hagiographie – Ses sources, ses méthodes, son histoire* (Paris, 1953); two works by Hippolyte Delhaye, S. J.: *Cinq leçons sur la méthode hagiographique* (Brussels, 1934, reprint 1968); and *The Legends of the Saints*, ed. by R. J. Schoeck, tr. V. M. Crawford (South Bend IN, 1961); André Vauchez, *La sainteté en Occident aux derniers siècles du Moyen Age* (Rome, 1981).

[11] The aim of hagiography is to "delight and to teach" (*delectare et docere*). Jacques Le Goff has differentiated between two hagiographic genres, *preexemplum* and *exemplum*. It is to the type he calls *preexumplum* that I am referring in this discussion because its aim is to inspire devotion to the saint. "Vita et pre-exemplum dans le deuxième livre des Dialogues de Grégoire le Grand," *Hagiographie, Cultures, et Sociétés, IVe–XIIe siècles. Actes du Colloque organisé à Nanterre et à Paris, 2–5 mai 1979*, Études Augustiniennes (Paris, 1981), pp. 110–11.

[12] Julio Caro Baroja, *Las formas complejas de la vida religiosa. Religión, sociedad y carácter en la España de los siglos XVI y XVII* (Madrid, 1978), p. 77.

[13] Pierre Delooz has outlined the usefulness of this distinction: "Pour une étude sociologique de la sainteté canonisée dans l'église catholique," *Archives de Sociologie des Religions* 13 (1962): 17–43; and his *Sociologie et canonisations* (Liège, 1969). See also Heinrich Günther, "Psicologia della legenda: aspetti e problemi" and Frantisek Graus, "Le funzioni del culto dei santi e della legenda," both in *Agiografia altomedievale*, ed. by Sofia Boesch Gajano (Bologna, 1976), pp. 73–84, 145–60.

Teresa), and their perceptions are therefore colored by the convictions, biases, and predispositions of their class, they should not be dismissed as unrepresentative of the total society, especially in regard to religiosity. The Roman Catholic Church may be a rigidly hierarchical institution, but Catholicism itself is not a monolithically hierarchical religion. In the complex process whereby devotion was fostered and sustained throughout Catholic Europe and in sixteenth-century Spain, "lay" and "clerical" piety were inseparably intertwined. Piety did not flow in only a downward direction from the ecclesiastical elite. To a considerable extent, as has been demonstrated in various recent studies, the piety of Catholic Europe was commonly shared by the clergy and the laity.[14]

I seek here to analyze the mythmaking mechanism itself, the values *perceived* and *promoted* through the hagiographic record, rather than the actual facts narrated within accounts of St. Teresa's death and afterlife. Like Weinstein and Bell, I will examine the collective mentality rather than the disputable empirical record. Consequently, my "facts" will be perceptions.[15] I will not strain to determine whether Teresa's body actually worked miracles or indeed whether she really paid visits to her sisters from the hereafter; instead, I will strive to discern how such accounts drew upon the collective mentality and how they might have influenced the development and perpetuation of Spanish attitudes toward death and the afterlife.

The best possible death

Because saints were human beings who inhabited heaven, they belonged as much to the temporal as to the eternal, to the material as to the spiritual. Catholic Christendom had long upheld the notion that when these special people died, they could peer beyond the boundary separating the earthly and heavenly realms. Their deaths were not endings but,

[14] See, for instance, John Bossy, *Christianity in the West, 1400–1700* (Oxford, 1987); Jean Delumeau, *Le catholicisme entre Luther et Voltaire* (Paris, 1971), English tr. *Catholicism Between Luther and Voltaire: A New View of the Counter-Reformation* (London/Philadelphia, 1977); Louis Châtellier, *L'Europe des dévots* (Paris, 1987). Trans, by Jean Birrell, *The Europe of the Devout: The Catholic Reformation and the Formation of a New Society* (Cambridge, 1989); and William Christian, Jr., *Local Religion in Sixteenth-Century Spain* (Princeton, 1981).

[15] Weinstein and Bell, *Saints and Society*, p. 10.

rather, beginnings: joyful transitions to a higher and more powerful state. Within the Catholic tradition, this belief had ritual confirmation, for the feast days of saints were supposed to be the anniversaries of their deaths. Saints were also always well prepared for their deaths, not only because of their holy lives but also because they were often capable of foreseeing future events, including their own deaths.[16] During the final moments, dying saints would sum up in word and deed the very essence of their holiness and offer proof positive of the most cherished truths of the Christian faith. Their deathbed statements were highly valued as revelations from the world beyond. To be present at the moment of their passing and to hear their final words was a privilege most often reserved solely for other virtuous mortals.[17]

Once dead, the corpse of the saint was unlike that of less virtuous Christians. Peter Brown has eloquently detailed how the bodies of the saints and their graves became the focal point of much of Christian piety from the fifth century onward, and how it came to be that Christians brought the living into contact with the dead, especially those among the dead who were regarded as holy. Brown argues that this occurred because the presence of the saints in heaven was believed somehow to affect their physical remains on earth.[18] Though their souls had departed to the celestial realm, their *praesentia*, or presence, and their *potentia*, or power, continued to be felt through their bodies and at their graves. The inscription on the grave of St. Martin of Tours said it clearly: "Here lies Martin the Bishop, of holy memory, whose soul is in the hand of God; but he is fully here, present and made plain in miracles of every kind."[19]

The miracle-working bodies of the saints, then, literally represented (or re-presented) their souls, which were enjoying their proximity to God's throne. The many miraculous attributes that came to be ascribed

---

16 Milton McCormick Gatch, *Preaching and Theology in Anglo Saxon England* (Toronto, 1967), p. 46; Guibert de Nogent, *Self and Society in Medieval France*, ed. J. Benton (New York, 1970), pp. 142–3; D. Gutmann, "Dying to Power: Death and the Search for Self-Esteem," in H. Feifeil, *New Meanings of Death* (New York, 1977), pp. 340–1.

17 Gregory the Great, *Dialogues*, IV, 20, 26, 27, 36, 40.

18 Peter Brown, *The Cult of the Saints: Its Rise and Function in Late Antiquity* (Chicago, 1981).

19 E. Le Blant, *Les inscriptions chrétiennes de la Gaule* (Paris, 1856), 1: 240; cited by Brown, *Saints*, p. 3.

to the saints' bodies – incorruption, luminescence, sweetness of smell, and so on – negated death itself and its putrefaction. Instead of rotting and dissolving, the bodies of the saints made manifest the central promise of the Christian faith: immortality and incorruption.[20]

By the time of Teresa's death in 1582, the Christian tradition of the excellent saintly death was already ancient. The hagiographic literature read by Teresa, her fellow nuns, and her biographers was replete with accounts of exquisite holy deaths that extolled the splendor of the joyous death that came at the end of a good and virtuous life.[21] In this tradition, the death of the saint was portrayed as the culmination of a lifelong quest. Conversely, the saint's life was summed up as a gradual and painful catharsis, a purification that led precisely to that single instant when soul and body were sundered and the saint entered heaven. The death of the saint was thus perceived as a hierophany and an apotheosis, as an irruption of the sacred into the most profane of events and an exalted transformation of the human into the divine. An *Ars Moriendi* manual published in Spain at the time of St. Teresa's canonization proceedings summed up this tradition, which had been imbibed by Teresa and her contemporaries:

Though death is terrible and horrific in and of itself, it is not feared by those who are good, but rather welcomed. . . . For the just, death is but the end point of misery, and the beginning of felicity. . . . Behold, my soul, how different the death of the just is from the death of sinners. . . . May I die the death of the just! If you desire to attain to this, attempt to live the life of the just: imitate them in life, if you wish to imitate them in death.[22]

---

[20] Finucane, "Sacred Corpse," p. 60: "The function of the body as symbol for the soul is most evident in rites associated with the saints." See also J. M. Sallman, "I poteri del corpo santo: rappresentazione e utilizzazione," *Forme i potere e pratica di carisma*, ed. P. Levillain and J. M. Sallman (Naples, 1984).

[21] Jerónimo Gracián de la Madre de Dios, "Dialogos del tránsito de la Madre Teresa de Jesús," (1584), cited over two dozen such accounts from patristic and medieval sources as a means of confirming the pattern followed by Teresa's death. FHM, pp. 45–7.

[22] Fray Alonso de Alvarado, *Arte de buen vivir, y camino del Cielo*, first published in 1608 (Valladolid, 1613), pp. 718, 720.

Teresa as exemplar

In a land brimming over with holy men and women, such as sixteenth-century Spain, one could study many exemplary saintly deaths: Ignatius Loyola (1491–1556), Francis Xavier (1506–52), Francis Borgia (1510–72), Peter of Alcántara (1499–1562), and John of the Cross (1542–91). With so many possibilities, why choose Teresa of Avila?

St. Teresa lends herself supremely well for the role of the "model" Spanish saintly death during this period for four reasons. First, she was regarded in her own day (and continues to be so regarded in some circles) as typically "Spanish," as an exemplar of *españolidad*. Second, there is a very rich and diverse pool of sources available for the study of her death and afterlife. Third, she was one of the best-known, best-loved, and most influential saints of the Catholic Reformation, not only within Spain and its empire but also throughout Catholic Europe. Finally, her own life and work and her mysticism were suffused with a longing for death.

St. Teresa as paradigm for Spain

In regard to her "Spanishness," Teresa seems to be unequaled among her fellow contemporary saints. Perhaps only the fictional character of Don Quixote can rival her *españolidad*. This is most convincingly evidenced by the fact that in 1627, six years after her official canonization, King Philip IV had Teresa officially proclaimed Patroness of Spain, an honor she was to share with Santiago, or St. James.[23] One of the sermons preached in Madrid during the celebration of Teresa's promotion to patroness of Spain summed up the public's attitude: "Everything about this saint is Spanish: her life, her *death*, her holiness, her religious order, her miracles, her teachings, and the fame she has earned throughout the world, all of these are Spanish [emphasis added]."[24]

---

[23] The issue of Teresa's patronage is discussed at length by Américo Castro, *España en su historia* (Buenos Aires, 1948), pp. 175–87.

[24] Sermon by Fray Tomás de San Vicente, *Relación sencilla y fiel de las fiestas que el Rey Don Felipe IIII nuestro Señor hizo al Patronato de sus Reinos de España Corona de Castilla, que dió a la gloriosa Virgen Santa Teresa de Jesús, año de 1627* (Madrid, 1627), p. 13. For

Teresa's new rank was opposed by some, especially by the influential military order of Santiago, which spearheaded its protest through the pen of the great Francisco de Quevedo, himself a knight of this order, in his two works, *His Sword for Santiago,* and *A Brief for the Patronage of Santiago.*[25] Yet, even those who resisted never denied the "Spanishness" of Teresa (in spite of the fact that they could have resurrected the then-forgotten fact of Teresa's Jewish ancestry). Those who protested did so mainly on account of the prominence of St. James and his unique status as patron of the *Reconquista* and defender of the nation. Quevedo especially also questioned the wisdom and propriety of assigning such an exalted and manly role to a woman.[26] Eventually, the defenders of Santiago would gain the ear of Pope Urban VIII and convince him to decree that St. James should be the sole patron of Spain, but this reversal in no way affected Teresa's reputation as an exemplar of everything Spanish.[27]

Teresa may not have gained the rank of patroness in the seventeenth century, but she certainly continued to elicit the strongest devotion from her fellow Spaniards in the following centuries.[28] As anticlericalsim

a discussion of the content of these sermons, see Francis Cerdan, "Santa Teresa en Los Sermones del Patronato (1627)," in *Santa Teresa y la literatura mística hispánica,* ed. Manuel Criado de Val (Madrid, 1984), pp. 601–8.

[25] Francisco de Quevedo, *Su espada por Santiago* (1628); *Memorial por el Patronato de Santiago* (1628). See Edmund Schramm, "Quevedo und das Patrozinium des heiligen Jakob," *Jarbuch für das Bistum Mainz* 5 (1950): 349–56; T. D. Kendrick, *Saint James in Spain* (London, 1960), chap. 4; Américo Castro, *La realidad histórica de España,* 3rd ed. (Mexico, 1966), pp. 394–9; Doris L. Baum, *Traditionalism in the Works of Francisco de Quevedo y Villegas* (Chapel Hill NC, 1970), esp. p. 102. A bibliography of the literature on this debate is included in Isaías Rodriguez's, *Santa Teresa de Jesús y la espiritualidad española* (Madrid, 1972), pp. 133–7.

[26] For a perceptive analysis of the impact of misogyny on Teresa and on her public image, see Alison Weber, *Teresa of Avila and the Rhetoric of Femininity* (Princeton, 1990), esp. chap. 1.

[27] For a detailed narrative and analysis of these events, see Francisco Lopez Estrada, "Cohetes para Teresa. La relación de 1627 sobre las Fiestas de Madrid por el Patronato de España de Santa Teresa de Jesús y la pólemica sobre el mismo," *Actas del Congreso Internacional Teresiano, 4–7 Octubre 1982,* 2 vols., ed. by T. Egido Martinez et al. (Salamanca, 1983), vol. I, pp. 637–81.

[28] These developments are outlined by Teófanes Egido in "El tratamiento historiográfico de Santa Teresa: Inercias y revisiones," *Perfil historico de Santa Teresa,* ed. by T. Egido (Madrid, 1981), esp. pp. 13–19; also published in *Revista de Es-*

flourished in the 1700s and 1800s and as the attacks on the Spanish Catholic Church and Catholicism intensified, St. Teresa's "Spanishness" gained significance among the defenders of tradition.[29] In the first part of the twentieth century, as Spain was plunged into the Civil War of 1936–9, with its attending iconoclasm and its anticlerical carnage, St. Teresa was conscripted into service on the side of Fascism and the church as *La Santa de la Raza,* or the saint of the Spanish "race," (with implicit and explicit connotations of the xenophobic concept of "purity of blood").[30] Generalissimo Francisco Franco promoted the cult of St. Teresa as protectress of the army of Catholic Spain and went as far as to award a medal, *La Cruz Laureada de San Fernando,* in 1940 to a relic of the hand of St. Teresa that he had rescued from the Republican "bolsheviks" and kept nearby thereafter.[31] In his zeal for Teresa, Francisco Franco was no innovator; he was guided by a long-standing tradition. Already in 1921, during the third centennial of Teresa's canonization, she had been praised as follows by the poet Aniceto de Castro Albarrán:

> Glory to you, Seraph of Carmel!
> You are the purest honor of Spain!
> In your breast God another heaven made,
> and within your heart a whole people enshrined.
> Glory, glory to Teresa, who shines
> as bright as the Sun of the Race on her altar!
> Come to Castile, you pilgrims,
> to kiss her cradle and grave!

piritualidad 40 (1962): 171–89. And by the same author, "Santa Teresa y las tendencias de la historiografía actual," *Ephemerides Carmeliticae* 23 (1982): 160–80.

[29] Antonio (Flórez) de San Joaquín, *Año Teresiano: Diario historico, panegirico moral, en que se describen las virtudes, sucesos, y maravillas de la seráfica y mística doctora de la Iglesia, Santa Teresa de Jesús,* 12 vols. (Madrid, 1733–69), esp. vol. II, pp. 147–248; Manuel (Traggia) de Santo Tomás, *La mujer grande. Vida meditada de Santa Teresa de Jesús, enseñando como madre, maestra, y doctora universal, con ejemplos y doctrina,* 3 vols. (Madrid, 1807). See also A. Pacho, *Del Antiguo Régimen a la España moderna. Manuel (Traggia) de Santo Tomás, O.C.D., protagonista e intérprete del tránsito* (Burgos, 1979), esp. pp. 347 ff.

[30] Gabriel de Jesús, *La Santa de la Raza. Vida gráfica de Santa Teresa de Jesús,* 4 vols. (Madrid, 1929–35); Silverio de Santa Teresa, *Santa Teresa de Jesús, síntesis suprema de la Raza* (Madrid, 1939).

[31] This is fully detailed by Giuliana di Febo in *Teresa d'Avila: Un culto barocco nella Spagna franchista (1937–62)* (Naples, 1988), esp. pp. 53 ff.

The saint's heavenly corpse

That light which illumines your face,
splendor of a triumphant Race,
is the fire of your soul divine,
aflame in the ardor of love.
Emblem of glory Teresa is,
wherein Spain her own soul sees;
alone, she sums up your history,
your valor, your honor, your faith!
In ascending to the altar, Oh Teresa!
Crowned in light as the sun,
It was not only the saint from Avila who rose,
but the soul of Spain.[32]

Sources for the death of St. Teresa

St. Teresa's death lends itself so well for study because her contemporaries themselves seized upon the significance of her passing, turned it into an event of epic proportions, and produced a voluminous record. Though much of this documentation is repetitive, dependent on a limited kernel of narratives and not originally intended for publication, the sheer bulk of the materials conveys a sense of the subject's prominence through its massiveness.

In the chronicling of any saint's life – and death – there is always a complex interdependence between oral and written accounts, and Teresa's case is no exception. Reports of her death began to circulate among the nuns of her order immediately through personal contact and correspondence. These letters and oral stories circulated freely and rapidly, influenced one another, and eventually gave shape to a narrative tradition. Furthermore, within three years of Teresa's passing, some of those who had worked most closely with her were asked by their Carmelite superiors to write brief accounts of her life and death.[33]

---

[32] *Tercer Centenario de la Canonización de Santa Teresa de Jesús*, 2 (1922), p. 190. Cited by Giulana di Febo, *Culto barocco*, pp. 75–6. On other centennial celebrations see Juan Bosco Sanromán, "Anteriores centenarios de la muerte de Santa Teresa," in T. Egido, ed., *Perfil histórico*. pp. 173–95.

[33] Julián Urkiza, introduction to Ana de San Bartolomé's "Ultimos años de la madre Teresa de Jesús," *Obras Completas de la Beata Ana de San Bartolomé*, 2 vols., Monu-

Biographies: Fray Luis de León, an Augustinian poet, mystic, and scripture scholar, was the first to embark on a biography of St. Teresa, having been asked to do so by the sister of King Philip II, the Empress Maria, but his project was never completed.[34] Fray Luis was also the first to edit and publish the mystical writings of St. Teresa in 1588. His brief biographical note on Teresa in the introduction to her *Opera* went only as far as 1561, however, and thus contained no account of her death.[35] Similarly, the unpublished *Life* by Teresa's onetime confessor, Julián de Avila, written in the closing years of the sixteenth century, took the narrative of the saint's life only to 1562 and thus did nothing to publicize her death.[36]

The first *published* biography of Teresa, which made an account of her death available to a wider public, did not appear until 1590, eight years after her death.[37] By then, the oral and written accounts used by the biographer (or more properly, hagiographer), the Jesuit priest Francisco de Ribera, contained the kernel of all subsequent accounts. Ribera's *Vida de la Madre Teresa de Jesús* focused a great deal of attention on Teresa's death, her subsequent apparitions, and the miracles associated with her body.[38] This hagiographic account, in turn, gave shape to all future narratives, oral as well as written.

menta Historica Carmeli Teresiani 5 (Rome, 1981), vol. I, pp. 3–4. (Hereafter cited as OCASB.)

[34] Fidel Fita, "Cuatro biógrafos de Santa Teresa en el siglo XVI: El Padre Francisco de Ribera, Fray Diego de Yepes, Fray Luis de León y Julián de Avila," *Boletín de la Real Academia de Historia* 67 (1915): 550–61.

[35] The title of Fray Luis's unfinished and unpublished manuscript indicates that he intended to focus considerable attention on Teresa's death: *De la vida, muerte, virtudes y milagros de la Santa Madre Teresa de Jesús.* This was first published in *Revista Augustiniana*, vol. 5 (1883), and was subsequently included in *Obras Completas Castellanas de Fray Luis de León*, ed. Félix Garcia, O.S.A., 2 vols., 4th ed. (Madrid, 1967).

[36] *Vida de Santa Teresa de Jesús, por el maestro Julián de Avila, primer capellán de la santa.* From the unpublished manuscript, ed. Vicente de la Fuente (Madrid, 1881).

[37] Francisco de Ribera, S. J., *La vida de la Madre Teresa de Jesús, fundadora de las Descalças y Descalços* (Salamanca, 1590). Fidel Fita argues that Ribera began his *Vida* in 1587 and that he knew that Luis de León was also engaged in the same project: "Nuevos datos biográficos del Padre Francisco de Ribera y de Fray Luis de León, primeros biógrafos de Santa Teresa," *Boletín de la Real Academia de Historia* 68 (1916).

[38] I have used the most recent edition (Barcelona, 1908), ed. Jaime Pons, S. J., in which roughly 10 percent of the total pages are devoted to Teresa's death and afterlife.

A second *Life* of Teresa appeared in 1599. Its purported author, the Hieronymite friar Diego de Yepes, confessor to King Philip II, onetime prior of San Lorenzo el Real de el Escorial, and later bishop of Tarazona, relied heavily on Ribera's *Vida* but also tapped into the oral and unpublished written tradition.[39] Yepes, who also published a history of the persecution of Catholics in England and an account of the death of Philip II, might not have really written this *Life*. It has been argued – somewhat convincingly – that internal dissension within the Carmelite order made it necessary for the true author, Fray Tomás de Jesús, to hide his identity and for Yepes to lend his name to the enterprise.[40] Putting aside the question of authorship, what is significant about this account is that it further publicized the miracles associated with Teresa's death and afterlife, and it did so in a manner that complemented Ribera's *Vida*, for its author focused more attention on interpretation than narration and drew many "lessons" for his readers.[41] With the publication of "Yepes's" *Vida*, the narrative tradition assumed fixed contours; all subsequent baroque *Lives* of Teresa depended heavily upon its summation in this work and that of Ribera.[42]

[39] Fray Diego de Yepes, *Vida, virtudes, y milagros de la Bienaventurada Virgen Madre Teresa de Jesús* (Madrid, 1599). Félix Garcia claims that the author of this *Life* used the unfinished manuscript of Luis de León, *Obras Completas de Fray Luis de León*, vol. I, p. 921, n. 1.

[40] Otilio Rodriguez del Niño Jesús, O.C.D., "¿Quién es el autor de la Vida de Santa Teresa a nombre de Yepes?" *El Monte Carmelo* 64 (1956): 244–55; V. Macca di Santa Maria, "Il dottorato di Santa Teresa. Sviluppo storico di una idea," *Ephemerides Carmeliticae*, 21 (1970): 36–47; Tomás Alvarez, "El ideal religioso de Santa Teresa de Jesús y el drama de su segundo biógrafo," *El Monte Carmelo* 86 (1978): 203–38; Teófanes Egido, "El tratamiento historiográfico de Santa Teresa. Inercias y revisiones," *Perfil historico de Santa Teresa*, ed. T. Egido (Madrid, 1981), pp. 15–16.

[41] I have used the most recent edition of the "Yepes" *Life*, published under the abbreviated title *Vida de Santa Teresa de Jesús*, with the briefest of introductions by Ramón Gomez de la Serna (Buenos Aires, 1946). For the sake of continuity with tradition and for the sake of simplicity, I will refer to the author of this work as Yepes.

[42] Because the scope of this book is limited to the sixteenth century, and more specifically to the age of Philip II, I have not dealt with later hagiographies, such as that of Antonio de la Encarnación, O.C.D., *Vida i milagros de la esclarecida i seráfica virgen Santa Teresa, erectora de la nueva reformación de Carmelitas Descalços* (Salamanca, 1614), edited and reissued by Gerardo de San Juan de la Cruz, O.C.D. (Toledo, 1914); or Juan Eusebio Nieremberg, *Vida de Santa Teresa de Jesús* (1640), 14th ed. (Madrid, 1882).

Death and the saint

Other personal accounts: There was much more written about Teresa in other documents that remained unpublished until the nineteenth and twentieth centuries. Although these writings could not have had an effect outside of a very narrow group of people – mostly Carmelites and members of the church hierarchy – they reveal clearly the mentality of those close to Teresa. Often, too, they reflect the attitudes of Spanish society at large.

First, there are the personal accounts and reflections of two of Teresa's closest friends and associates, Father Jerónimo Gracián de la Madre de Dios (1545–1614) and Sister Ana de San Bartolomé (1549–1626). Among those who helped Teresa to establish her reform of the Carmelite order no one was more supportive, perhaps, than Father Gracián, whom she fervently cherished. Gracián joined Teresa's reform in 1572 and eventually served as Discalced Provincial from 1581 to 1585; after Teresa's death he became embroiled in an intra-Carmelite dispute over the path to "true" reform in the Teresian spirit.[43] Totally devoted to Teresa, deeply moved and influenced by her mysticism, Father Gracián wrote a series of manuscripts in which he meditated upon the significance of Teresa's death and afterlife.[44] These remarkable documents give us a glimpse not only of the way in which Teresa's death affected those around her but also allow us to see how the event and its aftermath were theologically interpreted within the Carmelite order and the Catholic Church. Gracián's writings, then, not only disclose parallel mentalities, the personal and the institutional, but also reveal parallel dimensions of response, the emotional and intellectual.

The earliest known written response to Teresa's death was written by Jerónimo Gracián eight days after her death. His "Dialogue between Angela and Eliseo," composed in October 1582, speaks not of the details of Teresa's death but of Gracián's own inner response and his attempt to come to terms with the event.[45] This dialogue was further

---

[43] E. Allison Peers, *Handbook to the Life and Times of St. Teresa and St. John of the Cross* (London, 1954), pp. 71–104, 174–6; Silverio de Santa Teresa, O.C.D., *Obras del Padre Jerónimo Gracián de la Madre de Dios*, ed. by him, 3 vols. (Burgos, 1932), p. viii.

[44] Collected and published together for the first time during the quadricentennial of Teresa's death in *Fuentes historicas sobre la muerte y el cuerpo de Santa Teresa de Jesús (1582–1596)*, Monumenta Historica Carmeli Teresiani 6, ed. J. L. Astigarrage, E. Pacho, and O. Rodriguez (Rome, 1982). (Hereafter cited as FHM.)

[45] "Diálogo de Angela y Eliseo," FHM, pp. 1–10.

expanded in the early months of 1583 in a piece entitled "The Death and Final Journey of Angela." Though this text contains more factual information about Teresa's passing, which Gracián had himself solicited through correspondence with the nuns who had witnessed it, it is still more of a theological reflection and meditation than a report.[46] After collecting more information on Teresa's death and her postmortem miracles (and after having been directly involved in the first exhumation of Teresa's body), Gracián attempted to interpret all this in yet another piece, "Dialogues on the Death of Mother Teresa de Jesús," in the latter part of 1584.[47] This lengthy examination of Teresa's death and afterlife makes a concentrated effort to place these events in context: It is replete with theological and spiritual "lessons" drawn from biblical, patristic, and medieval sources. Without a doubt, it is the single most extensive contemplation of the meaning of Teresa's death and afterlife and thus also the single most revealing document written by someone close to Teresa. The interweaving of narration and theological reflection in this "Dialogue" make it a window not only into Gracián's thoughts and emotions but also into the collective mentality of his day and age. Since much of the narrative provided by Gracián closely resembles that later provided by Ribera and Yepes – sometimes even word for word – Gracián may also be one of the principal sources consulted by Teresa's biographers.[48]

Sister Ana (García) de San Bartolomé might not have studied theology at the University of Alcalá, as did Father Gracián, but her accounts of the death and miraculous afterlife of Teresa are no less significant or revealing. The affection between these two women was intense. Ana had entered St. Joseph's convent in Avila in 1570 as a lay sister. Illiterate,

---

[46] "Tránsito y última jornada de Angela," FHM, pp. 11–36.

[47] "Diálogos del tránsito de la Madre Teresa de Jesús," FHM, pp. 36–184. This piece was first published by Silverio de Santa Teresa under the title *Diálogos sobre la muerte de la Madre Teresa de Jesús* (Burgos, 1913). This is an extremely rare book; I have not been able to locate it anywhere outside of Spain.

[48] A prolific writer, Jerónimo Gracián also dealt briefly with Teresa's death and afterlife in some of his published works: "Dialogos sobre el espíritu de Ana de San Bartolomé," the autobiographical "Peregrinación de Anastasio," and most notably in his "Historia de las fundaciones," chaps. 13 and 14. The text from this latter work is available in FHM, pp. 188–201; and in *Documenta primigenia*, Monumenta Historica Carmeli Teresiani 3, doc. 423, pp. 640–52.

she learned to read and write in order to serve as St. Teresa's assistant. From 1577 until 1582, when Teresa died in her arms, she was the saint's nurse and constant companion. After Teresa's death, Sister Ana gradually assumed a prominent role in Teresa's Carmelite reform, especially as it spread to France and Flanders.[49]

Ana de San Bartolomé wrote a brief account of Teresa's final years sometime in 1584–5, apparently at the request of her superiors.[50] Because it is quite similar to the later accounts of Ribera and Yepes, it is quite likely that this unpublished document played a significant role in the writing of the published biographies. Many years later (1615–24), at Antwerp, Sister Ana composed an autobiography that included some of this earlier material and added numerous other reports of Teresa's postmortem miracles.[51] Though much less learned than the accounts of Gracián – one might even call this work, in a positive sense, theologically naive – Ana's *Autobiografía* reaches deeply into her intellect and psyche and reveals to us the collective mentality of the cloister in a very immediate way. Since Ana views the events in her life without the benefit (or hindrance) of learned theological discourse, it is also plausible that this one-time shepherdess more closely approximates the popular piety of her own day than Gracián, Ribera, or Yepes.

Later published throughout Europe, where it apparently enjoyed some popularity, this document remained accessible in manuscript only among those who thought and wrote about Teresa in Spain. These limitations, however, do not lessen its significance.[52]

---

[49] Ana de San Bartolomé was made Prioress of the newly founded Carmelite convents of Pontoise and Paris, and herself founded a house at Tours (1608) and one at Antwerp (1612). E. A. Peers, *Life and Times*, pp. 118–19; Julián Urkiza, introduction to Ana's *Obras Completas* OCASB I, pp. 53–85, and bibliography, pp. 25–56.

[50] "Ultimos años de la Madre Teresa de Jesús," OCASB I.3–26; also included in Fortunato Antolín's edition of Ana's *Autobiografía* (Madrid, 1969) as "Relación sobre la fundación de Burgos," pp. 201–28; an abridged version can be found in FHM, pp. 185–8.

[51] A critical edition of the two slightly different manuscript versions is included in OCASB, I.278–479. The so-called "A," or Antwerp, manuscript is used in Antolin's 1969 *Autobiografía*. See also Julián Urkiza's synopsis of both of Ana's documents, "Con el mal de la muerte y la hora del dichoso tránsito," *Perfil histórico de Santa Teresa*, ed. T. Egido, pp. 153–72.

[52] Ana's autobiography enjoyed a rich publishing history but not in the original Castilian Spanish. Urkiza lists Flemish (1632, 1733, 1937, 1977); French (1646, 1708, 1869, 1872); German (1669); Italian (1725); and English (1917): OCASB I.281.

Ecclesiastical and civil records: An ascent other than that of Mt. Carmel is required from those who pursue the study of St. Teresa's death and afterlife. I am referring here to the mountains of paper produced by her beatification and canonization proceedings (1591–1610) and a civil and ecclesiastical dispute over custody of her body (1585–9), which have to be scaled with care and patience. Mind-numbing as these repetitious inquiries and depositions are, they disclose by their sheer bulk the magnitude of interest in Teresa's death, her remains, and her miracles, and the extent to which knowledge of these subjects had spread throughout Spain at the dawn of the Baroque era. Besides, these documents also contain significant information about the subject and about the way in which it was interpreted by her contemporaries.

To be officially declared a saint in the Catholic Church of the Counter-Reformation, a holy person needed truly extraordinary credentials, as well as devotées and friends in high places. Popular acclaim was no longer enough to set in motion the complicated machinery of saint-making within the Church of Trent; documentation of the most rigorous sort was now required, without exception.[53]

The official inquiries into Teresa's holiness were among the first to be undertaken after the Council of Trent. The resulting documentation proved to be not only the most thorough and voluminous ever seen then but even down to our own day. In all regards, then, the documents produced for Teresa's canonization set a standard that has not been exceeded.[54]

The beatification and canonization process for Teresa was initially funded by a bequest of 14,000 *ducados* left in his will for this purpose by Don Fernando de Toledo, of the family of the Dukes of Alba. The wheels were set in motion by the ecclesiastical hierarchy, with the support of King Philip II, whose interest in the cause of Teresa's canonization was piqued by reports of her incorruptible body in 1591. It was a lengthy and involved process: Four separate inquiries were undertaken over a span of nineteen years. The first Informative inquest was ordered

[53] Eric Waldram Kemp, *Canonization and Authority in the Western Church* (Oxford, 1948), esp. pp. 141–6.

[54] Weinstein and Bell, *Saints and Society*, p. 142 reaffirm this point but mistakenly date Teresa's canonization as 1671 rather than 1621. See also Romeo de Maio, *Riforme e miti nella Chiesa del Cinquecento* (Naples, 1973), pp. 257–8.

by the Bishop of Salamanca, Jerónimo Manrique, at the prompting of King Philip (1591–2); the second Informative inquest was directed by the papal nuncio, Camilo Gaetano (1595–7); the *in genere* Remissory inquest (1604), and the *in specie* Remissory inquest (1609–10) were directed from Rome. More than 400 people – mostly Carmelite nuns – were interviewed throughout the Iberian peninsula as part of this process.[55]

Because the very purpose of these inquests was to find signs of the miraculous in Teresa's life – to substantiate the claims being made for her heroic virtue and other-worldly power – it stands to reason that several questions were asked in every one of these investigations about Teresa's death and its attending wonders. Intended as they were to elicit proof, rather than to raise doubts, the questions were always phrased in a leading manner, and themselves contained some of the "facts" that the answers were supposed to hold. The sixth question asked of everyone in the 1591 inquest is typical:

Do you know that the said Mother, around her sixty-eighth year, died in the convent of the Incarnation in the village of Alba on the feast day of the glorious St. Francis, October the fourth of the year 1582, and that she was buried there, and that when three years had elapsed, more or less, her body was found to be uncorrupted and whole, and that it emitted, and still reportedly emits, the sweetest of odors along with a certain oil or balm that passes through and soaks all cloths that touch the body, and that everything said above is well known by the populace, and that it is openly discussed?[56]

By the time Teresa's beatification seemed assured, during the 1609–10 inquest, the process had grown more elaborate and the "questioning" even more leading. During this investigation, those who testified were presented with a lengthy *rótulo*, or prepared statement, that summarized in detail all the previous testimonies offered for Teresa's canonization, which they were asked to comment or elaborate upon. The *rótulo* in question contained 117 items (seventy pages of small print in the 1934–5 edition), thirteen of which dealt with Teresa's death and

[55] See the introduction by Silverio de Santa Teresa, O.C.D., ed. *Procesos de beatificación y canonización de Santa Teresa de Jesús*, 3 vols., Biblioteca Mistica Carmelitana 18–20 (Burgos, 1934), vol. I, pp. vii–xxviii. (Hereafter cited as PBC.)
[56] PBC I.3.

afterlife. This *rótulo* alone, without the further testimonies elicited by it, is a formidable digest of information.[57]

The narrative tradition represented in these documents is at once simple and complex. It is simple because it tells a story that never changes. It is complex in two ways: in its profusion of detailed information that is constantly repeated and in its circular dependence on previous testimonies (formal and informal). The canonization testimonies seem at times a hall of mirrors, a series of reflections in which the original image is endlessly multiplied. For it is not only the earlier proceedings that affect the later testimonies; it is also the stories told in person or through letters in the network of Carmelite convents and the published biographies that affect these testimonies. Many of those who testified simply referred to what they had heard from so-and-so or candidly admitted that what they knew was what they had read in Ribera's or Yepes's *Life* of Teresa.[58]

What can be gleaned for our purposes here from these canonization proceedings, with their seemingly endless repetition of details that are constantly elaborated upon and never disputed, is not so much the "facts" of Teresa's death and afterlife as attitudes toward it. What these witnesses – most of them Carmelite nuns wholly devoted to Teresa – wanted *on record* in the sacred process of canonization was what mattered most to them in their religion. (And it bears observing that what we call a "religious order" they simply called *religión*.) Teresa's perfect death and her wondrous continued presence were proof positive for these witnesses of the truths of the Catholic Christian faith in which they lived and moved and had their being. Though what is narrated in these documents may seem fantastic, it actually reveals what was *expected* by those who sought comfort in the death of saints.

A different sort of information is revealed by the legal documents pertaining to the dispute between Avila and Alba for possession of Teresa's uncorrupted body. These depositions, accusations, affidavits, and cross-examinations from the years 1585 to 1589 focus on "facts" in

---

[57] PBC III. ix–lxxx, esp. items 94–117, pp. lxv–lxxx.

[58] The 1592 testimonies of the Alba nuns read much like Ribera, at times using identical language (PBC I.80–138). Even St. Teresa's own niece, Beatriz de Jesús, deferred to Ribera's authority, PBC I.119. Inés de Jesús said in 1610 that the Alba nuns were immensely fond of Ribera's and Yepes's works, "los cuales han causado gran consuelo y devoción." PBC III.189.

the manner of the courtroom, as each of the two parties in the suit presented their case.[59] Though the amount of paper taken up by this dispute is far greater than the amount of information provided by it, these documents taken as a whole speak volumes about the *real* – as opposed to the *ideal* – history of Teresa's corpse. As with the canonization inquiries, here there are leading questions and answers based on hearsay. There is also the same monotonous, deadening repetition. The question at hand, however, has not been predetermined and begs to be resolved: Who gets to keep the body of Teresa? Christian charity gives way to disharmony, rancor, and recrimination. Though the cause of all this strife is a sacred object, the mood is regrettably unholy; though the protagonists are nuns devoted to selflessness, their intentions (and those of their lay benefactors and ecclesiastical superiors) are ultimately self-serving. Taken as a whole, these documents reveal the dark side of the death of the saint.

Beatification sermons: Finally, there are the sermons preached in 1615 at the beatification festivities held by many Carmelite communities throughout Spain.[60] Though these sermons are principally focused on Teresa's achievements in life, they do contain numerous references to her death and afterlife. More significantly, they contain in their flights of oratory, as did Philip II's funeral sermons, some of the most extreme and most revealing interpretations of the paradigmatic good death.

St. Teresa as a Counter-Reformation saint

Teresa lends herself well for this study because she has long been considered one of the most representative saints of the Catholic Reformation, or Counter-Reformation. Of the dozens of saints who were canonized by the post–Tridentine church, few can rival Teresa for public recognition. The impact of her role as exemplar thus becomes magnified

---

[59] These documents are available in *Relaciones biográficas inéditas de Santa Teresa de Jesús*, ed. José Gómez Centurión (Madrid, 1917). Selected documents can also be found in FHM, pp. 245–495.

[60] *Sermones predicados en la Beatificación de la B.M. Teresa de Jesús, Virgen, Fundadora de la Reforma de los Descalços de Nuestra Señora del Carmen.* Colegidos por orden del padre fray Joseph de Jesús Maria, General de la misma orden (Madrid, 1615). BNM 2-19512.

by her fame. As Jerónimo Gracián said, Teresa's case clearly demon-strated that "the just in Heaven do not all share the same glory, and do not receive equal rewards there, or equal grace here below."[61]

One of the clearest indications of Teresa's appeal to Catholic soci-eties is the publication record of her biographies. Beyond the Pyrenees, Ribera's *Vida* was translated and published widely: in French (Paris 1602, 1645; Lyons, 1628); Flemish (Antwerp, 1620); Italian (Rome, 1601, 1670); and Latin (Mainz, 1603; Cologne, 1620). Yepes's *Vida* appeared in French (Paris, 1643, 1644) and Portuguese (Lisbon, 1616).[62]

Printers throughout Europe were also busy producing stamps and images of Teresa. The canonization inquest of 1610 specifically asked for information regarding the public acceptance of Teresa as a saint. In addition to detailing the ways in which laypeople sought Teresa's inter-cession, many witnesses also spoke of the widespread distribution of images of the saint, some printed in Spain, others in Paris and Rome.[63] These small portable images were intended for private devotion: Their diffusion throughout Europe, then, is an indication of her growing inter-national reputation.[64]

Less mobile images of Teresa also proliferated after her canonization, as churches and chapels began to accommodate to her growing cult. Of all the images painted and sculpted in the Baroque age, none is more famous than Bernini's "Transverberation." Then, as now, this monu-ment to the mystic enraptured unto death seems a lesson in stone about the values of the Catholic Reformation.[65]

Teresa's fame may also be gauged by her influence on the literary arts. Within Spain, her beatification and canonization spawned various public celebrations in which poetry competitions were held. Accounts of

[61] Gracián, "Dialogos," FHM, p. 65.

[62] This is not an exhaustive bibliography but merely a summation of what can be found in the *Catalogue of the British Library* and in *The National Union Catalogue* of the Library of Congress.

[63] Juan Bautista Lejalde, PBC II.208–9; Catalina de San Angelo, PBC III.211 are but two examples.

[64] This has been analyzed by Eleanor Goodman in her MA thesis, "'What Has Earth to Do with Heaven?' The Relationship Between Teresa of Avila's Mystical Experience and Description of the Transverberation of Her Heart and the Iconography of Divine Love and Saintly Martyrdom." (Charlottesville VA, 1991).

[65] See Irving Lavin, *Bernini and the Unity of the Visual Arts*, 2 vols. (New York, 1980), vol. I, pp. 77–142.

these festivities were published shortly thereafter in major cities, making the poems and sermons available to an even wider public. The descriptive narratives printed in Barcelona,[66] Valladolid,[67] and Cordoba,[68] focused on local celebrations of her beatification; the one published in Madrid by Fray Diego de San José dealt with all of Spain.[69] In addition to judging the poetry competition of the Madrid celebration, the great playwright Lope de Vega produced two works for the stage: *Mother Teresa de Jesús* and *The Life and* Death *of Santa Teresa de Jesús* (emphasis mine). Two other baroque playwrights, Juan Bautista Diamante and José de Cañizares, also featured Teresa on the stage.[70]

As Lope de Vega saw it, Teresa the Spanish nun had become a truly Catholic saint, a universal exemplar:

> In lands, isles and seas, now
> incense is kindled,
> temples for you are readied,
> and altars are erected.[71]

This reference to temples and altars was no hyperbole. By 1615, even before her canonization, Teresa was already being hailed as the greatest virgin in all of Christian history and "the Queen among all the Brides"

---

[66] J. Dalmau, *Relación de la solemnidad con que se han celebrado en la ciudad de Barcelona las fiestas de la Beatificación de la Madre Santa Teresa de Jesús* (Barcelona, 1615).

[67] M. de los Rios Hevia Ceron, *Fiestas que hizo la insigne ciudad de Valladolid en la beatificación de la Madre Teresa de Jesús* (Valladolid, 1615).

[68] J. Paez de Valençuela y Castillejo, *Relación de las fiestas que en la ciudad de Cordoba se celebraron a la beatificación de la Madre Teresa de Jesús* (Cordoba, 1615).

[69] Fray Diego de San José, *Compendio de las solenes fiestas que en toda España se hicieron en la Beatificación de N.B.M. Teresa de Jesús, fundadora de la reformación de los Descalzos y Descalzas de N.S. del Carmen* (Madrid, 1615).

[70] de Vega, "La Madre Teresa de Jesús," and "Vida y muerte de Santa Teresa de Jesús"; Juan Bautista Diamante, "Santa Teresa de Jesús"; José de Cañizares, "A cuál mejor, confesada y confesor." These are discussed by Nicolás Marín, "Teresa de Jesús en el teatro barroco," *Congreso Internacional* II. 699–719; and Ignacio Elizalde, "Teresa de Jesús, protagonista de la dramática española del siglo XVII," *Letras de Deusto* XII.24:173–98.

[71] "Ya en tierras, islas y mares/aromas estan ardiendo,
 templos te están previniendo/y están erigiendo altares."
 Lope de Vega, *Vida y muerte de Santa Teresa de Jesús*, ed. Elisa Aragone Terni (Messina/Florence, 1970), p. 100.

of Christ.[72] Several of her beatification sermons likened her to the Virgin Mary. One compared her death to Mary's and went so far as to say that only Mary's assumption could rival the reception that Teresa received in heaven.[73] Two others identified Teresa as the woman described in the Book of Revelation, Chapter 12, with the moon under her feet and a crown of twelve stars – a profoundly Marian image.[74]

Teresa's lifelong immersion in death

For a mystic such as Teresa of Avila, death was not only some shadowy future moment but also a constant reality. "She desired to suffer and to die not just one death, but many," observed Julián de Avila.[75] Though death remained a frontier, a line between this world and the hereafter, Teresa claimed ownership of some territory beyond the border. In Teresa's writings, as in those of many Christian mystics, death and ecstasy were closely intertwined at various levels.[76]

To begin with, Teresa often spoke of self-renunciation as a form of death, as an emptying of the human will and a dying to the allure of the sensual world. Though this notion was as old as Christian asceticism itself, Teresa imbued it with her own vigor. In one of the best-known passages of the *Interior Castle*, Teresa employed the image of a worm turning into a butterfly to represent the transformation experienced by the true mystic on the path to God. "Let us hasten to perform this task and spin this cocoon," she advised. "Let us renounce our self-love and

---

[72] Juan de Arauz, O.F.M., preaching at the Carmelite convent of Alba de Tormes, where Teresa was buried, *Sermones*, fol. 161v.

[73] Jerónimo de Florencia, S. J., at the Carmelite Fathers of San Hermenegildo, Madrid, *Sermones*, fol. 37r.

[74] Nicolás Ricardi, O. P., at N. S. del Carmen, Madrid, *Sermones*, fol. 74r; and Paulo Zamora, at the Discalced Fathers of Zamora, fol. 194r.

[75] Julián de Avila, PBC I.226.

[76] Because Christianity is a religion centered on the crucifixion of its savior, Jesus Christ, it stands to reason that the mystery of death has always been a prominent theological and devotional concern of its saints and mystics. For a general overview of this subject, see Alois M. Haas's article "Mort Mystique" in *Dictionnaire de Spiritualité, Ascetique, et Mystique* (Paris, 1980), vol. 10, pp. 1777–91. The same author has published a more detailed study: "*Mors Mystica:* Thanatologie der Mystik, unbesonders der Deutschen Mystik," *Freiburger Zeitschrift für Philosophie und Theologie*, 23 (1976): 304–92.

self-will, let us be detached from all earthly things . . . let the worm die
. . . let it die, as it does when it has completed its work."[77]

On another level, Teresa looked upon death itself much as did
Shakespeare's Hamlet, as "a consummation devoutly to be wished."[78]
"How miserable is this life which we live," she protested.[79] For Teresa,
death was dearer than life itself, and she took immense delight in this
paradox. "Oh, death, oh death," she once exclaimed, "I do not know
why you are so feared, since it is you who contain life!"[80] Indeed, Teresa
once revealed to her confessor that she had put the question to God
Himself: "How can we endure this life without you, Lord? How can we
live while dying" (*como se puede vivir muriendo*)? According to Diego de
Yepes, her confessor, even the amorous text of the *Song of Songs* spoke of
death to Teresa: "Why even ask for comfort in this life, my spouse? Do
you not long to die? . . . What better death could you hope for, than to
die from love?"[81] In one of her most famous poems, "Aspirations of
Eternal Life," Teresa summed up her anguish.

Vivo sin vivir en mi	I live without life in me
Y tan alta vida espero,	And such exalted living await,
Que muero porque no muero.	For I am dying to die.[82]

Because she longed for eternal life, Teresa openly confessed that she
desired death and observed that at one point in her life this yearning had
seemed overwhelming.[83] The advice she gave her sisters was painfully
simple: "It ought to be our deepest wish to die and suffer."[84] For those
who followed Teresa's advice, death should also be a joyous occasion.
Teresa was believed to have confirmed this in an apparition to a gravely

---

[77] "Moradas," 5.2.6, Santa Teresa de Jesús, *Obras Completas*, ed. by Efrén de la Madre
de Dios, O.C.D. 3 vols. (Madrid, 1954), vol. II, p. 400. Hereafter cited as *OCST*.
[78] William Shakespeare, *Hamlet*, III.1.63–4. [79] "Moradas," 1.2.13, *OCST* II.351.
[80] "Exclamaciones," *OCST* II.644. [81] Fray Diego de Yepes, PBC I.283.
[82] *OCST* II.955. St. John of the Cross paid homage to Teresa by using the same refrain
and enlarging upon this theme in one of his poems. See *Vida y Obras de San Juan de la
Cruz*, 6th ed., Crisógono de Jesus, O.C.D., et al., eds. (Madrid, 1972), pp. 390–1.
[83] *Vida*, 29.8, *OCST* I, p. 772–3: "Víame morir con deseo de ver a Dios y no sabía
adónde havía de buscar esta vida si no era con la muerte." In "Cuentas de Conciencia" *OCST* II, p. 562, Teresa admitted, however: "El deseo y impetus tan grande de
morir se me han quitado."
[84] "Apuntaciones," *OCST* II.572.

ill nun at Salamanca who was fearful of dying. "Calm down, my friend," she said, "do not be so foolish, you have nothing to fear, for tonight you shall go to see God."[85] Teresa's advice was also very much in keeping with Tridentine Catholic teaching: Because salvation itself hinged on the final moments of one's life, all of life should be a preparation for death. "Keep in mind that you have but one soul, and that you shall die but once, and that you only have one brief life, and only one chance to enter eternal glory."[86]

On a higher plane, in that realm of experience reserved for advanced mystics, Teresa linked ecstasy and death.[87] No single vision of Teresa's is better known than the so-called transverberation, immortalized in marble by Bernini, in which an angel pierced Teresa's heart and entrails with a flaming arrow. Though strictly speaking this was an experience of God's love rather than of death, its rich symbolism suggests a painful ecstasy on the verge of death.[88] During many of her other ecstasies, Teresa said she felt her soul leaving her body.[89] In the *Interior Castle,* Teresa hesitantly but explicitly described one kind of mystical trance, or *arrobamiento* as "the flight of the spirit." These were instances when the soul was suddenly and rapidly taken to a higher realm beyond the body. "I am not really sure how to say this," she cautioned before employing a dramatic metaphor, "what happens is that the soul rises interiorly in flight, and goes far outside of itself, very quickly, as fast as a bullet shot out from a gun."[90]

So overwhelming was the power of this spiritual phenomenon that the

[85] Maria de la Encarnación, PBC I.331–32.
[86] "Avisos," n. 68, *OCST* II.932. Teresa also confessed this attitude to Diego de Yepes, PBC I.283.
[87] Tomás de la Cruz, "L'Extase chez Sainte Thérèse D'Avila," *Dictionnaire de Spiritualité, Ascetique, et Mystique* (Paris, 1960), vol. 4, pp. 2100–60, analyzes the terms employed by Teresa to describe mystical ecstasy (*suspensión, levantamiento, éxtasis, arrobamiento, rapto, arrebatamiento, vuelo de espíritu, ímpetu*). The author concludes that "les descriptions Thérèsiennes n'ont rien de systématique."
[88] *Vida,* 29.13, OCST I, p. 775.
[89] Teresa's own understanding of mystical experience and of the relation between the natural and supernatural is a subject in need of further research. See Mauricio Martín del Blanco, *Santa Teresa de Jesús: Mujer de ayer para el hombre de hoy* (Bilbao, 1975), pp. 343–64; and the "scientific" study of Arturo Perales y Gutiérrez, *El supernaturalismo de Santa Teresa y la filosofía médica* (Madrid, 1894).
[90] "Moradas," 6.5.9, *OCST* II.440.

physical realm could not help but also respond. According to Teresa, these flights of the spirit caused her to levitate: As the soul was pulled upward, the body followed in its wake.[91] Teresa calmly reported that all attempts by her sisters to restrain her during these levitations proved fruitless; in spite of their physical efforts and her own repeated protestations, God saw fit to continue lifting Teresa's soul and body.[92] Elsewhere, Teresa called this kind of rapture an *enajenamiento,* a word that implies separation or alienation (*ajeno* = alien, different) and described it as physically painful.[93] After one such experience, Teresa complained that she had trouble writing: "My body felt so bruised, and my hands hurt so much, they seemed to be sprained."[94] Jerónimo Gracián would later disclose that Teresa had described these experiences as being "harder to take than death itself."[95]

Moreover, mystical ecstasy was not far from death or at least from its threshold. At the instant when she was enraptured by God's love, Teresa claimed that her body and soul were sundered. "Do not think, my daughters, that I exaggerate when I speak of dying [in ecstasy], because – as I have told you – it really does happen."[96] While the soul was passively suspended in ecstasy, the body began to grow cold and languished in a fatal torpor, wholly detached from the mystic's control.[97] Though the soul in ecstasy recognized this experience as a taste of death itself, it remained both unwilling and unable to reunite with the body.

---

[91] One of Teresa's confessors, Julián de Avila, had the same explanation for these phenomena. As he said in his 1604 *Life:* "Cuando el arrobamiento es perfecto, es tan fácil el levantar el cuerpo, y llevarle tras sí, como es fácil a el aire levantar una pluma." *Vida de Santa Teresa de Jesús,* ed. Don Vicente de la Fuente (Madrid, 1881), p. 68.

[92] "Moradas," 6.5.1, *OCST,* II.437.

[93] Julián de Avila used this term to describe Teresa's final mystical rapture at the moment of her death, *Vida,* p. 364.

[94] "Cuentas de Conciencia," *OCST,* II.547. In her autobiography, *Vida,* 20.6, OCST I.707, Teresa said she felt as if she had been cut to pieces after such raptures ("quedava hecha pedazos") but also added that she could feel a temporary respite from her many natural aches and pains, *Vida,* 20.21, OCST I.713.

[95] Gracián, "Dialogos," FHM, p. 124.

[96] "Meditaciones Sobre Los Cantares," 7.2, OCST II.629.

[97] "*Vida,*" 20.3, OCST I.706: "En estos arrobamientos parece no anima el alma en el cuerpo y ansí se siente muy sentido faltar de el calor natural, vase enfriando, aunque con grandísima suavidad y deleite."

This is a delectable death [*una muerte sabrosa*], a wrenching away of the soul from all the functions it possesses while it is in the body; a delightful death, because in order to be with God more fully, the soul truly seems to withdraw so far from the body that I still do not know if it is left with enough life to be able to breathe.[98]

Though she wondered how bodily functions could be sustained during such raptures and boldly compared the experience to dying, Teresa asserted that the mystic did not actually die at such moments. "The spirit truly does leave the body, and it seems obvious that one does not die."[99] Nonetheless, she seemed convinced that to remain in such a state would be to die, and in the *Interior Castle* she warned that ecstatic raptures could bring one dangerously close to death. Because Teresa had nearly died herself earlier in life from natural causes, she felt well qualified to compare death and mystical ecstasy.[100]

The reunion of soul and body after such ecstasy was always a disappointment for Teresa. Viewed against the backdrop of heaven itself, death seemed preferable to life. Only the knowledge that God willed for her to continue living in this world made life itself tolerable for the mystic. Embodiment became a "most grievous prison," a separation from God.[101] "Oh, life, life," she exclaimed, "how can you be sustained when you are so far from your Life, in such loneliness?"[102] "Woe to me, woe to me, Lord! This exile is too long, and I endure it sorrowfully, deeply yearning for You, my God."[103]

---

[98] "Moradas," 5.1.3, OCST II.393. In the "*Vida*," 29.8, Teresa said that during some ecstasies "me parecía se me arrancava el alma," and described this as "una muerte tan sabrosa que nunca el alma querría salir de ella." OCST I.773.

[99] "Moradas," 6.5.7, OCST II.439.

[100] "*Vida*," 20.14, OCST I.711. "Moradas," 6.11.11, OCST II.471–72: "En este camino espiritual [hay] peligro de muerte . . . de muy excesivo gozo y deleite, que es en tan grandísimo estremo, que verdaderamente parece que desfallece el alma de suerte que no le falta tantito para acabar de salir del cuerpo."

[101] "Exclamaciones," XV, OCST II.653: "Señor, que hará un alma metida en esta carcel?" Alonso de Orozco said saints should feel this way, for heaven was their true homeland, *Victoria de la Muerte*, pp. 257–8.

[102] "Exclamaciones," I, "Apartada de mi Dios?", OCST II.639.

[103] "Exclamaciones," XV, OCST II.653. This text continues: "Oh, Jesús, que larga es la vida del hombre, aunque se dice que es breve! Breve es, mi Dios, para ganar con ella vida que no se puede acabar; mas muy larga para el alma que se desea ver en la presencia de su Dios."

Death and the saint

Teresa's melancholy eagerness for death verged on the brink of desperation, and this anxiety fueled a mystical dialectic in which ultimate values were transmuted, inverted, and spun into a web of contradiction. Life was the ultimate horror, death the ultimate blessing; living was a form of nonexistence, dying the only authentic way of being; zest for death was zest for life. Lamenting, exulting in paradox, revealing that her deepest fears were but the shadow of her immeasurable yearning, Teresa summed up in poetry her mystic attitude toward death.[104]

¡Ay, que larga es esta vida,	Oh, how long is this life,
Que duros estos destierros,	How harsh these banishments,
Esta carcel, estos hierros	This prison, these irons
En que el alma está metida!	Into which the soul is crammed!
Solo esperar la salida	Simply waiting for my exit
Me causa dolor tan fiero,	Causes pain ever so fierce,
Que muero porque no muero.	For I am dying to die.
¡Ay, que vida tan amarga	Oh, how bitter is this life
Do no se goza al Señor!	Where the Lord cannot be owned!
Porque si es dulce el amor,	For the sweeter the love,
No lo es la esperanza larga:	The more bitter the long delay:
Quíteme Dios esta carga	May God rid me of this burden
Más pesada que el acero.	Which is weightier than steel.
Que muero porque no muero.	For I am dying to die.
Solo con la confianza	Solely with the promise
Vivo de que he de morir,	That I shall die can I live,
Porque muriendo el vivir	For it is in dying that living
Me asegura mi esperanza.	My hopes can ensure.
Muerte do el vivir se alcanza,	Death, you who impart life,
No te tardes que te espero,	Tarry not, I await you,
Que muero porque no muero.	For I am dying to die.
Mira que el amor es fuerte;	Behold how mighty is love;
Vida no me seas molesta,	Stand not in my way, life,
Mira que sólo te resta,	Fathom that all you need,
Para ganarte, perderte;	To be gained, is to be lost;
Venga ya la dulce muerte,	Come now, sweet death,

[104] OCST II.955–6.

399

The saint's heavenly corpse

Venga ya el morir muy ligero,   Come now, swift dying,
Que muero porque no muero.   For I am dying to die.

Throughout most of her life, Teresa yearned for death. When the moment finally arrived, how did she meet it? How did those around her interpret her passing?

~~~~~~

2

Come, sweet death, come, swift dying
The final days of Teresa of Avila

We should not be astonished that, as God accomplished wondrous things through her life, He should also have worked wonders at her death.[1]

Fatal ecstasy: Teresa's last journey

Although many would claim that Teresa of Avila predicted her own death, the actual event seemed to surprise everyone around her.[2] In 1582, Teresa founded yet another Discalced Carmelite convent in Burgos. She had been showing signs of physical deterioration for some time but pressed on as usual, undeterred by her poor health. Having completed her work in Burgos, Teresa left the city in late July 1582 and headed back to her own convent of St. Joseph in Avila, along with her inseparable companion, sister Ana de San Bartolomé, and her niece, Teresita.[3] After prolonged visits to the convents at Palencia and Valladolid, the three women resumed their journey in early September.

---

[1] Gracián, "Dialogos," FHM, p. 47.

[2] Several testimonies speak of predictions. Some of the less cryptic are: Inés de Jesús, PBC I.424, and I.430; Isabel de Cristo, PBC I.451; and Maria de San José, PBC I.504; Jerónimo Gracián, "Dichoso transito," FHM, p. 17; "Dialogos," FHM, p. 56; "Historia de las fundaciones," FHM, pp. 192–3. According to Weinstein and Bell, *Saints & Society*, p. 147, the saint's prediction of his or her own death was the most common prophecy attributed to holy people in hagiography. Gracián knew this and provided a long list of precedents in "Dialogos," FHM, pp. 55–8.

[3] St. Teresa was eager to reach Avila so her niece could take her final vows at the convent of St. Joseph. See testimony of Teresa de Jesús (Teresita), PBC I.195.

When they arrived at Medina del Campo, which was roughly two-thirds of the way home, they were surprised to find their provincial, Fray Antonio de Jesús, waiting for them. He had come to Medina to intercept Teresa and order her immediately to visit the Discalced Carmelite convent she had founded at Alba de Tormes, near Salamanca, where the Duchess of Alba, Doña Maria Enriquez, had requested the presence of Teresa. Because the duchess had been a great benefactress of the Carmelite order, Fray Antonio de Jesús was eager to accommodate her wishes.[4]

Teresa, who was ill and weak and felt worn out from her recent efforts at Burgos, desired nothing more than to return to Avila and rest. The provincial's command tested not only Teresa's endurance but also her capacity for self-denying obedience as well.[5] She now had to change her route, head southwest, and delay her return home for an indeterminate number of days, perhaps even weeks.

Fray Antonio de Jesús found a coach for Teresa and immediately dispatched her toward Alba without any provisions.[6] This proved to be a very rough journey. Feverish, hungry, and exhausted, Teresa soon fainted. Ana de San Bartolomé desperately searched for food in some of the villages along the road so that Teresa might build up her strength, but could find only figs, onions, and boiled greens.[7] Ana de San Bartolomé later said:

This final journey from Burgos . . . was a prolonged martyrdom. . . . It is only fair to report what I heard [from Teresa], which, given her great strength and courage, must have been most difficult for her to say: that in spite of all the many travails she had endured through her life, she had never been as distressed and afflicted as she was at that moment.[8]

---

[4] Some sources say instead that Teresa received these orders at Valladolid. See Efrén de la Madre de Dios and Otger Steggink, *Tiempo y Vida de Santa Teresa*, 2nd ed., (Madrid, 1978), pp. 968–70.

[5] Ana de San Bartolomé, "Ultimos años de la Madre Teresa de Jesús," OCASB I.23: "Nunca la ví sentir tanto, cosa que los prelados la mudasen como esta." Also related by her niece Teresita, PBC I.195.

[6] Ribera, p. 333.

[7] Ana de San Bartolomé, "Ultimos años," OCASB I.23. In her autobiography (OCASB I.306) Sister Ana said; "La santa iba ya mala de mal de muerte . . . y estaba con calentura."

[8] Ana de San Bartolomé, "Ultimos años," OCASB I.26.

Ana de San Bartolomé was greatly vexed by all this but later wrote about it as a lesson in Christian patience and resignation in the face of death:

I could not look at the Saint [Teresa] without weeping, because her face seemed half dead. I cannot exaggerate how much sorrow this caused me, because it seemed as if my heart was breaking. When I realized the seriousness of our situation, all I could do was to weep, because I was watching her die, and could do nothing to help her. And she said to me with the patience of an angel: "Do not weep, my daughter, because this is what God wills now." As the hour of her blessed death approached, the Lord continued to try her even further, but she bore it all in her usual saintly manner.[9]

Sister Ana was not the only one who interpreted this difficult journey as a "prolonged martyrdom." Francisco de Ribera would go as far as to suggest that Teresa's obedience and her subsequent torments were reminiscent of Christ's sacrifice on the cross.

She felt a great contradiction when she received the order from Fray Antonio . . . and it is incredible how much distress this caused her; but, since she had always obeyed so perfectly throughout her life, she also obeyed at that moment when she was near death, because she so resembled Him who was obedient, even unto death on a cross.[10]

As far as Ribera was concerned, Teresa's selflessness and obedience made her a martyr.[11] Diego de Yepes, another interpreter of Teresa's death, also concurred: "Though she was not a martyr in blade and blood, she was one in spirit, and her travails earned her the crown that others have earned through the sword."[12]

---

[9] Ana de San Bartolomé, *Autobiografía*, OCASB I.306.

[10] Ribera, *Vida*, p. 333.

[11] Ribera consciously employed conventional martyriological typology in reference to Teresa's death. Compare with St. Bonaventure's description of the death of St. Francis in his "Minor Life," chap. 7.1: "Francis now hung body and soul upon the cross with Christ." *St. Francis of Assisi, Writings and Early Biographies. English Omnibus of the Sources for the Life of St. Francis*, ed. Marion A. Habig (Chicago, 1973), p. 826.

[12] Yepes, p. 23. A sentiment shared by Isabel de Santo Domingo, PBC II.505, and Nicolás Ricardi, *Sermones*, fol. 70r-v. This was an acceptable theological opinion. Antonio de Guevara had said: "No fueron mártires los mártires por los trabajos que padecieron, sino por la paciencia que en ellos tuvieron." *Epistolas familiares*, p. 13, p. 211.

When she finally arrived at Alba on 20 September, after two days on the road with hardly anything to eat, Teresa looked so haggard that the prioress and nuns asked her to retire to bed immediately.[13] Even though it was hours before her customary bedtime, Teresa excused herself, saying "Oh God, how weary I feel; I have not retired to bed this early in over twenty years, but must do it now."[14]

During the next few days, Teresa rose from her sickbed to pray with her sisters, attend mass, and receive communion.[15] Ever the hard-working mother, Teresa also received visitors and conducted some business in spite of her severely weakened condition.[16] On the feast of St. Michael, 29 September, immediately after communion, she collapsed in bed and began to hemorrhage vaginally.[17] Now totally bedridden, Teresa asked that she be taken to a room on the upper floor of the convent, from which she could see the main altar in the chapel and follow the mass. As she waited for death over the next five days, Teresa prayed fervently, even through the night. According to Fray Diego de Yepes, it seemed certain to Teresa and all the nuns at Alba that the end was imminent: "She spent all day and night totally absorbed and enraptured

---

[13] There is some disagreement about this date. Some sources place her arrival on the following day. See FHM, p. 13, n. 5.

[14] Ribera, p. 334. The same words are quoted by Fray Diego de Yepes in his *Vida*, p. 410.

[15] Gracián, "Dialogos," FHM, p. 51.

[16] Ana de San Bartolomé, "Declaración sobre la traslación del cuerpo de la Madre Teresa de Jesús," OCASB I.38, said that Teresa received a visit from her sister, Juana de Ahumada, a resident of Alba. Agustín de los Reyes, PBC II.174, testified that he had spent three hours conducting business with Teresa about eight days before her death. For further documentation see *Tiempo y Vida de Santa Teresa*, pp. 974–8.

[17] Attempts have been made to diagnose Teresa's final illness: César Fernandez Ruiz, "La medicina y los medicos en la vida y la obra de la madre Teresa de Jesús," *Clinica y Laboratorio* 76 (1963): 129–60; Juan Paulís Pages, "La ultima enfermedad de la Mística Doctora Teresa de Jesús," *Clinica y Laboratorio* 75 (1962): 448–68. A full discussion of the medical literature can be found in Marcella Biró Barton, "Saint Teresa of Avila. Did She Have Epilepsy?," *Catholic Historical Review*, 68 (1982): 581–98.

in prayer, and thus learned from Our Lord that the hour of her rest was near."[18]

If Teresa had not been a nun, she would have probably called for a notary at this point, to write her last will and testament. In this respect, her experience was different from that of the vast majority of people for whom the visit from the notary was indispensable and as much a sign of resignation as the last rites administered by the priest. Monks and nuns went through this death ritual earlier in their lives, at the time they made their vows, as a confirmation of their "death" to the world.[19]

Throughout these final moments Teresa remained very much in control of the situation. Her physicians feigned optimism, but the dying saint had no need for their deception.[20] She knew she was dying and rejoiced at the prospect of crossing over into heaven. After all, as Yepes observed, her entire life had been a preparation for death:

Undoubtedly, this was the best news she had ever heard, since it was what she most wanted in life. . . . The troubled life of the just would be intolerable without the hidden promise of death, because for them it is not the end of life, but rather its beginning, when they reach the haven of that realm where they shall find everlasting repose and bliss.[21]

After eight days had passed, her condition worsened considerably. On 1 October, Teresa requested that the provincial Father Antonio de Jesús come and hear her confession. The nuns in the convent became apprehensive when they heard Father Antonio praying after this confession, "Please, Lord, do not take her from us now, not so soon."[22] Teresa also exclaimed she was no longer needed in this world and began to give

---

[18] Yepes, p. 410, adds: "Que aunque había mas de ocho años la había revelado el Señor el año que habia de morir, y lo traía escrito en cifras en su breviario . . . y así lo tenian entendido casi todas las monjas de aquella casa."

[19] R.C. Finucane, "Sacred Corpse," pp. 44–5, comments on this practice: "To speak of a dead monk is something of a tautology, for in theory monks were already dead to the world. . . . The monk was reborn into a place of protracted transition, the monastery."

[20] Gracián, "Dialogos," FHM, p. 52, reports Teresa waved off the doctors with her hands, saying, "Quítense de ahí, que lo que no es, no es."

[21] Yepes, p. 410.

[22] Ribera, p. 334; Constancia de los Angeles, PBC I.104–5.

advice to the nuns. The physicians ordered that she be moved back downstairs to a warmer room, and they applied *ventosas sajadas,* or cupping, a painful bleeding procedure that involved scarring the skin and placing a heated glass over the treated area. Teresa suffered gladly and smiled during all of this, knowing how pointless these ministrations really were.[23] Fray Diego de Yepes did not fail to draw a central lesson in the art of dying well from Teresa's composure. Because patient acceptance of suffering had been an integral part of the saint's life, it was only natural that the same be true in her death. "She who gloried in suffering throughout her life could not act differently at this hour, because as one lives, so does one die."[24]

By 3 October Teresa was so ill and weak she could no longer turn over in bed by herself.[25] At five in the afternoon she asked to receive communion. As she waited for the sacrament, she said: "My daughters and my ladies, for the love of God, I ask you to pay close attention to the observance of the [Discalced Carmelite] Rule and the constitutions, and not to follow the poor example that this bad nun has given you, which I ask you to forgive."[26] According to Diego de Yepes, Teresa also spoke of herself as "the worst sinner in the world."[27] Through this humbly penitent gesture, the saint further confirmed her holiness. Because absolute remorse was required of every *moriens,* or dying Christian, Teresa here exemplified the proper attitude, speaking of herself as sinful and in need of forgiveness, even though she had lived an exemplary life.[28]

---

[23] Yepes, p. 411. Teresa's obedience and self-denial were also confirmed through her acceptance of these futile attempts to cure her.

[24] Ibid.

[25] Constancia de los Angeles, PBC I.105; Juana del Espíritu Santo, PBC I.101.

[26] Ana San Bartolomé, "Ultimos años," OCASB I.24; Ribera, p. 335.

[27] Yepes, p. 412: "Hijas mías y señoras mías, perdónenme el mal ejemplo que les he dado, y no aprendan de mí, que he sido la mayor pecadora del mundo, y la que más mal ha guardado sus reglas y constituciones." Yepes and others report that Teresa kept repeating such protests throughout her final illness. See also Mariana de la Encarnación, PBC I.83; Catalina Bautista, PBC I.94.

[28] This was further confirmation of the dictum "in death as in life," since Teresa had constantly spoken of her "wretchedness." Alison Weber has analyzed this life-long tendency of Teresa's, which Weber calls "affected modesty": *Rhetoric of Femininity,* pp. 48–56. Even as fervent an admirer of Teresa as E. Allison Peers found this trait disturbing, saying this was "self-abasement carried to excess and suggestive of something the reverse of humility." *Studies of the Spanish Mystics,* 1st ed., 3 vols. (London, 1927), vol. I, pp. 149–50.

Although none of those around her would have failed to recognize this gesture as extreme, none also would have failed to see the lesson behind it. By calling herself "the worst sinner in the world," Teresa undoubtedly wanted to call attention to the radical sinfulness of human nature and the constant need all humans have for forgiveness, especially at the moment of death. Teresa apparently knew her *Ars Moriendi* very well, because she not only expressed contrition but also called on those around her to help her at this crucial moment. Although she expressed confidence that she would be saved through the merits of Jesus Christ (and none around her seemed to doubt she would enter heaven imminently), she asked her sisters to pray for her salvation. Once again, Teresa confirmed the value of another important Catholic teaching by means of example, even when it seemed evident that she did not really need what she requested.[29]

When the consecrated host was brought into her room, Teresa made an astonishing recovery and rose from her bed without help. Her face suddenly looked brighter, younger, and more beautiful.[30] Teresa exclaimed:

Oh my Lord and my spouse, the desired hour has finally arrived, it is now time to see one another! It is now time to begin our journey . . . may your will be done! The hour has finally come for me to leave this exile, and for my soul to rejoice as one with you in this, its deepest longing.[31]

In addition, Teresa thanked God for having made her a daughter of the church, and for allowing her to die in the church.[32] This was further confirmation, again, of the dictum "in death as in life." Teresa had cared so much for the church in her life that it was only natural that she should find such great comfort in the church at the moment of death. Even on

[29] Antonio de Caceres, Bishop of Astorga and royal preacher, made much of this point in his beatification sermon, *Sermones*, fols. 150r-153r.

[30] The accounts of Ana de San Bartolomé ("Ultimos años," OCASB I.23–25) and Diego de Yepes (p. 412) are nearly identical. Some of the Alba nuns thought she looked more manly. Mariana de Jesús, for instance, described Teresa's face as "un rostro que parecía mas de un hombre muy venerable que de mujer," PBC I.83.

[31] Ribera comments (p. 335): "Comenzó aquel blanquísimo cisne a cantar al fin de su vida, con mayor dulzura que en toda ella habia cantado."

[32] Yepes, p. 412. Ribera, p. 335, says she often said, "En fin, Señor, soy hija de la Iglesia."

her deathbed, Teresa did more than teach by example; she also recapitulated the need for obedience in the church and the Carmelite reform. When the nuns asked for advice and comfort from her, she simply told them to obey their Rule and constitutions and to follow the commands of their superiors. These words and gestures were welcomed by her sisters, though they did little to lessen their sorrow.[33]

During these final hours Teresa found comfort in some verses from Psalm 51, which she constantly intoned in Latin, as a litany. "The sacrifice acceptable to God is a broken spirit; a broken and contrite heart, Oh God, thou wilt not despise" (Ps. 51.17). "Cast me not away from your presence, and take not your Holy Spirit from me" (Ps. 51.11). "Create in me a clean heart, Oh God" (Ps. 51.10). Of these verses, Teresa most often repeated the seventeenth, "*Cor contritum et humiliatum, Deus, non despicies,*" which she kept reciting until she lost her voice.[34] At nine that night she requested and received the last rites. As soon as she had been anointed with the holy chrism, she again thanked God for having made her a daughter of the church, further confirming the value of Catholic sacramental theology.[35]

Soon afterward, Fray Antonio de Jesús asked her a most important, yet practical question: Did she want to be buried there at Alba, or would she prefer burial at her convent of St. Joseph in Avila? Teresa's answer was intended as yet another confirmation of her detachment, but it would cause no end of confusion in years to come: "Should I have something of my own? Can they not give me here a little earth?"[36] In this

---

[33] Ana de San Bartolomé, "Ultimos años," OCASB I.24. Also Yepes, p. 412: "Enternecíanse sus hijas como era razón, lloraban unas, gemían y suspiraban otras, y todas se compungían de ver la humildad de la santa, y de oir las palabras que decía."

[34] "Sacrificium Deo spiritus contribulatus. Cor contritum et humiliatum, Deus, non despicies" (Ps. 51.17). "Ne projicias me a facie tua, et Spiritum Santum tuum ne auferas a me" (Ps. 51.11). "Cor mundum crea in me Deus" (Ps. 51.10). Ribera, p. 336; Yepes, p. 413; Ana de San Bartolomé, "Ultimos años," OCASB I.24; Mariana de Jesús, PBC I.83; Juana del Espiritu Santo, PBC I.101; Constancia de los Angeles, PBC I.105.

[35] Yepes, p. 413, does not fail to spell out the meaning of Teresa's participation in the last rites: "El sacramento . . . con que el alma se acaba de fortalecer y dar un baño en la sangre del Cordero, para con más libertad juntarse con el y gozarle eternamente."

[36] Ribera, p. 336: "Tengo you de tener cosa propia? Aquí no me daran un poco de tierra?" An acrimonious quarrel arose concerning the location of Teresa's remains, as will be seen later in this narrative. The voluminous ecclesiastic and civil documenta-

way, as Yepes observed, "She who had always been a teacher of poverty proved how unattached and free she was from anything at that hour."[37]

Throughout that night Teresa continued to pray fervently, intoning the verses from Psalm 51, even though it was evident to all that she was in great pain. At seven the next morning, 4 October, the feast of St. Francis, Teresa assumed a serene demeanor that her sisters recognized as a mystical trance. Firmly clutching a crucifix to her breast, the dying saint withdrew from her immediate surroundings. "Her face was aflame," Ribera observed, "and she remained thus immersed in prayer, extremely calm and serene, without further movement."[38] This mystical experience, Teresa's last, would continue for the next fourteen hours, until nine that night.

Those around Teresa had no doubt that she was experiencing some kind of communication with God. For Yepes, the lesson was clear: Because death had been Teresa's goal in life, the moment of crossing over into the afterlife was her ultimate rapture, the supreme mystical experience. She who had longed to unite with God for eternity and who had enjoyed so many foretastes of life in paradise was now finally comforted by God Himself at the gates of heaven. Employing bridal imagery in a way that would have pleased Teresa herself, Yepes described the saint's final moments as follows:

She remained wholly absorbed in God, with the greatest serenity and stillness, totally enraptured with the novelty of what she was beginning to discover, rejoicing, and enjoying her nearness to that which she had so keenly desired. . . . Who can tell what transpired during that time between that holy soul and her sweet Spouse: the visions, the conversations, the expressions of love, as she now approached the bridal bed she had so intensely longed for, the flowery bed of her beloved? . . . Who would doubt that the King of Glory attended on her there?, revealing a thousand new joyful things, and calling her to Himself

---

tion created by this dispute (AHNM, Sección de codices, 168-B) was carefully collected, edited, and published by José Gómez Centurion, under the title *Relaciónes biográficas-inéditas de Santa Teresa de Jesús* (Madrid, 1917). Selected documents are also included in FHM, pp. 245–495.

[37] Yepes, pp. 413–14.

[38] Ribera, p. 336, says Teresa assumed a posture of repentance reminiscent of the iconography for Mary Magdalene, "con un Crucifijo en la mano, el cual tuvo hasta que se le quitaron para enterrarla." See also Constancia de los Angeles, PBC I.105, and Isabel de la Cruz, PBC I.111.

with those sweet words: "Come, my beloved, my dove, hurry, my friend, for the winter of this life is now over, and the beautiful flowers of my eternity and my glory are starting to bloom."[39]

Sometime in the late afternoon or early evening, Teresa became slightly agitated when Sister Ana de San Bartolomé momentarily left her bedside. After Sister Ana returned, Teresa lapsed back into a trance, "so much aflame with the love of her Bridegroom, that it seemed she could not wait for the moment when she would leave her body to enjoy him." At nine o'clock that evening of 4 October, Teresa died in the arms of Sister Ana de San Bartolomé.[40] Father Yepes described this moment with a phrase that neatly summarized Teresa's own attitude toward death: "This was the hour," he said, "in which that blessed soul left the prison of her body."[41]

By coincidence, this day also happened to be the feast of St. Francis of Assisi, one of Teresa's patron saints. The following day, by another coincidence, happened to be the first day of the new amended calendar promoted by Pope Gregory XIII, which now skipped a full ten days. Officially, then, according to the new Gregorian calendar, 5 October became 15 October. Even the calendar, it seemed, marked her passing in a most extraordinary way.[42]

Teresa's death was portrayed as the perfect death and as a most extraordinary confirmation of the dictum *como vive muere* (in death as in life).[43] Throughout her final ordeal, Teresa had displayed the virtues that had made her life holy. She had been calm, even joyful, in the face

---

[39] Yepes, p. 414. As will be seen presently, many came to believe that Teresa's death was not ultimately due to the severity of her natural illness but to the intensity of this supernatural rapture.

[40] Ana de San Bartolomé, *Autobiografía*, OCASB I.307–8, suggests that Teresa was not totally immobilized: "Y viniendo que me vió, *se río* y me mostró tanta gracia y amor, que *me tomó con sus manos y puso en sus brazos su cabeza*, y allí la tube abrazada hasta que expiró [my emphasis]." Neither Ribera (p. 336) nor Yepes (p. 415) makes mention of this. According to their accounts, Teresa remained totally immobile and enraptured throughout the final hours.

[41] Yepes, p. 415. Gracián described it more colorfully: "Dió un salto de la tierra al cielo y acabó sus dichosas peregrinaciones." "Dichoso transito," FHM, p. 13.

[42] Gracián, "Dichoso transito," FHM, p. 17.

[43] It was also a confirmation of Teresa's own advice: "Acuérdate que no tienes más de un alma, ni has de morir más de una vez, ni tienes más de una vida breve, y una, que es particular, ni hay más de una gloria, y esta eterna." "Avisos," n. 68, OCST, II, 938.

of death. The moment of transition itself was as uncommon as the saint: This woman who had devoted her life to prayer and who was believed to have received numerous mystical experiences culminated her life in an intense act of prayer. Her death had been very peaceful; so calm, in fact, that the nuns could not be sure she had stopped praying.[44]

Death as hierophany

Fray Diego de Yepes saw Teresa's death in a supernatural light, as the ultimate mystical experience. According to him, Teresa had not died of natural causes but as the result of a divine rapture that had sundered her soul from her body. Although the physicians attending to Teresa attributed her death to loss of blood, Yepes had a different diagnosis.

It would certainly be impossible to deny that these ailments greatly contributed towards severing the thread of her life, but the knife that finally killed her was the great force of God's mighty and powerful love, which wrested not only her spirit from her soul, but also her soul from her body.[45]

During her final fourteen-hour ecstasy, according to this interpretation, Teresa was aflame with the ardor of God's love for her. Yepes used imagery reminiscent of that which had earlier been used in the case of Catherine of Genoa, another saint who was believed to have been consumed inwardly by the *incendium amoris*, or divine flame of love.[46]

She was thus ignited and burned by love because of what she now experienced, through the enjoyment of what she had longed for. . . . Like a phoenix, she died in that fortunate fire in which she had always lived.[47]

[44] Ribera, p. 337: "Su muerte fué tan sosegada, que a las que muchas veces la habian visto en oración no las parecia sino que estaba todavia en ella."

[45] Yepes, pp. 416–17. Yepes thought the bleeding was not the *cause* of death but an effect of her mystical rapture: "Pues de esta violencia grande e ímpetu de amor fué su alma tan fuertemente arrebatada, que no sólo se enajenó de los sentidos, sino también del cuerpo, porque de la mucha fuerza con que estaba abrazada, unida con su divino y celestial Esposo, le provino un flujo de sangre, y de él la muerte."

[46] The notion of mystical love as a consuming fire can be found in the work of Richard Rolle of Hampole (d. 1349), *Incendium Amoris* (1340?). St. Catherine of Genoa (d. 1510) took this notion to new heights. See her posthumously published *Spiritual Dialogues* and *Treatise on Purgatory* (1551); available in English, *Catherine of Genoa: Purgation and Purgatory, Classics of Western Spirituality* (Mahwah NJ, 1982).

[47] Yepes, p. 416; Ana de San Bartolomé, *Autobiografía*, OCASB I.308: "Tan encendida en el amor de su Esposo que parecía no veía la hora de salir del cuerpo para gozarle."

Though he tried to be poetic, Yepes did not intend for this description to be simply metaphorical. According to him, Teresa herself had revealed the true cause of her death from beyond the grave to another saintly Carmelite, Catalina de Jesús. Teresa's own diagnosis, as revealed to Sister Catalina, was that she died from "the force [*ímpetu*] of the love of God, which thrust out her soul." In another apparition Teresa also revealed that these powerful supernatural forces (*ímpetus*) had directly caused her death, because her natural, physical body had been unable to tolerate them.[48]

Yepes thought that this supernatural explanation made perfect sense. Quoting Teresa herself, Yepes called attention to some earlier episodes from Teresa's life when the love of God literally pulled her soul toward heaven, away from her body.[49] One time, upon hearing a hymn about the soul's longing for God, Teresa had come close to death: The force drawing her away from her body had been so intense that, if the singing had not stopped, her soul would never have returned to her body.[50] Yepes also recalled that Teresa's companions had often said that she looked dead when she was absorbed in mystical transports. The peaceful look on her face when she died, many observed, was the same look she often had while in ecstasy. Yepes was not the only one to promote this interpretation. The beatification sermons show that by 1615 no natural explanation of Teresa's death was acceptable. Teresa could not have undergone the *agonía* that befalls all humans at the last moment, said one sermon.[51] Bridal imagery abounded. This was no death, said another sermon, but a love embrace: "Her soul was wrenched loose by the force of God's love, amidst the delight of his hugs and kisses."[52]

This attempt to interpret Teresa's death as a supernatural event, rather than as a natural occurrence, was very much in keeping with the hagiographical intentions of Yepes, Ribera, and others close to the saint,

---

[48] Ribera, p. 540; Yepes, p. 416. This interpretation quickly became well known. See testimony of Teresa de Jesús (Teresita), PBC I.195.

[49] See "Vida," Chap. 20, OCST I, 705–16; and "Moradas," 6.5, OCST, I, 437–41.

[50] Teresa's own account can be found in "Meditaciónes sobre los Cantares," 7.1–2, OCST, II, 628–9.

[51] Antonio de Caceres, *Sermones*, fol. 150 ff.

[52] Jaime Rebullosa, O. P., at the Discalced Carmelite convent of Barcelona, *Sermones*, fol. 366r. He added: "¡O muerte mas que dichosa!, muerte felicísima, muerte ya no muerte, sino vida, y glorioso principio de la que no ha de tener fín."

who wanted to idealize her death and to make it as *uncommon* as possible. The bare clinical facts of Teresa's final illness and death called for interpretation and elaboration not so much because they were themselves unusually unpleasant or horrifying (as in the case of Philip II) but because the saint herself had led a most unusual life. Guided by the dictum, "As one lives, so shall one die," these interpreters sought to find a correspondence between her entire life and the moment of her death. An extraordinarily holy woman who had already experienced glimpses of heaven on earth surely could not depart from this life in an ordinary way. In the case of a saint, the mundane is eclipsed by the extraordinary, and there is no longer any tension between the real and the ideal; in fact, the two *become* one and the same. Consequently, the images presented to us in these accounts are not so much descriptive as pedagogical and devotional. Teresa's death was thus portrayed as something that could inspire admiration and, to some extent, imitation, perhaps even envy.

In sum, those who wrote about Teresa's death sought to idealize it on three levels. First, the physical and emotional pain of death was raised beyond the mundane: In the case of Teresa, her patient suffering earned her a martyr's crown. Second, her behavior during this final ordeal was more than exemplary and more than a confirmation of the *Ars Moriendi* tradition. Teresa's blissful acceptance of death as the best single moment of her entire life left little or no room for fear and temptation: The only emotion felt by this *moriens* was a confident joy. Third, Teresa was not allowed a natural death: It was not her physical ailments that killed her but a mystical rapture. Because many of her numerous mystical experiences had been foretastes of death and the afterlife, in which her soul had ostensibly departed from her body, it was only to be expected that its final departure would occur in a similar manner. In other words, according to the maxim *como vive muere*, it was only natural for her death to be supernatural.[53]

Signs and portents at Teresa's death

The death of a great saint should be more than exemplary: It should also be an irruption of the sacred, a moment during which heaven and earth

---

[53] Gracián, "Dialogo," FHM, p. 53: "Quánto más que la buena vida es principio de buena muerte, y la buena muerte fin y premio de la buena vida."

intersect, and the glory and power of God are revealed. Consequently, the passing of the saint's soul from its earthly body to its new celestial home should be marked by unmistakable signs of divine approval as confirmation of a holy life well rewarded.[54]

Given such expectations, it is not surprising that most of the eyewitnesses present at the death of Teresa claimed to have seen all sorts of wonders, even before the event itself. Many nuns later recalled having seen a large bright star over their chapel a considerable time before Teresa's death. In 1582, some time before Teresa's arrival at Alba, one of the nuns had seen "a most lovely crystalline flash of light" streak across the window of the room in which Teresa would later die. Another nun reported seeing two "most resplendent" lights at this same window. Several times during matins that year, 1582, the nuns also saw bright lights in the choir.[55] At the time, the nuns could not explain these phenomena but interpreted them as portents of some great event to come. During the summer of 1582, as the nuns were engaged in prayer, they often heard a "low and oddly pleasant" moan. When Teresa died, she made the same sound, and the nuns realized this was the moan they had heard during prayer.[56]

If such portents could precede the saint's arrival and death, much greater signs would later appear at the time of her crossing over into heaven. Inés de Jesús reported seeing a brilliant flash of light as Teresa was dying.[57] Ana de San Bartolomé reported seeing Christ and a great multitude of angels, in great splendor, at the foot of Teresa's deathbed, "awaiting the soul of the holy mother, so they could lead her to glory." Though she had been despondent up to that moment – "deader than the Saint herself," as she put it – Ana immediately welcomed the inevitable and even asked Christ to take Teresa's soul, saying, "Now that I

---

[54] Examples in Gregory the Great, *Dialogues* II.37; IV.7–36; Caesarius of Heisterbach, *Miracles*, XI.1–35. Gracián intentionally made reference to numerous other examples, and cited Gregory of Tours and some sixteenth-century hagiographies, including Lorenzo Surio, *De probatis sanctorum historiis* (1570–81), and Aloysius Lipomanus, *Sanctorum priscorum patrum vitae* (1551–60). "Dialogos," FHM, p. 47, n. 21; p. 49, n. 29.

[55] Inés de Jesús, PBC III.178; Isabel de Santo Domingo, PBC II.94. Isabel de Cristo, a nun at Segovia, recalled having received a letter from Alba that spoke of these lights (PBC I.448).

[56] Ribera, p. 341.   [57] Inés de Jesús, PBC III.178.

have seen her in glory, do not leave her here for one more instant."[58] Another sister reported seeing a great crowd of "replendent" people, all dressed in brilliant white garments, walking through the cloister on the way to Teresa's cell at the moment of her death. Although she could not imagine how they would all fit into such a small room (unlike Ana de San Bartolomé, who seemed comfortable in the company of the throng at the foot of Teresa's bed), it was evident to her that they "had come for her soul, to accompany it" to heaven.[59] At the very moment when Teresa expired, one sister saw a large white butterfly fluttering over the saint's body,[60] another saw a small white dove flying upward from the saint's mouth.[61] Outside Teresa's window, a barren fruit tree suddenly filled with blossoms, "white as snow," despite the frigid weather.[62]

Simultaneously, far from Alba, other miracles took place. At the Discalced Carmelite convent of Valladolid, a wonderful odor suddenly began to emanate from any item that had been touched by Teresa during her visits. One of the nuns there was also surprised at prayer by a bright light. Looking up to heaven, she saw "something like an opening, and within it a great swirling of lights, very joyful and resplendent," which she interpreted as a sign of someone crossing over into eternal bliss.[63] Another nun at Valladolid received a vision in which she saw Teresa and

---

[58] As related in Yepes, pp. 414–15. In the *Autobiografía,* Ana herself says: "Y como el Señor es tan bueno y veía mi poca paciencia para llevar esta cruz, se me mostró con toda la majestad y compañia de los bienaventurados sobre los pies de la cama, que venían por su alma" (OCASB I.308). See also Ana's testimony in PBC I. 169–71.

[59] Ribera, p. 341; Catalina de San Angelo, PBC III.205. Yepes (p. 415) adds that these visitors were very joyful, rejoicing at the death of Teresa. Gracián provides a long list of hagiographic precedents for this phenomenon in "Dialogos," FHM, pp. 65–69.

[60] As reported to Juan Carillo, PBC I.389, FHM, p. 238, who also states that this same nun saw the butterfly over Teresa's grave three years later, one day before the saint's body was taken from Alba to Avila.

[61] Ribera (p. 341) interprets this as a visual reference to the biblical text, "Song of Songs," 2.13–14, "Arise, my love, my fair one, and come away, O my dove." Ana de San Bartolomé, *Autobiografía,* OCASB I.308, was more figurative: "Y con esto expiró, y se fué esta dichosa alma a gozar de Dios como una paloma." This was a common motif in hagiographical literature. For instance, Gregory the Great, *Dialogues,* II.34.1, IV.11.4; Caesarius of Heisterbach, *Miracles,* XII.45.

[62] Catalina de San Angelo (PBC III.205) said she noticed this miracle the following morning. According to her, the tree never bloomed again.

[63] Francisca de Jesús, PBC II.34.

St. Francis of Assisi together in heaven.[64] At Burgos, Gracia de Alaba reported having seen Teresa in church, ascending to heaven from the altar along with Christ and St. Joseph (her patron), "in great splendor."[65] At the Discalced convent of Segovia, one of the nuns experienced a strange sensation, as if someone were sighing nearby. Her puzzlement was resolved the following day when Teresa appeared to her and said, telepathically, "Daughter, I have not died, I live in eternity."[66] Far to the south, in Granada, Teresa also suddenly appeared to Ana de Jesús, who was gravely ill. Enveloped in a bright light that made it difficult to see her face clearly, Teresa approached sister Ana, cured her, and promised to assist the Carmelite reform from heaven.[67] At Veas, in yet another apparition, Teresa revealed to a Discalced prioress that she had just died as a result of a too intense mystical experience.[68]

Ribera paused at this juncture in his narrative to interpret the significance of these phenomena. According to him, these marvels were to be expected during the deaths of great saints. For instance, Ribera continued, at the death of St. Gertrude, Jesus and Mary stood at her right hand, St. John at her left, along with "a throng of virgins," all dressed in white. "And thus I thought that this throng dressed in white must have been the many virgins who came to retrieve this virgin [Teresa] who was so pure and the mother of so many other virgins."[69]

Ribera interpreted these apparitions as confirmation of two truths: first, that Teresa must have been an especially favored saint because such wonders were common only among the greatest of saints; second,

---

[64] Casilda de San Angelo, PBC III.327–8. This vision began at the moment of Teresa's passing, on the feast of St. Francis, and lasted for some time, until the news of her death reached Valladolid.

[65] From Jerónimo Gracián's marginal notes to Ribera's *Vida*, edited by Carmelo de la Cruz, O.C.D., "Un manuscrito inédito del Padre Gracián, 'Scholias y adiciones al libro de la vida de la Madre Teresa de Jesús'," *El Monte Carmelo* 68 (1960): 99–156, pp. 121–2. Sections of Gracián's notes are included in FHM 201–17.

[66] Inés de Jesús, PBC I.425; Isabel de Santo Domingo, PBC II.97.

[67] Ana de Jesús, PBC I.476–7.

[68] The prioress was Catalina de Jesús (Ribera, p. 540). Ana de Jesús describes this apparition at some length. PBC I.479.

[69] Ribera, p. 342. Ribera was certain that these must have been the Ten Thousand virgin martyrs, because Teresa was intensely devoted to them, and earlier in life, she had had a vision in which they appeared to her and revealed that they would accompany her to heaven at the hour of her death.

that Teresa had not only lived a pure life as a virgin but had also earned the crown of martyrdom through her many sacrifices and thus deserved the reverence owed to martyr-virgins.[70] Yepes predictably agreed with Ribera but thought that these apparitions confirmed two additional truths: first, that a good life on earth would always be rewarded with entrance into heaven; second, that the souls of saints never crossed over alone into heaven but were joined by a great many of the blessed, as if in a triumphal procession.[71]

Although Yepes took it for granted that his readers would believe these extraordinary accounts, Ribera seemed more cautious about the possibility of skepticism among his readers, pausing briefly at this point to assure them that such wonders really took place and could be verified by many reliable witnesses. Ribera employed circular reasoning to prove his point. If one is a faithful Christian, he argued, then one must believe that certain revelations of God are true and that He must at some time intervene and communicate with humanity. What better time than at the death of saints, he asked. "What signs could be more credible than these, which we see at these times, when some great servant of God dies and He confirms their sanctity?" Such signs should be believed by virtue of their revelatory content alone. Furthermore, no one should ever suspect Satan to be behind any of these deathbed apparitions. The devil, Ribera said, would never want to promote devotion to the saints; the last thing Satan would want to do is to glorify their obedience to God.[72]

Suspecting that some of his readers might be inclined to scoff at such marvels, Ribera tried to mount an argument for the truth of their existence. His tautological reasoning, however, did not aim to disarm hardened skeptics. According to Ribera, the miraculous events surrounding Teresa's death were proven true by the fact that they conformed exactly to the patterns previously established by medieval Christian hagiography. In other words, he argued that belief in these miracles should rest on the affinity between Teresa's death and the standards promoted by medieval hagiographers. If one could find great ancient authorities, such as Pope Gregory I, who described deathbed miracles in the sixth century

---

[70] Ribera, p. 342.
[71] Yepes, p. 415. Another common motif in hagiography: Gregory the Great, *Dialogues* IV.11–16; Caesarius of Heisterbach, *Miracles* XI.5–10.
[72] Ribera, p. 342.

that were identical to those of Teresa a thousand years later, should not one believe that all said about Teresa was true and consequently that these miracles convincingly proved that she had been immediately received into heaven? Ribera drew a tight circle: "Whoever reads these chapters carefully, will thus see that St. Gregory did not arrive at his belief through any more reliable or trustworthy testimony than that which we have before us now, and which I am writing about." The many wonders associated with the deaths of saints, ancient as well as recent, proved for Ribera that there was a seamless, constant pattern in Christian salvation.[73]

Teresa's hasty burial

If Teresa's contemporaries believed that "as one lives, so one dies" (*como vive muere*), they certainly also believed that "as one dies, so is one buried" (*como muere entierran*). The extraordinary death of the saint required an extraordinary burial, and in this respect Teresa also conformed to tradition.

Sixteenth-century Spanish wills often contained a preamble in which testators offered up the soul to God, "who had created and redeemed it," and commended the body to the earth "from which it was formed." Although this divorce between soul and body at the moment of death could be expected for ordinary Christians, it was not considered appropriate for great saints whose bodies had already attained a high degree of purification. For these remarkable men and women there could be no total separation of body and soul at death. Like all mortals, they too would have to commend their body to the earth from which it had been formed, but unlike all other mortals, these saints did not have to expect the earth to take back what it had given. Their bodies had already been offered up to God and had already transcended the purely material realm. In brief, the flesh of great saints could become imperishable because, in the fulness of salvation, their bodies already enjoyed the

---

[73] Ribera, p. 343, cites some similar accounts from St. Gregory's *Dialogues* IV.11–16: Abba Spes (IV.11), St. Stephanus (IV.12), St. Probus (IV.13), St. Servulus (IV.15), and St. Romula (IV.16). Ribera also cites examples from other hagiographies (pp. 342–3), and argues that Teresa's miracles also conform to more recent models.

promise of the resurrection. Once more, Teresa conformed to hagiographic expectations.

According to all reports, Teresa's body began to transform itself immediately at the moment of death. "Her face became most beautiful," said Ribera, "and without a single wrinkle, in spite of the fact that she had many before her death; her body was also free of wrinkles and very white, like alabaster; her flesh became very soft, and as tractable as that of a two- or three-year-old child."[74] According to some eyewitnesses, Teresa's flesh also took on a glass-like radiance.[75] True to his circular reasoning, Ribera cited Bonaventure's *Life of Francis* to support his claim that this could happen to a saint. Because the flesh of Francis had undergone a similar transformation (whiteness, softness), this miracle confirmed Teresa's sanctity and her direct entrance into heaven. As in the case of Francis and other great saints, the body of Teresa now began to show signs of its promised resurrection: "Her complexion became very white, a sign of the glory it would enjoy." This whiteness and softness were interpreted as "manifest signs" of the saint's innocence and purity.[76]

In addition, Teresa's body began to exude a wonderful, indescribable odor that was so strong that the window to her room had to be opened to relieve the headaches it caused in some nuns.[77] This fragrance quickly permeated the entire convent and also began to waft from every single object that had come into contact with Teresa's body before her death, such as her clothes and bedlinens.[78] One nun, detecting a very strong

[74] Ribera, p. 339. See also Constancia de los Angeles, PBC I.105; and Maria de San Francisco, PBC III.219. Caroline Walker Bynum singles this out as a common motif in the hagiography of women saints, *Holy Feast and Holy Fast*, p. 211.

[75] Catalina de San Angelo described the flesh as "blanca . . . a manera de cristal." PBC III.205. Ana de San Bartolomé said: "Las manos parecía se podía mirar en ellas." PBC I.170.

[76] Ribera, p. 339. A sentiment also voiced by Teresa's niece, Teresa de Jesús, PBC I.196. For comparison with Francis see Bonaventure, "Major Life," Part I, ch. 15 (*Omnibus*, p. 743); also Thomas of Celano, "First Life," Book II, ch. 9 (*Omnibus*, p. 326).

[77] Catalina de San Angelo, PBC III.195. Isabel de la Cruz, PBC I.111, says that the door, too, had to be opened.

[78] The same phenomenon was later reported at the Discalced convent of Valladolid by Casilda de San Angelo, PBC III.327.

presence of this odor in the kitchen, began to look about for its source. Following her nose, literally, she found a little salt dish that Teresa had used, with the imprint of her fingers still visible on the salt. The potency of this aroma was overwhelming and irrepressible. When the nuns tried to clean the dishes used by Teresa, they discovered that the water itself picked up the smell, instead of washing it off. The same thing happened in the laundry, even to rags she had touched. One of the nuns who prepared her body for burial was later unable to wash away the perfume that clung to her hands. "One of the sisters carelessly began to wash up after she had finished dressing the corpse, when she detected a very strong fragrance rising up from her hands; yet, it was also so sweet she thought it must be from heaven, since she had never experienced anything like it here below."[79] This miraculous scent even had the power to unclog noses. Another nun who had completely lost her sense of smell and was distressed by her inability to enjoy this saintly fragrance was miraculously cured when she kissed Teresa's feet.

Ribera interpreted the fragrance as a sign from God, a means by which He revealed Teresa's holiness to others. Because the saint's life, and not just her death, had been holy, Ribera insisted that the odor of sanctity had been detectable even before her death. "It is a fact that she often exuded a marvelous fragrance . . . which was perceived by the sisters in the convent and also by outsiders."[80] Diego de Yepes confessed, with shame, that the wonderfully sweet fragrance that could be detected in Teresa's breath had once led him to suspect – unfairly – that she might have been indulging in candies.[81] Yepes interpreted the continued presence of this fragrance after Teresa's death as a marvelous juxtaposition of opposites and as a testimony of the redemptive power of God:

This is a great marvel, that a corpse (which in and of itself is no more than foulness, and the most nauseating thing in this life, ordinarily belching forth a

---

[79] Ribera, pp. 339–40. Yepes (p. 418) seemed to have no doubt about the origins of this odor: "verdaderamente era olor del cielo."

[80] Ribera, p. 340: One child blessed by her remarked to his mother "Ay, madre, como huelen las manos de aquella santa!" See also the testimony of Maria de Jesús, a Discalced nun of Toledo, PBC I.257.

[81] Yepes, p. 419: "Me vino sospecha si acaso tomaba algunas pastillas de alcorzas conficionadas con olores, que suelen llamar pastillas de boca."

powerful stench that pollutes the air in such a way as to cause plagues and other contagious diseases), should emit such an excessively pleasing scent.[82]

Four nuns prepared Teresa's body for burial, washing and dressing it in a fresh Discalced habit.[83] The crucifix Teresa had been clutching at the moment of death was still so firmly in her grip that it had to be pried loose with force.[84] The entire convent of Alba then held vigil over Teresa's body for thirteen hours, from nine on the night of 4 October until ten in the morning the following day, as their Rule demanded.[85] With mixed emotions, the nuns at Alba grieved over their loss and rejoiced over Teresa's certain entrance into heaven.[86]

Although Teresa's soul had entered heaven, her presence at Alba continued to be felt intensely by the nuns. Her body, which, as Ribera says, "had been for so long a temple of the Holy Spirit," now worked wonders. Miraculous cures began to take place as the sisters kissed her hands and feet repeatedly.[87] One nun who suffered from chronic headaches was immediately healed when she kissed the feet; another who had long endured a blinding pain in her eyes was quickly cured when she took the saint's hand and pressed it against her face; the sister of the Duchess of Alba, Doña Bernardina de Toledo y Enriquez, who had been ill with a fever for two months, suddenly recovered when she touched a garment of Teresa's.[88] Ana de San Bartolomé, who was placed in charge of dressing Teresa's body for burial, attributed a less dramatic but no less remarkable miracle to the saint. Since, by her own admission, she loved Teresa "more than it is possible to love someone," she was too griefstricken to carry out the necessary preparations. After asking for Teresa's help in this matter, she quickly regained her compo-

---

[82] Yepes, p. 419.

[83] Ana de San Bartolomé, *Autobiografía*, OCASB I.308; Maria de San Francisco, PBC III.219; Catalina de San Angelo, PBC III.194, III.208; Isabel de la Cruz, PBC I.111.

[84] Francisca de Jesús, PBC II.34.

[85] Constituciones, 8.2, OCST II.888: "Por las difuntas se hagan sus honras y enterramiento cada una con vigilia y Misa cantada."

[86] Ana de San Bartolomé, "Ultimos años," OCASB I.24–25: "Quedando todas con tanta tristeza y trabajo." Yepes, p. 420: "Fué grande el sentimiento que hicieron sus hijas, y toda la orden, como la que quedaba huérfana sin ella . . . sin embargo, que todos entendían la mucha razón que había para holgarse, entendiendo la gloria y felicidad que gozaba."

[87] Ribera, p. 340.   [88] Ribera, p. 340; Yepes, p. 421.

sure: "My will was strengthened so I could prepare her holy body, and I was able to do it, untroubled by her death."[89] Even the emotions, then, could be miraculously touched by Teresa immediately after her death.

Teresa's burial was solemn but hasty. At ten the following morning, a requiem mass began in the convent chapel, where Teresa's body would be buried. According to many eyewitnesses, nearly all the inhabitants of Alba thronged the chapel, eager to kiss the feet and habit of Teresa.[90] Aside from this veneration, Teresa received the same kind of funeral that any notable resident of Madrid might have requested in 1582, proving that, even for a saint, certain obsequies were required. In addition to all the secular clerics and civil officials of the town of Alba, many nobles were also in attendance, a number of whom had coincidentally arrived at Alba to celebrate the baptism of the duchess's grandson. Moreover, Teresa also did not lack the intercessory presence of Franciscan and Hieronymite friars and several confraternities. Although some would later accuse the duke and duchess of having buried Teresa with insufficient pomp, many eyewitnesses would deny the charge. Father Pedro Sanchez, a secular priest at the parish of San Andrés in Alba, recalled the funeral as follows:

This eyewitness saw Teresa de Jesús buried by the prioress and nuns of the convent of the Incarnation after her death . . . she was interred there with great pomp and veneration. Many of the leading citizens of Alba were in attendance, as were also the clergy and magistrates from that said place . . . and they offered up many masses, exequies, and sacrifices.[91]

Inés de Jesús, later prioress of the convent of the Incarnation at Alba, would testify that the chapel was sumptuously decorated and illuminated and that in addition to the requiem mass, a *novenario* and some anniver-

[89] Ana de San Bartolomé, *Autobiografía*, OCASB I.308.
[90] Yepes, p. 422: "Concurrió al entierro de la santa madre toda la gente de aquella villa, y hízose con toda la solemnidad que en aquel lugar se podía esperar, besándola sus santos pies y hábito toda la gente con mucha devoción, teniendose por dichoso el que podía llegar a tocar aquel cuerpo santo." Also Mariana de Jesús, PBC I.83; Constancia de los Angeles, PBC I.105–6; Catalina Bautista, PBC I.95; Francisca de Fonseca, PBC I.136–7.
[91] *Relaciones biográficas inéditas*, p. 206. See also the testimonies of Simón de Garza, p. 202; Diego Gonzalez, p. 210. Garza recalls seeing "mucha gente principal de condes y marqueses é otras gentes con la clerecía a la dicha villa y frailes Franciscos y Jerónimos y confradías." Also Mariana de la Encarnación, PBC I.90.

sary masses were also said for Teresa.[92] Elsewhere throughout Spain, as news of the death of Teresa arrived at other Carmelite convents, funeral effigies were erected and other masses were offered for her soul.[93]

The sisters at Alba knew they had a treasure in their midst and were eager to keep it there for years to come. Their lay benefactress and foundress, Teresa de Laiz, who herself planned to be buried there and undoubtedly relished the thought of being so close to a great saint in the afterlife, ordered that Teresa's body be buried in such a way as to make its exhumation difficult.[94] A deep grave was dug in the ground beneath a grille-covered archway that separated the nun's choir from the rest of the chapel, "so that those within the convent and those from outside could both enjoy her presence." Dressed in a Carmelite habit, its face covered by a black veil, the body of Teresa was moved from a brocade-covered bier into a simple wooden coffin and lowered into the grave. Finally, great quantities of stone, brick, soil, lime, and water were hurled on top of it and packed firmly to form a tight seal.[95] The immense weight of this load crushed the coffin and filled it with debris. Many would later conjecture that the foundress Teresa de Laiz had done this "because she thought this was the best way to protect the body and to make sure that no one would try to disturb it."[96] Although such pos-

---

[92] *Relaciones Biográficas Inéditas*, p. 162: "Y que el noveno de la Madre Teresa de Jesús lo hizo la Duquesa muy solemne y con mucha cera y se colgó la iglesia ricamente y en la sepultura se puso los paños de brocado é hizo fiesta cada año, hasta que el Prelado mandó que no se hiciese." The thirty Gregorian masses recommended for Carmelite funerals were apparently dispensed with. "Constituciones," 8.2, OCST, II, 888.

[93] Gracián, "Angela y Eliseo," FHM, p. 8, speaks of a *bulto* set up at Veas and of the masses he said for Teresa.

[94] E. Alison Peers, *Handbook to the Life and Times*, p. 186, says that Teresa de Laiz sometimes interfered "unduly" in the convent's affairs. St. Teresa's own account of this laywoman's role in the establishment of the Alba convent is in her *Libro de las Fundaciones*, chap. 20, OCST II.770–75. See also José de Lamano y Beneite, *Santa Teresa de Jesús en Alba de Tormes*, pp. 47–61, esp. p. 56 for a photograph of Teresa de Laiz's grave.

[95] Maria de San Francisco Baraona estimated that the grave was between five and six feet deep, PBC II.65. Ana de San Bartolomé testified that the workmen dumped two wagonloads of stone and lime into the grave, PBC I.170. Catalina Bautista said that "un paredón muy recio" was constructed over the coffin, PBC I.95. Similarly, Inés de Jesús complained that this seal over Teresa's remains was so large and sturdy that it could have served as the foundation for a building, PBC III.181.

[96] Ribera, p. 341. Yepes (p. 422) observes that the nuns buried Teresa quickly "porque

sessiveness might have seemed unbecoming of Discalced Carmelite nuns, Yepes considered it to be divinely inspired.

This was not their own idea, but rather God's, who guided them and made them do this . . . so He could honor His own by all possible ways and means, and thus prove how much He cares for them in life and in death, because this act helped to further ensure the preservation of her body.[97]

Fray Diego, it seems, could extract magnificence from any event connected with Teresa's death: Even this final humiliation served a divine purpose.

se recataban no les hurtasen el cuerpo para el monasterio de Avila." Also: Mariana de Jesús, PBC I.84; Maria de San Francisco Baraona, PBC II.65.
[97] Yepes, p. 422.

3

~~~~~~

Imperishable flesh, incomparable wonder

What St. Augustine said about the death of his mother in the *Confessions* could also have been said of St. Teresa by her devotées: "She was neither unhappy in her death, nor altogether dead."[1] Teresa was believed to have died a blissful death and to have immediately gained heaven. Though she was no longer living and breathing on earth, she was by no means believed to have ceased caring for those she left behind. On the contrary, Teresa's entrance into heaven had simply made her a more powerful friend and ally. Moreover, it was also believed that her body was no more earthbound than her soul.

The saintly death in hagiography

In traditional Christian hagiography, sanctity is conclusively proven through miracle. In fact, miracles *must* occur in order for anyone to be acclaimed as a saint, because nothing proves the saint's access to heaven more convincingly than a supernatural intervention in human affairs.[2] All the literature published about Teresa into the eighteenth century and most of that published to this day assumes that Teresa's sanctity was immediately confirmed by miracles. Ribera relied once again on St. Gregory the Great to prove this point:

[1] St. Augustine of Hippo, *Confessions*, 9.12.29: "At illa nec misere moriebatur nec omnino moriebatur." Migne, *Patrologia Latina* (Paris, 1878–90), vol. 27. p. 150.

[2] Weinstein and Bell, *Saints and Society*, pp. 142–3, have indicated that the cult of the saints rests squarely on "evidence" of supernatural power in the lives of holy people.

St. Gregory says that just as the life of the soul is revealed through the movement of one's limbs, while it is still in the body, so is the life of the soul revealed through the virtue of miracles, once it is released from the body.[3]

Ribera had a firm didactic purpose in mind when he wrote this hagiography: He hoped his readers would seek to imitate Teresa's virtues. He considered these miracle stories to be a crucial part of Teresa's story, because they proved that the saint's life was genuinely holy, but he did not think that they deserved center stage. As Ribera put it: "Miracles cannot be imitated, but virtues can." For him, what mattered most was the moral transformation of his readers. Those who sought to imitate Teresa, especially within her Carmelite order, could be assured a place in heaven: "We too can attain the glory enjoyed by the saints in heaven if we imitate them perfectly here below."[4]

The significance of this point cannot be overstressed. By underscoring the necessity of mimetic behavior, Ribera was driving home one of the central points of the Catholic Reformation and of the Baroque era that was then unfolding. Spontaneous behavior was antithetical to the spirit of Tridentine and Baroque Catholicism. In spite of its exuberant aesthetics and its exaggerated sense of pomp and circumstance, this was an age that sought to rigidly conform all gestures to established norms, especially in piety. The Tridentine reform planned to educate through example, offering ideal archetypes as models and conformity as a goal. Only those who conformed could hope to see God. Small wonder, then, that the seventeenth century becomes the golden age of "mirror" literature, with mirrors for every member of society from the monarch to the priest and the housewife.

As one Spanish scholar has observed, a distinctive trait of this age was the way in which it sought to depersonalize death and to make each individual death correspond to preconceived patterns.[5] No wonder, then, that Teresa's death and her miracles were so important to Ribera. Though few might be able to imitate Teresa fully, especially in her death and afterlife, her shining example was held aloft by Ribera as a means of enticing others at least to make the effort to fit the proper mold. Teresa's

---

[3] Ribera, p. 526; Gregory the Great, *Dialogues*, IV.6.2.

[4] Ribera, p. 526. Gracián drove home the same lesson, "Dialogos," FHM, p. 72.

[5] José Luis Sanchez Lora, *Mujeres, conventos y formas de la religiosidad barroca* (Madrid, 1988), pp. 371–2.

miracles, in addition, could help prove better than any other argument the ability of her particular pattern to ensure success in the pursuit of heaven.

Testimonies of heavenly power

Numerous wonders began to be reported immediately after Teresa's burial, not only at Alba, where she was buried, but almost anywhere that one could find Discalced Carmelites. At Alba, Teresa continued to exert a forceful presence. For some time, whenever any of the sisters fell asleep at prayer in the chapel, she would be woken up by a noise emanating from Teresa's grave. The sweet fragrance never disappeared either and even grew stronger on the feast days of Teresa's favorite saints.[6] The scent was unmistakable, yet changeable, smelling sometimes like lillies, at others like jasmine, or violets, or other flowers. Often, it could not be compared to anything else.[7]

As the weeks and months passed and the miracles continued, the sisters at Alba grew increasingly impatient, even uncomfortable, with the concealment of Teresa's body. In part, the sisters felt some slight remorse over the untidy manner in which their mother had been buried.[8] In part, also, the sisters continued to be dazzled by Teresa's miracles, especially the loud knocking they occasionally heard emanating from her grave. Yepes commented that "it was as if the holy body [of Teresa] could not refrain from showing some signs of the miracle enclosed at that spot by God." Nonetheless, he concluded, it was the sweet fragrance, more than anything else, which made them eager to open Teresa's grave.[9]

---

[6] Ribera (p. 452) lists over thirty feast days favored by Teresa, not counting those dedicated to Carmelite saints. Some relics of Teresa in Segovia also reportedly became more fragrant on certain feast days (Maria de la Concepción, PBC I.452).

[7] Maria de San Angelo, PBC I.54; Miguel de Carranza, PBC II.139.

[8] Yepes (p. 429): "Parece que las religiosas se reprehendían no haber puesto desde el principio aquel santo cuerpo con la veneración y reverencia debida a tan esclarecida santa." A priest from Alba, Pablo Gonzalez, later confessed he felt great sorrow over the method of burial, PBC III.242. Teresa's own family would protest that the body was not decently buried: Gomez Centurión, *Relaciones biográficas inéditas*, p. 40.

[9] Yepes, p. 430. This is confirmed numerous times in the testimonies of the nuns at Alba, PBC I.80–120; III.167–239, passim.

The curiosity of the nuns at Alba intensified as these prodigies continued: Was Teresa's body uncorrupted, even after nine months in the grave? The fragrance led the sisters to suspect it probably remained intact. Visitors from the outside also detected this special fragrance and wondered about the condition of Teresa's body. Nonetheless, no one could be certain unless the grave was opened. Ana de San Bartolomé would later admit some doubt, not only in herself but also in the convents at Alba and Avila, "where they feared . . . uncovering her holy body . . . not knowing in what condition it might be." Sister Ana's doubts were resolved while she slept, in a dream in which angels carried her to Teresa's grave and showed her Teresa's uncorrupted body, but the curiosity of those other nuns who had not been so singularly gifted could be resolved only during the waking hours, with picks and shovels.[10]

Finally, after nine months had elapsed, the sisters at Alba seized their opportunity when their provincial, Father Jerónimo Gracián, came to visit, and they prevailed upon him to inspect Teresa's corpse. Father Gracián, who had formerly served as Teresa's confessor, seemed as eager as the sisters to look inside the grave. Helped by another male Carmelite with whom he was traveling, and also by the nuns, who did as much as they could, Gracián set about the arduous task of digging.[11] The job was made more difficult by two special circumstances. First, the stones over the coffin formed a great *paredón*, or bulwark, against gravediggers. Second, the work had to be carried out as stealthily as possible, so that the duke and his family, who had already begun to think of Teresa's body as "the best jewel in their estate," would not be upset by the exhumation.

The deeper they dug, the stronger the fragrance became.[12] After four days of strenuous labor, in which they dislodged many fragrant stones, Father Gracián and his assistant finally reached Teresa's coffin on 4 July 1583, exactly nine months since the saint's death.

At first sight, the coffin seemed to offer little hope. The top had been

---

[10] Ana de San Bartolomé, *Autobiografía*, OCASB I.310.

[11] Mariana de Jesús, who claimed to have helped with the digging, left a detailed account of the event, PBC I.84. Curiously enough, Gracián reveals no unique details about this event. See "Dialogos," FHM, pp. 73 ff.; "Historia," FHM, pp. 196–8.

[12] Yepes, p. 430.

smashed in, and the rotting, moss-covered wood suggested an advanced state of decay. But as soon as the cover was lifted, a great wonder was revealed: Although Teresa's habit had begun to molder and her skin was badly soiled and partially encrusted with soil and moss, the saint's appearance remained unchanged from the day of her burial.[13] The sisters then undressed and washed Teresa's uncorrupted corpse, scraping off some of the dirt with knives,[14] "and the strongest and most marvelous fragrance wafted through the entire house, and remained present for many days later."[15] According to one witness, this scent overwhelmed those who got close to the body and seemed powerful enough to "set their brains on fire."[16] Gracián found it overpowering and said "it could barely be tolerated" and that breathing it involved "risking damage to one's head."[17]

This sweet aroma adhered to anything that had come in contact with Teresa's body, even indirectly. For instance, many eyewitnesses reported that the stones from her grave gave off so strong a scent that it was even imparted to the straw on which the stones rested. When this straw was used to stuff a mattress, the room itself filled with Teresa's fragrance. The soil from Teresa's grave also gave off a very strong scent and was apparently gathered and distributed by the nuns. Ribera himself attests that he received some of it and that "it had a most wonderful odor, which no one was able to compare with any other scent."[18] This otherworldly aroma was also detected in a miraculous oil that oozed not only from Teresa's body but also from anything that had come in contact with it.[19]

---

[13] Yepes (p. 431) described it thus: "Estaba sin que le faltase un cabello todo entero, como si entonces le acabaran de enterrar."

[14] Diego de Yepes, PBC I.285. In his *Life* of Teresa, Yepes (p. 431) adds that the habit had to be pried off carefully with knives as well. This was not done in disregard of the prohibition of ritual corpse washing, which applied only to the newly dead. In Teresa's case the cleaning was obviously necessary. On this subject, see M. del Arbol Navarro, *Spanisches funeralbrauchtum*, p. 57.

[15] Ribera, p. 528.

[16] Domingo Bañez, O.P., former confessor of St. Teresa, and professor of theology at the University of Salamanca, PBC I.11. Teresita, niece of St. Teresa, later testified (PBC I.197) that this odor was so strong, "que a veces no había fuerza para estar allí." She also observed that the odor was most intense on hot days.

[17] Gracián, "Dialogos," FHM, p. 74. [18] Ribera, p. 528.

[19] Yepes (p. 432) reported seeing and smelling this miraculous oil more than twenty

Father Gracián and the sisters marveled at all this but seemed most intensely affected by the uncorrupted state of Teresa's corpse. "They all fell to their knees," said Yepes, "and, shedding many tears, they revered the body with great devotion, all the time praising Our Lord, who is so wondrous in all His works."[20] For Ribera, this miracle attested to Teresa's purity, and he associated this absence of corruption with Teresa's virginity:

As Our Lord protected her entirely from all impurity during her life, granting her the most perfect virginity, so did He also guard her against all corruption after her death, and He did not allow the worms to touch that flesh which had not been stained by immodesty.[21]

It seemed clear to Ribera, then, that virginity materially effected the purification of Teresa's flesh not just in life but also in the afterlife.[22] This was also the explanation favored in the beatification sermons.[23]

Fray Diego de Yepes drew a similar lesson from this incorruption and thought it all the more marvelous given that natural circumstances seemed to work against it:

It is no small marvel to see this in a corpse that was buried whole, with its entrails, especially in the case of a female (and even more so in the case of this saint, who was stout and corpulent), because they are more susceptible to corruption due to their greater moisture.[24]

At the same time, Yepes also seemed to think that it was only natural that this virgin's incorruptible flesh should smell so good: Flesh that had

years after Teresa's burial, at Zaragoza, where it oozed from a belt once worn by her corpse. Also see Ana de la Encarnación, PBC I.23–4; Maria de San José, PBC I.325; Luisa de Reynaltes, PBC I.410; and Inés de Jesús, PBC I.426.

[20] Yepes, p. 431. One nun who claimed to have embraced Teresa's body for a long while ("un gran rato") described it as "tratable y ligero, como si no fuera de carne y hueso . . . y con muy bien color y olor." Juana del Espíritu Santo, PBC I.102.

[21] Ribera, p. 528.

[22] On the significance of virginity and chastity in the cult of the saints, see Weinstein and Bell, *Saints and Society*, chap. 3; and Peter Brown, *The Body and Society: Men, Women, and Sexual Renunciation in Early Christianity* (New York, 1988).

[23] For instance, Gerónymo de Tiedra, O.P., royal preacher, at Discalced Carmelite Fathers of Madrid, *Sermones*, fol. 5v; and Juan de Arauz, O.S.F., at Alba, fol. 161v, who argued that virginity "spiritualized" the body.

[24] Yepes, p. 431. Similar observations were made by the physician Luis Vazquez, PBC I.233–4.

avoided sexual experiences should somehow escape corruption and indicate its exalted status. Fray Diego intentionally juxtaposed the most vivid bridal imagery with his tribute to Teresa's virginal purity: "It was only fitting that she who had run with such great swiftness after the fragrance of her Spouse's ointments, and on whom so much of this fragrance had rubbed off, should not lose it after her death."[25]

The paradox of Teresa's remains

Because Teresa's uncorrupted body was a hierophany, a manifestation of divine power, it quickly became the fulcrum of paradox.[26] Though it continued to remain very much as it once had been, it obviously had become *something else*; though it still occupied a limited physical space, its presence was desired everywhere; though its integrity was its preeminent distinction, its mutilation and dispersal became most desirable.

A splendid treasure such as Teresa's body could not for long remain intact or localized, especially in a place as remote as Alba de Tormes. Because her incorruption proved beyond a doubt that she was now in heaven, Teresa now belonged to the whole world. Many of Teresa's companions and admirers concluded that her presence would be more keenly felt through its diffusion.[27] Ironically, then, the very same purity that ensured the preservation of Teresa's flesh also prompted a very different kind of disintegration. Little by little, the saint would be carved up, and pieces of her would be distributed throughout the globe. Nature had seemed unable to efface her presence on earth, but Teresa's devotées almost succeeded where nature had failed.

[25] Yepes, p. 431. Caroline Walker Bynum contends that the "closure" of women's bodies through fasting and celibacy is a necessary condition for exuding corpses. She also conjectures that women saints account for the majority of cases of bodies that exuded sweet odors or looked young and beautiful at death. *Holy Feast and Holy Fast*, pp. 145, 211. The phenomenon of exuding women becomes central to Bynum's thesis (pp. 274–5): the goal of feminine asceticism through "closure," which leads to exuding, was the imitation of Christ, especially as present in the eucharist.

[26] As Mircea Eliade has written: "It is impossible to overemphasize the paradox represented by every hierophany, even the most elementary." *The Sacred and the Profane*, p. 12.

[27] Peter Brown (*The Cult of the Saints*, p. 86) has singled out "particularity" as a distinguishing feature of Christian devotion to the saints. "*Hic locus est. . . .* The holy was available in one place, and in each such place it was accessible to one group in a manner in which it could not be accessible to anyone situated elsewhere."

This was nothing new, of course. Since early Christian times, the faithful had sought the physical presence of the saints through the dispersal of small fragments from their bodies. Peter Brown has eloquently described this process as the summation of the "imaginative dialectic" that gave rise to the cult of the saints.[28] Throughout the Middle Ages, belief in the full sacred power of even the smallest of relic fragments continued unabated and perhaps also intensified. Some have argued that by the end of the medieval era, this belief had led to a frenzied cutting up – a *découpage millimetrique* – of saints' bodies.[29] What is remarkable about Teresa's case is *not* that it is novel or unusual but that it is so much a part of this long tradition at a time when it had already been rejected elsewhere in Europe.

Parceling out Teresa

The gradual dismemberment of the saint's body began at this first exhumation, when Father Gracián cut off her left hand and the little finger from the right hand. Gracián kept the finger for himself and carried it with him for the rest of his life.[30] The left hand he ostensibly cut off so he could return at least some part of Teresa to her own house, the convent of St. Joseph of Avila, where the nuns had been clamoring for the return of their Mother's body. To the nuns at Alba, this might have seemed a conciliatory gesture toward their sisters in Avila, but Father Gracián's intentions were not so simple, as his actions would later reveal. Because he was planning to return the entire body to Avila at some future date and feared that the ducal family of Alba would block

---

[28] Ibid., p. 78. Brown's "imaginative dialectic" and Eliade's inescapable "paradox" are very similar: Both assume there is something inherently complex and enigmatic in religious experience because it seeks to reconcile extremes. "How better to suppress the fact of death," says Brown, "than to remove part of the dead from its original context in the all too cluttered grave? How better to symbolize the abolition of time in such dead, than to add to that an indeterminacy of space? Furthermore, how better to express the paradox of the linking of Heaven and Earth than by an effect of 'inverted magnitudes', by which the object around which boundless associations clustered should be tiny and compact?"

[29] Jacques Toussaert, *Le sentiment religieux en Flandre à le fin du Moyen Age* (Paris, 1963), p. 291.

[30] Gracián's marginal notes on Ribera's *Vida*, FHM 209, note "f"; also available in *El Monte Carmelo*, 68 (1960): 99–156. See also Ana de San Bartolomé, PBC I.171.

any such effort, Father Gracián chose to dissemble, shrouding his own actions in secrecy. Although he took the hand directly to St. Joseph's in Avila, he presented this gift to the nuns in a sealed coffer, refused to reveal its contents, and ordered that it not be opened. The sisters at Avila suspected that the coffer could contain some relic from their beloved Mother, but they could not confirm it without breaking their vow of obedience.[31] The dismemberment thus remained a secret, and Father Gracián ensured some degree of victory for Avila. If Avila won the dispute, then the entire body would be reunited in one location; if Alba won, then the sisters at St. Joseph's would at least have part of Teresa.[32]

After Father Gracián had cut off Teresa's left hand, the body was dressed in a fresh Carmelite habit, wrapped in a winding sheet, placed in a new coffin, and reburied in the same location. To facilitate future exhumations – and the planned translation of the body to Avila – the grave was not packed tightly.[33] Gracián dissembled further: To allay the suspicion of the Duke of Alba, great care was taken to make it look as if the grave had not been disturbed.[34] The sisters at Alba were overjoyed at their good fortune and displayed their gratitude by offering constant devotion to Teresa's miraculous presence. Their gladness would not last undisturbed for long, however. Others who coveted this prize and had even anticipated its value before the saint's death, would do their best to take it away from them.

The miracle at Alba remained hidden from the public at large, but it could not easily remain a secret within the Carmelite order. Almost

---

[31] According to Yepes, p. 433, Teresa herself circumvented this order by appearing to the prioress and revealing what was in the box: "Tengan cuenta con aquel cofrecito," she said, "que en el está una mano de mi cuerpo."

[32] Yepes, p. 433. Some time later, when it seemed Avila would win its case, Father Gracián would take this hand to the new Carmelite convent in Lisbon. Ribera (p. 528) incorrectly reports that Gracián took the hand directly to Lisbon.

[33] Catalina Bautista, PBC I.95.

[34] Yepes (p. 433) again focuses attention on Gracián's attempts at deception: "La pusieron . . . con la mayor decencia que pudieron, pero cubierta y secreta, de suerte que pareciese que no se había llegado a el, teniendo consideración el padre provincial a que, si los duques de Alba entendían aquella nueva maravilla, no habían de dar lugar a sus intentos, que eran llevar el cuerpo a Avila, como el lo tenía prometido al obispo don Alvaro de Mendoza."

exactly three years after the death of Teresa, on 18 October 1585, Father Gracián succeeded in his plan to have Teresa's body moved to Avila. On that day, a general chapter of the Discalced Carmelite Fathers meeting at Pastrana ordered that the holy remains be quietly removed from Alba and returned to Teresa's convent of St. Joseph at Avila. This decision was prompted in part by the Bishop of Palencia, Don Alvaro de Mendoza, who had formerly served as Bishop of Avila and had recognized the value of Teresa's reforming work when many others still opposed it.[35] Bishop Alvaro de Mendoza had a legitimate claim. He had earlier reached an agreement with the Carmelites concerning funerary arrangements for himself and Teresa and had donated a considerable sum of money for the construction of the chapel at St. Joseph's. This bequest stipulated that the chapel must be constructed with two centrally located tombs in the chapel, one for Teresa, to whom he was very devoted, and the other for himself.[36] As Ribera wryly observed, "He [the bishop] was so devoted to her that he did not want, even in death, to be far from her."[37] Because Don Alvaro was well acquainted with Teresa and knew of her constant travels, he had been careful enough in 1577 to obtain a signed pledge from Jerónimo Gracián, then Carmelite provincial, ordering that if Teresa were to die somewhere else, her body should be brought back to Avila for burial.[38]

At seven-thirty in the evening of 18 October 1585, then, this Carmelite chapter signed a patent letter, ordering the sisters at Alba to surrender the body of Teresa to Fray Gregorio Nacienceno, Provincial Vicar of Old Castile.[39] At that same moment, Ribera reports, the recreational hour of the sisters at Alba was interrupted by three loud knocking noises coming from the chapel. It did not take long for the nuns to discern, after three additional knocks, that the sounds emanated from Teresa's grave. Although they did not know how to interpret this marvel at the time, they soon found out from Fray Gregorio himself, when he came to claim their precious relic, that the letter enabling him to bring

---

[35] Julián de Avila, *Vida*, p. 216. For more details on the bishop's role in Teresa's reform see Jodi Bilinkoff, *The Avila of St. Teresa: Religious Reform in a Sixteenth Century City* (Ithaca/London, 1989), pp. 147–50.

[36] Correspondence to and from Bishop Alvaro de Mendoza related to these arrangements is included in FHM, pp. 219–43.

[37] Ribera, p. 528.   [38] This document can be read in FHM, pp. 245–6.

[39] Letter of Juan Carrillo, FHM, p. 232; this decree itself is in FHM, pp. 246–7.

them such sorrow had been signed just as the noises were being heard. Teresa, it seems, could not help but alert her sisters to such a momentous decision, or perhaps, as Yepes thought, even bid them farewell.[40]

Fray Gregorio Nacienceno planned and executed a stealthy raid on Alba with all the cunning of a character in a picaresque novel. After procuring a wagon and casket, secretly renting rooms across the street from the Alba convent, and finding out when the ducal family would be away from town, Gregorio Nacienceno and Jerónimo Gracián showed up at Alba, much to the nuns' surprise, on 24 November 1585, "with great circumspection and secrecy."[41] After attending to some business matters related to the convent, Fathers Gregorio and Jerónimo suddenly announced they would like to see Teresa's body, making no mention of the fact that what they intended to do was to take it away. Dissembling, they said, "Let us open the casket and see how the body of our Mother looks."[42] To lessen the chance of resistance and to divert attention from what was about to happen, they ordered all the sisters, save the prioress and two or three of the oldest ones, to go upstairs to pray.[43] When Father Gregorio and his assistants exhumed Teresa's body, they discovered that Teresa's appearance had remained largely unchanged after three years in the grave.

Stealthily and quickly they removed the body, which was as whole as when it was first buried, and exuded the same fragrance as before, even though it was a bit leaner and its garments had almost rotted away.[44]

The shroud in which her body had been wrapped was totally soaked with the substance that seeped from her body, "as if it had been dipped in oil."[45] The coffin, too, was smeared with oil.[46]

---

[40] Ribera, p. 529, Yepes, p. 435. Also: Juan Carillo, PBC I.389; Ines de Jesús, PBC III.183–4.

[41] Letter of Gregorio Nacienceno, FHM, pp. 234–5; letter of Juan Carrillo, an assistant of Bishop Alvaro de Mendoza, who participated in this raid on Alba, FHM, p. 235. Gracián's own account is skimpy on details, "Historia," FHM pp. 198 ff.

[42] Testimony of Juan de Errie, servant to the Duke of Alba, FHM, pp. 252–3.

[43] Juan Carrillo, FHM, p. 236, says the nuns were sent upstairs *after* they had viewed the body. Other accounts differ – for example, Maria de San Francisco, PBC III.220.

[44] Ribera, p. 529.

[45] Yepes, p. 436; Juan de Jesús Maria, PBC I.353.

[46] Many oil-soaked splinters from this coffin would be distributed as relics. Inés de Jesús, PBC III.182.

On closer inspection, another marvel was uncovered that might have been overlooked at the first exhumation.[47] When Teresa was first prepared for burial in 1582, her bleeding had not yet fully ceased. To stem the flow of blood, a cloth dressing had been applied and buried with her. Now, three years later, this dressing was still soaked in blood, "with a vivid color, as fresh as if it had flowed from her veins on that same day."[48] The fabric from this dressing not only exuded a wonderful fragrance and passed it on to whatever touched it but also transferred the blood to other cloths, turning them red.

I have seen a piece of this cloth, and I have also seen many other cloths that have been tinted in its color, without the aid of soaking or any other procedure, save simply by placing them together for a day; and it is a wondrous thing, to see how beautiful is the color of that blood.[49]

Only after night had fallen and the body had been exhumed and examined did the two Carmelite fathers reveal their true intent to the prioress, telling her they had come to take away the body.[50] To appease the sisters at Alba and to compensate them for the loss of their treasure, Father Gregorio had been ordered by his superiors to cut off Teresa's left arm and leave it with them. This was a great test for Father Gregorio. Later, he confessed to Ribera that "this was the greatest sacrifice he had ever offered up to Our Lord, in order to fulfill his vow of obedience."[51] As he reluctantly drove his knife into Teresa's shoulder joint, another miracle occurred:

It was marvelous. Using no more force than would be needed to cut a melon, or some soft cheese, so to speak, he instantly severed the arm at the shoulder joint.

---

[47] This is one of the very few discrepancies in the canonization testimonies. Though Mariana de Jesús and others at Alba claimed this was uncovered during the first exhumation (PBC I.84), other nuns agreed with the accounts of Yepes and Ribera, claiming it had been overlooked: Mariana de la Encarnación, PBC I.89; Catalina Bautista, PBC I.96; Ana de San Bartolomé, PBC I.171; Teresa de Jesús, PBC I.196; Ana de los Angeles, PBC I.186; Gracián, "Historia," FHM, p. 198.

[48] Yepes, p. 436; also Mariana de la Encarnación, PBC I.89.

[49] Ribera, p. 529; also Guiomar del Sacramento, PBC I.78.

[50] Juan Carrillo, FHM, p. 236, says the nuns were shaken by this surprise: "les causó infinita turbación y pena."

[51] Ribera, p. 529. Father Gregorio also conveyed this in person to Yepes (p. 436).

Though he had not spent a long time trying to do it, the arm was cleanly separated from the body.[52]

According to Yepes, "Her bones were white, and her flesh was soft, white, and red. The shoulder remained dense and solid, as if she had just died a few moments before."[53]

Although Teresa evidently did not object to this dismemberment, yielding her arm so easily, the nuns at Alba were less unselfish. As the miraculous fragrance wafted upstairs, to where the sisters were praying, they soon realized that they were about to lose "the most valuable jewel they possessed on earth."[54] Although they interrupted their prayer and rushed downstairs to bid farewell to their treasured Mother's body, it was too late. Father Gregorio had already hastily dressed the body in a fresh habit, wrapped it in a shroud, and dashed with it directly across the street from the convent's *portería*, to a room he had rented specifically for this purpose, where the cloistered nuns could not follow.[55] "So they became immensely sad, having now retained only the arm and a piece of the bloody cloth."[56]

According to a request made by Don Alvaro de Mendoza, who apparently wanted to ensure the protection of Teresa's body on its way to his burial chapel in Avila, Father Gregorio was joined and accompanied by Father Julián de Avila, former confessor of Teresa, and Don Juan Carillo, a cathedral canon and secretary to Bishop de Mendoza. The body was again quickly inspected in Father Gregorio's room before it was taken, under cover of night, to another inn a bit farther from the convent, where Julián de Avila and Juan Carrillo were staying. After spending a night with Teresa's body in their room, Carillo and Julián de Avila

---

[52] Ribera, pp. 529–30. Mariana de San Angelo said it seemed as easy as slicing a loaf of bread, PBC I.55.

[53] Yepes, pp. 436–7. Domingo Bañez, O. P., who saw the body the next day in Avila, claimed the wound looked fresh, "como podia estar el de una persona que de repente le hubieran cortado el brazo." PBC I.11.

[54] Yepes, p. 437. A sense of panic is conveyed in the testimonies of the Alba nuns: PBC I.80–120; III.167–239, passim.

[55] Juan Carrillo, FHM, pp. 236–37.

[56] Ribera, p. 530. Inés de Jesús later confessed that she wept over this and that all the nuns remained "muy solas y desconsoladas en tal ocasión." PBC III.184.

teamed up with Fathers Jerónimo and Gregorio very early the next morning, when they all left for Avila. Carrillo would later testify that his room had filled with the saint's fragrance. He would also marvel at how the weather had suddenly turned very warm for that time of the year, as if Teresa were somehow responsible.[57]

The nuns of St. Joseph's welcomed the uncorrupted remains of their beloved former prioress with delight, as could be expected. The body was placed on a bier, "very decently," so that all the nuns could enjoy its presence. Eventually, it would be transferred to an ornate coffin decorated in silver and gold and lined with silk and velvet. In death, then, Teresa could enjoy the luxuries she had so carefully avoided in life.[58] Bishop Alvaro de Mendoza was not there in person to join the celebration; he was at Valladolid and quite ill at the time. His secretary Juan Carrillo wrote him an exultant letter in which he said, "God be praised for His having brought such a guest to your chapel, through whose intercession Your Holiness can be certain to be granted a full and perfected life to enjoy her presence here, and later to join her in heaven."[59]

In seeking the company of Teresa's body − a privilege that had been duly granted to him − Bishop Alvaro de Mendoza acted to protect his interests. He miscalculated on two accounts, however. First, he underestimated the power of the Duke of Alba and his family, who refused to relinquish the body without a fight. Second, he had acted in a way that seemed to violate the sacredness of Teresa's body, and this would weaken Avila's case against Alba. In the Christian cult of the saints, an ancient tradition placed great significance on the "translation," or reburial of holy bodies, as a ceremony that highlighted the saint's elevation to a higher status. It was a highly charged moment that required great preparation and much pomp and circumstance. Usually, a three-day fast would precede translations; nobles and other exalted figures, along with the populace, would be present during the ceremony.[60] Removed from

[57] Juan Carrillo, PBC I.388–9; FHM, pp. 236–7.
[58] Ribera, p. 530. In an apparition, Teresa herself defended her right to be buried "con más decencia." Gracián, "Dialogos," FHM, p. 149.
[59] Juan Carrillo, FHM, p. 238.
[60] R. C. Finucane, "Sacred Corpse," pp. 53, 60: "A saint's corpse represented his soul even more clearly in rites of translation. . . . The corpse moved to the holiest, highest position within the church, for the soul had 'arrived', moved near to the centre and highest source of all holiness."

her original grave unceremoniously in the dark of night, under secrecy, without adequate preparations, Teresa had suffered a violation of her sanctity. She may not have yet been canonized, but those involved *knew* they were dealing with a saint. When Alba sued Avila for possession of the body, the ignominious translation of November 1585 would weigh heavily in their favor.[61]

Profane contention over Teresa's sacred flesh

For three years, the miracle of Teresa's preservation had remained a well-kept secret. Now that the body had been moved, the news apparently traveled fast, even beyond the confines of the Carmelite community. Within the order, plans were drawn up for an official investigation. By late December 1585, even King Philip II had become involved.[62]

On New Year's eve, 1585, three envoys from the king arrived in Avila after a difficult journey from Madrid. This commission was headed by Fray Diego de Yepes, prior of the royal monastery of San Jerónimo in Madrid, confessor to King Philip, and biographer of St. Teresa.[63] Fray Diego was accompanied by Don Pablo de Laguna and Don Francisco de Contreras, both members of the Royal Council. With the cooperation of the Carmelite superiors and of the Bishop of Avila, Pedro Fernandez de Temiño, the royal emissaries assembled about eighteen civil and ecclesiastic authorities and two physicians.[64] On New Year's day, 1586, the bishop and these official examiners met at St. Joseph's. The ensuing scene resembled more a solemn liturgy than a clinical examination. Teresa's body was taken to the *portería*, reverently placed on a rug, and uncovered for inspection. Candles aloft, the bishop and the examiners approached; suddenly, every man dropped to his knees, uncovered his head, and gazed upon the body "with great admiration, and many tears." The two physicians then examined it "with great curiosity" and con-

---

[61] See the "Interrogatorio de preguntas . . . formulado en nombre del Duque de Alba," question 6, *Relaciones biográficas inéditas*, p. 188.

[62] Gracián, "Historia," FHM, p. 198; Yepes, p. 437.

[63] Yepes (p. 438) says of his own involvement: "En este mesmo tiempo, estando yo en Madrid, supe, aunque en secreto, el milagro, y con el mayor silencio y prisa que fué posible, partimos de Madrid."

[64] Ribera, p. 531; Ana de los Angeles, PBC I.185.

firmed that this could not be a natural phenomenon, and thus must be something truly miraculous.[65]

Later in the day, the two physicians submitted an official report to the bishop in which they outlined their reasons for declaring this phenomenon a miracle. The descriptions found in all the published and unpublished documents are not much different from that of Yepes:

The body had remained whole, without a hint of decomposition, and it gave off a very pleasant odor; the bones and sinews were still so taut that the body could be stood on its feet without much external support when it was taken out of the coffin. Her breasts were firm and fleshly, her abdomen remained as ample as when she expired. Her flesh was so tractable that it would dent and spring back when pressed with a finger; and even though she had been a corpulent woman, the body did not weigh more than that of a two-year-old child. It gave the appearance of being already clothed not only with incorruptibility and fragrance, but also with the agility of the resurrected bodies of the blessed.[66]

Ribera murmured that the medical report was superfluous: Common sense dictated to all that this could be nothing else but "the work of God's right hand." How could it be possible for any corpse not to undergo corruption, he asked rhetorically, especially one that had not been embalmed? "They were no less astonished to see the cloth stained with blood so fresh and fragrant."[67]

Convinced that the nuns of St. Joseph did indeed possess a miraculous treasure, the bishop cautioned them to treat the body most reverently and never again to use the rug upon which it had been placed. "You could not ask for anything better in this life," he unnecessarily reminded the sisters of St. Joseph. Wishing to keep news of this miracle secret a while longer, the bishop enjoined everyone from speaking about it, under pain of excommunication. But the miracle could not be hidden for long: The protest from the other members of the commission was so strong, that he soon relented. The city of Avila rejoiced as news of this wonder began to spread throughout Spain and even abroad.[68]

This jubilation, however, did not last for long. While the people and

---

[65] Ibid., p. 532.

[66] Yepes, p. 439; Domingo Bañez, PBC I.11; Ana de la Encarnación, PBC I.24; Guiomar del Sacramento, PBC I.77–8; Maria de San Jerónimo, PBC I.159; Luis Vazquez, PBC I.233–4.

[67] Ribera, p. 532.   [68] Ibid.

the authorities in Avila celebrated the city's good fortune, the Duke of Alba was furiously endeavoring to have the body returned to its original resting place. Don Antonio de Toledo, the duke, had been away in Navarre when Teresa's body was taken from Alba. Hurt by the loss of such treasure and angered by the stealthy way in which the Carmelites at Avila had carried it off, Don Antonio set out to prove that the honor of Teresa's presence rightfully belonged to him, his family, and the convent of Alba. Because very few other families in Spain could rival the power and influence wielded by the Dukes of Alba, Don Antonio was able to prevail over all the arguments that seemed to favor St. Joseph's, even the agreement reached between the Bishop of Avila and the Carmelite provincial before Teresa's death.[69] Letters and envoys were quickly sent to Rome. Before long, Pope Sixtus V intervened, ordering the immediate return of Teresa's body to Alba.[70]

The Carmelite provincial who received the pope's order, Fray Nicolás de Jesús Maria, promptly obeyed. Neither he nor the sisters at St. Joseph had any say in this matter, at least for the time being. On 23 August 1586 Teresa's body was once again exhumed and unceremoniously transported back to Alba.[71] Because he was already planning an appeal of this decision, the Carmelite provincial cautioned the sisters at Alba not to rejoice: As far as he was concerned, this was but a temporary move. Nonetheless, Teresa's body received a tumultuous welcome, not just from the sisters but also from everyone at Alba, including the duke and his wife, the Countess of Lerín.[72] When the body was exhibited in the chapel, behind the grille that separated the public and cloistered areas, a great crowd surged forward to catch a glimpse. Ribera himself had to wait patiently for his chance to kiss the saint's feet and complained that the laity (*los de fuera*) filled the church to overflowing, creating no small disturbance.

---

[69] On Don Antonio's immediate predecessor, who died the same year as St. Teresa and who was later reportedly found uncorrupted, see William Maltby, *Alba: A Biography of Fernando Alvarez de Toledo, Third Duke of Alba* (Berkeley CA, 1983), esp. p. 306.

[70] The pertinent documentation is reproduced in Gomez Centurión, *Relaciones biográficas inéditas*, pp. 240–86. Some of the more significant documents are also available in FHM, pp. 245–495.

[71] Yepes (p. 440) reports that even under these circumstances, Teresa's body called attention to itself through its fragrance, which was noticed by those along the road.

[72] Catalina de San Angelo, PBC III.209.

It was necessary to keep the body behind bars, because so many pressed to see it, with so much force and devotion, that if it had been outside, they would have torn the habit to shreds, in order to obtain relics, and the body itself would have been imperiled. The church remained so packed with visitors who had come to see that marvel, that no one could move. Those of us who were in front, nearer to the grille, were trapped there for a very long time, due to the fact that no one seemed to tire of looking at her.[73]

As the Carmelite superiors petitioned Rome for a reversal of the pope's decision, the townspeople at Alba took no risks. Fearing that the body might once again be carried off suddenly in the night, they stationed guards outside the convent and even attempted to make the nuns promise that they would never again obey any orders to surrender the body.[74]

The two Carmelite fathers who had obediently returned Teresa's body to Alba departed immediately, taking with them the relic of Teresa's habit, which they had once again changed before leaving. On their way back to Avila, they crossed paths at an inn with Father Ribera. The intensity with which the continued presence of Teresa could be felt is revealed in Ribera's account of his encounter with these two Carmelites. As could be expected, Ribera marveled at the fragrance exuded by the habit. Although the Carmelites had spent no more than forty-five minutes at the inn and had kept the habit wrapped in a large cloak, the scent of Teresa lingered long after they left.[75]

The nuns of St. Joseph's convent at Avila, aided by their superiors, continued to press for a reversal of the papal order but were never successful in overriding the influence of the Duke of Alba and his uncle, the prior of the order of San Juan. Despite their best efforts, Pope Sixtus V never ruled in their favor. At first, he relegated the matter to one of his nuncios, Cesar Speciano, the Bishop of Novara. In December 1588 Bishop Speciano ruled that the body of Teresa should forever remain at Alba. When this ruling was appealed, Pope Sixtus decided not to overturn his nuncio's decision. On 10 July 1589, nearly seven years after Teresa's death, Sixtus V formally decreed that Alba should be her final resting place.[76] By then, Bishop Alvaro de Mendoza had been dead and

---

[73] Ribera, p. 533; Inés de Jesús, PBC III.184–5; Catalina de San Angelo, PBC III.209.
[74] Ribera, p. 533.   [75] Ibid., p. 534.
[76] Gomez Centurión, *Relaciones biográficas inéditas*, pp. 284–6; FHM, pp. 490–5.

buried for three years, alone in the grave he had hoped would be next to Teresa's.[77] The nuns at St. Joseph's remained ever hopeful Teresa's body would be returned to them, and they kept the coffin on display. Ribera would later see the empty coffin and remark that "although the body was no longer present, the fragrance still remained."[78]

While Avila mourned, Alba rejoiced. The nuns of Alba claimed that God had clearly indicated his preference in this case. A month before the body was returned to Alba, one of the nuns had seen some bright lights in the choir. One seemed like a very bright star, over the very same spot where Teresa's body finally came to rest. "It was so bright that, in comparison, the other stars seemed to give off no light at all."[79] A new sumptuous tomb was constructed for Teresa by the ducal family of Alba. Many other notables began to donate decorative items for this shrine, which quickly became a pilgrimage center. Even before her official canonization, Teresa was sought out by all classes of people as an intercessor through whom miracles could be obtained. The intensity of this devotion was itself a reason for her canonization, but it proved to be something of a burden on the nuns at Alba, who sometimes felt besieged by pilgrims.[80]

In spite of the triumph of Alba in this dispute, the sisters at St. Joseph's in Avila continued to claim that God was on their side. Ana de San Bartolomé, who remained troubled by Teresa's burial place until the end of her own life, even while residing in far-off Paris and Flanders, claimed numerous visions and apparitions in which she had been assured that Avila had the proper claim and that Teresa would eventually return to St. Joseph's.[81] One of the most dramatic of these visions occurred while the body was still in Avila, and no news had yet been heard about the pope's decision to return it to Alba. Sister Ana says she asked God about the pope's verdict and heard him respond, "Sentence has already been passed against justice; but do not grieve. Let them have their own way for now, I will have mine in due time."[82] Sister

---

[77] FHM, p. 243, n. 1.   [78] Ribera, p. 530.   [79] Ribera, p. 535.

[80] Inés de Jesús confessed that the Alba nuns were "molestadas" by the pilgrims, PBC III.188. She also provides a good description of the shrine and of a list of the gifts received, PBC III.189–90, as does Catalina de San Angelo, PBC III.212. See also the account of Mariana de Jesús, PBC I.85.

[81] Ana de San Bartolomé, PBC I.171–2.

[82] Ibid., *Autobiografía*, OCASB I.325. See also OCASB I.310.

Ana waited impatiently for God's promises to come true, but Teresa's body remained at Alba. Though puzzled, she continued to hope, as no doubt did the sisters at Avila: "The Lord must not want it to happen during my lifetime. . . . I continue always to have hope. . . . If it was indeed His Majesty who spoke to me, His promise will come true, even if it is too late for me."[83]

Others who wanted to see Teresa buried at Avila came to terms with reality more quickly than did Sister Ana. Isabel de Santo Domingo, who was confused and upset by this dispute, prayed for guidance. In a vision, Teresa appeared to her, touched her face, and said: "Do not be so foolish. Do you think it makes any difference whether I am at Alba or Avila?"[84]

On the one hand, the acrimonious dispute over Teresa's body reveals how, in one significant respect, saints were not much different from other Christians. In sixteenth-century Spain, the location of an individual's burial could on occasion be disputed within the family. Teresa's case was no exception. In death as well as in life, saints were never fully exempted from the harsh social realities of a fractious world. On the other hand, however, this controversy discloses how different the death of a saint could be from the death of the average Christian. Burials were very much a family concern, but the graves of holy men and women were never strictly the property of the immediate family – even a family as large as a religious order. Access to the grave could remain in the order's hands, but the grave itself usually became a public, universal asset of the church. Saints were too special to leave in the hands of a few close "relatives."[85] Consequently, conflict could arise between the kin and the community at large, as well as between rival systems of patronage, with each party seeking to manipulate the sacred corpse for their own ends.[86] The tug of war in Teresa's case was especially intense. On one level, the interests of individual convents were pitted against each other, and

---

[83] Ana de San Bartolomé, *Autobiografía*, OCASB I.326.

[84] Isabel de Santo Domingo, PBC II.100.

[85] Brown, *Cult of the Saints*, p. 73, speaks of an "uneasy dialectic" between the graves of saints and the graves of others: "The difference between their graves and the thousands of ordinary graves that surrounded them could seem as irremovable as the ancient fault between the earth and the untouchable glow of the Milky Way."

[86] R. C. Finucane, "Sacred Corpse," p. 58; Brown, *Cult of the Saints*, p. 24.

against the Carmelite order as a whole. On another level, the patronage of the secular clergy, represented by Bishop Alvaro de Mendoza, was pitted against that of rich and powerful laypeople, the ducal family of Alba and the foundress Teresa de Laiz. At the center of the fury lay Teresa's imperishable flesh.

4

~~~~~~

Earthbound no longer

But the Lord had not worked such wonders so they could remain hidden and unknown; he had accomplished them in order to demonstrate and increase His glory, and that of His servant.[1]

The miracle of Teresa's corpse

In an age marked by the Protestant rejection of the cult of the saints, Teresa's uncorrupted body was assigned great value, not only as a nexus between heaven and earth but also as a heuristic device, a palpable confirmation of the truth of Catholic teachings. Much of what was said or written about the death of Teresa focused attention on this marvel, highlighting even the most minute details, as if description alone were the most convincing argument. Such an attitude toward the miraculous and its role in the afterlife demands that we, too, linger over the body.

Diego de Yepes identified four separate miracles in the marvel of Teresa's body: (1) its incorruption; (2) its fragrance; (3) its ability to exude blood and oil; (4) its weightlessness.[2] Because the sources themselves also isolate each of these phenomena to some extent, Yepes's taxonomy suggests a way of structuring our own approach to the miracle accounts.

[1] Diego de Yepes, p. 438.   [2] Ibid., PBC I.285.

Incorruption

The most significant marvel, according to all who viewed Teresa's body, was the fact that its flesh showed no signs of decomposition.[3] Even under the worst conditions, such as extreme heat, it never stank or showed the slightest blemish. On the contrary, the more adverse the circumstances, the more incorruptible the flesh appeared.[4] It was an otherworldly marvel. "This flesh will not submit to decomposition, in any natural way," Ribera said, "it seems stronger than steel."[5]

Ribera's attitude toward Teresa's remains was one of extreme affection, not disgust or morbid fascination. He had seen Teresa's body twice.[6] The first time, in August 1586, on the day when the body was returned to Alba, the crowd prevented him from getting a good look. The second time, in March 1588, he studied it carefully as part of his research for Teresa's biography. This viewing made a tremendous impression on him: "It was such a great delight to behold this hidden treasure, that, to my mind, I cannot remember ever having a better day in my entire life. I never tired of looking at it."[7]

When Ribera viewed the body in 1588, it was displayed upright, "though it leaned forward slightly, the same way an old person would walk." Teresa's complexion had browned and taken on the color of dates, but not uniformly. The face was darkest, as a result of the soil that had fallen on it when the first casket broke.[8] The skin resembled dried beef (*cecina*) and was slightly wrinkled, "as in someone who has lost

---

[3] Report of Dr. Martín Arias, PBC I.144–5, who reiterates that this was a greater miracle in the case of a woman, because women are more "humid" and prone to corruption.

[4] Teresa de Jesús (Teresita), PBC I.197; Dr. Luis Vazquez, PBC I.234; Ana de San Bartolomé, PBC I.172.

[5] Ribera, p. 536. Gracián was well aware of the hagiographic precedents and cited the case of Catherine of Genoa, whose body also displayed such characteristics. "Dialogos," FHM, pp. 163–4.

[6] Although he describes only two viewings, Ribera (p. 536) also says "Yo lo he tenido muchas veces en mis manos . . . y le he visto muchas veces."

[7] Ibid., p. 537.

[8] Ibid. Juan de Jesús Maria, PBC I.353, described the complexion as "de color de datil claro." Teresa de Jesús (Teresita), PBC I.197, implied no substantial change had taken place: "El color tostado, como pudiera tener cuando viva."

weight."[9] Overall, as others also reported, the flesh was soft and malleable, yet light to the touch.[10]

The left arm, which had been severed in 1585, was enshrined in its own reliquary. Though slightly leaner than the rest of Teresa's body, this arm also remained uncorrupted.[11] Aside from missing its left arm, the body was still largely intact in 1588 and had a full head of hair. The back, especially, still looked very fleshy. "Nothing is missing, not even from the tip of her nose . . . the warts on her face still have hairs in them." The eyes remained in their sockets, though somewhat sunken; the mouth was firmly closed and could not be opened.[12] For the nuns at Alba, this body seemed not much different from that of a crippled sister: "They dress and undress it, as if it were alive."[13]

The right arm was bent at the elbow, its hand upraised as in a gesture of blessing. Some fingers were missing, however: Someone, no doubt, had desired the more tangible blessing brought by relics.[14] This angered Ribera: "They acted quite badly in removing them, because a hand that worked such great miracles, and which God preserved intact, should have always remained whole." Fearing an even worse assault on the body by relic hunters, Ribera launched into an impassioned plea. It would be a terrible shame, he cautioned, if this body were ever to be further dismembered. Whether it be requested by powerful people or other monasteries, it should never be done under any circumstances. No true heir of Teresa would ever desire to further carve up her body, or worse, actually allow it to happen. The body should remain

[9] Ribera, p. 536. Juan Carrillo, FHM, p. 237, said the skin resembled "cuerecillos."

[10] Juan de Jesús Maria, PBC I.353: "la carne fresca y tratable." Diego Nuñez de Godoy, PBC I.456: "La carne blanda y tan tratable como si estuviera viva; solo había la diferencia que sonaba la carne un poquito a hueca."

[11] Ribera, p. 536, was careful to explain that this was Teresa's lame arm, which she had broken in a fall. Father Jaime Pons, S. J., includes an account of a miracle attributed to the arm during the Napoleonic occupation of Spain in the early nineteenth century. See his edition of Ribera's *Vida*, pp. 614–19.

[12] Perucho de Villareal, PBC I.147–8, testified that when he had seen the body in 1592 the eyes, nose, and mouth seemed "consumidos."

[13] Ribera, p. 537.

[14] Three priests confessed to having fingers, or parts of fingers of Teresa: the Dominican Juan de las Cuevas, PBC I.368; Francisco Aguilar, preacher to King Philip II, PBC I.394; and Jerónimo Gracián, as related by Ribera, p. 548. See also Ana de San Bartolomé, "Dialogos sobre su espíritu," OCASB I.258.

as God Himself had left it, "testifying to the grandeur of God, and to the most pure virginity and admirable sanctity of Mother Teresa de Jesús."[15]

Nonetheless, the relic hunters prevailed: Merely four years after the publication of Ribera's *Vida*, the body had already been significantly mutilated. Sometime around 1592 the body cavity was cut open to verify that no embalming had taken place.[16] At this time the heart was removed and placed in its own reliquary.[17] This separation of the heart from the body gave rise to various legends over the years – all of which sought to confirm the physical truth of Teresa's mystical experiences. When the heart developed some calcified excretions, they were taken to be thorns.[18] Tradition also claimed that Teresa's heart had been scarred by the wound of the transverberation, that mystical rapture in which an angel pierced her heart with a flaming spear.[19] The beatification sermons testify to two other legends. One claimed that Teresa's heart had been torn to shreds by the final mystical rapture of her death.[20] The other, oddly enough, claimed that God had taken Teresa's heart for Himself at the transverberation and that she had lived without it until her death.[21]

Those who opposed Alba's custody of the body eagerly furnished testimony of her further dismemberment. Ana de San Bartolomé testified that when she had last seen Teresa's body in 1594, "there was a great deal of flesh missing from the back, and almost half the belly was gone."[22] Another witness who viewed the body around the same time

---

[15] Ribera, p. 537.

[16] Antonio de la Trinidad, PBC I.151, claimed to have seen the body still intact in March 1592.

[17] Catalina de San Angelo, PBC III.207–8; Inés de Jesús, PBC III.185–6; Pablo Gonzalez, PBC III.246.

[18] See the 1872 report by the medical faculty of the University of Salamanca and other documents related to the heart in Pons's edition of Ribera's *Vida*, pp. 609–13. See also Nemesio Cardellac, *Santa Teresa di Gesù e le spine del suo cuore* (Venice, 1882).

[19] See J. Lamano y Beneite, *Santa Teresa en Alba de Tormes*, pp. 353–62 (which includes a photograph of the heart); and Montague Summers, *The Physical Phenomena of Mysticism* (New York, 1950), p. 192.

[20] Juan Gonzalez, O. P., Prime Chair of Theology at the University of Alcalá, *Sermones*, fol. 128r.

[21] Gerónymo de Florencia, S. J., royal preacher, *Sermones*, fols. 26r ff.

[22] Ana de San Bartolomé, PBC I.172.

testified that only Teresa's legs and feet remained undisturbed.[23] Teresita (Teresa's niece) lashed out against the convent at Alba: "I have been told that the body is all cut up, and that they parcel out pieces of flesh to those who ask for them out of devotion."[24]

Fragrance

Those who approached Teresa's body continued to marvel at its fragrance for many years. When Teresa's remains were unceremoniously transferred from Avila back to Alba, even those who did not know what was happening were alerted to the saint's presence by her scent. Near the village of Peñaranda (coincidentally, the spot where Teresa had stopped to rest on her final journey to Alba) local farmers came running to meet the cortege as Teresa's body passed by, drawn out into the road by the marvelous fragrance that had suddenly filled their homes.[25] Ribera and others reported that the odor had not diminished but, rather, had intensified over the years.[26] In addition, this fragrance continued to adhere to any object or person who touched Teresa's body or even some other relic of hers.[27] Far from Alba, away from the body, relics of Teresa reportedly became more fragrant on her favorite feast days.[28] It was also claimed that foul-smelling objects would lose their odor when they came in contact with Teresa's hand[29] or with her bed linens.[30] Ribera claimed that musk from an African civet – a substance potent enough to use in the manufacture of perfumes – could lose its pungency completely when rubbed against Teresa's hand. The fragrance could

---

[23] Juan de Jesús Maria, PBC I.353. In 1617, however, the right foot was given to the Carmelites of the convent of La Scala in Rome. (In 1908 Father Jaime Pons, S. J., compiled a list of all the major relics of St. Teresa, which clearly suggests the further dismemberment of the saint's body. See his edition of Ribera's, *Vida*, p. 538.)

[24] Teresa de Jesús, PBC I.197. Inés de Jesús, PBC I.I.182, testified in 1610 that relics of flesh from Teresa's body had been distributed to "many diverse people," and that they had been dispersed to many places.

[25] Yepes, p. 440.

[26] Ribera, p. 537; Ana de San Bartolomé, PBC I.172.

[27] Ribera, pp. 534, 537; Guiomar del Sacramento, PBC I.78; Jerónimo de Gracián in Ana de San Bartolomé's "Dialogos sobre su espiritu," OCASB I.257–8, and *Autobiografía*, OCASB I.312.

[28] Maria de la Concepción, PBC I.452; Maria de San José, PBC I.507.

[29] Maria de San José, PBC I.506.   [30] Francisca de Cristo, PBC I.361.

not be contained, either: The hand at Lisbon was hermetically sealed in a reliquary, yet its scent was distinctly noticeable.[31] Even objects that were merely associated with Teresa but had not come in contact with her body could also emit this perfume: Gracián, for instance, reported smelling it when he approached Teresa's funeral effigy at Veas.[32]

Though potent and somewhat changeable, Teresa's odor of sanctity was immensely pleasing; many thought it to be otherworldly.[33] This fragrance also endured like no other. Ribera relates how the very first time he held the arm in his hands it was shortly before dinner time. "Since its fragrance stayed on my hands, and it gave me such delight, I did not want to wash up before eating." Yet, after eventually washing his hands, the scent remained on them for fifteen days.[34]

None of these miracles were considered novel; on the contrary, these phenomena very much conformed to hagiographic models established in the patristic era. Gregory of Tours, for instance, had noticed that the odor of sanctity at the graves of martyrs filled everyone's nostrils with the aroma of lilies and roses.[35] The discovery of the body of St. Stephen near Jerusalem had elicited the following report from Lucianus:

At that instant the earth trembled and a smell of sweet perfume came from the place such as no man had ever known of, so much that we thought that we were standing in the sweet garden of Paradise. And at that very hour, from the smell of that perfume, seventy-three persons were healed.[36]

But Teresa's hagiographers did not need to hark back to antiquity. Medieval Spain had its share of incorruptible, sweet-smelling saints. Two prominent examples came from the Madrid area: Saint Isidore the Laborer (ca. 1080–1130) and Saint Diego of Alcalá (1400?–1463). Saint Isidore's corpse, which was buried at the church of San Andrés, was

---

[31] Ribera, p. 547. [32] Gracián, "Angela y Eliseo" FHM, p. 8.

[33] Yepes, p. 418; Gracián, "Dialogos," pp. 74–75; Maria de San Angelo, PBC I.54; Miguel de Carranza, PBC II.139; Teresa de Jesús (Teresita), PBC I.197; Domingo Bañez, PBC, I.11; Juan Carrillo, FHM, p. 237.

[34] Ribera, p. 537.

[35] Gregorii episcopi Turonensis, "Liber in gloria confessorum," *Miracula et opera minora*, ed. B. Krusch, *Monumenta Germaniae Historica: Scriptores Rerum Merovingicarum*, 2 vols. (Hanover, 1885), 40, 323.

[36] *Epistola Luciani* 2, J. G. Migne, *Patrologiae cursus completus: Patrologia Latina* (PL) 41.809; trans. Brown, *Cult of the Saints*, p. 92.

known for its miraculous preservation and otherworldly fragrance and became a favored relic of the royal family.[37] Diego's incorruptible body exhibited some of the same qualities as Teresa's. It, too, became a royal favorite: He was credited with having saved the life of the prince Don Carlos in 1562, and when his canonization was celebrated in 1589, King Philip II had both of Diego's legs severed below the knee and claimed them for himself and his family.[38] Teresa's contemporaries were familiar with these paradigmatic phenomena and expected such miracles from a great saint.[39]

Blood and oil

Teresa's fragrance was inseparably connected to the oil that continually oozed from her body, which some described as "perspiration" (*sudor*), or "dewdrops" (*granicos de aljófar*),[40] and which felt slippery to the touch.[41] This oil flowed constantly and copiously. It had not only soaked through all the shrouds and habits used to bury Teresa but also adhered to her coffins and to splinters taken from them.[42] The left arm was continually wrapped in new cloths, which were changed frequently, because the fabric very quickly became stained. Ribera said of the cloth: "It looks as if it had been dipped in oil, or something similar." These cloths always

[37] Canonized in 1622, he was named the patron of Madrid. Though long revered as a local saint, it was not until 1593 that his canonization was set in motion by Philip II. On Isidore see Juan Diacono de San Andrés, *Vida y milagros del glorioso san Isidro Labrador, hijo, abogado, y patrono de la Real Villa de Madrid*, con adiciones de Jaime Bleda (Madrid, 1622); and Manuel Rosell, *Disertación histórica sobre la aparición de San Isidro Labrador, patrón de Madrid* (Madrid, 1789).

[38] On Diego see Antonio Rojo, *Historia de San Diego de Alcalá* (Madrid, 1663); and "Documentos sobre la curación del Principe Don Carlos y la canonización de San Diego de Alcalá, *Archivo Iberoamericano*, vols. 2, 4, 5 (1914–16).

[39] Many of the older religious orders had long traditions of incorruptible, sweet-smelling saints. José de Sigüenza listed several from the late fifteenth and early sixteenth centuries in his *Historia de la Orden de San Jerónimo*, modern ed. by Juan Catalina Garcia, 2 vols. *Nueva Biblioteca de Autores Españoles* (Madrid, 1909). See vol. II (Tercera Parte), pp. 180, 184, 229.

[40] Ana de los Angeles, PBC I.185; Teresa de Jesús (Teresita), PBC I, 197; Ana de San Bartolomé, PBC I.172, said the body always had "el mismo sudor como de aceite."

[41] Juan de Jesús Maria, PBC I.353, "palpándola con los dedos se deslizan algún tanto."

[42] Yepes, p. 436; Juan de Jesús Maria, PBC I.353; Inés de Jesús, PBC III.182; Antonio de Zamora, FHM 562.

exuded a wonderful fragrance. "Many cloths have been stained in this manner, and have been distributed as relics. Every day more are stained and given away."[43] Sancho Davila, Bishop of Jaén, had a small piece of Teresa's arm which exhibited all these miraculous qualities, and he attributed them to the fact that Teresa's body had been a receptacle for God's love.[44]

Wherever relics of Teresa were kept, one could hope to find this oil; far from Alba, even the smallest pieces of Teresa's flesh would continually furnish it.[45] When the flesh was cut, the oil would flow more copiously.[46] But this miracle was not limited to Teresa's flesh: It could also be produced by objects she had simply touched. At Zaragoza, for instance, drops of oil issued from the belt with which Teresa had been buried.[47] One Discalced nun reported having seen a letter written by Teresa that was totally soaked in oil, even though it had not been brought into contact with Teresa's body or any other relic. This wonder was caused, she thought, solely because Teresa "had written the letter and passed her hand over it."[48]

Oil was not the only fluid that issued from Teresa's body and relics. Because Teresa's incorruption was believed to be so complete, it is not surprising to find reports that claimed she could still bleed. Several priests and nuns testified they had seen blood flowing from Teresa's back,[49] and one of them claimed to have a piece of cloth stained by it.[50] Blood could also ooze from very small pieces of Teresa's flesh or from objects she had touched. At the Discalced convent of Madrid the following story was related by Maria de San José: Once, when some of the soil scraped off of Teresa was distributed among all the nuns at Avila,

---

[43] Ribera, p. 536. Maria de San José, PBC I.506, testified that she had soaked "dos varas de holanda y dos cobadas de tafetán" in the oil that seeped from Teresa's hand at Lisbon.

[44] Sancho Davila, *Sermones*, fol. 317v.

[45] Juan de las Cuevas, PBC I.368; Francisco Aguilar, PBC I.394.

[46] Maria de San José, PBC I.325; Luisa de Reynaltes, PBC I.410.

[47] Yepes, p. 432.   [48] Maria de San José, PBC I.102.

[49] Dr. Francisco Ramirez, PBC I.141–2; Maria de la Encarnación, PBC I.243; Diego de Yepes, PBC I.289; Jerónima del Espíritu Santo, PBC I.297; Juan de Jesús Maria, PBC I.352; Inés de Jesús, PBC III.183.

[50] Juan de Jesús Maria, PBC I.352, testified that another cloth dipped in this blood was in the possession of Fray Diego de Yepes.

one of the sisters received a tiny piece of skin along with the soil. Unaware of this, she wrapped the relic in a piece of paper. Later, much to her surprise, she discovered that blood had soaked through all the folds of the wrapping paper. The same nun who related this story also claimed that Teresa's belt at Zaragoza did not drip oil but blood.[51]

As in the case of the odor of sanctity, this exuding miracle conformed perfectly to medieval hagiographic models. Gregory of Tours had spoken of "oil the odor of nectar" that flowed from the tomb of St. Andrew on his feast day.[52] Throughout the Middle Ages, many holy men and women were believed to exude miraculous fluids, substances, or odors. The three best-known myroblytes, or exuding saints, were Catherine of Alexandria (who bled milk when beheaded), Elizabeth of Hungary,[53] and Nicholas of Myra,[54] but there were many others as well, and many of them were women: Walburga, Hedwig of Silesia, Agnes of Montepulciano, Lutgard of Aywières, Mary of Oignies, Christina the Astonishing, Lidwina of Schiedam, and Rose of Viterbo.[55] The account of St. Walburga (d. 779) is typical: Her body secreted an aromatic oil that was thought to issue from her breastbone or from the stone on which her relics rested. This oil was still effecting miraculous cures 1,000 years after her death. One hagiographer, Philip of Eichstätt, claimed he was once cured by this oil, and he also observed that it seemed to flow more copiously during mass.[56]

When it came to exuding, then, Teresa was in very good company.

---

[51] Maria de San José, PBC I.326–7.

[52] Nicole Hermann-Mascard contends that this exuding, or *vinage*, as she calls it, dates from about the fourth century, and she cites Gregory of Tours, *De gloria martyrum*, L.I.31, in *Les reliques des saints. Formation coutumière d'un droit* (Paris, 1975), pp. 48–9.

[53] Albert Huyskens, *Quellenstudien zur Geschichte der heiligen Elisabeth Landgräfin von Thüringen* (Marburg, 1908), pp. 51–2.

[54] Charles W. Jones, *Saint Nicolas of Myra, Bari, and Manhattan: Biography of a Legend* (Chicago, 1978).

[55] Caroline Walker Bynum discusses myroblytes throughout *Holy Feast, Holy Fast*, pp. 122–3, 135–6, 145, 211, 274. A list of myroblytes is also contained in Herbert Thurston, *The Physical Phenomena of Mysticism* (Chicago, 1952), pp. 268–70. See also Nicole Hermann-Mascard, *Les reliques des saints*, pp. 68–9.

[56] Francesca M. Steele, *The Life of Walburga* (London, 1921), pp. 133–6; Philip of Eichstätt, *Life of Walburga*, chap. 7, pp. 37–8; J. Bollandus and G. Henschenius, *Acta Sanctorum . . . editio novissima*, ed. J. Carnandet et al. (Paris, 1863), February, vol. 3 (Paris, 1865), pp. 567–8.

Weightlessness

Numerous witnesses who examined Teresa's uncorrupted body testified that its flesh had little density. Juan Carrillo testified that the body "weighed little."[57] Diego Nuñez de Godoy thought that Teresa's flesh looked and felt like living flesh but had a hollow sound.[58] Juana del Espiritu Santo said it was "so light it did not seem to be flesh and bone."[59] Francisco de Ribera claimed that the body could be very easily lifted and held up with a single hand.[60] Diego de Yepes insisted that Teresa's body weighed no more than that of a two-year-old child, even though the saint remained "corpulent," and he interpreted this as proof that her flesh already enjoyed the benefits of the Resurrection.[61] Luis Vazquez, one of the physicians who examined Teresa's body at Avila, testified that he was especially impressed by the ease with which he was able to lift Teresa's uncorrupted body, which seemed nearly weightless. (He claimed to have lifted the body almost by himself, because the other physician who helped him, Dr. Ramos, was "old and frail".) Like Yepes, he also expected this from a holy body: "It did not have the weight of normal flesh," he averred, "but rather of sanctified flesh."[62]

Miracles performed by Teresa's relics

Teresa's uncorrupted body was coveted not only because it was a marvel in itself, a testament to the manner in which the saints were exempted from a normal death, but also because it could radiate the full healing power of salvation.

According to Ribera, God wanted to honor Teresa for all the honor she had shown him and for her service to Him.[63] What better way to show this reciprocal esteem than by now granting the favors that the

---

[57] Juan Carrillo, FHM, p. 237. [58] Diego Nuñez de Godoy, PBC I.456.

[59] Juana del Espíritu Santo, PBC I.102.

[60] Ribera, p. 537; Antonio de la Trinidad, PBC I.150–1; and Perucho de Villareal, PBC I.147–8, who added that the body stood up straight on its own, without bending at the waist.

[61] Yepes, p. 439; PBC I.285.

[62] Luis Vazquez, PBC I.234. Also attested to by Juan de Jesús Maria, another examiner, PBC I.353.

[63] Ribera, p. 545.

faithful on earth sought through her agency? What better way to show the power of salvation than by imparting the full healing of the Resurrection to come through her miraculously incorruptible flesh? Thinking perhaps of Gregory the Great, Ribera argued that miracles were the best possible demonstration of the power of the saints.[64]

The many hundreds of miracles attributed to Teresa can be classified according to the agency through which they were believed to have been granted: (1) her body, or relics of her body; (2) representative, or contact relics; (3) her image; (4) prayers that sought her intercession.

A complete list of all the miracles attributed to relics from Teresa's body in the first thirty years following her death would be immensely long and unnecessary for our purposes. A brief sample of the different kinds of miracles reported is sufficient to give us a clear picture of the way in which Teresa's uncorrupted remains were approached. Though these are bizarre tales by late twentieth-century standards, they are nonetheless revealing. What Caroline Walker Bynum has said about her fourteenth-century sources also holds true here:

> Their extravagant details tend to suggest to readers either pathology on the part of their subject or uncontrolled imagination on the part of their authors. Yet it is from these late texts . . . that we get our sense of the crystalline structure underlying not merely the behavior of saintly women but also the expectations of ordinary women and men, which shaped that behavior.[65]

What we follow in this section is the way in which the miracles attributed to Teresa's relics reflected and reinforced certain prevailing attitudes toward death and the afterlife. More specifically, by looking at what the saints were thought capable of doing, we might be able to get a clearer picture of what was expected from heaven by those who remained on earth, afflicted by pain and suffering.

Corporeal relics

Fragments of Teresa's body were widely distributed and fervently approached. One Discalced nun testified that she knew of families who owned relics of Teresa and prized them so highly that they threatened to

---

[64] Gregory the Great, *Dialogues*, IV.1.5–6.
[65] Bynum, *Holy Feast and Holy Fast*, p. 146.

disown any heir who would allow these relics to leave their estate.[66] Those who were not fortunate enough to possess relics sought them eagerly. Teresa's hand at Lisbon was frequently approached for cures.[67] One of the Discalced sisters at Madrid declared that her convent was greatly comforted by the presence of relics and also admitted that they generated income for the house (*hacen limosnas*) from many people who came to ask for them and who gave alms.[68] The nuns at Alba were constantly pressed to lend Teresa's arm and did so reluctantly.[69] One man who claimed to have been cured by Teresa's arm, which he was allowed to embrace on his sickbed for several hours, testified that he knew of many others who had also been healed by the arm, in spite of the fact that the nuns lent out the relic only "with great secrecy, not wanting people to know about it."[70] News of this arm reached other communities. A paralyzed nun at Caravaca, we are told, "intensely desired to have in her possession some flesh from this holy arm, and she also had great faith in its power to cure her." Ultimately, she was healed by one of Teresa's fingers.[71]

The most common type of miracle reported is the healing of some physical illness or infirmity. Father Baeza, a Franciscan from Alba who was suffering from an ear ailment, was instantly cured when the arm of Teresa was pressed against his ear.[72] Francisco Gomez, a carpenter from Alba, was cured of a painful and immobilizing eye disease when the Carmelite sisters allowed him to touch his face and eyes to Teresa's arm.[73] A Carmelite nun at Lisbon regained her sense of smell when Teresa's hand was displayed: "A hot vapor rose up her nostrils and

---

[66] Beatriz del Sacramento, PBC III.115.

[67] Ribera, p. 547: "Hay en aquella ciudad mucha devoción con ella, y pídenla muchas personas graves en sus necesidades." Isabel de la Cruz claimed that the hand at Lisbon had worked more miracles than the body itself at Alba, PBC I.33.

[68] Francisca de Cristo, PBC I.360.

[69] For the remarkable history of this arm in the twentieth century, see Guilana Di Febo, *Culto barocco*, pp. 104–22.

[70] Licenciado Juan Casquer, PBC I.148–9.

[71] Ribera adds that the nuns at Alba eventually sent some flesh from the arm to Caravaca, p. 548.

[72] Father Diego Nuñez de Godoy claimed he had been the one who held the relic for Father Baeza, PBC I.456.

[73] Isabel de la Cruz, PBC I.113.

opened them, and smelling the hand, she recovered that sense."[74] Some nuns from Low Countries "who had suffered greatly among the heretics" were taken in by the Carmelites of Lisbon, at the convent where Father Gracián had taken Teresa's hand. One of them suffered from a painful stomach disorder and was touched with this relic. At first her pain intensified, but then she was suddenly cured and could later eat all the foods that had previously troubled her.[75] The frequency of miracle reports is difficult to gauge, but many individuals testified they had either experienced or witnessed multiple miracles within a short span of time.[76]

Though large relics such as the arm and hand attracted much attention, even the smallest particles of Teresa's skin would suffice for a miraculous cure.[77] Ribera himself reported a miracle, claiming to have been cured of insufferable pains in his feet and legs. In this miracle, a relic of Teresa became a substitute for continual medication. Apparently, Ribera had grown dissatisfied with his physicians' prescribed remedies for this pain, even though the medicine offered partial relief. After coming in contact with "a small box containing a bit of [Teresa's] flesh," Ribera gave up his medications and was cured, though not completely. The pain would return occasionally, but on such occasions he would merely seek out the relic again, and the pain would go away.[78]

Pregnancy and childbirth posed many dangers for women, so it is not surprising that relics of the virgin Teresa were also solicited for help with this condition.[79] The hand of Teresa at Lisbon was credited with

[74] Ribera, p. 546; Yepes, p. 434; Maria de San José, PBC I.507. A similar miracle was reported at Segovia by Maria de la Concepción, PBC I.453.

[75] Ribera, p. 547. In our own century, the hand of Teresa played a prominent role in the life of Generalisimo Francisco Franco. See Giulana di Febo, *Culto barocco*, pp. 53–61; and Silverio de Santa Teresa O.C.D., "La mano de la Santa redimida de la esclavitud bolchevique" *El Monte Carmelo*, 45 (1937).

[76] For instance, Teresa de Bobadilla y Cerda, Countess of Lemos, testified she had witnessed three miraculous cures, PBC I.373.

[77] Isabel de la Cruz, PBC I.113; Beatriz del Espíritu Santo, PBC I.441.

[78] Ribera, p. 551. This miracle first occurred in April 1589 and was still in effect as Ribera finished his biography of Teresa in July 1590.

[79] William Christian, Jr., *Apparitions in Late Medieval and Renaissance Spain* (Princeton, 1981), p. 92, mentions "La Santa Cinta," or the holy belt of Tortosa, reportedly given by the Virgin Mary to a priest in 1178, which was used as an aid in childbirth. Similar belts, girdles, and "ceintures" of Mary could be found throughout France, Italy, England, and Flanders.

having saved some women from complications in giving birth. One woman even claimed she gave birth without any pain whatsoever.[80]

Mental and emotional ailments could also be cured by Teresa's corporeal relics. Placing a relic over one's heart, for instance, could bring about relief from anxiety or ease a troubled conscience.[81] Madness, too, could be cured.[82] Even crimes of passion could be prevented. A man in Lisbon suspected that his wife was betraying him and was overcome by the desire to kill her. Troubled by this temptation, however, he came to the Carmelite convent, seeking the aid of Teresa's hand. When the prioress placed Teresa's relic over his heart, he lost his inclination to violence and desisted from murdering his spouse.[83]

Moreover, one did not even have to establish physical contact with Teresa's body; mere proximity to it could also ensure a miracle. These kinds of miracles, however, were usually other than cures and more open to interpretation as natural occurrences. For instance, a nun at Avila choked on a fish bone during dinner and could not dislodge it from her throat. Realizing her danger, she immediately rushed to the chapel, knelt before Teresa's body, and commended herself to the saint. Then, without much difficulty, she reached into her throat and pulled out the stubborn fish bone.[84] Likewise, when a chimney fire was successfully extinguished by one of the nuns in the kitchen at Alba, her efforts were interpreted as a miracle because she had invoked the aid of Teresa.[85] These two people had been fortunate enough to be near Teresa's grave at the time of their accidents; those who were far from the saint's body had to seek its beneficial presence through more circuitous routes. One

---

[80] Ribera, p. 547; Maria de San José, PBC I.327; I.506; Ana de San Agustín, PBC I.513–14, spoke of pregnant women seeking the aid of Teresa's belt at Villanueva de la Jara. At Madrid, similar assistance was provided by Teresa's bed linens: Maria del Nacimiento, PBC I.314; Maria de la Encarnación, PBC I.332; and Elena de la Cruz, PBC I.338.

[81] Maria de la Concepción, PBC I.452.

[82] Maria de San José, PBC I.506; Isabel de la Cruz, PBC I.113.

[83] Ribera, p. 548; Isabel de la Cruz, PBC I.33.

[84] Ribera, p. 564. Ana de la Encarnación, a cousin of St. Teresa, claimed she had resolved an identical problem by wrapping one of Teresa's belts around her throat, PBC I.24.

[85] Catalina de Bautista, PBC I.96–7, makes no mention of any effort on her part to put out the fire. Gracián, however, says she reached up the chimney with a pole, "Dialogos," FHM, p. 77.

of the more remarkable narratives tells of a French priest who wrote letters to Teresa, "as if she were alive," to be placed over her body, in which he "pleaded with her to intercede with Our Lord to bring about the conversion of heretics in his kingdom." An ardent supporter of Teresa's reforms, this cleric eventually oversaw the foundation of seven Discalced convents in France. The nuns at Alba always complied with the requests of this fervent devotée, who also came in person to visit the body twice, and they attributed his successes in France to his peculiar method of correspondence with the dead Teresa.[86]

Because Teresa's corporeal relics no longer belonged strictly to the natural world but, rather, to the supernatural, they had to be approached with the proper reverence. Those who were truly devoted to Teresa but who handled her relics improperly could be reprimanded by the relics themselves, which were thought capable of manifesting their own holiness and power.[87] Once, when a Discalced priest kissed Teresa's arm at Alba, he also surreptitiously bit off a particle of skin. After wrapping this relic in a piece of paper, he discovered eight days later that a drop of fresh blood had soaked through all the folds of the paper. Frightened, he rewrapped it in fresh paper, only to have the same thing happen again. These papers themselves, in turn, became important relics.[88] Similarly, Maria de San José testified that she had once seen someone cutting off "some of the Mother's flesh" with less than the proper reverence. In this case, a drop of oil gushed forth, larger than the particle that had been cut off, and afterward soaked several sheets of paper.[89]

Skepticism, too, could evince a miracle. Luisa de Reynaltes, wife of the court painter Alonso Sanchez Coello, testified that when she and another woman were shown a relic of Teresa they doubted its authenticity because it seemed to them "too large a piece" of the saint's flesh.

---

[86] Inés de Jesús, PBC III.187–8; Maria de San Francisco, PBC III.237. The priest is identified as "Juan Quintanadueños . . . una persona principal del reino de Francia." He was a member of a family of Spanish merchants from Rouen and had studied in Seville from 1562 to 1570. See *Quintanadueñas. Lettres de Jean de Bretigny, 1556–1634*, ed. by Pierre Sereouet (Louvain, 1971).

[87] This trait was commonly attributed to all relics. See, for instance, the story of St. Bartholomew's tooth in Caesarius of Heisterbach, *Miracles*, VIII.60.

[88] Ribera, p. 548.

[89] Maria de San José, PBC I.325. Similar account in Inés de Jesús, PBC I.426. Both accounts involve fourteen or fifteen layers of paper.

When a fragment was cut off, it subsequently soaked some paper "the color of blood."[90] Others who were disrespectful received stronger reprimands. Maria de la Encarnación testified that when she had once tried to pinch off a particle of skin from Teresa's arm, her offending finger began to swell painfully and did not return to normal until she promised never to do such a thing again.[91]

Teresa's flesh could also prove its sanctity through its fragrance. Father Jerónimo Gracián once displayed Teresa's finger, which he always carried with him, to the Carmelite nuns of Malagón. "Behold how wonderfully it smells," he told the sisters. One of the nuns, who was described as "irreligious" and who had in the past been reprimanded by St. Teresa, murmured to herself, "They say it smells good, but it really stinks." Immediately, the fragrance intensified to such an extent that the disrespectful nun was knocked off her feet. Repentant, she cried out, "Now it smells good indeed!"[92]

Those who related these miracle accounts were convinced that Teresa's flesh was now imbued with a supernatural quality: Teresa now resided in heaven, therefore her body on earth shared in her celestial glory. Heaven itself could not remain silent in the face of irreverence, doubt, or carelessness. Francisca de Cristo testified that when she inadvertently lost a corporeal relic of Teresa at the convent in Madrid, she was able to locate it by its fragrance, which had intensified and filled the room where she had dropped it. To her mind, it was not Teresa, but God Himself who had intervened. "It seemed," she said, "that Our Lord was not pleased to see a part of the sainted Mother lying about indecently."[93]

Contact relics

From the earliest days of the Christian faith, it was commonly believed that the divine power inherent in holy people radiated from their bodies

---

[90] Luisa de Reynaltes, PBC I.410.

[91] Maria de la Encarnación, PBC I.90.

[92] Jerónima del Espíritu Santo, PBC I.296.

[93] Francisca de Cristo, PBC I.361. Teresa's relics defended their holiness in a most benign manner, especially when compared to some medieval legends that told of physical injuries and even deaths inflicted by relics on the disrespectful. See R. C. Finucane, "Sacred Corpse," p. 52.

and could be transferred to objects touched by them.[94] Although distinctions were made in nomenclature between noncorporeal "real" relics (items touched by the saints during their life on earth) and the "representative" or "contact" relics (items touched by the saint's presence after their death), which were generally called *brandea* and could also be named *sanctuaria, pignora,* or *beneficia,* no practical distinction is discernible concerning the ways in which they were venerated or used.[95] As Gregory the Great had put it, the saints and martyrs were as fully present in church through their *brandea* as through their bodies. "Contact" relics were thus believed to contain the full presence and power of the saint.[96] Given such a tradition, it is only natural that it be reflected in Teresa's case. Headdresses, belts, pieces of cloth, even soil from her grave or splinters from her coffin, were sought out for miracles. Because such objects could be subdivided and distributed more readily than her body, the miracles attributed to them were more numerous.[97]

Virtually every kind of miracle attributed to Teresa's body was also ascribed to relics that had touched it, which leads one to conclude that corporeal relics, though highly prized, were not necessarily regarded as more holy or potent than noncorporeal relics.[98] The nuns, priests, and laypeople who testified for Teresa's canonization inquests mentioned hundreds of miracles effected by these relics; Ribera carefully listed about forty miracles ascribed to Teresa's clothing alone.[99]

[94] Acts of the Apostles, 5.15: St. Peter's shadow could heal those touched by it; 19.11–12. Pieces of cloth were touched to the body of St. Paul and distributed among the sick for healing.

[95] For a full discussion of this topic see Nicole Hermann-Mascard, *Reliques des saints,* pp. 41–70, esp. 42–6.

[96] Gregory the Great, *Dialogues,* II.38; also Gregory of Tours, *De miraculis sancti Martini,* I.2 (PL 71.923–5), and *Liber in gloria martyrum,* 27.54; and Paul the Deacon, *S. Gregorii magni vita* 24 (PL 75.53–5). See J. M. McCulloh, "The Cult of Relics in the Letters and Dialogues of Pope Gregory the Great: A Lexicographical Study," *Traditio* 32 (1975): 158–61.

[97] Maria de San José, PBC I.506, testified in 1610 that she alone had dipped large quantities of cloth ("dos varas de holanda y dos cobados de tafetán") in the oil from Teresa's hand at Lisbon.

[98] Father Miguel de Carranza, PBC II.139, testified he always carried with him a piece of Teresa's oil-soaked burial shroud, and claimed it protected him from all sorts of harm, even from a fall off a horse.

[99] Ribera, pp. 552–9.

As in the case of corporeal relics, most of the miracles involved cures of one sort or another. Again, it is not necessary to detail or tabulate the entire catalogue of reported miracles. Instead, let us turn our attention to a few of the narratives that help to shed more light on Spanish attitudes toward the afterlife and, more specifically, toward the place of the holy dead as a nexus between this life and the next.

In the vast majority of the miracle narratives, a simple message is driven home: Faith in Teresa's relics is better than any earthly medicine. The following three examples are typical. Beatriz de Mendoza, a noble laywoman, proudly confessed that she owned a headdress of Teresa's and that she regularly pressed it against her head whenever her migraine headaches assailed her.[100] A Carmelite nun at Medina who suffered from gout, a chronic fever, and chest pains could not improve in spite of medical attention. As the pain intensified, she began to ask her nurse for a relic of Teresa. Finally, a piece of Teresa's girdle was touched to her body, and she was immediately healed.[101] Catalina Bautista, the same nun who had miraculously regained her sense of smell at Alba, once stepped on a nail. As her foot swelled alarmingly, a surgeon was called in. Disregarding his ministrations, she took off the dressings, knelt in her cell, and applied a relic from Teresa's clothing to her foot. "If I have faith in Mother Teresa de Jesús, what need have I of any other remedy but this," she declared. Immediately the swelling subsided and her wound healed.[102]

By far the greatest number of miracles reported concerned small pieces of cloth (*pañitos*) that had come in contact with Teresa's body, or some corporeal relic or some other item soaked in her blood and oil.[103] Most of these accounts simply relate a healing: a layman cured of colic; a little girl cured of a high fever and bloody vomiting; an important laywoman cured of deafness and liberated from terrible, noisy headaches; a

---

[100] Beatriz de Mendoza, PBC I.397, was nonetheless careful to specify that she used this relic for only the most severe headaches.

[101] Gracián, "Historia," FHM, p. 199; Ribera, pp. 554–5; Maria de San José, PBC I.326.

[102] Ribera, p. 555; Catalina Bautista, PBC I.97.

[103] These *pañitos* (or *pañicos*) figure prominently, for instance, in the testimony of the Discalced nuns of Toledo, PBC I.247–64. Bishop Alvaro de Mendoza, who desperately wanted to visit Teresa's body when it first came to Avila, but was so ill he could not travel, also asked for *pañicos*, FHM, p. 243.

Discalced nun cured from melancholy and chest pains.[104] Other narratives tell of wondrous, startling cures. One of the most dramatic by far involved Pedro de Vallejo, a counselor to the Duke of Alba, who sought help for his dying two-year-old son. The boy was severely dehydrated, and his doctors had given up hope. Don Pedro and his wife left their boy's bedside and went to pray in church. In the meantime, however, someone had managed to obtain a *pañito* soaked with Teresa's blood and applied it to the boy's forehead, rapidly curing him. Upon regaining consciousness, the first thing the boy did was to grab the cloth and say "This is mine." Clutching the *pañito* and refusing to relinquish it, the boy was taken to the church where his parents were praying. Don Pedro and his wife were as astonished as they were grateful to see their son alive, and from that day forward they were fervently devoted to Teresa.[105]

The curative power of these cloths could also be passed on to water. At Salamanca, miracles were often attributed to the water in which oil- and water-stained *pañitos* had been soaked.[106] A similar phenomenon was reported in Peñaranda, near Alba (where Teresa finally collapsed during her final illness). A certain Isabel Martinez came down with a fever. One of her neighbors, whose daughter, a nun at Alba, had given her a small piece of cloth soaked with Teresa's oil, came to the rescue of Doña Isabel. After washing the relic in water, she gave Doña Isabel the water to drink, and her fever immediately vanished.[107]

So powerful was the holiness of Teresa and so irrepressible her presence that even the smallest fragments connected with her person could effect miracles. Splinters from her coffin worked wonders in Madrid.[108] Particles of soil from her grave could not only effect cures but also bring about apparitions. In Cuerva, near Toledo, a Discalced nun suffered from intense pain in one of her arms. Soil from Teresa's grave was applied to her arm, but because it immediately intensified her pain, she

---

[104] Ribera, pp. 549–50.

[105] Ibid., p. 549; Licenciado Pedro de Vallejo, PBC I.121–2.

[106] Maria de los Santos, PBC I.39.

[107] Ribera, p. 558. Bynum, *Holy Feast and Holy Fast*, n. 87, p. 392, points out that large numbers of cures were attributed to the wash water of saints, and she concludes: "This would suggest that water was viewed as an extension of the body." See also Hermann-Mascard, *Reliques des saints*, p. 274, n. 21.

[108] Luisa de Reynaltes, PBC I.410.

refused it. "Do not be foolish, sister," implored the other nuns, "put on the soil again." Later that day, as the nun slept, Teresa appeared in a dream, applied the soil herself, and cured her. This dream/vision was so vivid that the nun was convinced for some time that Teresa was still alive and had actually been present in her cell.[109]

These noncorporeal relics did not always effect cures, as the narratives carefully point out. Sometimes death was inevitable, but if God willed for someone to die, these relics could help bring about a good death. Orofrisia de Mendoza claimed that Teresa's headdress always had an immediate effect on the sick: "Those who were meant to live, improved noticeably; those who were meant to die would take some time to worsen."[110] In one case, Teresa's headdress was used to revive a dying nun so that she would not pass away unconscious. This story reveals the fear many people had of not being able to make a full repentance immediately before the moment of death. According to Ribera, a certain Bernardina de Toledo fell ill and lapsed into unconsciousness. Fearing that she would die in such a state, her sisters tried to keep her awake "through the power of cudgels and torments." Although these beatings succeeded in keeping her awake, they were not enough to bring her out of a delirium and into full consciousness. Only Teresa's headdress could do that: As soon as it was touched to her head, she awakened. Though the relic did not cure her illness, it did allow her to regain full consciousness, make a full confession, and die a good death.[111]

As in the case of corporeal relics, these holy items could also wondrously announce their sacredness and power in the face of disrespect. One case revealed this clearly. Juan de Ovalle, who was married to Juana de Ahumada, St. Teresa's sister, suffered from gout. He asked his wife to bring home a relic of Teresa to cure this ailment. When Juana brought her husband a *pañito* from the Alba convent, he raised his foot and asked to have the relic rubbed on the spot that hurt him the most. Much to everyone's surprise, instead of relieving his pain, the relic made him tremble violently. Realizing that this was a punishment for irrever-

---

[109] Maria del Nacimiento, PBC I.313. Other accounts tell of pains changing location in the ill person's body. Ribera, p. 551, tells of a man with a festering head wound who was healed by a *pañito* stained with Teresa's oil.

[110] Orofrisia de Mendoza, PBC I.402.

[111] Ribera, p. 554. A similar story is told about a Dominican friar at Salamanca: Maria de San José, PBC I.325.

ence to the relic, he asked that it be removed from his foot. As soon as it was applied to his face instead of his foot, the shaking stopped, and the pain disappeared permanently.[112]

One set of miracles, in which Ribera himself was involved, shows clearly how quickly these relics could become popular and how many different kinds of ailments they were believed to cure. In June 1588, a fellow Jesuit, Martin Gastiatiguí, asked Ribera for some relics of Teresa. Ribera gave him small pieces of the habit and tunic and another small piece of the cloth in which the arm had been wrapped. Gastiatiguí, a Basque, then returned to his native Vizcaya with these relics. As he was passing through the town of Manaria, near Durango, he was asked if he happened to have any relics in his possession that might possibly help a local man who had been suffering from a severe case of quartan fever for three years. Gastiatiguí gladly came to the rescue with Teresa's relics. Before long, news of this healing had spread over the region, and devotion to Teresa's relics quickly intensified.

As soon as this news became known, many people sought out this brother and asked him to give them these relics, pleading tearfully and with great devotion. He was especially beseiged by those who had been sorely tempted by the devil to kill themselves.[113]

Five or six of these who had been tempted to commit suicide were immediately cured and never again troubled by such a thought.

Henceforward, Father Gastiatiguí apparently could not go anywhere without being besieged. After giving away two of his three relics, he was accosted in the plaza of Durango by a certain Maria de Galarraga, the wife of one of the town's *regidores*. She pleaded with the Jesuit to let her have one of Teresa's relics so that she could take it to her husband, who was deathly ill. Gastiataguí explained that he had only one relic left and that he very much wanted to keep it. The woman persisted: "She said that if they had brought health to so many others, they would also bring it to her husband. . . . She asked for this with much weeping, and in the end, he gave in to her."[114]

Thirty days later, Father Gastiataguí passed again through Durango.

---

[112] Ribera, p. 554. Juan de Ovalle, PBC I.129–30, changes a few details but essentially corroborates Ribera's account.
[113] Ribera, p. 556.   [114] Ibid.

Again, Maria de Galarraga approached him in public, thanked him, and praised the relics of Teresa. Her husband's recovery had been remarkable. Within twenty-four hours of having touched Teresa's relic, the ailing *regidor*, who had been given up for dead by his doctors, could already eat and talk; within four or five days, he was completely cured, much to the astonishment of his doctors. Father Gastiataguí himself went to visit the man and found him hale and hearty. "All of these people said that the relics had a strong fragrance. And in that land they have remained quite eager to obtain these relics."

Among those who maintained a great desire for Teresa's relics was Father Gastiataguí himself. Having given away his three relics, the Jesuit sought to replace them. Apparently, he was able to obtain a fourth relic from someone in Burgos, "a tiny little piece of the Mother's tunic," which served him well by curing him of a bothersome toothache. Fearing he would not be able to hold on to this relic, either, he made another request of Ribera. This time, he left a piece of cloth with Ribera and asked him to wrap it around Teresa's arm for a few days, so it could soak up her holy oil. Ribera reveals that this request was made "with caution," because Gastiataguí had come to appreciate the full value of such relics and knew how difficult it was to keep them to oneself.[115] In his narration of all these miracles, Ribera revealed something about the tension created by Teresa's relics *before* her canonization. One must remember that as he was writing his biography of Teresa, she had not yet been officially proclaimed a saint by the church. Yet, popular devotion, both lay and clerical, already approached her as a mediatrix. How did this process of popular acceptance fit into the scheme of canonization? According to Ribera, Teresa herself calmed the consciences of those who were troubled by her lack of *de jure* canonization, as evidenced by the following story.

A Carmelite prior placed a cloth relic of Teresa with some other saints' relics that he carried about with him. One day, as he was preparing to say mass, he suddenly felt troubled over the fact that he had put all these relics together, even though Teresa had not yet been canonized. Was this not a lack of proper reverence for the relics of officially canonized saints? Later, as he was saying mass, this reservation caused him to be overcome by guilt. "Within his soul," says Ribera, "he felt severely

[115] Ibid., p. 557.

reprimanded . . . and it seemed someone was harshly saying to him, 'You are ungrateful, and do not deserve to carry about this relic.'" This reprimand produced in him a great affection toward Teresa, which caused him to weep. "He acquired such a great devotion towards the saint [Teresa] and her relics, even to the point of wanting to open his heart and place her inside." From that moment forward, this priest became one of her staunchest advocates and dedicated much of his time to collecting reports of miracles performed by Teresa and her relics.[116]

Images and letters

Teresa's ability to reach beyond the grave also extended to her literary output. Beatríz del Sacramento testified in 1610 that "it was not only the flesh and vestments of the said Mother that were venerated as relics but also her very own letters and writings."[117] Some also reported having witnessed miracles caused by Teresa's published works.[118]

Not surprisingly, Teresa's miraculous power ranged yet further, beyond anything she had produced or that had come in contact with her person. She could also work wonders through her pictures. Images of Teresa could be produced and distributed through the medium of printing much more rapidly and widely than any relic. By 1610, images of Teresa could be found nearly everywhere throughout Catholic Europe, in churches and convents as well as in the homes of lay people.[119] Numerous testimonies affirmed that the faithful everywhere sought aid from these images, "in their travails, illnesses, and tribulations."[120] Though the images could work healings, most of the miracles ascribed to them were displays of power and bordered more on the fantastic than the mundane.[121]

---

[116] Ibid., p. 559.   [117] Beatríz del Sacramento, PBC III.115.

[118] One example: Jerónima del Espíritu Santo, PBC I.297.

[119] The canonization inquest of 1610 specifically asked for information regarding the cult of images that had sprung up around Teresa. Two sample testimonies are Juan Bautista Lejalde, PBC II.208–9: "Se han estampado y se estampan muchos retratos de la dicha beata Madre"; and Catalina de San Angelo, who said she had seen engravings of Teresa printed in Paris and Rome and many images of her in various places, PBC III.211.

[120] One of many possible examples is Inés de Jesús, PBC III.188.

[121] Two examples of cures are Guiomar del Sacramento, PBC I.78, and Maria del Nacimiento, PBC I, 314.

Teresa's images could cure spiritual infirmities and hold sway over the forces of evil. Hernando de Trejo, a devout layman in Seville, was greatly troubled by demons who not only tempted him interiorly but also appeared to him in visible form. On one occasion, when these demonic attacks were peculiarly intense, he reached for an image of the Virgin Mary to ward off his diabolical tormentors. Unintentionally, he picked up an image of Teresa and, without realizing his mistake, showed it to the demons. Immediately, the demons shrieked and ran away, "as if some great force were expelling them from there." From that day forward, he wore Teresa's likeness around his neck and was no longer subjected to any of these onslaughts. Whenever illness threatened his family, he used Teresa's images as medicine, "having great faith in their power to heal."[122]

In addition to dispersing evil spirits, Teresa could also reach into the hearts of others and continue to fulfill her function as a spiritual director. A Discalced nun who was once tempted to leave the convent changed her mind after gazing at a picture of Teresa.[123] Another nun who was once subjected to some intense spiritual affliction sought comfort in an image of Teresa, which she contemplated fervently and with which she conversed, "as if *la Madre* were present." Gazing at the image made her feel as if Teresa's eyes were fixed on her, within her soul, filling her with the presence of God. Teresa conveyed to the troubled nun a sense of resignation and filled her with great comfort, advising her to surrender to her spiritual suffering.[124]

Ribera tells of an even more astonishing miracle in the case of a priest from Palencia. This cleric, who had known Teresa while she was alive, also suffered from spiritual turmoil, even to the point of thinking himself incapable of saying mass. Desperate for relief, he invoked the aid of Teresa; immediately, she appeared to him. He prostrated himself at her feet and asked for her blessing. After referring to herself as *La de Dios* (she who is from God, or belongs to God), Teresa handed the priest an image of herself. As could be expected, the priest was cured of his

---

[122] Ribera, p. 560; Maria de San José, PBC I.508.

[123] Ana de la Madre de Dios, PBC I.526, said she felt as if a chain were being wrapped around her ankle.

[124] Ribera, pp. 560–1. Images of Teresa could also produce spiritual comfort in lay people: Francisca de las Llagas, PBC I.346.

affliction. From that day forward he began to carry this picture on his person and to show it to everyone, telling the story of his miracle.[125]

The power inherent in images of Teresa was so strong that it could even affect those who unintentionally came near them. Ever the good teacher, Teresa once reached out to convey a lesson through one of her images. Ribera tells of a priest who was experiencing some difficulty in preparing a sermon. As he paced up and down, searching for something to say about a certain gospel passage, he happened to pass a portrait of Teresa, and at that very instant, he grasped some totally new meaning of the passage in question. This insight came so suddenly and was so unlike anything he had ever thought of that it seemed to him not to have come from his own mind. After preaching one of the best sermons of his life, this priest became very devoted to Teresa and credited her with this miracle.[126]

Teresa could also effect much more through her images than these wholly interior miracles. One of the most fantastic narratives was provided by Sister Inés de Jesús. While serving as sacristan in her convent, Sister Inés once accidentally dropped and seriously dented a new silver chalice. According to her, this disfigured chalice was miraculously restored to its original condition after she prayed to an image of Teresa.[127]

If Teresa could grant favors to those who showed great reverence toward her images and relics, she could also take away favors from those who were irreverent. Genoveva de Toledo, a Franciscan nun in Palencia, had once received a letter from Teresa. She greatly treasured this relic, which gave off the same sweet fragrance as all others, and one day, as a means of seeking relief from a stomach ache, decided to carry it about on her person. After she was cured, she resolved to continue carrying the letter for the rest of her life. In rereading the letter, however, she noticed that it contained some detail about her life that she did not want ever to be made public, so she attempted to erase it. Although she was overcome by a great fear as she erased, she continued to do it until she finished with the passage in question. Suddenly, she noticed that the fragrance had vanished. Some time later, a visiting Franciscan priest noticed the fragrance as he was speaking to her. "You cannot deny that you are carrying some relic of Mother Teresa de Jesús, because I have caught a whiff of that fragrance connected with her and all her

[125] Ribera, p. 561. [126] Ibid. [127] Inés de Jesús, PBC I.428–9.

things." At that moment, she became aware of what had happened to her: God had punished her for erasing part of Teresa's letter by making her unable to smell its fragrance. Though all others were still overwhelmed by its odor, this nun was never again able to smell the letter.[128]

Token of the resurrection

To touch Teresa's body or anything that had come in contact with it was to knock on heaven's door. Through her death, Teresa had now entered the realm of God and could serve as an advocate before Him. Furthermore, Teresa's relics now transcended space and time. Space was transcended through her relics in two ways: by the joining of heaven and earth, and by the scattering of her presence, through *découpage millimetrique*, beyond the grave at Alba. Time itself collapsed before the relics as the boundaries were erased between past, present, and future. Teresa's relics could work miracles because of what she *had* accomplished in the *past*, where she was at *present*, and how she already enjoyed the promised Resurrection *to come*. It was precisely this "pushing forward into the present of God's power to remake the human body at the Resurrection" that had made St. Augustine marvel when he contemplated the miracles wrought by the flesh of the saints. As another church father put it, the great wonder of it all was the way in which every fragment of a saint's body was "linked by a bond to the whole stretch of eternity."[129]

The relics of the saints, then, did more than cure when they worked miracles, they served as a denial of death itself,[130] as evidence of the Resurrection to come, and as a negation of "the full horror of the dissolving body."[131]

---

[128] Ribera, pp. 561–2. Isabel de la Ascención, PBC I.568, testified that a letter of Teresa's that had been mistakenly thrown into the garbage was not at all soiled.

[129] Brown, *Cult of the Saints*, p. 77, citing St. Augustine, *City of God* 22.9, and Victritious of Rouen, *De laude sanctorum* 11; J. G. Migne, *Patrologiae cursus completus. Patrologia Latina* (Paris, 1844), PL 20.454B.

[130] André Grabar, *Martyrium* (Paris, 1946), 2: 39, has said: "The imagery of a martyr's relics is never in any case an imagery of the *memento mori;* rather it strives by all means in its power to proclaim the suppression of the fact of death." Cited by Brown, *Cult of the Saints*, p. 75.

[131] Brown, *Cult of the Saints*, p. 83.

5

~~~~~~

Saint Teresa's apparitions

Whenever a message from the hereafter is conveyed to someone in this life, it should never be disregarded, even if it turns out to be an illusion or a figment of the imagination; rather, its content should always be carefully appraised.[1]

Another ancient tradition

Teresa's miracles were not the only messages she conveyed from beyond the grave. After death, Teresa also maintained a constant presence in the world of the living and further confirmed her presence in heaven through numerous visitations and apparitions.[2]

Being an essential component of Christian hagiography, this, too, was expected of great saints. Throughout the Middle Ages, this commerce between the dead and the living was generally accepted as a fact of life, by both the clergy and laity.[3] Merely the briefest of glances at Book IV of Gregory the Great's (540–604) *Dialogues* confirms the weighty presence of apparition stories in medieval piety.[4] The monastic clergy were espe-

---

[1] Gracián, "Transito y Ultima Jornada de Angela," FHM, p. 18.

[2] The only existing study of this phenomenon is descriptive rather than analytic and seems to have been written as an attempt to prove that the apparitions took place exactly as they are described. See Olivier Leroy, "Apparitions de Sainte Thérèse de Jésus: Recherche Critique," *Revue d'Ascetique et de Mystique* 134 (1958): 165–84.

[3] For a wide-ranging discussion of the place of apparitions, visions, and visionaries in Catholic piety, past and present, see Carlos Maria Staehlin, S. J., *Apariciones* (Madrid, 1954).

[4] I have used the Sources Chrétiennes edition, no. 260, ed. by Adalbert de Vogüe, 2 vols. (Paris, 1979).

cially prone to visions and apparitions. The frequency of visions reported by members of religious orders can be gauged from the *Dialogue on Miracles* (1223) of Caesarius of Heisterbach.[5] This Cistercian collected stories of miracles and visions that had been experienced by clerics, monks, or nuns who were virtuous. In this clerical culture, familiarity with divine spirits was assumed. Much of this was passed over to lay culture, particularly through preachers who mined this narrative tradition for use in their sermons.

Stories of visions, apparitions, and miracles, such as those contained in Caesarius's work, were widely circulated throughout Europe in the late Middle Ages through collections of *exempla*, or sermon illustrations. In Spain many such collections were in use, including that of Caesarius. One popular collection was compiled between 1400 and 1420 by Clemente Sanchez, *El Libro de los exemplos por a.b.c.*[6] Another was the *Legenda Aura* or *Golden Legend* of Jacobus de Voragine (1264), which had been enlarged through the centuries and enjoyed a wide circulation in manuscript and print.[7] Though these exempla collections did not include many Spanish miracles or apparitions, they did provide Spanish preachers and their audiences with patterns and motifs that gave shape to subsequent vision accounts.[8] For instance, the visions and apparitions in José de Siguenza's *History of the Order of St. Jerome* adhere closely to the paradigms established in the earlier literature.[9]

[5] English translation by H. von E. Scott and C. C. Swinton Bland, 2 vols. (New York, 1929).

[6] On exempla see Clemente Sánchez de Vercial, *El Libro de los exemplos por a.b.c.*, ed. John Esten Keller (Madrid, 1961). Also John Esten Keller, *Motif-Index of Mediaeval Spanish Exempla* (Knoxville, 1949); Claude Bremond, Jacques Le Goff, and Jean-Claude Schmitt, *L'"Exemplum," Typologie des sources du Moyen Age Occidental*, 40 (Belgium, 1982); Fredric C. Tubach, *Index Exemplorum: A Handbook of Medieval Religious Tales* (Helsinki, 1969); and J. Th. Welter, *L'Exemplum dans la litterature religiuese et didactique du Moyen Age* (Paris/Toulouse, 1927).

[7] Numerous editions and translations are available. I have consulted the modern Spanish translation by Fray José Manuel Macías, 2 vols. (Madrid, 1982). For more on this hagiographical classic see Sherry L. Reames, *The Legenda Aurea: A Reexamination of its Paradoxical History* (Madison WI, 1985); and M. von Nagy, *Die Legenda Aurea und ihr Verfasser Jacobus de Voragine* (Munich, 1971).

[8] The cultural context of Spanish visions is superbly analyzed by William A. Christian, Jr., *Apparitions*, pp. 4 ff.

[9] Siguenza, *Historia*, pp. 372 ff.

Teresa's apparitions cannot be fully understood apart from the context of this rich visionary tradition, especially in view of the fact that her apparitions were promoted as exemplary and as conclusive proof of her orthodoxy and sanctity. Her apparition scenarios were inextricably bound to this long tradition of miracle stories and *exempla:* They built on one another, borrowing motifs of previous visions and combining them in new ways.[10] Teresa's apparitions fully conformed to the tradition, and in a relatively brief time they became legends of their own. What William Christian has said about Spanish apparition accounts is certainly true of Teresa's case: There was a symbiotic relation between apparitions and all prior accounts. "The different legend items are like beads; the assembled legends like necklaces. Familiar items are rearranged in apparitions into new patterns. The repetition of individual items maintains a recognizable continuity in divine behavior."[11] This mimetic pattern was consciously and unconsciously apprehended by those who reported visions of Teresa. Ribera, for one, straightforwardly laced his narrative with references to established hagiographical patterns taken from this narrative tradition as a means of making his own account seem more credible.[12]

In my analysis of these apparitions, I do not pass judgment on their veracity. Instead, I accept the narratives on their own terms, guided by William Christian's definition of a vision that "really takes place" as one where the people who were present seemed convinced of its truth.[13] As in the case of Teresa's miracles, I seek to understand better the mentality disclosed by these sources, for by revealing the expectations of the narrators, these accounts also ultimately reveal much about popular and official attitudes toward the afterlife and about the way in which Teresa's contemporaries sought to experience the interrelation between this world and the next.

[10] Gracián was very much aware of this and always made an effort to cite hagiographic precedents in his "Dialogos," FHM, esp. pp. 47–49.

[11] Christian, *Apparitions*, p. 92; see also p. 208.

[12] Ribera, p. 539.

[13] Christian, *Apparitions*, p. 6. Christian describes his approach on p. 9: "This book investigates the world of images in the minds of the people. . . . Rather than explaining away the visions, or even explaining them, I have tried to learn from them how people experienced both the world they knew and the world they had to imagine. These were extraordinary moments when the two intersected."

Discerning the nature of apparitions

Overall, Teresa's apparitions fulfilled the four functions intrinsic in all medieval apparition accounts. By paying visits from the hereafter, Teresa accomplished the following: first, she confirmed and strongly reinforced accepted beliefs in life after death; second, she reiterated teachings about punishment and reward after death, according to Catholic doctrine and dogma; third, she clarified and nourished belief in purgatory; fourth, she called attention to significant tasks or developments that needed attention.[14]

The largest number of reported apparitions of Teresa describe her as being corporeally visible.[15] In some instances, she even touched or embraced those to whom she appeared.[16] Other apparitions were less graphic but no less vivid. Sometimes Teresa would appear in dreams,[17] or conceal herself in a bright light.[18] At times she would reveal only a sense of her presence,[19] or fill a room with her holy fragrance.[20] Some of her visitations were locutions, that is, instances when she merely spoke without being visible.[21]

Before proceeding any further, it needs to be pointed out that a very wide range of experiences were considered as apparitions by Teresa's contemporaries. Although most apparition reports made no effort to distinguish between various phenomena, Jerónimo Gracián took great

[14] These four functions have been identified by R. C. Finucane, *Appearances of the Dead: A Cultural History of Ghosts* (New York, 1984), pp. 85–6. Finucane also provides a superb history of the development of this tradition, pp. 29–152.

[15] Ana de Jesús, PBC I.476–7, said Teresa sometimes appeared "gloriosa y llena de resplandor," and at other times "no gloriosa, sino como en la vida la vimos."

[16] For instance, in one of the apparitions reported by Mother Catalina de Jesús, Teresa performed a healing miracle by touching her. Yepes, p. 424; Ines de Jesús, PBC I.427.

[17] Ana de San Bartolomé, *Autobiografía*, OCASB, I.374–5; Yepes, p. 429; Maria de San Francisco, PBC III.232.

[18] Maria de San Francisco, PBC III.232, describes a "bulto de luz."

[19] Ana de San Bartolomé, *Autobiografía*, OCASB, I.311, p. 76: "Otras veces, muchas, me confortaba con un amor y un olor como si su santo cuerpo estuviera a par de mí, aunque no se mostraba, sentía su olor y favor, que estaba cerca de mí." The paradox of Teresa's invisible, yet nearly corporeal presence made Sister Ana feel freed from the limitations of her own body: "Mi cuerpo era como si fuera todo espíritu."

[20] Teresa de Jesús (Teresita), PBC I.198; Isabel de Santo Domingo, PBC II.99–100.

[21] Gracián, "Transito," FHM, p. 26; "Dialogos," FHM, p. 98.

care to outline the various ways in which someone could experience a visitation from the hereafter. His taxonomy of visions and locutions helps put some of the reported apparitions into perspective.

In his *Dialogues on the Death of Mother Teresa de Jesús*, Gracián classified three distinct sorts of visionary experiences: sensible, imaginative, and intellectual. This was a more streamlined elaboration of six categories he had earlier identified in his *Dialogo de Angela y Eliseo*.[22] Sensible phenomena were the most dramatic irruptions of the sacred, because they involved an apprehension of some supernatural apparition through the five physical senses of sight, sound, smell, taste, and touch. Imaginative events were more "interior" and involved the mental processes of memory and imagination. Intellectual experiences were those that took place strictly in the reasoning faculty.

Within each of these three types of experiences, Gracián further distinguished between "ordinary" and "extraordinary" phenomena. Ordinary events were those that involved the routine functions of the senses or faculties involved. For instance, seeing an object that stood before one's vision would be an ordinary sensible experience; seeing an object with one's eyes that was not physically present would be an extraordinary vision. Gracián's taxonomy in the *Dialogos* made even further distinctions between different kinds of ordinary and extraordinary experiences and are far too involved to discuss here in detail. Suffice it to say at this point that all these further distinctions blur rather than clarify the line between the vision and the visionary, between natural and supernatural processes, and between reality and imagination.[23]

Gracián reported experiencing frequent and numerous apparitions but was careful enough to explain that none of these had been "with the eyes." His description of one of the types of apparitions he experienced reveals how complex an interaction he discerned between the act of perceiving and the thing perceived.

Sometimes, when a soul is praying, without any image in its imagination, it feels the presence and company of whoever is being addressed in prayer. Even though this is not seen with the eyes of the imagination, this presence is

[22] Gracián, "Angela y Eliseo," FHM, pp. 3–4. This taxonomy eventually appeared in print, in his "Dilucidario del verdadero espiritu" (1608), part II, chaps. 11 and 12, *Obras* I.177–86.
[23] Gracián, "Dialogos," FHM, pp. 84–7.

definitely ascertained by the soul, and it feels very much as if a friend is talking to me in the dark: for this presence is sensed, and something is heard, even though the darkness prevents the eyes from seeing. So it comes to pass with this presence in the imagination, which is later sustained in the intellect with interior concepts and words that come from who-knows-where.[24]

Gracián also described another type of visitation that was totally interior and that he seems to have elicited, rather than received, as he meditated upon the memory of Teresa while traveling with some nuns in a crowded coach between Veas and Caravaca:

Angela [a pseudonym for Teresa] came to me and entered in my soul, and we remained together, two souls in one body, embraced in Christ; and in that manner we prayed the Hours together with the others in the coach, and often repeated the *Gloria Patri*.[25]

Often, Gracián's visitations were limited to interior locutions, which, as he put it, "seemed to come into my intellect,"[26] "came without any words," or were received inwardly "without any noise, as if they were being written there inside."[27] The complexity of these phenomena, as explained by Gracián, can seem bewildering. It would not be entirely inappropriate to hint at a vague resemblance between postmodern deconstructive critical theory and Gracián's explications of apparitions, for he established the reality of each apparition *within* the visionary rather than in the vision itself. After all, Gracián certainly thought it possible for several people to simultaneously experience an apparition in different ways. One time, for instance, while he was receiving an inward locution from an invisible Teresa during Chapter at a convent, one nun actually saw Teresa sitting next to him, and her sisters in turn noticed that this nun was in some kind of trance, as if "astonished and transfixed."[28]

Ultimately, Gracián was at a loss for words as to how to best describe the different possible types of apparitions and locutions. As long as the experiences were truly from God and beneficial, he did not much care how they were explained.[29] One thing is clear, nonetheless: A very wide

[24] Ibid., p. 110. [25] Ibid., p. 22. [26] Ibid., p. 26.
[27] Ibid., pp. 98–9. [28] Ibid., p. 115.
[29] Ibid., pp. 27–8: "Da Dios a un alma un buen pensamiento o un alto espiritu; no ande pidiendo a Dios como se llama, ni quiera sabiduría de sus interiores."

range of experiences could be considered to be apparitions, from the otherworldly to the mundane. Gracián was willing to admit a substantial, active role to the perceiver.

Despite these divergent types of visions, all reported apparitions of Teresa greatly resemble one another. This stems from the fact that the reported apparitions conform so precisely to established patterns in hagiographic literature. To begin with, Teresa's apparitions were never indiscriminate. On the contrary, her visitations always served a purpose and were portrayed as gifts of God intended for specific individuals, toward the accomplishment of some divine end in the life of some person. Yepes makes this clear many times, for instance, when he says "*Our Lord willed it* [emphasis mine] that the holy mother [Teresa] should appear to" so and so.[30] This personalized, individually oriented nature of the apparitions placed them entirely within the realm of divine providence and further enhanced the image of Teresa as God's obedient servant.

Because Teresa appeared only for specific purposes in the lives of certain individuals, it was possible for her to be visible to only those for whom the vision was intended. Even in crowded convents, then, it was possible for only one or a few nuns to report having seen Teresa when many others were in the same room, oblivious to the apparition. Such was the case of Isabel de Santo Domingo, Discalced prioress at Segovia, who had been very close to Teresa and had loved her very much. This prioress became increasingly discouraged as she heard of Teresa's apparitions to other Carmelite nuns. "Why not to me?" she grumbled out loud, letting her sisters know that she felt slighted by Teresa. Finally, after some time had passed, "with her corporeal eyes" she saw Teresa standing by the choir in the convent chapel. As she looked about the chapel, she marveled that no one else seemed to be reacting to Teresa's presence, and she soon realized that the vision was intended for her alone. Teresa then embraced her and said, telepathically, "Daughter, do not think that my failure to visit you stems from a lack of love, on the contrary, you are among my most beloved."[31] Teresa thus confirmed

---

[30] Yepes, p. 425. Isabel de Santo Domingo, PBC II.100–1, is but one of many who make this clear. This functional approach to apparitions can also be found in Venegas, *Agonía*, p. 203.

[31] Yepes, p. 425. Inés de Jesús claimed that Teresa also touched her face during this

what the other sisters had been telling this prioress whenever she had complained – that she had not been visited because she was one of the strongest nuns and did not really *need* an apparition. It was only when the absence of apparitions became a problem for Isabel that God saw fit to send her a visitation from Teresa.

Although Teresa appeared only to specific persons who somehow *needed* to see her, her apparitions always served not so much the individual as the larger needs of her Discalced Carmelite reform. It is no accident that the reported apparitions came almost exclusively from Carmelites. Contemporary interpreters of these apparitions did not suspect some Carmelite connivance behind this exclusivity; on the contrary, they saw it as only natural and fitting for Teresa to keep working among those she had known in life. For Yepes, the identity of those who claimed visions made the reports more credible:

Almost all of them are, or have been, superiors [*perladas*] and companions of the sainted Mother, and are among those who first worked for the [Carmelite] reform, true daughters and followers of her spirit. . . . Thus we can easily believe that God bestowed these favors after her death for their consolation, so some could witness the glory now being enjoyed by their Mother; and so others could be advised by her about what they needed to do, and be helped in their many uncertainties and spiritual trials.[32]

Yepes knew fully well that this argument was necessary. The fact that Teresa's apparitions were reported mainly by Carmelites rather than laypeople made Teresa's visitations seem more credible in the eyes of his contemporaries; more important, it legitimized them. Apparitions reported by laypeople had come under increasing scrutiny by the Inquisition and had precipitously declined after 1525. In fact, by the end of the sixteenth century, when Yepes was writing, nonclerical apparitions were extremely rare and had long been considered disreputable by church authorities.[33]

---

apparition, PBC I.427. Francisca de la Encarnación did not see the apparition but did notice a change in the faces of those who were experiencing it, PBC I.446.

[32] Yepes, p. 423; Ana de Jesús, PBC I.476–7, 479. In the twentieth century this argument has also been offered as conclusive proof of the veracity of the accounts. See Leroy "Apparitions de St. Thérèse," p. 184.

[33] Christian, *Apparitions*, p. 183, comments on the situation after 1525: "Visions themselves were no longer respectable; and with the Inquisition periodically soliciting de-

This decrease in lay visions was not a symptom of skepticism or rationalism. Many other nonapparitional miracles were reported and believed in Spain at this time: a crucifix that bled in 1575, a painting of Veronica that exuded sweat during Holy Week in 1644, not to mention the many cures effected by Teresa's relics. What lay behind this "clericalization" of visions was the church's desire to regulate lay piety more closely. After the closing of the Council of Trent in 1563, when the church embarked on a vigorous mission to expand further the role of the clergy in public religious life, visions by laypeople could have been greeted only with suspicion. Obedient nuns who were totally dedicated to a life of prayer – and who were also carefully regulated – were the best witnesses to apparitions that one could hope for in the late sixteenth or early seventeenth century. Trances and visions were their stock in trade, the fruit of an unquestionably holy life and a sound, pure faith.[34]

Nary an idle apparition

The purpose of Teresa's apparitions was revealed from the very start. On the day of Teresa's burial she appeared to Catalina de Jesús, the foundress of the Discalced Carmelite convent at Veas, and revealed to her that she had died and gone to heaven, and that Catalina should not grieve, because she would now be better able to assist the order from the hereafter.[35] Catalina continued to report numerous apparitions under various circumstances. The list of intended reasons behind these apparitions is a fairly comprehensive catalogue of the various kinds of visits reported by Carmelite nuns: "consoling some, encouraging some, reprimanding some for specific faults, teaching others and providing them with very profitable instructions."[36] As Diego de Yepes put it, Teresa appeared for a number of objectives: to defend absolute poverty, encourage charity, quell disorder, mend disputes, and break up harmful friendships. "And thus, like a true mother she has always responded to

nunciations, it may have been seen as suspicious even to believe in a new one, much less have one."

[34] Christian, *Apparitions*, pp. 183–7.

[35] Gracián, "Dialogos," FHM, p. 120.

[36] Yepes, p. 424. Teresa affirmed in another vision that she would now work for her reform from heaven and console those sisters who missed her. Maria de San José, PBC I.325.

the needs of her convents, and promoted their increase."[37] Consequently, all who reported seeing Teresa were never frightened by her
presence but consoled and more eager to observe the Discalced Rule.[38]

Teresa, then, did much more than comfort and guide the nuns from
heaven. She also continued to exert her authority. In one apparition
alone, Teresa reportedly disclosed twelve ways in which a certain prioress could improve her convent; on another occasion she listed no
fewer than fifteen instructions concerning the duties of Carmelite pro-
vincials.[39] One of the first apparitions was reported by Ana de San
Bartolomé, who wanted to remain at Alba with Teresa's body but was
ordered to go back to Avila. "I was a bit perplexed," she later wrote,
"and the Saint appeared to me and said: 'Obey your orders, daughter,
and go [to Avila].'"[40] The nuns at Alba also reported numerous inter-
ventions by Teresa in which she corrected their observance of the reformed Carmelite rule. For instance, whenever any of the nuns spoke
during times of total silence, in disregard for Teresa's Rule, three loud
knocks would be heard, "as if Mother were there, advising them to keep
quiet."[41] At other times, these knocks would remind distracted nuns to
pay more attention to their prayers.[42]

Teresa not only kept the sisters in line; she also continued to expand
the order, gaining new recruits for the Carmelite reform. One good
example is the case of her niece Beatriz de Ovalle, to whom she appeared in a dream and asked "How much longer do you think you can
postpone becoming a nun?" Although Beatriz had feared the severity of
the Discalced rule, she was persuaded by her aunt's apparition and
joined the convent at Alba. Simultaneously, Teresa also appeared to one
of the Alba nuns, who had been praying for a change of heart in Beatriz,
to let her know that her prayers had been answered. Later, Beatriz
would prove to be a model nun.[43]

Teresa could also strengthen the wavering vocations of new recruits.

[37] Yepes, p. 428; Maria de San José, PBC I.325.
[38] Ana de San Agustín, PBC I.517.
[39] Gracián, "Transito," FHM, pp. 15–16; "Dialogos," FHM, pp. 139–41.
[40] Ana de San Bartolomé, *Autobiografía*, OCASB, I.308; PBC I.171.
[41] Ribera, p. 539.
[42] Inés de Jesús, PBC III.180; Gracián, "Dialogos," FHM, p. 77.
[43] Ribera, p. 541. Oddly enough, this story is also told by another Avila nun, Petronila Bautista, PBC I.182, but it is not related by Beatriz herself, PBC I.176–80.

One Carmelite nun who had difficulty surrendering herself completely to God received help from Teresa in the following manner: One day she suddenly saw Teresa standing before her, surrounded by flowers and a very bright light, holding an open book on her breast. "Read it, daughter," said Teresa. The young nun, however, was terrified and could not open her eyes. Teresa then touched her eyes. The nun lifted her head and read the golden letters on the page: "My Spouse has taken your will to use it according to His will, and always against your own." When the nun complained to Teresa that she could not surrender her will completely, Teresa reassured her that she most certainly could and that she was already well on the way to perfection. On another occasion, Teresa appeared to this same nun, who was troubled by temptation, and chased away a demon who was troubling her.[44]

Teresa continued to take an intense interest in the Discalced Rule from beyond the grave. In one of her first apparitions to Gracián, Teresa declared that superiors should zealously enforce the Rule and never shrink back from punishing offenders, and she reprimanded Gracián himself for being too lenient.[45] During another apparition she also reminded Gracián that God would judge all superiors harshly, sending them to purgatory for the slightest laxity, or to hell for sins they had allowed others to commit under their supervision.[46] Ana de San Bartolomé, who reported numerous apparitions, claimed she frequently received messages concerning the interpretation of the Rule, particularly at times when she felt that Teresa's reform was being compromised. For instance, when an attempt was made to restructure the order and place it under the direction of a governing board consisting of a Discalced vicar and six other non-Carmelite councillors, Ana experienced a spectacular vision.

La Santa showed herself to me, weeping copiously, her face covered by a black veil that did not prevent me from recognizing her as *la Santa Madre*. I asked her, "Mother, why do you weep, since you now reside where there can be no sorrow?" And she responded: "Behold, daughter, how many nuns are leaving my

---

[44] Ribera, p. 542. Teresa was credited with having saved many vocations after her death. Two other dramatic examples were Maria del Nacimiento, PBC I.314, and Constanza de la Cruz, PBC I.523.

[45] Gracián, "Angela y Eliseo," FHM, p. 10.   [46] Gracián, "Dialogos," FHM, p. 141.

Order." And she showed me many nuns gathered in a convent parlor who were talking to secular clergy and to clerics from other orders, and as they conversed with them, the nuns became as black as crows, and grew beaks, as if they were really crows, and the outsiders sprouted horns. And she said to me: "Daughter, do not think that this [proposed change] is good for our Order; should it ever be implemented, it would be most wretched."[47]

Sister Ana's nightmarish story conveyed a simple message: Teresa had not ceased caring about her reform in the hereafter. Even in heaven, where sadness should be impossible, Teresa could shed tears over proposed alterations in the Discalced Carmelite order. Teresa's vigilance and concern were meticulous, and she watched over her Rule like a good mother superior, ensuring that it would not be changed in any way, neither toward laxity nor toward severity.[48]

At the convent of Villanueva de la Jara she appeared to a nun who was insincerely using poor health as an excuse to eat red meat and fowl. "Do you know who I am?" she asked the frightened sister. "What kind of relaxation [of the Rule] is this? Who are you to come along now and relax that which I established with so much difficulty?" The shamed nun then hurled her meal onto the floor, where it was devoured by a cat. Henceforward, she refused to eat forbidden food, except when some genuine illness required it. In addition, we are told, her health also improved.[49] Similarly, when Ana de San Agustín once failed to perform a task ordered by her superior, Teresa not only appeared and scolded the wayward nun but also took her by the hand and watched over her until the task was completed.[50]

Teresa would brook no compromises toward excessive rigor, either. A good case in point is that of a Carmelite nun in the Madrid convent who

---

[47] Ana de San Bartolomé, *Autobiografía*, OCASB, I.312–13. For a description of internal conflicts among the Carmelites after the death of Teresa, see E. Allison Peers, *Handbook*, pp. 71–104.

[48] Teresa also revealed her displeasure with proposed changes in the Discalced Rule (though less dramatically) to Isabel de la Cruz, PBC I.303, and Inés de Jesús, PBC I.425.

[49] Yepes, p. 427; Ana de San Agustín, PBC I.515. Ana de San Bartolomé told of numerous apparitions in which Teresa scolded and directed wayward Carmelites, PBC I.515–17.

[50] Ana de San Agustín, PBC I.513.

was "inclined toward penance and greatly devoted to it," and performed austerities that went beyond those required by the Rule. The result of this infraction was predictably tragic: After fasting to excess, this nun went mad. Since this nun's behavior rapidly deteriorated into fits of violence, her sisters locked her in a cell and bound her with chains. Routine beatings were also administered in an attempt to restrain her, but nothing seemed to help. After seven months, the madness worsened, and her seizures became so violent that she would break her chains. Sadly, this only served to increase the severity of her beatings. One night after an especially rough seizure and lashing had taken place, Teresa appeared to Ana de San Bartolomé and silently led her to the door of this nun's cell. "Come in, do not be afraid, I am well," said a voice from inside. Upon turning the key and entering, Sister Ana found the mad nun sitting up, "sane and very happy." "The Mother of God and our sainted mother were both here," she said, "and they cured me." According to Ana de San Bartolomé, this nun never again gave in to excessive penance and remained sane.[51] This story sought to illustrate not only what could happen to those who broke the Rule but also how solicitous and benevolent *La Santa Madre* could be toward those who suffered the consequences. It is significant that in this apparition Teresa was accompanied by the Virgin Mary and that both are addressed by the title "Mother" rather than by their names.[52]

Ana de San Bartolomé confessed that she came to depend on Teresa's apparitions as a constant means of interpreting the Rule. Whenever any conflict emerged between Sister Ana and her superiors, Teresa would appear to Ana and somehow settle the question. During one especially trying time in Paris, when Sister Ana was trying to decide if she should cease being a lay sister and take her final vows, Teresa appeared and told her to obey her male superiors, even though their orders disagreed with those of her prioress.[53] After Ana took the veil and eventually became a prioress herself, she continued to rely on Teresa's apparitions on a regular basis. Sometimes, she claimed, Teresa would

[51] Ana de San Bartolomé, *Autobiografía*, OCASB, I.318; PBC I.174.
[52] According to Maria de la Concepción, the Discalced sisters at Segovia would always be warned by loud knocking sounds when one of them was exceeding the penance required by the Rule, PBC I.453.
[53] Ana de San Bartolomé, *Autobiografía*, OCASB, I.338.

reveal what needed to be done in dreams; at other times she would appear corporeally to advise her and even take her hand as she showed her what needed to be amended in the convent.[54] Ana knew she was not the only one guided by Teresa's apparitions. She recalled that Teresa had appeared so often to the prioress of the Madrid convent, Maria de San Jerónimo, that the sisters came to say that it was really Teresa "who presided, and ruled, and gave advice."[55]

Diego de Yepes marveled at the way in which Teresa had predicted that she would better serve the interests of her order from beyond the grave:

The holy mother [Teresa] has convincingly proven through these accomplishments what she had promised numerous times during her life, that she would attend to her order much better after her death: While she was alive she could only be in one convent, but after she died she could respond to the spiritual needs of many, advising the superiors, reproving the sisters, and preventing any attempts to relax the Rule.[56]

Indeed, Teresa often reassured her sisters that she was now capable of offering supernatural aid.[57] Teresa's heavenly power could even be felt in hell. In one case, for instance, the demons tormenting one sister were forced to admit that Teresa now waged war on them more stubbornly and effectively.[58] No longer confined to a single place at any given time, Teresa had now become an even more energetic and intrusive reformer. In this case, death had effected a reversal of normal expectations: The more fervently that Teresa's sisters believed in her presence in heaven, the more intensely they felt her company on earth.

[54] Ana de San Bartolomé, *Autobiografía*, OCASB, I.374–5.

[55] Ana de San Bartolomé, PBC I.175. Gracián would say that he had experienced so many visitations by Teresa that he would never be able to recount them all. "Dialogos," FHM, p. 125.

[56] Yepes, pp. 426–7. Gracián, "Transito," FHM, p. 17, explained: "Mas estando con Dios, como Dios está en todo lugar, El le está presente en espíritu cabo todas sus hijas y en todos conventos."

[57] Inés de Jesús, PBC I.484–5, claimed Teresa had revealed to her that she would be "más madre que nunca" from heaven. Ana de Jesús heard Teresa say during an apparition: "No dejó de ser la Iglesia por haber muerto San Pedro y San Pablo en un día, y así no cesará nuestra Orden, antes crecerá más, que desde el cielo os podré ayudar mejor." PBC, I.476.

[58] Ana de San Agustín, PBC I.514.

Teresa's apparitions also served the vital function of relaying messages from the afterlife, preparing her sisters for death or confirming someone's entrance into heaven. Whenever one of the sisters at Alba died, lights would be seen around Teresa's grave, signaling, as it were, God's favorable judgment.[59] A year after Teresa's death, one of the nuns at Alba saw "the holy Mother" emerging from her grave in great splendor, holding a beautiful cross in one hand and accompanied by another nun she could not recognize. Teresa then entered the cell of Catalina de la Concepción, a nun who was deathly ill. After receiving a blessing from Teresa, Catalina died.[60] On another occasion, Teresa was also seen leading a nun out of purgatory and into heaven.[61]

Teresa could also intervene directly in the deaths of her sisters and benefactors. Soon after the saint's burial at Alba, the foundress Teresa de Laiz became ill. Even though the physicians declared that she was in no immediate danger, she saw the saint at her bedside, cheerfully beckoning her with hand gestures. The foundress said: "Mother, I wish to die, is this finally the hour?" Immediately, Teresa disappeared, and the foundress began to worsen. "I want to die," repeated Teresa de Laiz, "because our Mother has called me, and ordered my soul to leave." A few hours later, she died.[62] Comparable stories abound. In Zaragoza Teresa appeared to Pedro Juan Casa de Monte, a merchant who had contributed to Teresa's reform, and warned him he would die that very same day. Heeding Teresa's message, in spite of optimistic reports from his physicians, this merchant was able to confess his sins, receive extreme unction, and die a good death.[63] A similar visitation in 1610 would also help Teresa's niece, Teresita, to die a saintly death.[64]

Teresa was not only interested in those whose hour of reckoning had arrived. She could also appear to encourage the despondent, especially within the Carmelite order. Maria de Jesús, a Discalced nun at Toledo, reported having been instantly cured of a grave illness after an "interior"

---

[59] Ribera, p. 539.   [60] Ibid., p. 541; Inés de Jesús, PBC III.179.

[61] Gracián, "Dialogos," FHM, p. 539.

[62] Ribera, p. 540: Inés de Jesús, PBC III.180; Catalina de San Angelo, PBC III.206.

[63] Yepes, p. 428. In gratitude for this apparition, says Yepes, Don Pedro left his entire estate to the Discalced Carmelites of Zaragoza.

[64] Ana de San Bartolomé, *Autobiografía*, OCASB, I.312. Although Sister Ana was in France at the time, she claimed she saw Teresa leading her niece to heaven by the hand at the exact moment of death.

visitation by Teresa in which the sainted Mother reassured her it was God's will that she keep on living.[65] Ana de San Bartolomé, who had enormous difficulties establishing the Carmelite reform in Paris, often longed for death as an escape from her troubles. One year, on the anniversary of her death, Teresa appeared to Sister Ana, along with numerous other Carmelite nuns who had died and joined her in heaven.

Upon seeing her, I thought she had come to rescue me from so many dangers, and I said to her with great joy, "Mother, take me with you." She said nothing, and the other sisters [who were with her] turned to her and begged that she take me along because I was suffering so much. But she answered them sternly, "She should not come with us, because it is necessary that she continue to live and complete what I began."[66]

Teresa's visitations on behalf of her order were not limited to Discalced nuns; she could also appear to potential benefactors. One case was that of an Italian nobleman residing in Madrid, who appealed to Teresa for aid during a serious illness. According to numerous testimonies, Teresa appeared at the bedside of this count from Milan, along with several other deceased Carmelites, touched him and healed him. In gratitude, the nobleman and his wife became generous patrons of the Discalced order, not only in Madrid but also in their native land.[67] The devotion of this noble family to Teresa and her order greatly impressed many Carmelites and seems to have given rise to other miracle stories.[68]

Messages from heaven

Teresa proved herself a diligent teacher after death, confirming essential Catholic teachings and always making sure that the proper inter-

---

[65] Maria de Jesús, PBC I.259. Similar experiences were also reported by Teresa de la Concepción, PBC I.262, and Maria de la Concepción, PBC I.452.

[66] Ana de San Bartolomé, *Autobiografía*, OCASB, I.361–62. A similar vision is reported on another occasion, p. 373.

[67] Margarita Lasso, Countess of Tiburcio and wife of the nobleman in question, was interviewed during the canonization inquiries, PBC I.364–5. Guiomar del Sacramento, PBC I.78, is but one of many who speak of this apparition. This story is repeated often in the Madrid testimonies, PBC I.276–415, passim.

[68] Beatriz de Jesús (a cousin of St. Teresa), PBC I.179, reported that the countess had calmed a storm at sea by tossing a relic of Teresa into the waves. The countess herself makes no mention of this miracle, PBC I.364–5.

pretation be given to certain facts. At the time of her death, many believed she had died either from the hemorrhage or from the rigors of her trip from Burgos to Alba. Soon after her death, Teresa herself made it known that she had not died of natural causes.[69] Similarly, Teresa also appeared to the prioress of St. Joseph's convent at Avila to let her know that the small box brought there by Father Jerónimo Gracián contained something very special: "Be especially careful with that little coffer," she said, "because it contains one of my hands."[70]

Always the good teacher, Teresa also ensured that her apparitions and messages did not become too distracting to her brothers and sisters. When she appeared for the second time to Catalina de Jesús at the convent of Veas, Catalina was somewhat reluctant to accept the apparition as real. Teresa responded with a lesson on the true value of such signs and wonders. "It is good that you are not easily inclined to believe this vision," Teresa said to Catalina, "because I want these convents to pay much more attention to true virtues than to visions and revelations." To prove that this was no false vision, Teresa reached out and touched a lesion under Catalina's breast and another sore on her hand, and both immediately disappeared.[71]

As a result of Teresa's continued presence, the boundary between heaven and earth became blurred. At the same time, however, the lessons in Catholic soteriology seemed to get clearer, particularly about the capacity of the human will to determine one's place in the afterlife. In several of Teresa's apparitions she indicated that there was a continuum between this life and the next and that one's moral effort formed the link between the two states of existence.

Jerónimo Gracián reported an apparition that conveyed a very stern and very *Catholic* message:

A certain nun asked Our Lord one day in prayer to let her know which book He would best like for her and the sisters to read. Suddenly, it seemed to her that she could see the holy Mother [Teresa] with her eyes, holding a booklet in her hand, and that she said, "This is the book I would best like to have my

---

[69] Ribera, p. 540; Yepes, p. 416; Teresa de Jesús (Teresita), PBC I.195.
[70] Yepes, p. 433; Gracián, "Historia," FHM, p. 197. Father Gracián, it might be remembered, had secretly brought this relic to Avila and had also intentionally hidden its identity from the nuns.
[71] Ribera, p. 541; Yepes, p. 424.

daughters read, meditating night and day on the Law of God." Then the Mother's face seemed to burst into flame, and she began to say such things about Judgment Day, that this nun remained frightened for many days, and henceforward she intensely desired to amply serve God, strive for purity, and do penance.[72]

An even more spectacular revelation was reported by Ana de San Agustín, a Discalced nun at Segovia. One night, Teresa appeared to sister Ana in a dream, standing at the shore of a lake filled with fish. The lake was divided into three sections: one part was pure and clear, the second red with blood, the third turbid and swampy. As sister Ana gazed at the fish that wallowed in the quagmire, Teresa made clear the meaning of this vision: "For those in this Order, and for everyone else, there is heaven, or purgatory, or hell." Teresa then ordered sister Ana to tell her confessor about this vision. Ana neglected to follow this order, however, and the dream returned the following night. This time, Teresa scolded her, taking her by the shoulders and threatening to cast her into the lake if she did not do as told. Ana obeyed Teresa after this revelation, but the dream returned again. This third time Teresa commanded that Ana and her confessor spread the news of this vision. "It was not just for you two," said Teresa, "but so it can be known by all." After Ana and her confessor began to tell others of this revelation, the dreams stopped.[73]

Another revelation about the hereafter took place at the convent in Segovia when Teresa appeared to Isabel de Santo Domingo, offering her a glimpse of heaven and a lesson on how to get there.

She saw herself immersed in such wondrous bliss and glory that it seemed impossible for her to describe it. There she saw the holy Mother [Teresa] in glorious splendor, girded by a ribbon that bound her to God; and she saw great beams of light flowing to Him from her mouth, eyes, and heart. And she seemed to hear the mother say that the ribbon signified how God had rewarded her purity and her zeal for the improvement of souls.[74]

---

[72] Gracián, "Dialogos," FHM, pp. 129–30. Gracián's gloss on this message is even more forbidding: "¡Oh, válame Dios, quán estrecho y riguroso será aquel escrutinio, pues no se contenta el Señor con escudriñar con sus ojos el alma, sino dice que buscará candelas para mirar los rincones del alma!"

[73] Ana de San Agustín, PBC I.513.

[74] Yepes, p. 426, is a faithful description of the vision reported by Isabel de Santo Domingo, PBC II.97–8; and Gracián, "Dialogos," FHM, p. 143.

On another occasion, Teresa appeared to a Discalced Carmelite priest and scolded him for missing her. The message was clear: Teresa had earned heaven through her many labors and now could better encourage her brothers and sisters to join her. She informed him that she did not like it when anyone thought of her as absent or when people were saddened by their trials on earth. "It is only because of my many labors in the world that I have been so richly rewarded in heaven," she said, "and if anything at all makes me wish to return to earth, it would be to suffer even more."[75] A similar conclusion was reached by Ana de San Bartolomé during one of the many visions in which she saw Teresa in heaven. "I was so very grateful to see the glory enjoyed by *la Santa* [Teresa]," she said, "that I did not cease to thank God, and I became eager to suffer for Him, because He so well rewards His own."[76]

In another apparition, Teresa manifested herself dramatically to Jerónimo Gracián as he was sleepily praying at three in the morning to reaffirm his belief in the ethical bond between heaven and earth and to point out the relation between this soteriology and the Catholic Eucharist. Raising his head from prayer, Gracián reported, he suddenly saw a beam of light leading up to heaven that widened as it moved upward; at the very top he saw Teresa, clad in a resplendent white robe and enveloped in an unearthly light. She said to him:

> Those here in heaven and those there on earth ought to be as one in love and purity. Those here in heaven can contemplate the divine Essence, those there on earth can venerate the Most Holy Sacrament, through which you there can approximate what we here enjoy through the Essence. Tell this to my daughters.[77]

Speaking from heaven, Teresa confirmed the relation between Catholic eschatology and sacramentology. When Ribera recounted this story, the message contained a further lesson. According to him, Teresa also said to Gracián that a significant difference between heaven and earth was

---

[75] Ribera, p. 540.
[76] Ana de San Bartolomé, *Autobiografía*, OCASB, I.311. In another document, Sister Ana reported a similar vision, and said it had made her regret how long she had yet to live and increased her desire to die. "Relaciones de gracias místicas," OCASB, I.503.
[77] Gracián, "Dialogos," FHM, pp. 96–97. This very same message had already been recorded by Gracián in one of his very first apparition accounts, "Angela y Eliseo," FHM, p. 9.

that "while we rejoice, you suffer; and the more you suffer, the more you will later rejoice." Ribera and Yepes both pointedly added that Gracián retained but two words in his mind afterward, the same two words that the Council of Trent hoped would drown out the Protestant message of salvation through faith alone: sacrament and effort (*sacramento y trabajos*).[78]

This Tridentine message was even more clearly revealed in an apparition to Antonia del Espíritu Santo at Granada, one of Teresa's first recruits for the Carmelite reform. When Teresa appeared to her, she not only revealed "the great glory she was enjoying" in heaven but provided a detailed, concise analysis of the connection between the Carmelite reform, the Tridentine Reformation, and the traditional Catholic teaching on salvation by works (rather than strictly faith, as proposed by Lutheran and Reformed theology). With remarkable succinctness, Teresa took aim in this apparition against the heresy of Protestantism and its interpretation of salvation.

She revealed the wondrous glory she now enjoyed, and the surpassing graces which had been awarded to her as recompense for the zeal she had shown for God's honor while she lived on earth, and for the pity she had felt for the souls of those impious heretics who were heading towards damnation. Since she had ordered her convents to beseech God for their conversion, Our Lord granted her this reward: that she would now be the special patroness and advocate for this cause in heaven. Thus did God pay her back with ample glory for all the work she had carried out on earth.[79]

If reward is one side of the coin of salvation, punishment is the other, and it is precisely the fear of punishment that had led Martin Luther as an anguished Augustinian monk to find comfort in the doctrine of salvation through faith alone and nothing but horror in what he called "works righteousness." What Luther had railed against figured prominently in Teresa's apparitions to Jerónimo Gracián. Shortly after Gracián learned

---

[78] Ribera, p. 540, does not mention Gracián by name but indicates he took the information from a letter that had been written by a very high-ranking Carmelite. Yepes, p. 426, does not have Ribera's addendum, but he, too, hides Gracián's identity.

[79] Yepes, p. 427. Ana de Jesús, PBC I.479, testified that Teresa had appeared to her and asked that all the nuns pray for the church and its clergy, for the reduction of heretics, and for the conversion of infidels.

of Teresa's death, for instance, she appeared and warned him: "Though our imperfections may seem few and insignificant on earth, they are judged otherwise in heaven."[80]

Affection, grief, and consolation

Teresa's apparitions were regarded as *purposeful* because they were always aimed toward the betterment of individuals and institutions. But beyond, or perhaps beneath this very pragmatic dimension lay another consideration: Her apparitions also served as a testimony of the affection that could exist between the living and the dead. Teresa's sisters and admirers expressed their love and esteem for the "holy Mother" by continuing to seek – and heed – her advice from beyond the grave. In turn, Teresa was also believed to show her affection and continued concern for those she had left behind, proving true a common assumption of her time, "that those who are with God do not lose the fondness that they have for those they love on earth."[81]

Those who reported having seen or heard Teresa after her death very much wanted to have her present among them. The desire to *visualize* Teresa ran strong among her followers, as is evidenced by Gracián's order that one seat be left vacant for her in every Carmelite choir.[82] Again, the paradoxical nature of religious belief becomes evident: Teresa's absence could signify her continued presence, or, conversely, her apparitions could be a constant reminder of her absence. Apparitions may not have been the only reminders of her presence or of the affection felt for her, but they were certainly preferable to empty choir stalls.

Finally, Teresa's apparitions were also a means for coping with grief. Though this function is obliquely suggested in many accounts, it is most fully and poignantly revealed by Gracián in his "Dialogue Between Angela and Eliseo," which he wrote immediately after Teresa's death, while his grief was painfully fresh. Gracián made no attempt to hide the fact that he was crushed by news of Teresa's death, even though he knew as a theologian that such feelings were not appropriate, especially

---

[80] Gracián, "Angela y Eliseo" FHM, p. 7, admitted that this made him tremble. He also confessed to feeling great shame when he realized that Teresa could now see all his sins from heaven, FHM, p. 4.

[81] Gracián, "Transito," FHM, p. 21.

[82] Gracián, "Angela y Eliseo," FHM, p. 6; "Dialogos," FHM, p. 115.

in the case of someone so manifestly holy. "I was stunned, I felt cold and I trembled," he confessed. "I wanted to lie in bed and stay there, but I did not dare to be alone, or to be swept away by that grief, lest I anger her Spouse and his Mother the Virgin." Seeking solace as he thought Teresa would have, Gracián immersed himself in prayer and contemplation before the "Most Blessed Sacrament," in adoration of the consecrated host. Though this calmed him some, it did not quell his anguish.

Outwardly, my body remained cold and quaking; inwardly, a fog descended on me, and such great loneliness that I felt as if a great weight had fallen upon me. . . . And for many hours I had no consolation, and I could not dare to remove myself from that place or to stop what I was doing, in fear of being crushed by that great burden.[83]

As wave after wave of grief beat upon Gracián, the memory of Teresa seemed to grow more painful for him. "I could not stop remembering her, or imagining her: all I could do was to plead with God to have her with Him in His glory." Suddenly, he thought he saw Teresa indistinctly, as if from far away, and inwardly, not with his eyes. She spoke to him: "Here I am. Why miss your Mother? I am your Mother." Though this calmed him, his grief soon returned in full force. "Troubled and afflicted," he fell asleep for a short while only to wake up with a start. "From my bed it seemed to me I was seeing my Angela [Teresa] over me, and she was happy."[84]

These were but the first of many apparitions recorded over the next several days by Gracián, and they established a pattern in his narrative. Each episode of grief would prompt an apparition. Some memory of Teresa would trigger a fit of weeping, for instance, only to be immediately followed by a locution.[85] Another vivid memory would make him long for her presence as he tried to fall asleep, and he would find Teresa seated next to his bed.[86] As the visions increased, the memories grew sweeter and the sorrow lessened, and a calm resignation eventually surfaced in Gracián. By 1 November, All Saints Day, these visions had healed him substantially, and he seemed to have grown familiar enough with Teresa's continued presence to ask her never to depart from his

---

[83] Gracián, "Angela y Eliseo," p. 2.   [84] Ibid., p. 3.
[85] Ibid., pp. 6–7.   [86] Ibid., pp. 7–8.

side. "Never withdraw from God," responded Teresa, "and I will always be with you, since I am with Him."[87]

No other source discloses so clearly the interrelation between grief and apparitions. Though others were not as frank or eloquent, there can be little doubt that this dynamic could have also been at work among them.

Closing the circle of faith

A certain ambivalence can be detected in most of these apparition narratives. On the one hand, the apparitions are interpreted as splendid testimonies to the truth of Catholic Christianity and as a confirmation of Teresa's moral triumph. On the other hand, however, cautionary statements are often inserted because it was also believed that visions and apparitions could call too much attention to themselves. Even worse, there could also be false apparitions, produced by demonic delusions. One of Teresa's messages to Catalina de Jesús contained the following warning:

> These convents should not pay any attention whatsoever to visions or revelations, because though some are true, many are false and full of lies, and it is immensely difficult and dangerous to separate truth from falsehood. The more that one pays attention to these things, the more that one strays from the faith.[88]

Diego de Yepes thought that human beings were naturally inclined to overestimate the value of extraordinary phenomena, especially of visions and apparitions, thinking that they somehow confirmed holiness or signified an assurance of salvation. The risks were even more intense for women. "Since women are more gullible and not as intelligent," he cautioned, "they can easily be fooled." Only obedience to God's law could bring true holiness and virtue. The final lesson to be drawn here was deceptively simple: "The reward that Teresa enjoyed in heaven was not granted her because of her visions but, rather, because of her virtues."[89]

Yepes was fully aware of the dark side of visions and apparitions, for in his lifetime many nuns and beatas throughout Spain had been con-

---

[87] Ibid., p. 9.   [88] Yepes, p. 424; Gracián, "Dialogos," FHM, pp. 126, 139.
[89] Yepes, pp. 424–5.

demned as fraudulent visionaries.[90] Gracián, for one, had painted a grim picture of the spiritual climate of the day. "In our times," he said, "there exist a multitude of hoaxes, hypocrisies, and enlightenments [*alunbramientos* – a reference to the heresy of the *Alumbrados*]. For every true miracle, there are twenty false, phony, and deceiving ones."[91] Yepes had also probably read enough about this problem to know he was dealing with a potentially explosive subject. The practice of discerning "true" visions had a very long tradition. As in so many matters that concerned the commerce between the spiritual and material realms, Gregory the Great had established clear guidelines in the sixth century: Only the virtuous and humble could be considered true visionaries.[92] The evaluation of visions received attention in the late Middle Ages, particularly from Jean Gerson. His *De Distinctione Verarum Visiounum a Falsis* (1400) outlined a more detailed set of criteria. A genuine visionary, he argued, must possess the five virtues displayed by Mary at the Annunciation: humility, docility, patience, correctness, and charity. Gerson was especially suspicious of female visionaries because of the "natural" instability of women, and he strongly advised that all their visions be cautiously examined by men.[93]

Because Spain had its lion's share of mystics and visionaries, it is not surprising that it contributed to this literature of discernment. In the Middle Ages, the *Libro de los exemplos por a.b.c.* had warned of demonic deception, as had Vincent Ferrer in his *Tractatus de vita spirituali*.[94] In *A*

---

90 See *Monjas y beatas embaucadoras*, ed. Jesús Imirizaldu (Madrid, 1977); Richard Kagan, *Lucrecia's Dreams: Politics and Prophecy in Sixteenth Century Spain* (Berkeley CA, 1990); and Staehlin, *Apariciones*, pp. 53–4.

91 Gracián, "Dialogos," FHM, p. 78. Saint Teresa herself had been intensely aware of this. See Alison Weber, "Saint Teresa, Demonologist," in *Culture and Control in Counter-Reformation Spain*, ed. A. J. Cruz and M. E. Perry (Minneapolis, 1991), pp. 171–95.

92 Gregory the Great, *Dialogues*, I.2.

93 In 1415, as he was passing an unfavorable judgment on the visions of Bridget of Sweden, Gerson wrote another treatise, *De Probatione Spiritum*, which further defined the guidelines for the discernment of visions. See Paschal Boland, *The Concept of Discretio Spiritum in John Gerson's "De Probatione Spiritum" and "De Distinctione Verarum Visionum a Falsis"* (Washington DC, 1959); and Christian, *Apparitions*, pp. 191–8.

94 Sanchez de Vercial, *Exemplos*, no. 424 (378), "Visionibus non omnibus est credendum," Keller edition, pp. 329–30; Vicente Ferrer, *Tractatus de vita spirituali*, chap. 14 (Madrid, 1956), p. 517.

Condemnation of Superstition and Sorcery (1530), Pedro Ciruelo warned against the many ways in which the devil could counterfeit apparitions or in which seers could become demon-possessed.[95] Juan de Horozco also warned against this possibility in 1588. He was especially wary of females because of their greater susceptibility for deception.[96] Jerónimo Gracián was familiar with the problem of the discernment of spirits and cautioned against too readily accepting the visions of women.[97]

Teresa's apparitions touched on yet another potentially troublesome subject: how a dead holy person should be approached by the faithful before he or she has been officially declared a saint. During the canonization process, a certain degree of friction can arise between *popular* devotion and *official* church recognition. Despite her being almost universally acclaimed as a saint after her death, Teresa was not put forward as a candidate for sainthood until the 1590s and was not canonized until 1621. Consequently, for nearly forty years Teresa's *official* status as a saint remained unconfirmed. Though her miraculous apparitions came to be considered as one of the most dramatic proofs of her sainthood, conflicts were unavoidable in the interval between her death and her canonization.

Gracián had been troubled by this quandary: If Teresa was indeed a saint (and every fiber in his being told him she was, because Teresa herself had revealed as much to him in apparitions), should he say masses for her soul? Doubts momentarily flickered in his mind. What if the devil had tempted her at the moment of death? Was there any chance of her being in purgatory?[98] Though these were the briefest of doubts, Gracián chose to say masses for her anyway, in keeping with church teaching. Even if there were 100,000 apparitions that revealed someone's presence in heaven, he cautioned, one should still do what the church requires for all of the faithful. Full and absolute certainty about someone's sanctity could come only through official canonization.[99]

---

[95] *Reprobación de las supersticiones y hechizerias* (1530), Book III, chap. 8. Modern edition (Madrid, 1952).

[96] Juan de Horozco, *Tratado de la verdadera y falsa prophecia* (Segovia, 1588), 57 rv.

[97] Gracián, "Dialogos," FHM, pp. 42, 89, 90–4, 153. See also his "Dilucidario del verdadero espiritu," part II, chap. 13, *Obras*, I.187–94.

[98] Gracián, "Angela y Eliseo," FHM, pp. 6, 8; "Transito," FHM, p. 23; "Dialogos," FHM, p. 119.

[99] Gracián, "Dialogos," pp. 119–120.

Ana de San Bartolomé provides a glimpse into some of the difficulties that could be caused by these apparitions. Immediately following Teresa's death and her first apparition, Sister Ana began to invoke the *Santa Madre* in prayer as an intercessor. When she revealed this to her confessor, he ordered her to stop praying to Teresa because she had not yet been canonized. As usual for Ana, Teresa herself intervened from heaven to resolve this dilemma. Through yet another apparition she testified on her own behalf, against Ana's confessor.

While I slept that night *La Santa* appeared to me, wondrously resplendent and most glorious, and she said, "Daughter, ask me for whatever you might desire, and I will obtain it all for you." I awoke saying, "I ask that the spirit of God may always reside in my soul," and then she vanished, leaving me convinced that my opinion concerning her sainthood was correct. Before, I had been saddened by my confessor's order, but now, after this vision, my burden was lifted.[100]

The vast majority of those who reported apparitions or commented on them seemed eager to believe that they were true, even while they admitted that they were extraordinary events. Whereas a modern reader would immediately raise questions about the credibility of these reports, most of Teresa's contemporaries seemed eager to believe in them.

It has been argued that belief in miracles was one of the essential components of early modern religion in Spain. As Julio Caro Baroja put it, "The 'will to miracle' ruled the day." In hagiography and sermons, miracle was essential; disbelief was an improbability. The few clerics who tried to downplay miracles were not at all successful. Fray Hortensio Félix Paravicino, who preached at San Salvador in Madrid, found his congregation most unreceptive when he told them that miracles might have been important for the early church but were no longer appropriate for the present.[101]

Official theology and popular piety moved in tandem, propelled by faith in miracle and guided by hagiography. In this mentality the natural order was constantly subverted or invaded by the supernatural: The laws of the physical world were malleable, subject to the supernatural power

---

[100] Ana de San Bartolomé, *Autobiografía*, OCASB, I.308–9; PBC I.174.
[101] "La 'voluntad del milagro' está a la orden del día." Caro Baroja, *Formas complejas*, p. 92.

of God and his saints. It was commonly believed that passage from one world to the other was indeed possible. "Reality" was defined according to such an understanding: Matter and flesh seemed but a gossamer veil that frequently revealed the brilliance of a stronger, brighter force. This was a worldview constructed on faith rather than reason, a perpetual motion machine that hungrily required miracles.[102]

Nonetheless, the arguments against skepticism raised by some of those who wrote about Teresa suggest that not all Spaniards were equally ready to believe in the miraculous dimension of her death and afterlife. After publishing his first edition of Teresa's works, Luis de León found it necessary to write an "apology," to be included in subsequent editions, in which he openly challenged doubters and skeptics and in which he said: "You do not want to believe? Go ahead and doubt, you are free; you are lord and master of your own judgment; no one is forcing you; go ahead, then, be skeptical, be know-it-alls, let there be as many of you unbelievers as you want."[103] Francisco de Ribera, too, apparently suspected that his testimony might be doubted and proffered the same disdainful advice:

> There will be some who shall ask me why they should believe what I relate in this chapter, because all of these accounts come only from certain people who were quite fond of *la Madre* [Teresa], and could have imagined it all in order to fulfill their wishes. To these I reply: believe only as much as you want to believe; I cannot push you any further, and I have no desire to do so anyway.[104]

This literature was not aimed at skeptics anyway, but at believers. Though Ribera was willing to entertain the possibility of doubt, he seemed impatient with the subject.

Gracián seems to have been keenly aware of the shadow of doubt that lurked among the learned, and he used this shadow as an artifice in his "Dialogos," to make the outline of faith seem clearer by contrast. One of the characters in this work, named Anastasio, personifies skepticism. Acting as a gadfly to two other unskeptical characters who are eager to

---

[102] Sanchez Lora, *Religiosidad barroca*, p. 258, calls early modern Spain "una república de hombres encantados que viven fuera del orden natural." See also his observations on pp. 306 ff., and 448 ff. Taken from Gonzalez de Cellorigo. This is also cited by Gerald Brennan, *The Literature of the Spanish People* (Cambridge MA, 1951), p. 270.
[103] Luis de León, *Obras Completas*, I.915–20.   [104] Ribera, p. 543.

believe in miracles and apparitions, Anastasio constantly tries to cast doubt on their assumptions. Wherever Cirilo and Eliseo find some supernatural event, Anastasio usually sees some natural process at work.

Anastasio does not disagree that there are different kinds of apparitions but maintains that they are really figments of the imagination. Illness, melancholy, bad humors, and the "thick vapors that rise from the heart to the brain" produce some of the visions that are taken for apparitions.[105] Fantasy and wish-fulfillment are another likely cause he mentions. Many reported apparitions, he argues, can be easily attributed to overactive imaginations.[106] And it was not only apparitions that could be explained away: Doubt could also be cast on all the other miracles associated with Teresa. "In our ignorance of the way in which many natural things work, they seem miraculous to us." There could be some natural cause for Teresa's incorruption, for the bodies of some obviously unholy people, such as the pagan Cicero's daughter, had been found uncorrupted. Sick people "cured" with relics might have been recovering naturally when the relics were taken to them. Loud knocking noises heard in the night might be caused by unknown natural causes or by overheated imaginations. In this way, says Anastasio, "Miracles are made from nothing." Finally, he raises the same argument leveled against Catholic miracles by Reformed Protestants: They occurred only in the Apostolic age when they were needed to lend credibility to the Gospel, and they can no longer take place.[107]

Gracián, however, used Anastasio's arguments as a foil. Ultimately, the other two characters prevail by raising doubts of their own about Anastasio's logic, making faith and credulity seem more acceptable than disbelief.[108]

Yepes did not seem much concerned by the possibility of skepticism and merely asserted that those who thought that God no longer worked miracles could be proved wrong by Teresa's case. He did, however, have two arguments against those few who might have wanted to doubt Teresa's holiness and to ascribe the apparitions to the devil. Demonic cau-

---

[105] Gracián, "Dialogos," FHM, p. 43.
[106] Ibid., pp. 44, 63. Anastasio passes the following judgment on the apparitions described by the character Eliseo, p. 110: "No lo tengo por sobrenatural, sino por natural, y muy ordinario . . . y desta manera entenderemos mejor estas tus ymaginaciones, que no ay que hacer mucho dellas."
[107] Gracián, "Dialogos," FHM, pp. 77–8.   [108] Ibid., p. 44.

sation was out of the question, he thought, because the devil would never want to credit and honor any saint and also because it would be impossible for the devil to have sufficient power to delude so many devout, holy, and respectable witnesses.[109]

The potentially self-destructive circularity of these arguments against skepticism suggests that Teresa's hagiographers were more interested in bolstering the faith of believers than in changing the minds of skeptics. Ribera, Yepes, and Luis de León thought that the evidence presented by them could convince any "dispassionate" reader. Reports of Teresa's apparitions had to be true because they conformed to hagiographic tradition; anyone who chose to doubt these reports or who thought them to be delusions would also have to disbelieve "many similar things, which fill the histories of ancient and modern saints." This argument was as ancient as the hagiographies used in its construction and as simple as a perfect circle.[110]

To illustrate this point, Ribera launched into a close comparison of Teresa's miracles with those reported in Gregory's *Dialogues* (Book 2, Ch. 34). As far as Ribera was concerned, Gregory's reports confirmed the truth of Teresa's miracles. For instance, Gregory related that when St. Scholastica died, her brother St. Benedict had seen a dove leaving her mouth. Was this not identical to some of the reports about Teresa's death? Did this not prove that Teresa was as holy as St. Scholastica and that reports about her must be true? Ribera found little room for doubt in his perfect circle.

Certainly, St. Benedict could have been mistaken concerning some revelations, no matter how saintly he was. But in the case of these revelations, which were intended for the credit and approbation of these holy souls, no one will say he was mistaken. And we can say the same thing about others who were not as holy as Benedict.[111]

---

[109] Yepes, pp. 18, 423.

[110] Ribera, p. 543. Ribera's circular reasoning can be found in Gregory of Tours. "For, as Gregory frequently repeats, if healing and mercy did not happen in his own days, who would believe that they had ever happened or ever would happen again?" Brown, *Cult of the Saints*, p. 82, citing Gregory of Tours, *Libri I–IV de virtutibus sancti Martini episcopi* 1 praef.: 135; *Libri in gloria confessorum* 6.302.

[111] Ribera, p. 543.

As further proof, Ribera cited other hagiographical classics, such as Bonaventure's *Life of St. Francis*, Cyril of Jerusalem's *Life of St. Jerome*, Sulpicious Severus's *Life of St. Martin*, and Paulinus of Nola's *Life of St. Ambrose*. All the miracles reported in these venerable hagiographies were true historical events, argued Ribera, not delusions or lies.

These and countless other things that are related in the most authentic histories of the saints were seen only by certain people, and it was only through them that the knowledge was passed on. Yet, no sane person would say that their affection caused them to imagine these apparitions.[112]

Luis de León made the same vertiginous wager. If one did not believe in the wonders effected by God through Teresa, he huffed, then one would have to doubt it possible for God to work miracles in human history. "Out with revelations, then! Let us not believe in visions or read about them!"[113] It would seem, then, that Ribera and Luis de León knew that these reports had to be believed within a context of faith, and that they intentionally raised the tautological argument to enhance the credibility of Teresa's miracles. Suspecting that few, if any, would be willing to carry their skepticism to its logical conclusion, these hagiographers wagered that the credibility of Christianity itself depended on belief in Teresa's apparitions. If one was ready to doubt the truth of Teresa's apparitions, then one would also have to concede that the truthfulness of the Christian faith itself was questionable.[114]

---

[112] Ibid., p. 544. To further substantiate the credibility of the Christian hagiographic tradition, Ribera points to the continuity of classical patterns into his own day and cites some recent hagiographies, such as Fray Vicente Justiniano, O.P., *Historia del santo Fray Luis Beltrán* (chaps. 20, 21); Fray Cristobal Moreno, O.F.M., *Historia del santo Fray Pedro Nicolás* (chaps. 50, 51, 52).

[113] Luis de León, *Obras Completas*, I.920.

[114] Julian de Avila presented a similar argument in his testimony for Teresa's canonization, PBC I.232.

Conclusion

In this manner do God's servants die, and dying they give off light, so that others may live in Christ.[115]

Interpreters of Teresa's death and afterlife saw all these miracles as more than ends in themselves. According to Ribera, the wonders associated with Teresa after her death served a purpose: God worked these wonders "To make the world understand how highly He esteems His faithful servant, and how much He wants others to esteem her; and to make it known that He will grant many favors to those who seek her holy intercession."[116]

Ribera's life of Teresa was written to promote her canonization. One does not have to read between the lines to realize this; on the contrary, Ribera himself made it clear.

Since her death, I see that Our Lord has made an effort to honor this saintly woman and make her known by all; and every day He performs many miracles, because He wants to see her canonized quickly, for her greater fame and honor, and for the benefit of many more souls.[117]

Nothing revealed the sanctity of Teresa better than her uncorrupted body. For Ribera and others, this miracle was God's seal of approval on the spiritual and moral perfection of Teresa. Although the proper church procedures still needed to be followed in having her declared a saint, God Himself had already given sufficient proof that she was with

---

[115] Gracián, "Dialogos," FHM, p. 62.   [116] Ribera, p. 539.   [117] Ibid., p. 564.

Him in heaven and should be approached for assistance.[118] It was not incorrect, argued Ribera, to call Teresa *la Santa Madre* or to speak of her body as *el santo cuerpo*. After all, postmortem miracles were one of the requirements for canonization, and here one had an abundance of them.[119] Through these arguments, Ribera attempted to legitimize the devotion that already surrounded Teresa. In this way, his biography became instrumental in the canonization process: It was the first major public recognition of the cult of Teresa.

Ribera was careful to point out, however, that the glory enjoyed by Teresa in the afterlife was a gift of God, not something inherently deserved by the saint. Teresa certainly exercised her free will correctly and thus "earned" her salvation, but her perfection could ultimately be attributed only to the power of God's grace.

You, Our Lord and Savior of the world, are the source and endpoint of all holiness. These beautiful and fragrant flowers that have sprung and continue to spring up in Your holy Church would not be roses, but only thorns and thistles, if they had not been irrigated with Your most precious blood. Your saints are Your most perfect creation; praise be to You eternally through them.[120]

The key lesson to be learned from Teresa's life – as from any saint's life – was that God's grace could transform human nature and that humans had the ability to *respond* to this gift of grace. Teresa's accomplishments, astounding as they were, *could* be imitated to some extent. As Gracián put it, "The wonders and the extraordinary spiritual gifts of this servant of God may delight us, but what we must pay closest attention to is knowledge of her virtues."[121] Ribera argued that to broadcast the news about her sanctity was to make known the power of God that was in fact already available to every individual through the church.[122]

---

[118] Ibid.: "Aunque a mi parecer, entretanto que la Iglesia la canoniza, la tiene Dios en alguna manera canonizada, con el milagro que se ve en su cuerpo, cuando otro ninguno hubiera." The same argument was made by Luis de León, *Obras Completas*, I.910.

[119] Weinstein and Bell, *Saints and Society*, pp. 141, 159, list the three essential attributes of sainthood as doctrinal purity, heroic virtue, and miraculous intercession after death. Other attributes are supernatural grace, asceticism, good works, worldly power, and evangelical activity.

[120] Ribera, p. 565.   [121] Gracián, "Dialogos," FHM, p. 48.

[122] Ribera, p. 566: "Deseado he que no se pierda la memoria de tus gloriosas obras, y

In his day and age, Ribera could not overstress this profoundly Catholic message. In the immensely popular *Flos Sanctorum,* his contemporary Alonso de Villegas had singled out this theme as the principal aim of the hagiographer: "What I aim to do in this book is to prove that all those who are good and desire to go to heaven ought to earn it through meritorious works, founded on grace, and that through the example of some, imitation might be inspired in others."[123]

Yepes, too, thought that the life and death of Teresa could inspire others to do great things, but he did not seem to think that it would be possible for many to reach the same level of sanctity. Monarchs always like some servants better than others, and parents often have a favorite child, he observed. God, too, had his favorites. In fact, Yepes began his biography of Teresa with the following observation: "God is glorious in His majesty, and wondrous in His saints, through whom He displays His kindness and greatness, even though His love and mercy are not distributed equally among them."[124]

Teresa's corpse served as a heuristic device in yet another way, as tangible proof of certain metaphysical principles rejected by Protestants, especially those of the Reformed tradition. Teresa's corpse and grave blurred the lines between heaven and earth or, perhaps even more, served as a nexus between the two spheres. Juan de Arauz, preaching at Alba, in the same chapel where Teresa was buried, praised that place as having an exceptional polemical value. Alba, he said, was "the greatest glory of our nation, and the greatest defense and bulwark of the Faith and the Church." And this preeminence stemmed precisely from the fact that Teresa was buried there and worked so many miracles. "This is no sepulcher, but a sanctuary," he said, possibly pointing to Teresa's grave, "it is heaven, and it rains mercy."[125] Likewise, Paulo Zamora proclaimed that the little pieces of Teresa scattered throughout the

---

para esto he hecho todas las diligencias que me ha sido posible, para que seas siempre conocida y alabada e imitada; y, en ti y por ti, sea alabado este gran Señor, que tan maravillosa te hizo."

[123] Alonso de Villegas, *Flos Sanctorum. Tercera parte y Historia General en que se escriven las vidas de Santos Extravagantes y de varones ilustres en virtud* (1588), later edition (Madrid, 1675), "Prólogo al lector," no page number.

[124] Yepes, p. 13. This statement is very similar to the first sentence of Luis de León's unfinished and unpublished *Vida.* See his *Obras Completas,* I.921.

[125] Juan de Arauz, *Sermones,* fol. 168v.

world did not seem to be "flesh taken from a woman, but rather brought down from heaven."[126] Whereas Luther had stressed the *unlikeness* between the human and the divine, and Calvin and Zwingli the *gulf* between the spiritual and the material, Teresa's corpse now proved them wrong. No such chasm existed as the Protestants claimed. "She was totally permeated by God, and barely seemed to show her womanhood, even though she was made of flesh," said one preacher of Teresa. "She seemed a human angel, a divine woman, a spirit almost wholly divinized."[127] In brief, her body itself *was* heaven.[128]

Yepes seems to have had a heightened awareness of the polemical dimensions of his work. He maintained that God's special love for Teresa was rooted in His love for the Roman Catholic Church and in His desire to demonstrate to the world the "errors" of Protestantism and the need for reform within Catholicism. Teresa's exceptional life and death could be best appreciated, he thought, when viewed against the backdrop of the Protestant Reformation, that wayward child of the Renaissance.

It should cause ceaseless admiration to see the birth of a new resplendent sun during these miserable times, in these most wretched centuries during which the darkness of heresy and other sins have seemed intent on blotting out the light of the Church.[129]

According to Yepes, Teresa was herself an impressive weapon in God's hand, and she was most effective because of her commitment to prayer and her conscious desire to counteract the "offenses" being committed against God by "miserable" heretics in her own time.[130] In brief, Teresa was God's answer to Luther.

---

[126] Paulo Zamora, *Sermones*, fol. 197v.

[127] Marco Antonio Miravall, at Discalced Carmelite Fathers, Zaragoza, *Sermones*, fol. 402r.

[128] "Su cuerpo cielo," Francisco de Soto, S. J., at Discalced Carmelite Sisters of Málaga, *Sermones*, fol. 345v.

[129] Yepes, p. 14.

[130] Ibid., p. 17: "La tomó por instrumento para hacer guerra a los herejes, no con la espada y lanza, sino con armas más poderosas y fuertes, que son las de la oración . . . con el gran sentimiento que había en su alma de las ofensas que los herejes le hacían, con la mucha lástima que tenía a las almas de estos perdidos y miserables, con particular acuerdo del Espíritu Santo instituyó sus monasterios."

This, too, was planned by God, that at almost the same time that the wicked Luther began to plot his lies and deceptions, and to concoct the poison with which he would later kill so many, He should be forming this sainted woman so she could serve as an antidote to this poison; so that whatever was withdrawn from God on one side by Luther should be gathered and collected on another side by her.[131]

Yepes was not alone in thinking this way. The Jesuit Juan de Herrera exclaimed that Teresa had crushed Luther's head with the rock of Christ.[132] Similarly, the Dominican Juan Gonzalez thought that Teresa had effectively waged war against those Protestants in far-off lands who had burned holy images and relics, vilified the sacraments, and profaned holy places.[133] Luis de León summed it up in his preface to the collected works of Teresa (1588):

God willed at this time – when it seems that the devil is triumphant among the throng of infidels who follow him, and in the obstinacy of so many heretical nations who take his side, and in the many vices of the faithful who belong to his camp – to disgrace and ridicule him by putting before him not some valiant and learned man, but a lone poor woman, to sound the challenge and raise the battle flag, and to openly beget people who can trámple, humble, and defeat him. Furthermore, in order to demonstrate His power at this time, when so many thousands of men threaten His Kingdom with their erring minds and damnable morals, God also undoubtedly willed it that a woman should foster the repair of this damage by enlightening the intellects and reforming the behavior of many, whose numbers keep growing.[134]

Luis de León also saw the life and death of Teresa, and her miracles, as proof positive of the continuity of salvation history, and he took great pride in pointing out that Teresa's life was "a picture of the holiness of the early church."[135] More specifically, he thought that all of this con-

---

131 Ibid., pp. 17–18. For an entirely different modern assessment, see D. Nugent, "What Has Wittenberg to Do with Avila? Martin Luther and St. Teresa," *Journal of Ecumenical Studies* 23 (1986): 650–58.

132 Juan de Herrera, S. J., at Teresa's own convent of St. Joseph, Avila, *Sermones*, fol. 172r. Herrera chose an allusion from a biblical book rejected by the Protestants, comparing Teresa to Judith, and Luther to Holofernes. See Judith 13.6–12, where the heroine cuts off the head of the Assyrian Holofernes.

133 Juan Gonzalez, O. P., *Sermones*, fol. 123r-v.

134 Luis de León, *Obras Completas*, I.905. 135 Ibid., I.906.

firmed the legitimacy of the Roman Catholic Church as God's elect. This was one of the principal aims of hagiography. As another Luis – Luis de Granada – put it, the continuity of the miraculous proved that the church was still under the same divine protection that had assisted God's people in scripture and Christian history, that "it is the same God at work now as then," and that "one should not think it incredible that He should do now what He did back then."[136] In this respect, Teresa served as a bright, shining weapon against Protestantism and Renaissance skepticism, two movements that were never considered separable in Spain, where church authorities despised Erasmians as much as or perhaps even more than Lutherans.[137]

The polemical dimension of Teresa's apparitions cannot be overlooked. Though we have grown accustomed to speak of a Catholic Reformation rather than a Counter-Reformation, there is no denying the grain of truth that remains embedded in the latter term. The Catholic church that struggled to regain lost ground in the latter half of the sixteenth century was certainly a less corrupt, more vigorous institution, but it was also very belligerent and exceedingly mindful of its need to confront Protestantism and unbelief. Every positive affirmation made in this age carried with it some reflection of the fear of heresy and skepticism.[138] In fact, what makes Teresa's hagiography distinctly *postmedieval* and gives it a distinctly modern feel is that it openly acknowledges disbelief.

The clerical elite of Spain seized upon the cult of the saints as a means of revitalizing the present through the past and of further distinguishing Catholicism from Protestantism, making this age an *era sancto-*

---

[136] Luis de Granada, *Historia de Sor Maria de la Visitación y Sermón de las caídas públicas*, ed. Juan Flors (Barcelona, 1962), p. 154. Similar statements on pp. 26, 148–9, 156.

[137] Nicolás Ricardi, O. P., preaching at the Calced Carmelite monastery of Madrid, listed some "agents of the devil" who had been let loose by the Reformation: Luther, Calvin, Zwingli, Brenz, Oecolampadius, and Melanchton; and then added to their ranks "la otra vil canalla de Escribas, gramaticones, puros, y humanistas, un espiritu parlero y endemoniado." *Sermones*, fol. 67v. See Marcel Bataillon, *Erasme et L'Espagne* (1991), vol. I, pp. 467–532, 743–80.

[138] Sanchez Lora, *Religiosidad barroca*, p. 217, has said that this age "representa tanto lo proprio como lo contrario, retrata en si mismo el objeto del miedo, negándolo, y afirma al refljarlo en un juego de antísesis."

rum.[139] The preeminence of the cult of the saints in the Catholic culture of post–Tridentine Spain can be confirmed in part through bibliography, by tallying the number of hagiographies published in Spain. According to the records kept by a bibliophile from Seville, Nicolás Antonio, hagiographical publications increased dramatically around the time of St. Teresa's death and peaked at the time of her canonization, growing from a mere twenty-three titles in 1500–59 to 350 in 1600–39![140] One of the clearest indications of Teresa's appeal to Catholic societies is the publication record of her hagiographies. Beyond the Pyrenees, Ribera and Yepes were widely distributed.[141] The following list gives the production of hagiographies from 1500 to 1679:

1500–09	4	1560–69	10	1620–29	124
1510–19	1	1570–79	11	1630–39	50
1520–29	5	1580–89	36	1640–49	35
1530–39	5	1590–99	46	1650–59	58
1540–49	1	1600–09	79	1660–69	43
1550–59	7	1610–19	97	1670–79	41

These figures suggest that one of the most vigorous and massive Catholic responses to the Protestant challenge may very well have been in hagiography, for this genre was not only attuned to popular piety but could also convey through narrative the many lessons of the Catechism of Trent. It was at once a didactic tool *and* a form of devotion. The Tridentine hagiographer wasted little time on subtlety. Every event, every gesture in the narrative was imbued with meaning and purpose. One of the most popular post-Tridentine hagiographers, the Jesuit Ped-

---

[139] Ibid., p. 366, thinks this is a fitting label for the seventeenth century. I think it can also apply to the latter half, and especially the latter third, of the sixteenth century.

[140] *Bibliotheca Hispana Nova sive Hispanorum Scriptorum Qui ab anno D. A. MDCLXXXIV Floruere Notitia*, 2 vols. (Madrid, 1783–8), as cited by Sanchez Lora, *Religiosidad Barroca*, p. 374.

[141] A quick glance at the *National Union Catalogue* and the *British Library Catalogue* reveals that Ribera's *Vida* was translated and published in French (Paris, 1602, 1645; Lyons, 1628); Flemish (Antwerp, 1620), Italian (Rome, 1601, 1670); and Latin (Cologne, 1620). Yepes's *Vida* appeared in French (Paris, 1643, 1644), and Portuguese (Lisbon, 1616). A more careful bibliographical search may reveal several others as well.

ro de Ribadeneyra, succinctly outlined the advantages of hagiography as follows:

It is the greatest glory for the entire Catholic Church to make known her countless illustrious progeny. For if one distinguished child is all it takes to bring honor to an entire family, what will so many remarkable children do for their Mother? Moreover, they are a mighty shield, and a defense against the unfaithful . . . and a hammer, and a dagger against heretics. Nothing can undermine their error and folly better than the examples of the saints; for teaching through accomplishment is far superior to teaching by mere words, and the deeds of the saints are holy, and totally contrary to all the delusions and falsehoods of the heretics.[142]

Within this tradition, models of behavior were created and promoted in a series of infinite reflections. Hagiography sought to link past and present, but its aim was ahistorical rather than historical, for it aspired to find a miraculous continuum through past, present, and future. The more an event conformed to established patterns, the more convincing its holiness.[143] The more that time was abolished through the imitation of paradigms and the repetition of prototypical gestures, the closer one came to the truth.[144]

One of the more prominent paradigms singled out for imitation in Counter-Reformation hagiography is the model of the good, saintly death. Many saints' lives routinely dedicated several chapters to postmortem *mirabilia* and recount miracles, apparitions, and wonders similar to those found in Teresa's case.[145] The death of Teresa offered much

[142] Pedro de Ribadeneyra, S. J., *Flos Sanctorum de las Vidas de los Santos* (1599–1601), later edition (Madrid, 1761), vol. I, "Al cristiano lector." Cited by Sanchez Lora, *Religiosidad Barroca*, p. 377.

[143] Julio Caro Baroja, *Formas complejas*, p. 82, calls this the "traditionalist" approach and praises its capacity to mold the present in reference to past and future.

[144] Mircea Eliade has identified this kind of thinking as typical of "archaic" or "primitive" religion. One significant difference separates Christian hagiography from primitive religion, however. Whereas archaic religion seeks to replicate *cosmic* events from the realm of the divine and from outside of time, Christian hagiography seeks to imitate the deeds of virtuous men and women within human history. *The Myth of the Eternal Return, or Cosmos and History*, trans. Willard R. Trask (Princeton, 1954), p. 35.

[145] Sanchez Lora, *Religiosidad Barroca*, p. 448–50, quotes twelve examples from Baroque

ammunition against Protestantism and unbelief, and it also served a purpose within a Catholic society such as Spain at the dawn of the Baroque era. This was an age during which those in power began to make a conscious effort to offer paradigms and models of behavior. Of the two groups of elites that dominated early Baroque society, the political and the ecclesiastic, it was the religious elite who exercised the more powerful didactic muscle, offering sacred models to be followed that even kings tried to imitate. And few other saints could even come close to Teresa when it came time to offer up models of behavior. After all, as Maravall has observed, the Baroque was an age in which moralists and politicians became preoccupied with *conservation* and *preservation* and the desire to prolong all endings.[146] In an age that raged against flux and decay, what more fitting paradigms could be found than Teresa's incorruptible flesh and her constant, forceful presence after death?

hagiographies that greatly resemble Teresa's case; on pp. 450–3 he also provides nine examples of miracle-working bodies and relics.

[146] José Antonio Maravall, *Culture of the Baroque: Analysis of a Historical Structure* (Manchester UK, 1986), chap. 5, esp. pp. 127–8, 180; original Spanish edition *La cultura del barroco: analisis de una estructura historica* (Espluges de Llobregat, 1975).

EPILOGUE

‹‹

In death as in life
From the daily rounds of hell
to the vestibule of heaven

"I go to seek a great Perhaps," François Rabelais supposedly said as he lay dying in 1553. Fitting words for a progenitor of modern Western skepticism. Fitting, yet insufficient, for he is also credited with three other wisecracks: "Ring down the curtain, the farce is over!"; "I am greasing my boots for the final journey," after receiving extreme unction; and *Beati qui in domino moriuntur*, as he wrapped himself in a hooded cloak called a *domino* ("Blessed are they who die in the Lord/in a domino").[1] In death as in life, this satirist approached Christianity with suspicion and mocked its beliefs through the irreverent use of tradition.[2]

Since the time of Rabelais, Western skeptics have made humor in the face of death a virtue and a means of allaying anxiety.[3] In fact, comedy has so much become the currency with which modern culture seeks to pay its fee to Charon that flippant remarks are constantly coined, circulated, and collected.[4] Yet, it would not have been possible for any leading cultural figure in early modern Spain to promote a "great Perhaps," or to crack jokes in the final hour. This is not to say it would have been unthinkable but only that it would not have been allowed. Surely, there

---

[1] Cited in D. J. Enright, ed., *The Oxford Book of Death* (Oxford, 1987), p. 330.

[2] See Lucien Febvre, *Le problème de l'incroyance au XVIe siècle. La religion de Rabelais* (Paris, 1942, 1968). Trans. Beatrice Gottlieb, *The Problem of Unbelief in the Sixteenth Century. The Religion of Rabelais* (Cambridge MA, 1982).

[3] See John McManners, "Death and the French Historians," in *Mirrors of Mortality*, pp. 106–30.

[4] Malcolm Forbes, with Jeff Bloch, *They Went That-a-way: How the Famous, the Infamous, and the Great Died* (New York, 1988).

were skeptics across the Pyrenees who might have softened the hard edge of their anxieties through humor, as did Rabelais, but they remained silent or were silenced. In Spain, the Inquisition was ever vigilant for false belief, and everyone had to guard their speech carefully. We know that one of the principal activities of Inquisitors during their local visitations was to discipline those who had made utterances against the faith.[5] In Valencia, for instance, the Inquisition processed a peak number of cases for "ill speaking" (*hablar mal*) in 1575–89. Quite a few of these cases concerned the denial of purgatory. In Castile, the number of such cases at this time was even higher.[6] We also know that denial of the afterlife was a standard charge included in the so-called Edicts of Grace, the lists of heresies posted by the Holy Office before any local investigation.[7] The assertion, "There is no God, only birth and death" was a favorite target of the Inquisitors.[8] Yet, even among the worst criminals processed by the civil courts one could find a high degree of conformity to the official beliefs promoted by church and state. Outcasts and sociopaths who were about to be hanged, strangled, or burned alive seemed to fear showing a disrespect for death even more than they feared the executioner.[9]

Death was a somber subject in sixteenth-century Spain, perhaps the most serious subject of all. Anxiety over death usually found outlets other than humor in the culture of early modern Spain. As Venegas pointed out in his somberly entitled *The Agony of Crossing Over at Death*, laughter at the deathbed was a certain sign that the devil had gained the

---

[5] Henry Kamen, *Inquisition and Society in Spain in the Sixteenth and Seventeenth Centuries* (Bloomington IN, 1985), p. 202.

[6] Ricardo Garcia Carcel, *Herejía y sociedad en el siglo XVI: La Inquisición en Valencia, 1530–1569* (Barcelona, 1980), pp. 343–44.

[7] P. J. Hanken, ed., *The Spanish Inquisition* (New York, 1969), p. 56.

[8] *El tribunal de la Inquisición en Mallorca. Relación de causas de fé 1576–1806*, ed. by L. Perez, L. Montaner, and M. Colom (Palma de Mallorca, 1986), vol. I, pp. 188, 192 195, 197.

[9] The Jesuit priest Pedro de León, who ministered to the condemned prisoners of Seville from 1578 to 1616, seeking their conversion and repentance, admitted very few failures, recording only a few cases of *valentones*, or braggarts – most of them *Moriscos* – whose final words were irreverent or blasphemous. See Antonio Domínguez Ortiz, *Crisis y decadencia de la España de los Austrias* (Madrid, 1965).

upper hand.[10] Even the fictional character of Don Quixote knew that death was serious business. As Cervantes had him say on his deathbed, "I fear I am dying quickly, sirs, leave all joking aside . . . for at a grave moment such as this no man ought to jest with his soul."[11]

Having said this, I must insert a word of caution. The last thing I want to do in this epilogue is to make absolute claims about early modern Spanish culture. After ten years of work on this project, I have become convinced that the study of Spanish attitudes toward death requires an open, reflexive frame. This is not a topic that can be exhausted in one or many books, and it is in large part the still unanswered and perhaps ultimately unanswerable questions about any culture's stance in the face of death that remain most intriguing. I do not intend these concluding remarks – perhaps a better word might be suggestions – on the Spanish character to be understood as definitive assertions. My hope here is to engage the reader in a dialectic that will foment thinking, prompt questions, and open the possibility of further inquiry and dialogue. As I see it, there is no way I can ignore the question of Spanish exceptionalism when it comes to attitudes toward death, for it is a subject that has been raised far too often by others. Though it would be more prudent to steer clear of this minefield, it is an unavoidable risk. This was bluntly pointed out to me at an earlier stage by a perceptive reader who commented on my manuscript: "This is disappointing," he said of an early draft that contained no introduction or conclusion. "I expected you to say *something* about the uniqueness of Spanish attitudes toward death."

Which brings us back to sixteenth-century Spain. A contemporary of Rabelais, St. John of Avila (1499–1569), is a superb foil to Rabelais and an articulate spokesman for his culture's attitudes toward death and the afterlife. St. John was a reformer, an Erasmian who criticized abuses in the church and society without Erasmus's sarcasm and humor. Uneasy with the status quo, often willing to question fundamental assumptions, John of Avila was denounced to the Inquisition in 1531 on account of his preaching against corruption and privilege. But John of Avila was no rebel, for he earnestly desired to remain within the fold of the Roman Catholic church and had never strayed from orthodoxy. He was acquit-

---

[10] Venegas, *Agonía*, "Breve declaración," p. 274.
[11] *Don Quixote*, Book II, ch. 74 (Barcelona, 1975), p. 1035.

ted two years later and went on to establish numerous schools throughout Spain, including some seminaries. In our own century he was canonized and named the patron saint of the Spanish secular clergy.[12]

John of Avila proposed something in 1565 that probably sounded as
scandalous to his countrymen as any irreverent Rabelaisian witticism:
He asked King Philip II to do away with bullfighting. Though iconoclastic, his reasoning was firmly grounded on traditional attitudes toward
death and the afterlife. St. John was not concerned with the welfare of
the bulls or the cruelty of the spectacle, as one might expect nowadays,
but rather with the eternal fate of the men killed by the bulls. Many
souls, he argued, were going straight from the bullring to hell: "Since
those who take part in this neither go to confession first, nor take communion, nor prepare for death as one should, what happens to them?
We should fear and weep, with good reason, for he who dies like that is
forever damned."[13]

For St. John there was no "great Perhaps." On the contrary, he was
quite certain about the otherworldly destination of those killed in bull-
fights, and that certainty was strong enough to make him ask for radical
changes in his world. But St. John probably knew that bullfighting could
no more easily be abolished in Spain than death itself. Because his worry
was the dangers of the bullfight, rather than the spectacle itself, he
proposed a compromise. Perhaps bulls could have their horns sawn off
or padded in some way that would prevent lethal injuries. His warning to
King Philip was as stern as it was full of conviction: Because it was the
monarch's duty to protect his subjects from harm, those souls sent to
hell from the bullring were Philip's responsibility, and they would continually petition God for vengeance upon him who neglected to outlaw
such dangerous spectacles.[14] Despite its urgency and despite King Philip's own preoccupation with the afterlife, Saint John's plea went un-
heard.

Hell, purgatory, and heaven were very real places for St. John. At just
about the same time as Rabelais was trying to elicit laughter from those

[12] The most complete biography of John of Avila is that of Luis Sala Balust, in *Obras
Completas del Santo Maestro Juan de Avila*, ed. Luis Sala Balust and Francisco Martín
Hernandez, 6 vols. (Madrid, 1970), vol. I, pp. 3–392. See also Florencio Sanchez
Bella, *La Reforma del clero en San Juan de Avila* (Madrid, 1981).

[13] *Advertencias necesarias para los reyes, Obras Completas*, vol. 6, p. 216.

[14] Ibid., vol. 6, p. 217.

who gathered around his deathbed, John of Avila was trying to frighten his readers to death:

Think of how you will collapse in bed one day, how you will perspire the sweat of death; think of how your chest will heave, how your eyes will dim, how your face will grow pale; think how painful will be the sundering of that intimate bond between body and soul. Your corpse will then be shrouded, borne on a litter, and taken to be buried, accompanied by laments and mournful songs. You will be cast into a narrow grave, covered with earth, and, after the soil has been stamped down, you will be all alone, and soon forgotten.[15]

Thinking the unthinkable was necessary, taught St. John, for those who ignored death would pay a high price when their time came. "Remember," he cautioned,

that the more you flee from death and the less that you meditate upon it, the greater will be your torment and distress when you die. It is beneficial to spend time preparing for that final hour, and experiencing it with our mind.[16]

And living through death in one's mind involved nothing less than contemplating the putrefaction of one's flesh and pondering the ultimate futility of all carnal pursuits. This acute dualism pervaded not only St. John's meditation but Spanish Catholicism itself. It was an ancient tradition dating back to the desert hermits of the second and third centuries, now renewed and strengthened in face of the Protestant challenge. Faced with the inevitability of death, the best one could do was to turn one's eyes away from temporality and toward eternity. Embodiment in the material world was both painful and perilous. This was a mentality that conceived of bodily pleasures as fleeting illusions bathed in light from the flames of hell: "How deceived are they that give themselves over to the body and follow its appetites; for all they are doing is cooking a meal for the worms that will feed upon it, exchanging a few brief pleasures for everlasting torments."[17]

---

[15] *Audi, Filia* (1556), *Obras Completas*, vol. I, p. 707.

[16] *Obras Completas*, vol. 3, sermon 82, p. 355. As Martín de Castro observed in his funeral sermon for Philip II: "Justo juyzio de Dios, que quien mientras vive no se acuerde de la muerte, en la muerte no se acuerde de Dios para pedirle perdon de sus pecados, y assi se valla con ellos y tenga que pagar por siempre en el Infierno." *Sermones funerales*, fol. 243r.

[17] *Audi, filia*, ch. 60, *Obras Completas*, vol. I, p. 708. This tradition reached its apogee in

Properly nauseated by one's own body after such a meditation, added St. John, one would be more easily disposed to flee from temptation and to make the right moral choices. And so much was riding on each human deed. Unlike the Protestants, who taught that one's salvation depended on faith rather than good works, Catholics believed that heaven could be gained or lost by one's actions. This was precisely the point emphasized by John of Avila. If one desired to gain heaven, one had better behave in a certain way.[18] No single human act and no other single instant was so crucial for one's fate as behavior at the moment of death, for it was then that the consequences of one's choices in life would be revealed: It was Judgment Day. When a person was poised on a razor's edge between salvation and damnation, the deathbed became the ultimate battleground. And even more dreadful than the wrenching away of the soul from the body, more harrowing than the approaching dissolution of the flesh, was the presence of the devil, who hovered over the dying, eager to snatch them away to hell. When John of Avila spoke of the demons that lurked at the deathbed, "as ravenous wolves around a lamb," tempting the dying, claiming their souls from God, eagerly listing for Him every sin they had committed, he was merely reminding his readers of what they already knew. This was the ultimate fright. As St. John bluntly put it, "You have every reason to fear."[19]

Death was made all the more frightful because this mentality perceived the entire human race, and thus every individual, as worthy of eternal damnation. Indeed, demons had every right to claim one's soul. In his meditation on death, John of Avila sought to elicit despondency: "The objective of this exercise," he admitted, "is not only to make you realize that you are evil but to make you taste and feel it willingly, to compel you to accept your depravity and unworthiness, like someone who admits that he has a dead dog right under his nose."[20]

This attitude was pervasive. We can find it reflected, for instance, in St. Teresa's deathbed confession, when she spoke of herself as "the

the seventeenth century, especially in the writings of Juan Eusebio Nierenberg, S. J., (1595–1658), *Partida a la eternidad y preparación para la muerte* (Madrid, 1645), and *De la diferencia entre lo temporal y lo eterno* (Lisbon, 1653).

[18] *Obras Completas*, vol. III, sermon 82, p. 355.

[19] *Audi, filia, Obras Completas*, vol. I, p. 709–10.

[20] Ibid., chap. 61, *Obras Completas*, vol. I, p. 710.

worst sinner in the world,"[21] and in Philip II's will in which he implored "The Divine Majesty" for mercy, calling himself "the greatest of all sinners."[22] We can also see it reflected in the anxious gesture of Luis de León, who, fearing he might die suddenly, prepared a written confession lest he die without publicly admitting his sinfulness:

I confess before heaven and earth that . . . I have lived as a lawless man, full of ingratitude and disobedience, and of an infinite number of grave, enormous sins, for which I confess that I truly deserve Hell many times over, having nothing that could excuse or justify me on my own.[23]

Pedro de Medina admitted that whenever he thought of "the dreadful and terrifying draught of the hour of death," he immediately thought of judgment and of being cast into "strange regions" filled with horrendous demons who would accuse him before God, listing every sin he had committed.[24] Likewise, Alonso de Orozco, Philip II's chaplain, warned that God was not only a stern judge but also a witness to all of one's sins. There was no hiding from Him. "There you will see the sword of divine justice threatening you," he said of the divine tribunal, "and you will see the Hell deserved by your evil deeds . . . and not only the judge, but also the angels will be indignant with you." Examine your conscience each night, he advised, and think of yourself as buried in your own grave, for there "you will see the hand of God passing sentence against you."[25]

Hell was no vague destination in the Spanish mentality but, rather, a vividly pictured place of unspeakable horror 1,193 leagues beneath the earth's surface.[26] Ecclesiastics were fond of graphic depictions of hell that were very much in keeping with the accepted medieval tradition and that were no less frightening. In fact, the shock value of these images was intensified. If there is any difference at all between the hell of Dante and that of Ignatius Loyola, it is not so much in the imagined torments as in the way in which these horrors were internalized: Loyola's hell is not a place for others but a place for oneself. In the 1520s a vivid sort of

[21] Yepes, p. 412.   [22] *Testamento de Felipe II*, pp. 2–3.
[23] *Protestación de Fray Luis sobre si le tomare la muerte subitamente, Obras Completas Castellanas de Fray Luis de Leon*, ed. by Felix Garcia, 4th ed. (Madrid, 1967), vol. I, p. 966.
[24] Medina, *Libro de la Verdad*, III.6, pp. 450–3.
[25] Orozco, *Victoria de la muerte*, pp. 5; 94–5.
[26] This was Venegas's exact calculation, *Agonía*, p. 202.

meditation had already gained popularity in Spain. Antonio de Guevara, for instance, thought it advisable to hang a picture of hell in one's chamber and distinctly to imagine the punishments meted out for each of the seven deadly sins. "Blessed be the soul that daily makes the rounds of hell," he said. For Guevara, it was better to descend to hell regularly in this life through meditation than to end up there for real at death. As far as he was concerned, the fear of hell was a much more potent antidote to sin than the love of God.[27] When Ignatius Loyola devised his influential *Spiritual Exercises,* he made it an absolute necessity to imagine the sensory as well as the spiritual torments of hell: seeing the flames and the suffering souls in their fire-bodies (*cuerpos ygneos*); feeling the pain; smelling the smoke, sulphur, and putrefaction; tasting one's tears and the worm of conscience; hearing the woeful screams and blasphemies of the damned.[28] This kind of meditation was never short on details. Pedro de Medina drew verbal images of demons worthy of Hieronymus Bosch: They were black and disfigured, with huge mouths, long nails, and sharp teeth; they spewed out flames from their eyes and every orifice in their vile bodies. "They are so horribly ugly," he warned, "that simply to look at them is a grave torment." Like Loyola, Medina asked his readers to place themselves there, and to realize that this is precisely what one deserved for eternity.[29] No wonder, then, that when Teresa of Avila received a vision of hell, she found herself in a cramped and filthy niche that had been specially carved out for her and that she later spoke of this experience as one of the greatest gifts she had received from God.[30]

Youth and good health were no buffer against the fear of hell. Death was everywhere to be seen: in the streets, where funerals, *viaticum* processions, and the tolling of bells were routine events; and inside the churches, where the dead were relentlessly buried under the worshipers'

[27] Guevara, *Epistolario familiar,* esp. 15 (1524), p. 100.

[28] Ignatius Loyola, Fifth Exercise, *Texte Autographe des Exercices Spirituels et Documents Contemporains,* ed. Edouard Gueydan, S. J. (Paris, 1985), pp. 89–90. These graphic meditations reached their zenith in the seventeenth century, in a vast corpus of literature. For an overdramatic account of these later developments in Europe, see Piero Camporesi, *The Fear of Hell: Images of Damnation and Salvation in Early Modern Europe* (University Park PA, 1992); for Spain see Ana Maria Arancón, *Geografía de la eternidad* (Madrid, 1987), pp. 55–124.

[29] Medina, *Libro de la verdad,* pp. 486–90.

[30] Teresa, *Vida,* chap. 32, OCST, I.796–98.

feet.[31] Everyone was also painfully aware of the death of children and youths.[32] As the royal preacher Aguilar de Terrones phrased it, the more offspring one had, the greater the chances that one would have to bury several of them before they reached the age of thirty. Out of 500 yearly burials in any busy parish, he estimated, "fifty will be old, four hundred and fifty young." Preachers and devotional writers elicited despair by harping upon this awful fact.[33]

Such despair was essential: It was a key assumption of Christian soteriology. Without it, the promise of salvation held little meaning. Consequently, to despair was to hope, for it was sin itself that had prompted the incarnation of God, His crucifixion, and His resurrection. Luis de León knew all this when he appealed to Christ:

Prostrate on the ground, I beseech and implore His Majesty to have mercy and forgive me, for, even though He is my judge and must pass sentence, He should recall He is also my most kind and gentle brother. Inasmuch as I acknowledge and confess the vast quantity and gravity of my sins, I also offer and present before Him, for their remission, the infinite treasure and virtue of His own blood, of His sacred passion, of His divine and inexhaustible merits, which I entreat Him to make my own as a divine gift; and though my heart is the most sinful in the whole world, it rests secure in Him, believing in Him, hoping in Him, and loving Him above all else.[34]

Such was the dialectic of redemption: God, ever gracious, ever merciful, could forgive the sins of evil men and women through the merits of Christ.

But sixteenth-century Spanish Catholicism was too profoundly convinced of human corruption to engage in a simple dialectic of forgive-

---

[31] Aguilar de Terrones, *Sermones funerales*, fol. 281v: "Vemos morir tantos, doblense las campanas tan amenudo por los muertos." Juan Bernal went as far as to exclaim: "¿O dónde podrá poner los ojos [el hombre], que no vea rastros de muerte, y que en todo lugar tiene Dios puesta suhorca y chuchillo?" Funeral sermon for Philip II, appendix to Ariño, *Sucesos de Sevilla*, p. 540.

[32] In parts of early modern Spain, children accounted for up to half of all deaths. The death rate was highest for children under one year of age and next highest for those between one and three years old. See Vicente Perez Moreda, *La crisis de la mortalidad en la España interior, siglos XVI–XIX* (Madrid, 1980), p. 161; and Martinez Gil, *Toledo*, pp. 35–37.

[33] For instance, Orozco, *Victoria de la muerte*, p. 94.

[34] *Protestación, Obras Completas*, vol. I, p. 967.

ness. In a society with nearly unattainable goals of behavior, everyone was doomed to moral failure. The guilt, the despair, were far too intense in the collective psychology; the polarities of culpability and absolution were not evenly balanced and could attain no full equilibrium. Anxiety could be lessened, but it could never be totally dissipated. Though theology proclaimed a message of forgiveness, outright pardon seemed improper, even impossible. Redemption could not be simply effected in beings so thoroughly evil. Deep within, the collective psyche ached for punishment.

Hence, purgatory. A place of temporal rather than eternal punishment, a way station to heaven, purgatory allowed God to be both merciful and just – to be both brother and judge. Though a place of torment, it gave sinners a chance for redemption beyond the confines of material existence. Viewed against the yawning abyss of hell, which all human beings deserved as their eternal fate, purgatory seemed a merciful reprieve. Purgatory was the vestibule of heaven. John of Avila knew how to offer hope to his readers after he had driven them to despair:

On that hour when the soul is commanded by God to leave the body, its fate shall be decided, eternal perdition or eternal salvation. One shall then hear from the mouth of God: "Depart from me to the eternal flames," or "Remain with me in a state of *salvation* [emphasis added] in purgatory or paradise."[35]

In that final moment when one's soul was in the balance, literally, the scales could be tipped by God toward purgatory. And this was a marvelous gift, an infinitely compassionate gesture by the Almighty, for purgatory was in fact an undeserved, albeit unprecipitous entrance into heaven. John of Avila juxtaposed what was truly deserved with what was graciously granted, urging his readers to consider that they merited nothing but rejection and torment. "If you truly know yourself as a sinner and worthy of hell," he advised, "you should say to yourself, 'whatever evil comes my way is very little indeed, for I deserve hell'." In other words, purgatory was relatively benign punishment. As he put it, "Who shall complain about insect bites, knowing they deserve eternal torment?"[36]

Belief in purgatory lessened anxiety over death by means of paradox and by setting in motion a dialectic between terror and confidence. On

[35] *Audi, filia, Obras Completas*, vol. I, p. 709.   [36] Ibid., p. 711.

the one hand, as a place of torment, it was something to be feared; on the other hand, as a place of gradual cleansing, it offered hope for redemption and made the landscape of the afterlife seem less daunting and unfamiliar. The route from Madrid to purgatory was not an easy one to traverse, but it was a spacious highway, open to any Christian who would pay its tolls. Passage could be gained through effort and expense. As has been shown, sixteenth-century Madrileños seemed eager to do what was needed for this journey, either for themselves or for their beloved dead. And the language used to deal with death reveals precisely that it was thought of in terms of a journey, for death was often called a *tránsito.* Whether king, saint, courtier, artisan, or prostitute, one faced this inevitable common passage into the hereafter. Certain gestures and modes of behavior were invested with meaning by clergy and laity alike, as means for conveyance and as currency on this road to heaven. Except for saints, those rare spiritual athletes who could scale the fine high trail to paradise, the vast majority of baptized Catholics expected to voyage through purgatory, and they routinely made use of the means of travel offered to them by the church. Chief among these were prayers and masses for the dead.

In death as in life, sixteenth-century Spaniards thought of prayer as a communal responsibility. Surely, there was much that individuals could – and should – do for themselves, but there was also much that needed to be done by others. Whether it was thousands of masses, as in the case of King Philip II, or a simple *novenario,* suffrages for the dead were the responsibility of the living. For each individual, it was usually the immediate family that sought to hasten the purification process in the afterlife; for all of the dead, it was the community as a whole that interceded. In a tangible way, the living cared for the dead, and the dead remained very much a part of the living community; each generation interceded for its forebears, secure in the knowledge that, in turn, it too would be cared for by its descendants as they continued the chain of intercession. If masses for the dead are viewed as an industry – a system of labor and production into which capital is invested and in which workers are paid to perform assigned tasks – then one has to admit that it was one of the most important and most rapidly growing industries in sixteenth-century Spain.

Maintaining such close contact between the living and the dead had obvious social and psychological benefits, but it also had a price. Caring for the souls in purgatory became an increasingly heavy responsibility in the sixteenth century, as the evidence from Madrid indicates. For individual and community alike, the dead made heavy demands in economic as well as emotional terms, and as the century progressed these demands spiraled ever higher, along with Spain's economic inflation. Moreover, alongside the inflation in the cost and in the number of masses, a certain relativism took hold of the suffrage system itself, so that the benefits of the suffrages became linked to one's commitment to them. As José de Siguenza saw it, for instance, the value of suffrages was proportional to the investment made by each individual in the care of the dead. In other words, the more intensely that one had prayed and offered masses for the souls in purgatory while in this life, the more one would benefit from each suffrage made by others on one's behalf in the afterlife; conversely, the less one had cared for the dead while in this life, the less one would enjoy from each suffrage in the hereafter.[37]

No wonder, then, that levity toward death seems lacking from the Spain of Philip II; no wonder, also, that Rabelais's skepticism would seem so foreign there. Among the elite as well as among the common people, death and the hereafter could hold little mystery. At the end of life there was no "great Perhaps," no *terra incognita.* The hereafter was *not* that "undiscover'd country from whose bourn no traveler returns."[38] Alejo Venegas had not only calculated the distance from the earth's surface to hell as an exact 1,193 leagues but had also mapped out the entire cosmos for his readers. His description was very much in the tradition of medieval Christian cosmology: The universe was composed of concentric spheres.[39] Earth was at the lowest point, at the center of this spherical pre-Copernican cosmos. Hell, purgatory, and limbo were at the earth's core. Hell, of course, was the lowest point of all, a place of utter desolation and eternal fire, the abode of the devil and his minions. Purgatory was above hell, its cleansing flames derived from the infernal

---

[37] José de Siguenza, *Historia de la Orden de San Jeronimo,* vol. II, p. 189.

[38] Shakespeare, *Hamlet,* 3.1.79.

[39] On conceptions of the Christian cosmos, see Colleen McDannell and Bernhard Lang, *Heaven: A History* (New Haven/London, 1988), pp. 1–180; Edward Grant, *Planets, Stars, and Orbs: The Medieval Cosmos, 1200–1687* (Cambridge/New York, 1993); Gregor Maurach, *Coelum Empyreum: Versuch einer Begriffsgeschichte* (Wiesbaden, 1968); Jacques Le Goff, *The Birth of Purgatory;* and Eilen Gardiner, ed., *Visions of Heaven and Hell Before Dante* (New York, 1989).

regions. Above this there were two limbos: the one in which the souls of the pre-Christian just had awaited Christ's redemption and which was now empty; and the one in which the souls of unbaptized infants would languish for eternity. Above the earth there were ten mobile heavenly spheres where the celestial bodies moved in harmony. Venegas had little to say about these. What interested him was the immobile empyrean heaven, the highest of all the spheres, the abode of God and His Celestial Court. This was also the destination for which God had created human beings, their true home. Venegas's view of the empyrean heaven was detailed enough to include a description of the posture that resurrected human bodies would have there for eternity: According to him, everyone would be forever on their feet, standing erect before God, without any need for rest.[40]

Pedro de Medina, too, gave his readers a tour of the afterlife in his *Book of Truth*. Despite saying that heaven was beyond imagination or description, he went on to describe a celestial realm that was analogous to his own society, arranged spatially in a rigid hierarchy where everyone would have his or her proper station for eternity. At the very summit of the Celestial Court, the Triune God reigned as a supreme monarch. Below the trinity, the Virgin Mary reigned as Queen of Heaven, gloriously clad in superb apparel, "according to the dignity and worthiness that belong to such a high lady."[41] Below Mary, the angelic hosts were hierarchically arranged like army and government officials. Medina unreflectively described the function of each of the angelic choirs with terms familiar to all Spaniards: *caballeros, oficiales reales, tesoreros, regidores,* and so on. Below the angels, the saints, too, would be eternally arranged according to their merit.[42] In such a heaven egalitarianism was as alien a concept as in early modern Spain.[43]

It is no mere coincidence that at a time when Spain dominated the seas and the Counter-Reformation, the same man who wrote an influential manual for sailors without much seafaring experience of his own should have also turned his attention to death and the afterlife. Pedro de

---

[40] Venegas, *Agonía*, pp. 200–2. [41] Medina, *Libro de la verdad*, p. 494.

[42] Ibid., pp. 494–500.

[43] The royal preacher Gerónymo de Florencia, said that Saint Teresa had been given a grander reception into the Celestial Court than anyone else but the Virgin Mary and that her presence was eagerly sought by all: "Todos los Angeles y Santos la piden y pleytean sobre quedarse con ella." *Sermones*, fol. 37r.

Medina's *Art of Navigation* and his *Book of Truth* shared a similar purpose in the author's mind: They both aimed to show how to steer a course through known dangers to a safe haven. The two books also shared in a similar kind of expertise, for Medina had derived his knowledge of both subjects more from personal study and technical mastery than from actual experience (Medina was a cleric as well as a cartographer and maker of navigational instruments).[44] By century's end, the hereafter was a clearly defined place in the Spanish mentality. Much like Spain's overseas colonies, the hereafter had a presence that was not diminished by distances. Gold from the New World and masses for the dead were equally "real" for someone who had seen neither Mexico nor purgatory. Moreover, much like the empire abroad, the hereafter was a destination reached by travel, and that voyaging could be mapped. In 1599, Pedro Sanchez could therefore publish a treatise entitled, *Book of the Kingdom of God, and of the Road by Which It Is Reached.*[45] Mapping out the hereafter could also become a science, as in the case of Cristóbal Ponce de Leon's *Book of the Natural Science of Heaven.*[46] This type of literature would steadily gain popularity in Spain throughout the seventeenth century.[47]

One of the favorite maxims of this society was *como vive muere* (in death as in life) – a most revealing aphorism.[48] On a broad level this maxim discloses the attitude that death is not something unto itself,

[44] Pedro de Medina (1493–1567), also known for his geographical survey, *Libro de las grandezas y cosas memorables de España* (1548), was sharply criticized by the leading navigators of Spain for all the errors included in his *Arte de Navegar* (1545). Nonetheless, this manual was translated into all the major Western European languages before the end of the sixteenth century. In 1552, after interviewing many sailors, he published a revised version entitled *Regimiento de Navegación*. See the introduction by Angel Gonzalez Palencia to the *Obras de Pedro de Medina, Clasicos Españoles*, vol. 1 (Madrid, 1944): xii–xix.

[45] Pedro Sanchez, *Libro del Reyno de Dios, y del camino por do se alcança* (Madrid, 1599).

[46] Cristóbal Ponce de Leon, *Libro de la ciencia natural del cielo, con cuatro repertorios del* (Alcalá, 1598).

[47] See the ample bibliography in Martinez Arancón, *Geograffía de la eternidad*, pp. 265–77.

[48] Bartolomé Bennassar has rightfully called attention to the significance of this Spanish maxim: "In his manner of dying a man reveals his innermost value, his deepest nature, his courage, the respect that he owes to himself, his mastery of himself." *The Spanish Character. Attitudes and Mentalities from the Sixteenth to the Nineteenth Century*, trans. Benjamin Keen (Berkeley CA, 1979), p. 241.

something "other" but, rather, a part of life, a point on a continuum. Sixteenth-century Spaniards thought of death and the afterlife in familiar and mundane terms, as a continuation of the realities of this world. On a personal and moral level, death was a moment that summed up a lifetime of behavior; consequently, one's afterlife was determined by one's deeds on earth. On a social and political level, death and the afterlife were but an extension of the intricately intertwined obligations of family and community life and of the bonds that linked each individual to his or her society.

The maxim "in death as in life" was grounded on a mimetic conception of reality and was intended as a confirmation of paradigmatic metaphysics, epistemology, and ethics. To accept this truism, one had to conceive of reality as a series of reflections. On a metaphysical level, this maxim proposed a continuity and a mirroring between different spheres of existence: the seen and the unseen, the material and the spiritual, the earthly and the postearthly. On an epistemological level, it contended that one thing can be understood only in terms of another, that is, namely, that death and the afterlife cannot be conceived of in any other way than as a reflection of earthly life and vice versa. On an ethical level, it suggested that one's moral choices in life determined one's fate in the hereafter and that patterns of behavior cannot be easily or quickly altered. This implied three things: that all behavior is mimetic; that the range of each individual choice is determined by the paradigms or models that have been previously employed; and that "good" paradigms should always be followed. Moreover, this mimetic conception of death and the afterlife, linked as it was to the notion of some final judgment being passed on one's behavior, was central to a repressive society such as Spain, where conformity was an ultimate virtue. To fashion conduct for the afterlife was also to control behavior in this world.

No wonder, then, that paradigmatic "good" deaths were so vigorously publicized in early modern Spain. No wonder that the Hapsburg monarchs of the seventeenth century carefully imitated and recapitulated the deaths of Charles V and Philip II. No wonder that St. Teresa's corpse remained as wondrously incorruptible as those of earlier saints, and that her apparitions so closely paralleled those described by Gregory the Great and Caesarius of Heisterbach. No wonder, also, that funeral practices and postmortem devotions in Madrid increased in cost and complexity after the court moved there and inflation gripped the economy. Inasmuch as they interwove life with death and actions with paradigms, sixteenth-century Spaniards found it difficult, on the whole, to segregate their attitudes toward death from their attitudes toward life in general. The ultimate paradox – and therefore also the uniqueness – of early modern Spanish attitudes toward death might very well reside in this apparent inability to approach death as something "other," or even a "perhaps." By focusing so intently on death and by making the hereafter so familiar, the subjects of Philip II could make death more mundane and life more otherworldly.[49]

If there was any "perhaps" at all in early modern Spanish attitudes toward death and the afterlife, it was not likely to be of a speculative or irreverent sort but, rather, of a functional nature. The prevailing Spanish approach to death was above all practical, for dying was not a passive experience. Though death was unavoidable, dying was a problem with solutions: There was much one could and should do concerning death and the hereafter, both for oneself and for others. Furthermore, it was generally agreed upon that emotional, economic, and ritual strategies for death and the afterlife could and should be codified. This is not to say that the Spanish were free from anxiety and uncertainty.[50] On the contrary, their practicality in the face of death was itself an attempt to confront doubt and fear, for the rigid order of death rituals and the apparent confidence invested in their value betray a deep-seated anxiety. After all, every sixteenth-century Madrileño who wrote a will had to assent to the routine confession that they were "fearing death, which is a natural thing, common to all human creatures."

In the Spain of Philip II, most attempts to alleviate mortal fright centered on the outward cultural forms surrounding death, that is, on ritual gestures made by the living, whether on the deathbed or in postmortem suffrages. In death as in life, the Spanish thrived on conventional gestures to carry them through to appointed goals. That rituals and paradigms became more rigidly codified and that their perceived value was ever more stridently proclaimed as the century wore on suggest that

[49] Américo Castro thought this was true of Spanish culture in general: "El alma española corrió como bisectriz entre una tierra divinizada y un cielo humanizado." *España en su historia*, p. 35.

[50] Bennassar stresses the pervasiveness of the early modern Spanish fear of death, and provides some examples, *Spanish Character*, pp. 244–5.

their supposed efficacy was in need of greater resolution. This means, of course that doubts lingered close at hand. But these were doubts about practical matters rather than about core beliefs. Because the world of the dead was so closely intertwined with the world of the living, these doubts concerning the specific value of certain gestures reflected the preoccupations of society at large. As the inflation in mass requests is related to the economic inflation, so are the "good" deaths related to specific anxieties, that of Philip II to fears of a declining monarchy and that of Teresa to the Protestant challenge. In death as in life, uncertainties cry out for resolution. What makes the Spain of Philip II seem unique is its ability to focus on the smaller functional uncertainties rather than on the "great Perhaps."

It stands to reason, then, that the preeminent metaphorical archetype for the early modern Spanish mentality should be Don Quixote, that character whose life was consumed with paradigms and mimetic behavior and whose deeds were always invested with a transcendent purpose. It is also reasonable that this archetype should be a character who blurred the lines between the mundane and the otherworldly and who always sought to correct some perceived problem through practical means. Given the acumen of Cervantes and his genius for allegory, it is reasonable, too, that one episode in *Don Quixote* should brilliantly capture attitudes toward death and the hereafter in the form of parable. I refer here to that point in the narrative where Don Quixote and Sancho Panza encounter a funeral cortege on a deserted road in the middle of the night. Cervantes describes a cortege much like the ones requested in Madrid wills, only in greater detail, and with an emphasis on its haunting eeriness. It was a long cortege, obviously of a person of means, consisting of about twenty people, twelve of whom were clerics. The deceased was being taken from Baeza, where he had died and been temporarily "deposited," to his native Segovia, where he had requested permanent burial. The clerics and mourners were attired in long dark robes, their blazing torches held aloft, their steeds draped in mourning gear. As the lights drew nearer, their spectral appearance was made all the more frightening by the surrounding gloom and the remoteness of the location. This so unnerved Don Quixote that his hair stood on end and so terrified Sancho that he could not stop his teeth from chattering. Unable, as always, to distinguish the real from the illusory, Don Quixote mistook the mourners for demons and charged them with his lance to prevent them from taking the deceased to hell. The members of the cortege then fled the assault, they too fearing that Don Quixote was a demon who had come to claim the corpse. Not until the dust had settled and he had confronted a fallen cleric whose leg he had broken did Don Quixote and his victim realize what had really happened. Aware that he now faced excommunication for having harmed a priest but undaunted by the prospect, Don Quixote defended his actions, saying:

You brought this damage upon yourself, *señor bachiller* Alonso López, by appearing at night as you did, dressed in those surplices, with your torches lit, praying, shrouded in mourning, for you truly seemed to be an evil thing from the other world (*cosa mala y del otro mundo*).[51]

A remarkable aspect of this episode is the way in which Cervantes has reality and illusion dissolve into each other, not only for Don Quixote and Sancho but also for the members of the funeral cortege. For all involved, *the other world* and this world impinged on each, and a funeral was a most likely place for the two worlds to converge. For all involved, too, and not just for Don Quixote, it seemed conceivable to do something for the dead. Both Don Quixote and the members of the funeral cortege deemed it possible – and necessary – to rescue the dead man from an awful fate. The significant difference, of course, is that whereas the mourners and clerics did so through their prayers, their "murmuring among themselves, in a low, compassionate voice," Don Quixote did so through brute physical force. Hence the irony and the humor. Hence the unphilosophical humor, so different from that of Rabelais's final words. Hence, also, the acumen and the allegorical potential of Cervantes's parable. For the narrator and reader, certain facts are observable and describable. But the external acts of the characters alone do not tell the full story. To comprehend the action, narrator and reader must enter into the minds of the characters, gain hold of their perceptions, and see the congruity between what they *think* is happening and what is actually taking place. For all those involved in this episode, sane and insane alike, the dead man was much more than a corpse that needed burial: He was a soul who needed assistance from the living. For them, as for most Spaniards, the *aquí* (the here) and the *mas allá* (the hereafter)

---

[51] Miguel de Cervantes, *El ingenioso hidalgo Don Quijote de la Mancha* (1605), Bk I, chap. 19 (Barcelona, 1976), p. 213.

were of one piece: Every practical act could vibrate with transcendent purpose, and every road in Spain could lead to *the other world.* As the road from Baeza to Segovia could suddenly become a highway to hell, so could the Calle Mayor and every other street reveal the brief ephemeral distance from Madrid to purgatory.

This collapsing of boundaries came at a high price for Spain, however. Mounting evidence indicates that the amount of money and resources invested in death ritual by Spaniards *might* have had a profound impact on the economy and the social fabric. As we have seen, many Madrileños were spending much more on funerals and postmortem rituals than their grandparents ever had. And this phenomenon was only part of a much larger and more complex picture, for it was only the beginning of a long and steep inflationary ascent in the seventeenth century and only a local reflection of a peninsular phenomenon. Spain's preoccupation with death ritual at this time *seems* to be unique, not just because Protestant Europe had done away with purgatory and the need for postmortem ritual but because even in other neighboring Catholic societies, such as France and Italy, far less money seems to have been spent on the dead.[52]

Again, however, I must insert a word of caution. The comparative evidence is far too scanty at present for definitive conclusions. Recent work on popular religion suggests that there could be substantial local variations in piety within nation states, and even within the same church. All I am saying here is that the evidence to date suggests that Spain as a whole probably differed from the rest of Europe in its approach to death ritual. Much more research is still needed on this subject.

Much can be inferred about the cost of Spain's peculiar obsession with death ritual from Sara Nalle's findings in Cuenca. Between 1591 and 1654, the population of Cuenca declined by 40 percent. During this period, Cuenca's economy also took a nose dive: Woolen cloth production (1600–31) declined by 93 percent, and tax revenues (1590–1640) declined by 60 percent.[53] At the same time, however, the cult of the dead expanded. Despite their shrinking population and economy, the people of Cuenca doubled their number of mass requests between 1585 and 1645 and continued building chapels and churches. Also, despite a

---

[52] Bartolomé Bennassar concurs, *Spanish Character*, p. 71.
[53] Nalle, *God in La Mancha*, pp. 173–4.

dwindling population, the number of priests in Cuenca increased by 30 percent between 1591 and 1654, doubling the priest-to-laity ratio! This heavy investment in ritual, which was usually funded by rents on land or gifts of land to the churches, led to an imbalance in the economic and social framework of Cuenca. By 1752 the ecclesiastics had become the principal landowners and employers in Cuenca, owning 57 percent of all city property and 44 percent of the surrounding land, and employing about two-fifths of the total population. As Nalle sums it up, "After generations of investing in salvation, the city had become a vast monument to the dead."[54]

Bringing up the subject of Spain's decline is even more perilous than talking about Spanish exceptionalism, but, as I see it, there is no way for me to steer clear of the issue of the decline of Spain and its relation to death ritual. By the end of the sixteenth century, Spain was not yet an empire of the dead, but it was a dying empire and a culture very much aware of its own oddness and decline.[55] A reformer who was quite sensitive to Spain's *declinación*, Martín Gonzalez de Cellorigo, said in 1600: "It seems as if one had wished to reduce these kingdoms to a republic of enchanted beings, living outside the natural order of things."[56] Seventeenth-century Spain would become the land of *desengaño*, or disillusionment, in which perceptions were radically inverted. Life would be seen as an illusion or dream and death as an awakening.[57] In such a culture the paradigms of Philip II and Teresa of

---

[54] Ibid., pp. 175, 188, 202–5. "In the end," she also suggests, "the reallocation of Cuenca's dwindling economic resources to the service of the dead may well have contributed to the decline of the city as well as to the impoverishment of its spiritual life."

[55] See John H. Elliott, "Self-Perception and Decline in Early Seventeenth-Century Spain," *Past and Present* 74 (1977): 41–61; also available in J. H. Elliott, *Spain and its World, 1500–1700* (New Haven/London, 1989), pp. 241–62.

[56] Martín Gonzalez de Cellorigo, *Memorial de la política necesaria y util restauración a la república de España* (Valladolid, 1600), trans. J. H. Elliott, "Art and Decline in Seventeenth-Century Spain," *Spain and Its World*, pp. 262–86.

[57] The Marquis of Valparaiso, Francisco de Irarrazábal y Andia, entitled his paean to Charles V's death-obsessed days at Yuste, *El perfecto desengaño* (1638); Francisco de Miranda y Paz published *El desengañado: Philosophia moral* (1663); Juan Eusebio Nierenberg gave the subtitle *Crisol de desengaños* to his *Diferencia entre lo temporal y lo eterno* (1640); and Pedro Calderón de la Barca staged his world-renowned play, *La Vida es sueño* (1636).

Avila reigned supreme, and the dead made off with much of the nation's wealth.

This is not to say that Spain's decline was a direct result of its fervent interest in death and its rituals. I am not saying here that I see a simple causal relation between Spain's investment in death ritual and its decline. What I am saying is that there seems to have been some *vague* dialectical relation between Spain's funerary inflation and its decline. I am not here formulating some inverse of Weber's controversial thesis about the relation between mentalities and capitalist success.[58] A vast mental and spiritual gulf separated the societies of this-worldly Calvinist ascetics and other-worldly Spanish Catholics, but their different approaches to the creation of wealth cannot be reduced to such a simple formula. Economic historians may someday tell us with more precision how this siphoning of time, energy, and wealth into the cult of death contributed to Spain's tailspin – along with numerous weightier factors. In the sixteenth century, this behavior seems to have been more a symptom than a cause of decline. It was an appropriate coping mechanism in an age of gathering gloom, a means of ordering an increasingly incomprehensible world, a way of focusing beyond immediate disappointments and frustrations. Whether this behavior turned deadly in the seventeenth century, becoming a contributing cause of decline, remains to be determined. My observations here apply more to the Spanish mentality than the Spanish economy. I am more than happy to leave the more definitive conclusions to economic historians.

This is not to say that early modern Spain developed a fascination with death that was morbid or to suggest that the brittle negative stereotypes of yesteryear should be sustained. Three decades have passed since Christian Dedet complained: "We are still faced with that tiresome heresy maintained for more than two centuries by a horde of bigots, bores, and squint-eyed academicians, which represents Spain as a land of mourning, of funereal love, and eternal grief."[59] Dedet's irritation,

---

[58] Max Weber, *Die Protestantische Ethik und der Geist des Kapitalismus*, vol. 1 of *Gesammelte Aufsätze zur religionssoziologie* (Tübingen, 1924), Trans. Talcott Parsons, *The Protestant Ethic and the Spirit of Capitalism* (New York, 1958).

[59] Christian Dedet, *La Fuite en Espagne* (Paris, 1965), p. 9. Some Spaniards themselves have favored the negative stereotypes. Américo Castro, *España en su historia*, p. 181, cites José Ortega y Gasset, who said that Spain not only suffered from an "enfer-

though legitimate, rests on the mistaken assumption that devotion to the cult of death was necessarily a negative, pathological attitude. Sixteenth-century Spain's immersion in death and its rituals can be viewed in quite another light.

Ritual is a means of imposing order on a seemingly disorderly, painful, and indifferent universe. Experts remind us that ritual speaks in the subjunctive mood: It is an attempt to turn the world as it is into the world as it should be, a fusing together of the imagined and the real into a unified vision.[60] Ritual is multidimensional. It is an expression and confirmation of a society's myths through symbolic behavior. It is a means of transcending and redeeming mundane reality *as well as* a process of social interaction and control. Death rituals in particular are a dense amalgam of coping mechanisms, arranged not just against the ultimate terror offered up by the universe but also against more immediate threats to one's society and family as well as to oneself. The fear of death – the ultimate disintegration – incorporates fears of all lesser dissolutions, social, political, and economic. The greater the menace of dissolution, the more valuable that ritual can become. It is no coincidence, then, that in an era of crisis and decline the Spanish should have sought solace in myths, symbols, and rituals associated with death. Because the disintegration of the body politic could not be disassociated from the dissolution of each human body within it, the integrative power of ritual seems to have been enhanced. If one keeps in mind that the Catholic death rituals observed in Spain stressed *order, stability,* and *continuity* on multiple interdependent levels of meaning (encompassing both the sacred and the profane), then their appeal to this unstable society might be better understood. Instead of seeming odd or morbidly pathological, this Spanish fixation might then appear downright practical, or even gallant.

Baroque is a French word that means "bizarre" or "odd." It was originally used as a period label to show contempt for a certain mentality

---

medad cronica," but that "su existir es radicalmente patológico," *España invertebrada* (1922), in *Obras* (Madrid, 1936), p. 800.

60 Victor Turner, *From Ritual to Theatre* (New York, 1982), pp. 82ff.; Clifford Geertz, "Religion as a Cultural System," *Anthropological Approaches to the Study of Religion,* ed. Michael Banton (New York/London, 1966), p. 28.

and an entire culture. Spain's immersion in death and its rituals has long been considered typically Baroque in that disdainful sense. Certain early modern Spanish attitudes toward death and the afterlife might seem bizarre or even morbid to modern observers: the proximity of the living and the dead in Madrid's churches, the attention lavished on the dissolving body of Philip II, the fervor shown for St. Teresa's incorruptible flesh. Given the long distance that we have from that culture, mental images of Teresa's corpse being carved up and of men and women toting pieces of her *carne* can be most disquieting. I use the Castilian *carne* intentionally, for, unlike English which has two words – "flesh" and "meat" – Castilian has but one word for the substance of animal bodies. Those who sought Teresa's bodily relics said they hankered after her *carne*, using the same word that they would have used at a butcher's shop.

This brings us back to the bullring, where we began. Bullfighting, too, is a death ritual: a mythic summation of the struggle for survival on earth reenacted time and time again in a highly structured ceremonial setting. It is a social artifice, a means of imposing order and control – and even a sense of transcendence – on what is at bottom a fierce, chaotic struggle for survival. In more colloquial terms, it is a way of looking one's meat in the eye with gallantry. Bullfighting is all about embodiment and its perils. It is an unflinching acknowledgment of the effort and pain involved in the consumption of flesh, of the way in which one body survives through feeding upon another. The paradigms and rituals of death so favored in sixteenth-century Spain also dealt with embodiment: social and political as well as individual. By focusing so intently on death at this time, the Spanish elected to stare down life's most vexing quandary, much in the same way that a *matador* ("killer" or "slayer") braves his dangerous prey. In fixing upon such a predicament and in seeking to subdue it ritually, they also chose to transcend it.

The paradoxical complexity of the early modern Spanish mentality certainly did not exclude gloominess or fatalism but it also engendered a certain aplomb and a healthy measure of optimism. To die well in sixteenth-century Spain could also be to live well. To be buried well could also be to ensure a lasting remembrance of oneself. To invest in postmortem rituals could be to maintain and reinforce the social ties that bound families and communities together. To invest in purgatory could be to expand the economy of salvation, to bridge the gap between saints and sinners, and to hope for a nearly universal redemption from evil. To embrace dead flesh could be to preserve one's own for eternity. To make the daily rounds of hell could be to secure a place in heaven for eternity. And to stare at death and the sun could be to prevail in the face of the ultimate terror.

Bibliography

Primary sources

Ariño, Francisco de. *Sucesos de Sevilla de 1592 a 1604, Sociedad de Bibliófilos Andaluces* series 1 (Seville, 1873).

Aznar Gil, Federico Rafael. *Concilios provinciales y sinodos de Zaragoza de 1215 a 1563* (Zaragoza, 1982).

Blois, Louis de. *Opera quae quidem conscripsit omnia* (Cologne, 1572).

Obras. Traduzidas por Fray Gregorio de Alforo (Barcelona, 1609).

The Works of Louis de Blois, trans. Bertrand A. Wilberforce, 7 vols. (London, 1925–30).

Cabrera, Alonso. *Sermones funerales en las honras del Rey Nuestro Señor don Felipe Segundo*, recogidos por Juan Iñiguez de Lequerica (Madrid, 1601), BNM 2–57997.

Canons and Decrees of the Council of Trent, trans. H. J. Schroeder (Rockford, 1978).

Carranza, Bartolomé de. *Comentarios sobre el catecismo Cristiano* (1558), ed. J. L. Tellechea, 2 vols. (Madrid, 1972).

Castanega, Martin de. *Tratado de las supersticiones, hechicerias y varios conjurs y abusiones y de la posibilidad y remedio dellos* (Logroño, 1529).

Cervera de la Torre, Luis. *Testimonio Autentico y Verdadero de las cosas que pasaron en la dichosa muerte del Rey Nuestro Señor Don Felipe Segundo* (Valencia, 1599).

Ciruelo, Pedro. *Reprobación de las supersticiones y hechicerias* (1530), ed. Francisco Tolsada (Madrid, 1952).

Los códigos españoles concordados y anotados, ed. M. Rivadeneyra, 12 vols. (Madrid, 1847–51).

Collado, Francisco Gerónimo. *Descripción del Túmulo relación de las exequias que hizo la ciudad de Sevilla en la muerte del Rey don Felipe II* (1598), *Sociedad de Bibliófilos Andaluces* (Seville, 1869): series 2, vol. 22.

Compendio de las solenes fiestas que en toda España se hicieron en la Beatificación de N.B.M. Teresa de Jesús, fundadora de la reformación de los Descalzos y Descalzas de N.S. del Carmen, por Fray Diego de San José (Madrid, 1615).

"Constituciones sinodales de la diocesis de Canarias" (1497), in *El Museo Canario* 15 (1945).

Constituciones sinodales del obispado de Segovia, del Consejo de Su Majestad y electo Arçobispo de Çaragoza en el año 1586.

Dalmau, J. *Relación de la solemnidad con que se han celebrado en la ciudad de Barcelona las fiestas de la Beatificación de la Madre Teresa de Jesús* (Barcelona, 1615).

De Vega, Lope. *Vida y muerte de Santa Teresa de Jesús* (1638), ed. Elisa Aragone Terni (Messina/Florence, 1970).

Diaz, Nicolás. *Tratado del juyzio final en el cual se hallarán muchas cosas prove- chosas y curiosas* (Valladolid, 1588).

Erasmus of Rotterdam. *De praeparatione ad mortem* (Basel, 1534), in *Opera Omnia Desiderii Erasmi Roterodami* (Amsterdam/Oxford, 1969), Ordinis V, vol. I, pp. 321–92.

Fiestas que hizo la insigne ciudad de Valladolid en la beatificación de la Madre Teresa de Jesús, por M. de los Rios Hevia Ceron (Valladolid, 1615).

Francisco Gonzalez de Audia, Marqués de Valparaiso. *El Perfecto Desengaño* (1638), Modern edition (Madrid, 1983).

Fuentes historicas sobre la muerte y el cuerpo de Santa Teresa de Jesús (1582–1596), Monumenta Historica Carmeli Teresiani, ed. J. L. Astigarraga, E. Pacho, and O. Rodriguez (Rome, 1982).

Garcia Polanco, Juan. "Memoria de las misas que en sus testamentos y por las animas del purgatorio y por otros negocios gravísmos o devociones partic- ulares se dicen" (1625), BNM ms. 18728, n. 9.

Gonzalez de Cellorigo, Martín. *Memorial de la política necesaria y util restauración a la república de España* (Valladolid, 1600).

Gracián de la Madre de Dios, Jerónimo. "Dialogos del tránsito de la Madre Teresa de Jesús" (1584). *Fuentes históricas sobre la muerte y cuerpo de la Santa Teresa de Jesús (1582–1596),* ed. J. L. Astigarraga, E. Pacho, and O. Rodriguez (Rome, 1982).

Granada, Luis de. *Libro de la oración y meditación* (1554). Modern edition (Madrid, 1979).

Horozco, Juan de. *Tratado de la verdadera y falsa prophecia* (Segovia, 1588).

La Rochefoucauld, Francois VI, duc de. *Maximes et réflexions diverses* (Paris, 1975).

Bibliography

Lhermite, Jehan. *Le Passetemps* (1602 manuscript), ed. Charles Ruelens, 2 vols. (Antwerp, 1890–6; rpt. Geneva, 1971).

Libros de acuerdos del Consejo Madrileño (1464–1600), 4 vols. (Madrid, 1932).

Libro de las bulas y pragmaticas de los Reyes Catolicos, 2 vols. Facsimile edition (Madrid, 1973).

Lopez de Hoyos, Juan. *Hystoria y relación verdadera de la enfermedad, felicissimo transito y sumptuosas exequias funebres de la Serenisima Reyna de España doña Isabel de Valoys nuestra señora* (Madrid, 1569), *Fuentes para la Historia de Madrid y su Provincia*, ed. Jose Simon Diaz, vol. 1.

Manuel, Nicholas. *Niklaus Manuels Spiel Evangelischer Freiheit: Die Totenfresser. "Vom Papst und Seiner Priestschaft," 1523*, ed. F. Vetter (Leipzig, 1923).

Mariana, Juan de, S. J. *Historiae de rebus Hispaniae* (Toledo, 1592).

Medina, Pedro de. *Libro de la Verdad* (Valladolid, 1555), thirteen editions, 1563–1626. Modern edition: *Obras de Pedro de Medina*, ed. Angel Gonzalez Palencia, *Clasicos Españoles*, vol. I (Madrid, 1944).

Montañes, Jaime. *Libro intitulado espejo de buen vivir. Con otro tratado para ayudar a buen morir, en el incierto dia y hora de la muerte* (Madrid, 1573).

Nierenberg, Juan Eusebio, S. J. *Hechos politicos y religiosos del que fué Duque Quarto de Gandía, Virey de Cataluña y despues tercero General de la Compañia de Jesús, el Beato Francisco de Borja* (1643). Later edition (Barcelona, 1882), 2 vols.

Obras Completas Castellanas de Fray Luis de León, ed. Félix Garcia, O.S.A., 2 vols., 4th ed. (Madrid, 1967).

Obras Completas de la Beata Ana de San Bartolomé, 2 vols., *Monumenta Historica Carmeli Teresiani 5* (Rome, 1981).

Obras del Padre Jerónimo Gracián de la Madre de Dios, ed. Silverio de Santa Teresa, O.C.D., 3 vols. (Burgos, 1932).

Obras Completas del Santo Maestro Juan de Avila, ed. Luis Sala Balust and Francisco Martin Hernandez, 6 vols. (Madrid, 1970).

Orozco, Alonso de. *Victoria de la Muerte* (Burgos, 1583). Modern editions by Gil Blas (Madrid, 1921 and 1975).

Paez de Valençuela y Castillejo, J. *Relación de las fiestas que en la ciudad de Cordoba se celebraron a la beatificación de la Madre Teresa de Jesús* (Cordoba, 1615).

Perez de Herrera, Cristóbal. *Elogio a las esclarecides virtudes del Rey Nuestro Señor Don Felipe II, que está en el cielo y de su exemplar y cristianísima muerte* (Valladolid, 1604), included as an appendix to Luis Cabrera de Cordoba, *Felipe II, Rey de España*, 4 vols. (Madrid, 1877), vol. 4.

Bibliography

Polanco, Juan, S. J. *Methodus ad eos adiuvandos, qui moriuntur* (Burgos, 1578). *Regla y orden para ayudar a bien morir a los que se parten de esta vida* (Zaragoza, 1578).

Ponce de Leon, Cristóbal. *Libro de la ciencia natural del cielo, con cuatro repertorios del* (Alcalá, 1598).

Porreño, Baltasar. *Dichos y Hechos del Rey Don Felipe II* (1628). Modern edition (Madrid, 1942).

Procesos de beatificación y canonización de Santa Teresa de Jesús, ed. Silverio de Santa Teresa, O.C.D., 3 vols. *Biblioteca Mistica Carmelitana* 18–20 (Burgos, 1934).

Quaderno de las leyes, ordenanzas, provisiones y pragmaticas hechas a la suplicación de los tres estados del Reyno de Navarra, 1562 (Pamplona, 1563).

Raulin, Juan. *Libro de la muerte temporal y eterna* (Madrid, 1596).

Rebolledo, Luis de. *Primera parte de cien oraciones funebres en que se considera la vida, y sus miserias: la muerte y sus provechos* (Madrid, 1600).

Relaciones biográficas inéditas de Santa Teresa de Jesús, ed. José Gómez Centurión (Madrid, 1917).

Ribadeneyra, Pedro de, S. J. *Flos Sanctorum de las Vidas de los Santos (1599–1601)*.

Ribera, Francisco de, S. J. *Vida de la Madre Teresa de Jesús, fundadora de las Descalças y Descalços* (Salamanca, 1590). Nueva Edición, aumentada con una introducción, copiosas notas y apendices por el P. Jaime Pons, S. J. (Barcelona, 1908).

Rodriguez de Monforte, Pedro. *Descripción de las honras que se hicieron a la Catholica Magestad de Don Phelippe quarto Rey de las Españas y del nuevo mundo en el Real Convento de la Encarnación* (Madrid, 1666).

Rojo, Antonio. *Historia de San Diego de Alcalá* (Madrid, 1663).

St. Francis of Assisi, Writings and Early Biographies: English Omnibus of the Sources for the Life of St. Francis, ed. Marion A. Habig (Chicago, 1973).

San Andrés, Juan Diacono de. *Vida y milagros del glorioso San Isidro Labrador, hijo, abogado, y patrono de la Real Villa de Madrid*, con adiciónes de Jaime Bleda (Madrid, 1622).

Sanchez, Pedro. *Libro del Reyno de Dios, y del camino por do se alcança* (Madrid, 1599).

Sánchez de Vercial, Clemente. *El Libro de los exemplos por a.b.c.* Modern edition by John Esten Keller (Madrid, 1961).

San Vicente, Fray Tomás de. *Relación sencilla y fiel de las fiestas que el Rey Don Felipe IIII nuestro Señor hizo al Patronato de sus Reinos de España Corona de Castilla, que dió a la gloriosa Virgen Santa Teresa de Jesús, año de 1627* (Madrid, 1627).

Bibliography

Sepulveda, Jerónimo de. *Documentos para la historia del monasterio de San Lorenzo del Escorial* (Madrid, 1924, 1964–65).

Serrano, Luciano, ed., 3 vols. *Fuentes para la historia de Castilla,* (Valladolid, 1906–10).

Sermones funerales en las honras del Rey Nuestro Señor don Felipe II, recogidos por Juan Iñiguez de Lequerica (Madrid, 1601).

Sermones predicados a las honras del Rey Nuestro Señor Don Philipo Segundo este año de 1598 (Seville, 1599).

Sermones predicados en la Beatificación de la B.M. Teresa de Jesús, Virgen, Fundadora de la Reforma de los Descalços de Nuestra Señora del Carmen. Colegidos por orden del Padre Fray Joseph de Jesús Maria, General de la misma orden (Madrid, 1615).

Siguenza, José de. *Historia de la Orden de San Jerónimo* (1605). Modern edition, *Nueva Biblioteca de Autores Españoles* 8 and 12 (Madrid, 1907).

Tejada y Ramiro, Juan. *Colección de canones y de todos los concilios de la Iglesia Española,* 5 vols. (Madrid, 1855).

Testamento de Carlos V, facsimile edition (Madrid, 1982).

Testamento de Felipe II, facsimile edition (Madrid, 1982).

El tribunal de la Inquisición en Mallorca. Relación de causas de fé 1576–1806, ed. L. Perez, L. Montaner, and M. Colom (Palma de Mallorca, 1986).

Valdés, Alfonso de. *Dialogo de Mercurio y Carón* (1530). Modern edition (Madrid, 1954).

Venegas, Alejo. *Agonía del tránsito de la muerte. Con avisos y consuelos que cerca della son provechosos* (1536). *Escritores Misticos Españoles,* ed. Miguel Mir, vol. I, which is vol. XVI of the *Nueva Biblioteca de Autores Españoles* (Madrid, 1911).

Vida de Santa Teresa de Jesús, por el maestro Julián de Avila, primer capellán de la santa. From the unpublished manuscript, ed. Vicente de la Fuente (Madrid, 1881).

Vigil, Ciríaco Miguel. *Colección histórico-diplomática del Ayuntamiento de Oviedo* (Oviedo, 1889).

Villegas, Alonso de. *Flos Sanctorum. Tercera parte y Historia General en que se escriven las vidas de Santos Extravagantes y de varones ilustres en virtud* (Toledo, 1588).

Yepes, Diego de. *Relación de algunas particularidades que pasaron en los vecinos dias de la enfermedad de que murío nuestro Catolico Rey Don Phelipe II* BNM 1504 F154.

Vida, virtudes y milagros de la Bienaventurada Virgen Teresa de Jesús (Madrid, 1599). Modern edition published under the title *Vida de Santa Teresa de Jesús* (Buenos Aires, 1946).

Bibliography

Prologue

Ariès, Philippe. *L'homme devant la mort* (Paris, 1977), trans. Helen Weaver, *The Hour of Our Death* (New York, 1981).

Ayuso Rivera, Juan. *El concepto de la muerte en la poesía romantica española* (Madrid, 1959).

Banker, James R. *Death in the Community: Memorialization and Confraternities in an Italian Commune in the Late Middle Ages* (Athens GA/London, 1988).

Bennassar, Bartolomé. *L'Homme Espagnol: Attitudes et mentalités du XVIe au XIXe siècle* (Paris, 1975), trans. Benjamin Keen, *The Spanish Character* (Berkeley, 1979).

Brown, Jonathan. *Images and Ideas in Seventeenth-Century Spanish Painting* (Princeton, 1978).

Camacho Guizado, Eduardo. *La elegía funeral en la poesía española* (Madrid, 1969).

Casero, Antonio. *De Madrid al Cielo* (Madrid, 1968).

Castro, Américo. *España en su historia: Cristianos, moros y judíos* (Buenos Aires, 1948).

An Idea of History, Selected Essays of Américo Castro, ed. S. Gilman and E. L. King (Columbus OH, 1977).

Chaunu, Pierre. *La Mort à Paris, XVIe–XVIIIe siècles* (Paris, 1981).

Chiffoleau, Jacques. *La comptabilité de l'au delà: Les hommes, la mort et la religión dans la region d'Avignon a la fin du Moyen Age* (Rome, 1980).

Durkheim, Emile. *The Elementary Forms of Religious Life,* trans. J. S. Swain (New York, 1912).

Eliade, Mircea. *The Sacred and the Profane: The Nature of Religion,* trans. W. R. Trask (New York, 1959).

Evans-Pritchard, E. E. *Theories of Primitive Religion* (Oxford, 1965).

Fernald, James C. *The Spaniard in History* (New York, 1898).

Fernandez Alonso, Maria del Rosario. *Una visión de la muerte en la lírica española: la muerte como amada* (Madrid, 1971).

Gachard, Louis-Prosper. *Sur le séjour de Charles Quint au Monastère de Yuste* (Brussels, 1843).

Geertz, Clifford. "Religion as a Cultural System," in *Anthropological Approaches to the Study of Religion,* ed. Michael Banton (London/New York, 1966).

Goody, Jack. "Religion and ritual: The definitional problem," *British Journal of Sociology* 12 (1961): 148–62.

Jimenez Vasco, Felipe. *Como nace un monasterio y muere un César* (Caceres, 1969).

Le Goff, Jacques. "Les mentalités, une histoire ambigue," in *Faire de l'histoire:*

Bibliography

nouveaux problèmes, ed. by J. Le Goff and P. Nora (Paris, 1974), part 3, pp. 76–94.

Malinowski, Bronislaw. "Magic, Science, and Religion" (1925), in *"Magic, Science and Religion, and Other Essays"* (Glencoe IL, 1948).

Maltby, William. *The Black Legend in England* (Durham NC, 1971).

Martín Gonzalez, Juan José. "En torno al tema de la muerte en el arte español," *Boletín del Seminario de Estudios de Arte y Arqueología* 38 (1972): 267–85.

Maxwell, William Stirling. *The Cloister Life of the Emperor Charles V* (London, 1853).

Mignet, François A. A. *Charles Quint, son abdicatión, son séjour, et sa mort au monastère de Yuste* (Paris, 1854).

Mirrors of Mortality: Studies in the Social History of Death, ed. Joachim Whaley (London, 1981).

Mitchell, Timothy. *Blood Sport: A Social History of Spanish Bullfighting* (Philadelphia, 1991).

Passional Culture: Emotion, Religion and Society in Southern Spain (Philadelphia, 1990).

Poschman, Adolf. *Kaiser Karl V in Yuste* (Leppstadt, 1960).

Ray, Benjamin C. *Myth, Ritual, and Kingship in Buganda* (New York/Oxford, 1991).

Sanchez Camargo, Manuel. *La muerte y la pintura española* (Madrid, 1954).

Suau, Pedro, S. J. *Historia de San Francisco de Borja, tercer General de la Compania de Jesús* (Zaragoza, 1963).

Turner, Victor. *Dramas, Fields, and Metaphors: Symbolic Action in Human Society* (Ithaca NY/London, 1974).

Vives Suria, José. *El tema de la vida y la muerte a través de algunos de nuestros principales literatos* (Folletones de Mision, s.d., s.l.).

Vovelle, Michel. "Les attitudes devant la mort: Problèmes de methode, approches et lectures différentes," *Annales, E.S.C.* 1976.

"L'histoire des hommes au miroir de la mort," in *Death in the Middle Ages*, ed. Herman Braet and Werner Verbrecke (Louvain, 1983), pp. 1–18.

Piété baroque et déchristianisation en Provence au XVIIIe siècle (Paris, 1973).

(with Gaby Vovelle). *Vision de la mort et l'au-delà en Provence du XVe au XXe siècle* (Paris, 1970).

Book One

Adeva Martín, I. *El maestro Alejo Venegas de Busto, su vida y sus obras* (Toledo, 1987).

"Los Artes de Bien Morir en España antes del Maestro Venegas," *Scripta Teologica* (1984), pp. 405–16.

Bibliography

Alvar Ezquerra, Alfredo. *Felipe II, la corte y Madrid en 1561* (Madrid, 1985).

Alvarez de Baena, José Antonio, *Compendio histórico de las grandezas de la coronada villa de Madrid, corte de la monarquía de España* (1786). Modern edition (Madrid, 1978).

Arbol Navarro, Miguel del. *Spanisches Funeralbrauchtum unter Berücksichtigung Islamischer Einflüsse* (Bern/Frankfurt, 1974).

Archivo Histórico de Protocolos de Madrid. *Indice de Testamentos y Documentos Afines*, Primera Serie, ed. Antonio Matilla Tascon (Madrid, 1980).

Banker, James R. *Death in the Community* (Athens GA/London, 1988).

Bataillon, Marcel. *Erasme et l'Espagne* (Paris, 1937), 3rd ed., 3 vols. (Geneva, 1991).

Beaty, N. L. *The Craft of Dying. A Study in the Literary Tradition of the* Ars Moriendi *in England* (New Haven, 1970).

Bernard, A. *La sepulture en droit canonique du Décret de Gratien au Concile de Trente* (Paris, 1933).

Black, Christopher F. *Italian Confraternities in the Sixteenth Century* (Cambridge UK, 1989).

Bono y Huerta, J. "Los formularios notariales españoles de los siglos xvi, xvii, y xviii," *Anales de la Academia Matritense del Notariado* (1978): 22.1.

La Vida Privada Española en el Protocolo Notarial (Madrid, 1950).

Braudel, Ferdinand. *The Mediterranean in the Age of Philip II*, 2 vols., trans. Siân Reynolds (New York, 1972).

Camara y Castro, Tomás. *Vida y escritos del Beato Alonso de Orozco* (Valladolid, 1882).

Cannadine, David, and Simon Price. *Rituals of Royalty* (Cambridge UK, 1987), p. 14.

Carbajo Isla, M. F. *La población de la villa de Madrid desde finales del siglo XVI hasta mediados del siglo XIX* (Madrid, 1987).

Castro, Américo. *España en su historia* (Buenos Aires, 1945).

Cattaneo, E. *Introduzione alla storia della liturgia occidentale* (Milan, 1969).

Chartier, Roger. "Les Arts de Mourir, 1450–1600," *Annales, E.S.C.* 31 (1976): 51–76.

Châtellier, Louis. *L'Europe des devots* (Paris, 1987), trans. J. Birrel, *The Europe of the Devout: The Catholic Reformation and the Formation of a New Society* (Cambridge UK, 1989).

Christian, Jr., William. *Apparitions in Late Medieval and Renaissance Spain* (Princeton, 1981).

Local Religion in Sixteenth-Century Spain (Princeton, 1981).

Cipolla, Carlo M., in "La prétendue 'révolution des prix', réflexions sur l'experience italienne," *Annales, E.S.C.* Oct.–Dec., (1955): 513–16.

Bibliography

Cohn, Samuel S., Jr. *Death and Property in Siena, 1205–1800. Strategies for the Afterlife* (Baltimore, 1988).

Coster, R. *Antonio de Guevara, sa vie* (Bordeaux, 1925).

La documentación notarial y la historia: Actas del Segundo Coloquio de metodología histórica aplicada (Santiago de Compostela, 1984).

Douglas, Mary. *Implicit Meanings: Essays in Anthropology* (London, 1975).

Études sur l'histoire de la pauvreté (Moyen Age – XIVe siècle), ed. Michel Mollat, 2 vols. (Paris, 1974).

Farmer, Sharon. "Personal Perceptions, Collective Behavior: Twelfth-Century Suffrages for the Dead," in *Persons in Groups: Social Behavior as Identity Formation in Medieval and Renaissance Europe*, ed. Richard Trexler (Binghamton NY, 1985).

Fernández Alvarez, M. *El establecimiento de la capitalidad de España en Madrid* (Madrid, 1960).

El Madrid de 1586 (Madrid, 1962).

Flynn, Maureen. *Sacred Charity: Confraternities and Social Welfare in Spain, 1400–1700* (Ithaca NY, 1989).

Gómez Nieto, Leonor. *Ritos funerarios en el Madrid medieval* (Madrid, 1991).

Garcia Mercadal, José. *España vista por los extranjeros*, 3 vols. (Madrid, 1917–21).

Viajes de extranjeros por España y Portugal, 3 vols. (Madrid, 1952–62).

Gluckman, M. "Les rites de passage," in *Essays on the Ritual of Social Relations*, ed. by M. Gluckman (Manchester UK, 1962).

Gonzalez Novalín, José Luis. "Las misas 'artificiosamente ordenadas' en los misales y escritos renascentistas," in *Doce consideraciones sobre el mundo hispano-italiano en tiempos de Alfonso y Juan de Valdés. Coloquio interdisciplinar, Bologna, Abril 1976*, ed. by Francisco Ramos Ortega (Rome, 1979).

"Misas supersticiosas y misas votivas en la piedad popular del tiempo de la reforma," in *Miscelania José Zunzunegui* (Vitoria, 1975).

"Religiosidad y Reforma del Pueblo Cristiano," in *Historia de la Iglesia en España*, ed. Ricardo García-Villoslada (Madrid, 1980), vol. III.1.

Goody, Jack. *Death, Property, and the Ancestors* (Stanford CA, 1962).

Gutierrez Nieto, J. I. "En torno al problema del establecimiento de la capitalidad de la monarquía hispanica en Madrid," *Revista de Occidente*, special issue, "Madrid, villa, y communidad" (1983): 53–65.

Hamilton, Earl J. *American Treasure and the Price Revolution in Spain 1501–1650* (Cambridge UK, 1934).

Huarte Echenique, Amalio. "Origenes del Archivo de Protocolos de Madrid," *Revista de la Biblioteca, Archivo y Museo del Ayuntamiento de Madrid* 7 (1930): 194–9.

Bibliography

Kany, Charles E. *Life and Manners in Madrid, 1750–1800* (Berkeley CA, 1932).

LeGoff, Jacques. *La Civilisation de l'Occident Medieval* (Paris, 1964), p. 240.
La naissance du purgatoire (Paris, 1981), trans. Arthur Goldhammer, *The Birth of Purgatory* (Chicago, 1984).

Las leyes del Reyno de Navarra, hechas en Cortes Generales a suplicación de los tres estados del, desde el año 1512 hasta el de 1612, ed. by Pedro de Sada and Miguel de Murillo y Ollacarizqueta (Pamplona, 1614).

Lopez Alonso, Carmen. *Los rostros, la realidad de la pobreza en la sociedad castellana medieval (siglos XIII–XV)* (Madrid, 1983).
La pobreza en la España medieval. Estudio histórico-social (Madrid, 1986).

Lopez i Miguel, O. *Actituds colectives davant la mort i discurs testamentari al Mataro del sigle XVIII* (Mataro, 1987).

Lopez Lopez, Roberto J. *Comportamientos religiosos en Asturias durante el Antiguo Régimen* (Gijón, 1989), pp. 38 and 41.

Lorenzo Pinar, Francisco J. *Actitudes religiosas ante la muerte en Zamora en el siglo XVI: Un estudio de mentalidades* (Zamora, 1989), p. 28.

Madrid en el Archivo Histórico de Protocolos, ed. Ana Duplá del Moral (Madrid, 1990), pp. 151–52.

Maertens, T., and L. Heuschen. *Doctrine et pastorale de la liturgie de la mort* (Bruges, 1957).

Maldonado y Fernández del Torco, José. *Herencias a favor del alma en el derecho español* (Madrid, 1944).

Martines, Lauro. "Ritual Language in Renaissance Italy: The Worldly Aspect," to be published: *Rites et rituels dans les sociétés médiévales (XIII–XVIe siècles)*, ed. A. Paravicini Bagliani and J. D. Maire-Vigeur (Erice, Sicily).

Martinez Arancón, Ana. *Geografía de la eternidad* (Madrid, 1987).

Martinez Gil, Fernando. *Actitudes ante la muerte en el Toledo de los Austrias* (Toledo, 1984).

Martz, Linda. *Poverty and Welfare in Hapsburg Spain* (Cambridge UK, 1984).

Matilla Tascón, Antonio. "Escribanos, notarios y Archivos de Protocolos en España," *Archivum* 12 (1962).

Meslin, Michel. *Aproximación a una ciencia de las religiones* (Madrid, 1978).

Mesonero Romanos, Ramon de. *El Antiguo Madrid* (Madrid, 1861).

Molinié-Bertrand, Annie. *Au siècle d'or. L'Espagne et ses hommes: La population du royaume de Castille au XVIe siècle* (Paris, 1985).

Mollat, Michel. *Les pauvres au Moyen Age* (Paris, 1978).

Montero Vallejo, Manuel. *El Madrid Medieval* (Madrid, 1987).

Morell Pequero, B. *La contribución etnográfica del Archivo de Protocolos* (Salamanca, 1981).

Bibliography

Nadal Oller, J. "La revolución de los precios españoles del siglo XVI," *Hispania* 19 (1959): 503–29.

Nalle, Sara T. *God in La Mancha: Religious Reform and the People of Cuenca, 1500–1650* (Baltimore, 1992).

O'Connor, Sister M. C. *The Art of Dying Well: The Development of the Ars Moriendi* (New York, 1942).

Odriozola, A. "Liturgia: Libros liturgicos impresos," in *Diccionario de historia eclesiastica de España*, 4 vols., plus supplement (Madrid, 1972), vol. 2, pp. 1326–30.

Orlandis, A. "Sobre la elección de sepultura en la España medieval," *Anuario de Historia del Derecho Español* (1950): 5–49.

Pascua, M. J. de la. *Actitudes colectivas ante la muerte en el Cadiz de la primera mitad del siglo XVIII* (Cadiz, 1984).

Paxton, Fredrick. *Christianizing Death: The Creation of a Ritual Process in Early Medieval Europe* (Ithaca NY, 1990).

Paz, Julián. "Noticias de Madrid y de las familias madrileñas de su tiempo, por Gonzalo Fernández de Oviedo," *Revista de la Biblioteca, Archivo, y Museo del Ayuntamiento de Madrid* (1947), pp. 273–326.

Peñafiel Ramón, Antonio. *Testamento y buena muerte: Un estudio de mentalidades en la Murcia del siglo XVIII* (Murcia, 1987).

Pintor, Hector. *Imagen de la vida Cristiana, ordenada por dialogos* (Madrid, 1573).

A pobreza e a assistencia aos pobres na peninsula Iberica durante a Idade Media. Actas das Ias jornadas luso-espanholas de historia medieval, 2 vols. (Lisbon, 1973).

Primer Encuentro sobre religiosidad popular (Seville, 1987).

Quintana, Jerónimo de la. *Historia de la antiguedad, nobleza, y grandeza de la villa de Madrid* (Madrid, 1954).

Reder Gadow, Marion. *Morir en Málaga: Testamentos Malageños del siglo XVIII* (Málaga, 1986).

La religiosidad popular, eds. C. Alvarez Santaló, M. J. Buxó, and S. Rodriguez Becerra, 3 vols. (Barcelona, 1989), vol. II, *Vida y Muerte: La imaginación religiosa*.

Ringrose, David. "Imigración, estructuras demográficas, y tendencias económicas en Madrid a comienzos de la Epoca Moderna," *Moneda y Credito*, 138, pp. 9–55.

Rivas Alvarez, José A. *Miedo y Piedad: Testamentos Sevillanos del siglo XVIII* (Seville, 1986).

Romero, Juan Ramón. "Asistencia a los pobres y caridad en Madrid en la segunda mitad del siglo XV," *Anales el Instituto de estudios Madrileños* (1987): 123–31.

Rosenthal, Joel T. *The Purchase of Paradise: Gift Giving and the Aristocracy, 1307–1485* (London, 1972).

Bibliography

Ruiz, Teofilo. "Feeding and Clothing the Poor: Private Charity and Social Distinction in Northern Castille Before the Black Death." Unpublished paper.

Rush, A. C. *Death and Burial in Christian Antiquity* (Washington DC, 1941).

Sainz de Robles, F. C. *Motivos que determinaron la exaltación de Madrid a capitalidad de España* (Madrid, 1932).

¿Porqué es Madrid capital? (Madrid, 1961).

Sanchez Herrero, José. *Concilios provinciales y sinodos toledanos de los siglos xiv y xv: La religiosidad cristiana del clero y pueblo* (Laguna, 1976).

Sills, Edward. "Ritual and Crisis," in *Center and Periphery: Essays in Macrosociology, Selected Papers of Edward Sills*, vol. II (Chicago, 1975).

Strocchia, Sharon T. *Death and Ritual in Renaissance Florence* (Baltimore, 1992).

Tenenti, A. *Il Senso della morte e l'amore della vita nel Rinascimento (Francia e Italia)* (Turin, 1957).

Turner, Victor. *The Forest of Symbols* (Ithaca NY, 1967).

The Ritual Process (Chicago, 1969).

Van Gennep, Arnold. *Les rites de passage* (1909), trans. M. B. Vizedom and G. L. Caffee, *The Rites of Passage* (London, 1960).

Varela, Javier. *La muerte del rey: El ceremonial funerario de la monarquía Española, 1500–1885* (Madrid, 1990).

Wagstaff, Grayson. *Music for the Dead: Settings of the Missa and Officium pro defunctis by Spanish and Latin American Composers before 1700*. Ph.D. dissertation, in progress (Austin, TX).

Weissman, R. F. *Ritual Brotherhood in Renaissance Florence* (London/New York, 1982).

Book Two

Alvarez Turienzo, Saturnino. *El Escorial en las letras españolas* (Madrid, 1985).

Arco, R. *Sepulcros de la casa real de Castilla* (Madrid, 1954).

Bloch, Marc. *Les rois thaumaturges* (Paris, 1961).

Brown Jonathan, and John Elliott. *A Palace for a King: The Buen Retiro and the Court of Philip IV* (New Haven/London, 1980).

Cabrera de Cordoba, Luis. *Felipe II, Rey de España*, 4 vols. (Madrid, 1877), vol. 4.

Calí, Maria. *Da Michelangelo all'Escorial. Momenti del dibattito religioso nell'arte del Cinquecento* (Turin, 1980).

Catalano, G. *Controversie giurisdizionali tra Chiesa e Stato nell'etá di Gregorio XIII e Fillipo II* (Palermo, 1955).

Chueca, Fernando. *Casas Reales en Monasterios y Conventos Españoles* (Madrid, 1966).

Bibliography

Cuartero y Huerta, Baltasar. *El monasterio de San Jerónimo el Real: protección y dádivas de los Reyes de España a dicho Monasterio* (Madrid, 1966).

Cuervo, J. *Biografía de Fray Luis de Granada* (Madrid, 1895).

Diez Borque, José Maria. *La vida Española en el Siglo de Oro según los extranjeros* (Barcelona, 1990).

Eire, Carlos, M. N. *War Against the Idols: The Reformation of Worship from Erasmus to Calvin* (New York, 1986).

Eliade, Mircea. *Images and Symbols. Studies in Religious Symbolism* (New York, 1969).

Elliott, J. H. "Self Perception and Decline in Early Seventeenth Century Spain," *Past and Present*, 74 (1977): 47.

"Power and Propaganda in the Spain of Philip IV," in *Rites of Power: Symbolism, Ritual, and Politics Since the Middle Ages*, ed. by Sean Wilentz (Philadelphia, 1985).

The Revolt of the Catalans: A Study in the Decline of Spain, 1598–1640 (Cambridge, 1963); and *The Count-Duke of Olivares: The Statesman in an Age of Decline* (New Haven/London, 1986).

"The Court of the Spanish Habsburgs: a peculiar institution?" in *Politics and Culture in Early Modern Europe: Essays in Honor of H. G. Koenigsberger*, ed. by Phyllis Mack and Margaret C. Jacob (Cambridge UK, 1987).

Estal, Juan Manuel del, O. S. A. "Felipe II y su archivo hagiografico de El Escorial," *Hispania Sacra*, XXIII (1970): 1–96.

Monasterio de San Lorenzo el Real, "Curioso memorial del mayor traslado de reliquias de Alemania al Escorial (1597–98)" (Escorial, 1964): 403–49.

Frazer, James G. *The Golden Bough*, 12 vols. (London, 1911–15).

Gallego, Julian. *Vision et symboles dans la peinture Espagnole du siècle d'or* (Paris, 1968).

Geertz, Clifford. "Centers, Kings, and Charisma," in *Rites of Power: Symbolism, Ritual, and Politics Since the Middle Ages*, ed. Sean Wilentz (Philadelphia, 1985).

Giesey, Ralph E. *Royal Funeral Ceremony in Renaissance France* (Geneva, 1960). *If not, not: The Oath of the Aragonese and the Legendary Laws of Sobrarbe* (Princeton, 1968).

Hofmann, Christina. *Das Spanische Hofzeremoniell von 1500–1700* (Frankfurt am Main, 1985).

Kantorowicz, Ernst. *The King's Two Bodies* (Princeton, 1957).

Kubler, George. *Building the Escorial* (Princeton, 1982).

Lagomarsino, David. "The Hapsburg Way of Death." Unpublished paper.

Lemaire, L. "La mort de Philippe le Bon," *Revue du Nord* 1 (1910): 321–6.

Llaneza, M. *Bibliografía de Fray Luis de Granada*, 4 vols. (Salamanca, 1926–28).

Bibliography

Longas, Pedro. "La Coronación Liturgica del Rey en la Edad Media," *Anuario de Historia del Derecho Español* 23 (1953): 371–81.

Mackay, Angus. "Ritual and Propaganda in Fifteenth-Century Castile," *Past and Present* 107 (1985): 19–20.

Menjot, Denis. "Les funérailles des souverains castillans du Bas Moyen Age racontées par les chroniqueurs: Une image de la souveraineté," *Annales de la Faculté des Lettres et Sciences Humaines de Nice* 39 (1985): 3–43.

Morena, Aurea de la. "El Monasterio de San Jerónimo el Real, de Madrid," *Anales del Instituto de Estudios Madrileños* 10 (1974): 47–78.

Moxey, Keith. "Interpreting Pieter Aertsen: The Problem of 'Hidden Symbolism'," *Nederlands Kunsthistorisch Jaerboek* 40 (1989).

Nieto Soria, José Manuel. *Iglesia y poder real en Castilla: El episcopado, 1250–1350* (Madrid, 1988).

Fundamentos ideologicos del poder real en Castilla, siglos XIII–XVI (Madrid, 1985).

Oakley, Francis. *The Western Church in the Later Middle Ages* (Ithaca/London, 1979).

Les obsèques de Philippe le Bon, ed. by E. Lory (Dijon, 1869).

O'Kane, Eleanor. *Refranes y frases proverbiales españolas de la Edad Media* (Madrid, 1959).

Orso, Steven N. *Art and Death at the Spanish Court: The Royal Exequies for Philip IV* (Columbia MO, 1989).

Pfandl, Ludwig. *Cultura y costumbres del pueblo español de los siglos xvi y xvii*, first Spanish edition (Barcelona, 1929).

Philippe II, trans. M. E. Lepointe (Paris, 1942).

Phillips, William D. *Enrique IV and the Crisis of Fifteenth Century Castile, 1425–1480* (Cambridge MA, 1978).

Quarto Centenario del Monasterio de El Escorial (Madrid, 1986).

Rosenthal, Earl E. "The Invention of the Columnar Device of Emperor Charles V at the Court of Burgundian Flanders in 1516," *Journal of the Warburg and Courtauld Institutes* 36 (1973): 198–230.

Ruiz, Teofilo F. "Unsacred Monarchy: The Kings of Castile in the Late Middle Ages," in Sean Wilentz, ed., *Rites of Power: Symbolism, Ritual, and Politics Since the Middle Ages* (Philadelphia, 1985).

Sánchez, Maria Leticia. "El sentido de la muerte en El Escorial," in *IV Centenario del monasterio de El Escorial. Las casas reales, el palacio* (Madrid, 1986).

Sánchez Perez, Aquilino. *La literatura emblemática española (Siglos XVI y XVII)* (Madrid, 1977).

Schramm, Percy Ernst. *Herzschaftszeichen und Staatsymbolik* (Stuttgart, 1956).

Shils, Edward, and Michael Young. "The Meaning of the Coronation," in Shils, *Center and Periphery* (Chicago, 1975), pp. 135–52.

Taylor, René. "Architecture and Magic: Considerations on the Idea of the Escorial," in *Essays in the History of Architecture Presented to Rudolf Wittkower* (New York, 1967).

Turner, Victor. *Revelation and Divination Among the Ndembu* (Ithaca NY, 1967), pp. 31–2.

Unamuno, Miguel de. *Andanzas y visiones españolas*, in *Obras*, vol. I (Madrid, 1966), p. 392.

Valdevellano, Luis G. *Curso de historia de las instituciones españolas: de los órigines al final de la edad media* (Madrid, 1968), p. 431.

Valgoma y Díaz Varela, Dalmiro de la. "Honras fúnebres regias en tiempo de Felipe II," in *El Escorial 1563–1963* (Madrid, 1963).

Vaughan, R. *Philip the Good* (New York, 1970).

Valois Burgundy (London, 1974).

Von Cartellieri, O. *The Court of Burgundy* (London, 1929).

Von der Osten Sacken, Cornelia. *San Lorenzo el Real de el Escorial. Studien zur baugeschichte und ikonologie* (Mittenwand-München, 1979).

Book Three

Aigrain, René. *L'Hagiographie – Ses sources, ses méthodes, son histoire* (Paris, 1953).

Alvarez, Tomás. "El ideal religioso de Santa Teresa de Jesús y el drama de su segundo biógrafo," *El Monte Carmelo* 86 (1978): 203–38.

Bilinkoff, Jodi. *The Avila of St. Teresa: Religious Reform in a Sixteenth-Century City* (Ithaca/London, 1989).

Boland, Paschal. *The Concept of Discretio Spiritum in John Gerson's "De Probatione Spiritum," and "De Distinctione Verarum Visionum a Falsis,"* (Washington DC, 1959).

Bossy, John. *Christianity in the West, 1400–1700* (Oxford, 1987).

Bremond, Claude, Jacques Le Goff, and Jean-Claude Schmitt. *L'"Exemplum," Typologie des sources du Moyen Age Occidental* 40 (Belgium, 1982).

Brown, Peter. *The Cult of the Saints: Its Rise and Function in Late Antiquity* (Chicago, 1981).

The Body and Society: Men, Women, and Sexual Renunciation in Early Christianity (New York, 1988).

Cardellac, Nemesio. *Santa Teresa di Gesù e le spine del suo cuore* (Venice, 1882).

Caro Baroja, Julio. *Las formas complejas de la vida religiosa. Religión, sociedad y carácter en la España de los siglos XVI y XVII* (Madrid, 1978).

Bibliography

Centre de Recherches sur l'Antiquité et le Haut Moyen Age. *Hagiographie, Cultures, et Sociétès, IVe–XIIe siècles. Actes du Colloque organisé à Nanterre et à Paris, 2–5 mai 1979* (Paris, 1981).

Cerdan, Francis. "Santa Teresa en Los Sermones del Patronato (1627)," in *Santa Teresa y la literatura mística hispánica*, ed. Manuel Criado de Val (Madrid, 1984).

Cruz, Tomás de la. "L'Extase chez Sainte Thérèse D'Avila," *Dictionnaire de Spiritualité, Ascetique, et Mystique* (Paris, 1960), vol. 4, pp. 21–60.

Delhaye, Hippolyte S. J. *Cinq leçons sur le méthode hagiographique* (Brussels, 1934; reprint, 1968).

The Legends of the Saints, ed. by R. J. Schoeck, trans. V. M. Crawford (South Bend, 1961).

Delooz, Pierre. "Pour une étude sociologique de la sainteté canonisée dans l'église catholique," *Archives de Sociologie des Religions* 13 (1962): 17–43.

Sociologie et canonisations (Liège, 1969).

Delumeau, Jean. *Le catholicisme entre Luther et Voltaire* (Paris, 1971), English tr. *Catholicism Between Luther and Voltaire: A New View of the Counter-Reformation* (London/Philadelphia, 1977).

Egido, Teófanes. "El tratamiento historiográfico de Santa Teresa: Inercias y revisiones," *Perfil historico de Santa Teresa*, ed. T. Egido (Madrid, 1981); also published in *Revista de Espiritualidad* 40 (1981): 171–89.

"Santa Teresa y las tendencias de la historiografía actual," *Ephemerides Carmeliticae* 23 (1982): 160–80.

Eliade, Mircea. *The Myth of the Eternal Return, or Cosmos and History*, tr. by Willard R. Trask (Princeton, 1954).

Febo, Giuliana di. *Teresa d'Avila: Un culto barocco nella Spagna franchista (1937–62)* (Naples, 1988).

Finucane, R. C. "Sacred Corpse, Profane Carrion: Social Ideals and Death Rituals in the Later Middle Ages," in *Mirrors of Mortality: Studies in the Social History of Death*, ed. by Joachim Whaley (London, 1981; New York, 1982).

Appearances of the Dead: A Cultural History of Ghosts (New York, 1984).

Fita, Fidel. "Cuatro biógrafos de Santa Teresa en el siglo XVI: El Padre Francisco de Ribera, Fray Diego de Yepes, Fray Luis de León y Julián de Avila," *Boletín de la Real Academia de Historia* 67 (1915): 550–61.

Graus, Frantisek. "Le funzioni del culto dei santi e della legenda," in *Agiografia altomedievale*, ed. by Sofia Boesch Gajano (Bologna, 1976).

Gutmann, D. "Dying to Power: Death and the Search for Self-Esteem," in H. Feifeil, *New Meanings of Death* (New York, 1977).

Huyskens, Albert. *Quellenstudien zur Geschichte der heiligen Elisabeth Landgräfin von Thüringen* (Marburg, 1908).

Bibliography

Jesús, Gabriel de. *La Santa de la Raza. Vida gráfica de Santa Teresa de Jesús*, 4 vols. (Madrid, 1929–35).

Jones, Charles W. *Saint Nicholas of Myra, Bari, and Manhattan: Biography of a Legend* (Chicago, 1978).

Kagan, Richard. *Lucrecia's Dreams: Politics and Prophecy in Sixteenth-Century Spain* (Berkeley, 1990).

Keller, John Esten. *Motif-Index of Mediaeval Spanish Exempla* (Knoxville, 1949).

Kemp, Eric Waldram. *Canonization and Authority in the Western Church* (London, 1948).

Kendrick, T. D. *Saint James in Spain* (London, 1960).

Lamano y Beneite, J. *Santa Teresa en Alba de Tormes* (Salamanca, 1914).

Lavin, Irving. *Bernini and the Unity of the Visual Arts*, 2 vols. (New York, 1980).

Le Goff, Jacques. "Vita et pre-exemplum dans le deuxième livre des *Dialogues* de Grégoire le Grand," in *Hagiographie, Cultures, et Sociétès, IVe–XIIe siècles. Actes du Colloque organisé à Nanterre et à Paris, 2–5 mai 1979* (Paris, 1981).

Leroy, Olivier. "Apparitions de Sainte Thérèse de Jésus: Recherche Critique," *Revue d'Ascetique et de Mystique* 134 (1958): 165–84.

Lopez Estrada, Francisco. "Cohetes para Teresa. La relación de 1627 sobre las Fiestas de Madrid por el Patronato de España de Santa Teresa de Jesús y la pólemica sobre el mismo," *Actas del Congreso Internacional Teresiano, 4–7 Octubre 1982*, 2 vols., ed. by T. Egido Martinez, V. Garcia de la Concha, and O. Gonzalez de Cardenal (Salamanca, 1983).

Macca di Santa Maria, V. "Il dottorato di Santa Teresa. Sviluppo storico di una idea," *Ephemerides Carmeliticae*, 21 (1970): 36–47.

Madre de Dios, Efrén de la, and Otger Steggink. *Tiempo y Vida de Santa Teresa*, 2nd ed., (Madrid, 1978).

Maltby, William. *Alba: A Biography of Fernando Alvarez de Toledo, Third Duke of Alba* (Berkeley CA, 1983).

Martin del Blanco, Mauricio. *Santa Teresa de Jesús: Mujer de ayer para el hombre de hoy* (Bilbao, 1975).

Mascard, Hermann. *Les reliques des saints. Formation coutumière d'un droit* (Paris, 1975).

Mecklin, John M. *The Passing of the Saint: A Study of a Culture Type* (Chicago, 1941).

Monjas y beatas embaucadoras, ed. by Jesús Imirizaldu (Madrid, 1977).

Nugent, D. "What has Wittenberg To Do With Avila? Martin Luther and St. Teresa," *Journal of Ecumenical Studies* 23 (1986): 650–8.

Peers, E. Allison. *Handbook to the Life and Times of St. Teresa and St. John of the Cross* (London, 1954).

Bibliography

Perales y Gutiérrez, Arturo. *El supernaturalismo de Santa Teresa y la filosofía médica* (Madrid, 1894).

Reames, Sherry L. *The Legenda Aurea: A Reexamination of its Paradoxical History* (Madison WI, 1985).

Rodriguez del Niño Jesús, Otilio, O.C.D. "¿Quién es el autor de la Vida de Santa Teresa a nombre de Yepes?" *El Monte Carmelo* 64 (1956): 244–55.

Rodriguez, Isaías. *Santa Teresa de Jesús y la espiritualidad española* (Madrid, 1972), pp. 133–7.

Romeo de Maio, *Riforme e miti nella Chiesa del Cinquecento* (Naples, 1973).

Rosell, Manuel. *Disertación histórica sobre la aparición de San Isidro Labrador, patrón de Madrid* (Madrid, 1789).

Sallman, J. M. "I poteri del corpo santo: rappresentazione e utilizzazione," *Forme i potere e pratica di carisma*, ed. by P. Levillain and J. M. Sallman (Naples, 1984).

Sanchez Lora, José Luis. *Mujeres, conventos y formas de la religiosidad barroca* (Madrid, 1988).

San Joaquín, Antonio (Flórez) de. *Año Teresiano: Diario historico, panegirico moral, en que se describen las virtudes, sucesos, y maravillas de la seráfica y mística doctora de la Iglesia, Santa Teresa de Jesús* 12 vols. (Madrid, 1733–69).

Santa Teresa, Silverio de, O.C.D. *Santa Teresa de Jesús, síntesis suprema de la Raza* (Madrid, 1939).

"La mano de la Santa redimida de la esclavitud bolchevique," *El Monte Carmelo*, 45 (1937).

Schramm, Edmund. "Quevedo und das Patrozinium des heiligen Jakob," *Jarbuch für das Bistum Mainz* 5 (1950): 349–56.

Staehlin, Carlos Maria, S. J. *Apariciones* (Madrid, 1954).

Summers, Montague. *The Physical Phenomena of Mysticism* (New York, 1950).

Toussaert, Jacques. *Le sentiment religieux en Flandre à le fin du Moyen Age* (Paris, 1963).

Tubach, Fredric C. *Index Exemplorum: A Handbook of Medieval Religious Tales* (Helsinki, 1969).

Vauchez, André. *La sainteté en Occident aux derniers siècles du Moyen Age* (Rome, 1981).

Vida y Obras de San Juan de la Cruz, 6th ed., Crisogono de Jesús, O.C.D. et al., eds., (Madrid, 1972).

Von Nagy, M. *Die Legenda Aurea und ihr Verfasser Jacobus de Voragine* (Munich, 1971).

Walker Bynum, Caroline. *Holy Feast and Holy Fast: The Religious Significance of Food to Medieval Women* (Berkeley CA, 1987).

Bibliography

Weber, Alison. "Saint Teresa, Demonologist," in *Culture and Control in Counter-Reformation Spain*, ed. by A. J. Cruz and M. E. Perry (Minneapolis, 1991). *Teresa of Avila and the Rhetoric of Femininity* (Princeton, 1990).

Weinstein, Donald, and Rudolph M. Bell, *Saints and Society. The Two Worlds of Western Christendom, 1000–1700* (Chicago, 1982).

Welter, J. Th. *L'Exemplum dans la litterature religieuse et didactique du Moyen Age* (Paris/Toulouse, 1927).

Epilogue

Camporesi, Piero. *The Fear of Hell: Images of Damnation and Salvation in Early Modern Europe* (University Park PA, 1992), trans. Lucinda Byatt *La casa dell'Eternità* (Milan, 1987).

Dedet, Christian. *La Fuite en Espagne* (Paris, 1965).

Domínguez Ortiz, Antonio. *Crisis y decadencia de la España de los Austrias* (Madrid, 1965).

Febvre, Lucien. *Le problème de l'incroyance au XVIe siècle. La religion de Rabelais* (Paris, 1942, 1968). English translation by Beatrice Gottlieb, *The Problem of Unbelief in the Sixteenth Century. The Religion of Rabelais* (Cambridge MA, 1982).

Forbes, Malcolm with Jeff Bloch, *They Went That-a-way: How the Famous, the Infamous, and the Great Died* (New York, 1988).

Garcia Carcel, Ricardo. *Herejía y sociedad en el siglo XVI: La Inquisición en Valencia, 1530–1569* (Barcelona, 1980), pp. 343–44.

Gardiner, Eilen. ed. *Visions of Heaven and Hell Before Dante* (New York, 1989).

Geertz, Clifford. "Religion as a Cultural System," *Anthropological Approaches to the Study of Religion*, ed. by Michael Banton (New York/London, 1966), p. 28.

Grant, Edward. *Planets, Stars, and Orbs: The Medieval Cosmos, 1200–1687* (Cambridge/New York, 1993).

Hanken, P. J., ed. *The Spanish Inquisition* (New York, 1969).

Kamen, Henry. *Inquisition and Society in Spain in the Sixteenth and Seventeenth Centuries* (Bloomington IN, 1985).

Loyola, Ignatius. *Texte Autographe des Exercices Spirituels et Documents contemporains*, ed. by Edouard Gueydan, S. J. (Paris, 1985), pp. 89–90.

McDannell, Colleen, and Bernhard Lang. *Heaven: A History* (New Haven/London, 1988).

Maurach, Gregor. *Coelum Empyreum: Versuch einer Begriffsgeschichte* (Wiesbaden, 1968).

The Oxford Book of Death, ed. by D. J. Enright (Oxford, 1987).

Bibliography

Perez Moreda, Vicente. *La crisis de la mortalidad en la España interior, siglos XVI–XIX* (Madrid, 1980).

Sanchez Bella, Florencio. *La Reforma del clero en San Juan de Avila* (Madrid, 1981).

Turner, Victor. *From Ritual to Theatre* (New York, 1982).

Weber, Max. *Die Protestantische Ethik und der Geist des Kapitalismus*, vol. 1 of *Gesammelte Aufsätze zur religionssoziologie* (Tübingen, 1924), English tr. by Talcott Parsons, *The Protestant Ethic and the Spirit of Capitalism* (New York, 1958).

Index

Note: Canonized saints and monks and nuns who gave up their surnames are indexed by their first names.

Index

Index

Index

Index

Index

Index

Index

Printed in the United Kingdom
by Lightning Source UK Ltd.
119936UK00001B/345